'This **grim** masterpiece, shot thr[...] ... The personal details are rivet[...]

'This **fascinating** book ... [Montefiore] concentrates, as any good historian should, on pushing forward the boundaries of our knowledge of the subject ... [He] provides rich detail of daily life and family relationships in a world of human values turned inside out ... scrupulously fair in the way he describes Stalin's qualities – including his ability to charm, his uncanny grasp of geopolitical issues, his brilliant handling of foreign statesmen and his genuine passion for literature' Antony Beevor, *Sunday Times*

'His **masterful** and terrifying account of Stalin ... seldom has the picture been put in finer focus than by Sebag Montefiore. It is partly through his diligent interviews with the children of survivors and his admirable combination of history and gossip that one sees the awful banality, the brutal crudity of the men who carelessly sent so many millions to their senseless deaths' Alistair Horne, *The Times*

'This magnificent portrait ... Simon Sebag Montefiore has mined the rich veins of recent Russian writing on the Stalin age and of newly opened archives to give us an intimate history ... The stifling, contiguous life of the Soviet elite in and around the Kremlin is wonderfully conveyed, in some of the most striking and literary passages in the book ... Striking the balance between political narrative and personal biography is a difficult one ... Montefiore keeps both in perspective ... a wonderfully rich and vibrant portrait of the Stalinist elite who lived in the shadow of a remarkable and dangerous colossus'

Richard Overy, *Literary Review*

'Everyone in Westminster has been reading [*Stalin*] during these turbulent leadership times. I've met Labour ministers and Tory backbenchers reeling from stories ... reading this book for tips on how to become an efficient fighting machine ... Everyone is mugging up on Stalin' Alice Thomson, *Daily Telegraph*

'Read it or face social Siberia ... a cross-over success. Academically and intellectually rigorous, it's also a riveting read ... it takes a

great writer to make it seem fresh. And Sebag Montefiore certainly does that … Sebag Montefiore's greatest achievement has been to "humanise" Stalin. Uncle Joe was a mass murderer and a paranoid sociopath. But he was also charming, friendly and flirtatious'
100 Best Things in the World Right Now, GQ magazine

'Grimly brilliant'   Andrew Marr, *Daily Telegraph*

'Excellent … This book is like a vast Russian novel full of characters, colour, terror, passion and treachery … love affairs, marriages, divorces, imprisonments and killings'
Susannah Tarbush, *Al-Hayat*

'Montefiore's masterful study of Stalin and his entourage provides the best personal portrait to date of the man and his group'   Daniel Beer, *Jewish Chronicle*

'Montefiore has managed to get inside the mind of the 20th century's worst mass murderer. What he has found there will affect your view of human nature … a thoughtful book of first-class scholarship as well as a transfixing narrative … all … vividly recreated by Montefiore's caustically witty prose'
Andrew Roberts, *Daily Telegraph*

'Its extraordinary revelation of the evil – the complete amorality – at the heart of the dictator's court will change the way historians approach the great historical questions about the Stalinist regime'
Orlando Figes, *Sunday Telegraph*

'An astonishingly good and important book … he provides a remarkably fresh and exciting account of one of history's darkest periods'   Simon Heffer, *Country Life*

'This is no ordinary scholarly life, it's ultra reader-friendly, lively, gossipy, and packed with revelations about the intimacies and intrigues of Stalin the man and his courtiers. Brilliant'
Evening Standard, Metro Life magazine

'For anyone with the slightest interest in 20th-century history, this is essential, utterly compelling, page-turning reading. The book is a masterpiece of horror'   Robert Harvey, *The Tablet*

'I did not think I could learn anything new about Stalin but I was wrong. A stunning performance' Dr Henry Kissinger

'Sebag Montefiore paints a detailed and fascinating picture of the complex interactions and intrigues that characterized Kremlin life under Stalin ... [he] has done a valuable service in drawing our attention to a hitherto little-studied aspect of Stalinism. As his *Stalin* demonstrates, the personal relationships of those who ran the Kremlin provided an essential dynamic for the development of the Stalinist system' Amy Knight, *TLS*

'This fascinating account of the dictator's reign ... Montefiore provides a riveting portrait of the man and his ruling circle ... this book gives us an unprecedented glimpse into his intimate life, the inner workings of his government and the relations between the members of his junta, many of whom have remained shadowy figures until now ... The result is a much finer and nuanced understanding of the Bolshevik phenomenon than we have had before. Using his sources with great skill, Montefiore has succeeded in placing Stalin and the Bolsheviks in the context of their time' Marc Lambert, *Scotsman*

'This magisterial new biography of Stalin ... Sebag Montefiore makes some interesting new assertions about Stalin's psychology ... well-written; he evidently has a superb grasp of Russian, and can operate well in that still-difficult country'
Lesley Chamberlain, *Independent*

'Montefiore drives his story forward with breathless enthusiasm ... in a work of great importance. Scholars will read it for the valuable new evidence it assembles. Others will enjoy it as a fascinating page-turner and an everyday saga of extraordinary Kremlin folk' Rodric Braithwaite, *Financial Times*

'Gripping and timely ... [Montefiore] ... had the bright idea of examining the letters, telegrams and diaries of [Stalin's] intimate associates. As a result, this is a book based on extraordinary primary research ... one of the few recent books on Stalinism that will be read in years to come. The devil is in the detail'
Robert Service, *Guardian*

'Montefiore's master work charts in compelling detail the story of Georgia's two most infamous sons, the all-powerful dictator and Beria' Andrew Cook, *The Times*

'No summary can do justice to the wealth of this book, which leaves little to be desired ... Nevertheless, this work should be read by anyone interested in Stalin's life and times, or in the workings of a highly developed tyranny' Clive Foss, *History Today*

'Marvellous' Allan Massie, *Sunday Times*

BOOK OF THE YEAR 2003

'Montefiore's *Stalin*, I should imagine, will be the standard work on this twentieth-century monster for years to come'
Jeremy Paxman, *Sunday Telegraph*

'Enormously readable and even grimly amusing ... the details of the cruelty and depravity ... are incredible'
Miriam Gross, *Sunday Telegraph*

'Packed with details about a man who was brilliant, often charming, sometimes kind, but also terrorised his own people ... The story of a monster' Charles Guthrie, *Sunday Telegraph*

'Montefiore's *Stalin* showed us the century's worst dictator wasn't merely a paranoid narcissist but also anxious, uncertain, even charming ... Now we can see him as a human being too'
John Simpson, *Daily Telegraph*

'One of the two outstanding books of the year, *Stalin* by Simon Sebag Montefiore ... was the most civilised and elegant chronicle of brutality and ruthlessness I have ever read, its prose cool and clear but never indifferent' Ruth Rendell, *Daily Telegraph*

'Outstanding ... Unforgettable' Antony Beevor, *Daily Telegraph*

'Montefiore's *Stalin* ... full of wonderful detail, a more convincing portrait of the charm of wickedness than Gitta Sereny's sober studies' Sarah Sands, *Daily Telegraph*

'Simon Sebag Montefiore had one of the literary triumphs of the year in *Stalin: Court of the Red Tsar*' David Robson, *Sunday Telegraph*

'Montefiore's *Stalin* uses newly available archival materials to paint a picture – simultaneously fascinating and repulsive – of the homelife of [these] jolly psychopaths. Book of the Year'
T. J. Binyon, *Evening Standard*

'The most revealing account of the inner circles of tyranny since Albert Speer's inside story of Hitler's bunker. Book of the Year'
Norman Lebrecht, *Evening Standard*

'Enlivened by sharp pen portraits and grisly anecdotes, Montefiore's study ... was admired for its elegant prose as well as its grotesque cavalcade of monsters' Books of the Year, *The Week*

'Montefiore's *Stalin* captivated me'
Rod Little, Cultural Highlights of the Year, *The Times*

'Montefiore's *Stalin* ... horrific, revelatory and sobering ... triumph of research and should be required reading in Russia. Book of the Year' John le Carré, *Observer*

'Brings alive that many-sided monster ... the first book that has given me grounds for thinking it might be possible to understand how Stalin's got away with his enormities. Book of the Year'
David Pryce-Jones, *Spectator*

'The most insightful account of the regime I have yet read. Book of the Year' Oliver Letwin, *Guardian*

'Superb ... Obligatory reading!'
Ronald Harwood, 'My 6 Best Books', *The Week*

'Illuminates the complexities of Stalinism. Book of the Year'
Neil Tennant, *The Times*

Simon Sebag Montefiore, who was born in 1965, read history at Gonville & Caius College, Cambridge. He spent much of the nineties travelling through the ex-Soviet Empire, particularly the Caucasus, Ukraine and Central Asia, and wrote widely on Russia, especially for the *Sunday Times*, *New York Times* and *Spectator*. *Prince of Princes: the Life of Potemkin* was published in 2000 and shortlisted for the Samuel Johnson, Duff Cooper and Marsh Biography prizes. *Stalin: The Court of the Red Tsar* won the History Book of the Year Award at the British Book Awards. A Fellow of the Royal Society of Literature, the author of two novels and presenter of television documentaries, he lives in London with his wife, the novelist Santa Montefiore, and their two children.

Stalin

The Court of the Red Tsar

SIMON SEBAG MONTEFIORE

PHOENIX

A PHOENIX PAPERBACK

First published in Great Britain in 2003
by Weidenfeld & Nicolson
This paperback edition published in 2004
by Phoenix,
an imprint of Orion Books Ltd,
Orion House, 5 Upper St Martin's Lane,
London WC2H 9EA

Fourth impression 2004

A CIP catalogue record for this book
is available from the British Library.

ISBN 0 75381 766 7

Typeset by Selwood Systems, Midsomer Norton

Printed and bound in Great Britain by
Clays Ltd, St Ives plc

www.orionbooks.co.uk

To Lily Bathsheba

Contents

Part Four: Slaughter: Yezhov the Poison Dwarf, 1937–1938

Part Five: Slaughter: Beria Arrives, 1938–1939

Part Six: 'The Great Game': Hitler and Stalin, 1939–1941

Part Seven: War: The Bungling Genius, 1941–1942

Part Eight: War: The Triumphant Genius, 1942–1945

Illustrations

General Vasily Stalin: over-promoted, alcoholic, unstable, cruel and terrified.[1]

After the war, General Vasily Stalin persuaded General Vlasik to give him his exquisite townhouse not far from the Kremlin.[10]

At the end of the war, a tired but cheerful Stalin sits between the two rivals, Malenkov and Zhdanov.[2]

Section 4: 1945–1953

After victory, Stalin fell ill with a series of minor strokes or heart attacks.[3]

On 12 August 1945, Generalissimo Stalin cheerfully leads his magnates for the parade.[8]

Zhdanov and the charlatan Trofim Lysenko.[10]

The exhausted Stalin gloomily leads Beria, Mikoyan and Malenkov through the Kremlin to the Mausoleum for the 1946 May Day parade.[4]

Stalin leads the mourning at Kalinin's funeral in 1946.[2]

Stalin, Voroshilov and Kaganovich follow Zhdanov's coffin at his funeral.[2]

In late 1948, Stalin sits with the older generation, Kaganovich, Molotov and Voroshilov, while an intrigue is being prepared behind them amongst the younger.[2]

Mikoyan and others at Stalin's house in the summer.[3]

At his seventieth birthday gala, on stage at the Bolshoi, Stalin stands between Mao Tse-tung and Khrushchev.[10]

Stalin's restless last holiday in 1952: his new house at New Athos;[10] the Likani Palace, which once belonged to Tsar Nicholas II's brother Grand Duke Michael;[10] his remote house at Lake Ritsa, where he spent weeks;[10] green metal boxes containing phones were built by his guards so that Stalin could call for help if he was taken ill on his daily strolls.[10]

The sofa at Kuntsevo on which Stalin died on 5 March 1953.[10]

The ageing but determined Stalin watches Malenkov give the chief report at his last public appearance at the Nineteenth Congress in 1952.[6]

Khrushchev, Bulganin, Kaganovich, Mikoyan, Beria, Malenkov, Molotov and Voroshilov face each other over Stalin's body.[4]

Stalin at the 1927 Congress: in his prime.[2]

The author and the publishers offer their thanks to the following for their kind permission to reproduce images:

1 Alliluyev Family Collection
2 RGASPI
3 Vlasik Family Collection
4 AKG
5 Poskrebyshev Family Collection
6 David King Collection
7 Camera Press
8 Stalin Museum, Gori, Republic of Georgia
9 Hugh Lunghi Collection
10 Photographs by the author/Author's own collection
11 Victoria Ivleva-Yorke

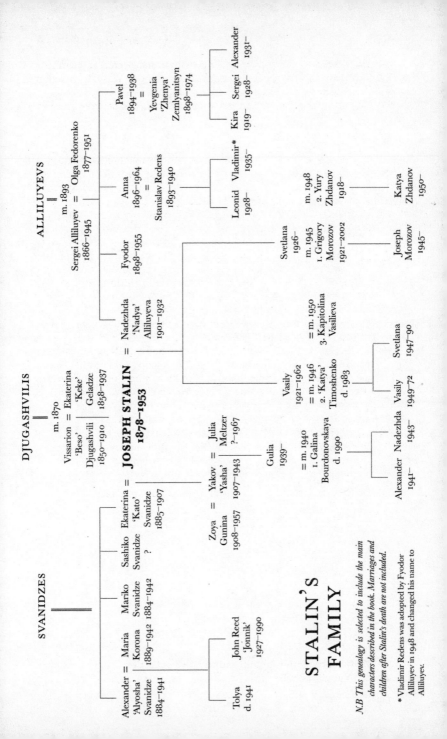

SVANIDZES

DJUGASHVILIS

m. 1870

Vissarion 'Beso' Djugashvili 1850–1910 = Ekaterina 'Keke' Geladze 1858–1937

ALLILUYEVS

m. 1893

Sergei Alliluyev 1866–1945 = Olga Fedorenko 1877–1951

Alexander 'Alyosha' Svanidze 1884–1941 = Maria Korona 1889–1942

Mariko Svanidze 1884–1942

Sashiko Svanidze ?

Ekaterina 'Kato' Svanidze 1885–1907 = **JOSEPH STALIN 1878–1953** = Nadezhda 'Nadya' Alliluyeva 1901–1932

Fyodor 1898–1955

Anna 1896–1964 = Stanislav Redens 1893–1940

Pavel 1894–1938 = Yevgenia 'Zhenya' Zemlyanitsyn 1898–1974

Tolya d. 1941

John Reed 'Jonnik' 1927–1990

Zoya Gunina 1908–1957

Yakov 'Yasha' 1907–1943 = Julia Meltzer ?–1967

Gulia 1939–

Vasily 1921–1962 = m. 1940 1. Galina Bourdonovskaya d. 1990 = m. 1946 2. 'Katya' Timoshenko d. 1983

Svetlana 1926– = m. 1945 1. Grigory Morozov 1921–2002 = m.1950 3. Kapitolina Vasilieva = m. 1948 2. Yury Zhdanov 1918–

Leonid 1928–

Vladimir* 1935–

Kira 1919–

Sergei 1928–

Alexander 1931–

Alexander 1941–

Nadezhda 1943–

Vasily 1949–72

Svetlana 1947–90

Joseph Morozov 1945–

Katya Zhdanov 1950–

STALIN'S FAMILY

N.B This genealogy is selected to include the main characters described in the book. Marriages and children after Stalin's death are not included.

* Vladimir Redens was adopted by Fyodor Alliluyev in 1948 and changed his name to Alliluyev.

The Soviet Union under Stalin 1929–1953

Territory won in Finnish War 1940

Territories added 1939/1940 after Molotov–Ribbentrop Pact

German and Czech territory annexed by USSR in 1945

Extent of the German invasion January – July 1942

SWEDEN

FINLAND

Leningrad

ESTONIA

Baltic Sea

LATVIA

LITHUANIA

• Gorky (Nizhny-Novgorod)

• Moscow

• Smolensk

SOVIET UNION

• Minsk
BELORUSSIA

• Kuibyshev (Samara)

POLAND

• Kursk

• Kiev

Kharkov

• Stalingrad (Tsaritsyn)

CZECHOSLOVAKIA

HUNGARY

UKRAINE

Rostov-on-Don

YUGOSLAVIA

RUMANIA

Kerch

Yalta

Caspian Sea

BULGARIA

Black Sea

GEORGIA
Tbilisi •

ARMENIA

Baku •

AZERBAIJAN

GREECE

TURKEY

IRAN

Teheran
•

Mediterranean Sea

Selected cities named after Stalin's comrades:

Molotov (Perm)
Zhdanov (Mariupol)
Kalinin (Tver)
Voroshilov (Lugansk)
Ordzhonikidze (Vladikafkaz)
Kirov (Viatka)
Gorky (Nizhny-Novgorod)

Kuibyshev (Samara)
Vorashilovsk (Stavropol)
Stalingrad (Tsaritsyn)
Stalino (Yuzhovka)
Stalinabad (Dushanbe)
Kirovabad (Elizavetpol)

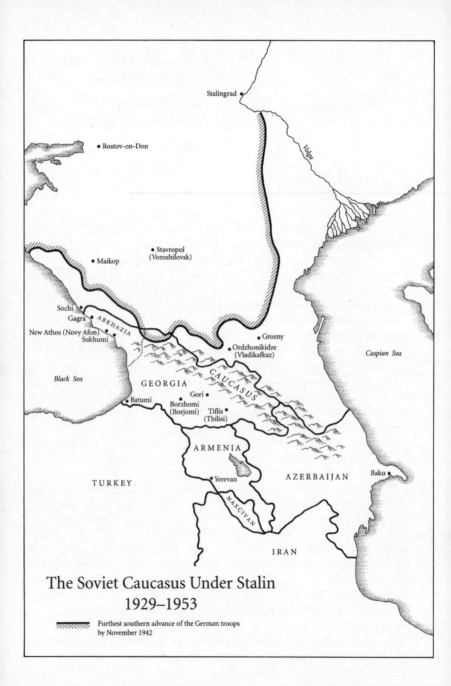

The Soviet Caucasus Under Stalin
1929–1953

///////// Furthest southern advance of the German troops
by November 1942

Introduction and Acknowledgements

I have been helped generously by many people in this enterprise from Moscow and St Petersburg to Sukhumi, from Tbilisi to Buenos Aires and Rostov-on-Don. My aim here was simply to write a portrait of Stalin, his top twenty potentates, and their families, to show how they ruled and how they lived in the unique culture of his years of supreme power. This does not pretend to be a history of his foreign and domestic policies, his military campaigns, his youth or the struggle with Trotsky. This is a chronicle of his court from his acclamation as 'the leader' in 1929 to his death. It is a biography of his courtiers, a study of high politics and informal power and customs. In a way, this is a biography of Stalin himself through his relationships with his magnates: he is never off-stage.

My mission was to go beyond the traditional explanations of Stalin as 'enigma', 'madman' or 'Satanic genius', and that of his comrades as 'men without biographies', dreary moustachioed sycophants in black-and-white photographs. Deploying the arsenal of new archives and unpublished memoirs, my own interviews, and well-known materials, I hope Stalin becomes a more understandable and intimate character, if no less repellent. I believe the placing of Stalin and his oligarchs in their idiosyncratic Bolshevik context as members of a military-religious 'order of sword-bearers' explains much of the inexplicable. Stalin was utterly unique but many of his views and features, such as dependence on death as a political tool, and his paranoia, were shared by his comrades. He was a man of his time, so were his magnates.

Molotov and Beria are probably the most famous of them but many are not well known in the West. Yezhov and Zhdanov gave their names to epochs yet remain shadowy. Some, such as Mekhlis, have hardly been covered even by academics. Mikoyan was admired by many; Kaganovich widely despised. They may have presented a grey mask to the outside world but many were flamboyant, dynamic and larger-than-life. The new access to their correspondence and even their love letters will at least make them live.

In telling their stories, this is inevitably a cautionary tale: of the many mass murderers chronicled here, only Beria and Yezhov were prosecuted (and not for their true crimes). The temptation has been to blame all the crimes on one man, Stalin. There is an obsession in the West today with the cult of villainy: a macabre but inane competiton between Stalin and Hitler to find the 'world's most evil dictator' by counting their supposed victims. This is demonology not history. It has the effect of merely indicting one madman and offers us no lesson about either the danger of utopian ideas and systems, or the responsibility of individuals.

Modern Russia has not yet faced up to its past: there has been no redemption, which perhaps still casts a shadow over its development of civil society. Many modern Russians will not thank me for the intimate frankness of a history they would prefer to forget or avoid. While this book certainly does not diminish Stalin's paramount guilt, it may discourage the convenient fiction of his sole responsibility by revealing the killings of the whole leadership, as well as their own sufferings, sacrifices, vices and privileges.

I have been enormously fortunate in those who have helped me: this book was inspired by Robert Conquest, who has been the most patient, generous supporter and adviser throughout. I am superlatively grateful to Robert Service, Professor of Russian History, Oxford University, who has 'supervised' my book with generous encouragement and outstanding knowledge, and whose detailed reading and editing of the text have been invaluable. In Russia, I have been 'supervised' by the most distinguished scholar of Stalinist high politics, Oleg Khlevniuk, Senior Researcher at the State Archive of the Russian Federation (GARF) who has steered and helped me throughout. I am fortunate too that on matters of the NKVD/MGB, I have been helped by Nikita Petrov, Vice-Chairman of Moscow's Memorial Scientific Research Centre, the finest scholar of the secret police working in Russia today. On military matters, I was guided and helped, in both interpretation and archival research, by Professor Oleg Rzheshevsky and his associates. On diplomatic questions, I have treasured the knowledge, checking and charming acquaintance of Hugh Lunghi, who attended Teheran, Yalta and Potsdam, and meetings with Stalin during the later 1940s. Sir Martin Gilbert has been generous with both his knowledge and contacts in Russia. On Georgian matters, my guides have been Zackro Megrelishvili, Professor (American Studies), Tbilisi Ilia Chavchavadze State University of Language and Culture, and Gela Charkviani. On Abkhazian affairs, I must thank the top scholar in Sukhumi, Professor Slava Lakoba. I am also grateful for the guidance and ideas of the following: Geoffrey Hosking, Professor of Russian History at the University of London; Isabel de Madariaga, Professor Emeritus of Slavonic Studies at the University of London; and Alexander Kamenskii, Professor of Early and Early-Modern Russian History at Moscow's Russian State University for the Humanities. Roy Medvedev, Edvard Radzinsky, Arkady Vaksberg and Larissa Vasilieva also advised and helped me. I am most fortunate to be aided by such a towering cast and I can only humbly thank them; any wisdom is theirs; any mistakes my own.

I was most fortunate in my timing, for the opening of a chunk of the Presidential Archive in the Russian State Archive of Social and Political History (RGASPI) in 1999 meant that I was able to use a large amount of new, fascinating papers and photographs, containing the letters of Stalin, his entourage and their families, which made this book possible. In addition, I was able to access new military material in the Russian State War Archives (RGVA) and the Central Archives of the Ministry of Defence of the Russian Federation (TSAMO RF) in Podolsk. Oleg Khlevniuk was my original sponsor in both RGASPI and GARF. My greatest thanks go to Larisa A. Rogovaya, Head of Section at RGASPI, the expert on Stalin's papers and the pre-eminent interpreter of his handwriting, who helped me every step of the way. Thanks also to Dr Ludmilla Gatagova, Researcher in the Institute of Russian History. But above all, I owe thanks to the uniquely talented scholar of the History Department of the Russian State Humanities University, Galina Babkova, who helped me as much here as she did on *Potemkin*.

I have been lucky to gain access to many witnesses of this time and often to their family papers, including their fathers' unpublished memoirs. I am enormously grateful for this to Mikhail Fridman, Ingaborga Dapkunaite and Vladimir Grigoriev, Deputy Minister of Press, Television and Radio of the Russian Federation, proprietor of Vagrius publishing house; Galina Udenkova of

RGASPI, who shared her unique contacts with me; Olga Adamishina, who arranged several of my interviews; and Rosamond Richardson, who generously gave me access to her Alliluyev family contacts and her tapes of her interviews with Svetlana Alliluyeva. Kitty Stidworthy allowed me to use Vera Trail's unpublished reminiscence of Yezhov. My thanks to Dr Luba Vinogradova for her efficiency, charm, empathy and patience in helping with many of my interviews. Special thanks to Alan Hirst and Louise Campbell for their introductions to the Molotovs. Lieut.-Gen. Stepan Mikoyan and his daughter Askhen were charming, hospitable, helpful and generous. The following also proffered their memories and their time: Kira Alliluyeva, Vladimir Alliluyev (Redens), Natalya Andreyeva, Nikolai Baibakov, Nina Budyonny, Julia Khrushcheva, Tanya Litvinova, Igor Malenkov, Volya Malenkova, Sergo Mikoyan, Joseph Minervin (Kaganovich's grandson), Stas Namin, Vyacheslav Nikonov (Molotov's grandson), Eteri Ordzhonikidze, Martha Peshkova, Natalya Poskrebysheva, Leonid Redens, Natalya Rykova, Lieut.-Gen. Artyom Sergeev, Yury Soloviev, Oleg Troyanovsky, Yury Zhdanov, Nadezhda Vlasik. I am grateful to my researcher Galina Babkova for arranging the interviews with Tina Egnatashvili and Gulia Djugashvili. I must thank the admirable Mark Fielder of Granada Productions, with whom it was a pleasure to work on the BBC2 Stalin documentary. In St Petersburg, thanks to the Director and staff of the SM Kirov Museum.

In Tbilisi, Professor Megrelishvili arranged many interviews, recalled his memories of his stepfather Shalva Nutsibidze and introduced me to Maya Kavtaradze who shared her father's unpublished memoirs with me. Gela Charkviani told me his memories of his youth and, above all, most generously gave me access to his father's unpublished memoirs. I also grateful to the following: Nadya Dekanozova, Alyosha Mirtskhulava, Eka Rapava, Nina Rukhadze. Thanks to Lika Basileia for accompanying me to the Likani Palace and Gori, and to Nino Gagoshidze and Irina Dmetradze for their energetic help; Nata Patiashvili for her help in translation and arranging interviews; Zurab Karumidze; Lila Aburshvili, Director of the Stalin Museum, Gori.

For my trip to Abkhazia, I must thank HM Ambassador to Georgia, Deborah Barnes Jones; Thadeus Boyle, Field Service Administrator, UNOMIG; the Abkhazian Prime Minister, Anri Djirgonia. It would not have been possible without Victoria

Ivleva-Yorke. Thanks to Saida Smir, Director of the Novy Afon dacha and staffs of Stalin's other residences at Sukhumi, Kholodnaya Rechka, Lake Ritsa, Museri and Sochi. In Buenos Aires, thanks to Eva Soldati for interviewing Leopoldo Bravo and his family.

Thanks for having me to stay during my visits to Moscow and elsewhere: Masha Slonim, who turned out to be Maxim Litvinov's granddaughter; Marc and Rachel Polonsky who live in Marshal Koniev's apartment on Granovsky where many events in the book happened; Ingaborga Dapkunaite, David Campbell, Tom Wilson in Moscow; the Hon. Olga Polizzi and Julietta Dexter in St Petersburg.

A special thank-you to two of the wisest historical minds: my father Dr Stephen Sebag-Montefiore MD who has been as brilliant in reading the psychology of Stalin as he was with Potemkin; and my mother April Sebag-Montefiore for her flawless gifts of language and psychology.

I must thank my agent Georgina Capel; Anthony Cheetham; my publisher Ion Trewin; and Lord and Lady Weidenfeld. Thanks for answering questions and helping in small or large ways to: Andy Apostolou, Anne Applebaum, Joan Bright Astley, Professor Derek Beales, Antony Beevor, Vadim Benyatov, Michael Bloch, Dr David Brandenburger, Pavel Chinsky, Winston Churchill, Bernadette Cini, Lady Dahrendorf, Dr Sarah Davies, Yelena Durden-Smith, Ellen, Lisa Fine, Sergei Degtiarev Foster, Mark Franchetti, Levan and Nino Gachechiladze, Professor J. Arch Getty, Nata Gologre, Jon Halliday, Andrea Dee Harris, Mariana Haseldine, Dr Dan Healy, Laurence Kelly, Dmitri Khankin, Maria Lobanova, V. S. Lopatin, Edward Lucas, Ambassador of the Republic of Georgia and Mrs Teimuraz Mamatsashvili, Neil McKendrick, the Master, Gonville & Caius College, Cambridge, Catherine Merridale, Princess Tatiana Metternich, Professor Richard Overy, Charles and Patty Palmer-Tomkinson, Martin Poliakoff, Alexander Prozverkin, David Pryce-Jones, Julia Tourchaninova and Ernst Goussinksi, Professor E. A. Rees, Count Fritz von der Schulenburg, Hugh Sebag-Montefiore, Lady Soames, Professor Boris Sokolov, Geia Sulkanishvili, Lord Thomas of Swynnerton, Count Nikolai Tolstoy, Prince George Vassiltchikov, Dr D. H. Watson, Adam Zamoyski. I owe much to my Russian tutor, Galina Oleksiuk. Thanks to Jane Birkett, my valiant copy editor, to John Gilkes for the maps, to Douglas Matthews for the index and mountainous thanks to Victoria Webb for the heroic job of collating the proofs.

Last but first, I must lovingly thank my wife Santa Montefiore, not only for translating materials on Leopoldo Bravo from the Spanish, but above all, for tolerating and even sometimes welcoming, for years on end, the brooding presence of Stalin in our lives.

List of Characters

Joseph Stalin born Djugashvili known as 'Soso' and 'Koba'. Secretary of Bolshevik Party 1922–1953 and Premier 1941–53. Marshal. Generalissimo

Family
Keke Djugashvili, Stalin's mother
Kato Svanidze, Stalin's first wife
Yakov Djugashvili, son of Stalin's first marriage to Kato Svanidze. Captured by Germans
Nadya Alliluyeva, Stalin's second wife
Vasily Stalin, Stalin's son by Nadya Alliluyeva, pilot, General
Svetlana Stalin now known as Alliluyeva, Stalin's daughter
Artyom Sergeev, Stalin and Nadya's adopted son
Sergei Alliluyev, Nadya's father
Olga Alliluyeva, Nadya's mother
Pavel Alliluyev, Nadya's brother, Red Army Commissar married to
Zhenya Alliluyeva, Nadya's sister-in-law, actress, mother of Kira
Alyosha Svanidze, brother of Kato, Georgian, Stalin's brother-in-law, banking official married to
Maria Svanidze, diarist, Jewish Georgian opera singer
Stanislas Redens, Nadya's brother-in-law, secret policeman, married to Anna Redens, Nadya's elder sister

Allies
Victor Abakumov, secret policeman, head of Smersh, MGB Minister
Andrei Andreyev, Politburo member, CC Secretary, married to
Dora Khazan, Nadya's best friend, Deputy Textiles Minister, mother of Natasha Andreyeva
Lavrenti Beria, 'Uncle Lara', secret policeman, NKVD boss, Politburo member in charge of nuclear bomb, married to
Nina Beria, scientist, Stalin treated her 'like a daughter', mother of
Sergo Beria, scientist, married to

Martha Peshkova Beria, granddaughter of Gorky, daughter-in-law of Beria

Semyon Budyonny, cavalryman, Marshal, one of the Tsaritsyn Group

Nikolai Bulganin, 'the Plumber', Chekist, Mayor of Moscow, Politburo member, Defence Minister, heir apparent

Candide Charkviani, Georgian Party chief and Stalin's confidant

Semyon Ignatiev, MGB Minister, master of the Doctors' Plot

Lazar Kaganovich, 'Iron Lazar' and 'the Locomotive', Jewish Old Bolshevik, Stalin's deputy early 1930s, Railways chief, Politburo member

Mikhail Kalinin, 'Papa', the 'Village Elder', Soviet President, peasant/ worker

Nikita Khrushchev, Moscow, then Ukrainian First Secretary, Politburo member

Sergei Kirov, Leningrad chief, CC Secretary, Politburo member and Stalin's close friend

Valerian Kuibyshev, economic chief and poet, Politburo member

Alexei (A. A.) Kuznetsov, Zhdanov's deputy in Leningrad; post-WW2, CC Secretary and curator of MGB, Stalin's heir apparent as Secretary

Nestor Lakoba, Abkhazian boss

Georgi Malenkov, nicknamed 'Melanie' or 'Malanya', CC Secretary, allied to Beria

Lev Mekhlis, 'the Gloomy Demon' and 'Shark', Jewish, Stalin's secretary, then *Pravda* editor, political chief of Red Army

Akaki Mgeladze, Abkhazian, then Georgian boss; Stalin called him 'Wolf'

Anastas Mikoyan, Armenian Old Bolshevik, Politburo member, Trade and Supply Minister

Vyacheslav Molotov, known as 'Iron-Arse', and 'our Vecha', Politburo member, Premier, Foreign Minister, married to

Polina Molotova née Karpovskaya, known as Comrade Zhemchuzhina, 'the Pearl', Jewish, Fishery Commissar, perfume boss

Grigory Ordzhonikidze, known as Comrade Sergo and as 'Stalin's Arse', Politburo member, Heavy Industry chief

Karl Pauker, ex-barber of Budapest Opera, Stalin's bodyguard and head of Security

Alexander Poskrebyshev, ex-medical orderly, Stalin's *chef de cabinet*, married to

Bronka Metalikova Poskrebysheva, doctor, Jewish

Mikhail Riumin, 'Little Misha', 'the Midget', MGB Deputy Minister and manager of the Doctors' Plot

Nikolai Vlasik, Stalin's bodyguard and head of Guards Directorate

Klim Voroshilov, First Marshal, Politburo member, Defence Commissar, veteran of Tsaritsyn married to

Ekaterina Voroshilova, diarist

Nikolai Voznesensky, Leningrad economist, Politburo member, Deputy Premier, Stalin's anointed heir as Premier

Genrikh Yagoda, NKVD chief, Jewish, in love with Timosha Gorky

Abel Yenukidze, 'Uncle Abel', Secretary of Central Executive Committee, Georgian, bon viveur, Nadya's godfather

Nikolai Yezhov, 'Blackberry' or 'Kolya', NKVD boss, married to

Yevgenia Yezhova, editor, socialite, Jewess

Andrei Zhdanov, 'the Pianist', Politburo member, Leningrad boss, CC Secretary, Naval chief, Stalin's friend and heir apparent, father of

Yury Zhdanov, CC Science Dept chief, married Svetlana Stalin

Generals

Grigory Kulik, Marshal, Artillery chief, womaniser and bungler, veteran of Tsaritsyn

Boris Shaposhnikov, Marshal, Chief of Staff, Stalin's favourite staff officer

Semyon Timoshenko, Marshal, victor of Finland, Defence Commissar, veteran of Tsaritsyn; his daughter married Vasily Stalin

Alexander Vasilevsky, Marshal, Chief of Staff, priest's son

Georgi Zhukov, Marshal, Deputy Commander-in-Chief, Stalin's best general

Enemies and Former Allies

Nikolai Bukharin, 'darling of the Party', 'Bukharchik', theorist, Politburo member, Stalin's co-ruler 1925–9, friend of Nadya, Rightist. Chief defendant in last show trial

Lev Kamenev, Leftist Politburo member, defeated Trotsky with Stalin, with whom ruled 1924–5, Jewish. Defendant in first show trial

Alexei Rykov, 'Rykvodka', Rightist Politburo member, Premier and co-ruler with Stalin and Bukharin 1925–8. Defendant in last show trial

Leon Trotsky, genius of the Revolution, Jewish, War Commissar and creator of Red Army, 'operetta commander' in Stalin's words

Grigory Zinoviev, Leftist Politburo member, Leningrad boss, Jewish. Triumvirate with Stalin and Kamenev 1924–5. Defendant in first show trial

'Engineers of the Human Soul'

Anna Akhmatova, poet, 'harlot-nun,' said Zhdanov

Isaac Babel, author of *Red Cavalry* and friend of Eisenstein, Mandelstam

Demian Bedny, 'the proletarian poet', boon companion of Stalin

Mikhail Bulgakov, novelist and playwright, Stalin saw his *Days of the Turbins* fifteen times

Ilya Ehrenburg, Jewish writer and European literary figure

Sergei Eisenstein, Russia's greatest film director

Maxim Gorky, Russia's most famous novelist, close to Stalin

Ivan Kozlovsky, Stalin's court tenor

Osip Mandelstam, poet: 'Isolate but preserve,' said Stalin

Boris Pasternak, poet, 'cloud dweller', said Stalin

Mikhail Sholokhov, novelist of Cossacks and collectivization

Konstantin Simonov, poet and editor, friend of Vasily Stalin, favourite of Stalin

The Holiday Dinner: 8 November 1932

At around 7 p.m. on 8 November 1932, Nadya Alliluyeva Stalin, aged thirty-one, the oval-faced and brown-eyed wife of the Bolshevik General Secretary, was dressing for the raucous annual party to celebrate the fifteenth anniversary of the Revolution. Puritanical, earnest but fragile, Nadya prided herself on her 'Bolshevik modesty', wearing the dullest and most shapeless dresses, draped in plain shawls, with square-necked blouses and no make-up. But tonight, she was making a special effort. In the Stalins' gloomy apartment in the two-storey seventeenth-century Poteshny Palace, she twirled for her sister, Anna, in a long, unusually fashionable black dress with red roses embroidered around it, imported from Berlin. For once, she had indulged in a 'stylish hairdo' instead of her usual severe bun. She playfully placed a scarlet tea rose in her black hair.

The party, attended by all the Bolshevik magnates, such as Premier Molotov and his slim, clever and flirtatious wife, Polina, Nadya's best friend, was held annually by the Defence Commissar, Voroshilov: he lived in the long, thin Horse Guards building just five steps across a little lane from the Poteshny. In the tiny, intimate world of the Bolshevik élite, those simple, cheerful soirées usually ended with the potentates and their women dancing Cossack jigs and singing Georgian laments. But that night, the party did not end as usual.

Simultaneously, a few hundred yards to the east, closer to Lenin's Mausoleum and Red Square, in his office on the second floor of the triangular eighteenth-century Yellow Palace, Joseph Stalin, the General Secretary of the Bolshevik Party and the *Vozhd* – the leader – of the Soviet Union, now fifty-three, twenty-two years Nadya's senior, and the father of her two children, was meeting his favoured secret policeman. Genrikh

Yagoda, Deputy Chairman of the GPU,* a ferret-faced Jewish jeweller's son from Nizhny Novgorod with a 'Hitlerish moustache' and a taste for orchids, German pornography and literary friendships, informed Stalin of new plots against him in the Party and more turbulence in the countryside.

Stalin, assisted by Molotov, forty-two, and his economics chief, Valerian Kuibyshev, forty-five, who looked like a mad poet, with wild hair, an enthusiasm for drink, women and, appropriately, writing poetry, ordered the arrest of those who opposed them. The stress of those months was stifling as Stalin feared losing the Ukraine itself which, in parts, had descended into a dystopia of starvation and disorder. When Yagoda left at 7.05 p.m., the others stayed talking about their war to 'break the back' of the peasantry, whatever the cost to the millions starving in history's greatest man-made famine. They were determined to use the grain to finance their gargantuan push to make Russia a modern industrial power. But that night, the tragedy would be closer to home: Stalin was to face a personal crisis that was the most wounding and mysterious of his career. He would replay it over and over again for the rest of his days.

At 8.05 p.m., Stalin, accompanied by the others, ambled down the steps towards the party, through the snowy alleyways and squares of that red-walled medieval fortress, dressed in his Party tunic, baggy old trousers, soft leather boots, old army greatcoat and his wolf *shapka* with earmuffs. His left arm was slightly shorter than the other but much less noticeable than it became in old age – and he was usually smoking a cigarette or puffing on his pipe. The head and the thick, low hair, still black but with specks of the first grey, radiated the graceful strength of the mountain-men of the Caucasus; his almost Oriental, feline eyes were 'honey-coloured' but flashed a lupine yellow in anger. Children found his moustache prickly and his smell of tobacco acrid but, as Molotov and his female admirers recalled, Stalin was still attractive to women with whom he flirted shyly and clumsily.

---

* The Soviet secret police was first called the Extraordinary Commission for Combating Counterrevolution and Sabotage, known as the Cheka. In 1922, it became the State Political Administration (GPU) then the United GPU: OGPU. In 1934, it was subsumed into the People's Commissariat of Internal Affairs (NKVD). However, secret policemen were still known as 'Chekists' and the secret police itself as 'the Organs'. In 1941 and 1943, State Security was separated into its own Commissariat, the NKGB. From 1954 to 1991, it became a Committee of State Security, the KGB.

This small, sturdy figure, five feet, six inches tall, who walked ponderously yet briskly with a rough pigeon-toed gait (which was studiously aped by Bolshoi actors when they were playing Tsars), chatting softly to Molotov in his heavy Georgian accent, was only protected by one or two guards. The magnates strolled around Moscow with hardly any security. Even the suspicious Stalin, who was already hated in the countryside, walked home from his Old Square office with just one bodyguard. Molotov and Stalin were walking home one night in a snowstorm 'with no bodyguards' through the Manege Square when they were approached by a beggar. Stalin gave him ten roubles and the disappointed tramp shouted: 'You damned bourgeois!'

'Who can understand our people?' mused Stalin. Despite assassinations of Soviet officials (including an attempt on Lenin in 1918), things were remarkably relaxed until the June 1927 assassination of the Soviet Ambassador to Poland, when there was a slight tightening of security. In 1930, the Politburo passed a decree 'to ban Comrade Stalin from walking around town on foot'. Yet he continued his strolling for a few more years. This was a golden age which, in just a few hours, was to end in death, if not murder.

Stalin was already famous for his Sphinxian inscrutability, and phlegmatic modesty, represented by the pipe he ostentatiously puffed like a peasant elder. Far from being the colourless bureaucratic mediocrity disdained by Trotsky, the real Stalin was an energetic and vainglorious melodramatist who was exceptional in every way.

Beneath the eerie calm of these unfathomable waters were deadly whirlpools of ambition, anger and unhappiness. Capable both of moving with controlled gradualism and of reckless gambles, he seemed enclosed inside a cold suit of steely armour but his antennae were intensely sensitive and his fiery Georgian temper was so uncontrollable that he had almost ruined his career by unleashing it against Lenin's wife. He was a mercurial neurotic with the tense, seething temperament of a highly strung actor who revels in his own drama – what his ultimate successor, Nikita Khrushchev, called a *litsedei*, a man of many faces. Lazar Kaganovich, one of his closest comrades for over thirty years who was also on his way to the dinner, left the best description of this 'unique character': he was a 'different man at different times ... I knew no less than five or six Stalins.'

However, the opening of his archives, and many newly available sources, illuminate him more than ever before: it is no longer enough to describe him as an 'enigma'. We now know how he talked (constantly about himself, often with revealing honesty), how he wrote notes and letters, what he ate, sang and read. Placed in the context of the fissiparous Bolshevik leadership, a unique environment, he becomes a real person. The man inside was a super-intelligent and gifted politician for whom his own historic role was paramount, a nervy intellectual who manically read history and literature, a fidgety hypochondriac suffering from chronic tonsillitis, psoriasis, rheumatic aches from his deformed arm and the iciness of his Siberian exile. Garrulous, sociable and a fine singer, this lonely and unhappy man ruined every love relationship and friendship in his life by sacrificing happiness to political necessity and cannibalistic paranoia. Damaged by his childhood and abnormally cold in temperament, he tried to be a loving father and husband yet poisoned every emotional well, this nostalgic lover of roses and mimosas who believed the solution to every human problem was death, and who was obsessed with executions. This atheist owed everything to priests and saw the world in terms of sin and repentance, yet he was a 'convinced Marxist fanatic from his youth'. His fanaticism was 'semi-Islamic', his Messianic egotism boundless. He assumed the imperial mission of the Russians yet remained very much a Georgian, bringing the vendettas of his forefathers northwards to Muscovy.

Most public men share the Caesarian habit of detaching themselves to admire their own figures on the world stage, but Stalin's detachment was a degree greater. His adopted son Artyom Sergeev remembers Stalin shouting at his son Vasily for exploiting his father's name. 'But I'm a Stalin too,' said Vasily.

'No, you're not,' replied Stalin. 'You're not Stalin and I'm not Stalin. Stalin is Soviet power. Stalin is what he is in the newspapers and the portraits, not you, no not even me!'

He was a self-creation. A man who invents his name, birthday, nationality, education and his entire past, in order to change history and play the role of leader, is likely to end up in a mental institution, unless he embraces, by will, luck and skill, the movement and the moment that can overturn the natural order of things. Stalin was such a man. The movement was the Bolshevik Party; his moment, the decay of the Russian monarchy.

After Stalin's death, it was fashionable to regard him as an aberration but this was to rewrite history as crudely as Stalin did himself. Stalin's success was not an accident. No one alive was more suited to the conspiratorial intrigues, theoretical runes, murderous dogmatism and inhuman sternness of Lenin's Party. It is hard to find a better synthesis between a man and a movement than the ideal marriage between Stalin and Bolshevism: he was a mirror of its virtues and faults.

* * *

Nadya was excited because she was dressing up. Only the day before at the Revolution Day parade, her headaches had been agonizing but today she was cheerful. Just as the real Stalin was different from his historical persona, so was the real Nadezhda Alliluyeva. 'She was very beautiful but you can't see it in photographs,' recalls Artyom Sergeev. She was not conventionally pretty. When she smiled, her eyes radiated honesty and sincerity but she was also po-faced, aloof and troubled by mental and physical illnesses. Her coldness was periodically shattered by attacks of hysteria and depression. She was chronically jealous. Unlike Stalin, who had a hangman's wit, no one recalls Nadya's sense of humour. She was a Bolshevik, quite capable of acting as Stalin's snitch, denouncing enemies to him. So was this the marriage of an ogre and a lamb, a metaphor for Stalin's treatment of Russia itself? Only in so much as it was a Bolshevik marriage in every sense, typical of the peculiar culture that spawned it. Yet in another way, this is simply the commonplace tragedy of a callous workaholic who could not have been a worse partner for his self-centred and unbalanced wife.

Stalin's life appeared to be a perfect fusion of Bolshevik politics and family. Despite the brutal war on the peasants and the increasing pressure on the leaders, this time was a happy idyll, a life of country weekends at peaceful dachas, cheerful dinners in the Kremlin, and languid warm holidays on the Black Sea that Stalin's children would remember as the happiest of their lives. Stalin's letters reveal a difficult but loving marriage:

'Hello, Tatka ... I miss you so much Tatochka – I'm as lonely as a horned owl,' Stalin wrote to Nadya, using his affectionate nickname for her, on 21 June 1930. 'I'm not going out of town on business. I'm just finishing up my work and then I'm going out of town to the children tomorrow ... So goodbye, don't be too long, come home sooner! My kisses! Your Joseph.' Nadya was away taking treatment for her headaches in Carlsbad, Germany. Stalin missed her and was keeping an eye on the children, like any other husband. On another occasion, she finished her letter:

'I ask you so much to look after yourself! I am kissing you passionately just as you kissed me when we were saying goodbye! Your Nadya.'

It was never an easy relationship. They were both passionate and thin-skinned: their rows were always dramatic. In 1926, she took the children to Leningrad, saying she was leaving him. But he begged her to return and she did. One feels these sorts of rows were frequent but there were intervals of a kind of happiness, though cosiness was too much to hope for in such a Bolshevik household. Stalin was often aggressive and insulting but it was probably his detachment that made him hardest to live with. Nadya was proud and severe but always ailing. If his comrades like Molotov and Kaganovich thought her on the verge of 'madness', her own family admit that she was 'sometimes crazed and oversensitive, all the Alliluyevs had unstable Gypsy blood.' The couple were similarly impossible. Both were selfish, cold with fiery tempers though she had none of his cruelty and duplicity. Perhaps they were too similar to be happy. All the witnesses agree that life with Stalin was 'not easy – it was a hard life.' It was 'not a perfect marriage', Polina Molotova told the Stalins' daughter Svetlana, 'but then what marriage is?'

After 1929, they were often apart since Stalin holidayed in the south during the autumn when Nadya was still studying. Yet the happy times were warm and loving: their letters fly back and forth with secret-police couriers and the notes follow each other in such quick succession that they resemble emails. Even among these ascetic Bolsheviks, there were hints of sex: the 'very passionate kisses' she recalled in her letter quoted above. They loved each other's company: as we have seen, he missed her bitterly when she was away and she missed him too. 'It's very boring without you,' she wrote. 'Come up here and it'll be nice together.'

They shared Vasily and Svetlana. 'Write anything about the children,' wrote Stalin from the Black Sea. When she was away, he reported: 'The children are good. I don't like the teacher, she's running round the place and she lets Vasya and Tolika [their adopted son, Artyom] rush around morning till night. I'm sure Vaska's studies will fail and I want them to succeed in German.' She often enclosed Svetlana's childish notes. They shared their health worries like any couple. When Stalin was taking the cure at the Matsesta Baths near Sochi, he reported to her: 'I've had two baths and I will have ten ... I think we'll be seriously better.'

'How's your health?' she inquired.

'Had an echo on my lungs and a cough,' he replied. His teeth were a perennial problem:

'Your teeth – please have them treated,' she told him. When she took a cure in Carlsbad, he asked caringly: 'Did you visit the doctors – write their opinions!' He missed her but if the treatment took longer, he understood.

Stalin did not like changing his clothes and wore summer suits into winter so she always worried about him: 'I send you a greatcoat because after the south, you might get a cold.' He sent her presents too: 'I'm sending you some lemons,' he wrote proudly. 'You'll like them.' This keen gardener was to enjoy growing lemons until his death.

They gossiped about the friends and comrades they saw: 'I heard Gorky [the famous novelist] came to Sochi,' she wrote. 'Maybe he's visiting you – what a pity without me. He's so charming to listen to ...' And of course, as a Bolshevik handmaiden living in that minuscule wider family of magnates and their wives, she was almost as obsessed about politics as he was, passing on what Molotov or Voroshilov told her. She sent him books and he thanked her but grumbled when one was missing. She teased him about his appearances in White émigré literature.

The austerely modest Nadya was not afraid of giving orders herself. She scolded her husband's saturnine *chef de cabinet* Poskrebyshev while on holiday, complaining that 'we didn't receive any new foreign literature. But they say there are some new ones. Maybe you will talk to Yagoda [Deputy GPU boss] ... Last time we received such uninteresting books ...' When she returned from the vacation, she sent Stalin the photographs: 'Only the good ones – doesn't Molotov look funny?' He later teased the absurdly stolid Molotov in front of Churchill and Roosevelt. He sent her back his own holiday photographs.

However by the late twenties, Nadya was professionally discontented. She wanted to be a serious Bolshevik career woman in her own right. In the early twenties, she had done typing for her husband, then Lenin and then for Sergo Ordzhonikidze, another energetic and passionate Georgian dynamo now responsible for Heavy Industry. Then she moved to the

International Agrarian Institute in the Department of Agitation and Propaganda where, lost in the archives, we find the daily work of Stalin's wife in all its Bolshevik dreariness: her boss asks his ordinary assistant, who signs herself 'N. Alliluyeva', to arrange the publication of a shockingly tedious article entitled 'We Must Study the Youth Movement in the Village'.

'I have absolutely nothing to do with anyone in Moscow,' she grumbled. 'It's strange though I feel closer to non-Party people – women of course. The reason is they're more easy going ... There are a terrible lot of new prejudices. If you don't work, you're just a *baba*!'* She was right. The new Bolshevik women such as Polina Molotova were politicians in their own right. These feminists scorned housewives and typists like Nadya. But Stalin did not want such a wife for himself: his Nadya would be what he called a *'baba'*. In 1929, Nadya decided to become a powerful Party woman in her own right and did not go on holiday with her husband but remained in Moscow for her examinations to enter the Industrial Academy to study synthetic fibres, hence her loving correspondence with Stalin. Education was one of the great Bolshevik achievements and there were millions like her. Stalin really wanted a *baba* but he supported her enterprise: ironically, his instincts may have been right because it became clear that she was really not strong enough to be a student, mother and Stalin's wife simultaneously. He often signed off:

'How are the exams? Kiss my Tatka!' Molotov's wife became a People's Commissar – and there was every reason for Nadya to hope she would do the same.

* * *

Across the Kremlin, the magnates and their wives converged on Voroshilov's apartment, oblivious of the tragedy about to befall Stalin and Nadya. None of them had far to come. Ever since Lenin had moved the capital to Moscow in 1918, the leaders had lived in this isolated secret world, behind walls thirteen feet thick, crenellated burgundy battlements and towering fortified gates, which, more than anything, resembled a 64-acre theme park of the history of old Muscovy. 'Here Ivan the Terrible used to walk,' Stalin told visitors. He daily passed the Archangel Cathedral

---

* She certainly cared for Stalin like a good *baba*: 'Stalin has to have a chicken diet,' she wrote to President Kalinin in 1921. 'We've only been allocated 15 chickens ... Please raise the quota since it's only halfway through the month and we've only got 5 left ...'

where Ivan the Terrible lay buried, the Ivan the Great Tower, and the Yellow Palace, where he worked, had been built for Catherine the Great: by 1932, Stalin had lived fourteen years in the Kremlin, as long as he had in his parental home.

These potentates – the 'responsible workers' in Bolshevik terminology – and their staff, the 'service workers', lived in high-ceilinged, roomy apartments once occupied by Tsarist governors and major-domos, mainly in the Poteshny* or Horse Guards, existing so closely in these spired and domed courtyards that they resembled dons living in an Oxford college: Stalin was always popping into their homes and the other leaders regularly turned up at his place for a chat, almost to borrow the proverbial cup of sugar.

Most of the guests only needed to walk along the corridor to get to the second floor apartment of Kliment Voroshilov and his wife Ekaterina in the Horse Guards (nominally the Red Guards Building but no one called it that). Their home was reached through a door in the archway that contained the little cinema where Stalin and his friends often decamped after dinner. Inside it was cosy but spacious, with dark wood-panelled rooms looking out over the Kremlin walls into the city. Voroshilov, their host, aged fifty-two, was the most popular hero in the Bolshevik pantheon – a genial and swaggering cavalryman, once a lathe turner, with an elegant, almost d'Artagnanish moustache, fair hair and cherubic rosy-cheeked face. Stalin would have arrived with the priggish Molotov and the debauched Kuibyshev. Molotov's wife, the dark and formidable Polina, always finely dressed, came from her own flat in the same building. Nadya crossed the lane from the Poteshny with her sister Anna.

In 1932, there would have been no shortage of food and drink but these were the days before Stalin's dinners became imperial banquets. The food – Russian *hors d'oeuvres*, soup, various dishes of salted fish and maybe some lamb – was cooked in the Kremlin canteen and brought hot up to the flat where it was served by a housekeeper, and washed down with vodka and Georgian wine in a parade of toasts. Faced with unparalleled disaster in the regions where ten million people were starving, conspiracy in his Party, uncertain of the loyalty of his own entourage – and with the added strain of a troubled wife, Stalin felt beleaguered and at war.

---

* The Poteshny Palace, where the Stalins lived, means 'Amusement Palace' since it once housed actors and a theatre maintained by the Tsars.

Like the others at the centre of this whirlwind, he needed to drink and unwind. Stalin sat in the middle of the table, never at the head, and Nadya sat opposite him.

* * *

During the week, the Stalin household was based in the Kremlin apartment. The Stalins had two children, Vasily, eleven, a diminutive, stubborn and nervous boy, and Svetlana, seven, a freckly red-haired girl. Then there was Yakov, now twenty-five, son of Stalin's first marriage, who had joined his father in 1921, having been brought up in Georgia, a shy, dark boy with handsome eyes. Stalin found Yakov irritatingly slow. When he was eighteen, he had fallen in love with, and married, Zoya, a priest's daughter. Stalin did not approve because he wanted Yasha to study. In a 'cry for help', Yasha shot himself but only grazed his chest. Stalin regarded this 'as blackmail'. The stern Nadya disapproved of Yasha's self-indulgence: 'she was so appalled by Yasha,' Stalin mused. But he was even less sympathetic.

'Couldn't even shoot straight,' he quipped cruelly. 'This was his military humour,' explains Svetlana. Yasha later divorced Zoya, and came home.

Stalin had high, and given his own meteoric success, unfair expectations of the sons – but he adored his daughter. In addition to these three, there was Artyom Sergeev, Stalin's beloved adopted son, who was often in their house, even though his mother was still alive.* Stalin was more indulgent than Nadya, even though he smacked Vasily 'a couple of times'. Indeed, this woman portrayed as angelic in every history was, in her way, even more self-centred than Stalin. Her own family regarded her as 'utterly self-indulgent', recalls her nephew Vladimir Redens. 'The nanny complained that Nadya was not remotely interested in the children.' Her daughter Svetlana agreed that she was much more committed to her studies. She treated the children sternly and never gave Svetlana a 'word of praise'. It is surprising that she rowed most with Stalin, not about his evil policies, but about his spoiling the children!

---

* One of the few attractive traditions of Bolshevism was the adoption of the children of fallen heroes and ordinary orphans. Stalin adopted Artyom when his father, a famous revolutionary, was killed in 1921 and his mother was ill. Similarly Mikoyan adopted the sons of Sergei Shaumian, the hero of Baku; Voroshilov adopted the son of Mikhail Frunze, the War Commissar who died suspiciously in 1925. Later both Kaganovich and Yezhov, harsh men indeed, adopted orphans.

Yet it is harsh to blame her for this. Her medical report, preserved by Stalin in his archive, and the testimonies of those who knew her, confirm that Nadya suffered from a serious mental illness, perhaps hereditary manic depression or borderline personality disorder though her daughter called it 'schizophrenia', and a disease of the skull that gave her migraines. She needed special rest cures in 1922 and 1923 as she experienced 'drowsiness and weakness'. She had had an abortion in 1926 which, her daughter revealed, had caused 'female problems'. Afterwards she had no periods for months on end. In 1927, doctors discovered her heart had a defective valve – and she suffered from exhaustion, angina and arthritis. In 1930, the angina struck again. Her tonsils had recently been taken out. The trip to Carlsbad did not cure her mysterious headaches.

She did not lack for medical care – the Bolsheviks were as obsessively hypochondriacal as they were fanatically political. Nadya was treated by the best doctors in Russia and Germany. But these were not psychiatrists: it is hard to imagine a worse environment for a fragile girl than the cruel aridity of this Kremlin pressure-cooker pervaded by the martial Bolshevism that she so worshipped – and the angry thoughtlessness of Stalin whom she so revered.

She was married to a demanding egotist incapable of giving her, or probably anyone, happiness: his relentless energy seemed to suck her dry. But she was also patently the wrong person for him. She did not soothe his stress – she added to it. He admitted he was baffled by Nadya's mental crises. He simply did not possess the emotional resources to help her. Sometimes her 'schizophrenia' was so grievous, 'she was almost deranged'. The magnates, and the Alliluyevs themselves, sympathized with Stalin. Yet, despite their turbulent marriage and their strange similarity of passion and jealousy, they loved each other after their own fashion.

After all, it was Stalin for whom Nadya was dressing up. The 'black dress with rose pattern appliqué ...' had been bought as a present for her by her brother, slim brown-eyed Pavel Alliluyev who had just returned with his usual treasure chest of gifts from Berlin, where he worked for the Red Army. With Nadya's proud Gypsy, Georgian, Russian and German blood, the rose looked striking against her jet-black hair. Stalin would be surprised because, as her nephew put it, he 'never encouraged her to dress more glamorously'.

* * *

The drinking at dinner was heavy, regulated by a *tamada* (Georgian toastmaster). This was probably one of the Georgians such as the flamboyant Grigory Ordzhonikidze, always known as Sergo, who resembled 'a Georgian prince' with his mane of long hair and leonine face. Some time during the evening, without any of the other revellers noticing, Stalin and Nadya became angry with one another. This was hardly a rare occurrence. Her evening began to crumble when, among all the toasts, dancing and flirting at table, Stalin barely noticed how she had dressed up, even though she was one of the youngest women present. This was certainly ill-mannered but not uncommon in many marriages.

They were surrounded by the other Bolshevik magnates, all hardened by years in the underground, blood-spattered by their exploits in the Civil War, and now exultant if battered by the industrial triumphs and rural struggles of the Stalin Revolution. Some, like Stalin, were in their fifties. But most were strapping, energetic fanatics in their late thirties, some of the most dynamic administrators the world has ever seen, capable of building towns and factories against all odds, but also of slaughtering their enemies and waging war on their own peasants. In their tunics and boots, they were macho, hard-drinking, powerful and famous across the Imperium, stars with blazing egos, colossal responsibilities, and Mausers in their holsters. The boisterous, booming and handsome Jewish cobbler, Lazar Kaganovich, Stalin's Deputy, had just returned from presiding over mass-executions and deportations in the North Caucasus. Then there was the swaggering Cossack commander Budyonny with his luxuriant walrus moustaches and the dazzling white teeth, and the slim, shrewd and dapper Armenian Mikoyan, all veterans of brutal expeditions to raise grain and crush the peasants. These were voluble, violent and colourful political showmen.

They were an incestuous family, a web of long friendships and enduring hatreds, shared love affairs, Siberian exiles and Civil War exploits: Mikhail Kalinin, the President, had been visiting the Alliluyevs since 1900. Nadya knew Voroshilov's wife from Tsaritsyn (later Stalingrad) and she studied at the Industrial Academy with Maria Kaganovich and Dora Khazan (wife of another magnate, Andreyev, also present), her best friends along with Polina Molotova. Finally there was the small intellectual Nikolai Bukharin, all twinkling eyes and reddish beard, a painter, poet and philosopher whom Lenin had once called the 'darling of the Party' and who had been Stalin and Nadya's closest friend. He was a charmer, the Puck of the Bolsheviks. Stalin had defeated him in 1929 but he remained friends with Nadya. Stalin himself half-loved and half-hated 'Bukharchik' in that deadly combination of admiration and envy that was habitual to him. That night, Bukharin was readmitted, at least temporarily, to the magic circle.

Irritated by Stalin's lack of attention, Nadya started dancing with her louche, sandy-haired Georgian godfather, 'Uncle Abel' Yenukidze, the official in charge of the Kremlin who was already shocking the Party with his affairs with teenage ballerinas. 'Uncle Abel's' fate would illustrate the deadly snares of hedonism when private life belonged to the Party. Perhaps Nadya was trying to make Stalin angry. Natalya Rykova, who was in the Kremlin that night with her father, the former Premier, but not at the dinner, heard the next day that Nadya's dancing infuriated Stalin. The story is certainly credible because other accounts mention her flirting with someone. Perhaps Stalin was so drunk, he did not even notice.

* * *

Stalin was busy with his own flirtation. Even though Nadya was opposite him, he flirted shamelessly with the 'beautiful' wife of Alexander Yegorov, a Red Army commander with whom he had served in the Polish War of 1920. Galya Yegorova, née Zekrovskaya, thirty-four, was a brash film actress, a 'pretty, interesting and charming' brunette well known for her affairs and risqué dresses. Among those drab Bolshevik matrons, Yegorova must have been like a peacock in a farmyard for, as she herself admitted in her later interrogation, she moved in a world of 'dazzling company, stylish clothes … flirtatiousness, dancing and fun'. Stalin's style of flirting alternated between traditional Georgian chivalry and, when drunk, puerile boorishness. On this occasion, the latter triumphed. Stalin always entertained children by throwing biscuits, orange peel and bits of bread into plates of ice-cream or cups of tea. He flirted with the actress in the same way, lobbing breadballs at her. His courtship of Yegorova made Nadya manically jealous: she could not tolerate it.

Stalin was no womanizer: he was married to Bolshevism and emotionally committed to his own drama in the cause of Revolution. Any private emotions were bagatelles compared to the betterment of mankind through Marxism-Leninism. But even if they were low on his list of priorities, even if he was emotionally damaged, he was not uninterested in women – and women were definitely interested in him, even 'enamoured' according to Molotov. One of his entourage later said that Stalin complained that the Alliluyev women 'would not leave him alone' because 'they all wanted to go to bed with him'. There was some truth in this.

Whether they were the wives of comrades, relations or servants, women buzzed around him like amorous bees. His newly opened archives reveal how he was bombarded with fan letters not unlike those received by modern pop stars. 'Dear Comrade Stalin ... I saw you in my dreams ... I have hopes of an audience ...' writes a provincial teacher, adding hopefully like a starry-eyed groupie: 'I enclose my photograph ...' Stalin replied playfully if negatively:

'Comrade Unfamiliar! I ask you to trust that I have no wish to disappoint you and I'm ready to respect your letter but I have to say I have no appointment (no time!) to satisfy your wish. I wish you all the best. J Stalin. PS Your letter and photograph returned.' But sometimes he must have told Poskrebyshev that he would be happy to meet his admirers. This gels with the story of Ekaterina Mikulina, an attractive, ambitious girl of twenty-three who wrote a treatise, 'Socialist Competition of Working People', which she sent to Stalin, admitting it was full of mistakes and asking for his help. He invited her to visit him on 10 May 1929. He liked her and it was said she stayed the night at the dacha in Nadya's absence.* She received no benefits from this short liaison other than the honour of his writing her preface.

Certainly, Nadya, who knew him best, suspected him of having affairs and she had every reason to know. His bodyguard Vlasik confirmed to his daughter that Stalin was so besieged with offers that he could not resist everyone: 'he was a man after all,' behaving with the seigneurial sensuality of a traditional Georgian husband. Nadya's jealousy was sometimes manic, sometimes indulgent: in her letters, she lovingly teased him about his female admirers as if she was proud of being married to such a great man. But at the theatre, she had recently ruined the evening by throwing a tantrum when he flirted with a ballerina. Most recently, there was the female hairdresser in the Kremlin with

---

* She later became director of a gramophone factory from which she was sacked many years later for taking bribes. She lived until 1998 but never spoke about her short friendship with Stalin.

whom Stalin was evidently conducting some sort of dalliance. If he had merely visited the barber's shop like the other leaders, this anonymous girl would not have become such an issue. Yet Molotov remembered the hairdresser fifty years later.

Stalin had had his share of affairs within the Party. His relationships were as short as his spells in exile. Most of the girlfriends were fellow revolutionaries or their wives. Molotov was impressed by Stalin's 'success' with women: when, just before the Revolution, Stalin stole a girlfriend named Marusya from Molotov, the latter put it down to his 'beautiful dark brown eyes', though luring a girlfriend away from this plodder hardly qualifies Stalin as a Casanova. Kaganovich confirmed that Stalin enjoyed affairs with several comrades including the 'plump, pretty' Ludmilla Stal.* One source mentions an earlier affair with Nadya's friend Dora Khazan. Stalin may have benefited from revolutionary sexual freedom, even in his diffident way, enjoying some success with the girls who worked on the Central Committee secretariat, but he remained a traditional Caucasian. He favoured liaisons with discreet GPU staff: the hairdresser fitted the bill.

As so often with jealousy, Nadya's manic tantrums and bouts of depression encouraged the very thing she dreaded. All of these things – her illness, disappointment about her dress, politics, jealousy and Stalin's oafishness – came together that night.

* * *

Stalin was unbearably rude to Nadya but historians, in their determination to show his monstrosity, have ignored how unbearably rude she was to him. This 'peppery woman', as Stalin's security chief, Pauker, described her, frequently shouted at Stalin in public which was why her own mother thought her a 'fool'. The cavalryman Budyonny, who was at the dinner, remembered how she was 'always nagging and humiliating' Stalin. 'I don't know how he puts up with it,' Budyonny confided in his wife. By now her depression had become so bad that she confided in a friend that she was sick of 'everything, even the children'.

The lack of interest of a mother in her own children is a flashing danger signal if ever there was one, but there was no one to act on

---

* Another of his sweethearts was a young Party activist, Tatiana Slavotinskaya. The warmth of his love-letters from exile increased in proportion to his material needs: 'Dearest darling Tatiana Alexandrovna,' he wrote in December 1913, 'I received your parcel but you really didn't need to buy new undergarments … I don't know how to repay you, my darling sweetheart!'

it. Stalin was not the only one puzzled by her. Few of this rough-hewn circle, including Party women like Polina Molotova, understood that Nadya was probably suffering from clinical depression: 'she couldn't control herself,' said Molotov. She desperately needed sympathy. Polina Molotova admitted the *Vozhd* was 'rough' with Nadya. Their roller-coaster continued. One moment, she was leaving Stalin, the next they loved each other again.

At the dinner, some accounts claim, it was a political toast that inflamed her. Stalin toasted the destruction of the Enemies of the State and noticed Nadya had not raised her glass.

'Why aren't you drinking?' he called over truculently, aware that she and Bukharin shared a disapproval of his starvation of the peasantry. She ignored him. To get her attention, Stalin tossed orange peel and flicked cigarettes at her, but this outraged her. When she became angrier and angrier, he called over, 'Hey you! Have a drink!'

'My name isn't "hey"!' she retorted. Furiously rising from the table, she stormed out. It was probably now that Budyonny heard her shout at Stalin: 'Shut up! Shut up!'

Stalin shook his head in the ensuing silence:

'What a fool!' he muttered, boozily not understanding how upset she was. Budyonny must have been one of the many there who sympathized with Stalin.

'I wouldn't let my wife talk to me like that!' declared the Cossack bravo who may not have been the best adviser since his own first wife had committed suicide or at least died accidentally while playing with his pistol.

Someone had to follow her out. She was the leader's wife so the deputy leader's wife had to look after her. Polina Molotova pulled on her coat and followed Nadya outside. They walked round and round the Kremlin, as others were to do in times of crisis. Nadya complained to Polina,

'He grumbles all the time ... and why did he have to flirt like that?' She talked about the 'business with the hairdresser' and Yegorova at the dinner. The women decided, as women do, that he was drunk, playing the fool. But Polina, devoted to the Party, also criticized her friend, saying 'it was wrong of her to abandon Stalin at such a difficult time'. Perhaps Polina's '*Partiinost*' – Partymindedness – made Nadya feel even more isolated.

'She quietened down,' recalled Polina, 'and talked about the

Academy and her chances of starting work … When she seemed
perfectly calm', in the early hours, they said goodnight. She left
Nadya at the Poteshny Palace and crossed the lane, home to the
Horse Guards.

Nadya went to her room, dropping the tea rose from her hair at
the door. The dining room, with a special table for Stalin's array
of government telephones, was the main room there. Two halls
led off it. To the right was Stalin's office and small bedroom where
he slept either on a military cot or a divan, the habits of an
itinerant revolutionary. Stalin's late hours and Nadya's strict
attendance at the Academy meant they had separate rooms.
Carolina Til, the housekeeper, the nannies and the servants were
further down this corridor. The left corridor led to Nadya's tiny
bedroom where the bed was draped in her favourite shawls. The
windows opened on to the fragrant roses of the Alexandrovsky
Gardens.

* * *

Stalin's movements in the next two hours are a mystery: did he
return home? The party continued *chez* Voroshilov. But the
bodyguard Vlasik told Khrushchev (who was not at the dinner)
that Stalin left for a rendezvous at his Zubalovo dacha with a
woman named Guseva, the wife of an officer, described by
Mikoyan, who appreciated feminine aesthetics, as 'very beautiful'.
Some of these country houses were just fifteen minutes' drive
from the Kremlin. If he did go, it is possible he took some boon
companions with him when the women went to bed.
Voroshilov's wife was famously jealous of her husband. Molotov
and President Kalinin, an old roué, were mentioned afterwards to
Bukharin by Stalin himself. Certainly Vlasik would have gone
with Stalin in the car. When Stalin did not come home, Nadya is
said to have called the dacha.

'Is Stalin there?'

'Yes,' replied an 'inexperienced fool' of a security guard.

'Who's with him?'

'Gusev's wife.'

This version may explain Nadya's sudden desperation.
However, a resurgence of her migraine, a wave of depression or
just the sepulchral solitude of Stalin's grim apartment in the early
hours, are also feasible. There are holes in the story too: Molotov,
the nanny, and Stalin's granddaughter, among others, insisted
that Stalin slept at home in the apartment. Stalin certainly would

not have entertained women in his Zubalovo dacha because we
know his children were there. But there were plenty of other
dachas. More importantly, no one has managed to identify this
Guseva, though there were several army officers of that name.
Moreover Mikoyan never mentioned this to his children or in his
own memoirs. Prim Molotov may have been protecting Stalin in
his conversations in old age – he lied about many other matters,
as did Khrushchev, dictating his reminiscences in his dotage. It
seems more likely that if this woman was the 'beautiful' wife of a
soldier, it was Yegorova who was actually at the party and whose
flirting caused the row in the first place.

We will never know the truth but there is no contradiction
between these accounts: Stalin probably did go drinking at a
dacha with some fellow carousers, maybe Yegorova, and he
certainly returned to the apartment in the early hours. The fates
of these magnates and their women would soon depend on their
relationship with Stalin. Many of them would die terrible deaths
within five years. Stalin never forgot the part they each played
that November night.

* * *

Nadya looked at one of the many presents that her genial brother
Pavel had brought back from Berlin along with the black
embroidered dress she was still wearing. This was a present she
had requested because, as she told her brother, 'sometimes it's so
scary and lonely in the Kremlin with just one soldier on duty'. It
was an exquisite lady's pistol in an elegant leather holster. This is
always described as a Walther but in fact it was a Mauser. It is little
known that Pavel also brought an identical pistol as a present for
Polina Molotova but pistols were not hard to come by in that
circle.

Whenever Stalin came home, he did not check his wife but
simply went to bed in his own bedroom on the other side of the
apartment.

Some say Nadya bolted the bedroom door. She began to write a
letter to Stalin, 'a terrible letter', thought her daughter Svetlana.
In the small hours, somewhere between 2 and 3 a.m. when she
had finished it, she lay on the bed.

* * *

The household rose as normal. Stalin always lay in until about
eleven. No one knew when he had come home and whether he
had encountered Nadya. It was late when Carolina Til tried

Nadya's door and perhaps forced it open. 'Shaking with fright', she found her mistress's body on the floor by the bed in a pool of blood. The pistol was beside her. She was already cold. The housekeeper rushed to get the nanny. They returned and laid the body on the bed before debating what to do. Why did they not waken Stalin? 'Little people' have a very reasonable aversion to breaking bad news to their Tsars. 'Faint with fear', they telephoned the security boss Pauker, then 'Uncle' Abel Yenukidze, Nadya's last dancing partner, the politician in charge of the Kremlin, and Polina Molotova, the last person to see her alive. Yenukidze, who lived in Horse Guards like the others, arrived first – he alone of the leaders viewed the pristine scene, a knowledge for which he would pay dearly. Molotov and Voroshilov arrived minutes later.

One can only imagine the frantic uproar in the apartment as the oblivious ruler of Russia slept off his drink down one corridor while his wife slept eternally down the other. They also called Nadya's family – her brother Pavel, who lived across the river in the new House on the Embankment, and parents, Sergei and Olga Alliluyev. Someone called the family's personal doctor who in turn summoned the well-known Professor Kushner.

Peering at her later, this disparate group of magnates, family and servants, searching for reasons for this act of despair and betrayal, found the angry letter she left behind. No one knows what it contained – or whether it was destroyed by Stalin or someone else. But Stalin's bodyguard, Vlasik, later revealed that something else was found in her bedroom: a copy of the damaging anti-Stalinist 'Platform', written by Riutin, an Old Bolshevik who was now under arrest. This might be significant or it might mean nothing. All the leaders then read opposition and émigré journals so perhaps Nadya was reading Stalin's copy. In her letters to Stalin, she reported what she had read in the White press 'about you! Are you interested?' None the less, during those days in the country at large, the mere possession of this document warranted arrest.

No one knew what to do. They gathered in the dining room, whispering: should they wake up Stalin? Who would tell the Vozhd? How had she died? Suddenly Stalin himself walked into the room. Someone, most likely it was Yenukidze, Stalin's old friend who judging by the archives had assumed responsibility, stepped forward and said:

'Joseph, Nadezhda Sergeevna is no longer with us. Joseph, Joseph, Nadya's dead.'

Stalin was poleaxed. This supremely political creature, with an inhuman disregard for the millions of starving women and children in his own country, displayed more humanity in the next few days than he would at any other time in his life. Olga, Nadya's mother, an elegant lady of independent spirit who had known Stalin so long and always regretted her daughter's behaviour, hurried into the dining room where a broken Stalin was still absorbing the news. Doctors had arrived and they offered the heartbroken mother some valerian drops, the valium of the thirties, but she could not drink them. Stalin staggered towards her:

'I'll drink them,' he said. He downed the whole dose. He saw the body and the letter which, wrote Svetlana, shocked and wounded him grievously.

Nadya's brother, Pavel, arrived with his dimpled sunny wife Yevgenia, known to all as Zhenya, who would herself play a secret role in Stalin's life – and suffer for it. They were shocked not only by the death of a sister but by the sight of Stalin himself.

'She's crippled me,' he said. They had never seen him so soft, so vulnerable. He wept, saying something like this lament of many years later: 'Oh Nadya, Nadya ... how we needed you, me and the children!' The rumours of murder started immediately. Had Stalin returned to the apartment and shot her in a row? Or had he insulted her again and gone to bed, leaving her to kill herself? But the tragedy raised greater questions too: until that night, the existence of the magnates was a 'wonderful life', as described by Ekaterina Voroshilova in her diary. That night, it ended for ever. 'How,' she asks, 'did our life in the Party become so complex, it was incomprehensible to the point of agony?' The 'agony' was just beginning. The suicide 'altered history,' claims the Stalins' nephew, Leonid Redens. 'It made the Terror inevitable.' Naturally Nadya's family exaggerate the significance of her death: Stalin's vindictive, paranoid and damaged character was already formed long before. The Terror itself was the result of vast political, economic and diplomatic forces – but Stalin's personality certainly shaped it. Nadya's death created one of the rare moments of doubt in a life of iron self-belief and dogmatic certainty. How did Stalin recover and what was the effect of this humiliation on him, his entourage – and Russia itself? Did vengeance for this personal fiasco play its part in the coming Terror when some of the guests that night would liquidate the others?

Stalin suddenly picked up Nadya's pistol and weighed it in his hands: 'It was a toy,' he told Molotov, adding strangely, 'It was only fired once a year!'

The man of steel 'was in a shambles, knocked sideways', exploding in 'sporadic fits of rage', blaming anyone else, even the books she was reading, before subsiding into despair. Then he declared that he resigned from power. He too was going to kill himself:

'I can't go on living like this ...'

Part One

That Wonderful Time:
Stalin and Nadya, 1878–1932

1

The Georgian and the Schoolgirl

Nadya and Stalin had been married for fourteen years but it extended deeper and longer than that, so steeped was their marriage in Bolshevism. They had shared the formative experiences of the underground life, intimacy with Lenin during the Revolution, then the Civil War. Stalin had known her family for nearly thirty years and he had first met her in 1904 when she was three. He was then twenty-five and he had been a Marxist for six years.

Joseph Vissarionovich Djugashvili was not born on 21 December 1879, Stalin's official birthday. 'Soso' was actually born in a tiny shack (that still exists) to Vissarion or 'Beso' and his wife Ekaterina, 'Keke', née Geladze, over a year earlier on 6 December 1878. They lived in Gori, a small town beside the Kura River in the romantic, mountainous and defiantly unRussian province of Georgia, a small country thousands of miles from the Tsar's capital: it was closer to Baghdad than St Petersburg.* Westerners often do not realize how foreign Georgia was: an independent kingdom for millennia with its own ancient language, traditions, cuisine, literature, it was only consumed by Russia in gulps between 1801 and 1878. With its sunny climate, clannish blood feuds, songs and vineyards, it resembles Sicily more than Siberia.

Soso's father was a violent, drunken semi-itinerant cobbler who savagely beat both Soso and Keke. She in turn, as the child later recalled, 'thrashed him mercilessly'. Soso once threw a dagger at his father. Stalin reminisced how Beso and Father

---

* This was not lost on another peasant boy who was born only a few hundred miles from Gori: Saddam Hussein. A Kurdish leader, Mahmoud Osman, who negotiated with him, observed that Saddam's study and bedroom were filled with books on Stalin. Today, Stalin's birthplace, the hut in Gori, is embraced magnificently by a white-pillared marble temple built by Lavrenti Beria and remains the centrepiece of Stalin Boulevard, close to the Stalin Museum.

Charkviani, the local priest, indulged in drinking bouts together to the fury of his mother: 'Father, don't make my husband a drunk, it'll destroy my family.' Keke threw out Beso. Stalin was proud of her 'strong willpower'. When Beso later forcibly took Soso to work as a cobbling apprentice in Tiflis, Keke's priests helped get him back.

She took in washing for local merchants. Stalin's mother was pious and became close to the priests who protected her. But she was also earthy and spicy: she may have made the sort of compromises that are tempting for a penniless single mother, becoming the mistress of her employers. This inspired the legends that often embroider the paternity of famous men. It is possible that Stalin was the child of his godfather, an affluent innkeeper, officer and amateur wrestler named Koba Egnatashvili. After-wards, Stalin protected Egnatashvili's two sons who remained friends until his death and reminisced in old age about Egnatashvili's wrestling prowess. None the less, one sometimes has to admit that great men are the children of their own fathers. Stalin was said to resemble Beso uncannily. Yet he himself once asserted that his father was a priest.

Stalin was born with the second and third toes of his left foot joined. He suffered a pock-marked face from an attack of smallpox and later damaged his left arm, possibly in a carriage accident. He grew up into a sallow, stocky, surly youth with speckled honey-coloured eyes and thick black hair – a *kinto*, Georgian street urchin. He was exceptionally intelligent with an ambitious mother who wanted him to be a priest, perhaps like his real father. Stalin later boasted that he learned to read at five by listening to Father Charkviani teaching the alphabet. The five-year-old then helped Charkviani's thirteen-year-old daughter with her reading.

In 1888, he entered the Gori Church School and then, triumphantly, in 1894, won a 'five rouble scholarship' to the Tiflis Seminary in the Georgian capital. As Stalin later told a confidant, 'My father found out that along with the scholarship, I also earned money (five roubles a month) as a choirboy … and once I went out and saw him standing there:

'"Young man, sir," said Beso, "you've forgotten your father … Give me at least three roubles, don't be as mean as your mother!"

'"Don't shout!" replied Soso. "If you don't leave immediately,

I'll call the watchman!"' Beso slunk away.* He apparently died of cirrhosis of the liver in 1909.

Stalin sometimes sent money to help his mother but henceforth kept his distance from Keke whose dry wit and rough discipline resembled his own. There has been too much cod-psychology about Stalin's childhood but this much is certain: raised in a poor priest-ridden household, he was damaged by violence, insecurity and suspicion but inspired by the local traditions of religious dogmatism, blood-feuding and romantic brigandry. 'Stalin did not like to speak about his parents and childhood' but it is meaningless to over-analyse his psychology. He was emotionally stunted and lacked empathy yet his antennae were supersensitive. He was abnormal but Stalin himself understood that politicians are rarely normal: History, he wrote later, is full of 'abnormal people'.

* * *

The seminary provided his only formal education. This boarding school's catechismic teaching and 'Jesuitical methods' of 'surveillance, spying, invasion of the inner life, the violation of people's feelings' repelled, but impressed, Soso so acutely that he spent the rest of his life refining their style and methods. It stimulated this autodidact's passion for reading but he became an atheist in the first year. 'I got some friends,' he said, 'and a bitter debate started between the believers and us!' He soon embraced Marxism.

In 1899, he was expelled from the seminary, joined the Russian Social Democratic Workers' Party and became a professional revolutionary, adopting the *nom de revolution*, Koba, inspired by the hero of a novel, *The Parricide*, by Alexander Kazbegi, a dashing, vindictive Caucasian outlaw. He combined the 'science' of Marxism with his soaring imagination: he wrote romantic poetry, published in Georgian, before working as a weatherman at the Tiflis Meteorological Institute, the only job he held before becoming one of the rulers of Russia in 1917.

---

* I am grateful to Gela Charkviani for sharing with me the unpublished but fascinating manuscript of the memoirs of his father, Candide Charkviani, First Secretary of the Georgian Party, 1938–51. In old age, Stalin spent hours telling Charkviani about his childhood. Charkviani writes that he tried to find Beso's grave in the Tiflis cemetery but could not. He found photographs meant to show Beso and asked Stalin to identify him but he stated that these did not show his father. It is therefore unlikely that the usual photograph said to show Beso is correct. On Stalin's paternity, the Egnatashvili family emphatically deny that the innkeeper was Stalin's father.

'Koba' was convinced by the universal panacea of Marxism, 'a philosophical system' that suited the obsessive totality of his character. The class struggle also matched his own melodramatic pugnacity. The paranoid secrecy of the intolerant and idiosyncratic Bolshevik culture dovetailed with Koba's own self-contained confidence and talent for intrigue. Koba plunged into the underworld of revolutionary politics that was a seething, stimulating mixture of conspiratorial intrigue, ideological nitpicking, scholarly education, factional games, love affairs with other revolutionaries, police infiltration and organizational chaos. These revolutionaries hailed from every background – Russians, Armenians, Georgians and Jews, workers, noblemen, intellectuals and daredevils – and organized strikes, printing presses, meetings and heists. United in the obsessional study of Marxist literature, there was always a division between the educated bourgeois émigrés, like Lenin himself, and the rough men of action in Russia itself. The underground life, always itinerant and dangerous, was the formative experience not only of Stalin but of all his comrades. This explains much that happens later.

In 1902, Koba won the spurs of his first arrest and Siberian exile, the first of seven such exiles from which he escaped six times. These exiles were far from Stalin's brutal concentration camps: the Tsars were inept policemen. They were almost reading holidays in distant Siberian villages with one part-time gendarme on duty, during which revolutionaries got to know (and hate) each other, corresponded with their comrades in Petersburg or Vienna, discussed abstruse questions of dialectical materialism, and had affairs with local girls. When the call of freedom or revolution became urgent, they escaped, yomping across the taiga to the nearest train. In exile, Koba's teeth, a lifelong source of pain, began to deteriorate.

Koba avidly supported Vladimir Lenin and his seminal work, *What Is To Be Done?* This domineering political genius combined the Machiavellian practicality of seizing power, with mastery of Marxist ideology. Exploiting the schism that would lead to the creation of his own Bolshevik Party, Lenin's message was that a supreme Party of professional revolutionaries could seize power for the workers and then rule in their name in a 'dictatorship of the proletariat' until this was no longer necessary because socialism had been achieved. Lenin's vision of the Party as 'the advance detachment' of the 'army of proletarians ... a fighting group of leaders' set the militarist tone of Bolshevism.

In 1904, on Koba's return to Tiflis, he met his future father-in-law Sergei Alliluyev, twelve years his senior, a skilled Russian electrical artisan married to Olga Fedorenko, a strong-willed Georgian-German-Gypsy beauty with a taste for love affairs with revolutionaries, Poles, Hungarians, even Turks. It was whispered that Olga had an affair with the young Stalin who fathered his future wife, Nadya. This is false since Nadezhda was already three when her parents first met Koba, but his affair with Olga is entirely credible and he himself may have hinted at it. Olga, who, according to her granddaughter Svetlana, had a 'weakness for southern men', saying 'Russian men are boors,' always had a 'soft spot' for Stalin. Her marriage was difficult. Family legend has Nadya's elder brother Pavel seeing his mother making up to Koba. Such short liaisons were everyday occurrences among revolutionaries.

Long before they fell in love, Stalin and Nadya were part of the Bolshevik family who passed through the Alliluyev household: Kalinin and Yenukidze among others at that dinner in 1932. There was another special link: soon afterwards Koba met the Alliluyevs in Baku, and saved Nadya from drowning in the Caspian Sea, a romantic bond if ever there was one.

* * *

Koba meanwhile married another sprig of a Bolshevik family. Ekaterina, 'Kato', a placid, darkly pretty Georgian daughter of a cultured family, was the sister of Alexander Svanidze, also a Bolshevik graduate of Tiflis seminary who joined Stalin's Kremlin entourage. Living in a hut near the Baku oilfields, Kato gave him a son, Yakov. But Koba's appearances at home were sporadic and unpredictable.

During the 1905 Revolution, in which Leon Trotsky, a Jewish journalist, bestrode the Petersburg Soviet, Koba claimed he was organizing peasant revolts in the Kartli region of Georgia. After the Tsarist backlash, he travelled to a Bolshevik conference in Tammerfors, Finland – his first meeting with his hero, Lenin, 'that mountain eagle'. The next year, Koba travelled to the Congress in Stockholm. On his return, he lived the life of a Caucasian brigand, raising Party funds in bank robberies or 'expropriations': he boasted in old age of these 'heists ... our friends grabbed 250,000 roubles in Yerevan Square!'

After visiting London for a Congress, Koba's beloved, half-ignored Kato died 'in his arms' in Tiflis of tuberculosis on 25 November 1907. Koba was heartbroken. When the little procession reached the cemetery, Koba pressed a friend's hand and said, 'This creature softened my heart of stone. She died and with her died my last warm feelings for people.' He pressed his heart: 'It's desolate here inside.' Yet he left their son Yakov to be brought up by Kato's family. After hiding in the Alliluyevs' Petersburg apartment, he was recaptured and returned to his place of banishment, Solvychegodsk. It was in this remote one-horse town in January 1910 that Koba moved into the house of a young widow named Maria Kuzakova by whom he fathered a son.*

Soon afterwards, he was involved in a love affair with a school-girl of seventeen named Pelageya Onufrieva. When she went back to school, he wrote: 'Let me kiss you now. I am not simply sending a kiss but am KISSSSSING you passionately (it's not worth kissing otherwise).' The locals in the north russified 'Iosef' to 'Osip' and his letters to Pelageya were often signed by her revealing nickname: 'Oddball Osip'.

* * *

After yet another escape, Koba returned to Petersburg in 1912, sharing digs with a ponderous Bolshevik who was to be the comrade most closely associated with him: Vyacheslav Scriabin, just twenty-two, had just followed the Bolshevik custom of assuming a macho *nom de revolution* and called himself that 'industrial name' Molotov – 'the hammer'. Koba had also assumed an 'industrial' alias: he first signed an article 'Stalin' in 1913. It was no coincidence that 'Stalin' sounds like 'Lenin'. He may have been using it earlier and not just for its metallic grit. Perhaps he borrowed the name from the 'buxom pretty' Bolshevik named Ludmilla Stal with whom he had had an affair.

This 'wonderful Georgian', as Lenin called him, was co-opted by the Party's Central Committee at the end of the Prague conference of 1912. In November, Koba Stalin travelled from Vienna to Cracow to meet Lenin with whom he stayed: the leader

---

* The son Konstantin Kuzakov enjoyed few privileges except that it is said that during the Purges, when he came under suspicion, he appealed to his real father who wrote 'Not to be touched' on his file – but that may be simply because he was the son of a woman who was kind to Stalin in exile. In 1995, after a successful career as a television executive, Kuzakov, in an article headed 'Son of Stalin', announced: 'I was still a child when I learned I was Stalin's son.' There was almost certainly another child from a later exile.

supervised his keen disciple in the writing of an article expressing Bolshevik policy on the sensitive nationality question, henceforth Stalin's expertise. 'Marxism and the National Question', arguing for holding together the Russian Empire, won him ideological kudos and Lenin's trust.

'Did you write all of it?' asked Lenin (according to Stalin).

'Yes ... Did I make mistakes?'

'No, on the contrary, splendid!' This was his last trip abroad until the Teheran Conference in 1943.

In February 1913, Stalin was rearrested and given a suspiciously light exile: was he an agent of the Tsar's secret police, the Okhrana? The historical sensationalism of Stalin's duplicity shows a naïve misunderstanding of underground life: the revolutionaries were riddled with Okhrana spies but many were double or triple agents.* Koba was willing to betray colleagues who opposed him – but, as the Okhrana admitted in their reports, he remained a fanatical Marxist – and that is what mattered.

Stalin's final exile began in 1913 in the distant cold north-east of Siberia, where he was nicknamed 'Pock-marked Joe' by the local peasants. Fearing more escapes, exiles were moved to Kureika, a desolate village in Turukhansk, north of the Arctic Circle where his fishing prowess convinced locals of magical powers and he took another mistress. Stalin wrote pitiful letters to Sergei and Olga Alliluyev: 'Nature in this cursed region is shamefully poor' and he begged them to send him a postcard: 'I'm crazy with longing for nature scenes if only on paper.' Yet it was also strangely a happy time, perhaps the happiest of his life for he reminisced about his exploits there until his death, particularly about the shooting expedition when he skied into the *taiga*, bagged many partridges and then almost froze to death on the way back.

The military blunders and food shortages of the Great War inexorably destroyed the monarchy which, to the surprise of the Bolsheviks, collapsed suddenly in February 1917, replaced by a Provisional Government. On 12 March, Stalin reached the capital

---

* The recent *Secret File of Stalin* by Roman Brackman claims the entire Terror was Stalin's attempt to wipe out anyone with knowledge of his duplicity. Yet there were many reasons for the Terror, though Stalin's character was a major cause. Stalin liquidated many of those who had known him in the early days yet he mysteriously preserved others. He also killed over a million victims who had no knowledge of his early life. However, Brackman also gives an excellent account of the intrigues and betrayals of underground life.

and visited the Alliluyevs: once again, Nadya, a striking brunette, sixteen, her sister Anna and brother Fyodor, questioned this returning hero about his adventures. When they accompanied him by tram towards the offices of the newspaper *Pravda*, he called out,

'Be sure to set aside a room in the new apartment for me. Don't forget.' He found Molotov editing *Pravda*, which job he immediately commandeered for himself. While Molotov had taken a radical anti-Government line, Stalin and Lev Kamenev, né Rosenfeld, one of Lenin's closest comrades, were more conciliatory. Lenin, who arrived on 4 April, overruled Stalin's vacillations. In a rare apology to Molotov, Stalin conceded,

'You were closer to Lenin ...' When Lenin needed to escape to Finland to avoid arrest, Stalin hid him *chez* Alliluyev, shaved off his beard and escorted him to safety. The sisters, Anna, who worked at Bolshevik headquarters, and Nadya waited up at night. The Georgian entertained them, mimicking politicians and reading aloud Chekhov, Pushkin or Gorky, as he would later read to his sons. On 25 October 1917, Lenin launched the Bolshevik Revolution.

* * *

Stalin may have been a 'grey blur' in those days, but he was Lenin's own blur. Trotsky admitted that contact with Lenin was mainly through Stalin because he was of less interest to the police. When Lenin formed the new Government, Stalin founded his Commissariat of Nationalities with one secretary, young Fyodor Alliluyev, and one typist – Nadya.

In 1918, the Bolsheviks struggled for survival. Faced with a galloping German advance, Lenin and Trotsky were forced to make the pragmatic Brest-Litovsk agreement, ceding much of Ukraine and the Baltics to the Kaiser. After Germany's collapse, British, French and Japanese troops intervened while White armies converged on the tottering regime, which moved its capital to Moscow to make it less vulnerable. Lenin's beleaguered Empire soon shrunk to the size of medieval Muscovy. In August, Lenin was wounded in an assassination attempt, avenged by the Bolsheviks in a wave of Terror. In September, Lenin, recovered, declared Russia 'a military camp'. His most ruthless troubleshooters were Trotsky, the War Commissar, creating and directing the Red Army from his armoured train, and Stalin, the only two leaders allowed access without appointment to Lenin's study. When Lenin formed an executive decision-making organ with just five members called the Political Bureau – or Politburo – both were members. The bespectacled Jewish intellectual was the hero of the Revolution, second only to Lenin himself, while Stalin seemed a rough provincial. But Trotsky's patronising grandeur offended the plain-spoken 'old illegals' of the regions who were more impressed with Stalin's hard-nosed practicality. Stalin identified Trotsky as the main obstacle to his rise.

The city of Tsaritsyn played a decisive role in Stalin's career – and his marriage. In 1918, the key strategic city on the Lower Volga, the gateway to the grain (and oil) of the North Caucasus and the southerly key to Moscow, looked as if it was likely to fall to the Whites. Lenin despatched Stalin to Tsaritsyn as Director-General of Food Supplies in south Russia. But the latter soon managed to get his status raised to Commissar with sweeping military powers.

In an armoured train, with 400 Red Guards, Fyodor Alliluyev and his teenage typist Nadya, Stalin steamed into Tsaritsyn on 6 April to find the city beset with ineptitude and betrayal. Stalin showed he meant business by shooting any suspected counter-revolutionaries: 'a ruthless purge of the rear,' wrote Voroshilov, 'administered by an iron hand.' Lenin ordered him to be ever more 'merciless' and 'ruthless'. Stalin replied:

'Be assured our hand will not tremble.' It was here that Stalin grasped the convenience of death as the simplest and most effective political tool but he was hardly alone in this: during the Civil War, the Bolsheviks, clad in leather boots, coats and holsters, embraced a cult of the glamour of violence, a macho brutality that Stalin made his own. It was here too that Stalin met and befriended Voroshilov and Budyonny, both at that dinner on 8 November 1932, who formed the nucleus of his military and political support. When the military situation deteriorated in July, Stalin effectively took control of the army: 'I must have military powers.' This was the sort of leadership the Revolution required to survive but it was a challenge to Trotsky who had created his Red Army with the help of so-called 'military experts', ex-Tsarist officers. Stalin distrusted these useful renegades and shot them whenever possible.

He resided in the plush lounge carriage that had once belonged to a Gypsy torch singer who decorated it in light blue silk. Here Nadya and Stalin probably became lovers. She was seventeen, he

was thirty-nine. It must have been a thrilling, terrifying adventure
for a schoolgirl. When they arrived, Stalin used the train as his
headquarters: it was from here that he ordered the constant
shootings by the Cheka. This was a time when women accompanied their husbands to war: Nadya was not alone. Voroshilov
and Budyonny's wives were in Tsaritsyn too.

Stalin and these swashbucklers formed a 'military opposition'
against Trotsky whom he revealingly called an 'operetta
commander, a chatterbox, ha-ha-ha!' When he arrested a group of
Trotsky's 'specialists' and imprisoned them on a barge on the
Volga, Trotsky angrily objected. The barge sank with all
apparently aboard. 'Death solves all problems,' Stalin is meant to
have said. 'No man, no problem.' It was the Bolshevik way.*

Lenin recalled Stalin. It did not matter that he had probably
made things worse, wasted the expertise of Tsarist officers and
backed a crew of sabre-waving daredevils. Stalin had been ruthless
– the merciless application of pressure was what Lenin wanted.
But the *kinto* had glimpsed the glory of the Generalissimo. More
than that, the enmity with Trotsky and the alliance with the
'Tsaritysn Group' of cavalrymen were seminal: perhaps he
admired Voroshilov and Budyonny's macho devil-may-care
courage, a quality he lacked. His loathing for Trotsky became one
of the moving passions of his life. He married Nadya on his
return, moving into a modest Kremlin flat (shared with the whole
Alliluyev family) and, later, a fine dacha named Zubalovo.

In May 1920, Stalin was appointed Political Commissar to
the South-Western Front after the Poles had captured Kiev. The
Politburo ordered the conquest of Poland to spread the
Revolution westwards. The commander of the Western Front
pushing on Warsaw was a brilliant young man named Mikhail
Tukhachevsky. When Stalin was ordered to transfer his cavalry to
Tukhachevsky, he refused until it was already too late. The
vendettas reverberating from this fiasco ended in slaughter
seventeen years later.

---

* Stalin later seemed to confirm the story of the sinking barge in a fascinating letter
to Voroshilov: 'The summer after the assassination attempt on Lenin we … made a
list of officers whom we gathered in the Manege … to shoot en masse … So the
Tsaritsyn barge was the result not of the struggle against military specialists but
momentum from the centre …' Five future Second World War marshals fought at
Tsaritsyn: in ascending competence – Kulik, Voroshilov, Budyonny, Timoshenko and
Zhukov (though the latter fought there in 1919 after Stalin's departure).

In 1921, Nadya showed her Bolshevik austerity by walking to hospital where she gave birth to a son, Vasily, followed five years later by a daughter, Svetlana. Nadya meanwhile worked as a typist in Lenin's office where she was to prove very useful in the coming intrigues.

* * *

The 'vanguard' of Bolsheviks, many young and now blooded by the brutality of that struggle, found themselves a tiny, isolated and embattled minority nervously ruling a vast ruined Empire, itself besieged in a hostile world. Contemptuous of the workers and peasants, Lenin was none the less surprised to discover that neither of these classes supported them. Lenin thus proposed a single organ to rule and oversee the creation of socialism: the Party. It was this embarrassing gap between reality and aspiration that made the Party's quasi-religious fidelity to ideological purity so important, its military discipline so obligatory.

In this peculiar dilemma, they improvised a peculiar system and sought solace in a uniquely peculiar view of the world. The Party's sovereign organ was the Central Committee (CC), the top seventy or so officials, who were elected annually by Party Congresses which, later, were held ever less frequently. The CC elected the small Politburo, a super-War Cabinet that decided policy, and a Secretariat of about three Secretaries to run the Party. They directed the conventional government of a radically centralized, vertical one-Party State: Mikhail Kalinin, born in 1875, the only real peasant in the leadership known as the 'All-Union peasant elder', became Head of State in 1919.* Lenin ran the country as Premier, the Chairman of the Council of People's Commissars, a cabinet of ministers which executed the Politburo's orders. There was a sort of democracy within the Politburo but after the desperate crises of the Civil War, Lenin banned factions. The Party frantically recruited millions of new members but were they trustworthy? Gradually, an authoritarian bureaucratic dictatorship

* Stalin was never the titular Head of State of the Soviet Union, nor was Lenin. Kalinin's title was the Chairman of the Central Executive Committee, technically the highest legislative body, but he was colloquially the 'President'. After the 1936 Constitution, his title was Chairman of the Presidium of the Supreme Soviet. Only with the Brezhnev Constitution did the Secretary-General of the Party add the Presidency to his titles. The Bolsheviks created a whole new jargon of acronyms in their effort to create a new sort of government. People's Commissars (*Narodny Komissar*) were known as *Narkoms*. The Council (Soviet) of Commissars was known as *Sovnarkom*.

took the place of the honest debates of earlier days but in 1921, Lenin, that superlative improviser, restored a degree of capitalism, a compromise called the New Economic Policy (NEP), to save the regime.

In 1922, Lenin and Kamenev engineered the appointment of Stalin as General Secretary – or *Gensec* – of the CC to run the Party. Stalin's Secretariat was the engine-room of the new state, giving him sweeping powers which he demonstrated in the 'Georgian Affair' when he and Sergo annexed Georgia, which had seceded from the Empire, and then imposed their will on the independent-minded Georgian Party. Lenin was disgusted but his stroke in December 1922 prevented him moving against Stalin. The Politburo, taking control of the health of the Party's greatest asset, banned him from working more than ten minutes a day. When Lenin tried to do more, Stalin insulted Lenin's wife Krupskaya, a tantrum that could have ended his career.*

Lenin alone could see that Stalin was emerging as his most likely successor so he secretly dictated a damning Testament demanding his dismissal. Lenin was felled by a fatal stroke on 21 January 1924. Against the wishes of Lenin and his family, Stalin orchestrated the effective deification of the leader and his embalming like an Orthodox saint in a Mausoleum on Red Square. Stalin commandeered the sacred orthodoxy of his late hero to build up his own power.

An outsider in 1924 would have expected Trotsky to succeed Lenin, but in the Bolshevik oligarchy, this glittery fame counted against the insouciant War Commissar. The hatred between Stalin and Trotsky was not only based on personality and style but also on policy. Stalin had already used the massive patronage of the Secretariat to promote his allies, Molotov, Voroshilov and Sergo; he also supplied an encouraging and realistic alternative to Trotsky's insistence on European revolution: 'Socialism in One Country'. The other members of the Politburo, led by Grigory

---

*Stalin's row with Lenin's wife, Krupskaya, outraged Lenin's bourgeois sentiments. But Stalin thought it was entirely consistent with Party culture: 'Why should I stand on my hindlegs for her? To sleep with Lenin does not mean you understand Marxism-Leninism. Just because she used the same toilet as Lenin ...' This led to some classic Stalin jokes, in which he warned Krupskaya that if she did not obey, the Central Committee would appoint someone else as Lenin's wife. That is a very Bolshevik concept. His disrespect for Krupskaya was probably not helped by her complaints about Lenin's flirtations with his assistants, including Yelena Stasova, the one whom Stalin threatened to promote to 'wife'.

Zinoviev, and Kamenev, Lenin's closest associates, were also terrified of Trotsky, who had united all against himself. So when Lenin's Testament was unveiled in 1924, Kamenev proposed to let Stalin remain as Secretary, little realizing that there would be no other real opportunity to remove him for thirty years. Trotsky, the Revolution's preening panjandrum, was defeated with surprising ease and speed. Having dismissed Trotsky from his powerbase as War Commissar, Zinoviev and Kamenev discovered too late that their co-triumvir Stalin was the real threat.

By 1926, Stalin had defeated them too, helped by his Rightist allies, Nikolai Bukharin and Alexei Rykov, who had succeeded Lenin as Premier. Stalin and Bukharin supported the NEP. But many of the regional hardliners feared that compromise undermined Bolshevism itself, putting off the reckoning day with the hostile peasantry. In 1927, a grain crisis brought this to a head, unleashed the Bolshevik taste for extreme solutions to their problems, and set the country on a repressive martial footing that would last until Stalin's death.

In January 1928, Stalin himself travelled to Siberia to investigate the drop in grain deliveries. Replaying his glorious role as Civil War commissar, Stalin ordered the forcible gathering of grain and blamed the shortage on the so-called kulaks, who were hoarding their harvest in the hope of higher prices. Kulak usually meant a peasant who employed a couple of labourers or owned a pair of cows. 'I gave a good shaking to the Party Organs,' Stalin said later but he soon discovered that 'the Rightists didn't like harsh measures ... they thought it the beginning of civil war in the villages.' On his return, Premier Rykov threatened Stalin: 'Criminal charges should be filed against you!' However the rough young commissars, the 'committee men' at the heart of the Party, supported Stalin's violent requisitioning of grain. Every winter, they headed into the hinterlands to squeeze the grain out of the kulaks who were identified as the main enemies of the revolution. However, they realized the NEP had failed. They had to find a radical, military solution to the food crisis.

Stalin was a natural radical and now he shamelessly stole the clothes of the Leftists he had just defeated. He and his allies were already talking of a final new Revolution, the 'Great Turn' leftwards to solve the problem of the peasantry and economic backwardness. These Bolsheviks hated the obstinate old world of the peasants: they had to be herded into collective farms, their grain forcibly collected and sold abroad to fund a manic gallop to create an instant industrial powerhouse that could produce tanks and planes. Private trade of food was stopped. Kulaks were ordered to deliver their grain and prosecuted as speculators if they did not. Gradually, the villagers themselves were forced into collectives. Anyone who resisted was a kulak enemy.

Similarly, in industry, the Bolsheviks unleashed their hatred of technical experts, or 'bourgeois specialists' – actually just middle-class engineers. While they trained their own new Red élite, they intimidated those who said Stalin's industrial plans were impossible with a series of faked trials that started at the Shakhty coalmine. Nothing was impossible. The resulting rural nightmare was like a war without battles but with death on a monumental scale. Yet the warlords of this struggle, Stalin's magnates and their wives, still lived in the Kremlin like a surprisingly cosy family.

2

The Kremlin Family

'Oh what a wonderful time it was,' wrote Voroshilov's wife in her diary. 'What simple, nice, friendly relationships.' The intimate collegiate life of the leaders up until the mid-thirties could not have been further from the cliché of Stalin's dreary, terrifying world. In the Kremlin, they were always in and out of each other's houses. Parents and children saw each other constantly. The Kremlin was a village of unparalleled intimacy. Bred by decades of fondness (and of course resentments), friendships deepened or frayed, enmities seethed. Stalin often dropped in on his neighbours the Kaganoviches for a chess game. Natasha Andreyeva remembers Stalin frequently putting his head round their door looking for her parents: 'Is Andrei here or Dora Moisevna?' Sometimes he wanted to go to the cinema but her parents were late, so she went with Stalin herself. When Mikoyan needed something, he would simply cross the courtyard and knock on Stalin's door, where he would be invited in for dinner. If he was not at home, they pushed a note under the door. 'Your leaving's most unfortunate,' wrote Voroshilov. 'I called on your apartment and no one answered.'

When Stalin was on holiday, this merry band continually dropped in on Nadya to send her husband messages and catch up on the latest political gossip: 'Yesterday Mikoyan called in and asked after your health and said he'll visit you in Sochi,' Nadya wrote to Stalin in September 1929. 'Today Voroshilov is back from Nalchik and he called me ...' Voroshilov in turn gave her news of Sergo. A few days later, Sergo visited her with Voroshilov. Next she talked to Kaganovich who sent his regards to Stalin. Some families were more private than others: while the Mikoyans were highly sociable, the Molotovs, on the same floor as them, were more reserved and blocked up the door between their apartments. If Stalin was the undoubted headmaster of this chatty, bickering school, then Molotov was its prissy prefect.

* * *

The only man to shake hands with Lenin, Hitler, Himmler, Göring, Roosevelt and Churchill, Molotov was Stalin's closest ally. Nicknamed 'Stone-Arse' for his indefatigable work rate, Molotov liked to correct people ponderously and tell them that Lenin himself had actually given him the soubriquet 'Iron-Arse'. Small, stocky with a bulging forehead, chilling hazel eyes blinking behind round spectacles, and a stammer when angry (or talking to Stalin), Molotov, thirty-nine, looked like a bourgeois student, which he had indeed been. Even among a Politburo of believers, he was a stickler for Bolshevik theory and severity: the Robespierre of Stalin's court. Yet he also possessed an instinct for the possible in power politics: 'I am a man of the Nineteenth Century,' said Molotov.

Born in Kukarla, a provincial backwater near Perm (soon renamed Molotov), Vyacheslav Scriabin was the son of a boozy salesman, a poor nobleman but no relation to the composer. He had played the violin for merchants in his home town and unusually, for Stalin's men, had a glancing secondary education though he became a revolutionary at sixteen. Molotov regarded himself as a journalist – he first met Stalin when they both worked on *Pravda*. He was cruel and vengeful, actually recommending death for those, even women, who crossed him, harsh to his subordinates, with whom he constantly lost his temper, and so disciplined that he would declare to his office that he would take 'a thirteen-minute nap', then wake up on the thirteenth minute. Unlike many of the Politburo's energetic showmen, Molotov was an uninspired 'plodder'.

A candidate Politburo member since 1921, 'our Vecha' had been Party Secretary before Stalin but Lenin denounced Molotov for the 'most shameful bureaucratism, and the most stupid'. When Trotsky attacked him, he revealed the intellectual inferiority complex he shared with Stalin and Voroshilov: 'We can't all be geniuses, Comrade Trotsky,' he replied. The chips on the shoulders of these home-grown Bolsheviks were mountainous.

Now Second Secretary after Stalin himself, Molotov admired Koba but did not worship him. He often disagreed with, and criticized, Stalin right up until the end. He could outdrink anyone in the leadership – no mean feat among so many alcoholics. He seemed to enjoy Stalin's teasing, even when he called him the Jewish 'Molotstein'.

His saving grace was his devotion to Polina Karpovskaya, his Jewish wife, known by her *nom de guerre* Zhemchuzhina, 'the Pearl'. Never beautiful but bold and intelligent, Polina dominated Molotov, worshipped Stalin and became a leader in her own right. Both devoted Bolsheviks, they had fallen in love at a women's conference in 1921. Molotov thought her 'clever, beautiful and above all a great Bolshevik'.

She was the consolation for the discipline, stress and severity of his crusade, yet Molotov was no automaton. His love letters show how he idolized her like a schoolboy in love. 'Polinka, darling, my love! I shan't hide that sometimes I'm overcome with impatience and desire for your closeness and caresses. I kiss you, my beloved, desired ... Your loving Vecha. I'm tied to you body and soul ... my honey.' Sometimes the letters were wildly passionate: 'I wait to kiss you impatiently and kiss you everywhere, adored, sweetie, my love.' She was his 'bright love, my heart and happiness, my pleasure honey, Polinka'.

Molotov's spoiled daughter, Svetlana, and the other Politburo children played in the courtyard but 'we didn't want to live in the Kremlin. We were constantly told by our parents not to be noisy. "You're not in the street now," they'd say. "You're in the Kremlin." It was like a jail and we had to show passes and get passes for our friends to visit us,' remembers Natasha, the daughter of Andreyev and Dora Khazan. The children constantly bumped into Stalin: 'When I was ten with long plaits playing hop, skip and jump with Rudolf Menzhinsky [son of the OGPU chief], I was suddenly lifted up by strong hands and I wriggled round and saw Stalin's face with its brown eyes and very intense, strict expression. "So who are you?" he asked. I said "Andreyeva." "Well, go on jumping then!" Afterwards, Stalin frequently chatted to her, particularly since the Kremlin's earliest cinema was reached by a staircase near their front door.

Often Stalin's dinner was simply a continuation of his meetings with workaholic comrades: soup was placed on the sideboard, guests could help themselves and they frequently worked until 3 a.m., recalls Stalin's adopted son Artyom. 'I saw Molotov, Mikoyan and Kaganovich all the time.' Stalin and Nadya often dined with the other Kremlin couples. 'Dinners were simple,' wrote Mikoyan in his memoirs. 'Two courses, a few starters, sometimes some herring ... Soup for first course then meat or fish and fruit for dessert – it was like anywhere else then.' There was a bottle of white wine and little drinking. No one sat at table for more than half an hour. One evening, Stalin who took a serious interest in political image, emulated Peter the Great's barbering exploits:

'Get rid of that beard!' he ordered Kaganovich, asking Nadya, 'Can I have some scissors? I'll do it myself.'* Kaganovich did it there and then. Such was the entertainment at Stalin and Nadya's for dinner.

The wives were influential. Stalin listened to Nadya: she had met a big-eared rotund young hobbledehoy, a fitter on the mines of the Donets, Khrushchev, at the Academy where he was energetically crushing the opposition. She recommended him to Stalin who launched his career. Stalin regularly had the young official to dinner with Nadya. Stalin always liked Khrushchev, partly because of Nadya's recommendation. This was, remembered Khrushchev, 'how I survived ... my lottery ticket'. He simply could not believe that here was Stalin, the demigod he worshipped, 'laughing and joking' with him so modestly.

Nadya was fearless about approaching Stalin about injustices: when an official, probably a Rightist, was sacked from his job, she pleaded for his career and told Stalin that 'these methods should not be used with such workers ... it's so sad ... He looked as if he'd been killed. I know you really hate me interfering but I think you should interfere in this case which everyone knows is unfair.' Stalin unexpectedly agreed to help and she was thrilled: 'I'm so glad you trust me ... it's a shame not to correct a mistake.' Stalin did not take such interference kindly from anyone else but he seemed to be able to take it from his young wife.

Polina Molotova was so ambitious that, when she decided her boss as Commissar for Light Industry was not up to the job, she asked Stalin during dinner if she could create a Soviet perfume industry. Stalin called in Mikoyan and placed her TeZhe perfume trust under him. She became the Tsarina of Soviet fragrance. Mikoyan admired her as 'capable, clever, and vigorous' but 'haughty'.

* * *

* Of course Kaganovich kept the moustache which remained fashionable. Even facial hair was then based on the leader cult: if a client wanted a goatee with beard and moustache, he would ask his barber for a 'Kalinin' after the Politburo member. When Stalin ordered another leader, Bulganin, to chop off his beard, he compromised by keeping a 'Kalinin' goatee.

Except for the snobbish Molotovs, these potentates still lived simply in the palaces of the Kremlin, inspired by their devout revolutionary mission with its obligatory 'Bolshevik modesty'. Corruption and extravagance were not yet widespread: indeed, the Politburo wives could barely afford to dress their children and the new archives show that Stalin himself sometimes ran out of money.

Nadya Stalin and Dora Khazan, the ascendant Andreyev's wife, daily caught the tram to the Academy. Nadya is always held up as a paragon of modesty for using her maiden name but Dora did the same: it was the style of the times. Sergo banned his daughter taking his limousine to school: 'too bourgeois!' The Molotovs on the other hand were already notoriously unproletarian: Natalya Rykova heard her father complain that the Molotovs never invited their bodyguards to eat at table with them.

At Stalin's, Nadya was in charge: Svetlana says that her mother managed the household on 'a modest budget'. They prided themselves on their Bolshevik austerity. Nadya regularly exhausted her housekeeping money: 'Please send me 50 roubles because I only get my money on 15 October and I've got none.'

'Tatka, I forgot to send the money,' replied Stalin. 'But I've now sent it (120 roubles) with colleagues leaving today ... Kiss you, Joseph.' Then he checked she had received it. She replied:

'I got the letter with the money. Thanks! Glad you're coming back! Write when you're arriving so I can meet you!'

On 3 January 1928, Stalin wrote to Khalatov, the chief of GIZ (the State Publishing House): 'I'm in great need of money. Would you send me 200 roubles!'* Stalin cultivated his puritanism out of both conviction and taste: when he found new furniture in his apartment, he reacted viciously:

'It seems someone from housekeeping or the GPU bought some furniture ... contrary to my order that old furniture is fine,' he wrote. 'Discover and punish the guilty! I ask you to remove the furniture and put it in storage!'

The Mikoyans had so many children – five boys plus some adopted children and, in the summer, the extended Armenian

---

* Stalin followed the same principle with his clothes: he refused to replace his meagre wardrobe of two or three much-darned tunics, old trousers and his favourite greatcoat and cap from the Civil War. He was not alone in this sartorial asceticism but he was aware that, like Frederick the Great whom he had studied, his deliberately modest old clothes only accentuated his natural authority.

family arrived for three months – that they were short of money even though Mikoyan himself was one of the top half-dozen men in Russia. So Ashken Mikoyan secretly borrowed money from the other Politburo wives who had fewer children. Mikoyan would have been furious if he had known about it, according to his sons. When Polina Molotova saw the shabby Mikoyan children, she reprimanded their mother, who retorted:

'I have five boys and I haven't got the money.'

'But,' snapped Polina, 'you're the wife of a Politburo member!'

3
The Charmer

This small group of idealistic, ruthless magnates, mainly in their thirties, were the engine of a vast and awesome Revolution: they would build socialism immediately and abolish capitalism. Their industrial programme, the Five-Year Plan, would make Russia a great power never again to be humiliated by the West, their war on the countryside would forever exterminate the internal enemy, the kulaks, and return to the values of 1917. It was Lenin who said, 'Merciless mass terror against the kulaks ... Death to them!' Thousands of young people shared their idealism. The Plan demanded a 110 per cent rise in productivity which Stalin, Kuibyshev and Sergo insisted was possible because everything was possible. 'To lower the tempo means to lag behind,' explained Stalin in 1931. 'And laggards are beaten! But we don't want to be beaten ... The history of old Russia consisted ... in her being beaten ... for her backwardness.'

The Bolsheviks could storm any fortress. Any doubt was treason. Death was the price of progress. Surrounded by enemies as they had been in the Civil War, they felt they were only just managing to keep control over the country. Hence they cultivated *tverdost*, hardness, the Bolshevik virtue.* Stalin was praised for it: 'Yes he vigorously chops off what is rotten ... If he didn't, he wouldn't be ... a Communist fighter.' Stalin wrote to Molotov about 'inspecting and checking by punching people in the face' and openly told officials he would 'smash their bones'.

---

* Yet their self-conscious brutality coexisted with a rigid code of Party manners: Bolsheviks were meant to behave to one another like bourgeois gentlemen. Divorces were 'frowned upon more severely than in the Catholic Church'. When Kaganovich wrote on the death sentence of an innocent general that he was a 'slut', he just put 's...'. Molotov edited Lenin's use of the word 'shitty', replacing it with '......' and talked prissily about using a 'name not used in Party circles'. When Kaganovich criticized the crude poetry of Demian Bedny, he told Stalin, 'Being a people's proletarian poet in no way means sinking to the level of the negative qualities of our masses.'

Bukharin resisted 'Stalin's Revolution' but he and Rykov were no match for either Stalin's patronage and charm, nor the Bolshevik taste for recklessly violent solutions. In 1929, Trotsky travelled into exile, with a look of stunned hauteur on his face, to become Stalin's mocking critic abroad, and his ultimate symbol of treason and heresy at home. Bukharin was voted off the Politburo. Stalin was the leader of the oligarchs but he was far from a dictator.

In November 1929, while Nadya studied for her exams at the Industrial Academy, Stalin returned refreshed from his holidays and immediately intensified the war on the peasantry, demanding 'an offensive against the kulaks ... to get ready for action and to deal the kulak class such a blow that it will no longer rise to its feet'. But the peasants refused to sow their crops, declaring war on the regime.

On 21 December 1929, at the exhilarating height of this colossal and terrible enterprise, the young magnates and their wives, weary but febrile from their remarkable achievements in building new cities and factories, blooded by the excitement of brutal expeditions against the obstinate peasants, arrived at Stalin's Zubalovo dacha to celebrate his official fiftieth birthday, the night our story really begins. That day, the magnates each wrote an article in *Pravda* hailing him as the *Vozhd*, the leader, Lenin's rightful heir.

* * *

Days after the birthday party, the magnates realized they had to escalate their war on the countryside and literally 'liquidate the kulaks as a class'. They unleashed a secret police war in which organized brutality, vicious pillage and fanatical ideology vied with one another to destroy the lives of millions. Stalin's circle was to be fatally tested by the rigours of collectivization because they were judged by their performance in this ultimate crisis. The poison of these months tainted Stalin's friendships, even his marriage, beginning the process that would culminate in the torture chambers of 1937.

Stalin spent half his letters to his men losing his temper, and the other half, apologizing for it. He treated everything personally: when Molotov had returned from a grain expedition to the Ukraine, Stalin told him, 'I could cover you with kisses in gratitude for your action down there' – hardly the dour Stalin of legend.

In January 1930, Molotov planned the destruction of the kulaks, who were divided into three categories: 'First category: ... to be immediately eliminated'; the second to be imprisoned in camps; the third, 150,000 households, to be deported. Molotov oversaw the death squads, the railway carriages, the concentration camps like a military commander. Between five and seven million people ultimately fitted into the three categories. There was no way to select a kulak: Stalin himself agonized,* scribbling in his notes: 'What does *kulak* mean?'

During 1930–31, about 1.68 million people were deported to the east and north. Within months, Stalin and Molotov's plan had led to 2,200 rebellions involving more than 800,000 people. Kaganovich and Mikoyan led expeditions into the countryside with brigades of OGPU troopers and armoured trains like warlords. The magnates' handwritten letters to Stalin ring with the fraternal thrill of their war for human betterment against unarmed peasants: 'Taking all measures about food and grain,' Mikoyan reported to Stalin, citing the need to dismiss 'wreckers': 'We face big resistance ... We need to destroy the resistance.' In Kaganovich's photograph album, we find him heading out into Siberia with his armed posse of leather-jacketed ruffians, interrogating peasants, poking around in their haystacks, finding the grain, deporting the culprits and moving on again, exhausted, falling asleep between stops. 'Molotov works really hard and is very tired,' Mikoyan told Stalin. 'The mass of work is so vast it needs horsepower ...'

Sergo and Kaganovich possessed the necessary 'horsepower': when the leaders decided on something, it could be done instantly, on a massive scale and regardless of waste in terms of human lives and resources. 'When we Bolsheviks want to get something done,' Beria, a rising Georgian secret policeman, said later, 'we close our eyes to everything else.' This pitiless fraternity lived in a sleepless frenzy of excitement and activity, driven by adrenalin and conviction. Regarding themselves like God on the

---

* His revealing thoughts on the kulaks on his scraps of paper include: 'kulaks – deserters' then, even more suggestively: 'villages and slaves'. One peasant revealed how kulaks were selected: 'Just between the three of us, the poor peasants of the village get together in a meeting and decide: "So and so had six horses ..." They notify the GPU and there you are: So-and-so gets five years.' Only novelists and poets are really capable of catching the brutish alienation of the villages: Andrei Platonov's novel *The Foundation Pit* is the finest of these.

first day, they were creating a new world in a red-hot frenzy: the big beasts of the Politburo personified the qualities of the Stalinist Commissar, 'Partymindedness, morality, exactingness, attentiveness, good health, knowing their business well' but above all, as Stalin put it, they required, 'bull nerves'.

'I took part in this myself,' wrote a young activist, Lev Kopelev, 'scouring the countryside, searching for hidden grain ... I emptied out the old folks' storage chests, stopping my ears to the children's crying and the women's wails ... I was convinced I was accomplishing the great and necessary transformation of the countryside.'

The peasants believed they could force the Government to stop by destroying their own livestock: the despair that could lead a peasant to kill his own animals, the equivalent in our world of burning down our own house, gives a hint of the scale of desperation: 26.6 million head of cattle were slaughtered, 15.3 million horses. On 16 January 1930, the government decreed that kulak property could be confiscated if they destroyed livestock. If the peasants thought the Bolsheviks would be obliged to feed them, they were mistaken. As the crisis worsened, even Stalin's staunchest lieutenants struggled to squeeze the grain out of the peasantry, especially in the Ukraine and North Caucasus. Stalin berated them but even though they were often twenty years younger, they replied with tantrums and threats of resignation. Stalin was constantly pouring unction on troubled waters. Andrei Andreyev, thirty-five, the boss of the North Caucasus, was close to Stalin (his wife Dora was Nadya's best friend). None the less, he said Stalin's demands were impossible: he needed at least five years. First Molotov tried to encourage him:

'Dear Andreievich, I got your letter on grain supplies, I see it's very hard for you. I see also that the kulaks are using new methods of struggle against us. But I hope we'll break their backs ... I send you greetings and best wishes ... PS: Hurrying off to Crimea for the holidays.' Then Stalin, overwrought, lost his temper with Andreyev who sulked until Stalin apologized:

'Comrade Andreyev, I don't think you do nothing in the field of grain supply. But the grain supplies from the North Caucasus are cutting us like a knife and we need measures to strengthen the process. Please remember, every new million poods is very valuable for us. Please remember, we have very little time. So to work? With Communist greetings, Stalin.' But Andreyev was still upset so Stalin scribbled him another letter, this time calling him by a pet name and appealing to his Bolshevik honour:

'Hello Andryusha, I'm late. Don't be angry. About strategy … I take my words back. I'd like to stress again that close people must be trusted and honourable until the end. I speak about our top people. Without this our Party will utterly fail. I shake your hand, J. Stalin.' He often had to take back his own words.

* * *

The foundation of Stalin's power in the Party was not fear: it was charm. Stalin possessed the dominant will among his magnates, but they also found his policies generally congenial. He was older than them all except President Kalinin, but the magnates used the informal 'you' with him. Voroshilov, Molotov and Sergo called him 'Koba'. They were sometimes even cheeky: Mikoyan, who called him Soso, signed one letter: 'If you're not lazy, write to me!' In 1930, all these magnates, especially the charismatic and fiery Sergo Ordzhonikidze, were allies, not protégés, all capable of independent action. There were close friendships that presented potential alliances against Stalin: Sergo and Kaganovich, the two toughest bosses, were best friends. Voroshilov, Mikoyan and Molotov frequently disagreed with Stalin. His dilemma was that he was the leader of a Party with no *Führerprinzip* but the ruler of a country accustomed to Tsarist autocracy.

Stalin was not the dreary bureaucrat that Trotsky wanted him to be. It was certainly true that he was a gifted organizer. He 'never improvised' but 'took every decision, weighing it carefully'. He was capable of working extraordinarily long hours – sixteen a day. But the new archives confirm that his real genius was something different – and surprising: 'he could charm people'. He was what is now known as a 'people person'. While incapable of true empathy on one hand, he was a master of friendships on the other. He constantly lost his temper, but when he set his mind to charming a man, he was irresistible.

Stalin's face was 'expressive and mobile', his feline movements 'supple and graceful', he buzzed with sensitive energy. Everyone who saw him 'was anxious to see him again' because 'he created a sense that there was now a bond that linked them forever'. Artyom said he made 'we children feel like adults and feel important'. Visitors were impressed with his quiet modesty, the puffing on the pipe, the calmness. When the future Marshal Zhukov first met him, he could not sleep afterwards: 'The appearance of JV Stalin, his quiet voice, the concreteness and depth of his judgements, the attention with which he heard the report made a great impression on me.' Sudoplatov, a Chekist, thought 'it was hard to imagine such a man could deceive you, his reactions were so natural, without the slightest sense of him posing' but he also noticed 'a certain harshness ... which he did not ... conceal'.

In the eyes of these rough Bolsheviks from the regions, his flat quiet public speaking was an asset, a great improvement on Trotsky's oratorical wizardry. Stalin's lack of smoothness, his anti-oratory, inspired trust. His very faults, the chip on the shoulder, the brutality and fits of irrational temper, were the Party's faults. 'He was not trusted but he was the man the Party trusted,' admitted Bukharin. 'He's like the symbol of the Party, the lower strata trust him.' But above all, reflected the future secret police chief, Beria, he was 'supremely intelligent', a political 'genius'. However rude or charming he was, 'he dominated his entourage with his intelligence'.

He did not just socialize with the magnates: he patronized junior officials too, constantly searching for tougher, more loyal, and more tireless lieutenants. He was always accessible: 'I'm ready to help you and receive you,' he often replied to requests. Officials got through directly to Stalin. Those lower down called him, behind his back, the *Khozyain* which is usually translated as 'Boss', but it means much more: the 'Master'. Nicholas II had called himself '*Khozyain* of the Russian lands'. When Stalin heard someone use the word, he was 'noticeably irritated' by its feudal mystique: 'That sounds like a rich landowner in Central Asia. Fool!'

His magnates saw him as their patron but he saw himself as much more. 'I know you're diabolically busy,' Molotov wrote to him on his birthday. 'But I shake your fifty-year-old hand ... I must say in my personal work I'm obliged to you ...' They were all obliged to him. But Stalin saw his own role embroidered with both Arthurian chivalry and Christian sanctity: 'You need have no doubt, comrades, I am prepared to devote to the cause of the working class ... all my strength, all my ability, and if need be, all my blood, drop by drop,' he wrote to thank the Party for acclaiming him as leader. 'Your congratulations, I place to the credit of the great Party ... which bore me and reared me in its own image and likeness.' Here was how he saw himself.

None the less, this self-anointed Messianic hero worked hard to envelop his protégés in an irresistible embrace of folksy intimacy that convinced them there was no one he trusted more. Stalin was mercurial but far from a humourless drone: he was convivial and entertaining, if exhaustingly intense. 'He was such fun,' says Artyom. According to the Yugoslav Communist Milovan Djilas, his 'rough ... self-assured humour' was 'roguish' and 'impish' but 'not entirely without finesse and depth' though it was never far from the gallows. His dry wit was acute but hardly Wildean. Once when Kozlovsky, the court tenor, was performing at the Kremlin, the Politburo started demanding some particular song.

'Why put pressure on Comrade Kozlovsky?' intervened Stalin calmly. 'Let him sing what he wants.' He paused. 'And I think he wants to sing Lensky's aria from *Onegin*.' Everyone laughed and Kozlovsky obediently sang the aria.*

When Stalin appointed Isakov Naval Commissar, the admiral replied that it was too arduous because he only had one leg. Since the Navy had been 'commanded by people without heads, one leg's no handicap', quipped Stalin. He was particularly keen on mocking the pretensions of the ruling caste: when a list of tedious worthies recommended for medals landed on his desk, he wrote across it:

'Shitters get the Order of Lenin!' He enjoyed practical jokes. During the Italian invasion of Ethiopia, he ordered his bodyguards to get 'Ras Kasa on the phone at once!' When a young guard returned 'half-dead with worry', to explain that he could not get this Abyssinian mountain chieftain on the line, Stalin laughed:

'And you're in security!' He was capable of pungent repartee. Zinoviev accused him of ingratitude: 'Gratitude's a dog's disease,' he snapped back.

Stalin 'knew everything about his closest comrades – EVERYTHING!' stresses the daughter of one of them, Natasha Andreyeva. He watched his protégés, educated them, brought them to Moscow and took immense trouble with them: he

---

* At the Bolshoi, Kozlovsky suddenly lost his voice during Rigoletto. The singer peered helplessly up towards Stalin's Box A, pointing at his throat. Quick as a flash, Stalin silently pointed at the left side of his tunic near the pocket where medals are pinned and painted a medal. Kozlovsky's voice returned. He got the medal.

promoted Mikoyan, but told Bukharin and Molotov that he thought the Armenian 'still a duckling in politics ... If he grows up, he'll improve.' The Politburo was filled with fiery egomaniacs such as Sergo Ordzhonikidze: Stalin was adept at coaxing, charming, manipulating and bullying them into doing his bidding. When he summoned two of his ablest men, Sergo and Mikoyan, from the Caucasus, they argued with him and each other but his patience in soothing (and baiting) them was endless.

Stalin personally oversaw their living arrangements. In 1913, when he stayed in Vienna with the Troyanovsky family, he gave the daughter of the house a bag of sweets every day. Then he asked the child's mother: to whom would the child run if they both called? When they tried it, she ran to Stalin hoping for some more sweets. This idealistic cynic used the same incentives with the Politburo. When Sergo moved to Moscow, Stalin lent him his apartment. When Sergo loved the apartment, Stalin simply gave it to him. When young, provincial Beria visited Moscow for the Seventeenth Congress, Stalin himself put his ten-year-old son to bed at Zubalovo. When he popped into the flats of the Politburo, Maya Kaganovich remembered him insisting they light their fire. 'No detail was too small.' Every gift suited the recipient: he gave his Cossack ally Budyonny swords with inscribed blades. He personally distributed the cars and latest gadgets.* There is a list in the archives in Stalin's handwriting assigning each car to every leader: their wives and daughters wrote thank-you letters to him.

Then there was money: these magnates were often short of money because wages were paid on the basis of the 'Party Maximum', which meant that a 'responsible worker' could not earn more than a highly-paid worker. Even before Stalin abolished this in 1934, there were ways round it. Food hampers from the Kremlin canteen and special rations from the GORT (government) stores were delivered to each leader. But they also

---

* Kirov, his Leningrad boss, lived in a huge apartment containing a dazzling array of the latest equipment. First there was a huge new American fridge – a General Electric – of which only ten were imported into the USSR. American gramophones were specially prized: there was a 'radiola' on which Kirov could listen to the Mariinsky Ballet in his apartment; there was a 'petiphone', a wind-up gramophone without a speaker, and one with a speaker, plus a lamp radio. When the first television reached Moscow just before the war, the Mikoyans received the alien object that reflected the picture in a glass that stuck out at forty-five degrees. As for Budyonny, Stalin wrote: 'I gave you the sword but it's not a very beautiful one so I decided to send you a better one inscribed – it's on its way!'

received *pakets*, secret gifts of money, like a banker's bonus or cash in a brown envelope, and coupons for holidays. The sums were nominally decided by President Kalinin, and the Secretary of the Central Executive Committee, the major-domo of all the goodies, Yenukidze, but Stalin took great interest in these *pakets*. In the archives, Stalin underlined the amounts in a list headed 'Money Gifts from Funds of Presidium for group of responsible workers and members of their families'. 'Interesting numbers!' he wrote on it. When he noticed that his staff were short of money, he secretly intervened to help them, procuring publishing royalties for his chief secretary, Tovstukha. He wrote to the publishing chief that if Tovstukha denied he was skint, 'he's lying. He's desperately short of money.' It used to be regarded as ironic to call the Soviet élite an 'aristocracy' but they were much more like a feudal service nobility whose privileges were totally dependent on their loyalty.

Just when these potentates needed to be harsher than ever, some were becoming soft and decadent, particularly those with access to the luxuries like Yenukidze and the secret policeman Yagoda. Furthermore, the regional bosses built up their own entourages and became so powerful that Stalin called them 'Grand Dukes'. But there was no Party 'prince' as beneficent as he himself, the patron of patrons.

The party was not just a mass of self-promoting groups – it was almost a family business. Whole clans were members of the leadership: Kaganovich was the youngest of five brothers, three of whom were high Bolsheviks. Stalin's in-laws were all senior officials. Sergo's brothers were both top Bolsheviks in the Caucasus where family units were the norm. A tangle of inter-marriage* complicated the power relationships and would have fatal results: when one leader fell, everyone linked to him disappeared with him into the abyss like mountaineers tied together with one safety rope.

The backs of the peasants, in Stalin and Molotov's chilling phrase, were indeed being broken but the scale of the struggle shook even their most ruthless supporters. In mid-February 1930, Sergo and Kalinin travelled to inspect the countryside and returned to call a halt. Sergo, who as head of the Party Control

---

* For example, Kamenev's wife was Trotsky's sister; Yagoda was married into the Sverdlov family; Poskrebyshev, Stalin's secretary, was married to the sister of Trotsky's daughter-in-law. Two top Stalinists, Shcherbakov and Zhdanov, were brothers-in-law. Later the children of the Politburo would intermarry.

Commission, had orchestrated the campaign against the Rightists, now ordered the Ukraine to stop 'socializing' livestock.

Stalin had lost control. The masterful tactician bowed before the magnates and agreed to retreat – with resentful prudence. On 2 March, he wrote his famous article 'Dizzy with Success', in which he claimed success and blamed local officials for his own mistakes, which relieved the pressure* in the villages.

Stalin had regarded his allies as his 'tightest circle' of 'friends', a brotherhood 'formed historically in the struggle against ... the opportunism' of Trotsky and Bukharin. But he now sensed the Politburo was riddled with doubt and disloyalty as the 'Stalin Revolution' turned the countryside into a dystopian nightmare. Even in stormy times, Politburo meetings, at midday on Thursday round the two parallel tables in the map-covered Sovnarkom Room in the Yellow Palace, could be surprisingly light-hearted. Stalin never chaired the Politburo, leaving that to the Premier, Rykov. He was careful never to speak first, according to Mikoyan, so that no one was tied by his opinion before they had stated their own.

There was much scribbling across the table at these meetings. Bukharin, before he lost his place, drew caricatures of all the leaders, often in ludicrous poses with rampant erections or in Tsarist uniforms. They were always teasing Voroshilov for his vanity and stupidity even though this hero of the Civil War was one of Stalin's closest allies. 'Hi friend!' Stalin addressed him fondly. 'Pity you're not in Moscow. When are you coming?'

'Vain as a woman', no one liked uniforms more than Voroshilov. This proletarian boulevardier who sported white flannels at his sumptuous dacha, and full whites for tennis, was a jolly Epicurean, 'amiable and fun-loving, fond of music, parties and literature,' enjoying the company of actors and writers. Stalin heard that he was wearing his wife's scarf because of a midsummer cold: 'Of course, he loves himself so much that he takes great care of himself. Ha! He even does exercises!' laughed Stalin. 'Notoriously stupid', Voroshilov rarely saw a stick without getting the wrong end of it.

A locksmith from Lugansk (renamed Voroshilov), he had, like many of Stalin's leaders, barely completed two years at school. A Party member since 1903, Klim had shared a room with Stalin in Stockholm in 1906 but they had become friends at Tsaritsyn.

---

* In Sholokhov's novel, *Virgin Soil Upturned*, the Cossacks call off their revolt when they read it. But they also withdraw from the collective farm.

Henceforth Stalin backed this 'Commander-in-Chief from the lathe' all the way to become Defence Commissar in 1925. Out of his depth, Voroshilov loathed more sophisticated military minds with the inferiority complex that was one of the moving passions of Stalin's circle. Ever since he had delivered mail on horseback to the miners of Lugansk, his mind was more at home with the equine than the mechanized.

Usually described as a snivelling coward before his master, he had flirted with the oppositions and was perfectly capable of losing his temper with Stalin whom he always treated like an old buddy. He was only slightly younger than Koba and continued to call a spade a spade even after the Terror. Fair-haired, pink-cheeked, warm eyes twinkling, he was sweet-natured: the courage of this *beau sabreur* was peerless. Yet beneath his cherubic affability, there was something mean about the lips that revealed a petulant temper, vindictive cruelty, and a taste for violent solutions.* Once convinced, he was 'narrow-minded politically', pursuing his orders with rigid obedience.

His cult was second only to Stalin's: even in the West, the novelist Denis Wheatley published a panegyric entitled *The Red Eagle* – 'the amazing story of the pitboy who beat professional soldiers of three nations and is now Warlord of Russia.'

In one note passed round the table, Voroshilov wrote: 'I cannot make the speech to the brake-makers because of my headache.'

'To let off Voroshilov, I propose Rudzutak,' replied Stalin, suggesting another Politburo member.

But Voroshilov was not escaping so easily: Rudzutak refused so Kalinin suggested letting him off, providing Voroshilov did the speech after all.

'Against!' voted Voroshilov, signing himself: 'Voroshilov who has the headache and cannot speak!'

If Stalin approved of a leader's speech, he sent an enthusiastically scatological note: 'A world leader, FUCK HIS MOTHER! I've read your report – you criticized everyone – fuck their mother!' he wrote approvingly to Voroshilov who wanted more praise:

'Tell me more clearly – did I fail 100% or only 75%?' Stalin retorted in his inimitable style: 'it was a good ... report. You

---

* 'You know Marapultsa,' Voroshilov wrote to Stalin in October 1930. 'He was condemned for five years ... I think you agree with me that he was condemned rightly.' On another occasion, Voroshilov appealed to Stalin for a 'semi-lunatic' he had known since 1911 who was in jail. 'What do I want you to do? Almost nothing ... but for you to consider for one minute the destruction of Minin and decide what to do with him ...'

smacked the arses of Hoover, Chamberlain and Bukharin. Stalin.'

Serious questions were decided too: during a budget discussion, Stalin verbally nudged Voroshilov to stand up for his department: 'They're robbing you but you're silent.' When his colleagues went back to discuss something Stalin thought had already been decided, they received this across the table: 'What does this mean? Yesterday we agreed one thing about the speech but today another. Disorganization! Stalin.' Appointments were made in this way too. Their tone was often playful: Voroshilov wanted to inspect the army in Central Asia:

'Koba, can I go ...? They say they're forgotten.'

'England will whine that Voroshilov has come to attack India,' replied Stalin, who wanted to avoid all foreign entanglements while he industrialized Russia.

'I'll be as quiet as a mouse,' Voroshilov persisted.

'That's worse. They'll find out and say Voroshilov came secretly with criminal intent,' scrawled Stalin. When it came to appointing Mikoyan to run Trade, Voroshilov asked,

'Koba, should we give Fishing to Mikoyan? Would he do it?' The members often bargained for appointments. Hence Voroshilov proposed to Kuibyshev, 'I was first to propose the candidature of Pyatakov in conversation with Molotov and Kaganovich, and I'll support you as your second ...'

The Politburo could sit for hours, exhausting even Stalin:

'Listen,' he wrote to Voroshilov during one session, 'let's put it off until Wednesday evening. Today's no good. Already it's 4.30 and we've still got 3 big questions to get through ... Stalin.' Sometimes Stalin wrote wearily: 'Military matters are so serious they must be discussed seriously but my head's not capable of serious work today.'

However, Stalin realized that the Politburo could easily unite to dismiss him. Rykov, the Rightist Premier, did not believe in his plans and now Kalinin too was wavering. Stalin knew he could be outvoted, even overthrown.* The new archives reveal how openly Kalinin argued with Stalin.

---

* They frequently disagreed with him, certainly on small matters such as a discussion about the Kremlin military school: 'Seems that after the objections of Comrade Kalinin and others (I know other Politburo members object too), we can forgive them because it's not an important question,' Stalin wrote to Voroshilov. Having defeated Bukharin in 1929, Stalin wanted to appoint him Education Commissar but as Voroshilov told Sergo in a letter, 'Because we were a united majority, we pushed it through (against Koba).'

"You defend the kulaks?' scribbled Stalin. He pushed it across the table to Papa Kalinin, that mild-mannered former peasant with round spectacles, goatee beard and droopy moustache.

'Not the kulaks,' Kalinin wrote back, 'but the trading peasant.'

'But did you forget about the poorest ones?' Stalin scrawled back. 'Did you ignore the Russian peasantry?'

'The middling sort are very Russian but what about non-Russians? They're the poorest,' argued Kalinin.

'Now you're the Bashkir President not the Russian one!' Stalin chided him.

'That's not an argument, that's a curse!' Stalin's curse did descend on those who opposed him during this greatest crisis. He never forgot Kalinin's betrayal. Every criticism was a battle for survival, a question of sin versus goodness, disease versus health, for this thin-skinned, neurotic egotist on his Messianic mission. During these months, he brooded on the disloyalty of those around him, for his family and his political allies were utterly interwoven. Stalin had every reason to feel paranoid. Indeed the Bolsheviks believed that paranoia, which they called 'vigilance', was an almost religious duty. Later Stalin was to talk privately about the 'holy fear' that kept even him on his toes.

His paranoia was part of a personal vicious circle that was to prove so deadly for many who knew him, yet it was understandable. His radical policies led to excessive repressions that led to the opposition he most feared. His unbalanced reactions produced a world in which he had reason to be fearful. In public he reacted to all this with a dry humour and modest tranquillity but one finds ample evidence of his hysterical reactions in private. 'You cannot silence me or keep my opinion confined inside,' Stalin wrote to Voroshilov during the struggles with the Rightists, 'yet you claim "I want to teach everyone." When will these attacks on me end? Stalin.' It extended to the family. One of his letters to Nadya went missing. Stalin was obsessed with the secrecy of his letters and travel plans. He impulsively blamed his mother-in-law but Nadya defended her: 'You unfairly accused Mama. It turns out the letter was never delivered to anyone … She's in Tiflis.'

Nadya laughed that the students at the Academy were divided into 'Kulaks, middle-peasants and poor peasants', but she was joking about the liquidation of over a million innocent women and children. There is evidence that Nadya happily informed

Stalin about his enemies, yet that was changing. The rural struggle divided their friends: her adored Bukharin and Yenukidze confided their doubts to her. Her fellow students had 'put me down as a Rightist,' she joked to Stalin, who would have been troubled that they were getting to his wife at a time when he was entering stormy waters indeed.

* * *

On holiday in the south, Stalin learned that Riutin, an Old Bolshevik who had been in charge of Cinema, was trying to create an opposition to dismiss him. He reacted fast to Molotov on 13 September: 'with regard to Riutin, it seems it's impossible to limit ourselves to expelling him from the Party ... he will have to be expelled somewhere as far as possible from Moscow. This counter-revolutionary scum* should be completely disarmed.' Simultaneously, Stalin arranged a series of show trials and 'conspiracies' by so-called 'wreckers'. Stalin redoubled the push for collectivization and race to industrialize at red-hot speed. As the tension rose, he stoked the martial atmosphere, inventing new enemies to intimidate his real opponents in the Party and among the technical experts who said it could not be done.

Stalin frantically ordered Molotov to publish all the testimonies of the 'wreckers' immediately and then 'after a week, announce that all these scoundrels will be executed by firing squad. They should all be shot.'

Then he turned to attacking the Rightists in the Government. He ordered a campaign against currency speculation which he blamed on Rykov's Finance Commissars, those 'doubtful Communists' Pyatakov and Briukhanov. Stalin wanted blood and he ordered the cultivated OGPU boss, Menzhinsky, to arrest more wreckers. He told Molotov 'to shoot two or three dozen saboteurs infiltrated into these offices'.

Stalin made a joke of this at the Politburo. When the leaders criticized Briukhanov, Stalin scribbled to Valery Mezhlauk, reporting on behalf of Gosplan, the economic planning agency:

'For all new, existing and future sins to be hung by the balls, and if the balls are strong and don't break, to forgive him and think him correct but if they break, then to throw him into the river.' Mezhlauk was also an accomplished cartoonist and drew a picture of this particular torture, testicles and all. Doubtless

* *Nechist* means an unclean devil in peasant folklore.

everyone laughed uproariously. But Briukhanov was sacked and later destroyed.

That summer of 1930, as the Sixteenth Congress crowned Stalin as leader, Nadya was suffering from a serious internal illness – so he sent her to Carlsbad for the best medical treatment and to Berlin to see her brother Pavel and his wife Zhenya. Her medical problems were complex, mysterious and probably psychosomatic. Nadya's medical records, that Stalin preserved, reveal that at various times, she suffered 'acute abdominal pains' probably caused by her earlier abortion. Then there were the headaches as fierce as migraines that may have been symptoms of synostosis, a disease in which the cranial bones merge together, or they may simply have been caused by her earlier stress of internal war within the USSR. Even though he was frantically busy arranging the Congress and fighting enemies in the villages and the Politburo, Stalin was never more tender.

4

Famine and the Country Set:
Stalin at the Weekend

'Tatka! What was the journey like, what did you see, have you been to the doctors, what do they say about your health? Write and tell me,' he wrote on 21 June. 'We start the Congress on the 26th ... Things aren't going too badly. I miss you ... come home soon. I kiss you.' As soon as the Congress was over, he wrote: 'Tatka! I got all three letters. I couldn't reply, I was too busy. Now at last I'm free ... Don't be too long coming home. But stay longer if your health makes it necessary ... I kiss you.'

* * *

In the summer, Stalin, backed by the formidable Sergo, guided one of his faked conspiracies, the so-called 'Industrial Party' to implicate President Kalinin, and seems to have used evidence that 'Papa', a ladies' man, was wasting State funds on a ballerina. The President begged for forgiveness.

Stalin and Menzhinsky were in constant communication about other conspiracies too. Stalin worried about the loyalty of the Red Army. The OGPU forced two officers to testify against the Chief of Staff, Tukhachevsky, that gifted, dashing commander who had been Stalin's bitter enemy since the Polish War of 1920. Tukhachevsky was hated by the less sophisticated officers who complained to Voroshilov that the arrogant commander 'makes fun of us' with his 'grandiose plans'. Stalin agreed they were 'fantastical', and so over-ambitious as to be almost counter-revolutionary.

The OGPU interrogations accused Tukhachevsky of planning a coup against the Politburo. In 1930, this was perhaps too outrageous even for the Bolsheviks. Stalin, not yet dictator, probed his powerful ally, Sergo: 'Only Molotov, myself and now you are in the know ... Is it possible? What a business! Discuss it with Molotov ...' However Sergo would not go that far. There would be no arrest and trial of Tukhachevsky in 1930: the commander 'turns out to be 100% clean', Stalin wrote disingenuously to Molotov in October. 'That's very good.' It is interesting that seven years before the Great Terror, Stalin was testing the same accusations against the same victims – a dress rehearsal for 1937 – but he could not get the support. The archives reveal a fascinating sequel: once he understood the ambitious modernity of Tukhachevsky's strategies, Stalin apologized to him: 'Now the question has become clearer to me, I have to agree that my remark was too strong and my conclusions were not right at all.'

* * *

Nadya returned from Carlsbad and joined Stalin on holiday. Brooding how to bring Rykov and Kalinin to heel, Stalin did not make Nadya feel welcome. 'I did not feel you wanted me to prolong my stay, quite the contrary,' wrote Nadya. She left for Moscow where the Molotovs, ever the busybodies of the Kremlin, 'scolded' her for 'leaving you alone', as she angrily reported to Stalin. Stalin was irritated by the Molotovs, and Nadya's feeling that she was unwelcome:

'Tell Molotov, he's wrong. To reproach you, making you worry about me, can only be done by someone who doesn't know my business.' Then she heard from her godfather that Stalin was delaying his return until October. Stalin explained that he had lied to Yenukidze to confuse his enemies:

'Tatka, I started that rumour ... for reasons of secrecy. Only Tatka, Molotov and maybe Sergo know the date of my arrival.'

Close to Molotov and Sergo, Stalin no longer trusted one of his closest friends who sympathized with the Rightists: Nadya's godfather, 'Uncle Abel' Yenukidze. Nicknamed 'Tonton', this veteran conspirator, at fifty three, two years older than Stalin, had known Koba and the Alliluyevs since the turn of the century. Another ex-Tiflis Seminarist, in 1904, he had created the secret Bolshevik printing press in Batumi. He was never ambitious and was said to have turned down promotion to the Politburo, but he was everyone's friend, bearing no grudges against the defeated oppositions, always ready to help old pals. This easy-going Georgian sybarite was well-connected in the military, the Party, and the Caucasus, personifying the incestuous tangle of Bolshevism: he had had an affair with Ekaterina Voroshilova before her marriage. Yet Stalin still enjoyed Yenukidze's companionship: 'Hello Abel! What the devil keeps you in Moscow? Come to Sochi ...'

Meanwhile, Stalin turned on Premier Rykov, whose drinking

was so heavy that in Kremlin circles, vodka was called 'Rykovka'.

'What to do about Rykov (who uncontestably helped them) and Kalinin ...?' he wrote to Molotov on 2 September. 'No doubt Kalinin has sinned ... The CC must be informed to teach Kalinin never to get mixed up with such rascals again.'

Kalinin was forgiven – but the warning was clear: he never crossed Stalin again, a political husk, a craven rubber stamp for all Stalin's outrages. Yet Stalin liked Papa Kalinin and enjoyed the pretty girls at his parties in Sochi. The success of his 'handsome' charms soon reached the half-indulgent, half-jealous Nadya in Moscow.

'I heard from a young and pretty woman,' she wrote, 'that you looked handsome at Kalinin's dinner, you were remarkably jolly, made them all laugh, though they were shy in your august presence.'

On 13 September, Stalin mused to Molotov that 'our summit of state is afflicted with a terrible sickness ... It is necessary to take measures. But what? I'll talk to you when I return to Moscow ...' He posed much the same thought to other members of the Politburo. They suggested Stalin for Rykov's job:

'Dear Koba,' wrote Voroshilov, 'Mikoyan, Kaganovich, Kuibyshev and I think the best result would be the unification of the leadership of Sovnarkom and to appoint you to it as you want to take the leadership with all strength. This isn't like 1918–21 but Lenin did lead the Sovnarkom.' Kaganovich insisted it had to be Stalin. Sergo agreed. Mikoyan wrote too that in the Ukraine 'they destroyed their harvest last year – very dangerous ... Nowadays we nead strong leadership from a single leader as it was in Illich [Lenin's] time and the best decision is you to be the candidate for the Chairmanship ... Doesn't all of mankind know who's the ruler of our country?'

Yet no one had ever held the posts of both General Secretary and Premier. Furthermore, could a foreigner,* a Georgian, formally lead the country? So Kaganovich backed Stalin's nominee, Molotov.

'You should replace Rykov,' Stalin told Molotov.

On 21 October, Stalin uncovered more betrayal: Sergei Syrtsov, candidate Politburo member and one of his protégés, was

---

* Lenin himself had governed as Premier (Chairman of Sovnarkom) from 1917 to 1924. On his death, his natural successor, Kamenev, had not succeeded to the post as a Jew not a Russian. Hence Rykov got the job.

denounced for plotting against him. Denunciation was already a daily part of the Bolshevik ritual and a duty – Stalin's files are filled with such letters. Syrtsov was summoned to the Central Committee. He implicated the First Secretary of the Transcaucasus Party, Beso Lominadze, an old friend of both Stalin and Sergo. Lominadze admitted secret meetings but claimed he only disapproved of comparing Stalin to Lenin. As ever, Stalin reacted melodramatically:

'It's unimaginable vileness ... They played at staging a coup, they played at being the Politburo and plumbed the lowest depths...' Then, after this eruption, Stalin asked Molotov: 'How are things going for you?'

Sergo wanted them expelled from the Party but Stalin, who understood already from his probings about Tukhachevsky, that his position was not strong enough yet, just had them expelled from the Central Committee. There is a small but important post-script to this: Sergo Ordzhonikidze protected his friend Lominadze by not revealing all his letters to the CC. Instead he went to Stalin and offered them to him personally. Stalin was shocked – why not the CC? 'Because I gave him my word,' said Sergo.

'How could you?' replied Stalin, adding later that Sergo had behaved not like a Bolshevik but 'like ... a prince. I told him I did not want to be part of his secret ...' Later, this would assume a terrible significance.

On 19 December, a Plenum gathered to consolidate Stalin's victories over his opponents. Plenums were the sittings of the all-powerful Central Committee, which Stalin compared to an 'Areopagus', in the huge converted hall in the Great Kremlin Palace with dark wood panelling and pews like a grim Puritan church. This was where the central magnates and regional viceroys, who ruled swathes of the country as First Secretaries of republics and cities, met like a medieval Council of Barons. These meetings most resembled the chorus of a vicious evangelical meeting with constant interjections of 'Right!' or 'Brutes!' or just laughter. This was one of the last Plenums where the old Bolshevik tradition of intellectual argument and wit still played a part. Voroshilov and Kaganovich clashed with Bukharin who was playing his role of supporting Stalin's line now that his own Rightists had been defeated:

'We're right to crush the most dangerous Rightist deviation,' said Bukharin.

'And those infected with it!' called out Voroshilov.

'If you're talking about their physical destruction, I leave it to those comrades who are ... given to bloodthirstyness.' There was laughter but the jokes were becoming sinister. It was still unthinkable for the inner circle to be touched physically, yet Kaganovich pressured Stalin to be tougher on the opposition while Voroshilov demanded 'the Procurator must be a very active organ ...'

The Plenum sacked Rykov as Premier and appointed Molotov.* Sergo joined the Politburo and took over the Supreme Economic Council, the industrial colossus that ran the entire Five-Year Plan. He was the ideal bulldozer to force through industrialization. The new promotions and aggressive push to complete the Plan in four years unleashed a welter of rows between these potentates. They defended their own commissariats and supporters. When they changed jobs they tended to change allegiances: as Chairman of the Control Commission, Sergo had backed the campaigns against saboteurs and wreckers in industry. The moment he took over Industry, he defended his specialists. Sergo started constantly rowing with Molotov, whom he 'didn't love much', over his budgets. There was no radical group: some were more extreme at different times. Stalin himself, the chief organizer of Terror, meandered his way to his revolution.

Stalin refereed the arguments that became so vicious that Kuibyshev, Sergo and Mikoyan all threatened to resign, defending their posts: 'Dear Stalin,' wrote Mikoyan coldly, 'Your two telegrams disappointed me so much that I couldn't work for two days. I can take any criticism ... except being accused of being disloyal to the CC and you ... Without your personal support, I can't work as Narkom Supply and Trade ... Better to find a new candidate but give me some other job ...' Stalin apologized to Mikoyan and he often had to apologize to the others too. Dictators do not need to apologize. Meanwhile Andreyev returned from Rostov to head the disciplinary Control Commission while Kaganovich, just thirty-seven, became Stalin's Deputy Secretary, joining the General Secretary and Premier Molotov in a ruling triumvirate.

---

* Stalin proudly advertised this to the novelist Maxim Gorky in Italy: 'He's a brave, clever, quite modern leader – his real name is Scriabin.' (Did Stalin, always an intellectual snob, add the 'Scriabin' to impress Gorky with Molotov's false association with the composer to whom he was not related?)

* * *

'Brash and masculine', tall and strong with black hair, long eyelashes and 'fine brown eyes', Lazar Moisevich Kaganovich was a workaholic always playing with amber worry beads or a key chain. Trained as a cobbler with minimal primary education, he looked first at a man's boots. If he was impressed with their workmanship, he sometimes forced them to take them off so he could admire them on his desk where he still kept a specially engraved tool set, presented to him by grateful workers.

The very model of a macho modern manager, Kaganovich had an explosive temper like his friend Sergo. Happiest with a hammer in his hand, he often hit his subordinates or lifted them up by their lapels – yet politically he was cautious, 'quick and clever'. He constantly clashed with plodding Molotov who regarded him as 'coarse, tough and straitlaced, very energetic, a good organizer, who floundered on ... theory' but was the leader 'most devoted to Stalin'. Despite the strong Jewish accent, Sergo believed he was their best orator: 'He really captured the audience!' A boisterous manager so tough and forceful that he was nicknamed 'The Locomotive', Kaganovich 'not only knew how to apply pressure', said Molotov, 'but he was something of a ruffian himself.' He 'could get things done,' said Khrushchev. 'If the CC put an axe in his hands, he'd chop up a storm' but destroy the 'healthy trees with the rotten ones'. Stalin called him 'Iron Lazar'.

Born in November 1893 in a hut in the remote village of Kabana in the Ukrainian-Belorussian borderlands into a poor, Orthodox Jewish family of five brothers and one sister, who all slept in one room, Lazar, the youngest, was recruited into the Party by his brother in 1911 and agitated in the Ukraine under the unlikely name of 'Kosherovich'.

Lenin singled him out as a rising leader: he was far more impressive than he seemed. Constantly reading in his huge library, educating himself with Tsarist history textbooks (and the novels of Balzac and Dickens), this 'worker-intellectual' was the brains behind the militarization of the Party state. In 1918 aged twenty-four, he ran and terrorized Nizhny Novgorod. In 1919 he demanded a tight dictatorship, urging the military discipline of 'Centralism'. In 1924, writing in clear but fanatical prose, it was he who designed the machinery of what became 'Stalinism'. After running the appointments section of the CC, 'Iron Lazar' was sent to run Central Asia then, in 1925, the Ukraine, before returning in 1928, joining the Politburo as a full member at the Sixteenth Congress in 1930.

Kaganovich and his wife Maria met romantically on a secret mission when these young Bolsheviks had to pretend to be married: they found their roles easy to play because they fell in love and got married. They were so happy together that they always held hands even sitting in Politburo limousines, bringing up their daughter and adopted son in a loving, rather Jewish household. Humorous and emotional, Lazar was an athlete who skied and rode, but he possessed the most pusillanimous instinct for self-preservation. As a Jew, Kaganovich was aware of his vulnerability and Stalin was equally sensitive in protecting his comrade from anti-Semitism.

Kaganovich was the first true Stalinist, coining the word during a dinner at Zubalovo. 'Everyone keeps talking about Lenin and Leninism but Lenin's been gone a long time … Long live Stalinism!'

'How dare you say that?' retorted Stalin modestly. 'Lenin was a tall tower and Stalin a little finger.' But Kaganovich treated Stalin far more reverently than Sergo or Mikoyan: he was, said Molotov disdainfully, '200% Stalinist'. He so admired the *Vozhd*, he admitted, that 'when I go to Stalin, I try not to forget a thing! I so worry every time. I prepare every document in my briefcase and I fill my pockets with cribs like a schoolboy because no one knows what Stalin's going to ask.' Stalin reacted to Kaganovich's school-boyish respect by teaching him how to spell and punctuate, even when he was so powerful: 'I've reread your letter,' Kaganovich wrote to Stalin in 1931, 'and realize that I haven't carried out your directive to master punctuation marks. I'd started but haven't quite managed it, but I can do it despite my burden of work. I'll try to have full-stops and commas in future letters.' He respected Stalin as Russia's own 'Robespierre' and refused to call him by the intimate 'thou': 'Did you ever call Lenin "thou"?'

His brutality was more important than his punctuation: he had recently crushed peasant uprisings from the North Caucasus to western Siberia. Succeeding Molotov as Moscow boss and the hero of a cult approaching Stalin's own, Iron Lazar began the vandalistic creation of a Bolshevik metropolis, enthusiastically dynamiting historic buildings.

By the summer of 1931, a serious shortage in the countryside was beginning to develop into a famine. While the Politburo softened its campaign against industrial specialists in mid-July, the rural struggle continued. The GPU and the 180,000 Party workers sent from cities used the gun, the lynch mob and the Gulag camp system to break the villages. Over two million were deported to Siberia or Kazakhstan; in 1930, there were 179,000 slaving in the Gulags; almost a million by 1935. Terror and forced labour became the essence of Politburo business. On a sheet covered in doodles, Stalin scrawled in a thick blue pencil:

1. Who can do the arrests?
2. What to do with ex-White military in our industrial factories?
3. Prisons must be emptied of prisoners. [He wanted them sentenced faster to make room for kulaks.]
4. What to do with different groups arrested?
5. To allow ... deportations: Ukraine 145,000. N. Caucasus 71,000. Lower Volga 50,000 (a lot!), Belorussia 42,000 ... West Siberia 50,000, East Siberia 30,000 ...'

On and on it goes until he totals it up to 418,000 exiles. Meanwhile he totted up the poods of grain and bread by hand on pieces of paper,* like a village shopkeeper running an empire.

* * *

'Let's get out of town,' scrawled Stalin, around this time to Voroshilov, who replied on the same note:

'Koba, can you see ... Kalmykov for five minutes?'

'I can,' answered Stalin. 'Let's head out of town and take him with us.' The war of extermination in the countryside in no way restrained the magnates' country-house existence. They had been assigned dachas soon after the Revolution where, often, the real power was brokered.

At the centre of this idyllic life was Zubalovo, near Usovo, 35 kilometres outside Moscow, where Stalin and several others had their dachas. Before the Revolution, a Baku oil nabob named Zubalov had built two walled estates, each with a mansion, one for his son, one for himself. There were four houses altogether, gabled Gothic dachas of German design. The Mikoyans shared the Big House at Zubalovo Two with a Red Army commander, a Polish

---

* Throughout his career, he would keep the crown jewels as it were, the Soviet gold reserve or the number of tanks in his reserve at the Battle of Moscow in 1941, scribbled in his personal notebook. He took a special interest in gold production, which was mostly by forced labour.

Communist and Pavel Alliluyev. Voroshilov and other commanders shared a Little House. Their wives and children constantly visited one another – the extended family of the Revolution enjoying a Chekhovian summer.

Stalin's Zubalovo One was a magical world for the children. 'It was a real life of freedom,' recalls Artyom. 'Such happiness,' thought Svetlana. The parents lived upstairs, the children downstairs. The gardens were 'sunny and abundant', wrote Svetlana. Stalin was an enthusiastic gardener though he preferred inspecting and clipping roses to real labour. Photographs show him taking his little children for strolls round the gardens. There was a library, a billiard room, a Russian bath and later a cinema. Svetlana adored this 'happy sheltered life' with its vegetable gardens, orchards and a farm where they milked cows and fed geese, chickens and guinea fowl, cats and white rabbits. 'We had huge white lilacs, dark purple lilacs, jasmine which my mother loved, and a very fragrant shrub with a lemony smell. We walked in the woods with nanny. Picked wild strawberries and blackcurrants and cherries.'

'Stalin's house,' remembers Artyom, 'was full of friends.' Nadya's parents Sergei and Olga were always there – though they now lived apart. They stayed at different ends of the house but bickered at table. While Sergei enjoyed mending anything in the house and was friendly with the servants, Olga, according to Svetlana, 'threw herself into the role of grand lady and loved her high position which my mother never did'.

Nadya played tennis with an immaculate Voroshilov, when he was sober, and Kaganovich, who played in his tunic and boots. Mikoyan, Voroshilov and Budyonny* rode horses brought from the army's cavalry. If it was winter, Kaganovich and Mikoyan skied. Molotov pulled his daughter in a sledge like a nag pulling a peasant's plough. Voroshilov and Sergo were avid hunters. Stalin

---

* The Red Army's Inspector of Cavalry, Semyon Budyonny, born on the Cossack Don, was a former sergeant in the Tsarist Dragoons, decorated during WWI with the St George Cavalryman's ribbon, the highest distinction available. He served first the Tsar, then the Revolution, and then Stalin personally for the rest of his life, distinguishing himself at Tsaritsyn in Voroshilov's Tenth Army and rising to worldwide fame as commander of the First Cavalry Army. When Babel published his *Red Cavalry* stories, telling of the cruelty, lyricism and machismo of the Cossacks and Budyonny's taciturn ruthlessness (and 'dazzling teeth'), the furious commander tried unsuccessfully to suppress them. Never rising to the Politburo, he remained one of Stalin's intimates until the war and, though always devoted to cavalry, studied hard to modernize his military knowledge.

preferred billiards. The Andreyevs were rock climbers which they regarded as a most Bolshevik pursuit. Even in 1930, Bukharin was often at Zubalovo with his wife and daughter. He brought some of his menagerie of animals – his pet foxes ran around the grounds. Nadya was close to 'Bukharchik' and they often walked together. Yenukidze was also a member of this extended family. But there was always business to be done too.

* * *

The children were used to the bodyguards and secretaries: the bodyguards were part of the family. Pauker, the head of the Guards Directorate, and Stalin's own bodyguard, Nikolai Vlasik, were always there. 'Pauker was great fun. He liked children like all Jews and did not have a high opinion of himself but Vlasik strutted around like a stuffed turkey,' says Kira Alliluyeva, Stalin's niece.

Karl Pauker, thirty-six, was the children's favourite, and important to Stalin himself. A symbol of the cosmopolitan culture of the Cheka of that time, this Jewish-Hungarian had been hairdresser at the Budapest Opera before being conscripted into the Austro-Hungarian army, captured by the Russians in 1916 and converted to Bolshevism. He was an accomplished actor, performing accents, especially Jewish ones, for Stalin. Rotund, with his belly held in by a (much-mocked) corset, bald, perfumed, with a scarlet sensuous mouth, this showman loved elaborate OGPU uniforms and pranced around on $1^{1}/_{2}$-inch-heeled boots. He sometimes returned to hairdressing, shaving Stalin like a valet, using talcum powder to fill the pock-marks. The font of delicacies, cars and new products for the Politburo, he kept the secrets of the magnates' private lives and was said to provide girls for Kalinin, Voroshilov and Stalin.

Pauker used to show off his Cadillac, a gift from Stalin, to the children. Long before Stalin officially agreed to bring back the Christmas tree in 1936, Pauker played Father Christmas, delivering presents round the Kremlin and running Christmas parties for the children. The secret policeman as Father Christmas is a symbol of this strange world.

The other figure who was never far away was Stalin's *chef de cabinet*, Alexander Poskrebyshev, thirty-nine, who scuttled round the garden at Zubalovo delivering the latest paperwork. Small, bald, reddish-haired, this bootmaker's son from the Urals had trained as a medical nurse, conducting Bolshevik meetings in his surgery. When Stalin found him working in the CC, he told him, 'You've a fearsome look. You'll terrify people.' This 'narrow-shouldered dwarf' was 'dreadfully ugly', resembling 'a monkey', but possessed 'an excellent memory and was meticulous in his work'. His Special Sector was the heart of Stalin's power machine. Poskrebyshev prepared and attended Politburos.

When Stalin exerted his patronage, helping a protégé get an apartment, it was Poskrebyshev who actually did the work: 'I ask you to HELP THEM IMMEDIATELY,' Stalin typically wrote to him. 'Inform me by letter about quick and exact carrying out of this request.' Lost in the archives until now is Stalin's correspondence with Poskrebyshev: here we find Stalin teasing his secretary: 'I'm receiving English newspapers but not German ... why? How could it be that you make a mistake? Is it bureaucratism? Greetings. J. Stalin.' Sometimes he was in the doghouse: in 1936, one finds on one of Stalin's list of things to do: '1. To forgive Poskrebyshev and his friends.'

The sad, twitchy face of this Quasimodo was a weather vane of the leader's favour. If he was friendly, you were in favour. If not, he sometimes whispered, 'You're in for it today.' The *cognoscenti* knew that the best way to get Stalin to read their letter was to address it to Alexander Nikolaievich. At work, Stalin called him Comrade but at home, he was 'Sasha' or 'the Chief'.

Poskrebyshev was part-buffoon, part-monster, but he later suffered grievously at Stalin's hands. According to his daughter Natalya, he asked if he could study medicine but Stalin made him study economics instead. But in the end, this half-trained nurse provided the only medical care Stalin received.

* * *

Stalin rose late, at about eleven, took breakfast and worked during the day on his piles of papers, which he carried around wrapped in the newspaper – he did not like briefcases. When he was sleeping, anxious parents begged children to be quiet.

The big daytime meal was an expansive 'brunch' at 3–4 p.m. with all the family and, of course, half the Politburo and their wives. When there were visitors, Stalin played the Georgian host. 'He was elaborately hospitable in that Asiatic way,' remembers Leonid Redens, his nephew. 'He was very kind to the children.' Whenever Stalin's brood needed someone to play with, there were their Alliluyev cousins, Pavel's children, Kira, Sasha and Sergei, and the younger boys of Anna Redens. Then there was the

Bolshevik family: Mikoyan's popular sons, whom Stalin nick-named the Mikoyanchiks, only had to scamper over from next door.

The children ran around together but Svetlana found there were too many boys and not enough girls to play with. Her brother Vasily bullied her and showed off by telling her sexual stories that she later admitted disturbed and upset her. 'Stalin was very loving to Svetlana but he did not really like the boys,' recalls Kira. He invented an imaginary girl named Lelka who was Svetlana's perfect alter ego. Weak Vasily was already a problem. Nadya understood this and gave him more attention. But Bolshevik parents did not raise their children: they were brought up by nannies and tutors: 'It was like an aristocratic family in Victorian times,' says Svetlana. 'So were the others, the Kaganoviches, Molotovs, Voroshilovs ... But the ladies of that top circle were all working so my mother did not dress or feed me. I don't remember any physical affection from her but she was very fond of my brother. She certainly loved me, I could tell, but she was a disciplinarian.' Once when she cut up a tablecloth, her mother spanked her hard.

Stalin kissed and squeezed Svetlana with 'overflowing Georgian affection' but she claimed later that she did not like his 'smell of tobacco and bristly moustache'. Her mother, whose love was so hard to earn, became the untouchable saint in her eyes.

* * *

The Bolsheviks, who believed it was possible to create a Leninist 'New Man', placed stern emphasis on education.* The magnates were semi-educated autodidacts who never stopped studying, so their children were expected to work hard and grew up much more cultured than their parents, speaking three languages which they had learned from special tutors. (The Stalin and Molotov children shared the same English tutor.)

The Party did not merely come *before* family, it was an *über*-family: when Lenin died, Trotsky said he was 'orphaned' and Kaganovich was already calling Stalin 'our father'. Stalin lectured

---

* Stalin's ex-secretary, now Editorial Director of *Pravda*, Lev Mekhlis, actually kept a 'Bolshevik diary' for his new born-son, Leonid, in which he confided the crazy fanatical faith in Communism for which he was creating 'this man of the future, this New Man'. On 2 January 1923, the proud father records how he has placed Lenin's portrait 'with a red ribbon' in the pram: 'The baby often looks at the portrait.' He was training the baby 'for the struggle'.

Bukharin that 'the personal element is ... not worth a brass farthing. We're not a family circle or a coterie of close friends – we're the political party of the working class.' They cultivated their coldness.* 'A Bolshevik should love his work more than his wife,' said Kirov. The Mikoyans were a close Armenian family but Anastas was a 'stern, exacting, even severe' father who never forgot he was a Politburo member and a Bolshevik: when he spanked his son, he said in time with the smacks:

'It's not YOU who's Mikoyan, it's ME!' Stepan Mikoyan's mother Ashken 'sometimes "forgot herself" and gave us a hug'. Once at a dinner in the Kremlin, Stalin told Yenukidze, 'A true Bolshevik shouldn't and couldn't have a family because he should give himself wholly to the Party.' As one veteran put it: 'If you have to choose between Party and individual, you choose the Party because the Party has the general aim, the good of many people but one person is just one person.'

Yet Stalin could be very indulgent to children, giving them rides around the estate in his limousine: 'I think "Uncle Stalin" really loved me,' muses Artyom. 'I respected him but I didn't fear him. He managed to make one's conversation interesting. He always made you formulate your thoughts like an adult.'

'Let's play the game of egg breaking – who can break theirs first?' Stalin asked his nephew Leonid when boiled eggs arrived. He entertained the children by throwing orange peel or wine corks into the ice-cream or biscuits into their tea. 'We children thought this was hilarious,' recalls Vladimir Redens.

It was the Caucasian tradition to let babies suck wine off the adults' fingers and when they were older, to give them little glasses of wine. Stalin often gave Vasily, and later Svetlana, sips of wine, which seems harmless (though Vasily died of alcoholism) but this infuriated the stern Nadya. They constantly argued about it. When Nadya or her sister told him off, Stalin just chuckled:

'Don't you know it's medicinal?'

Once Artyom did something that could have become serious because Stalin was already highly suspicious. 'When the leaders were working in the dining room', young Artyom noticed the soup which, as always, was on the sideboard. The boy crept

---

* Kirov, for example, had not seen his sisters for twenty years when he was assassinated and indeed he had not even bothered to tell them who or where he was. They only discovered when they read it in the papers that the famous Kirov was their brother Kostrikov.

behind the backs of Stalin, Molotov and Voroshilov and naughtily sprinkled Stalin's tobacco into the broth. He then waited to see if they would eat it. 'Molotov and Voroshilov tried it and found the tobacco. Stalin asked who did it. I said it was me.'

'Have you tried it?' asked Stalin.

Artyom shook his head.

'Well, it's delicious,' replied Stalin. 'You try it and if you like it, you can go and tell Carolina Vasilevna [Til, the housekeeper] to always put tobacco in the soup. If not, you better not do it again.'

The children were aware that it was a political household. 'We looked at everything with humour and irony,' says Leonid Redens. 'When Stalin dismissed a commissar, we regarded it with amusement.' This was a joke that would not remain funny for long.

This country set knew about the unspeakable depredations in the countryside. Stanislas Redens, Stalin and Nadya's brother-in-law, was the GPU boss of the Ukraine, at the centre of the famine, a job that entailed intimate knowledge and participation: there is no doubt that his wife talked to Nadya about the Ukraine's tragedy. Soon it had poisoned not only Stalin's marriage but the Bolshevik family itself.

5

Holidays and Hell:
the Politburo at the Seaside

In late 1931, Stalin, Nadya and most of the magnates were already on holiday as the hunger turned to famine. They took their holidays very seriously. Indeed, at least ten per cent of the letters between Stalin's circle, even during the worst years of famine, concerned their holidays. (Another twenty per cent concerned their health.) Networking on holiday was the best way to get to know Stalin: more careers were made, more intrigues clinched, on those sunny verandas than on the snowy battlements of the Kremlin.*

There was a fixed ritual for taking these holidays: the question was formally put to the Politburo 'to propose to Comrade Stalin one week's holiday' but by the late twenties, the holidays had expanded from 'twenty days' to one or two months 'on the suggestion of doctors'. Once the dates were arranged, Stalin's secretary sent a memorandum to Yagoda, giving him the schedule 'so bodyguards can be arranged appropriately'.

The potentates set off in private trains, guarded by OGPU troops, southwards to the Soviet Riviera – the Politburo's southern dachas and sanatoria were spread from the Crimea in the west to the Georgian spa of Borzhomi in the east. Molotov preferred the Crimea but Stalin favoured the steamy Black Sea coastline that ran from Sochi down into the semi-tropical towns of Sukhumi and Gagra in Abkhazia. All were state-owned but it was understood that whoever supervised their building had preferential rights to use them.

The magnates moved about to visit one another, asking permission so as not to wreck anyone else's holiday, but naturally they tended to cluster around Stalin. 'Stalin would like to come to

* These long holidays were formally proposed by his colleagues so the decrees in the archives often read: 'At the proposal of Ordzhonikidze' or 'To approve the proposition of Comrades Molotov, Kaganovich, Kalinin to grant Comrade Stalin twenty days holiday.'

Mukhalatka [in the Crimea]* but does not want to disturb anyone else. Ask Yagoda to organize bodyguards ...'

There was a dark side to their holidays. The OGPU carefully planned Stalin's train journey which, during the Hunger, was accompanied by a train of provisions. If, on arrival, the staff thought there was still a shortage of food for Stalin and his guests, his assistants rapidly sent 'a telegram to Orel and Kursk' to despatch more. They eagerly reported that during the journey they had successfully cooked Stalin hot meals. 'As for the GPU,' wrote one of his assistants, 'there's lots of work, massive arrests have taken place' and they were still working on hunting down 'those who remain ... Two bands of bandits have been arrested.'

Stalin's tastes in holiday houses changed but in the thirties, Dacha No. 9 in Sochi was his favourite. Krasnaya Polyana, Red Meadow, was 'a wooden house with a veranda around the whole outside', says Artyom, who usually holidayed with 'Uncle Stalin'.† Stalin's house stood high on the hill while Molotov and Voroshilov's houses stood symbolically in the valley below. When Nadya was on holiday with her husband, they usually invited a wider family, including Yenukidze and the obese proletarian poet, Demian Bedny. It was the job of Stalin's staff, along with the secret police and the local bosses, to prepare the house before his arrival: 'The villa ... has been renovated 100%,' wrote one of his staff, 'as if ready for a great party' with every imaginable fruit.

They enjoyed holidaying in groups, like an American university fraternity house, often without their wives who were with the children in Moscow. 'Molotov and I ride horses, play tennis, skittles, boating, shooting – in a word, a perfect rest,' wrote Mikoyan to his wife, listing the others who were with them. 'It's a male Bolshevik monastery.' But at other times they took their

---

* Mukhalatka was the favourite resort of Molotov and Mikoyan, though both also holidayed in orbit around Stalin at Sochi. It remained a Soviet favourite: the resort is close to Foros where Gorbachev was arrested during the 1991 *coup d'état*. Naturally, being Bolsheviks, the leaders were always sacking the local officials at these resorts: 'Belinsky was rude ... not for the first time,' Stalin wrote to Yagoda and Molotov. 'He should be removed at once from control of Mukhalatka. Appoint someone of the Yagoda type or approved by Yagoda.' If they did not find the holiday houses to their taste, they proposed new luxuries: 'There's no good hotel on the Black Sea for tourist and foreign specialists and working leaders,' wrote Kalinin to Voroshilov. 'To hurry it up, we must give it to the GPU.'

† In the mid-thirties, Miron Merzhanov, Stalin's architect, rebuilt the house in stone. The big, dark green house is still there: there is now a museum with a dummy of Stalin at his desk and a Café Stalin, a mini-Stalin theme park in the gardens.

wives and children too: when Kuibyshev went on holiday, the shock-haired economics boss and poet travelled round the Black Sea with a 'large and jolly troupe' of pretty girls and bon viveurs.

They competed to holiday with Stalin but the most popular companion was the larger-than-life Sergo. Yenukidze often invited his fellow womanizer Kuibyshev to party with him in his Georgian village. Stalin was half jealous of these men and sounded delighted when Molotov failed to rendezvous with Sergo: 'Are you running away from Sergo?' he asked. They always asked each other who was there:

'Here in Nalchik,' wrote Stalin, 'there's me, Voroshilov and Sergo.'

'I got your note,' Stalin told Andreyev. 'Devil take me! I was in Sukhumi and we didn't meet by chance. If I'd known about your intention to visit ... I'd never have left Sochi ... How did you spend your holidays? Did you hunt as much as you wanted?' Once they had arrived at their houses, the magnates advised which place was best: 'Come to the Crimea in September,' Stalin wrote to Sergo from Sochi, adding that Borzhomi in Georgia was comfortable 'because there are no mosquitoes ... In August and half of September, I'll be in Krasnaya Polyana [Sochi]. The GPU have found a very nice dacha in the mountains but my illness prevents me going yet ... Klim [Voroshilov] is now in Sochi and we're quite often together ...'

'In the south,' says Artyom, 'the centre of planning went with him.' Stalin worked on the veranda in a wicker chair with a wicker table on which rested a huge pile of papers. Planes flew south daily bringing his letters. Poskrebyshev (often in a neighbouring cottage) scuttled in to deliver them. Stalin constantly demanded more journals to read. He used to read out letters and then tell the boys his reply. Once he got a letter from a worker complaining that there were no showers at his mine. Stalin wrote on the letter that 'If there is no resolution soon and no water, the director of the mine should be tried as an Enemy of the People.'

Stalin was besieged with questions from Molotov or Kaganovich, left in charge in Moscow. 'Shame we don't have a connection with Sochi by telephone,'* wrote Voroshilov. 'Telephone would

---

* But this has been a boon for historians: their main communication was by letter until 1935 when a safe telephone link was set up between Moscow and the south. Trotsky had paraphrased Herzen's comment on Nicholas I, 'Genghiz Khan with a telegraph', to call Stalin 'Genghiz Khan with a telephone'. Yet it is a sobering thought that for several months a year, he ruled with no telephone at all.

help us. I'd like to visit you for 2–3 days and also have a sleep. I haven't been able to sleep normally for a long time.' But Stalin relished his dominance:

'The number of Politburo inquiries doesn't affect my health,' he told Molotov. 'You can send as many inquiries as you like – I'll be happy to answer them.' They all wrote Stalin long, handwritten letters knowing, as Bukharin put it, 'Koba loves to receive letters.' Kaganovich, in charge in Moscow for the first time, took full advantage of this though the Politburo still took most of the decisions themselves, with Stalin intervening from afar if he disapproved. The vain, abrasive, emotional magnates often argued viciously in Stalin's absence: after a row with his friend Sergo, Kaganovich admitted to Stalin, 'This upset me very much.' Stalin often enjoyed such conflicts: 'Well, dear friends … more squabbling …' None the less, sometimes even Stalin was exasperated: 'I can't and shouldn't give decisions on every possible and imaginable question raised at Politburo. You should be able to study and produce a response … yourselves!'

* * *

There was time for fun too: Stalin took a great interest in the gardens at the house, planting lemon bowers and orange groves, proudly weeding and setting his entourage to toil in the sun. Stalin so appreciated the gardener in Sochi, one Alferov, that he wrote to Poskrebyshev: 'it would be good to put [Alferov] in the Academy of Agriculture – he's the gardener in Sochi, a very good and honest worker …'

His life in the south bore no resemblance to the cold solitude that one associates with Stalin. 'Joseph Vissarionovich liked expeditions into nature,' wrote Voroshilova in her diary. 'He drove by car and we settled near some small river, lit a fire and made a barbecue, singing songs and playing jokes.' The whole entourage went on these expeditions.

'We often all of us get together,' wrote one excited secretary to another. 'We fire air rifles at targets, we often go on walks and expeditions in the cars, we climb into the forest, and have barbecues where we grill kebabs, booze away and then grub's up!' Stalin and Yenukidze entertained the guests with stories of their adventures as pre-revolutionary conspirators while Demian Bedny told 'obscene stories of which he had an inexhaustible reserve'. Stalin shot partridges and went boating.

'I remember the dacha in Sochi when Klim and I were invited

over by Comrade Stalin,' wrote Voroshilova. 'I watched him playing games such as skittles and Nadezhda Sergeevna was playing tennis.' Stalin and the cavalryman Budyonny played skittles with Vasily and Artyom. Budyonny was so strong that when he threw the skittle, he broke the entire set and the shield behind. Everyone laughed about his strength (and stupidity):

'If you're strong you don't need a brain.' They teased him for hurting himself by doing a parachute jump. 'He thought he was jumping off a horse!'

'Only two men were known as the first cavalrymen of the world – Napoleon's Marshal Lannes and Semyon Budyonny,' Stalin defended him, 'so we should listen to everything he says about cavalry!' Years later, Voroshilova could only write: 'What a lovely time it was!'

* * *

That September 1931, Stalin and Nadya were visited by two Georgian potentates, one she loved, one she hated. The popular one was Nestor Lakoba, the Old Bolshevik leader of Abkhazia which he ruled like an independent fiefdom with unusual gentleness. He protected some of the local princes and resisted collectivization, claiming there were no Abkhazian kulaks. When the Georgian Party appealed to Moscow, Stalin and Sergo supported Lakoba. Slim and dapper, with twinkling eyes, black hair brushed back, and a hearing aid because he was partially deaf, this player strolled the streets and cafés of his little realm, like a troubadour. As the maitre d' of the élite holiday resorts, he knew everyone and was always building Stalin new homes and arranging banquets for him – just as he is portrayed in Fasil Iskander's Abkhazian novel, *Sandro of Chegem*. Stalin regarded him as a true ally:

'Me Koba,' he joked, 'you Lakoba!' Lakoba was another of the Bolshevik family, spending afternoons sitting out on the veranda with Stalin. When Lakoba visited the dacha, bringing his feasts and Abkhazian sing-songs, Stalin shouted: 'Vivat Abkhazia!' Artyom says Lakoba's arrival 'was like light pouring into the house'.

Stalin allowed Lakoba to advise him on the Georgian Party, which was particularly clannish and resistant to orders from the centre. This was the reason for the other guest: Lavrenti (the Georgian version of Laurence) Pavlovich Beria, Transcaucasus GPU chief. Beria was balding, short and agile with a broad fleshy face, swollen sensual lips and flickering 'snake eyes' behind a glistening pince-nez. This gifted, intelligent, ruthless and tirelessly competent adventurer, whom Stalin would one day describe as 'our Himmler', brandished the exotic flattery, sexual appetites and elaborate cruelty of a Byzantine courtier in his rise to dominate first the Caucasus, then Stalin's circle, and finally the USSR itself.

Born near Sukhumi of Mingrelian parentage, probably the illegitimate son of an Abkhazian landowner and his pious Georgian mother, Beria had almost certainly served as a double agent for the anti-Communist Mussavist regime that ruled Baku during the Civil War. It was said that Stalin's ally, Sergei Kirov had saved him from the death penalty, a fate he had only escaped because there was no time to arrange the execution. Training as an architect at the Baku Polytechnic, he was attracted by the power of the Cheka, which he then joined and wherein he prospered, promoted by Sergo. Even by the standards of that ghastly organization, he stood out for his sadism. 'Beria is a man for whom it costs nothing to kill his best friend if that best friend said something bad about Beria,' said one of his henchmen. His other career as a sexual adventurer had started, he later told his daughter-in-law, on an architectural study trip to Romania when he had been seduced by an older woman – but while in prison during the Civil War, he fell in love with his cellmate's blonde, golden-eyed teenage niece, Nina Gegechkori, a member of a gentry family: one uncle became a minister in Georgia's Menshevik Government, another in the Bolshevik one. When he was twenty-two, already a senior Chekist, and she was seventeen, she asked for her uncle's release. Beria courted her and they finally eloped on his official train, hence the myth that he raped her in his carriage. On the contrary, she remained in love with her 'charmer' throughout her long life.

Beria was now thirty-two, the personification of the 1918 generation of leaders, much better educated than his elders in the first generation, such as Stalin and Kalinin, both over fifty, or the second, Mikoyan and Kaganovich, in their late thirties. Like the latter, Beria was competitive at everything and an avid sportsman – playing left-back for Georgia's football team, and practising ju-jitsu. Coldly competent, fawningly sycophantic yet gleaming with mischief, he had a genius for cultivating patrons. Sergo, then Caucasus boss, eased his rise in the GPU and, in 1926, introduced him to Stalin for the first time. Beria took over his holiday security.

'Without you,' Beria wrote to Sergo, 'I'd have no one. You're more than a brother or father to me.' Sergo steered Beria through meetings that declared him innocent of working for the enemy. In 1926, when Sergo was promoted to Moscow, Beria fell out with him and began to cultivate the most influential man in the region, Lakoba, importuning him to let him see Stalin again.

Stalin had been irritated by Beria's oleaginous blandishments on holiday. When Beria arrived at the dacha, Stalin grumbled,

'What, he came again?' and sent him away, adding, 'Tell him, here Lakoba's the master!' When Beria fell out with the Georgian bosses, who regarded him as an amoral mountebank, Lakoba backed him. Yet Beria aimed higher.

'Dear Comrade Nestor,' Beria wrote to Lakoba, 'I want very much to see Comrade Koba before his departure ... if you would remind him of it.'

But now Lakoba brought Beria to the *Vozhd*. Stalin had become infuriated by the insubordinate clans of Georgian bosses, who promoted their old friends, gossiped with their patrons in Moscow, and knew too much about his inglorious early antics. Lakoba proposed to replace these Old Bolshevik fat cats with Beria, one of the new generation devoted to Stalin. Nadya hated Beria on sight.

'How can you have that man in the house?'

'He's a good worker,' replied Stalin. 'Give me facts.'

'What facts do you need?' Nadya shrieked back. 'He's a scoundrel. I won't have him in the house.' Stalin later remembered that he sent her to the Devil:

'He's my friend, a good Chekist ... I trust him ...' Kirov and Sergo warned Stalin against Beria but he ignored their advice, something he later regretted. Now he welcomed his new protégé. None the less, 'when he came into the house', recalls Artyom, 'he brought darkness with him.' Stalin, according to Lakoba's notes, agreed to promote the Chekist but asked:

'Will Beria be okay?'

'Beria'll be fine,' replied Lakoba who would soon have reason to regret his reassurance.

After Sochi, Stalin and Nadya took the waters at Tsaltubo. Stalin wrote to Sergo from Tsaltubo to tell him about his new plan for their joint protégé. He joked that he had seen the regional bosses, calling one 'a very comical figure' and another 'now too fat'. He concluded, 'They agreed to bring Beria into the Kraikom [regional committee] of Georgia.' Sergo and the Georgian bosses were appalled at a policeman lording it over old revolutionaries. Yet Stalin happily signed off to Sergo, 'Greetings from Nadya! How's Zina?'

* * *

Taking the waters was an annual pilgrimage. In 1923, Mikoyan found Stalin suffering from rheumatism with his arm bandaged and suggested that he take the waters in the Matsesta Baths near Sochi. Mikoyan even chose the merchant's house with three bedrooms and a salon in which Stalin stayed. It was a mark of the close relationship between the two men. He often took Artyom with him 'in an old open Rolls-Royce made in 1911'. Only his personal bodyguard Vlasik accompanied them.*

Stalin seems to have been shy physically, either because of his arm or his psoriasis: among the leaders, only Kirov went to the baths with him. But he did not mind Artyom. As they soaked in the steam, Stalin told Artyom 'stories about his childhood and adventures in the Caucasus, and discussed our health'.

Stalin was obsessed with his own health and that of his comrades. They were 'responsible workers' for the people, so the preservation of their health was a matter of State. This was already a Soviet tradition: Lenin supervised his leaders' health. By the early thirties, Stalin's Politburo worked so hard and under such pressure that it was not surprising that their health, already undermined by Tsarist exile and Civil War, was seriously compromised. Their letters read like the minutes of a hypochondriacs' convention.†

'Now I'm getting healthy,' Stalin confided in Molotov. 'The waters here near Sochi are very good and work against sclerosis, neurosis, sciatica, gout and rheumatism. Shouldn't you send your wife here?' Stalin suffered the tolls of the poor diet and icy winters of his exiles: his tonsillitis flared up when he was stressed. He so liked the Matsesta specialist, Professor Valedinsky, that he often invited him to drink cognac on the veranda with his children, the

---

* The driver down south was named Nikolai Ivanovich Soloviev who was supposed to have been Nicholas II's driver. In fact Soloviev had been General Brusilov's chauffeur but had once during the First World War driven the Tsar.

† Beria was not the only future monster with whom Stalin concerned himself on this holiday. He also showed a special interest in Nikolai Yezhov, a young official who would be the secret police chief during the coming Terror: 'They say that if Yezhov extends his holidays for a month or two, it's not so bad. Yezhov himself is against this but they say he needs it. Let's prolong his holiday and let him stay in Abastuman for two more months. I'm voting "for".' Yezhov was clearly a man to watch.

novelist Maxim Gorky, and the Politburo. Later he moved Valedinsky to Moscow and the professor remained his personal physician until the war.

His dental problems might themselves have caused his aches. After his dentist Shapiro had worked heroically, at Nadya's insistence, on eight of his rotten and yellowed teeth, Stalin was grateful:

'Do you wish to ask me anything?' The dentist asked a favour. 'The dentist Shapiro who works a lot on our responsible workers asks me (now he's working on me) to place his daughter in the medical department of Moscow University,' Stalin wrote to Poskrebyshev. 'I think we must render such help to this man for the service he does daily for our comrades. So could you do this and fix it ... very quickly ... because we risk running out of time ... I'm awaiting your answer.' If he could not get the daughter into Moscow, then Poskrebyshev must try Leningrad.

Stalin liked to share his health with his friends: 'At Sochi, I arrived with pleurisy (dry),' he told Sergo. 'Now I feel well. I have taken a course of ten therapeutic baths. I've had no more complications with rheumatism.' They told theirs too.

'How's your nephritic stone?' Stalin asked Sergo who was holidaying with Kaganovich. The letters formed a hypochondriacal triangle.

'Kaganovich and I couldn't come, we're sitting on a big steamboat,' replied Sergo, telling 'Soso', 'Kaganovich's a bit ill. The cause isn't clear yet. Maybe his heart is so-so ... Doctors say the water and special baths will help him but he needs a month here ... I feel good but not yet rested ...'

Kaganovich sent a note too, from the Borzhomi Baths: 'Dear Comrade Stalin, I send you a steamy hello ... It's a pity the storm means you can't visit us.' Sergo also told Stalin about Kaganovich's health: 'Kaganovich has swollen legs. The cause isn't yet established but it's possible his heart is beating too faintly. His holiday ends on 30th August but it'll be necessary to prolong it ...' Even those in Moscow sent medical reports to Stalin on holiday: 'Rudzutak's ill and Sergo has microbes of TB and we're sending him to Germany,' Molotov reported to his leader. 'If we got more sleep, we'd make less mistakes.'

* * *

Term was starting so Nadya headed back to Moscow. Stalin returned to Sochi whence he sent her affectionate notes: 'We played bowling and skittles. Molotov has already visited us twice but as for his wife, she's gone off somewhere.' Sergo and Kalinin arrived but 'there's nothing new. Let Vasya and Svetlana write to me.'

Unlike the year before, Stalin and Nadya had got on well during the holidays, to judge by their letters. Despite Beria, her tone was confident and cheerful. Nadya wanted to report to her husband on the situation in Moscow. Far from being anti-Party, she remained as eager as ever to pass her exams and become a qualified manager: she worked hard on her textile designs with Dora Khazan.

'Moscow's better,' she wrote, 'but like a woman powdering to cover her blemishes, especially when it runs and runs in streaks.' Kaganovich's remodelling of Moscow was already shaking the city, such was his explosive energy. The destruction of the Christ the Saviour, the ugly nineteenth-century cathedral, to make way for a much more hideous Palace of the Soviets, was progressing slowly. Nadya began to report 'details' that she thought Stalin needed to know but she saw them from a very feminine aesthetic: 'The Kremlin's clean but its garage-yard's very ugly ... Prices in the shops are very high and stocks very high. Don't be angry that I'm so detailed but I'd like the people to be relieved of all these problems and it would be good for all workers ...' Then she turned back to Stalin himself: 'Please rest well ...' Yet the tensions in government could not be concealed from Nadya: indeed she was living at the heart of them, in the tiny world of the Kremlin where the other leaders visited her every day: 'Sergo called me – he was disappointed by your blaming letter. He looked very tired.'

Stalin was not angry about the 'details'. 'It's good. Moscow changes for the better.' He asked her to call Sergei Kirov, the Leningrad boss, of whom he was especially fond:

'He decided to come to you on 12th September,' she told him, asking a few days later, 'Did Kirov visit you?' Kirov soon arrived in Sochi where his house was one of those down in the valley beneath Stalin's. They played the games that perhaps reflected Stalin's spell as a weatherman:

'With Kirov, we tested the temperature in the valley where he lives and up where I live – there's a difference of two degrees.'*

---

* Later, the old dictator would preside over drinking contests in which his guests would have to drink a cup of vodka for every degree they got wrong.

Stalin was no swimmer, probably because of his bad arm though he told Artyom it was because 'mountain people don't swim'. But now he went swimming with Kirov.

'Good that Kirov visited you,' she wrote back, sweetly, to her husband who had once saved her life in the water. 'You must be careful swimming.' Later he had a special paddling pool built inside the house at Sochi, to precisely his height, so he could cool off in private.

Meanwhile the famine was gaining momentum: Voroshilov wrote to Stalin, encouraging the despatch of leaders into the regions to see what was happening.

'You're right,' Stalin agreed on 24 September 1931. 'We don't always understand the meaning of personal trips and personal acquaintance of people with affairs. We'd win a lot more often if we travelled more and got to know people. I didn't want to go on holiday but ... was very tired and my health's improving ...' He was not the only one on holiday while discussing the famine: Budyonny reported starvation but concluded, 'The building on my new country house is finished, it's very pretty ...'

'It's raining endlessly in Moscow,' Nadya informed Stalin. 'The children have already had flu. I protect myself by wrapping up warmly.' Then she teased him playfully about a defector's book about Lenin and Stalin. 'I read the White journals. There's interesting material about you. Are you curious? I asked Dvinsky [Poskrebyshev's deputy] to find it ... Sergo phoned and complained about his pneumonia ...'

There was a fearsome storm in Sochi: 'The gale howled for two days with the fury of an enraged beast,' wrote Stalin. 'Eighteen large oaks uprooted in the grounds of our *dacha* ...' He was happy to receive the children's letters. 'Kiss them from me, they're good children.'

Svetlana's note to her 'First Secretary' commanded:

'Hello *Papochka*. Come home quickly – it's an order!' Stalin obeyed. The crisis was worsening.

6

Trains Full of Corpses:
Love, Death and Hysteria

'The peasants ate dogs, horses, rotten potatoes, the bark of trees, anything they could find,' observed one witness, Fedor Belov, while, on 21 December 1931, in the midst of this crisis, Stalin celebrated his birthday at Zubalovo. 'I remember visiting that house with Kliment on birthdays and recall the hospitality of Joseph Vissarionovich. Songs, dances, yes, yes, dances. All were dancing as they could!' wrote the diarist Ekaterina Voroshilova, Jewish wife of the Defence Commissar, herself a revolutionary, once Yenukidze's mistress and now a fattening housewife. First they sang: Voroshilova recalled how they performed operatic arias, peasant romances, Georgian laments, Cossack ballads – and, surprisingly for these godless ruffians, hymns, learned in village churches and seminaries.

Sometimes they forgot the ladies and burst into bawdy songs too. Voroshilov and Stalin, both ex-choirboys, sang together: Stalin 'had a good tenor voice and he loved songs and music,' she writes. 'He had his favourite arias' – he particularly liked old Georgian melodies, arias from *Rigoletto*, and he always wanted to hear the hymn from the Orthodox liturgy, *Mnogaya leta*. He later told President Truman, 'Music's an excellent thing, it reduces the beast in men', a subject on which he was surely something of an expert. Stalin's pitch was perfect: it was a 'rare' and 'sweet' voice. Indeed, one of his lieutenants said he was good enough to have become a professional singer, a mind-boggling historical possibility.

Stalin presided over the American gramophone – he 'changed the discs and entertained the guests – he loved the funny ones'. Molotov was 'dancing the Russian way with a handkerchief' with Polina in the formal style of someone who had learned ballroom dancing. The Caucasians dominated the dancing. As Voroshilova describes it, Anastas Mikoyan danced up to Nadya Stalin. This Armenian who had studied for the priesthood like Stalin himself, was slim, circumspect, wily and industrious, with black hair, moustache and flashing eyes, a broken aquiline nose and a taste for immaculate clothes that, even when clad in his usual tunic and boots, lent him the air of a lithe dandy. Highly intelligent with the driest of wits, he had a gift for languages, understanding English and, in 1931, he taught himself German by translating *Das Kapital*.

Mikoyan was not afraid to contradict Stalin yet became the great survivor of Soviet history, still at the top in Brezhnev's time. A Bolshevik since 1915, he had managed to escape the fate of the famous Twenty-Six Commissars shot during the Civil War, and was now the overlord of trade and supply.* Svetlana, Stalin's daughter, thought him the most attractive of the magnates, 'youthful and dashing'. He was certainly the finest dancer and sharpest dresser. 'One was never bored with Mikoyan,' says Artyom. 'He's our cavalier,' declared Khrushchev. 'At least he's the best we've got!' But he warned against trusting that 'shrewd fox from the east'.

Though devoted to his modest, cosy wife Ashken, Mikoyan, perhaps trying to include Nadya in the festivities, 'for a long time scraped his feet before Nadezhda Sergeevna, asking her to dance the *lezginka* [a traditional Caucasian dance that she knew well] with him. He danced in very quick time, stretching up as if taller and thinner.' But Nadya was 'so shy and bashful' at this Armenian chivalry that she 'covered her face with her hands and, as if unable to react to this sweet and artistic dance, she slipped from his active approaches'. Perhaps she was aware of Stalin's jealousy.

Voroshilov was as light-footed a tripper on the dancefloor as he was a graceless blunderer on the political stage. He danced the *gopak* and then asked for partners for what his wife called 'his star-turn, the *polka*'. It was no wonder that the atmosphere among the magnates was so febrile. In the countryside, the regime itself seemed to be tottering.

* * *

By the summer, when Fred Beal, an American radical, visited a village near Kharkov, then capital of Ukraine, he found the inhabitants dead except one insane woman. Rats feasted on huts that had become charnel-houses.

---

* Mikoyan was the Vicar of Bray of Soviet politics. 'From Illich [Lenin] to Illich [Leonid Illich Brezhnev],' went the Russian saying, 'without accident or stroke!' A veteran Soviet official described Mikoyan thus: 'The rascal was able to walk through Red Square on a rainy day without an umbrella without getting wet.'

On 6 June 1932, Stalin and Molotov declared that 'no matter of deviation – regarding either amounts or deadlines set for grain deliveries – can be permitted.' On 17 June, the Ukrainian Politburo, led by Vlas Chubar and Stanislas Kosior, begged for food assistance as the regions were in 'a state of emergency'. Stalin blamed Chubar and Kosior themselves, combined with wrecking by enemies – the famine itself was merely a hostile act against the Central Committee, hence himself. 'The Ukraine,' he wrote to Kaganovich, 'has been given more than it should get.' When an official bravely reported it to the Politburo, Stalin interrupted: 'They tell us, Comrade Terekhov, that you're a good orator, but it transpires that you're a good story-teller. Fabricating such a fairy tale about famine! Thought you'd scare us but it won't work. Wouldn't it be better for you to leave the posts of ... Ukrainian CC Secretary and join the Writers' Union: you'll concoct fables, and fools will read them.' Mikoyan was visited by a Ukrainian who asked, 'Does Comrade Stalin – for that matter does anyone in the Politburo – know what is happening in Ukraine? Well if not, I'll give you some idea. A train recently pulled into Kiev loaded with corpses of people who had starved to death. It had picked up corpses all the way from Poltava ...'

The magnates knew exactly what was happening:* their letters show how they spotted terrible things from their luxury trains. Budyonny told Stalin from Sochi, where he was on holiday, 'Looking at people from the windows of the train, I see very tired people in old worn clothes, our horses are skin and bone ...' President Kalinin, Stalin's anodyne 'village elder', sneered at the 'political impostors' asking 'contributions for "starving" Ukraine. Only degraded disintegrating classes can produce such cynical elements.' Yet on 18 June 1932, Stalin admitted to Kaganovich what he called the 'glaring absurdities' of 'famine' in Ukraine.

The death toll of this 'absurd' famine, which only occurred to raise money to build pig-iron smelters and tractors, was between

---

* When Beal, the American, reported to the Chairman of Ukraine's Central Executive Committee (the titular President), Petrovsky, he replied: 'We know millions are dying. That is unfortunate but the glorious future of the Soviet Union will justify it.' By 1933, it is estimated that 1.1 million households, that is seven million people, lost their holdings and half of them were deported. As many as three million households were liquidated. At the start of this process in 1931, there were 13 million households collectivized out of roughly 25 million. By 1937, 18.5 million were collectivized but there were now only 19.9 million households: 5.7 million households, perhaps 15 million persons, had been deported, many of them dead.

four to five, and as high as, ten million dead, a tragedy unequalled in human history except by the Nazi and Maoist terrors. The peasants had always been the Bolshevik Enemy. Lenin himself had said: 'The peasant must do a bit of starving.' Kopelev admitted 'with the rest of my generation, I firmly believed the ends justified the means. I saw people dying from hunger.' 'They deny responsibility for what happened later,' wrote Nadezhda Mandelstam, wife of the poet, in her classic memoir, *Hope Abandoned*. 'But how can they? It was, after all, these people of the Twenties who demolished the old values and invented the formulas ... to justify the unprecedented experiment: You can't make an omelette without breaking eggs. Every new killing was excused on the grounds we were building a remarkable "new" world.' The slaughter and famine strained the Party but its members barely winced: how did they tolerate death on such a vast scale?

* * *

'A revolution without firing squads,' Lenin is meant to have said, 'is meaningless.' He spent his career praising the Terror of the French Revolution because his Bolshevism was a unique creed, 'a social system based on blood-letting'. The Bolsheviks were atheists but they were hardly secular politicians in the conventional sense: they stooped to kill from the smugness of the highest moral eminence. Bolshevism may not have been a religion, but it was close enough. Stalin told Beria the Bolsheviks were 'a sort of military-religious order'. When Dzerzhinsky, founder of the Cheka died, Stalin called him 'a devout knight of the proletariat'. Stalin's 'order of sword-bearers' resembled the Knights Templars, or even the theocracy of the Iranian Ayatollahs, more than any traditional secular movement. They would die and kill for their faith in the inevitable progress towards human betterment, making sacrifices of their own families with a fervour only seen in the religious slaughters and martyrdoms of the Middle Ages – and the Middle East.

They regarded themselves as special 'noble-blooded' people. When Stalin asked General Zhukov if the capital might fall in 1941, he said, 'Can we hold Moscow, tell me as a Bolshevik?' as an eighteenth-century Englishman might say, 'Tell me as a gentleman!'

The 'sword-bearers' had to *believe* with Messianic faith, to act with the correct ruthlessness, and to convince others they were *right* to do so. Stalin's 'quasi-Islamic' fanaticism was typical of the Bolshevik magnates: Mikoyan's son called his father 'a Bolshevik fanatic'. Most* came from devoutly religious backgrounds. They hated Judaeo-Christianity – but the orthodoxy of their parents was replaced by something even more rigid, a systematic amorality: 'This religion – or science, as it was modestly called by its adepts – invests man with a godlike authority ... In the Twenties, a good many people drew a parallel to the victory of Christianity and thought this new religion would last a thousand years,' wrote Nadezhda Mandelstam. 'All were agreed on the superiority of the new creed that promised heaven on earth instead of other worldly rewards.'

The Party justified its 'dictatorship' through purity of faith. Their Scriptures were the teachings of Marxism-Leninism, regarded as a 'scientific' truth. Since ideology was so important, every leader had to be – or seem to be – an expert on Marxism-Leninism, so that these ruffians spent their weary nights studying, to improve their esoteric credentials, dreary articles on dialectical materialism. It was so important that Molotov and Polina even discussed Marxism in their love letters: 'Polichka my darling ... reading Marxist classics is very necessary ... You must read some more of Lenin's works coming out soon and then a number of Stalin's ... I so want to see you.'

'Partymindedness' was 'an almost mystical concept', explained Kopelev. 'The indispensable prerequisites were iron discipline and faithful observance of all the rituals of Party life.' As one veteran Communist put it, a Bolshevik was not someone who believed merely in Marxism but 'someone who had absolute faith in the Party no matter what ... A person with the ability to adapt his morality and conscience in such a way that he can unreservedly accept the dogma that the Party is never wrong – even though it's wrong all the time.' Stalin did not exaggerate when he boasted: 'We Bolsheviks are people of a special cut.'

* * *

Nadya was not of 'a special cut'. The famine fed the tensions in Stalin's marriage. When little Kira Alliluyeva visited her uncle

---

* If anything, the Old Bolsheviks had a religious education: Stalin, Yenukidze and Mikoyan were seminarists, Voroshilov a choirboy; Kalinin attended church into his teens. Even Beria's mother spent so much time at church, she actually died there. Kaganovich's Jewish parents were *frum*: when they visited him in the Kremlin, his mother was not impressed – 'But you're all atheists!' she said.

Redens, GPU chief in Kharkov, she opened the blinds of her special train and saw, to her amazement, starving people with swollen bellies, begging to the train for food, and starving dogs running alongside. Kira told her mother, Zhenya, who fearlessly informed Stalin.

'Don't pay any attention,' he replied. 'She's a child and makes things up.'* In the last year of Stalin's marriage, we find fragments of both happiness and misery. In February 1932, it was Svetlana's birthday: she starred in a play for her parents and Politburo. The two boys Vasya and Artyom recited verses.

'Things here seem to be alright, we're all very well. The children are growing up, Vasya is ten now and Svetlana five … She and her father are great friends …' Nadya wrote to Stalin's mother Keke in Tiflis. It was hardly an occasion to confide great secrets but the tone is interesting. 'Altogether we have terribly little free time, Joseph and I. You've probably heard that I've gone back to school in my old age. I don't find studying difficult in itself. But it's pretty difficult trying to fit it in with my duties at home in the course of the day. Still, I'm not complaining and so far, I'm coping with it all quite successfully. …' She was finding it hard to cope.

Stalin's own nerves were strained to the limit but he remained jealous of her: he felt old friends Yenukidze and Bukharin were undermining him with Nadya. Bukharin visited Zubalovo, strolling the gardens with her. Stalin was working but returned and crept up on them in the garden, leaping out to shout at Bukharin:

'I'll kill you!' Bukharin naïvely regarded this as an Asiatic joke. When Bukharin married a teenage beauty, Anna Larina, another child of a Bolshevik family, Stalin tipsily telephoned him during the night: 'Nikolai I congratulate you. You outspit me this time too!' Bukharin asked how. 'A good wife, a beautiful wife … younger than my Nadya!'

At home, Stalin alternated between absentee bully and hectored husband. Nadya had in the past snitched on dissenters at the Academy: in these last months, it is hard to tell if she was denouncing Enemies or riling Stalin who ordered their arrest. There is the story of this 'peppery woman' shouting at him:

---

* The Alliluyevs had only recently returned from Germany and they were shocked by the changes: 'There were barriers and queues everywhere,' remembered Kira. 'Everyone was hungry and scared. My mother was ashamed to wear the dresses she brought back. Everyone made fun of European fashions.'

'You're a tormentor, that's what you are! You torment your own son, your wife, the whole Russian people.' When Stalin discussed the importance of the Party above family, Yenukidze replied: 'What about your children?' Stalin shouted, 'They're hers!' pointing at Nadya, who ran out crying.

Nadya was becoming ever more hysterical, or as Molotov put it, 'unbalanced'. Sergo's daughter Eteri, who had every reason to hate Stalin, explains, 'Stalin didn't treat her well but she like all the Alliluyevs was very unstable.' She seemed to become estranged from the children and everything else. Stalin confided in Khrushchev that he sometimes locked himself in the bathroom, while she beat on the door, shouting.

'You're an impossible man. It's impossible to live with you!' This image of Stalin as the powerless henpecked husband besieged, cowering in his own bathroom by the wild-eyed Nadya, must rank as the most incongruous vision of the Man of Steel in his entire career. Himself frantic, with his mission in jeopardy, Stalin was baffled by Nadya's mania. She told a friend that 'everything bored her – she was sick of everything'.

'What about the children?' asked the friend.

'Everything, even the children.' This gives some idea of the difficulties Stalin faced. Nadya's state of mind sounds more like a psychological illness than despair caused by political protest or even her oafish husband. 'She had attacks of melancholy,' Zhenya told Stalin, she was 'sick'. The doctors prescribed 'caffeine' to pep her up. Stalin later blamed the caffeine and he was right: caffeine would have disastrously exacerbated her despair.

* * *

Stalin became hysterical himself, feeling the vast Ukrainian steppes slipping out of his control: 'It seems that in some regions of Ukraine, Soviet power has ceased to exist,' Stalin scribbled to Kosior, Politburo member and Ukrainian boss. 'Is this true? Is the situation so bad in Ukrainian villages? What's the GPU doing? Maybe you'll check this problem and take measures.' The magnates again roamed the heartland to raise grain, more ferocious semi-military expeditions with OGPU troops and Party officials wearing pistols – Molotov headed to the Urals, the Lower Volga and Siberia. While he was there, the wheels of his car became stuck in a muddy rut and the car rolled over into a ditch. No one was hurt but Molotov claimed, 'An attempt was made on my life.'

Stalin sensed the doubts of the local bosses, making him more aware than ever that he needed a new, tougher breed of lieutenant like Beria whom he promoted to rule the Caucasus. Summoning the Georgian bosses to Moscow, Stalin turned viciously against the Old Bolshevik 'chieftains':

'I've got the impression that there's no Party organization in Transcaucasia at all,' Stalin played to the gallery. 'There's just the rule of chieftains – voting for whomsoever they drink wine with … It's a total joke … We need to promote men who work honestly … Whenever we send anyone down there, they become chieftains too!' Everyone laughed but then he turned serious: 'We'll smash all their bones if this rule of chieftains isn't liquidated …'

Sergo was away.

'Where is he?' whispered one of the officials to Mikoyan who answered:

'Why should Sergo participate in Beria's coronation? He knows him well enough.' There was open opposition to the promotion of Beria: the local chiefs had almost managed to have him removed to a provincial backwater but Stalin had saved him. Then Stalin defined the essence of Beria's career:

'He solves problems while the Buro just pushes paper!'*

'It's not going to work, Comrade Stalin. We can't work together,' replied one Georgian.

'I can't work with that charlatan!' said another.

'We'll settle this question the routine way,' Stalin angrily ended the meeting, appointing Beria Georgian First Secretary and Second Secretary of Transcaucasia over their heads. Beria had arrived.

* * *

In Ukraine, Fred Beal wandered through villages where no one was left alive and found heartbreaking messages scrawled beside the bodies: 'God bless those who enter here, may they never suffer as we have,' wrote one. Another read: 'My son. We couldn't wait. God be with you.'

Kaganovich, patrolling the Ukraine, was unmoved. He was more outraged by the sissy leaders there: 'Hello dear Valerian,' he wrote warmly to Kuibyshev, 'We're working a lot on the question of grain preparation … We had to criticize the regions a lot,

---

* Margaret Thatcher used a similar expression about her favourite minister, Lord Young: 'He brings me solutions: others bring me problems.' Every leader prizes such lieutenants.

especially Ukraine. Their mood, particularly that of Chubar, is very bad ... I reprimanded the regions.' But in the midst of this wasteland of death, Kaganovich was not going to spoil anyone's holidays: 'How are you feeling? Where are you planning to go for holidays? Don't think I'm going to call you back before finishing your holidays ...'

After a final meeting with Kaganovich and Sergo in his office on 29 May 1932, Stalin and Nadya left for Sochi. Lakoba and Beria visited them but the latter now had his access to Stalin. He ditched his patron, Lakoba, who muttered in Beria's hearing,

'What a vile person.'

We do not know how Stalin and Nadya got on during this holiday but, day by day, the pressure ratcheted up. Stalin governed a country on the edge of rebellion by correspondence, receiving the bad news in heaps of GPU reports – and the doubts of his friends.* While Kaganovich suppressed the rebellious textile workers of Ivanovo, Voroshilov was unhappy and sent Stalin a remarkable letter: 'Across the Stavropol region, I saw all the fields uncultivated. We were expecting a good harvest but didn't get it ... Across the Ukraine from my train window, the truth is it looks even less cultivated than the North Caucasus ...' Voroshilov finished his note: 'Sorry to tell you such things during your holiday but I can't be silent.'

Stalin later told Churchill this was the most difficult time of his life, harder even than Hitler's invasion: 'it was a terrible struggle' in which he had to destroy 'ten million. It was fearful. Four years it lasted. It was absolutely necessary ... It was no use arguing with them. A certain number of them had been resettled in the northern parts of the country ... Others had been slaughtered by the peasants themselves – such had been the hatred for them.'

The peasants understandably attacked Communist officials. Sitting on the terrace of the Sochi dacha in the baking heat, an angry, defensive Stalin seethed about the breakdown of discipline and betrayal in the Party. At times like this, he seemed to retreat

---

* Stalin felt the 'circle of friends', tempered by the fight with the oppositions, was falling apart under the pressure of crisis and rows between Sergo and Molotov, as he confided in Kaganovich: Comrade Kuibyshev, already an alcoholic, 'creates a bad impression. It seems he flees from work ... Still worse is the conduct of Comrade Ordzhonikidze. The latter evidently does not take into account that his conduct (with sharpness against Comrades Molotov and Kuibyshev) leads to the undermining of our leading group.' Furthermore, Stalin was dissatisfied with Kosior and Rudzutak among others in the Politburo.

into a closed melodramatic fortress surrounded by enemies. On 14 July, he put pen to paper ordering Molotov and Kaganovich in Moscow to create a draconian law to shoot hungry peasants who stole even husks of grain. They drew up the notorious decree against 'misappropriation of socialist property' with grievous punishments 'based on the text of your letter'.* On 7 August, this became law. Stalin was now in a state of nervous panic, writing to Kaganovich: 'If we don't make an effort now to improve the situation in Ukraine, we may lose Ukraine.' Stalin blamed the weakness and naïvety of his brother-in-law, Redens, Ukrainian GPU chief, and the local boss Kosior. The place 'was riddled with Polish agents, who 'are many times stronger than Redens or Kosior think'. He had Redens replaced with someone tougher.

* * *

Nadya returned early to Moscow, perhaps to study, perhaps because the tension in Sochi was unbearable. Her headaches and abdominal pains worsened. This in turn can only have added to Stalin's anxieties but his nerves were so much stronger. Her letters do not survive: perhaps he destroyed them, perhaps she did not write any, but we know she had been influenced against the campaign: 'she was easily swayed by Bukharin and Yenukidze.'

Voroshilov crossed Stalin, suggesting that his policies could have been resisted by a concerted effort of the Politburo. When a Ukrainian comrade named Korneiev shot a (possibly starving) thief and was arrested, Stalin thought he should not be punished. But Voroshilov, an unlikely moral champion, looked into the case, discovered the victim was a teenager and wrote to Stalin to support Korneiev's sentence, even if he only served a short jail term. The day he received Klim's letter, 15 August, Stalin angrily overruled Voroshilov, freed Korneiev, and promoted him.

Six days after Voroshilov's stand, on 21 August, Riutin, who earlier had been arrested for criticizing Stalin, met with some comrades to agree their 'Appeal to All Party Members', a devastating manifesto for his deposition. Within days, Riutin had been denounced to the GPU. Riutin's opposition, so soon after the Syrtsov–Lominadze affair and Voroshilov's waverings, rattled

---

* Just as the grain fuelled the industrial engine, so did the peasants themselves. The same week, Stalin and Sergo, on holiday in Sochi, ordered Kaganovich and Molotov to transfer another 20,000 slave labourers, probably kulaks, to work on their new industrial city, Magnitogorsk. The repression perhaps deliberately provided slave labour.

Stalin. On 27 August, he was back in the Kremlin meeting Kaganovich. Perhaps he also returned to join Nadya.

Whatever the ghastly situation in the country, her health alone would have been enough to undermine the morale of a strong person. She was terribly ill, suffering 'acute pains in the abdominal region' with the doctor adding on her notes: 'Return for further examination.' This was not just caused by psychosomatic tension due to the crisis but also by the aftermath of the 1926 abortion.

On 31 August, Nadya was examined again: did Stalin accompany her to the Kremlevka clinic? He had only two appointments, at 4 p.m. and 9 p.m. as if his day had been deliberately left open. The doctors noted: 'Examination to consider operation in 3–4 weeks' time.' Was this for her abdomen or her head? Yet they did not operate.

On 30 September, Riutin was arrested. It is possible that Stalin, supported by Kaganovich, demanded the death penalty for Riutin but the execution of a comrade – a fellow 'sword-bearer' – was a dangerous step, resisted by Sergo and Kirov. There is no evidence that it was ever formally discussed – Kirov did not attend Politburo sessions in late September and October. Besides, Stalin would not have proposed such a measure without first canvassing Sergo and Kirov, just as he had in the case of Tukhachevsky in 1930. He probably never proposed it specifically. On 11 October, Riutin was sentenced to ten years in the camps.

Riutin's 'Platform' touched Stalin's home. According to the bodyguard Vlasik, Nadya procured a copy of the Riutin document from her friends at the Academy and showed it to Stalin. This does not mean she joined the opposition but it sounds aggressive, though she might also have been trying to be helpful. Later it was found in her room. In the fifties, Stalin admitted that he had not paid her enough attention during those final months: 'There was so much pressure on me ... so many Enemies. We had to work day and night ...' Perhaps literary matters proved a welcome distraction.

7

Stalin the Intellectual

On 26 October 1932, a chosen élite of fifty writers were mysteriously invited to the art deco mansion of Russia's greatest living novelist, Maxim Gorky.* The tall, haggard writer with the grizzled moustache, now sixty-four, met the guests on the stairway. The dining room was filled with tables covered in smart white cloths. They waited in excited anticipation. Then Stalin arrived with Molotov, Voroshilov and Kaganovich. The Party took literature so seriously that the magnates personally edited the work of prominent writers. After some small talk, Stalin and his comrades sat down at the end table near Gorky himself. Stalin stopped smiling and started to talk about the creation of a new literature.

It was a momentous occasion: Stalin and Gorky were the two most famous men in Russia, their relationship a barometer of Soviet literature itself. Ever since the late twenties, Gorky had been so close to Stalin that he had holidayed with Stalin and Nadya. Born Maxim Peshkov in 1868, he had used his own bitter (hence his *nom de plume*, Gorky) experiences as an orphaned street Arab, who had survived 'vile abominations' living on scraps among outcasts in peasant villages, to write masterpieces that inspired the Revolution. But in 1921, disillusioned with Lenin's dictatorship, he went into exile in a villa in Sorrento, Italy. Stalin put out feelers to lure him back. Meanwhile Stalin had placed Soviet literature under RAPP (the Russian Association of Proletarian Writers), 'the literary wing of Stalin's Five-Year Plan for industry', which harassed and attacked any writers who did not depict the Great Turn with ecstatic enthusiasm. Gorky and Stalin began a complex *pas de deux* in which vanity, money and power

---

* None of the great writers, like Akhmatova, Mandelstam, Pasternak, Bulgakov or Babel, were there but Sholokhov, whom Stalin regarded as 'a great artistic talent', was present.

played their role in encouraging the writer to return. Gorky's experience of the savage backwardness of the peasantry made him support Stalin's war on the villages but he found the standard of RAPP literature to be dire. By 1930, Gorky's life was already oiled with generous gifts from the GPU.

Stalin concentrated his feline charms on Gorky.* In 1931, he returned to become Stalin's literary ornament, granted a large allowance as well as the millions he made from his books. He lived in the mansion in Moscow that had belonged to the tycoon Ryabushinsky, a large dacha outside the capital and a palatial villa in the Crimea along with numerous staff, all GPU agents. Gorky's houses became the headquarters of the intelligentsia where he helped brilliant young writers like Isaac Babel and Vasily Grossman.

The magnates embraced Gorky as their own literary celebrity while the Chekist Yagoda took over the details of running Gorky's household, spending more and more time there himself. Stalin took his children to see Gorky where they played with his grandchildren; Mikoyan brought his sons to play with Gorky's pet monkey. Voroshilov came for sing-songs. Gorky's granddaugher Martha played with Babel one day; Yagoda the next.

Stalin liked him: 'Gorky was here,' he wrote to Voroshilov in an undated note. 'We talked about things. A good, clever, friendly person. He's fond of our policy. He understands everything ... In politics he's with us against the Right.' But he was also aware of Gorky as an asset who could be bought. In 1932, Stalin ordered the celebration of Gorky's forty literary years. His home town, Nizhni Novgorod, was renamed after him. So was Moscow's main street, Tverskaya. When Stalin named the Moscow Art Theatre after the writer, the literary bureaucrat Ivan Gronsky retorted:

'But Comrade Stalin, the Moscow Art Theatre is really more associated with Chekhov.'

'That doesn't matter. Gorky's a vain man. We must bind him with cables to the Party,' replied Stalin. It worked: during the kulak liquidation, Gorky unleashed his hatred of the backward

---

* 'During the Congress I was busy with work,' he wrote to Gorky during 1930 in a friendly, confiding tone. 'Now things are different and I can write. It's not of course good, but now we have the opportunity to smooth out the fault. "No fault, no repentance, no repentance, no salvation." They say you're writing a play about the wreckers and you want new material. I'm gathering material and will send it to you ... When are you coming to the USSR?' He treated Gorky almost as a member of the Soviet Government, consulting him on Molotov's promotion. If he was late in his replies, Stalin apologized for his 'swinish' behaviour.

peasants in *Pravda*: 'If the enemy does not surrender, he must be exterminated.' He toured concentration camps and admired their re-educational value. He supported slave labour projects such as the Belomor Canal which he visited with Yagoda, whom he congratulated: 'You rough fellows do not realize what great work you're doing!'

Yagoda, the dominant secret policeman, followed in Stalin's wake. 'The first generation of young Chekists ... was distinguished by its sophisticated tastes and weakness for literature,' wrote Nadezhda Mandelstam. 'The Chekists were the avant-garde of the New People.' The *grand seigneur* of this avant-garde was Yagoda, thirty-nine, who now fell in love with Gorky's daughter-in-law, Timosha; she was 'young, very beautiful, merry, simple, delightful' and married to Max Peshkov.

Son of a jeweller, trained as a statistician and learning pharmacy as a chemist's assistant, Genrikh Yagoda (his real first name was Enoch), who had joined the Party in 1907, was also from Nizhny Novgorod, which gave him his calling card. 'Superior to' the creatures that followed him, according to Anna Larina, Yagoda became 'a corrupt ... careerist' but he was never Stalin's man. He had been closer to the Rightists but swapped sides in 1929. His great achievement, supported by Stalin, was the creation by slave labour of the vast economic empire of the Gulags. Yagoda himself was devious, short and balding, always in full uniform, with a taste for French wines and sex toys: another green-fingered killer, he boasted that his huge dacha bloomed with '2000 orchids and roses', while spending almost four million roubles decorating his residences.* He frequented Gorky's houses, courting Timosha with bouquets of his orchids. Gorky was appointed head of the Writers' Union and advised Stalin to scrap the RAPP, which was abolished in April 1932, causing both delight and confusion among the intelligentsia who eagerly hoped for some improvement. Then came this invitation.

* Voroshilov, another Bolshevik *seigneur*, regularly sent Yagoda gifts: 'I received the horse,' Yagoda thanked Voroshilov in one note. 'It's not just a horse but a full-blooded thoroughbred. Warmest thanks. GY.' But Yagoda was also married to revolutionary royalty: Ida, his wife, was the niece of Sverdlov, the organizing genius and first Head of State. By coincidence, Gorky had adopted Ida's uncle. Yagoda's brother-in-law was Leopold Averbakh, a proletarian writer, who had been Chairman of RAPP, who helped lure Gorky back to Moscow and who formed one of his circle when he arrived.

Playing ominously with a pearl-handled penknife and now suddenly 'stern', with a 'taste of iron' in his voice, Stalin proposed: 'The artist ought to show life truthfully. And if he shows our life truthfully he cannot fail to show it moving to socialism. This is, and will be, Socialist Realism.' In other words, the writers had to describe what life should be, a panegyric to the Utopian future, not what life was. Then there was a touch of farce, as usual provided unconsciously by Voroshilov:

'You produce the goods that we need,' said Stalin. 'Even more than machines, tanks, aeroplanes, we need human souls.' But Voroshilov, ever the simpleton, took this literally and interrupted Stalin to object that tanks were also 'very important'.

The writers, Stalin declared, were 'engineers of human souls', a striking phrase of boldness and crudity – and he jabbed a finger at those sitting closest to him.

'Me? Why me?' retorted the nearest writer. 'I'm not arguing.'

'What's the good of just not arguing?' interrupted Voroshilov again. 'You have to get on with it.' By now, some of the writers were drunk on Gorky's wine and the heady aroma of power. Stalin filled their glasses. Alexander Fadeev, the drunken novelist and most notorious of literary bureaucrats, asked Stalin's favourite Cossack novelist, Mikhail Sholokhov, to sing. The writers clinked glasses with Stalin.

'Let's drink to the health of Comrade Stalin,' called out the poet Lugovskoi. The novelist Nikoforov jumped up and said:

'I'm fed up with this! We've drunk Stalin's health one million one hundred and forty-seven thousand times. He's probably fed up with it himself ...' There was silence. But Stalin shook Nikoforov's hand:

'Thank you, Nikoforov, thank you. I am fed up with it.'

* * *

None the less Stalin never tired of dealing with writers. When Mandelstam mused that poetry was more respected in Russia, where 'people are killed for it', than anywhere else, he was right. Literature mattered greatly to Stalin. He may have demanded 'engineers of the human soul' but he was himself far from the oafish philistine which his manners would suggest. He not only admired and appreciated great literature, he discerned the difference between hackery and genius. Ever since the seminary in the 1890s, he had read voraciously, claiming a rate of five hundred pages daily: in exile, when a fellow prisoner died, Stalin purloined his library and refused to share it with his outraged comrades. His hunger for literary knowledge was almost as driving as his Marxist faith and megalomania: one might say these were the ruling passions of his life. He did not possess literary talents himself but in terms of his reading alone, he was an intellectual, despite being the son of a cobbler and a washerwoman. Indeed, it would be no exaggeration to say that Stalin was the best-read ruler of Russia from Catherine the Great up to Vladimir Putin, even including Lenin who was no mean intellectual himself and had enjoyed the benefits of a nobleman's education.

'He worked very hard to improve himself,' said Molotov. His library consisted of 20,000 well-used volumes. 'If you want to know the people around you,' Stalin said, 'find out what they read.' Svetlana found books there from the *Life of Jesus* to the novels of Galsworthy,* Wilde, Maupassant and later Steinbeck and Hemingway. His granddaughter later noticed him reading Gogol, Chekhov, Hugo, Thackeray and Balzac. In old age, he was still discovering Goethe. He 'worshipped Zola'.

The Bolsheviks, who believed in the perfectibility of the New Man, were avid autodidacts, Stalin being the most accomplished and diligent of all. He read seriously, making notes, learning quotations, like an omnipotent student, leaving his revealing marginalia in books varying from Anatole France to Vipper's *History of Ancient Greece*. He had 'a very good knowledge of antiquity and mythology', recalled Molotov. He could quote from the Bible, Chekhov and *Good Soldier Svejk*, as well as Napoleon, Bismarck and Talleyrand. His knowledge of Georgian literature was such that he debated arcane poetry with Shalva Nutsibidze the philosopher, who said, long after Stalin was no longer a god, that his editorial comments were outstanding. He read literature aloud to his circle – usually Saltykov-Shchedrin or a new edition of the medieval Georgian epic poem by Rustaveli, *The Knight in the Panther Skin*. He adored *The Last of the Mohicans*, amazing a young translator whom he greeted in *faux*-Red Indian: 'Big chief greets paleface!'

His deeply conservative tastes remained nineteenth century

---

* *The Forsyte Saga* by Galsworthy and Fenimore Cooper's *Last of the Mohicans* were probably the most popular foreign works for the entire Politburo who all seemed to be reading what they analysed as a damning indictment of a capitalist family, and of British imperialist repression in the Americas.

even during the Modernist blossoming of the twenties: he was always much happier with Pushkin and Tchaikovsky than with Akhmatova and Shostakovich. He respected intellectuals, his tone changing completely when dealing with a famous professor. 'I'm very sorry that I'm unable to satisfy your request now, illustrious Nikolai Yakovlevich,' he wrote to the linguistics professor, Marr. 'After the conference, I'll be able to give us 40–50 minutes if you'll agree ...'

Stalin could certainly appreciate genius but, as with love and family, his belief in Marxist progress was brutally paramount. He admired that 'great psychologist' Dostoevsky but banned him because he was 'bad for young people'. He enjoyed the satires of the Leningrad satirist Mikhail Zoschenko so much, even though they mocked Soviet bureaucrats, he used to read extracts to his two boys, Vasily and Artyom, and would laugh at the end: 'Here is where Comrade Zoschenko remembered the GPU and changed the ending!' – a joke typical of his brutal cynicism crossed with dry gallows humour. He recognized that Mandelstam, Pasternak and Bulgakov were geniuses, but their work was suppressed. Yet he could tolerate whimsical maestros: Bulgakov and Pasternak were never arrested. But woe betide anyone, genius or hack, who insulted the person or policy of Stalin – for the two were synonymous.

His comments are most fascinating when he was dealing with a master like Bulgakov whose Civil War play, *Days of the Turbins,* based on his novel *The White Guard,* was Stalin's favourite: he saw it fifteen times. When Bulgakov's play *Flight* was attacked as 'anti-Soviet and Rightist', Stalin wrote to the theatre director: 'It's not good calling literature Right and Left. These are Party words. In literature, use class, anti-Soviet, revolutionary or anti-revolutionary but not Right or Left ... If Bulgakov would add to the eight dreams, one or two where he would discover the international social content of the Civil War, the spectator would understand that the honest "Serafima" and the professor were thrown away from Russia, not by the caprice of Bolsheviks, but because they lived on the necks of the people. It's easy to criticize *Days of the Turbins* – it's easy to reject but it's hardest to write good plays. The final impression of the play is good for Bolshevism.' When Bulgakov was not allowed to work, he appealed to Stalin who telephoned him to say, 'We'll try to do something for you.'

Stalin's gift, apart from his catechismic rhythms of question and answer, was the ability to reduce complex problems to lucid simplicity, a talent that is invaluable in a politician. He could draft, usually in his own hand, a diplomatic telegram, speech or article straight off in the clearest, yet often subtle prose (as he showed during the war) – but he was also capable of clumsy crudity, though partly this reflected his self-conscious proletarian machismo.*

Stalin was not just supreme censor; he relished his role as imperial editor-in-chief, endlessly tinkering with other men's prose, loving nothing more than scribbling the expression that covers the pages of his library – that mirthless chuckle:

'Ha-ha-ha!'

* * *

Stalin's sneering did not help Nadya whose depression, stoked by caffeine and Stalin's own stress, worsened. Yet there were also moments of touching tenderness: Nadya took an unaccustomed drink which made her sick. Stalin put her to bed and she looked up at him and said pathetically:

'So you love me a little after all.' Years later, Stalin recounted this to his daughter.

At Zubalovo for the weekend, Nadya, who never gave Svetlana a word of praise, warned her to refuse if Stalin offered her wine:

'Don't take the alcohol!' If Nadya was taking Stalin's small indulgence of his children as a grave sin, one can only imagine how desperately she felt about his brusqueness, never mind the tragedy of the peasants. During those last days, Nadya visited her brother Pavel and his wife Zhenya, who had just returned from Berlin, in their apartment in the House on the Embankment: 'She said hello to me in the coldest way,' their daughter Kira noticed but then Nadya was a stern woman. Nadya spent some evenings working on designs with Dora Khazan, whispering in the bedroom of the latter's daughter, Natalya Andreyeva.

So we are left with a troubling picture of a husband and wife who alternated between loving kindness and vicious explosions

---

* Boris Pilniak, Russia's most respected novelist until Gorky's return, who had fallen into disfavour, wrote nervously to Stalin to ask if he could go abroad: 'Esteemed Comrade Pilniak,' replied the leader (sarcastically since he hated Pilniak for his short story 'Tale of the Unextinguished Moon', implying Stalin had arranged the medical murder of Defence Commissar Frunze in 1925), 'Inquiries show the bodies of control are not opposed to your going abroad. They doubted it but now cease to doubt. So ... your going abroad is decided. Good luck. Stalin.' Pilniak was executed on 21 April 1938.

of rage, parents who treated the children differently. Both were given to humiliating one another in public yet Nadya still seemed to have loved 'my man' as she called him. It was a tense time but there was one difference between this highly-strung, thin-skinned couple. Stalin was crushingly strong, as Nadya told his mother: 'I can say that I marvel at his strength and his energy. Only a really healthy man could stand the amount of work he gets through.' She on the other hand was weak. If one was to break, it was she. His stunted emotional involvement allowed him to weather the hardest blows.

Kaganovich again headed out of his Moscow fiefdom to crush dissent in the Kuban, ordering mass reprisals against the Cossacks and deporting fifteen villages to Siberia. Kaganovich called this 'the resistance of the last remnants of the dying classes leading to a concrete form of the class struggle'. The classes were dying all right. Kopelev saw 'women and children with distended bellies, turning blue, still breathing but with vacant lifeless eyes. And corpses – corpses in ragged sheepskin coats and cheap felt boots; corpses in peasant huts, in the melting snow of old Vologda, under the bridges of Kharkov.' 'Iron Lazar' arranged an array of executions of grain hoarders and was back in time for the fatal holiday dinner for the anniversary of the Revolution.

On 7 November, the potentates took the salute from atop Lenin's newly completed grey marble Mausoleum. They gathered early in Stalin's apartment in their greatcoats and hats for it was below freezing. Nadya was already taking her place in the parade as a delegate of the Academy. The housekeeper and nannies made sure Vasily and Artyom were dressed and ready; Svetlana was still at the dacha.

Just before 8 a.m., the leaders walked chatting out of the Poteshny Palace across the central square, past the Yellow Palace towards the steps that led up to the Mausoleum. It was bitterly cold up there; the parade lasted four hours.* Voroshilov and Budyonny waited on horseback at different Kremlin gates. As the Spassky Tower, Moscow's equivalent of Big Ben, tolled, they

---

* There were chairs hidden there for those of weak disposition to take a rest and, even better, there was a room behind with a bar for those who needed Dutch courage. The first Bolshevik Head of State, Yakov Sverdlov, died in 1919 after a freezing parade; the Politburo member Alexander Shcherbakov died after attending the 1945 victory parade; the Czech President Klement Gottwald died after enduring the icy hours of Stalin's funeral on the Mausoleum.

trotted out to meet in the middle in front of the Mausoleum, then dismounted to join the leadership.

Many people saw Nadya that day. She did not seem either depressed or unhappy with Stalin. She marched past, raising her oval face towards the leaders. Afterwards she met up with Vasily and Artyom on the tribune to the right of the Mausoleum, and bumped into Khrushchev, whom she had introduced to Stalin. She looked up at her husband in his greatcoat but, like any wife, she worried that Stalin's coat was open:

'My man didn't take his scarf. He'll catch cold and get sick,' she said – but suddenly she was struck with one of her agonizing headaches. 'She started moaning, "Oh my headache!"' remembers Artyom. After the parade, the boys requested the housekeeper to ask Nadya if they could spend the holiday at Zubalovo. It was easier to persuade the housekeeper than tackle the severe mother.

'Let them go to the dacha,' Nadya replied, adding cheerfully, 'I'll soon graduate from the Academy and then there'll be a real holiday for everyone!' She winced. 'Oh! My headache!' Stalin, Voroshilov and others were carousing in the little room behind the Mausoleum where there was always a buffet.

Next morning the boys were driven off to Zubalovo. Stalin worked as usual in his office, meeting Molotov, Kuibyshev and CC Secretary, Pavel Postyshev. Yagoda showed the transcripts of another anti-Stalin meeting of the Old Bolsheviks, Smirnov and Eismont, one of whom had asked, 'Don't tell me there's nobody in this whole country capable of removing him.' They ordered their arrest, then they walked over to the Voroshilovs' for dinner. Nadya too was on her way there. She looked her best.

Some time in the early hours, Nadya took the Mauser pistol that her brother Pavel had given her and lay on the bed in her room. Suicide was a Bolshevik death: she had attended the funeral of Adolf Yoffe, the Trotskyite who protested against Stalin's defeat of the oppositions by shooting himself in 1929. In 1930, the Modernist poet, Mayakovsky, also made that supreme protest. She raised the pistol to her breast and pulled the trigger once. No one heard the voice of that tiny feminine weapon; Kremlin walls are thick. Her body rolled off the bed on to the floor.

Part Two

The Jolly Fellows:
Stalin and Kirov, 1932–1934

8

The Funeral

Nadya died instantly. Hours later, Stalin stood in the dining room absorbing the news. He asked his sister-in-law Zhenya Alliluyeva 'what was missing in him'. The family were shocked when he threatened suicide, something they 'had never heard before'. He grieved in his room for days: Zhenya and Pavel decided to stay with him to make sure he did not harm himself. He could not understand why it had happened, raging what did it mean? Why had such a terrible stab in the back been dealt to him of all people? 'He was too intelligent not to know that people always commit suicide in order to punish someone ...' wrote his daughter Svetlana, so he kept asking whether it was true he had been inconsiderate, hadn't he loved her? 'I was a bad husband,' he confessed to Molotov, 'I had no time to take her to the cinema.' He told Vlasik, 'She's completely overturned my life!' He stared sadly at Pavel, growling, 'That was a hell of a nice present you gave her! A pistol!'

Around 1 p.m., Professor Kushner and a colleague examined the body of Nadezhda Stalin in her little bedroom. 'The position of the body,' the professor scrawled on a piece of squared paper ripped from one of the children's exercise books, 'was that her head is on the pillow turned to the right side. Near the pillow on the bed is a little gun.' The housekeeper must have replaced the gun on the bed. 'The face is absolutely tranquil, the eyes semi-closed, semi-open. On the right part of face and neck, there are blue and red marks and blood ...' There were bruises on her face: did Stalin really have something to hide? Had he returned to the apartment, quarrelled with her, hit her and then shot her? Given his murderous pedigree, one more death is not impossible. Yet the bruise could have been caused by falling off the bed. No one with any knowledge of that night has ever suggested that Stalin killed her. But he was certainly aware that his enemies would whisper that he had.

'There is a five-millimetre hole over the heart – an open hole,' noted the professor. 'Conclusion — death was immediate from an open wound to the heart.' This scrap of paper, which one can now see in the State Archive, was not to be seen again for six decades.

Molotov, Kaganovich and Sergo came and went, deciding what to do: as usual in such moments, the Bolshevik instinct was to lie and cover up, even though in this case, if they had been more open, they might have avoided the most damaging slanders. It was clear enough that Nadya had committed suicide but Molotov, Kaganovich and her godfather Yenukidze got Stalin's agreement that this self-destruction could not be announced publicly. It would be taken as a political protest. They would announce she had died of appendicitis. The doctors, a profession whose Hippocratic oath was to be as much undermined by the Bolsheviks as by the Nazis, signed the lie. Servants were informed that Stalin had been at his dacha with Molotov and Kalinin – but unsurprisingly, they gossiped dangerously.

Yenukidze drafted the announcement of her death and then wrote a letter of condolence, to be published next day in *Pravda*, signed by all the leaders' wives and then the leaders themselves, starting with Nadya's four greatest friends – Ekaterina Voroshilova, Polina Molotova, Dora Khazan and Maria Kaganovich: 'Our close friend, a person with a wonderful soul ... young, vigorous and devoted to the Bolshevik Party and the Revolution.' Even this death was seen by these singular dogmatists in terms of Bolshevism.

Since Stalin was barely functioning, Yenukidze and the magnates debated how to arrange this unique funeral. The Bolshevik funeral ritual combined elements of Tsarist funeral tradition with its own idiosyncratic culture. The deceased were beautified by the finest morticians, usually the professors in charge of Lenin's cadaver, then lay in state, snowy faces often heavily rouged, among the surreal *mise-en-scène* of lush tropical palms, bouquets, red banners, all unnaturally illuminated with arc lights. The Politburo bore the open coffin to, and from, the Hall of Columns where they also stood guard like knights of old. The rigorous eminence was then cremated and a plangent, military funeral was held, with the Politburo again bearing an elaborate catafalque enclosing the urn of ashes which they placed in the Kremlin Wall. But Stalin himself must have demanded an old-fashioned funeral.

Yenukidze presided over the Funeral Commission with Dora Khazan, Andreyev's wife, and Pauker, the Chekist who was so close to Stalin. They met first thing next morning and decided on the procession, the place of burial, the guard of honour. Pauker, the theatrical expert – ex-coiffeur of the Budapest Opera – was in charge of the orchestras: there were to be two, a military one and a theatrical one of fifty instruments.

Stalin could not speak himself. He asked Kaganovich, the Politburo's best speaker, to give the oration. Even that energetic bulldozer of a man, fresh from shooting droves of innocent Kuban Cossacks, was daunted by the burden of giving such a speech in front of Stalin himself, but as with so many other macabre chores, 'Stalin asked and I did it.'

The death of Nadya from appendicitis was broken to the children out at Zubalovo: Artyom was distraught but Vasily never recovered. Svetlana, six, did not grasp this finality. Voroshilov, who was so kind in all matters outside politics, visited her but could not talk for weeping. The older children were driven to Moscow. Svetlana remained in the country until the funeral.

When the body was removed from the apartment, some time on the morning of the 10th, a little girl in the Horse Guards, opposite Stalin's Poteshny Palace, sat glued to the window of her apartment. Natalya Andreyeva, daughter of Andreyev and Dora Khazan who was managing the funeral with Yenukidze, watched as a group of men carried down the coffin. Stalin walked beside it, wearing no gloves in the freezing cold, clutching at the side of the coffin with tears running down his cheeks. The body must have been taken to the Kremlevka to cover up the bruises.

The schoolboys, Vasily Stalin and Artyom, arrived at Stalin's flat where Pavel, Zhenya and Nadya's sister Anna, took turns watching over the widower who remained in his room and would not come out for dinner. The gloomy apartment was pervaded by whispers: Artyom's mother arrived and foolishly told her son the spellbinding truth about the suicide. Artyom rashly asked the housekeeper about it. Both he and his mother were reprimanded. 'The things I saw in that house!' recalls Artyom.

During the night, the body was delivered to the Hall of Columns close to Red Square and the Kremlin. It was to be the scene of some of the great trials and lying-in-states of Stalin's rule. At eight the next morning, Yagoda joined the Funeral Commission.

The three smaller children were taken to the hall where Nadezhda Alliluyeva Stalin lay in an open casket, her round face surrounded by bouquets, her bruises exquisitely powdered and rouged away by Moscow's macabre maestros. 'She was very beautiful in her coffin, very young, her face clear and lovely,' recalls her niece Kira Alliluyeva. Zina Ordzhonikidze, the plump half-Yakut wife of the irrepressible Sergo, took Svetlana's hand and led her up to the coffin. She cried and they rushed her out. Yenukidze comforted her, despatching her back to Zubalovo. She only learned of the suicide a decade later, incongruously from the *Illustrated London News*.

Stalin arrived accompanied by the Politburo who stood guard around the catafalque, a duty to which they were to grow accustomed in the deadly years ahead. Stalin was weeping. Vasily left Artyom and ran forward towards Stalin and 'hung on to his father, saying, "Papa don't cry!" ' To a chorus of sobs from Nadya's family and the hardmen of the Politburo and Cheka, the *Vozhd* approached the coffin with Vasily holding on to him. Stalin looked down at this woman who had loved, hated, punished and rejected him. 'I'd never seen Stalin cry before,' said Molotov, 'but as he stood there beside the coffin, the tears ran down his cheeks.'

'She left me like an enemy,' Stalin said bitterly but then Molotov heard him say: 'I didn't save you.' They were about to nail down the coffin when Stalin suddenly stopped them. To everyone's surprise, he leaned down, lifted Nadya's head and began to kiss her ardently. This provoked more weeping.

The coffin was carried out into Red Square where it was laid on a black funeral carriage with four little onion domes on each corner holding an intricate canopy, a cortège that seemed to belong in Tsarist times. There was an honour guard marching around it and the streets were lined with soldiers. Six grooms in black led six horses and ahead, a military brass band played the funeral march. Bukharin, who was close to Nadya but had tainted her politically, offered his condolences to Stalin. The widower insisted strangely that he had gone to the dacha after the banquet; he was not in the apartment. The death was nothing to do with him. So Stalin propagated an alibi.

The procession set off through the streets, the public held far back by police. Here was the first of many funerals in which the cause of death was concealed from most of the mourners. Stalin walked between Molotov and the shrewd, hawk-eyed Armenian

Mikoyan, themselves flanked by Kaganovich and Voroshilov. Pauker, resplendent in his uniform, belly buttressed by his invisible corset, kept pace to the side. Vasily and Artyom walked behind them along with the family, the cream of the Bolshevik movement and delegates from Nadya's Academy. Her mother Olga blamed Nadya:

'How could you do this?' she addressed her absent daughter. 'How could you leave the children?' Most of the family and leaders agreed, and sympathized with Stalin.

'Nadya was wrong,' declared the forthright Polina. 'She left him at such a difficult time.'

Artyom and Vasily fell behind the band and lost sight of Stalin. It has variously been claimed that Stalin either did not go to the funeral or that he walked all the way to the Novodevichy Cemetery. Neither is true. Yagoda insisted that it was not safe for Stalin to walk the whole route. When the procession reached Manege Square, Stalin, along with the deceased's mother, were driven to the cemetery.

At Novodevichy, Stalin stood on one side of the grave and the two boys, Vasily and Artyom, watched him from the other. Bukharin spoke, then Yenukidze announced the main speaker: 'It was so difficult,' Kaganovich remembered, 'with Stalin there.' The Iron Commissar, more used to tub-thumping broadsides, delivered his oration in that special Bolshevik language:

'Comrades, we are at the funeral of one of our best members of our Party. She grew up in the family of a Bolshevik worker ... organically connected with our Party ... she was the devoted friend of those who ruled ... fighting the great struggle. She distinguished herself by the best features of a Bolshevik – firmness, toughness in the struggle ...' Then he turned to the leader: 'We're close friends and comrades of Comrade Stalin. We understand the weight of Comrade Stalin's loss ... We understand we must share the burdens of Comrade Stalin's loss.'

Stalin picked up a handful of soil and threw it on to the coffin. Artyom and Vasily were asked to do the same. Artyom asked why it was necessary. 'So she can have some earth from your hand,' he was told. Later Stalin chose the monument that rested over her grave, with a rose to remember the one she wore in her hair and proudly emblazoned with the sacred words: 'Member of the Bolshevik Party.' For the rest of his life, Stalin ruminated on her death. 'Oh Nadya, Nadya, what did you do?' he mused in his old age, excusing himself: 'There was always so much pressure on me.' The suicide of a spouse usually affects the surviving partner, often leaving the bitter taste of guilt, betrayal and, above all, desertion. Nadya's abandonment of Stalin wounded and humiliated him, breaking one more of his meagre ties to human sympathy, redoubling his brutality, jealousy, coldness and self-pity. But the political challenges of 1932, particularly what Stalin regarded as betrayals by some of his comrades, also played their part. 'After 1932,' Kaganovich observed, 'Stalin changed.'

* * *

The family watched over Stalin, letting themselves into the apartment in case he needed anything. One night, Zhenya Alliluyeva visited him but there was no sound. Then she heard an ugly screeching and found the *Vozhd* lying on a sofa in the half-light, spitting on the wall. She knew he had been there a very long time because the wall was dripping with glistening trails of spit.

'What on earth are you doing, Joseph?' she asked him. 'You can't stay like that.' He said nothing, staring at the saliva rolling down the wall.

At the time, Maria Svanidze, the wife of Alyosha, his former brother-in-law, who now began to keep a remarkable diary,* thought Nadya's death had made him 'less of a marble hero'. In his despair, he repeated two questions:

'Never mind the children, they forgot her in a few days, but how could she do this to me?' Sometimes he saw it the other way round, asking Budyonny: 'I understand how she could do this to me, but what about the children?' Always the conversation ended thus: 'She broke my life. She crippled me.' This was a humiliating personal failure that undermined his confidence. Stalin, wrote Svetlana, 'wanted to resign but the Politburo said, "No, no, you have to stay!"'

He swiftly recovered the Messianic confidence in his mission: the war against the peasants and his enemies within the Party. His mind strayed on to the newly arrested Eismont, Smirnov and Riutin whose 'Platform' had been found in his wife's room. He was drinking a lot, suffering insomnia. A month after her death, on 17 December, he scrawled a strange note to Voroshilov:

---

* Maria 'Marusya' Svanidze was to become a vital figure in Stalin's entourage: her handwritten diary, which is one of the most revealing documents of the thirties, was preserved by Stalin in his own archive.

'The cases of Eismont, Smirnov and Riutin are full of alcohol. We see an opposition steeped in vodka. Eismont, Rykov. Hunting wild animals. Tomsky, repeat Tomsky. Roaring wild animals that growl. Smirnov and other Moscow rumours. Like a desert. I feel terrible, not sleeping much.' This letter shows how disturbed Stalin was after Nadya's death. It reeks of drink and despair.

He did not soften towards the peasants. On 28 December, Postyshev sent Stalin a note about placing GPU guards on grain elevators because so much bread was being stolen by starving people. Then he added, 'There've been strong elements of sabotage of bread supplies in the collective Machine Tractor Stations ... Let me send 2–300 kulaks from Dneipropetrovsk to the North by order of the GPU.'

'Right! *Pravilno!*' agreed Stalin enthusiastically in his blue pencil.

Nadya hung over Stalin until his own death. Whenever he met anyone who knew Nadya well, he talked about her. Two years later, when he met Bukharin at the theatre, he missed a whole act, talking about Nadya, how he could not live without her. He often discussed her with Budyonny.* The family met every 8th of November to remember her but he hated these anniversaries, remaining in the south – yet he always kept photographs of her, larger and larger ones, round his houses. He claimed he gave up dancing when Nadya died.

Thousands of letters of condolence poured into Stalin's *apparat* so the few he chose to keep are interesting: 'She was fragile as a flower,' read one. Perhaps he preserved it because it finished about him: 'Remember, we need you so take care of yourself.' Then he kept a poem sent to him, dedicated to her, that again appealed to his vision of self:

Night ocean, Wild storm ...
A haunted silhouette on the bridge of the ship.
It's the captain. Who is he?
A man of blood and flesh.
Or is he iron and steel?

When students wanted to name their institute after her, he did not agree but simply sent the request to Nadya's sister, Anna:

---

* Budyonny had lost his first wife in a possible suicide, perhaps when she discovered his relationship with his future second wife, the singer Olga. Ironically the other Soviet leader whose wife had committed suicide was the brilliant commander most hated by Stalin – Mikhail Tukhachevsky.

'After reading this note, leave it on my desk!' The pain of the subject was still fresh sixteen years later when a sculptor wrote to say that he wanted to give Stalin a bust of Nadya. Stalin wrote laconically to Poskrebyshev, his *chef de cabinet:* 'Tell him that you received the letter and you're returning it. Stalin.'

There was no time for mourning. The Party was at war.

* * *

At 4 p.m. on 12 November, the day after the funeral, Stalin arrived at his office to meet Kaganovich, Voroshilov, Molotov and Sergo. Alongside them was Stalin's closest friend, Sergei Mironich Kirov, First Secretary of Leningrad and Politburo member. 'After Nadya's tragic death', Maria Svanidze noticed that 'Kirov was the closest person who managed to approach Joseph intimately and simply, to give him that missing warmth and cosiness.' Stalin turned to Kirov who, he said, 'cared for me like a child'.

Always singing operatic arias loudly, brimming with good cheer and boyish enthusiasm, Kirov was one of those uncomplicated men who win friends easily. Small, handsome with deep-set brown, slightly Tartar eyes, pock-marked, brown-haired and high-cheekboned, women and men seemed to like him equally. Married without children, he was said to be a womanizer with a special eye on the ballerinas of the Mariinsky Ballet which he controlled in Leningrad.* Certainly he followed ballet and opera closely, listening to it in his own apartment by a special link. A workaholic like his comrades, Kirov liked the outdoors, camping and hunting, with his boon companion Sergo. Like Andreyev, Kirov was an avid mountaineer, an appropriate hobby for a Bolshevik. He was at ease in his own skin. It was perhaps this that made him so attractive to Stalin whose friendships resembled crushes – and, like crushes, they could turn swiftly into bitter envy. Now he wanted to be with Kirov all the time: Kirov was in and out of his office five times during the days after Nadya's funeral.

Born Sergei Kostrikov in 1886, the son of a feckless clerk who left him an orphan, in Urzhum, five hundred miles north-east of Moscow, Kirov was sent by charity to the Kazan Industrial School where he excelled. But the 1905 Revolution interfered with his plans for university and he joined the Social Democrat Party, becoming a professional revolutionary. In between exiles, he

---

* It was therefore entirely appropriate that the Mariinsky should be renamed the Kirov after his death.

married the daughter of a Jewish watchmaker but like all good Bolsheviks, his personal life 'was subordinated to the revolutionary cause', according to his wife. During the doldrums before the war, Kirov had worked as a journalist in the bourgeois press, which was strictly banned by the Party, and this was a black mark on his Bolshevik pedigree. Nineteen seventeen found him setting up power in the Terek in the North Caucasus. During the Civil War, Kirov was one of the swashbuckling commissars in the North Caucasus beside Sergo and Mikoyan. In Astrakhan he enforced Bolshevik power in March 1919 with liberal blood-letting: over four thousand were killed. When a *bourgeois* was caught hiding his own furniture, Kirov ordered him shot. He and Sergo, whose lives and deaths were parallel, engineered the seizure of Georgia in 1921, remaining in Baku afterwards, both brutal Bolsheviks of the Civil War generation. He had probably met Stalin in 1917 but got to know his patron on holiday in 1925:

'Dear Koba, I'm in Kislovodsk ... I'm getting better. In a week, I'll come to you ... Greetings to everyone. Say hello to Nadya,' he wrote. Kirov was a family favourite. Stalin inscribed a copy of his book *On Lenin and Leninism*: 'To SM Kirov, my friend and beloved brother.' In 1926, Stalin removed Zinoviev from his Leningrad power base and promoted Kirov to take over Peter the Great's capital, now the second largest Party in the State. He joined the Politburo in 1930.

When Kirov asked if he could fly south to join him for the 1931 holidays, Stalin replied: 'I have no right and would not advise anyone to authorize flights. I most humbly request you to come by train.' Artyom, often on these holidays, recalls, 'Stalin was so fond of Kirov, he'd personally meet Kirov's train in Sochi.' Stalin always had 'a lovely time with Kirov', even swimming and visiting the *banya*. Sometimes when Kirov swam, 'Stalin went to the beach and sat waiting for Kirov', says Artyom.

After Nadya's death, Stalin's friendship with 'my Kirich' became more insistent. Stalin often called him in Leningrad at any time of the night: the *vertushka* phone can still be seen by Kirov's bed in his apartment. When he came to Moscow, Kirov preferred to stay with Sergo who was so fond of his boon companion that his widow remembered how he once faked a car crash to ensure that Kirov missed his train.* Yet Stalin and Kirov were 'like a pair of

---

* Faked car crashes, often with fatal effects, were to become a bizarre feature of Stalin's rule.

equal brothers, teasing one another, telling dirty stories, laughing', says Artyom. 'Big friends, brothers and they needed one another.'

This did not mean that Stalin completely trusted Kirov. In the autumn of 1929, Stalin orchestrated *Pravda*'s criticism of Kirov. However fond he was of Kirov, Stalin could also be cross with him. In June 1928, one of his articles seemed to have been edited when it appeared in *Leningradskaya Pravda*, provoking a letter that revealed Stalin's thin-skinned paranoia on even small matters: 'I understand ... the technical reasons ... Yet I've heard no other such examples of articles by Politburo members ... It seems strange that the 40–50 words reduced are the brightest about how the peasantry are a capitalist class ... I await your explanation.'

Kirov did not regard Stalin as a saint: during the 1929 birthday celebrations that raised Stalin to *Vozhd*, the Leningraders dared to mention Lenin's views on Stalin's rudeness. Kirov knew Stalin's unusual mentality well: when a student sent him some questions on ideology, he forwarded them to Kirov with this note: 'Kirov! You must read the letter of student Fedotov ... an absolutely politically illiterate young man. Maybe you will telephone him and talk to him, probably he is a corrupted drunken "Party member". We must not introduce the GPU I think. By the way, the student is a very good trickster with an anti-Soviet face which he conceals artistically beneath a simple face that says "Help me understand. Maybe you understand all – I don't." Greetings! Stalin.' No doubt Kirov's intimacy with Sergo, Kuibyshev and Mikoyan worried Stalin. The challenges of 1932 – the Riutin Platform, Kirov's possible resistance to Riutin's execution, the famine, the suicide of Nadezhda – had shown Stalin needed firmer loyalty.

After Nadya's death, Kirov was almost part of the family: Stalin insisted he stay with him, not Sergo. Kirov stayed at Stalin's apartment so often he knew where the sheets and pillows were and he would bed down on the sofa. The children loved Kirov and sometimes when he was there, Svetlana would put on a doll show for him. Her favourite game was her own mock government. Her father was 'First Secretary'. This Stalinette wrote orders like: 'To my First Secretary, I order you to allow me to go with you to the theatre.' She signed it 'The Mistress or Boss (*khozyaika*) Setanka.' She hung the notes in the dining room above the telephone table. Stalin replied: 'I obey.' Kaganovich, Molotov and Sergo were Setanka's Second Secretaries, but 'she has a special friendship with

Kirov', noticed Maria Svanidze, 'because Joseph is so good and close with him'.

Stalin returned to the ascetic Bedouin life of the underground Bolshevik, with the tension and variety of the revolutionary on the run, except that now his restless progress more resembled the train of a Mongol Khan. Though a creature of routine, he needed perpetual movement: there were beds in his houses but there were also big, hard divans in every room. 'I never sleep on a bed,' he told a visitor. 'Always a divan' and on whichever one he happened to be reading. 'Which historical person had the same Spartan habit?' he asked, answering with that autodidactic omniscience: 'Nicholas I.' Nadya's death naturally changed the way Stalin and his children lived.

9

The Omnipotent Widower and his
Loving Family: Sergo the Bolshevik Prince

Stalin could not bear to go on living in the Poteshny Palace apartment and the Zubalovo mansion because Nadya's homes were too painful for him. Bukharin offered to swap apartments. Stalin accepted this comradely offer and moved into Bukharin's apartment on the first floor of the triangular Yellow Palace, the old Senate,* roughly beneath his office. Since his office stood where the two wings of the Senate met at an angle, it was known to the *cognoscenti* as the 'Little Corner'. Its polished floors, with their red and green carpets running down the centre, its wooden panelling up to shoulder height, its dreary drapes, were kept as clean and silent as a hospital. His secretary, Poskrebyshev, sat at the front of the anteroom, his desk immaculate, controlling access. Stalin's office itself was long, airy and rectangular, heavy with drapes, and lined with ornate Russian stoves against which he would lean to ease the aching in his limbs. A huge desk stood at the far right corner while a long green baize table, with straight-backed chairs in white covers, stood to the left beneath portraits of Marx and Lenin.

Downstairs, his 'formal', gloomy apartment with the 'vaulted ceilings' was to be his Moscow residence until his death. 'It was not like a home,' wrote Svetlana. It had once been a corridor. He expected the children to be there every evening when he returned for supper to review and sign their homework, like every parent.

---

* President Putin still rules from this building, the seat of power in Russia since Lenin. Putin's Chief of Staff works in Stalin's old office. Until 1930, Stalin kept his main office on the fifth floor of the grey granite edifice of the Central Committee building on Old Square, up the hill from the Kremlin, where he had been well served by his successive secretaries, Lev Mekhlis, who went on to greater things, and Tovstukha who died prematurely. It was here that Stalin planned his campaigns against Trotsky, Zinoviev and Bukharin. In 1930, Poskrebyshev and the Special Sector, the fulcrum of Stalin's dictatorship, moved into the Yellow Palace (also known as the Sovnarkom or Council of Ministers building) where the Politburo met, Stalin worked – and now lived.

Until the war, he maintained this dutiful routine – some of his parental reports to the children's teachers survive in the archive.

The children adored Zubalovo – it was their real home so Stalin decided not to uproot them but to build his own 'wonderful, airy modern one-storey' dacha at Kuntsevo, nine kilometres from the Kremlin. This now became his main residence, until he died there twenty years later, developing over the years into a large but austere two-storey mansion, painted a grim camouflage green, with a complex of guardhouses, guest villas, greenhouses, a Russian bath and a special cottage for his library, all surrounded by pinewoods, two concentric fences, innumerable checkpoints and at least a hundred guards.* Here he indulged his natural craving for privacy, the external expression of his emotional detachment: no guards or servants stayed in the house; unless friends came for the night, he henceforth closed himself in, quite alone. Stalin drove out to Kuntsevo after dinner – it was so close it was often called 'Nearby' by his circle because he also sometimes stayed at his other home, 'Faraway', at Semyonovskoe. The idyllic life went on at Zubalovo, Svetlana's 'paradise like an enchanted island'.

Stalin did not become a haunted hermit after Nadya's death. It was true he spent ever more time with his all-male magnates, almost like the segregated court of a seventeenth-century Tsar. But the all-powerful widower also found himself in the loving but overwhelming embrace of a newly reconstructed family. Pavel and Zhenya Alliluyev, recently returned from Berlin, became his constant companions. Nadya's sister Anna and her husband Stanislas Redens had returned from Kharkov for his new appointment as Moscow GPU boss. Redens, a handsome burly Pole with a quiff, always sporting his Chekist uniform, had been the secretary of the founder of the secret police, Dzerzhinsky. He and Anna fell in love during Stalin and Dzerzhinsky's expedition to investigate the fall of Perm in 1919. Redens had a reputation among austere Old Bolsheviks of 'putting on airs' and being a drinker because of an unfortunate incident. Until 1931, he had

---

* Kuntsevo was, like most of his other residences, built by Merzhanov: Stalin constantly ordered renovations and, after the war, the second floor. After his death, the contents were packed up but under Brezhnev, these were reassembled by Stalin's reunited staff. It remains today closed up under the aegis of the FSB security organ, but exactly as it was when Stalin lived, even down to his shaving brushes and gramophone.

been Georgian GPU boss. However, his deputy, Beria had, according to the family, outwitted Redens in a prank more worthy of a hearty stag night than a secret police intrigue – but it worked none the less. Beria got Redens drunk and sent him home naked. Family legends rarely tell the whole story: Stalin's letters reveal that Redens and local bosses tried to have Beria removed to the Lower Volga but someone, probably Stalin, intervened. Beria never forgave him. But it was Redens, not Beria, who left.

Stalin liked his cheerful brother-in-law but doubted his competence as a Chekist, removing him from the Ukraine. Anna, a loving mother to their two sons, was a good-natured but imprudent woman who, her own children admit, talked too much. Stalin called her 'a chatterbox'.

A third couple made up this sextet of loving relatives. Alyosha Svanidze, also just back from abroad, was the brother of Stalin's first wife, Kato, who died in 1907. 'Handsome, blonde, with blue eyes and an aquiline nose', he was a Georgian dandy, speaking French and German, who held high positions in the State Bank. Stalin loved him – 'they were like brothers,' wrote Mikoyan. His wife, Maria, was a Jewish Georgian soprano 'with a tiny upturned nose, peaches and cream complexion and big blue eyes', who was the *prima donna* in the full-time opera of her own life.* Svetlana said this glossy couple were brash, always bearing presents from abroad. That avid diarist, Maria, like all the ladies of Stalin's court, seemed somewhat in love with their *Vozhd*. There was constant, bitchy competition for his favour among these ladies who were so busy feeling superior to, and undermining, the others that they often missed dangerous signs of Stalin's seething moods.

Meanwhile, Yakov, now twenty-seven, was qualifying as an electrical engineer though Stalin had wanted him to be a soldier. Yasha 'resembled his father in voice and looks' but irritated him. Sometimes Stalin managed to show brisk affection: he sent him one of his books, *The Conquest of Nature*, inscribing it: 'Yasha read this book at once. J. Stalin.'

As Svetlana grew up into a freckly redhead, Stalin said she precisely resembled his mother, always the highest praise from him – but really, she was like him: intelligent, stubborn and determined. 'I was his pet. After mother's death, he tried to be

---

* They saddled their son with the absurd Bolshevik name Johnreed in honour of the author of *Ten Days That Shook the World*.

closer. He was very affectionate – he just wanted to see how I was doing. I do appreciate now that he was a very loving father ...' Maria Svanidze recorded how Svetlana buzzed around her father. 'He kissed her, admired her, fed her from his plate, selecting the best slices for her.' Svetlana, at seven, often declared: 'Providing daddy loves me, I don't care if the whole world hates me! If daddy told me, "fly to the moon," I'd do it!' Yet she found his affection stifling – 'always that tobacco smell, puffing clouds of smoke with moustache and he was hugging and kissing me.' Svetlana was really raised by her beloved nanny, the sturdy Alexandra Bychkova, and the stalwart housekeeper, Carolina Til.

A month after Nadya's death, Artyom remembers that she was still asking when her mother would be back from abroad. Svetlana was terrified of the dark, which she believed was connected to death. She admitted that she could not love Vasily who was either bullying her, spoiling her fun, or telling her disturbing sexual details that she believed damaged her view of sex.

Vasily, now twelve, was the most damaged: 'he suffered a terrible shock,' wrote Svetlana, 'ruining him completely.' He became a truculent, name-dropping, violent lout who swore in front of women, expected to be treated as a princeling and yet was tragically inept and unhappy. He ran riot at Zubalovo. No one told Stalin of his outrageous antics. Yet Artyom says Vasily was really 'kind, gentle, sweet, uninterested in material things; he could be a bully, but also defended smaller boys.' But he was terrified of Stalin whom he respected like 'Christ for the Christians'. In the absence of his disappointed father, Vasily grew up in the sad emotionally undernourished realm of bodyguards, rough and sycophantic secret policemen instead of loving but firm nannies. Pauker supervised this Soviet Fauntleroy. The Commandant of Zubalovo, Efimov, reported on him to Vlasik who then informed 'the Boss'.

Stalin trusted his devoted bodyguard, a brawny, hard-living but uncouth peasant, Nikolai Vlasik, thirty-seven, who had joined the Cheka in 1919 and guarded the Politburo, and then exclusively the *Vozhd*, since 1927. He became a powerful *vizier* at Stalin's side but remained the closest thing to Vasily's father-figure: Vasily introduced his girlfriends to Vlasik for his approval.

When his behaviour at school became impossible, it was Pauker who wrote to Vlasik that his 'removal to another school is absolutely necessary'. Vasily craved Stalin's approval: 'Hello father!' he wrote in a typical letter in which he talks in a childish version of Bolshevik jargon. 'I'm studying at the new school, it's very good and I think I'm going to become a good Red Vaska! Father, write to me how you are and how is your holiday. Svetlana is well and studies at school too. Greetings from our working collective. Red Vaska.' But he also wrote letters to the secret policemen:

'Hello Comrade Pauker. I'm fine. I don't fight with Tom [Artyom]. I catch a lot [of fish] and very well. If you're not busy, come and see us. Comrade Pauker, I ask you to send me a bottle of ink for my pen.' So Pauker, who was so close to Stalin that he shaved him, sent the ink to the child. When it arrived, Vasily thanked 'Comrade Pauker', claimed he had not reduced another boy to tears, and denounced Vlasik for accusing him of it. Already his life among schoolboys and secret policemen was leading the spoilt child to denounce others, a habit that could prove deadly for his victims in later life. The princely tone is unmistakable: 'Comrade Efimov has informed you that I asked you to send me a shotgun but I have not received it. Maybe you forgot so please send it. Vasya.'

Stalin was baffled by Vasily's insubordination and suggested greater discipline. On 12 September 1933, Carolina Til went on holiday, so Stalin, who was in the south, wrote the following instructions to Efimov at Zubalovo: 'Nanny will stay at the Moscow home. Make sure that Vasya doesn't behave outrageously. Don't give him free playtime and be strict. If Vasya won't obey Nanny and is offensive, keep him "in blinders",' wrote Stalin, adding: 'Take Vasya away from Anna Sergeevna [Redens, Nadya's sister] – she spoils him by harmful and dangerous concessions.' While the father was on holiday, he sent his son a letter and some peaches. 'Red Vaska' thanked him. Yet all was not well with Vasily. The pistol that had killed Nadya remained around Stalin's house. Vasily showed it to Artyom and gave him the leather holster as a keepsake.

It was only years later that Stalin understood how damaged the children had been by his absence and the care of bodyguards – what he called 'the deepest secret in his heart':

'Children growing up without their mother can be raised perfectly by nannies but they can't replace the mother ...'

* * *

In January 1933, Stalin delivered a swaggering Bolshevik rodomontade to the Plenum: the Five-Year Plan had been a remarkable success. The Party had provided a tractor industry, electric power, coal, steel and oil production. Cities had been built where none stood before. The Dnieper River dam and power station and the Turk-Sib railway had all been completed (built by Yagoda's growing slave labour force). Any difficulties were the fault of the enemy opposition. Yet this was Hungry Thirty-Three when millions more starved, hundred of thousands were deported.

In July 1933, Kirov joined Stalin, Voroshilov, OGPU Deputy Chairman Yagoda and Berman, boss of Gulag, the labour camp system, on the ship *Anokhin* to celebrate the opening of a gargantuan project of socialist labour: the Baltic–White Sea Canal or, in Bolshevik acronym, the Belomor,* a 227-kilometre canal begun in December 1931 and completed by the Pharaonic slavery of 170,000 prisoners, of whom around 25,000 died in a year and a half. Voroshilov later praised Kirov and Yagoda for their contributions to this crime.

By the summer, the magnates were exhausted after five years of Herculean labour in driving the triumphant Five-Year Plan, defeating the opposition and most of all, crushing the peasantry. After bearing such strain, they needed to relax if they were not going to crack – but even if the crisis of Hungry Thirty-Three had been weathered due to the massive repression, this was no time to rest. Sergo, who as People's Commissar for Heavy Industry, directed the Five-Year Plan, suffered heart and circulatory complaints – Stalin himself supervised his treatments. Kirov was also breaking under the pressure, suffering from 'irregular heartbeat ... severe irritability and very poor sleep'. The doctors ordered him to rest. Kirov's friend Kuibyshev, Gosplan boss, who had the impossible task of making the planning figures work, was drinking and chasing women: Stalin complained to Molotov, later muttering that he had become 'a debauchee'.

On 17 August, Stalin and Voroshilov set off in their special train.† We know from an unpublished note that the *Vozhd* was

---

* Belomor cigarettes now became one of the most popular brands, smoked by Stalin himself when his favourite Herzogovina Flor were not to hand. The Belomor Canal was one of the triumphs that were celebrated by writers and film-makers: Gorky, the novelist who had become a shameful apologist for the worst excesses of Bolshevism, edited a book, *The Canal Named for Stalin*, that amazingly praised the humanitarian aspects of Belomor.

† We are especially well-informed on this holiday because not only do we have Stalin's correspondence with Kaganovich, in charge in Moscow, but the GPU took photographs which they mounted in a special album for Stalin, and Lakoba, the host in Abkhazia, also kept notes: therefore we have both sound and vision.

already paranoid about his movements, fed up with his sister-in-law Anna Redens and keen for Klim to be more discreet:

'Yesterday, around my sister-in-law (a chatterbox) and near the doctors (they gossip), I did not want to say my exact departure. Now I'm informing you that I've decided to go tomorrow ... It's not good to talk widely. We're both tasty tidbits and we should not inform everyone by our openness. So if you agree, we go tomorrow at two. So I'll order Yusis [Stalin's Lithuanian bodyguard who shared duties with Vlasik] to ask immediately the chief of the railway station and order him to add one wagon, without information as to who it is for. Until tomorrow at two ...' It was to be a most eventful holiday: there was even an assassination attempt.

* * *

At Krasnaya Polyana, Sochi, he found Lakoba, the Abkhazian chief, waiting on the veranda along with President Kalinin and Poskrebyshev. When Stalin and Lakoba strolled in the gardens, Beria, now effective viceroy of the Caucasus, joined them. Lakoba and Beria, already enemies, had come separately. After breakfast on the verandas, the *Vozhd*, followed by this swelling entourage, which was soon joined by Yan Rudzutak, a Latvian Old Bolshevik who headed the Control Commission but was increasingly distrusted by Stalin, toured his gardens.

'Stop being idle,' said the green-fingered Stalin. 'The wild bushes here need to be weeded.' The leaders and the guards set to work, collecting wood and cutting brambles while Stalin in his white tunic with baggy white trousers tucked into boots, supervised, puffing on his pipe. Taking a fork, he even did some weeding himself. Beria worked with a rake while one of the leaders from Moscow hacked away with an axe. Beria seized the axe and, chopping away to impress Stalin, joked, with rather obvious *double entendre*:

'I'm just demonstrating to the master of the garden, Joseph Vissarionovich, that I can chop down any tree.' No leader was too big for Beria to fell. He would soon get the chance to wield his little axe.

Stalin sat down on his wicker chair and Beria sat behind him like a medieval courtier with the axe in his belt. Svetlana, who now called Beria 'Uncle Lara', was brought down to join them. When Stalin did some work on his papers, Lakoba listened to music on headphones while Beria called over to Svetlana, sat her on his knee and was photographed in a famous picture with his pince-nez glistening in the sun and his hands on the child, while the leader worked patiently in the background.

Voroshilov and Budyonny, who had also turned up, took Stalin, in the front seat of an open Packard, to inspect their horses bred by the army stud. They went on a cruise and then they went hunting, Stalin cheerfully carrying his rifle over his shoulder, with his hat on the back of his head, as his Chekist guard wiped the sweat off his forehead. After a day's hunting, they pitched tents for an *al fresco* picnic and barbecue. Later, Stalin went fishing. The informality of the whole trip is obvious: it was one of the last times he lived like this.

* * *

Meanwhile Stalin was outraged when, in his absence, Sergo managed to manipulate the Politburo against him. Kaganovich remained in charge as more and more leaders went on their holidays. He wrote to Stalin virtually every day, ending always with the same request: 'Please inform us of your opinion.' The magnates were constantly fighting one another for resources: the tougher the struggle for collectivization, the faster the tempo of industrialization, the more accidents and mistakes made in the factories, the greater the struggle within the Politburo for control over their own fiefdoms. 'Iron-Arse' Molotov, the Premier, rowed with Ordzhonikidze, the quick-tempered Heavy Industry Commissar, and Kaganovich who fought with Kirov who clashed with Voroshilov and so on. But suddenly, the Politburo united against Stalin's own wishes.

In the summer of 1933, Molotov received a report that a factory in Zaporozhe was producing defective combine harvester parts due to sabotage. Molotov, who agreed with Stalin that since their system was perfect and their ideology scientifically correct, all industrial mistakes must be the result of sabotage by wreckers, ordered Procurator-General Akulov to arrest the guilty. The local leaders appealed to Sergo. When the case came before the Supreme Court, the government case was represented by the Deputy Procurator, an ex-Menshevik lawyer, Andrei Vyshinsky, who would be one of Stalin's most notorious officials in the coming Terror. But with Stalin on holiday, Sergo passionately defended his industrial officials and persuaded the Politburo, including Molotov and Kaganovich, to condemn Vyshinsky's summing-up.

On 29 August, Stalin discovered Sergo's mischief and fired off a telegram of Pharisaical rage: 'I consider the position adopted by the Politburo incorrect and dangerous ... I find it lamentable that Kaganovich and Molotov were not capable of resisting bureaucratic pressure from the People's Commissariat of Heavy Industry.' Two days later, Kaganovich, Andreyev, Kuibyshev and Mikoyan officially annulled their resolution. Stalin brooded about the danger of Sergo's ability to use his undoubted prestige and force of personality to sway his potentates, letting off steam to Molotov:

'I consider Sergo's actions the behaviour of a hooligan. How can you have let him have his way?' Stalin was flabbergasted that Molotov and Kaganovich could have fallen for it. 'What's the matter? Did Kaganovich pull a fast one? ... And he's not the only one.' He fired off reprimands: 'I've written to Kaganovich to express to him my astonishment that he found himself, in this case, in the camp of reactionary elements.'

Two weeks later, on 12 September, he was still ranting to Molotov that Sergo was showing anti-Party tendencies in defending 'reactionary elements of the Party against the Central Committee'. He punished Molotov by calling him back from his holiday in the Crimea – 'neither I nor Voroshilov like the fact that you're vacationing for six weeks instead of two weeks' – and then felt guilty about it: 'I am a little uncomfortable with being the reason for your early return,' he apologized but then showed his continuing anger with Kaganovich and Kuibyshev: 'It's obvious it would be rash to leave the centre's work to Kaganovich alone (Kuibyshev may start drinking).' Molotov miserably returned to Moscow.

Stalin easily defeated Sergo but the vehemence of his attack on the 'hooligan' shows how seriously he took the strongest leader after himself. Moody and excitable, yet the very personification of the tough Stalinist administrator, Sergo Ordzhonikidze was born in 1886, the son of Georgian nobility. Orphaned when he was ten, he was barely educated but trained incongruously as a nurse.* He had already joined the Party at seventeen and was arrested at least

---

* After WW2, Stalin reminisced about how, in exile, 'I, as a peasant, was given 8 roubles monthly. Ordzhonikidze as a nobleman got 12 roubles so deported noblemen cost the Treasury 50% more than peasants.' The other trained male nurse in the leadership was Poskrebyshev.

four times before joining Lenin in Paris in 1911, one of the few Stalinists to experience emigration (briefly). A member of the Central Committee since 1912 (like Stalin), he was personally responsible in 1921 for brutally annexing and Bolshevizing Georgia and Azerbaijan where he was known as 'Stalin's Arse'. Lenin attacked him for slapping a comrade and for indulging in drunken orgies with hussies but also defended him for his aggressive shouting by joking, 'He does shout ... but he's deaf in one ear.'

In the Civil War, Sergo had been a dashing, leonine hero, at home on horseback (he was accused of riding a white horse through conquered Tiflis), so 'young and strong', it 'seemed as if he had been born in his long military coat and boots'. He was explosively temperamental. In the early twenties, he actually punched Molotov in a row over Zinoviev's book, *Leninism*, an incident that demonstrates how seriously they took matters of ideology: Kirov had separated them. Sergo's daughter, Eteri, recalls that this volcanic Georgian often got so heated that he slapped his comrades but the eruption soon passed – 'he would give his life for one he loved and shoot the one he hated,' said his wife Zina.

Promoted to run the Control Commission in 1926, Sergo was Stalin's most aggressive ally in the fight against the oppositions until he was placed in charge of Heavy Industry. He did not understand the subtleties of economics but he employed experts who did, driving them by charm and force. 'You terrorize comrades at work,' complained one of his subordinates who were constantly appealing against his tempers. 'Sergo really slapped them!' wrote Stalin approvingly to Voroshilov in 1928. 'The opposition were scared!'

Sergo, who had flirted with, then betrayed Bukharin, was a forceful supporter of Stalin's Great Turn – 'he accepted the policy heart and soul', said Kaganovich. Beloved by friends from Kaganovich to Bukharin and Kirov, Sergo was 'the perfect Bolshevik', thought Maria Svanidze, and 'chivalrous' too, according to Khrushchev. 'His kind eyes, grey hair and big moustache,' wrote Beria's son, 'gave him the look of an old Georgian prince.' Owing his career to Stalin, he remained the last big beast of the Politburo, sceptical about Stalin's cult, with his own clientele in industry and the Caucasus whom he was capable of defending. He was certainly never afraid to disagree with

Stalin* whom he treated like a prickly elder brother: sometimes he even gave him quasi-orders.

In September 1933, Sergo was holidaying in Kislovodsk, his favourite resort, whence he was soon in brisk correspondence with Stalin who resented this big-hearted 'prince'. Sergo was, Stalin complained, 'vain to the point of folly.'

* * *

'Here on vacation,' Stalin wrote, 'I do not sit in one place but move from one location to another ...' After a month, Stalin moved southwards to his newly-built house at Museri. Set atop a hill in a semi-tropical park, it was an ugly grey two-storey residence with his beloved wood-panelling, expansive verandas, large dining room and a beautiful view down to a harbour where Lakoba had constructed a special jetty. It was surrounded by walks along serpentine paths that led to a round summerhouse, where Stalin worked, and down steps to the sea. Often Lakoba and Stalin strolled down to a nearby village where the locals laid on *al fresco* Abkhazian feasts.

On 23 September, Lakoba arranged a boating and shooting trip: Stalin and Vlasik motored along the coast from the specially-built jetty on a motor yacht, *Red Star*, with their guns on their knees. Suddenly there was a burst of machine-gun fire from the coast.

* Stalin treated Sergo like an uncontrollable younger brother: 'You were trouble-making this week,' Stalin wrote typically to him, 'and you were successful. Should I congratulate you or not?' On another occasion: 'Tomorrow, the meeting on bank reform. Are you prepared? You must be.' When Stalin scolded him, he added, 'Don't dress me down for being rude ... Actually, tell me off as much as you like.' He usually signed himself 'Koba'. Sergo's notes almost always disagree with some decision of Stalin's: 'Dear Soso,' he carped in one note, 'is the new Russia being built by Americans?' He was quite capable of giving Stalin instructions too: 'Soso, they want to put Kaganovich on civil aviation ... Write to Molotov and Kaganovich and tell them not to!'

10

Spoiled Victory: Kirov, the Plot
and the Seventeenth Congress

Vlasik threw himself on to Stalin on the deck of the *Red Star*, requesting permission to return fire. Firing shots landwards, the boat turned to the open sea. Stalin initially thought it had just been Georgians firing a greeting but he changed his mind. He received a letter from the border guards admitting they had fired, mistaking it for a foreign vessel. Beria investigated personally, displaying his ruthlessness to get results which impressed Stalin, but he aroused suspicions that he had contrived the attack to undermine Lakoba, who was responsible for security inside Abkhazia. The guards were despatched to Siberia. Vlasik and Beria became closer to Stalin.

Back on dry land, the entourage progressed into Gagra, where the GPU had found a new dacha in the hills which Lakoba had started to rebuild. This became a favourite residence, Kholodnaya Rechka, Coldstream, a Stalinist eyrie built on a cliff with views of dazzling natural beauty.* Returning to Sochi, Svetlana stayed with Stalin but when she went back to school, he found himself 'like a lonely owl' and craved Yenukidze's company. 'What keeps you in Moscow?' he wrote to Abel. 'Come to Sochi, swim in the sea and let your heart rest. Tell Kalinin from me that he commits a crime if he doesn't send you on holiday immediately … You could live with me at the *dacha* … I've visited the new *dacha* at Gagra today … Voroshilov and his wife are enchanted with it … Your Koba.'

* * *

* The Gagra house is one of the most beautiful of Stalin's residences but also the least accessible. The children later got their own houses. A snake path of steps twists down to the sea. Yet it is invisible from the land. Like most of these houses, it is still under the control of the Abkhazian presidential security, hidden, eerie but perfectly preserved. Museri adjoins the same secret CC resort, Pitsunda, where Khrushchev had a house as First Secretary and where, in the eighties, Mikhail Gorbachev and Raisa his wife were criticized for building a multi-million-pound holiday house in the last Soviet years. All remain empty yet guarded in the steamy Abkhazian heat.

After this long holiday, the 'lonely owl' returned to Moscow on 4 November to plan the coming Congress of Victors which was to crown him for the triumphs of the last four years. Moscow felt as if it was waking up and stretching after a long nightmare. The famine was over. The harvest had improved. The starving millions were buried and forgotten in villages that had disappeared for ever off the map.

There was much to celebrate as the delegates started to arrive for the Seventeenth Congress in late January. It must have been an exciting and proud time for the 1,966 voting delegates to be visiting Moscow from every corner of the sprawling workers' paradise. The Congress was the highest Party organ, which theoretically elected the Central Committee to govern in its place until it met again, usually four years later. But by 1934, this was a pantomine of triumphalism, supervised by Stalin and Kaganovich, minutely choreographed by Poskrebyshev.

None the less, a Congress was not all business: the Great Kremlin Palace was suddenly filled with outlandish costumes as bearded Cossacks, silk-clad Kazakhs and Georgians paraded into the great hall. Here the viceroys of Siberia, the Ukraine, or Transcaucasia, renewed their contacts with allies in the centre while the younger delegates found patrons.* Lenin's generation, who regarded Stalin as their leader but not their God, still dominated but the *Vozhd* took special care of his younger protégés.

He invited Beria, his blonde wife Nina and their son to the Kremlin to watch a movie with the Politburo. Sergo Beria,† aged ten, and Svetlana Stalin, who would become friends, watched the cartoon, *Three Little Pigs*, with Stalin before they set off for Zubalovo where the Berias joined the magnates in feasting and singing Georgian songs. When Sergo Beria was cold, Stalin hugged him and let him snuggle into his coat lined with wolf fur before tucking him into bed. It must have been thrilling for Beria,

* These provincials wanted to meet their heroes and a great amount of time was spent posing for the photographers in the hall where they gathered in eager groups, beaming, in their boots, tunics and caps, around Stalin, Kalinin, Voroshilov, Kaganovich and Budyonny. At the Fifteenth Congress in 1927, Stalin was just one of the leaders who posed with his fans. At the Seventeenth, Stalin is always at the centre. The album is mutilated by the huge number of figures either crossed out or cut out as they were arrested and executed during the following four years: out of 1,966 delegates, 1,108 would be arrested. Few survived.

† Named, of course, after Beria's former patron, Ordzhonikidze, a friendship that had disintegrated into mutual hatred.

the ambitious provincial entering the inner portals of power.

'STALIN!' gasped *Pravda* when he attended the Bolshoi. 'The appearance of the ardently loved *Vozhd*, whose name is linked inseparably with all the victories scored by the proletariat, by the Soviet Union, was greeted with tumultuous ovations' and 'no end of cries of "Hurrah!" and "Long Live our Stalin!"' '

However, some regional bosses had been shaken by Stalin's brutal mismanagement. A cabal seems to have met secretly in friends' apartments to discuss his removal. Each had their own reasons: in the Caucasus, Orakhelashvili was insulted by the promotion of the upstart Beria. Kosior's cries for help in feeding the Ukraine had been scorned. Some of these meetings supposedly took place in Sergo's flat in the Horse Guards where Orakhelashvili was staying. But who was to replace Stalin? Kirov, popular, vigorous and Russian, was their candidate. In the Bolshevik culture with its obsession with ideological purity, the former Kadet and bourgeois journalist with no ideological credentials, who owed his career to Stalin, was an unlikely candidate. Molotov, as loyal to Stalin as ever, sneered that Kirov was never a serious candidate.

When he was approached in Sergo's apartment, Kirov had to consider fast what to do: he informed them that he had no interest in replacing Stalin but that he would be able to see that their complaints were heard. Kirov was still ill, recovering from flu, and his reaction shows that he lacked the backbone for this poisoned chalice. His immediate instinct was to tell Stalin, which he did, probably in his new apartment where he denounced the plot, repeated the complaints, and denied any interest in becoming leader himself.

'Thank you,' Stalin is supposed to have replied, 'I won't forget what I owe you.' Stalin was surely disturbed that these Old Bolsheviks considered 'my Kirich' his successor. Mikoyan, Kirov's friend, stated that Stalin reacted with 'hostility and vengefulness towards the whole Congress and of course towards Kirov himself'. Kirov felt threatened but showed nothing publicly. Stalin concealed his anxiety.

In the Congress hall, Kirov ostentatiously sat, joking, with his delegation, not up on the Presidium, the sort of demagoguery that outraged Stalin, who kept asking what they were laughing about. His victory had been spoiled. Yet this constant struggling against traitors also suited his character and his ideology. No political leader was so programmed for this perpetual fight against enemies as Stalin, who regarded himself as history's lone knight riding out, with weary resignation, on another noble mission, the Bolshevik version of the mysterious cowboy arriving in a corrupt frontier town.

There was no hint of any of this in the public triumph: 'Our country has become a country of mighty industry, a country of collectivization, a country of victorious socialism,' declared Molotov, opening the Congress on 26 January. Stalin enjoyed the satisfaction of watching his enemies, from Zinoviev to Rykov, old and new, praise him extravagantly: 'The glorious field marshal of the proletarian forces, the best of the best – Comrade Stalin,' declared Bukharin, now editor of *Izvestiya*. But when Postyshev, another Old Bolshevik hardman newly promoted to run the Ukraine, called Kirov, Congress gave him a standing ovation. Kirov rose to the occasion, mentioning Stalin ('the great strategist of liberation of the working people of our country and the whole world') twenty-nine times, ending excitedly:

'Our successes are really tremendous. Damn it all ... you just want to live and live – really, just look what's going on. It's a fact!' Stalin joined the 'thunderous applause'.

The last duty of a Congress was to elect the Central Committee. Usually this was a formality. The delegates were given the ballot, a list of names prepared by the Secretariat (Stalin and Kaganovich) who were proposed from the floor: Kirov had to propose Beria. The voters crossed out names they opposed and voted for the names left unmarked. As the Congress ended on 8 February, the delegates received their ballots but when the vote-counting commission started work, they received a shock. These events are still mysterious, but it seems that Kirov received one or two negatives while Kaganovich and Molotov polled over 100 each. Stalin got between 123 and 292 negatives. They were automatically elected but here was another blow to Stalin's self-esteem, confirming that he rode alone among 'two-faced double-dealers'.

When Kaganovich, managing the Congress, was informed by the voting commission, he ran to Stalin to ask what to do. Stalin almost certainly ordered him to destroy most of the negative votes (though naturally Kaganovich denied this, even in old age). Certainly 166 votes are still missing. On the 10th, the 71 CC members were announced: Stalin received 1,056 votes and Kirov 1,055 out of 1,059. The new generation, personified by Beria and

Khrushchev, became members while Budyonny and Poskrebyshev were elected candidates. The Plenum of this new body met straight afterwards to do the real business.

Stalin devised a plan to deal with Kirov's dangerous eminence, proposing his recall from Leningrad to become one of the four Secretaries, thereby cleverly satisfying those who wanted him promoted to the Secretariat: on paper, a big promotion; in reality, this would bring him under Stalin's observation, cutting him off from his Leningrad clientele. In Stalin's entourage, a promotion to the centre was a mixed blessing. Kirov was neither the first nor the last to protest vigorously – but, in Stalin's eyes, a refusal meant placing personal power above Party loyalty, a mortal sin. Kirov's request to stay in Leningrad for another two years was supported by Sergo and Kuibyshev. Stalin petulantly stalked out in a huff.

Sergo and Kuibyshev advised Kirov to compromise with Stalin: Kirov became the third Secretary but remained temporarily in Leningrad. Since he would have little time for Moscow, Stalin reached out to another newly elected CC member who would become the closest to Stalin of all the leaders: Andrei Zhdanov, boss of Gorky (Nizhny Novgorod), moved to Moscow as the fourth Secretary.

Kirov staggered back to Leningrad, suffering from flu, congestion in his right lung and palpitations. In March, Sergo wrote to him: 'Listen my friend, you must rest. Really and truly, nothing is going to happen there without you there for 10–15 days ... Our fellow countryman [their codename for Stalin] considers you a healthy man ... none the less, you must take a short rest!' Kirov sensed that Stalin would not forgive him for the plot. Yet Stalin was even more suffocatingly friendly, insisting that they constantly meet in Moscow. It was Sergo, not Stalin, with whom Kirov really needed to discuss his apprehensions. 'I want awfully to have a chat with you on very many questions but you can't say everything in a letter so it is better to wait until our meeting.' They certainly discussed politics in private, careful to reveal nothing on paper.

There were hints of Kirov's scepticism about Stalin's cult: on 15 July 1933, Kirov wrote formally to 'Comrade Stalin' (not the usual Koba) that portraits of Stalin's photograph had been printed in Leningrad on rather 'thin paper'. Unfortunately they could not do any better. One can imagine Kirov and Sergo mocking Stalin's vanity.

In private,* Kirov imitated Stalin's accent to his Leningraders.

When Kirov visited Stalin in Moscow, they were boon companions but Artyom remembers a competitive edge to their jokes. Once at a family dinner, they made mock toasts:

'A toast to Stalin, the great leader of all peoples and all times. I'm a busy man but I've probably forgotten some of the other great things you've done too!' Kirov, who often 'monopolized conversations so as to be the centre of attention', toasted Stalin, mocking the cult. Kirov could speak to Stalin in a way unthinkable to Beria or Khrushchev.

'A toast to our beloved leader of the Leningrad Party and possibly the Baku proletariat too, yet he promises me he can't read all the papers – and what else are you beloved leader of?' replied Stalin. Even the tipsy banter between Stalin and Kirov was pregnant with ill-concealed anger and resentment, yet no one in the family circle noticed that they were anything but the most loving of friends. However the 'vegetarian years', as the poetess Akhmatova called them, were about to end: 'the meat-eating years' were coming.

On 30 June, Adolf Hitler, newly elected Chancellor of Germany, slaughtered his enemies within his Nazi Party, in the Night of the Long Knives – an exploit that fascinated Stalin.

'Did you hear what happened in Germany?' he asked Mikoyan. 'Some fellow that Hitler! Splendid! That's a deed of some skill!' Mikoyan was surprised that Stalin admired the German Fascist but the Bolsheviks were hardly strangers to slaughter themselves.

---

* Amongst his possessions in his apartment, preserved in Leningrad, is one of his cigarette boxes emblazoned with a unprepossessing portrait of Stalin with a very long nose. The box is opened by pressing the nose.

11

Assassination of the Favourite

That summer, their own repression seemed to be easing. In May, the Chairman of the OGPU, Menzhinsky, a shadowy scholar who was permanently ill and spent most of his time in seclusion studying Persian manuscripts in any of the twelve languages of which he was master, died. The press announced that the hated OGPU had perished with him, swallowed by a new People's Commissariat of Internal Affairs – the NKVD. This aroused hopes that the dawning jazz age really did herald a new freedom in Russia – but the new Commissar was Yagoda who had been running the OGPU for some time.

The illusion of this thaw was confirmed when Yagoda came to Stalin and recited a poem by Osip Mandelstam, who, with his friend, the beautiful Leningrad poetess Anna Akhmatova, wrote verses with a searing emotional clarity which still shines through that twilight of humanity like beams of heart-rending honesty. Naturally they found it hard to conform with Soviet mediocrity.

Yagoda paid Mandelstam the back-handed compliment of learning the verse by heart, sixteen lines of poetry that damned and mocked Stalin as a bewhiskered 'Kremlin crag-dweller' and 'peasant-slayer' whose 'fat fingers' were 'as oily as maggots'. The poet Demian Bedny had complained to Mandelstam that Stalin left greasy fingermarks on the books he constantly borrowed. His fellow leaders were a 'rabble of thin-necked bosses', a line he wrote after noticing Molotov's neck sticking out from his collar and the smallness of his head. Stalin was outraged – but understood Mandelstam's value. Hence that heartless order to Yagoda that sounds as if it concerned a priceless vase: 'Preserve but isolate.'

On the night of 16–17 May, Mandelstam was arrested and sentenced to three years' exile. Meanwhile the poet's friends rushed to appeal to his patrons among the Bolshevik magnates.

His wife Nadezhda and fellow poet Boris Pasternak appealed to Bukharin at *Izvestiya*, while Akhmatova was received by Yenukidze. Bukharin wrote to Stalin that Mandelstam was a 'first class poet ... but not quite normal ... PS: Boris Pasternak is utterly flabbergasted by Mandelstam's arrest and nobody else knows anything.' Perhaps most tellingly, he reminded Stalin that 'Poets are always right, history is on their side ...'

'Who authorized Mandelstam's arrest?' muttered Stalin. 'Disgraceful.' In July, knowing that news of his interest would spread like ripples on a pond before the coming Writers' Congress, Stalin telephoned Pasternak. His calls to writers already had their ritual. Poskrebyshev called first to warn the recipient that Comrade Stalin wished to speak to him: he must stand by. When the call arrived, Pastemak took it in his communal apartment and told Stalin he could not hear well since there were children yelling in the corridor.

'Mandelstam's case is being reviewed. Everything will be all right,' Stalin said, before adding, 'If I was a poet and my poet-friend found himself in trouble, I would do anything to help him.' Pasternak characteristically tried to define his concept of friendship which Stalin interrupted: 'But he's a genius, isn't he?'

'But that's not the point.'

'What is the point then?' Pasternak, who was fascinated by Stalin, said he wanted to come for a talk. 'About what?' asked Stalin.

'About life and death,' said Pasternak. The baffled Stalin rang off. However, the most significant conversation took place afterwards, when Pasternak tried to persuade Poskrebyshev to put him through again. Poskrebyshev refused. Pasternak asked if he could repeat what had been said. The answer was a big yes.

Stalin prided himself on understanding brilliance: 'he's doubtless a great talent,' he wrote about another writer. 'He's very capricious but that's the character of gifted people. Let him write what he wants, and when!'

Pasternak's whimsy may have saved his life for, later, when his arrest was proposed, Stalin supposedly replied:

'Leave that cloud-dweller in peace.'

* * *

Stalin's intervention is famous but there was nothing new about it: as Nicholas I was for Pushkin, so Stalin was for all his writers. Stalin pretended he considered himself just a casual observer:

'Comrades who know the arts will help you – I am just a dilettante' but he was both gourmet and gourmand. His papers reveal his omnipotent critiques of writers, who wrote to him in droves.

Stalin's ultimate pet writer was 'the Proletarian Poet', Demian Bedny, a Falstaffian rhymester, with good-natured eyes gazing out of a head 'like a huge copper cauldron', whose works appeared regularly in *Pravda* and who holidayed with Stalin, rendering an endless repertoire of obscene anecdotes. Rewarded with a Kremlin apartment, he was a member of the literary Politburo. But Bedny began to irritate Stalin: he bombarded him with complaints, and his egregious poems, in a long and farcical correspondence, while engaging in drunken escapades inside the Kremlin: 'Ha-ha-ha! Chaffinch!' Stalin exclaimed on one such letter. Worse, Bedny stubbornly resisted Stalin's criticisms: 'What about the present in Russia?' Stalin scribbled to him. 'Bedny leaves in the mistakes!'

'I agree,' added Molotov. 'Must not be published without improvements.' Stalin was tired of his drunken poet and expelled him from the Kremlin:

'There must be no more scandals inside the Kremlin walls,' he wrote in September 1932. Bedny was hurt but Stalin reassured him: 'You must not see leaving the Kremlin as being sacked from the Party. Thousands of respected comrades live outside the Kremlin and so does Gorky!' Vladimir Kirshon was one of Gorky's circle and another recipient of GPU funds who liked to send Stalin everything he wrote. When he was in favour, he could do no wrong:

'Publish immediately,' Stalin scrawled on Kirshon's latest article when returning it to *Pravda*'s editor. When Kirshon sent in his new play, Stalin read it in six days and wrote back:

'Comrade Kirshon, your play's not bad. It must be put on in the theatre at once.' But Kirshon was being rewarded for his political loyalty: he was one of the hacks who viciously destroyed Bulgakov's career. However, after the creation of Socialist Realism, Kirshon wrote to Stalin and Kaganovich to ask if he was out of favour:

'Why are you putting the question of trust?' Stalin replied by hand. 'I ask you to believe the Central Committee is absolutely happy with your work and trusts you.' The writers also turned to Stalin to sort out their feuds: Panferov wrote to Stalin to complain that Gorky was mocking his work. Stalin's comment? 'Vain. File in my archive. Stalin.'

When he did not like a writer, he did not mince words: 'Klim,' he wrote to Voroshilov about an article, 'My impression: a first-rate chatterer who thinks he's the Messiah. Yeah! Yeah! Stalin.'* When the American novelist Upton Sinclair wrote to Stalin asking him to release an arrested movie-maker, Stalin commented: 'Green steam!' Stalin's favourite theatre was the Moscow Arts so he was gentler with its famous director, Stanislavsky, blaming his opinion on his colleagues. 'I didn't highly praise the play "Suicide" (by N. Erdman) ... My nearest comrades think it empty and even harmful ...'

His 'nearest comrades', much less literary than he, became unlikely literary tyrants too: Stalin, Molotov and Kaganovich (an uneducated cobbler) decided artistic matters. Molotov turned on Bedny, for example, with an absurd mixture of personal threat and literary criticism. Bedny, a gossip, even dared to play Stalin off against Molotov who lectured him gravely:

'I read Stalin's letter to you. I agree absolutely. It cannot be said better than by him ...' Molotov warned him about rumours of disagreements between the leaders – 'You did your bit too, Comrade Bedny. I didn't expect such things. It's not good for a proletarian poet ...' Molotov even gave poetical advice: 'It's very pessimistic ... you need to give a window through which the sun can shine (heroism of socialism).'

Stalin often informed Gorky and other writers that he was correcting their articles with Kaganovich, a vision that must have horrified them. At the theatres, Stalin evolved a pantomime of giving his judgement on a new play which was followed to the letter by Kaganovich and Molotov. In the Politburo's *loge* and the room behind it, the *avant-loge*, where they ate between acts, Stalin commented on the actors, plays, even the décor of the foyer. Every comment became the subject of rumours, myths and decisions that affected careers.

Stalin attended a new play on Peter the Great by Alexei Tolstoy, another newly returned émigré writer who, besides Gorky, was the richest author of the Imperium. Count Tolstoy, an illegitimate and renegade nobleman, had returned to Russia in 1923 where he was hailed as the 'Worker-Peasant-Count'. This literary gymnast

---

* When Stalin read Andrei Platonov's satire on the 'Higher Command' of collectivization, *For Future Use*, he supposedly wrote 'Bastard!' on the manuscript and told Fadeev, 'Give him a belt "for future use."' Platonov was never arrested but died, in great deprivation, of TB.

specialized in understanding Stalin, boasting, 'You really do have to be an acrobat.' His *On the Rack* was attacked by Bolshevik writers. Stalin left shortly before the end, accompanied to his car by the crestfallen director. Sensing Imperial disapproval, the play was attacked viciously inside the theatre until the director returned triumphantly to announce: 'Comrade Stalin, in speaking with me, passed the following judgement: "A splendid play. Only it's a pity Peter was not depicted heroically enough."' Stalin received Tolstoy and gave him 'the right historical approach' for his next project, a novel *Peter the Great*.

This pantomime was repeated exactly when Kaganovich rejected a new production by the avant-garde theatrical director Meyerhold and was pursued to his car by the disappointed artist. Yet he protected the Yiddish actor, Solomon Mikhoels. Like eighteenth-century *grands seigneurs*, the magnates patronized their own theatres, their own poets, singers and writers, and defended their protégés* whom they 'received' at their dachas and visited at home. 'Everyone goes to see someone,' wrote Nadezhda Mandelstam in her memoirs that provide a peerless moral guide to this era. 'There's no other way.' But when the Party turned against their protégés, the leaders abandoned them swiftly.

The artists were fascinated by Stalin: Pasternak longed to meet him. 'Can I meet you?' wrote the poet Gidosh eagerly. Meyerhold appealed to Stalin for a meeting which he said would 'lift my depression as an artist' and signed it 'Loving you.'

'Stalin not here now,' wrote Poskrebyshev.

* * *

On 30 July, a month after Hitler's Night of the Long Knives, Stalin headed down to the Sochi dacha where he was meeting his old favourite, Kirov, who had no wish to be there, and his new one, Andrei Zhdanov, who must have been honoured to be invited. There were four of them because Zhdanov brought along his son, Yury, Stalin's future son-in-law, a young man whom the *Vozhd* was

---

* There was one other returned émigré whom Stalin personally favoured. Ilya Ehrenburg, a Jewish Bohemian, friends with Picasso and Malraux, complained of persecution by the Party. His old schoolfriend Bukharin appealed for him. Stalin scrawled on the letter: 'To Comrade Kaganovich, pay attention to the attached document – don't let the Communists drive Ehrenburg mad. J. Stalin.' Molotov and Bukharin helped Mandelstam. Voroshilov aided his own stable as well as his 'court painter' Gerasimov. Kirov protected the Mariinsky Ballet, Yenukidze the Bolshoi. Yagoda patronized his own writers and architects, often meeting them at Gorky's mansion. Poskrebyshev received the tenor Kozlovsky at home.

to regard as an ideal Soviet man. They had gathered to write the new history of Russia.

Already ill and exhausted, Kirov was the sort of man who wanted to go camping and hunting with friends like Sergo. There was nothing relaxing about a holiday with Stalin. Indeed, escaping from holidays with Stalin was to become a common experience for all his guests. Kirov tried to get out of it but Stalin insisted. Kirov, realizing that 'Stalin was conducting a struggle of wills', could not refuse. 'I'm not in a happy mood,' he told his wife. 'I'm bored here ... At no time can I have a quiet vacation. To hell with it.' This was hardly the attitude Stalin needed or expected from 'my Kirich' but had he read such letters, they would have confirmed his already ambiguous feelings for Kirov.

The three leaders and the boy 'sat at a table on the balcony in gorgeous weather on the enclosed veranda' of the huge Sochi house with its courtyard and its small indoor pool for Stalin. Servants brought hors d'oeuvres and drinks. 'The four of us came and went,' says Yury Zhdanov. 'Sometimes we went into the study indoors, sometimes we went down the garden to the wooden summerhouse.' The atmosphere was relaxing and free and easy. In the breaks, Kirov took Yury picking blackberries which they brought back for Stalin and Zhdanov. Every evening Kirov returned to his dacha and the Zhdanovs to theirs. Sometimes the lonely Stalin went home with them. 'There were no bodyguards, no accompanying vehicles, no NKVD cars,' says Yury Zhdanov. 'There was just me in the front, next to the driver and my father and Stalin in the back.' They set off at dusk and when they turned on the lights, they saw two girls hitchhiking by the roadside.

'Stop!' said Stalin. He opened the door and let the girls get into the middle seats of the seven-seater Packard. The girls recognized Stalin:

'That's Stalin!' Yury heard one whisper. They dropped the girls off in Sochi. 'That was the atmosphere of the time.' It was about to change.

However informal it might have been, Zhdanov, like Beria, was one of the few magnates who could have brought his son to attend a meeting with Stalin even though the teenager had known him since he was five. 'Only Zhdanov received from Stalin the same kind of treatment that Kirov enjoyed,' explained

Molotov. 'After Kirov, Stalin loved Zhdanov best. He valued him above everyone else.'

Attractive, brown-eyed, broad-chested and athletic, though asthmatic, Zhdanov was always hearty and smiling, with a ready supply of jokes. Like Kirov, a sunny companion, he loved to sing and play the piano. Zhdanov already knew Stalin well. Born at the Black Sea port of Mariupol in 1896, Andrei Alexandrovich Zhdanov, a hereditary nobleman (like Lenin and Molotov), was the scion of Chekhovian intellectuals. Son of a Master of Religious Studies at the Moscow Religious Academy, who worked like Lenin's father as an inspector of public schools (his thesis was 'Socrates as Pedagogue'), and a mother who had graduated from the Moscow Musical Conservatoire and was herself the daughter of a rector of a religious academy, Zhdanov was the sole representative in top Party circles of the nineteenth-century educated middle-class. His mother, a gifted pianist, taught Zhdanov to play well too.

Zhdanov studied at a church school (like Stalin), dreamed of being an agriculturalist, then at twenty attended the Junior Officers' Training College in Tiflis. This 'acquainted him with Georgian culture and songs'. He grew up with three sisters who became Bolsheviks: two of them never married and became revolutionary maiden aunts who lived in his house, dominating Zhdanov and greatly irritating Stalin. Joining the Party in 1915, Zhdanov won his spurs in the Civil War as a commissar, like so many others. By 1922, he ran Tver, then Nizhny Novgorod, whence he was called to greater things.

Strait-laced and rigid in Party matters, his papers reveal a man of meticulous diligence who could not approach a subject without becoming an encyclopaedic expert on it. Despite never completing higher education though he attended Agricultural College, Zhdanov was another workaholic obessesive, who voraciously studied music, history and literature. Stalin 'respected Zhdanov', says Artyom, 'as his fellow intellectual', whom he constantly telephoned to ask:

'Andrei, have you read this new book?' The two were always pulling out Chekhov or Saltykov-Shchedrin to read aloud. Jealous rivals mocked his pretensions: Beria nicknamed him 'The Pianist'. Zhdanov and Stalin shared religious education, Georgian songs, a love of history and classical Russian culture, autodictactic and ideological obsessions, and their sense of humour – except that

Zhdanov was a prig.* He was personally devoted to Stalin whom he called 'Joseph Vissarionovich' but never Koba. 'Comrade Stalin and I have decided ...' was his favourite pompous way to begin a meeting.

On the veranda or in the summerhouse, they discussed history, epoch by epoch, on a table spread with revolutionary and Tsarist history textbooks. Zhdanov took notes. The supreme pedagogue could not stop showing off his knowledge.† Their mission was to create the new history that became the Stalinist orthodoxy. Stalin adored studying history, having such happy memories of his history teacher at the Seminary that he took the trouble in September 1931 to write to Beria:

'Nikolai Dmitrievich Makhatadze, aged 73, finds himself in Metechi Prison ... I have known him since the Seminary and I do not think he can present a danger to Soviet power. I ask you to free the old man and let me know the result.' He had been a history addict ever since. In 1931, Stalin decisively intervened in academia to create the historical precursor of 'Socialist Realism' in fiction: henceforth, history was not what the archives said but what the Party decreed on a holiday like this. 'You speak about history,' Stalin told his magnates. 'But one must sometimes correct history.' Stalin's historical library was read and annotated thoroughly: he paid special attention to the Napoleonic Wars, ancient Greece, nineteenth-century relations between Germany, Britain and Russia, and all Persian Shahs and Russian Tsars. A born student, he always mugged up on the history of that day's issue.

While Zhdanov was in his element in the discussions in Sochi, Kirov was out of his depth. It is said that Kirov tried to escape by saying,

'Joseph Vissarionovich, what kind of a historian am I?'

'Never mind. Sit down,' replied Stalin, 'and listen.' Kirov got so sunburnt he could not even play *gorodki*: 'However strange, for

---

* His wife Zinaida was even prissier: she once told Svetlana Stalin that the urbane novelist Ehrenburg 'loves Paris because there are naked women there'. It was Zinaida who was tactless enough to tell Svetlana her mother was mentally 'sick'.

† Yury Zhdanov, the boy at table with Stalin, Kirov and his father, is the main source for this account and now lives in Rostov-on-Don where he generously agreed to be interviewed for this book. The holiday became famous because of Kirov's fate soon afterwards: it forms a set piece in Anatoly Rybakov's novel *Children of the Arbat*. Yury Zhdanov remembers Stalin asking him: 'What was the genius of Catherine the Great?' He answered his own question. 'Her greatness lay in her choice of Prince Potemkin and other such talented lovers and officials to govern the State.'

most of the day, we are busy. This isn't what I expected for recreation. Well, to the devil with it,' he wrote to a friend in Leningrad. 'I'll just take to my heels as soon as possible.' Yet Yury Zhdanov recalled 'happy warmth' between Stalin and Kirov who swapped earthy jokes which Zhdanov received in prim silence. Yury still remembers Stalin's Jesus joke: they were working in the summerhouse, which stood under a big oak tree, when Stalin glanced at his closest friends:

'Look at you here with me,' he said, pointing at the tree. 'That's the Mamre tree.' Zhdanov knew from his Bible that the Mamre tree was where Jesus assembled his Apostles.*

There may have been a more sinister development that worried Kirov: some time when he was out of town, Moscow tried to remove his trusted NKVD boss in Leningrad, Medved, a close family friend, and replace him with a thuggish ex-criminal, Evdokimov, one of Stalin's rougher drinking pals on southern holidays. Stalin was trying to loosen Kirov's local patronage, and perhaps even control his security. Kirov refused to accept Evdokimov.

As Kirov headed back to Leningrad, Stalin despatched Zhdanov to Moscow to supervise the first Writers' Congress. This was Zhdanov's first test, which he passed with flying colours, managing, with Kaganovich's help, to cope with Gorky's demands and Bukharin's hysteria. Zhdanov reported every detail to Stalin in twenty-page letters in a fastidious hand that showed their close relationship and the younger man's new eminence. (There seems to have been an unspoken competition among his men to write the longest letters: if so, Zhdanov was the winner.) Like a schoolboy to his tutor, Zhdanov boasted of his good work: 'The opinion of all the writers – ours and foreigners – was good. All the sceptics who predicted failure now have to admit the colossal success. All the writers saw and understood the Party's attitude.' He admitted, 'the Congress cost me a lot in terms of my nerves but I think I did it well.' Stalin appreciated his openness about his weaknesses. Once the Congress was over, Zhdanov even had to apologize to Stalin that 'I didn't write to you. Congress took so much time ...' but he also apologized for writing 'such a long letter – I can't do it any other way'.

---

* When the writer Mikhail Sholokhov criticized the praise for the leader, Stalin replied with a sly smile, 'What can I do? The people need a god.'

By now the other leaders had gone off on holiday: 'Molotov, Kaganovich, Chubar and Mikoyan left today. Kuibyshev, Andreyev and me stayed.' Zhdanov, not even a Politburo candidate, and new in the Secretariat, was left in charge of the country, signing decrees himself. Here was another sign that the Politburo's importance was shrinking: proximity to Stalin was the source of real power.* Soviet Russia was enjoying its last months of oligarchy and approaching the first of dictatorship.

Zhdanov, one of the more fragile of Stalin's workhorses, was exhausted: 'I ask for one month's holiday in Sochi ... I feel very tired,' he wrote to Stalin. Of course he would work on their beloved history: 'During the holiday, I'd like to look through the textbooks on history ... I've already looked through the second level textbooks – not good. A big greeting to you, dear Comrade Stalin!'

What was Stalin's mood in this calm before the storm? He was frustrated by the NKVD's blunders and the 'whining' of Party bigwigs. On 11 September, Stalin complained to Zhdanov and Kuibyshev about misguided secret-police coercion: 'Find out all the mistakes of the deduction methods of the workers of the GPU ... Free persecuted persons who are innocent if they are innocent and ... purge the OGPU' of people with specific 'deduction methods' and punish them all – 'whoever they may be' [in Stalin's words: 'without looking at their faces']. A few days later, a sailor defected to Poland.

Stalin immediately ordered Zhdanov and Yagoda to enforce the punishment of the sailor's family: 'Inform me at once that 1. members of sailor's family were arrested and 2. if not, then who is guilty for the mistake [of not having done so] in our Organs and has the culprit been punished for this betrayal of the Motherland?' The tension was rising too in his relationship with Kirov.

* * *

On 1 September, Stalin despatched the Politburo around the countryside to check the harvest: Kirov was sent to Kazakhstan where there was a strange incident which might have been an

* After the Seventeenth Congress, formal Politburo meetings became gradually less frequent. Often a Politburo sitting was really just Stalin chatting with a couple of comrades: Poskrebyshev's minutes are simply marked 'Comrades Stalin, Molotov, Kaganovich – for' and the others were sometimes telephoned by Poskrebyshev who marked their votes and signed his 'P' underneath. By the end of the year, there was one meeting in September, none in October and one in November.

assassination attempt or meant to resemble one. The circumstances are murky but when he returned to Leningrad, four more Chekists were added to his NKVD guard, bringing it to about nine men who worked in shifts at different locations. This made Kirov one of the most guarded of all the Soviet leaders and he did not like it, sensing it was another attempt to separate him from his trusted local Chekists, particularly his bodyguard Borisov, middle-aged and overweight but loyal. After their tour, Sergo and Voroshilov joined Stalin on holiday while Zhdanov inspected Stalingrad, whence he managed another thirteen-page letter, showing his toughness by demanding, 'Some workers must be sent to trial here.' He signed off heartily: 'A hundred times: Devil curse the details!'

When Stalin returned to Moscow on 31 October, he again longed to see Kirov who was arguing against Stalin's plan to end bread rationing on which he depended to feed Leningrad's huge population. Kuibyshev was Kirov's ally: 'I need your support,' he wrote from Leningrad. On 3 November, Maria Svanidze recorded Stalin arriving in his apartment with Kaganovich while the 'absurd fat' Zhdanov ran along behind him. He rang a reluctant Kirov and invited him to Moscow 'to defend the interests of Leningrad'. Stalin gave the phone to Kaganovich who 'talked Kirov into coming down'. Maria said that Stalin really just wanted to 'go to the steambath and joke around with him'.

A few days later, Kirov drove out with Stalin and his son Vasily to Zubalovo to watch a puppet show put on by Svetlana, and then played billiards. Khrushchev, attending the Politburo as a rising star, witnessed 'an exchange of sharp words' between Stalin and Kirov. Khrushchev was shocked that the *Vozhd* behaved 'disrespectfully to another Party member'. Svanidze noticed Stalin was 'in a bad mood'. Kirov anxiously returned to Leningrad: he longed to discuss the rising tension with his friend: 'I haven't seen Sergo in such a long time.'

On 7 November, there was another sign of the apparent thaw. At the diplomatic reception in the Andreevsky Hall, presided over by Stalin, Kalinin and Voroshilov, the traditional Red Army oompah band packed up and were replaced, to the amazement of all, by Antonin Ziegler and his Jazz Revue. The wild swing music seemed completely out of place and no one knew whether they should dance or not. Then the light-footed Voroshilov, who was taking dancing lessons in cabaret jazz, started to foxtrot strenuously with his wife Ekaterina Davidovna.

On 25 November, Kirov rushed back to Moscow for the Plenum, hoping to consult with Ordzhonikidze. Sergo did not make it to the Plenum. Earlier that month, visiting Baku with Beria, he was suddenly taken ill after dinner. Beria took Sergo back to Tiflis by train. After the 7 November parade, Sergo fell ill again with intestinal bleeding, then suffered a serious heart attack. The Politburo sent three specialists down to examine him but they were confounded by his mysterious symptoms. Sergo was none the less determined to return for the Plenum but Stalin formally ordered him to 'strictly fulfil doctor's instructions and not return to Moscow before 26 November. Don't take your illness lightly. Regards. Stalin.'

When Beria was involved, it was indeed foolish to take one's illnesses lightly: Stalin perhaps did not want Sergo and Kirov to meet at the Plenum. Beria, who had offered to use his axe for Stalin, was already aware of the leader's disillusionment with Sergo. He was to prove adept with poisons. Indeed, the NKVD already boasted a secret department of medical poisoners under Dr Grigory Maironovsky but Beria needed little help in such matters. He truly brought the venom of the Borgias to the court of the Bolsheviks. But Stalin himself brooded about poison; reflecting on venomous intrigues at the eighteenth-century Persian court, which he was studying, he had earlier scribbled on his pad during a Politburo meeting: 'Poison, poison, Nadir Khan.'

After the Plenum, on the 28th, Stalin personally escorted Kirov to the Red Arrow train, embracing him in his compartment. Kirov was back at work in Leningrad the next day. On 1 December, he started work at home, preparing a speech, then, wearing his worker's peaked cap and raincoat, he set off from his apartment on foot to his office. He entered the grand neoclassical Smolny Institute by the public entrance. At 4.30 p.m. Kirov, followed by his bodyguard Borisov, walked up to his third-floor office. Old Borisov fell behind, either from unfitness or being strangely delayed by some Chekists from Moscow who appeared at the door.

Kirov turned right out of the stairwell and passed a dark-haired young man named Leonid Nikolaev, who pressed himself against the wall to let Kirov pass – and then trailed along behind him. Nikolaev pulled out a Nagan revolver and shot Kirov from three feet away in the back of the neck. The bullet passed through his cap. Nikolaev turned the pistol on himself and squeezed the trigger but an electrician working nearby somehow knocked him down and the second bullet hit the ceiling. Borisov the guard staggered up breathlessly, gun drawn impotently. Kirov fell face down, head turned to the right, his cap's peak resting on the floor, and still gripping his briefcase – a Bolshevik workaholic to the last.

Several minutes of chaos followed in which witnesses and police ran in every direction, seeing the same events differently and giving conflicting evidence: even the gun was variously seen on the floor and in the assassin's hand. There seems to be a special sort of miasma in the air at terrible events and this one was no different. What matters is that Kirov lay lifeless on the floor near the unconscious Nikolaev. Kirov's friend Rosliakov knelt beside him, lifting his head and whispering: 'Kirov, Mironich.' They lifted Kirov, with Rosliakov holding his lolling head, on to a conference table, with the blood seeping from his neck leaving a trail of heroic Bolshevik sacrament down the corridor. They loosened his belt and opened his collar. Medved, the Leningrad NKVD boss, arrived but was stopped at the door by Moscow Chekists.

Three doctors arrived, including a Georgian, Dzhanelidze. All declared Kirov dead but they still kept on giving him artificial respiration until almost 5.45 p.m. Doctors in totalitarian states are terrified of eminent dead patients – and with good reason. As the doctors surrendered, those present realized that someone would have to tell Stalin. Everyone remembered where they were when Kirov was assassinated: the Soviet JFK.

Part Three
On the Brink, 1934–1936

12

'I'm Orphaned':
the Connoisseur of Funerals

Poskrebyshev answered Stalin's telephone in his office. Kirov's deputy, Chudov, broke the terrible news from Leningrad. Poskrebyshev tried Stalin's phone line but he could not get an answer, sending a secretary to find him. The *Vozhd*, according to his journal, was meeting with Molotov, Kaganovich, Voroshilov and Zhdanov, but hurriedly called Leningrad, insisting on interrogating the Georgian doctor in his native language. Then he rang back to ask what the assassin was wearing. A cap? Were there foreign items on him? Yagoda, who had already called to demand whether any foreign objects had been found on the assassin, arrived at Stalin's office at 5.50 p.m.

Mikoyan, Sergo and Bukharin arrived quickly. Mikoyan specifically remembered that 'Stalin announced that Kirov had been assassinated and on the spot, without any investigation, he said the supporters of Zinoviev [the former leader of Leningrad and the Left opposition to Stalin] had started a terror against the Party.' Sergo and Mikoyan, who were so close to Kirov, were particularly appalled since Sergo had missed seeing his friend for the last time. Kaganovich noticed that Stalin 'was shocked at first'.

Stalin, now showing no emotion, ordered Yenukidze as Secretary of the Central Executive Committee to sign an emergency law that decreed the trial of accused terrorists within ten days and immediate execution without appeal after judgement. Stalin must have drafted it himself. This 1st December Law – or rather the two directives of that night – was the equivalent of Hitler's Enabling Act because it laid the foundation for a random terror without even the pretence of a rule of law. Within three years, two million people had been sentenced to death or labour camps in its name. Mikoyan said there was no discussion and no objections. As easily as slipping the safety catch on their Mausers, the Politburo clicked into the military emergency mentality of the Civil War.

If there was any opposition, it came from Yenukidze, that

unusually benign figure among these amoral toughs, but it was he who ultimately signed it. The newspapers declared the laws were passed by a meeting of the Presidium of the Central Executive Committee – which probably meant Stalin bullying Yenukidze in a smoky room after the meeting. It is also a mystery why the craven Kalinin, the President who was present, did not sign it. His signature had appeared by the time it was announced in the newspapers. Anyway the Politburo did not officially vote until a few days later.

Stalin immediately decided that he would personally lead a delegation to Leningrad to investigate the murder. Sergo wanted to go but Stalin ordered him to remain behind because of his weak heart. Sergo had indeed collapsed with grief and may have suffered another heart attack. His daughter remembered that 'this was the only time he wept openly'. His wife, Zina, travelled to Leningrad to comfort Kirov's widow.

Kaganovich also wanted to go but Stalin told him that someone had to run the country. He took Molotov, Voroshilov and Zhdanov with him along with Yagoda and Andrei Vyshinsky, the Deputy Procurator, who had crossed Sergo earlier that year. Naturally they were accompanied by a trainload of secret policemen and Stalin's own myrmidons, Pauker and Vlasik. In retrospect, the most significant man Stalin chose to accompany him was Nikolai Yezhov, head of the CC's Personnel Department. Yezhov was one of those special young men, like Zhdanov, on whom Stalin was coming to depend.

The local leaders gathered, shell-shocked, at the station. Stalin played his role, that of a Lancelot heartbroken and angry at the death of a beloved knight, with self-conscious and preplanned Thespianism. When he dismounted from the train, Stalin strode up to Medved, the Leningrad NKVD chief, and slapped his face with his gloved hand.

Stalin immediately headed across town to the hospital to inspect the body, then set up a headquarters in Kirov's office where he began his own strange investigation, ignoring any evidence that did not point to a terrorist plot by Zinoviev and the Left opposition. Poor Medved, the cheerful Chekist slapped by Stalin, was interrogated first and criticized for not preventing the murder. Then the 'small and shabby' murderer himself, Nikolaev, was dragged in. Nikolaev was one of those tragic, simple victims of history, like the Dutchman who lit the Reichstag fire with which this case shares many resemblances. This frail dwarf of thirty had been expelled from, and reinstated in, the Party but had written to Kirov and Stalin complaining of his plight. He was apparently in a daze and did not even recognize Stalin until they showed him a photograph. Falling to his knees before the jackbooted leader, he sobbed,

'What have I done, what have I done?' Khrushchev, who was not in the room, claimed that Nikolaev kneeled and said he had done it on assignment from the Party. A source close to Voroshilov has Nikolaev stammering, 'But you yourself told me ...' Some accounts claim that he was punched and kicked by the Chekists present.

'Take him away!' ordered Stalin.

The well-informed NKVD defector, Orlov, wrote that Nikolaev pointed at Zaporozhets, Leningrad's deputy NKVD boss, and said, 'Why are you asking me? Ask him.'

Zaporozhets had been imposed on Kirov and Leningrad in 1932, Stalin and Yagoda's man in Kirov's fiefdom. The reason to ask Zaporozhets was that Nikolaev had already been detained in October loitering with suspicious intent outside Kirov's house, carrying a revolver, but had been freed without even being searched. Another time, the bodyguards had prevented him taking a shot. But four years later, when Yagoda was tried, he confessed, in testimony filled with both lies and truths, to having ordered Zaporozhets 'not to place any obstacles in the way of the terrorist act against Kirov'.

Then the assassin's wife, Milda Draul, was brought in. The NKVD spread the story that Nikolaev's shot was a *crime passionnel* following her affair with Kirov. Draul was a plain-looking woman. Kirov liked elfin ballerinas but his wife was not pretty either: it is impossible to divine the impenetrable mystery of sexual taste but those who knew both believed they were an unlikely couple. Draul claimed she knew nothing. Stalin strode out into the anteroom and ordered that Nikolaev be brought round with medical attention.

'To me it's already clear that a well-organized counter-revolutionary terrorist organization is active in Leningrad ... A painstaking investigation must be made.' There was no real attempt to analyse the murder forensically. Stalin certainly did not wish to find out whether the NKVD had encouraged Nikolaev to kill Kirov.

Later, it is said that Stalin visited the 'prick' in his cell and spent an hour with him alone, offering him his life in return for testifying against Zinoviev at a trial. Afterwards Nikolaev wondered if he would be double-crossed.

The murkiness now thickens into a deliberately blind fog. There was a delay. Kirov's bodyguard, Borisov, was brought over to be interrogated by Stalin. He alone could reveal whether he was delayed at the Smolny entrance and what he knew of the NKVD's machinations. Borisov rode in the back of an NKVD Black Crow. As the driver headed towards the Smolny, the front-seat passenger reached over and seized the wheel so that the Black Crow swerved and grazed its side against a building. Somehow in this dubious car crash, Borisov was killed. The 'shaken' Pauker arrived in the anteroom to announce the crash. Such ham-handed 'car crashes' were soon to become an occupational hazard for eminent Bolsheviks. Certainly anyone who wanted to cover up a plot might have wished Borisov dead. When Stalin was informed of this reekingly suspicious death, he denounced the local Cheka: 'They couldn't even do that properly.'

The mystery will never now be conclusively solved. Did Stalin order Kirov's assassination? There is no evidence that he did, yet the whiff of his complicity still hangs in the air. Khrushchev, who arrived in Leningrad on a separate train as a Moscow delegate, claimed years later that Stalin ordered the murder. Mikoyan, a more trustworthy witness in many ways than Khrushchev and with less to prove, came to believe that Stalin was somehow involved in the death.

Stalin certainly no longer trusted Kirov whose murder served as a pretext to destroy the Old Bolshevik cliques. His drafting of the 1st December Law minutes after the death seems to stink as much as his decision to blame the murder on Zinoviev. Stalin had indeed tried to replace Kirov's friend Medved and he knew the suspicious Zaporozhets who, shortly before the murder, had gone on leave without Moscow's permission, perhaps to absent himself from the scene. Nikolaev was a pathetic bundle of suspicious circumstances. Then there were the strange events of the day of the murder: why was Borisov delayed at the door and why were there already Moscow NKVD officers in the Smolny so soon after the assassination? Borisov's death is highly suspect. And Stalin, often so cautious, was also capable of such a reckless gamble, particularly after admiring Hitler's reaction to the Reichstag fire and his purge.

Yet much of this appears less sinister on closer analysis. The lax security around Kirov proves nothing, since even Stalin often only had one or two guards. The gun is less suspicious when one realizes that all Party members carried them. Stalin's deteriorating relationship with Kirov was typical of the friction within his entourage. Stalin's swift reaction to the murder, and his surreal investigation, did not mean that he arranged it. When, on 27 June 1927, Voikov, Soviet Ambassador to Poland, was assassinated, Stalin had reacted with the same speed and uninterest in the real culprits. In that case, he told Molotov that he 'sensed the hand of Britain' and immediately ordered the shooting of scores of so-called 'monarchists'. The Bolsheviks always regarded justice as a political tool. The local NKVD, desperate to conceal their incompetence, may well have arranged Borisov's murder. So much can be explained by the habitual clumsiness of totalitarian panic.

However, it is surely naïve to expect written evidence of the crime of the century. We know that, in other murders, Stalin gave verbal orders in the name of the *Instantsiya*, an almost magical euphemism for the Highest Authority, with which we will become very familiar.* The direct involvement of Yagoda seems unlikely because he was not particularly close to Stalin but there were many Chekists, from Agranov to Zaporozhets, who were both personally trusted and amoral enough to do anything the Party asked of them. It is unlikely to have been a Henrician 'Rid me of this turbulent priest' because Stalin had to micromanage everything. So he may have read Nikolaev's letter to him and exploited his loser's resentment against Kirov.

Stalin's friendship with Kirov was one-sided and flimsy but there is no doubt that 'Stalin simply loved him,' according to 'Iron Lazar', who added that 'he treated everyone politically'. His friendships, like teenage infatuations, meandered between love, admiration and venomous jealousy. He was an extreme example of Gore Vidal's epigram that 'Every time a friend succeeds, a little bit of me dies.' He had adored Bukharin whose widow explains that Stalin could love and hate the same person 'because love and hate born of envy ... fought with each other in the same breast'. Perhaps Kirov's betrayal of his sincere friendship provoked a rage

---

* *Instantsiya* derives from the nineteenth-century German usage of *aller instanzen*, meaning to appeal to the highest court.

like a woman scorned, followed by terrible guilt after the murder. But even with his 'friends', Stalin cultivated his privacy and detachment: he wanted to be supremely elusive.

Stalin was always a more loyal friend to those he knew much less well. When a schoolboy of sixteen wrote to him, Stalin sent him a present of ten roubles and the boy wrote a thank-you letter. He was always indulging in bursts of sentimentality for the friends of his youth: 'I'm sending you 2,000 roubles,' he wrote to Peter Kapanadze, his friend from the Seminary who became a priest, then a teacher, in December 1933. 'I haven't got more now ... Your needs are a special occasion for me so I send my [book] royalties to you. You'll [also] be given 3,000 roubles as a loan ... Live long and be happy' and he signed the letter with his father's name, 'Beso.'

One strange unpublished letter illustrates this distant warmth: during 1930, Stalin received a request from the head of a collective farm in distant Siberia as to whether to admit a Tsarist policeman who claimed to have known Stalin. This old gendarme had actually been Stalin's guard in exile. But Stalin wrote a long, handwritten recommendation: 'During my exile in Kureika 1914–16, Mikhail Merzlikov was my guard/police constable. At that time he had one order – to guard me ... It's clear that I could not be in 'friendly' relations with Merzlikov. Yet I must testify that while not being friendly, our relations were not as hostile as they usually were between exile and guard. It must be explained why, it seems to me, Merzlikov carried out his duties without the usual police zeal, did not spy on me or persecute me, overlooked my often going away and often scolded police officers for barring his "orders" ... It's my duty to testify to all this. It was so in 1914–16 when Merzlikov was my guard, differing from other policemen for the better. I don't know what he did under Kolchak and Soviet power, I don't know how he is now.'

There, in a man who killed his best friends, was true friendship. Whether or not he killed Kirov, Stalin certainly exploited the murder to destroy not only his opponents but the less radical among his own allies.

* * *

Kirov lay in state in an open casket, wearing a dark tunic and surrounded by the red banners, inscribed wreaths and tropical palms of the Bolshevik funeral amidst the Potemkinian neoclassical grandeur of the Taurida Palace.* At 9.30 p.m. on 3 December, Stalin and the Politburo formed the honour guard, another part of Bolshevik necro-ritual. Voroshilov and Zhdanov appeared upset but Molotov was stony. 'Astonishingly calm and impenetrable was the face of JV Stalin,' noted Khrushchev, 'giving the impression that he was lost in thought, his eyes glazing over Kirov's bullet-struck corpse.' Before departing, Stalin appointed Zhdanov as Leningrad boss while remaining a CC Secretary. Yezhov also stayed behind to oversee the investigation.

At ten, Stalin and the others bore Kirov's coffin to a gun-carriage. The body travelled slowly through the streets to the station where it was loaded on to the train that was to take Stalin back to Moscow. Draped in garlands, this death train shunted into the darkness after midnight, leaving behind Kirov's brain where it was to be studied for signs of revolutionary brilliance in the Leningrad Institute.†

Even before the train arrived in Moscow, Agranov, the Chekist running the investigation, interrogated the assassin: 'Stubborn as a mule,' he reported to Stalin.

'Nourish Nikolaev well, buy him a chicken,' replied Stalin, who so enjoyed chicken himself. 'Nourish him so he will be strong, then he'll tell us who was leading him. And if he doesn't talk, we'll give it to him and he'll tell ... everything.'

At Moscow's October Station, the casket was again transferred to a gun carriage and deposited in the Hall of Columns for the funeral next day. Soon afterwards, Stalin briefed the Politburo on his unconvincing investigation. Mikoyan, who had loved Kirov, was so upset that he asked how Nikolaev had twice escaped arrest with a pistol and how Borisov had been killed.

'How could it happen?' Stalin agreed indignantly. 'Someone should answer for this, shouldn't they?' exclaimed Mikoyan,

---

* The Taurida Palace had been the scene of Prince Potemkin's extravagant ball for Catherine the Great in 1791 but it was also the home of the Duma, the Parliament gingerly granted by Nicholas II after the 1905 Revolution. In 1918, the palace housed the Constituent Assembly that Lenin ordered shut down by drunken Red Guards. It was thus both the birthplace and graveyard of Russia's first two democracies before 1991.

† This brain study was part of the rationalist-scientific ritual of the death of great Bolsheviks. Lenin's brain had been extracted and was now studied at the Institute of the Brain. When Gorky died, his brain was delivered there too. This was surely a scientific Marxist distortion of the tradition in the Romantic age for the hearts of great men, whether Mirabeau or Potemkin, to be buried separately. But the age of the heart was over.

focusing on the strange behaviour of the NKVD. 'Isn't the OGPU Chairman [Yagoda] responsible for Politburo security? He should be called to account.' But Stalin protected Yagoda, concentrating on his real targets, the Old Bolsheviks like Zinoviev. Afterwards, Sergo, Kuibyshev and Mikoyan were deeply suspicious: Mikoyan discussed Stalin's 'unclear behaviour' with Sergo, probably on their walks around the Kremlin, the traditional place for such forbidden chats. Both were 'surprised and amazed and could not understand it'. Sergo lost his voice with grief. Kuibyshev is said to have proposed a CC investigation to check the one being carried out by the NKVD. It is surely doubtful that Mikoyan, who still fervently admired Stalin and served him loyally until his death, believed at that time that his leader was responsible. These Bolsheviks were accustomed to self-delude and double-think their way out of such nagging doubts.

That night, Pavel Alliluyev replayed his role after Nadya's death by staying with Stalin at Kuntsevo. Leaning on his hand, Stalin murmured that after Kirov's death, 'I am absolutely an orphan.' He said it so touchingly that Pavel hugged him. There is no reason to doubt the sincerity of his anguish that someone had done this to Kirov – or that they had needed to do it.

At 10 a.m. on the 5th, with Gorky Street closed and tight security under the command of Pauker (as at Nadya's funeral), Stalin's entourage gathered in the Hall of Columns. The funeral was an extravaganza of Bolshevik sentimental kitsch – with burning torches, scarlet velvet curtains and banners hanging all the way from the ceiling and more palm trees – and modern media frenzy, with a press pack snapping their cameras and arc lights illuminating the body as if it was a prop in a neon-lit theatre. The orchestra of the Bolshoi played the funeral marches. It was not only the Nazis who could lay on a brilliant funeral for their fallen knights; even the colours were the same: everything was red and black. Stalin had already declared Kirov his closest martyred comrade: his home town, Viatka, Leningrad's Mariinsky Ballet and hundreds of streets were renamed 'Kirov'.

The coffin rested on scarlet calico, the face 'a greenish colour' with a blue bruise on his temple where he fell. Kirov's widow sat with the sisters he had not seen or bothered to contact for thirty years. Redens, Moscow NKVD chief, escorted his pregnant wife, Anna Alliluyeva, and the Svanidzes to their places beside the Politburo wives. Silence fell. Only the click of the sentry's boots echoed in the hall. Then Maria Svanidze heard the 'footsteps of that group of tough and resolute eagles': the Politburo took up position around the head of Kirov.

The Bolshoi orchestra broke into Chopin's Funeral March. Afterwards, in the silence, there was the clicking and whirring of cine-cameras: Stalin, fingers together across his stomach, stood beside the swaggering Kaganovich, with a leather belt around the midriff of his bulging tunic. The guards began to screw on the coffin lid. But just like at Nadya's funeral, Stalin dramatically stopped them by stepping up to the catafalque. With all eyes on his 'sorrowful' face, he slowly bent down and kissed Kirov's brow. 'It was a heart-breaking sight, knowing how close they were' and the whole hall burst into audible weeping; even the men were openly sobbing.

'Goodbye dear friend, we'll avenge you,' Stalin whispered to the corpse. He was becoming something of a connoisseur of funerals.

One by one the leaders wished Kirov adieu: a pale-faced Molotov, Zhdanov, Kaganovich leaned over but did not kiss Kirov, while Mikoyan placed his hand on the rim of the coffin and leaned in. Kirov's wife collapsed and doctors had to give her valerian drops. For Stalin's family, the loss of Kirov, 'this completely charming person loved by all', was linked to the death of Nadya because they knew he had 'transferred all the pain and burden of loss' of his wife on to this dear friend.

The leaders left and the coffin was closed up and driven away to the crematorium where Pavel and Zhenya Alliluyev watched the casket disappear into the furnace. The Svanidzes and others returned to Voroshilov's apartment in the Horse Guards, scene of Nadya's last supper, for a late dinner. Molotov and the other magnates dined with Stalin at Kuntsevo.

Next morning, Stalin, in his old greatcoat and peaked cap, Voroshilov, Molotov and Kalinin carried the urn of ashes, standing in an ornate mini Classical temple the size of a coffin, piled high with flowers, across Red Square where a million workers stood in the freezing silence. Kaganovich spoke – another parallel with Nadya's funeral, before trumpets blared out a salute, heads and banners were lowered, and that 'perfect Bolshevik', Sergo, placed the urn where it still rests in the Kremlin Wall. 'I thought Kirich would bury me but it's turned out the opposite,' he told his wife afterwards.

The executions had already started: by 6 December, sixty-six

'White Guardists' arrested for planning terrorist acts even before Kirov was assassinated, were sentenced to death by the Supreme Court's Military Collegium under the presidency of Vasily Ulrikh, a bullet-headed Baltic German nobleman who became Stalin's hanging judge. Another twenty-eight were shot in Kiev. On the 8th, Nikolai Yezhov, accompanied by Agranov, returned to Moscow from Leningrad to report for three hours on their hunt for the 'terrorists'.

Despite the tragedy and the dangerous signs that even Bolsheviks were soon to be shot for Kirov's murder, the life of Stalin's circle continued normally if sombrely. After the meeting with Yezhov, Molotov, Sergo, Kaganovich and Zhdanov dined with Stalin, Svetlana and Vasily, the Svanidzes and Alliluyevs at his flat as usual on 8 December. Svetlana received presents to help her recover from the loss of her beloved 'Second Secretary', Kirov. Stalin 'had got thinner, paler with a hidden look in his eyes. He suffers so much.' Maria Svanidze and Anna Alliluyeva bustled round Stalin. Alyosha Svanidze warned Maria to keep her distance. It was good advice but she did not take it because she thought he was just jealous of a relationship that possibly included an affair in the distant past. There was not enough food so Stalin called in Carolina Til and ordered her to rustle up more dinner. Stalin hardly ate. That night, he took Alyosha Svanidze, with Svetlana and Vasily, to spend the night at Kuntsevo while the others went on to Sergo's flat.

Since Stalin had declared within a couple of hours of Kirov's death that Zinoviev and his supporters were responsible, it was no surprise that Yezhov and the NKVD arrested a 'Leningrad Centre' and a 'Moscow Centre', lists drawn up by Stalin himself. Nikolaev, interrogated to 'prove' the connection with Zinoviev, admitted a link on 6 December. Zinoviev and Kamenev, Lenin's two closest comrades and both ex-Politburo members who had saved Stalin's career in 1925, were arrested. The Politburo were shown the testimonies of the 'terrorists'. Stalin personally ordered Deputy Procurator-General Vyshinsky and Ulrikh to sentence them to death.

All the witnesses remember that, as Yury Zhdanov puts it, 'everything changed after Kirov's death'. Security was massively tightened at a time when the informality of Stalin's court with its sense of fun, its bustling ambitious women, and scampering children, seemed more important than ever to comfort the

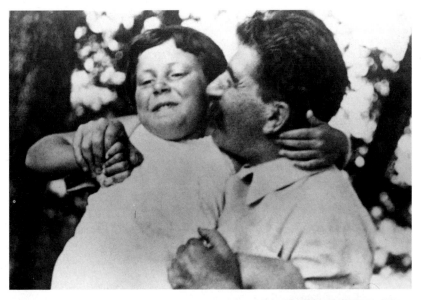

Stalin kisses his daughter Svetlana on holiday, early 1930s. He adored her: her freckles and red hair resembled his mother Keke, but her intelligence and obstinacy came from Stalin himself. He called her 'the Boss' and let her give mock orders to his henchmen. He was affectionate … until she started to grow up.

Nadya was much less affectionate, more strict and puritanical with the children: when she gave birth to their first son, she walked to hospital. She had a special relationship with the fragile and truculent Vasily – but she was primarily a Bolshevik career woman who left the upbringing of her children to nannies. Here she holds Svetlana, who longed for her love.

Top Stalin and his driver in the front with Nadya in the back of one of the Kremlin limousines: these were usually Packards, Buicks and Rolls-Royces. Nadya and Stalin lived ascetically, but he personally took great trouble to assign cars and apartments to his henchmen – and even sometimes to their children. Each family received about three cars.

Above left Stalin and Nadya enjoyed cosy, loving holidays on the Black Sea, though both had fiery tempers and there were often rows. The rulers of Soviet Russia were a tiny oligarchy who tended to holiday and dine constantly together: here are the Stalins on the right with the plodding Molotov and his clever, passionate Jewish wife, Polina. Stalin and Nadya laughed at Molotov. But the dictator never forgave Polina's friendship with Nadya.

Above right At Zubalovo, their country house near Moscow, the Stalins and the other top families enjoyed idyllic weekends. Here, Stalin comes in from the garden, carrying Svetlana.

Stalin built his power slowly, informally, and charmingly – despite the rigid façade of Party Congress, Central Committee and Politburo. The real business took place behind the scenes in the Kremlin's smoky corridors. Here in 1927, Stalin chats at a Party Congress with allies Sergo Ordzhonikidze and (right) Premier Alexei Rykov. But Rykov soon opposed Stalin's harsh policies – and paid the supreme penalty.

Stalin had been the dominant Soviet leader since the mid-Twenties – but not yet dictator. Many of his magnates were powerful in their own right. Here, at a Party Congress, Stalin holds court amongst his grandees: Sergo Ordzhonikidze (front left) and Klim Voroshilov turn to face him while the laughing Kirov (standing, to right of Stalin), along with Kaganovich and Mikoyan (far right) and Postyshev (second from left).

After her tragic death, Nadya lay in state. Stalin never recovered from her suicide and avenged himself on those whom he believed had encouraged her. 'She crippled me', he said. He sobbed when he saw her in her coffin. 'Don't cry Papa', said Vasily, who was holding his hand.

Nadya's funeral: Stalin walked for a while behind the surprisingly traditional coffin, but then drove on to the cemetery. His chief of personal security, Pauker, a Jewish former hairdresser from the Budapest Opera, arranged the orchestras that can be seen on the right.

Below Stalin leaving the Kremlin's Great Palace with two of his closest allies: Sergo Ordzhonikidze, the flamboyant, irascible and emotional scourge of his enemies, who was said to be 'the perfect Bolshevik', and to resemble a 'Georgian prince', stands in the middle. Mikhail 'Papa' Kalinin (with walking stick), the Soviet Head of State, was a genial, womanising ex-peasant. Kalinin opposed Stalin – he was lucky to survive. Sergo confronted Stalin and found himself cornered.

Above Lazar Kaganovich, a brawny and handsome Jewish cobbler, was Stalin's coarse, energetic, cruel and intelligent deputy in the 1930s. Here, during the famine that accompanied collectivisation, he personally leads an expedition into the Siberian countryside to search for grain hidden by peasants. The pace of Stalin's campaigns was punishing: Kaganovich (below, in middle) falls asleep afterwards surrounded by his officials and secret policemen.

Left The magnates were so close they were like a family: 'Uncle Abel' Yenukidze (left) was Nadya's godfather, Stalin's old friend, a senior official and a sybaritic bachelor with a taste for ballerinas. Stalin came to resent his familiarity. Voroshilov on the right, dapper, good-natured, stupid, envious and brutal, made his name in the Battle of Tsaritsyn and, in 1937, supervised the massacre of about 40,000 of his own officers.

In 1933, the first year after Nadya's death, Stalin's holiday was recorded by the secret police in a special private album given to him afterwards: it shows the surprising intimacy and informality of his life during the holiday months. He particularly enjoyed picnics. Here, he and Voroshilov (in braces) go camping (above). He adored gardening, weeding at his Sochi dacha (left) – he loved roses, but mimosas were his favourites. He was less keen on hunting, but here sets off with (from left) Budyonny, Voroshilov and his Chekist crony Evdokimov.

Holidays were the best time to get to know Stalin: there was frantic networking amongst the grandees – even the most trivial activities were politically significant if they brought the courtiers close to the Boss. Young Lavrenti Beria, Georgian leader and vicious sadist, offered to help weed the gardens: placing an axe in his belt (above), he told Stalin that there was no tree that he would not chop down. Stalin understood.

Stalin with Lakoba and Kirov, embarking on a fishing and shooting trip on the Black Sea which was to end in a mysterious assassination attempt – did Beria arrange it? *Above* Stalin inspects the fishing catch.

Molotov, Premier during the 1930s – and the second most important leader after Stalin, who enjoyed teasing him – was dominated by his wife Polina to whom he wrote passionate love letters. Here, on holidays he plays tennis with his family; in winter, he pulled his spoilt daughter on her sledge. But this Soviet Robespierre believed in terror and never regretted signing the death warrants of the wives of his friends. Stalin nicknamed him 'Molotstein' – or more fondly 'our Vecha'.

This is how Stalin ruled his Empire: with his family and friends around him, sitting out in the sun at the Sochi dacha, reading hundreds of pages and writing his orders in a red crayon, while his henchmen fight brutal duels for his favour. Beria stands like a guard behind him, having already fallen out with his patron Lakoba (right), while Svetlana (who called Beria 'Uncle Lara') plays around them. Within five years, Lakoba and his entire family were dead.

bereaved *Vozhd*. Yet the atmosphere had changed for ever: on 5 December, Rudzutak thought he saw Stalin pointing at him and accusing this proudly semi-educated Old Bolshevik of having 'studied in college so how could his father be a labourer?' Rudzutak wrote to Stalin 'I wouldn't bother you with such trifles but I hear so much gossip about me, it's sad, it's reached you.' Yan Rudzutak was an intelligent Latvian, a Politburo member and Stalin ally, an alumni of ten years in Tsarist prisons, with 'tired expressive eyes', a 'slight limp from his hard labour', and an enthusiastic nature photographer, but he clearly felt a chill from Stalin who no longer trusted him.

'You're wrong, Rudzutak,' Stalin replied, 'I was pointing at Zhdanov not you. I know well you didn't study at college. I read your letter in the presence of Molotov and Zhdanov. They confirmed you're wrong.'

Soon after the assassination, Stalin was walking through the Kremlin with a naval officer, past the security guards who were now posted at ten-yard intervals along the corridors, trained to follow every passer-by with their eyes.

'Do you notice how they are?' Stalin asked the officer. 'You're walking down the corridor and thinking, "Which one will it be?" If it's this one, he'll shoot you in the back after you've turned; if it's that one, he'll shoot you in the face.'

* * *

On 21 December, shortly before these executions, the entourage arrived at Kuntsevo to celebrate Stalin's fifty-fifth birthday. When there were not enough chairs at the table, Stalin and the men started moving the places and carrying in other tables, adding more place settings. Mikoyan and Sergo were elected '*tamada*'. Stalin was still depressed by the loss of Kirov but gradually regained his spirits. Yet when Maria Svanidze prepared a poem to read, Alyosha banned her from reading it, perhaps knowing that its sycophancy, or its obvious request for a ladies' trip to the West, would irritate Stalin.*

The dinner was *shchi*, cabbage soup, then veal. Stalin served soup for the guests, from the Molotovs, Poskrebyshev (with new

---

* Maria's poem's reveals both the devotion and cheekiness of Stalin's female courtiers: 'We wish much happiness to our Dear Leader and endless life. Let the enemies be scared off. Liquidate all Fascists ... Next year, take the world under your sway, and rule all mankind. Shame the ladies can't go West to Carlsbad. It's all the same at Sochi.'

wife) and Yenukidze to his children. 'Stalin ate his from his soup bowl, just taking his fork and taking the meat,' remembers Artyom. Beria, and his former patron, deaf Lakoba, master of Abkhazia, arrived in the middle of dinner.

Stalin toasted Sashiko Svanidze, sister of his first wife Kato and Alyosha. This infuriated Alyosha's wife, Maria Svanidze: there was a constant war among the women for Stalin's favour. Then Stalin noticed the children and 'he poured me and Vasily some wine', recalls Artyom, 'asking, "What's wrong with you two? Have some wine!"' Anna Redens and Maria Svanidze grumbled that it was not good for them, like Nadya, but Stalin laughed:

'Don't you know it's medicinal? It can cure all sorts of things!'

Now the evening took a maudlin turn: just as the family had thought of Nadya during Kirov's funeral, now this female Banquo turned up at this feast too. Toastmaster Sergo raised a glass for Kirov:

'Some bastard killed him, took him away from us!' The silence was broken by weeping. Someone drank to Dora Khazan, Andreyev's wife, who was one of Stalin's favourite women, and to her studies at the Academy. This reminded Stalin of Nadya for he stood up:

'Three times, we have talked about the Academy,' he said, 'so let us drink to Nadya!' Everyone rose with tears running down their faces. One by one, each walked silently round the table and clinked glasses with Stalin who looked agonized. Anna Redens and Maria Svanidze kissed him on the cheek. Maria thought Stalin was 'softer, kinder'. Later, Stalin played the disc jockey, putting his favourite records on the gramophone while everyone danced. Then the Caucasians sang laments with their all-powerful choirboy.

Afterwards, by way of relaxing after the sadness, Vlasik the bodyguard, who doubled as court photographer, assembled the guests for a photograph, a remarkable record of Stalin's court before the Terror: even this photograph would cause more rows among the competitive women.

Stalin sat in the middle surrounded by his worshipful women – on his right sat the pushy Sashiko Svanidze, then Maria Kaganovicha and the busty soprano Maria Svanidze, and on his left, the slim, elegant First Lady, Polina Molotova. Uniforms mixed with Party tunics: Voroshilov, always resplendent as the country's senior officer, Redens in NKVD blue, Pavel Alliluyev in his military Commissar's uniform. On the floor sat the laughing Caucasians Sergo, Mikoyan and Lakoba while Beria and Poskrebyshev just managed to squeeze in by lying almost flat. But at Stalin's feet, even more noticeable when he posed again with just the women, sat a Cheshire cat smiling at the camera as if she had got the cream: Zhenya Alliluyeva.

13

A Secret Friendship:
the Rose of Novgorod

'You dress so beautifully,' Stalin said admiringly to his sister-in-law Zhenya Alliluyeva. 'You should make designing your profession.'

'What! I can't even sew a button,' retorted the giggling Zhenya. 'All my buttons are sown on by my daughter.'

'So? You should teach Soviet women how to dress!' retorted Stalin.

After Nadya's death, Zhenya almost moved in to watch over him. In 1934, it seems, this relationship grew into something more. Statuesque and blue-eyed, with wavy blonde hair, dimples, an upturned nose and wide, beaming mouth, Zhenya, thirty-six, was a priest's daughter from Novgorod. She was not beautiful but this 'rose of the Novgorod fields' with golden skin and her quick mischievous nature, radiated health. When she was pregnant with her daughter Kira, she split some logs just before giving birth. While Dora Khazan dressed in austere shifts and Voroshilova got fatter, Zhenya was still young, fresh and completely feminine in her frilly dresses, flamboyant collars and silk scarves.

These women found Stalin all the more appealing because he was so obviously lonely after Nadya's and now Kirov's death: 'his loneliness is always on one's mind,' wrote Maria Svanidze. If power itself is the great aphrodisiac, the addition of strength, loneliness and tragedy proved to be a heady cocktail. However, Zhenya was different. She had known Stalin since marrying Nadya's brother, Pavel, around the Revolution, but they had been abroad a lot and returned from Berlin just before the suicide. Then a fresh relationship developed between Stalin the widower and this funny, blithe woman. The marriage of Pavel and Zhenya had not been easy. Unsuited to military life, Pavel was gentle but hysterical like Nadya. Zhenya grumbled about his weakness. Their marriage had almost ended in the early thirties, when Stalin ordered them to stay together. Despite having given the pistol to Nadya, Pavel often stayed with Stalin.

Stalin admired Zhenya's *joie de vivre*. She was unafraid of him: the first time she arrived at Zubalovo after her return from Berlin, she found a meal on the table and ate it all. Stalin then walked in and asked:

'Where's my onion soup?' Zhenya admitted she had eaten it. This might have provoked an explosion but Stalin merely smiled and said, 'Next time, they better make two.' She said whatever she thought – it was she, among others, who told him about the famine in 1932, yet Stalin forgave her for this. She was well read and Stalin consulted her about what he should read. She suggested an Egyptian history but joked that he 'started copying the Pharoahs'. Zhenya made him laugh uproariously with her earthy wit. Their conversation resembled his banter with rough male friends. She was an expert singer of the *chastushka*, bawdy rhymes with puns that resemble limericks. They do not translate well but Stalin's favourites were such gems as 'Simple to shit off a bridge, but one person did it and fell off' or 'Sitting in one's own shit, feels as safe as a fortress.'

Zhenya could not help tactlessly puncturing the balloons of the stiff Party women and Stalin always enjoyed playing off his courtiers. When Polina Molotova, mistress of the perfume industry, boasted to Stalin that she was wearing her latest product, Red Moscow, Stalin sniffed:

'That's why you smell so nice,' he said.

'Come on, Joseph,' interrupted Zhenya. 'She smells of Chanel No. 5!' Afterwards, Zhenya realized she had made a mistake: 'Why on earth did I say it?' This made the family enemies among the politicians at a time when politics was about to become a blood sport. None the less she alone could get away with these comments because Stalin 'respected her irreverence'.

When Stalin inaugurated the 1936 Constitution, Zhenya, who was late for everything, was late for that too. She crept in and thought no one had noticed until Stalin himself greeted her afterwards:

'How did you spot me?' she asked.

'I see everything, I can see two kilometres away,' replied Stalin whose senses were ferally acute. 'You're the only one who'd dare be late.'

Stalin needed female advice on his children. When Svetlana, maturing early, appeared in her first skirt, Stalin lectured her on 'Bolshevik modesty' but asked Zhenya:

'Can a girl wear a dress like that? I don't want her to bare her knees.'

'It's only natural,' replied Zhenya.

'And she asks for money,' said the father.

'That's all right, isn't it?'

'What's the money for?' he persisted. 'A person can live well on ten kopeks!'

'Come on, Joseph!' Zhenya teased him. 'That was before the Revolution!'

'I thought you could live on ten kopeks,' murmured Stalin.

'What are they doing? Printing special newspapers for you?' Only Zhenya could say this sort of thing to him.

Stalin and Zhenya probably became lovers at this time. Historians never know what happens behind bedroom doors, and Bolshevik conspiratorial secrecy and prudish morality make these matters especially difficult to research.* But Maria Svanidze observed their relationship and recorded it in her diary, which Stalin himself preserved: that summer, Maria spotted how Zhenya went out of her way to be alone with Stalin. The following winter, she records how Stalin arrived back in his apartment to find Maria and Zhenya. He 'teased Zhenya about getting plump again. He treated her very affectionately. *Now that I know everything I have watched them closely ...*'

'Stalin was in love with my mother,' asserts Zhenya's daughter Kira. Daughters perhaps tend to believe great men are in love with their mothers but her cousin Leonid Redens also believes it was 'more than a friendship'. There is other evidence too: later in the thirties, Beria approached Zhenya with an offer that sounds like Stalin's clumsy proposal of marriage. When she remarried after her husband's death, Stalin reacted with jealous fury.

Stalin himself was always gently courteous with Zhenya. While he barely telephoned Anna Redens or Maria Svanidze, Svetlana remembered how he often phoned her for a chat, even after their relationship was over.

Zhenya was far from the only attractive woman around Stalin. During the mid-thirties, he was still enjoying a normal social life with an entourage that included a cosmopolitan circle of young

---

* Even today, those that know such secrets persist in believing, in the words of Stalin's adopted son General Artyom Sergeev, now eighty, that his 'private life is secret and irrelevant to his place in history'. So far no love letters to anyone other than Nadya have emerged.

and flighty women. But for the moment, it was Zhenya who sat at Stalin's feet.

* * *

Just after the party, on 28 and 29 December the assassin Nikolaev and his fourteen co-defendants were tried by Ulrikh in Leningrad. That reptilian hanging judge called Stalin for orders.

'Finish it,' the *Vozhd* ordered laconically. Following the 1st December Law, they were shot within an hour – and their innocent families soon after. In the month of December, 6,501 people were shot. Stalin had no precise plan for the growing Terror, just the belief that the Party had to be terrorized into submission and that old enemies had to be eradicated. Opportunistic and supersensitive, Stalin meandered towards his goal. The NKVD could not link Leningrad to the 'Moscow Centre' of Zinoviev and Kamenev but it had the means to persuade its prisoners to do so. By mid-January, they had indeed encouraged a prisoner to implicate Zinoviev and Kamenev who were sentenced to ten and five years respectively. Stalin distributed a secret letter that warned that all the opposition had to be 'treated like White Guards' and 'arrested and isolated'. The flood of arrests was so huge that the camps were deluged by 'Kirov's Torrent', yet, simultaneously, Stalin orchestrated a jazz-playing 'thaw': 'Life has become merrier, comrades,' he said. 'Life has become better.'*

* * *

On 11 January, Stalin and most of the Politburo attended a gala celebration of the Soviet film industry at the Bolshoi which was a sort of 'Oscars without the jokes'. The directors were handed Orders of Lenin.

'For us,' Lenin had said, 'the most important of all the arts is cinema,' the art form of the new society. Stalin personally controlled a 'Soviet Hollywood' through the State Film Board, run by Boris Shumiatsky with whom he had been in exile. Stalin did not merely interfere in movies, he minutely supervised the directors and films down to their scripts: his archive reveals how he even helped write the songs. He talked about films with his entourage and passed every film before it was shown to the public, becoming his own supreme censor. Stalin was Joseph Goebbels combined with Alexander Korda, an unlikely pair united by love of celluloid, rolled into one.

---

* Here was Stalin's version of Harold Macmillan's 'You've never had it so good.'

He was an obsessional movie-buff. In 1934, he had already seen the new Cossack 'Eastern' *Chapaev* and *The Jolly Fellows* so often he knew them by heart. Directed by Grigory Alexandrov, the latter was personally supervised by Stalin. When this director finished *The Jolly Fellows*,* Shumiatsky decided to tantalize Stalin by showing only the first reel, pretending the second was unfinished. The *Vozhd* loved it:

'Show me the rest!' Shumiatsky summoned Alexandrov, nervously waiting outside:

'You're wanted at court!'

'It's a jolly film,' Stalin told Alexandrov. 'I felt I'd had a month's holiday. Take it away from the director. He might spoil it!' he quipped.

Alexandrov immediately started a series of these happy-go-lucky light musical comedies: *Circus* was followed by Stalin's all-time favourite, *Volga, Volga*. When the director came to make the last in the series, he called it *Cinderella* but Stalin wrote out a list of twelve possible titles including *Shining Path* which Alexandrov accepted. Stalin actually worked on the lyrics of the songs too: there is an intriguing note in his archive dated July 1935 in which he writes out the words for one of the songs in pencil, changing and crossing out to get the lyric to scan:

A joyful song is easy for the heart;
It doesn't bore you ever;
And all the villages small and big adore the song;
Big towns love the tune.

Beneath it, he scrawls the words: 'To spring. Spirit. Mikoyan' and then 'Thank you comrades.'

When the director Alexander Dovzhenko appealed for Stalin's help with his movie *Aerograd*, he was summoned to the Little Corner within a day and asked to read his entire script to Voroshilov and Molotov. Later Stalin suggested his next movie, adding that 'neither my words nor newspaper articles put you under any obligation. You're a free man ... If you have other plans, do something else. Don't be embarrassed. I summoned you

---

* The star was his wife Liuba Orlova and the songs were by the Jewish song writer Isaac Dunaevsky. The Russians, emerging from an era of starvation and assassination, flocked to see musicals and comedies – like Americans during the Depression. The style was singing, dancing and slapstick: a pig jumps on to a banqueting table, causing much messy hilarity with trotters and snout.

so you should know this.' He advised the director to use 'Russian folk songs – wonderful songs' which he liked to play on his gramophone.

'Did you ever hear them?' asked Stalin.

No, replied the director, who had no phonograph.

'An hour after the conversation, they brought the gramophone to my house, a present from our leader, that,' concluded Dovzhenko, 'I will treasure to the end of my life.'

Meanwhile, the magnates discussed how to manage Sergei Eisenstein, thirty-six, the Lavtian-German-Jewish *avant-garde* director of *Battleship Potemkin*. He had lingered too long in Hollywood and, as Stalin informed the American novelist Upton Sinclair, 'lost the trust of his friends in the USSR'. Stalin told Kaganovich he was a 'Trotskyite if not worse'. Eisenstein was lured back and put to work on *Bezhin Meadow*, inspired by the story of Pavlik Morozov, the boy-hero who denounced his own father for kulakism. The tawdry project did not turn out as Stalin hoped. Kaganovich loudly denounced his colleagues' trust:

'We can't trust Eisenstein. He'll again waste millions and give us nothing ... because he's against Socialism. Eisenstein was saved by Vyacheslav [Molotov] and Andrei Zhdanov who were willing to give the director another chance.' But Stalin knew he was 'very talented'. As tensions rose with Germany, he commissioned Eisenstein to make a film about that vanquisher of foreign invaders, *Alexander Nevsky*, promoting his new paradigm of socialism and nationalism. Stalin was delighted with it.

When Stalin wrote a long memorandum to the director Friedrich Emmler about his film *The Great Citizen*, his third point read: 'The reference to Stalin must be excluded. Instead of Stalin, mention the Central Committee.'

* * *

Stalin's modesty was in its way as ostentatious as the excesses of his personal cult. The leaders themselves had promoted Stalin's cult that was the triumph of his inferiority complex. Mikoyan and Khrushchev blamed Kaganovich for encouraging Stalin's concealed vanity and inventing Stalinism:

'Let's replace Long Live Leninism with Long Live Stalinism!' Stalin criticized Kaganovich but he knew Stalin better and he continued to promote 'Stalinism'.

'Why do you eulogize me as if a single person decides everything!' asked Stalin. Meanwhile he personally supervised the cult that was flourishing in the newspapers: in *Pravda*, Stalin was mentioned in half the editorials between 1933 and 1939. He was always given flowers and photographed with children. Articles appeared: 'How I got acquainted with Comrade Stalin.' The planes that flew over Red Square formed the word 'Stalin' in the skies. *Pravda* declared: 'Stalin's life is our life, our beautiful present and future.' When he appeared at the Seventh Congress of Soviets, two thousand delegates screamed and cheered. A writer described the reaction as 'love, devotion, selflessness'. A female worker whispered: 'How simple he is, how modest!'

There were similar cults for the others: Kaganovich was celebrated as 'Iron Lazar' and the 'Iron Commissar' and in thousands of pictures at parades. Voroshilov was honoured in the 'Voroshilov Rations' for the army and the 'Voroshilov Marksman's Prize' and his birthday celebrations were so grandiose that Stalin gave one of his most famous speeches at them. Schoolchildren traded picture postcards of these heroes like football players, the dashing Voroshilov trading at a much higher price than the dour Molotov.

Stalin's modesty was not completely assumed: in his many battles between vainglory and humility, he simultaneously encouraged eulogy and despised it. When the Museum of the Revolution asked if they could display the original manuscripts of his works, he wrote back: 'I didn't think in your old age, you'd be such a fool. If the book is published in millions, why do you need the manuscript? I burned all the manuscripts!' When the publishers of a Georgian memoir of his childhood sent a note to Poskrebyshev asking permission, Stalin banned Zhdanov from publishing it, complaining that it was 'tactless and foolish' and demanding that the culprits 'be punished.' But this was partly to keep control of the presentation of his early life.

He was aware of the absurdities of the cult, intelligent enough to know that the worship of slaves was surely worthless. A student at a technical college was threatened with jail for throwing a paper dart that struck Stalin's portrait. The student appealed to Stalin who backed him:

'They've wronged you,' he wrote. 'I ask ... do not punish him!' Then he joked: 'The good marksman who hits the target should be praised!' Yet Stalin needed the cult and secretly fostered it. With his trusted *chef de cabinet*, he could be honest. Two notes buried in Poskrebyshev's files are especially revealing: when a collective farm asked the right to name itself after Stalin, he gave Poskrebyshev blanket authority to name anything after himself:

'I'm not opposed to their wish to "be granted the name of Stalin" or to the others ... I'm giving you the right to answer such proposals with agreement [underlined] in my name.' One admirer wrote to say, 'I've decided to change my name to Lenin's best pupil, Stalin' and asked the titan's permission.

'I'm not opposed,' replied Stalin. 'I even agree. I'd be happy because this circumstance would give me the chance to have a younger brother. (I have no brother.) Stalin.' Just after the film prize-giving, death again touched the Politburo.

14

The Dwarf Rises; Casanova Falls

On 25 January 1935, Valerian Kuibyshev, who was forty-seven, died unexpectedly of heart disease and alcoholism, just eight weeks after his friend Kirov. Since he had questioned the NKVD investigation and allied himself with Kirov and Sergo, it has been claimed that he was murdered by his doctors, an impression not necessarily confirmed by his inclusion in the list of those supposedly poisoned by Yagoda. We are now entering a phase of such devious criminality and shameless gangsterism that all deaths of prominent people are suspect. But not every death cited as 'murder' in Stalin's show trials was indeed foul play: one has to conclude there were some natural deaths in the 1930s. Kuibyshev's son Vladimir believed his father was killed but this heroic drinker had been ill for a while. The magnates lived such an unhealthy existence that it is amazing so many survived to old age.

None the less it was well-timed for Stalin who took the opportunity on 1 February* to promote two younger stars who were the very spirit of the age. As Kaganovich took over the colossal job of running the railways, he handed over Moscow to Nikita Khrushchev, the semi-literate worker who would one day succeed Stalin.

Kaganovich met Khrushchev during the February 1917 Revolution in the Ukrainian mining town of Yuzovka. Despite a flirtation with Trotskyism, Khrushchev's patrons were unbeatable: 'Kaganovich liked me very much,' he recalled. So did both Nadya ('my lottery ticket,' said Khrushchev) and Stalin himself. Resembling a cannonball more than a whirlwind, Khrushchev's bright porcine eyes, chunky physique and toothy smile with its

---

* Mikoyan and Chubar, a senior official in Ukraine, as the two senior candidate members of the Politburo, were made full members, with Zhdanov and Eikhe, boss of West Siberia, taking their place as candidates.

golden teeth, exuded primitive coarseness and Promethean energy but camouflaged his cunning. As the capital's First Secretary, he drove the transformation of 'Stalinist-Moscow'; by a huge building programme, the destruction of old churches, and the creation of the Metro, he entered the élite. Already a regular at Kuntsevo, this pitiless, ambitious believer regarded himself as Stalin's 'son'. Born in 1894, son of a peasant miner, this meteoric bumpkin became Stalin's 'pet'.

It was Kaganovich's other protégé who suddenly emerged as the coming man. Yezhov was already the overlord of the Kirov case. Now he was promoted to Kirov's place as CC Secretary, and on 31 March was officially designated to supervise the NKVD. Soon to be notorious as one of history's monsters, 'the bloody dwarf', and a ghost whom no one remembered even knowing, Yezhov was actually liked by virtually everyone he met at this time. He was a 'responsive, humane, gentle, tactful man' who tried to help with any 'unpleasant personal matter', remembered his colleagues. Women in particular liked him. His face was almost 'beautiful', recalled one lady, his grin wide, his eyes a bright clever green-blue, his hair thick and black. He was flirtatious and playful, 'modest and agreeable'. Not only was he an energetic workaholic; this 'small slender man, always dressed in a crumpled cheap suit and a blue satin shirt' charmed people, chattering away in his Leningrad accent. He was shy at first but could be fun, exuberant with a keen sense of humour. He suffered from a slight limp but he had a fine baritone, played the guitar and danced the *gopak*. However, he was skinny and tiny: in a government of small men, he was almost a pygmy, 151 centimetres tall.

Born in 1895 to a forest warden, who ran a tearoom-cum-brothel, and a maid, in a small Lithuanian town, Yezhov, like Kaganovich and Voroshilov, only passed a few years at primary school before going to work in Petersburg's Putilov Works. No intellectual, he was another obsessive autodidact, nicknamed 'Kolya the book-lover' – but he possessed the Bolshevik managerial virtues: drive, hardness, organizational talent and an excellent memory, that bureaucratic asset described by Stalin as a 'sign of high intelligence'. Too short to serve in the Tsarist Army, he mended guns, joining the Red Army in 1919: in Vitebsk, he met Kaganovich, his patron. By 1921, he was working in the Tartar Republic where he aroused hatred by showing his contempt for the local culture and fell ill, the first of many signs of his fragility. He would now have met Stalin. In June 1925, he rose to be one of the secretaries of Kirgizia. After studying at the Communist Academy, he was promoted to work at the CC, then to Deputy Agriculture Commissar. In November 1930, Stalin received him in his office. At Kaganovich's suggestion, Yezhov began to attend the Politburo. In the early thirties, he headed the CC Personnel Assignments Department and helped Kaganovich purge the Party in 1933, flourishing in a frenzy of exhausting bureaucratic dynamism. Yet already there were signs of danger and complexity.

'I don't know a more ideal worker,' observed a colleague. 'After entrusting him with a job, you can leave him without checking and be sure he would do it,' but there was one problem: 'He does not know how to stop.' This was an admirable and deadly characteristic in a Bolshevik during the Terror but it also extended to Yezhov's personal life.

His humour was oafishly puerile: he presided over competitions to see which trouserless Commissar could fart away handfuls of cigarette ash. He cavorted at orgies with prostitutes, but was also an enthusiastic bisexual, having enjoyed avid encounters with his fellow tailoring apprentices, soldiers at the front and even high Bolsheviks like Filipp Goloshchekin, who had arranged the murder of the Romanovs. His only hobby apart from partying and fornicating was collecting and making model yachts. Unstable, sexually confused and highly strung, he was too weak to compete with bulldozers like Kaganovich, not to mention Stalin himself. Yezhov suffered constant nervous illnesses, including sores and itchy skin, TB, angina, sciatica, psoriasis (a nervous condition he probably shared with Stalin) and what they called 'neurasthenia'. He often sank into gloomy depression, drank too much and had to be nurtured by Stalin, just to keep him at work.

Stalin embraced him into his circle: Yezhov had exhausted himself so Stalin insisted on more rest cures. 'Yezhov himself is against this but they say he needs it,' he wrote in September 1931. 'Let's prolong his holiday and let him sit in Abastuman for two more months.' Stalin gave nicknames to his favourites: he called Yezhov 'my blackberry' (*yezhevika*). Stalin's notes were often curt personal questions: 'To Comrade Yezhov. Give him some work,' or 'Listen and help.' Yet he instinctively understood the essence of Yezhov: there is an unpublished note from August 1935 to his lieutenant in the archive that sums up their relationship. 'When you say something,' Stalin wrote, 'you always do it!' There was the heart of their partnership. When Vera Trail, whose memoir of her encounter remains unpublished, met him at his peak, she noticed Yezhov was so perceptive of the wishes of others that he could literally 'finish one's sentences'. Yezhov was uneducated, but also sly, able, perceptive and without moral boundaries.

Yezhov did not rise alone: he was accompanied by his wife who was to become the most flamboyant and, literally, fatal flirt of Stalin's entourage. It happened that Mandelstam, the poet, witnessed their courtship. In one of those almost incredible meetings, the encounter of Russia's finest poet with its greatest killer, Mandelstam found himself staying at the same sanatorium in Sukhumi as Yezhov and his then wife Tonya in 1930. The Mandelstams were in the attic of the mansion in Dedra Park that was shaped like a giant white wedding cake.*

Yezhov had married the educated and sincerely Marxist Antonina Titova in 1919. By 1930, Tonya was sunbathing in a deckchair at the Sukhumi mansion, reading *Das Kapital* and enjoying the attentions of an Old Bolshevik while her husband rose early every morning to cut roses for a girl, also married, who was staying there too. Cutting roses, pursuing adulterous romances, singing and dancing the *gopak*, one gets an idea of the incestuous world of the Bolsheviks on holiday. But Yezhov's new mistress was no Old Bolshevik but the Soviet version of a flapper who had already introduced him to her writer friends in Moscow. Yezhov divorced Tonya that year and married her.

Slim with flashing eyes, Yevgenia Feigenberg, at twenty-six, was a seductive and lively Jewess from Gomel. This avid literary groupie was as promiscuous as her new husband: she possessed the amorous enthusiasm of Messalina but none of her guile. She had first married an official, Khayutin, then Gadun, who was posted to the Soviet Embassy in London. She went too but when he was sent home, she stayed abroad, typing in the Berlin

---

* This dacha, built by a Jewish millionaire, later known as Dom (house of) Ordzhonikidze and now notorious as 'Stalin's house', was a favourite of the leadership: the founder of the Cheka, Felix Dzerzhinsky, often stayed there. Trotsky was recuperating there at the time of Lenin's death when Stalin and Ordzhonikidze managed to ensure he missed the funeral. Stalin (and Beria) stayed here after the war: the grand billiard room was installed specially for him and he took a great interest in the lush trees and flowers planted by local Party bosses up to his death. In one of the most sinister parts of the research for this book, the author stayed almost alone in this strange but historic house, probably in Mandelstam's attic.

legation. It was there that she met her first literary star, Isaac Babel, whom she seduced with the line of so many flirtatious groupies meeting their heroes:

'You don't know me but I know you well.' These words later assumed a dreadful significance. Back in Moscow, she met 'Kolya' Yezhov. Yevgenia yearned to hold a literary salon: henceforth Babel and the jazz star Leonid Utsesov were often *chez* Yezhov. It was she who asked the Mandelstams: 'Pilniak comes to see us. Whom do you go to see?' But Yezhov was also obsessionally devoted to Stalin's work – writers did not interest him. The only magnate who was a friend of both Yezhovs was Sergo, as was his wife Zina: photographs show the two couples at their *dachas*. Sergo's daughter Eteri remembers how Yevgenia 'was much better dressed than the other Bolshevik wives'.

By 1934, Yezhov was once again so weary that he almost collapsed, covered in boils. Stalin, on holiday with Kirov and Zhdanov, despatched Yezhov to enjoy the most luxurious medical care available in *Mitteleuropa* and ordered Poskrebyshev's deputy, Dvinsky, to send the Berlin Embassy this coded note:

'I ask you to pay very close attention to Yezhov. He's seriously ill and I cannot estimate the gravity of the situation. Give him help and cherish him with care ... He is a good man and a very precious worker. I will be grateful if you will inform the Central Committee regularly* on his treatment.'

No one objected to Yezhov's rise. On the contrary, Khrushchev thought him an admirable appointment. Bukharin respected his 'good heart and clean conscience' though he noticed that he grovelled before Stalin – but that was hardly unique. 'Blackberry' worked uneasily with Yagoda to force Zinoviev, Kamenev and their unfortunate allies to confess to being responsible for the murder of Kirov and all manner of other dastardly deeds.

* * *

*As Stalin wrote his history books with his dear friends Zhdanov and Kirov, he was receiving detailed reports on the health of his 'precious' comrade. The Yezhov case is a classic illustration of the Party's obsessive control over every detail of its leaders. 'The radioactive baths of Badgastein' had improved Yezhov's health, the Embassy reported after five days. A few days later, the patient was feeling energyless after the baths, he was following a diet but he was still chain smoking – and the sores on his thighs and legs had almost disappeared. The CC voted to send him the huge sum of 1,000 roubles. Next he had pains in his appendix, but having consulted Moscow doctors, Kaganovich sent an order that he was not to undergo surgery 'unless absolutely necessary'. After another rest in an Italian sanatorium, the Yezhovs returned that autumn.

It was not long before 'Blackberry's' chainmail fist reached out to crush one of Stalin's oldest friends: Abel Yenukidze. That genial sybarite flaunted his sexual affairs with ever younger girls, including teenage ballerinas. Girls filled his office, which came to resemble a sort of Bolshevik dating agency for future and cast-off mistresses.

Stalin's circle was already abuzz with his antics: 'Being dissolute and sensual', Yenukidze left a 'stench everywhere indulging himself to procure women, breaking up families, seducing girls', wrote Maria Svanidze. 'Having all the goodies of life in his hands .... he used this for his own filthy personal purposes, buying girls and women.' What is more, Yenukidze was 'sexually abnormal', picking up younger and younger girls and finally sinking to children of nine to eleven years old. The mothers were paid off. Maria complained to Stalin who surely began to listen: Stalin had not trusted him as early as 1929.

Nadya's godfather crossed the line between family and politics in Stalin's life and this proved a dangerous fence to straddle. A generous friend to Left and Right, he may have objected to the 1st December Law but he also personified the decadence of the new nobility. Abel was not the only one: Stalin felt himself surrounded by pigs at the trough. Stalin was always alone even among his convivial entourage, convinced of his separateness and often lonely. As recently as 1933, he had begged Yenukidze to holiday with him. In Moscow, Stalin often asked Mikoyan and Alyosha Svanidze, who was like 'a brother' to him, to stay overnight. Mikoyan stayed a few times but his wife was unhappy about it: 'How could she check whether I was really at Stalin's?' Svanidze stayed more often.

The catalyst for Yenukidze's fall was Stalin's favourite subject: personal history for the Bolsheviks was what genealogy was for the medieval knights. When his book *The Secret Bolshevik Printing Presses* was published, it was eagerly sent to Stalin by his weasel-faced *Pravda* editor, Mekhlis, with a note that 'some parts are ... marked'. Stalin's marginalia in his copy show his almost Blimpish irritation: 'That's false!', 'fibs' and 'balderdash!' When Yenukidze wrote an article about his activities in Baku, Stalin distributed it to the Politburo peppered with 'Ha-ha-ha!' Yenukidze made a grievous mistake in not lying about Stalin's heroic exploits. This was understandable because the outstanding part in the creation of the Baku movement had been played by himself.

'What more does he want?' Yenukidze complained. 'I am doing

everything he has asked me to do but it is not enough for him. He wants me to admit he is a genius.'

Others were not so proud. In 1934, Lakoba published a sycophantic history of Stalin's heroic role in Batumi. Not to be outdone, Beria mobilized an array of historians to falsify his *On the History of the Bolshevik Organizations in the Transcaucasus* which was published later in the year under his own name.

'To my dear, adored master,' Beria inscribed his book, 'to the Great Stalin!'

* * *

Now Nadya's death caught up with Yenukidze: a terrorist cell was 'uncovered' by Yezhov in the Kremlin, which Abel ran. Kaganovich raged, Shakespearean style, 'There was something rotten there.' The NKVD arrested 110 of Yenukidze's employees, librarians and maids, for terrorism. Stalinist plots always featured a wicked beauty: sure enough, there was a 'Countess', said to have poisoned book pages to kill Stalin. Two were sentenced to death and the rest from five to ten years in the camps. Like everything that happened around Stalin, this 'Kremlin Case' had various angles: it was partly aimed at Yenukidze, partly at clearing the Kremlin of possibly disloyal elements, but it was also somehow connected to Nadya. A maid, whose appeal to President Kalinin is in the archives, was arrested for gossiping with her friends about Nadya's suicide. Stalin had surely not forgotten that Yenukidze had 'swayed' Nadya politically, and been the first to see the body.

Yenukidze was sacked, made to publish a 'Correction of Errors', demoted to run a Caucasian sanatorium and viciously attacked by Yezhov (and Beria) at a Plenum. 'Blackberry' first raised the stakes: Zinoviev and Kamenev were not just *morally* responsible for Kirov's murder – they planned it. Then he turned to poor 'Uncle Abel' whom he accused of political blindness and criminal complacency in letting the 'counter-revolutionary Zinoviev-Kamenev and Trotskyite terrorists' feather their nests inside the Kremlin while plotting to kill Stalin. 'This nearly cost Comrade Stalin his life,' he alleged. Yenukidze was 'the most typical representative of the corrupt and self-complacent Communists, playing the "liberal" gentleman at the expense of the Party and State.' Yenukidze defended himself by blaming Yagoda:

'No one was hired for work without security clearance!'

'Not true!' retorted Yagoda.

'Yes it is! ... I – more than anyone else – can find a host of blunders. These may be indignantly characterized – as treason and duplicity.'

'Just the same,' intervened Beria, attacking Yenukidze for his generous habit of helping fallen comrades, 'why did you give out loans and assistance?'

'Just a minute ...' answered Yenukidze, citing an old friend who had been in the opposition, 'I knew his present and past better than Beria.'

'We knew his present situation as well as you do.'

'I didn't help him personally.'

'He's an active Trotskyite,' retorted Beria.

'Deported by the Soviet authorities,' intervened Stalin himself.

'You acted wrongly,' Mikoyan added.

Yenukidze admitted giving another oppositionist some money because his wife appealed to him.

'So what if she starves to death,' said Sergo, 'so what if she croaks, what does it have to do with you?'

'What are you? Some kind of child?' Voroshilov called out. The attacks on Yenukidze's lax security were also attacks on Yagoda: 'I admit my guilt,' he confessed, 'in that I did not ... seize Yenukidze by the throat ...'

On the question of how to punish Yenukidze, there was disagreement: 'I must admit,' Kaganovich said, 'that not everyone found his bearings in this matter ... but Comrade Stalin at once smelled a rat ...' The rat was finally expelled from the Central Committee and the Party (temporarily).

Days afterwards, at Kuntsevo, a grumpy Stalin suddenly smiled at Maria Svanidze:

'Are you pleased Abel's been punished?' Maria was delighted at his overdue cleansing of the suppurating wound of depravity. On May Day, Zhenya and the Svanidzes joined Stalin and Kaganovich for kebabs, onions and sauce but the *Vozhd* was tense until the women started bickering. Then they toasted Nadya: 'she crippled me,' reflected Stalin. 'After condemning Yasha for shooting himself, how could Nadya kill herself?'*

---

* Ignoring the fall of Uncle Abel, Svetlana decided she wanted to go to the dacha at Lipki, which had been Nadya's choice for a holiday home, all decorated in her style. Stalin agreed, even though 'it was hard for Joseph to be there', wrote Maria. The whole wider family, along with Mikoyan, set off in a convoy of cars. Stalin was very warm towards Mikoyan. Svetlana asked if she could stay up for dinner and Stalin let her. Vasily too was often at dinner with the adults.

15

The Tsar Rides the Metro

Amidst the Yenukidze Case, Stalin, Kaganovich and Sergo attended the birthday party of Svetlana's beloved nanny at his apartment. 'Joseph has bought a hat and wool stockings' for the nanny. He cheerfully and lovingly fed Svetlana from his own plate. Everyone was filled with excitement and optimism because the great Moscow underground, named the Kaganovich Metro, a magnificent Soviet showpiece with marble halls like palaces, had just opened. Its creator Kaganovich had brought ten tickets for Svetlana, her aunts and the bodyguards to ride the Metro. Suddenly Stalin, encouraged by Zhenya and Maria, decided he would go too.

This change of plan provoked a 'commotion' among Stalin's courtiers which is hilariously described in Maria's diary. They became so nervous at this unplanned excursion that even the Premier was telephoned; almost half the ruling Politburo was involved within minutes. All were already sitting in their limousines when Molotov scurried across the courtyard to inform Stalin that 'such a trip might be dangerous without preparation'. Kaganovich, 'the most worried of all, went pale' and suggested they go at midnight when the Metro was closed but Stalin insisted. Three limousines of magnates, ladies, children and guards sped out of the Kremlin to the station, dismounted and descended into Kaganovich's tunnels. Once they arrived on the platform, there was no train. One can only imagine Kaganovich's frantic efforts to find one fast. The public noticed Stalin and shouted compliments. Stalin became impatient. When a train finally arrived, the party climbed aboard to cheers.

They got out at Okhotny Ryad to inspect the station. Stalin was mobbed by his fans and Maria almost crushed against a pillar but the NKVD finally caught up with them. Vasily was frightened, Maria noticed, but Stalin was jovial. There was then a thoroughly Russian mix-up as Stalin decided to go home, changed his mind and got out at the Arbat where there was another near-riot before they all got back to the Kremlin. Vasily was so upset by the whole experience that he cried on his bed and had to be given valerian drops.

The trip marked another decline in relations between the leaders and the Svanidze and Alliluyev ladies, those unBolshevik actresses, all 'powder and lipstick' in Maria's words. Kaganovich was furious with the women for persuading Stalin to travel on the Metro without any warning: he hissed at them that he would have arranged the trip if only they had given him some notice. Only Sergo would have shaken his head at this ludicrous scene. Dora Khazan, working her way up the Light Industry Commissariat, thought they were 'trivial women who did nothing, frivolous time-wasters'. The family began to feel that 'we were just poor relations', said Kira Alliuyeva. 'That's how they made us feel. Even Poskrebyshev looked down on us as if we were in the way.' As for Beria, the family, with fatal misjudgement, made no bones of their dislike of him. The women interfered and gossiped in a way that Nadya never had. But in the stern Bolshevik world, and especially given Stalin's views of family, they went too far. Maria, who had sneaked to Stalin about Yenukidze's amours, boasted to her diary, 'They even say I'm stronger than the Politburo because I can overturn its decrees.'

Worse, the women pursued vendettas against each other: The photograph of the 1934 birthday party now caused another row that undermined Stalin's trust. When Sashiko Svanidze stayed with him at Kuntsevo, she found the photograph on Stalin's desk and borrowed it in order to print up some copies, the sort of pushy behaviour often found in ambitious women at imperial courts, suggesting that these ladies regularly read the papers on Stalin's desk. Maria, who loathed Sashiko's brazen climbing, discovered this, warning Stalin:

'You can't let her make a shop out of your house and start trading on your kind-heartedness.' It was a rare occasion indeed when Stalin was criticized for his big-heartedness. He became irritated, blaming his secretaries and Vlasik for losing the photographs. Eventually he said Sashiko could 'go to the devil' but his fury applied equally to all the family:

'I know she did wonderful things for me and other Old Bolsheviks ... but none the less, she always takes offence, writes letters to me at the drop of a hat, and demands my attention. I have no time to look after myself and I couldn't even look after my own wife ...' Nadya was constantly on his mind at this time.

Sashiko was dropped, to Zhenya and Maria's delight, yet they themselves took liberties. The Svanidzes still acted as if Joseph was their kind-hearted paterfamilias, not the Great Stalin. When Stalin invited the Svanidzes and Alliluyevs to join him for dinner after watching the Kirov Ballet, 'we badly miscalculated the time and did not arrive until almost midnight when the ballet ended at ten. Joseph does not like to wait.' This understates the case: it is hard to imagine anyone forgetting the time and leaving an American president waiting for two hours. Here we see Stalin through the eyes of his friends before the Terror turned him into a latter-day Ivan the Terrible: we find him 'stood up' by his dinner dates for two hours, left at Kuntsevo to play billiards with the bodyguards! Stalin, his sense of historic and sacerdotal mission despoiled, must have reflected on the disrespect of these Soviet aristocrats: they were not remotely afraid of him.

When they arrived, the men went off to play billiards with the disgruntled Stalin who was distinctly unfriendly to the women. But after the wine, he shone with pride about Svetlana, recounting her charming sayings like any father. None the less they would pay for their tardiness.

* * *

Stalin had loved his unscheduled Metro ride, telling Maria how moved he was 'by the love of the people for their leader. Here nothing was prepared and fixed. As he said ... the people need a Tsar, whom they can worship and for whom they can live and work.' He had always believed the 'Russian people are Tsarist'. At various times, he compared himself to Peter the Great, Alexander I and Nicholas I but this child of Georgia, a Persian satrapy for centuries, also identified with the Shahs. He named two monarchs as his 'teachers' in his own notes: one was Nadir Shah, the eighteenth-century Persian empire-builder of whom he wrote: 'Nadir Khan. Teacher'. (He was also interested in another Shah, Abbas, who beheaded a father's two sons and sent him their heads: 'Am I like the Shah?' he asked Beria.)

But he regarded Ivan the Terrible as his true *alter ego*, his 'teacher'* something he revealed constantly to comrades such as

---

* In his entourage, Stalin even called Bukharin 'Shuisky', according to Kaganovich, referring either to the Shuisky family of *boyars* who lorded it over the young Ivan, or the so-called *'Boyars' Tsar'* after Ivan's death. Either way, Stalin was identifying his own position with that of Ivan against his *boyars*.

Molotov, Zhdanov and Mikoyan, applauding his necessary murder of over-mighty *boyars*. Ivan too had lost his beloved wife, murdered by his *boyars*. This raises the question of how his grandees could have claimed to be 'tricked' by Stalin's real nature when he openly lauded a Tsar who systematically murdered his nobility.

Now, in late 1935, he also began to reproduce some of the trappings of Tsardom: in September, he restored the title Marshal of the Soviet Union (though not Field Marshal), promoting Voroshilov and Budyonny and three other heroes of the Civil War including Tukhachevsky whom he hated, and Alexander Yegorov, the new Chief of Staff, whose wife had so upset Nadya on the night of her suicide. For the NKVD, he created a rank equivalent to Marshal, promoting Yagoda to Commissar-General of State Security. Sartorial splendour suddenly mattered again: Voroshilov and Yagoda gloried in their uniforms. When Stalin sent Bukharin on a trip to Paris, he told him,

'Your suit is threadbare. You can't travel like that ... Things are different with us now; you have to be well dressed.' Such was Stalin's eye for detail that the tailor from the Commissariat of Foreign Affairs called that afternoon. More than that, the NKVD had access to the latest luxuries, money and houses. 'Permit me 60,000 gold Roubles to buy cars for our NKVD workers,' wrote Yagoda in a pink pen to Molotov on 15 June 1935. Interestingly Stalin (in blue) and Molotov (in red) signed it but reduced it to 40,000. But that was still a lot of Cadillacs. Stalin had already ordered that the Rolls-Royces in the Kremlin be concentrated in the 'special garage.'

Stalin had become a Tsar: children now chanted 'Thank you, Comrade Stalin, for our happy childhood' perhaps because he now restored Christmas trees. But unlike the bejewelled Romanovs, identified so closely with the old Russian village and peasantry, Stalin created his own special kind of Tsar, modest, austere, mysterious and urban. There was no contradiction with his Marxism.

Sometimes Stalin's loving care for his people was slightly absurd. In November 1935, for example, Mikoyan announced to the Stakhanovites in the Kremlin that Stalin was taking great interest in soap and had demanded samples, 'after which we received a special Central Committee decree on the assortment and composition of soap', he announced to cheers. Then Stalin moved from soap to lavatories. Khrushchev ran Moscow with Mayor Nikolai Bulganin, another rising star, a handsome but ruthless blond ex-Chekist with a goatee beard: Stalin nicknamed them the 'city fathers'. Now he summoned Khrushchev: 'Talk it over with Bulganin and do something ... People hunt around desperately and can't find anywhere to relieve themselves ...' But he liked to play the Little Father intervening from on high for his people. In April, a teacher in Kazakhstan named Karenkov appealed to Stalin about losing his job.

'I order you to stop the persecution of teacher Karenkov at once,' he ordered* the Kazakh bosses. It is hard to imagine either Hitler or even President Roosevelt investigating urinals, soap or that smalltown teacher.

The dim but congenial Voroshilov initiated another step deeper into the mire of Soviet depravity when he read an article about teenage hooliganism. He wrote a note to the Politburo saying that Khrushchev, Bulganin and Yagoda 'agree there is no alternative but to imprison the little vagabonds ... I don't understand why one doesn't shoot the scum.' Stalin and Molotov jumped at the chance to add another terrible weapon to their arsenal for use against political opponents, decreeing that children of twelve could now be executed.

* * *

On holiday in Sochi, Stalin was still infuriated by the antics of fallen friends and truculent children. The relentlessly convivial Yenukidze was still chattering about politics to his old pal, Sergo. Once a man had fallen, Stalin could not understand how any loyalist could remain friends with him. Stalin confided his distrust of Sergo to Kaganovich (Sergo's friend):

'Strange that Sergo ... continues to be friends with' Yenukidze. Stalin ordered that Abel, this 'weird fellow', be moved away from his resort. Fulminating against 'the Yenukidze group' as 'scum' and the Old Bolsheviks as ' "old farts" in Lenin's phrase', Kaganovich moved Abel to Kharkov.

Vasily, now fourteen, worried him too: the more absolute Stalin

---

* When he received no reply, again showing the attitude of the local bosses to the centre, Poskrebyshev chased up the Kazakh First Secretary: 'We have not received confirmation of our order.' This time, the local boss replied instantly. But this only illustrates how the local bosses ignored Moscow in small matters and great, following the old Russian tradition of apparent obedience while avoiding actual execution of orders.

became, the more delinquent Vasily became. This mini-Stalin aped his Chekist handlers, denouncing teachers' wives:

'Father, I've already asked the Commandant to remove the teacher's wife but he refused ...' he wrote. The harassed Commandant of Zubalovo reported that while 'Svetlana studies well, Vasya does badly – he is lazy.' The schoolmasters called Carolina Til to ask what to do. He played truant or claimed 'Comrade Stalin' had ordered him not to work with certain teachers. When the housekeeper found money in his pocket, Vasily would not reveal where he had come by it. On 9 September 1935, Efimov reported chillingly to Stalin that Vasily had written: 'Vasya Stalin, born in March 1921, died in 1935.' Suicide was a fact in that family but also in the Bolshevik culture: as Stalin cleansed the Party, his opponents began to commit suicide, which only served to outrage him more: he called it 'spitting in the eye of the Party'. Soon afterwards, Vasily entered an artillery school, along with other leaders' children including Stepan Mikoyan; his teacher also wrote to Stalin to complain of Vasily's suicide threats:

'I've received your letter about Vasily's tricks,' wrote Stalin to V. V. Martyshin. 'I'm answering very late because I'm so busy. Vasily is a spoilt boy of average abilities, savage (a type of Scythian), not always honest, uses blackmail with weak "rules", often impudent with the weak ... He's spoilt by different patrons who remind him at every step that he's "Stalin's son". I'm happy to see you're a good teacher who treats Vasily like other children and demands he obey the school regime ... If Vasily has not ruined himself until now, it's because in our country there are teachers who give no quarter to this capricious son of a baron. My advice is: treat Vasily MORE STRICTLY and don't be afraid of this child's false blackmailing threats of "suicide". I'll support you ...'

Svetlana, on holiday with her father, remained the adored favourite: 'my little sparrow, my great joy', as Stalin wrote so warmly in his letters to her. As one reads Stalin's letters to Kaganovich (usually about persecuting Yenukidze), one can almost see her sitting near him on the veranda as he writes out his orders in his red pencils, enthroned in his wicker chair at the wicker table with piles of papers wrapped in newspaper which were brought daily by Poskrebyshev. He often mentions her. Kaganovich seemed to have replaced Kirov as Svetlana's 'Party Secretary', greeting her in his letters to Stalin and adding:

'Hail to our Boss Svetlana! I await instructions ... on postponement by 15/20 days of the school term. One of the Secretaries LM Kaganovich.' Vasily was 'Svetlana the Boss's colleague'.

Three days later, Stalin informed Kaganovich that 'Svetlana the Boss* ... demands decisions ... in order to check on her Secretaries.'

'Hail Boss Svetlana!' replied Kaganovich. 'We await her impatiently.' When she was back in Moscow, she visited Kaganovich who reported to her father: 'Today our Boss Svetlana inspected our work ...' Indeed Stalin encouraged her interest in politics:

'Your little Secretaries received your letter and we discussed its contents to our great satisfaction. Your letter enabled us to find our way in complicated international and domestic political questions. Write to us often.' Soon she was commanding him in her 'Daily Order No. 3. I order you to show me what happens in the Central Committee! Strictly confidential. Stalina, the mistress of the house.'

Then Stalin heard from Beria that his mother Keke was getting frailer. On 17 October, he headed across to Tiflis to visit her for only the third time since the Revolution.

Beria had taken over the responsibility for caring for the old lady like a courtier looking after a dowager empress. She had lived for years in comfortable rooms in the servant's quarters of the palace of the nineteenth-century Tsarist Governor, Prince Michael Vorontsov, where she was accompanied by two old ladies. All of them wore the traditional black headdress and long dress of Georgian widows. Beria and his wife Nina called on Keke frequently, recalling her spicy taste for sexual gossip:

'Why don't you take a lover?' she asked Nina. Stalin was a negligent son but still wrote his dutiful notes:

'Dear mother, please live for 10,000 years. Kisses, Soso.' He apologized, 'I know you're disappointed in me but what can I do? I'm busy and can't write often.' Mother sent sweets; Soso, money; but, as the son who had replaced her husband as the man of the family, he always played the hero, revealing his dreams of destiny and courage:

'Hello my mama, the children thank you for the sweets. I'm healthy, don't worry about me ... I'll stand up for my destiny! You need more money? I sent you 500 roubles and photos of me and

---

* *Khozyaika* means mistress, the female of *Khozyain*, boss, master, Stalin's nickname amongst the bureaucracy, though it also usually means 'housewife'.

the children. PS the children bow to you. After Nadya's death, my private life is very hard but a strong man must *always* be valiant.'

Stalin took special trouble to protect the Egnatashvili brothers, the children of the innkeeper who was the benefactor of his mother. Alexander Egnatashvili, a Chekist officer in Moscow (supposedly Stalin's food-taster, nicknamed 'the Rabbit'), kept this old link alive:

'My dear spiritual mother,' Egnatashvili wrote in April 1934, 'yesterday I visited Soso and we talked a long time ... he's put on weight ... In the last four years, I had not seen him so healthy ... He was joking a lot. Who says he's older? No one thinks he's more than 47!' But she was ailing.

'I know you're ill,' Stalin wrote to her. 'Be strong. I'm sending you my children ...' Vasily and Svetlana stayed at Beria's residences and then visited the old lady in her 'tiny room', filled with portraits of her son. Svetlana remembered how Nina Beria chatted to her in Georgian but the old lady could not speak Russian.

Now Stalin recruited his old brother-in-law Alyosha Svanidze and Lakoba to visit his mother with him while Beria briskly made the arrangements. He did not stay long. If he had looked around the rooms, he would have noticed that not only did she have photographs of Stalin but also a portrait of Beria in her bedroom. Beria had his own cult of personality in Georgia but more than that, he must have become like a son to her.

Stalin's real feelings for his mother were complicated by her taste for beating him and alleged affairs with her employers. There is a clue to this possible saint–whore complex in his library where he underlined a passage in Tolstoy's *Resurrection* about how a mother is both kind and wicked. But she also had the tendency of making tactless, if drily witty, comments. She wondered why Stalin fell out with Trotsky: they should have ruled together. Now when Stalin sat smiling beside her, he revealingly asked her:

'Why did you beat me so hard?'

'That's why you turned out so well,' she replied, before asking: 'Joseph, what exactly are you now?'

'Well, remember the Tsar? I'm something like a Tsar.'

'You'd have done better to become a priest,' she said, a comment that delighted Stalin.

The newspapers reported the visit with the queasy sentimentality of a Bolshevik version of *Hello!* magazine:

'Seventy-five-year-old Keke is kind and lively,' gushed *Pravda*. 'She seems to light up when she talks about the unforgettable moments of their meeting. "The whole world rejoices when it looks upon my son and our country. What would you expect me, his mother, to feel?"'

Stalin was irritated by this outbreak of Stalinist *Hello!*-ism. When Poskrebyshev sent him the article, Stalin wrote back:

'It's nothing to do with me.' But then he penned another Blimpish note to Molotov and Kaganovich: 'I demand we ban *petit-bourgeois* tidbits that have inflitrated our press ... to insert the interview with my mother and all this other balderdash. I ask to be freed of the incessant publicity din of these bastards!' But he was glad his mother was healthy, telling her 'Our clan is evidently very strong' and sending some presents: a headdress, a jacket and some medicine.

Back in Moscow,* Stalin decided to reopen and expand the Kirov Case that had subsided with the shooting of Nikolaev and sentencing of Zinoviev and Kamenev in early 1935. Now the two Old Bolsheviks were reinterrogated and the net of arrests was spread wider. Then a former associate of Trotsky's named Valentin Olberg was arrested by the NKVD in Gorky. His interrogation 'established' that Trotsky was also involved in the murder of Kirov. More arrests followed.

---

* In case we have forgotten that this was a state based on repression, Zhdanov and Mikoyan were inspecting the NKVD's slave labour projects in the Arctic such as the Belomor Canal: 'the Chekists here have done a great job,' Zhdanov wrote enthusiastically to Stalin. 'They allow ex-kulaks and criminal elements to work for socialism and they may become real people ...'

16

Take Your Partners; Mount Your
Prisoners: the Show Trial

Oblivious of these lengthening shadows, Stalin's birthday party, attended by the magnates, Beria and the family, was 'noisy and cheerful'. Voroshilov was resplendent in his new white Marshal's uniform while his dowdy wife stared jealously at Maria Svanidze's dress from Berlin. After dinner, there were songs and dancing like old times: with Zhdanov on harmonies, they sang Abkhazian, Ukrainian, student and comic songs. Stalin decided to order a piano so Zhdanov could play. Amidst general hilarity, Postyshev, one of the Ukrainian bosses, slow-danced with Molotov – and 'this couple very much amused Joseph and all the guests'. Here was the first example of the notorious stag slow-dancing that was to become more forced after the war.

Stalin took over the gramophone and even did some Russian dancing. Mikoyan performed his leaping *lezginka*. The Svanidzes did the foxtrot and asked Stalin to join them but he said he had given up dancing since Nadya's death. They danced until four.

In the spring of 1936, the arrests of old Trotskyites spread further and those already in camps were resentenced. Those convicted of 'terror' offences were to be shot. But the real work was the creation of a new sort of political show: the first of Stalin's great trials. Yezhov was the supervisor of this case – this hopeful theoretician was even writing a book about the Zinovievites, corrected personally by Stalin. Yagoda, Commissar-General of State Security, who was sceptical about this 'nonsense', remained in charge but Yezhov constantly undermined him. This process exhausted frail Yezhov. Soon he was once again so debilitated that Kaganovich suggested, and Stalin approved, that he be sent on another special holiday for two months with a further 3,000 roubles.

The chief defendants were to be Zinoviev and Kamenev. Their old friends were arrested to help persuade them to perform. Stalin followed every detail of the interrogations. The NKVD interrogators were to devote themselves body and soul to achieving the confessions. Stalin's instructions to the NKVD were suggestive of this terrible process:

'Mount your prisoner and do not dismount until they have confessed.' The NKVD defector Alexander Orlov left the best account of how Yezhov rigged up this trial, promising the 'witnesses' their lives in return for testifying against Zinoviev and Kamenev who refused to co-operate. Stalin's office phoned hourly for news.

'You think Kamenev may not confess?' Stalin asked Mironov, one of Yagoda's Chekists.

'I don't know,' replied Mironov.

'You don't know?' said Stalin. 'Do you know how much our State weighs with all the factories, machines, the army with all the armaments and the navy?' Mironov thought he was joking but Stalin was not smiling. 'Think it over and tell me?' Stalin kept staring at him.

'Nobody can know that, Joseph Vissarionovich; it is the realm of astronomical figures.'

'Well, and can one man withstand the pressure of that astronomical weight?'

'No,' replied Mironov.

'Well then ... Don't come to report to me until you have in this briefcase the confession of Kamenev.' Even though they were not physically tortured, the regime of threats and sleeplessness demoralized Zinoviev, suffering from asthma, and Kamenev. The heating was turned up in their cells in midsummer. Yezhov threatened that Kamenev's son would be shot.

* * *

While the interrogators worked on Zinoviev and Kamenev, Maxim Gorky was dying of influenza and bronchial pneumonia. The old writer was now thoroughly disillusioned. The dangers of his Chekist companions became obvious when Gorky's son Maxim died mysteriously of influenza. Later, Yagoda would be accused, with the family doctors, of killing him. After his death, Maxim's daughter Martha remembers how Yagoda would visit the Gorky household every morning for a cup of coffee and a flirtation with her mother, on his way to the Lubianka: 'he was in love with Timosha and wanted her to return his affection,' said Alexei Tolstoy's wife.

'You still don't know me, I can do anything,' he threatened the distraught Timosha: the writer Alexander Tikhonov claimed they began an affair; her daughter denies it. When Stalin visited, Yagoda lingered, still in love with Timosha and increasingly worried about himself. After the Politburo had left, he asked Gorky's secretary: 'Did they come? They've left now? What did they talk about? ... Did they say anything about us ...?'

Stalin had asked Gorky to write his biography, but he recoiled from the task. Instead he bombarded Stalin and the Politburo with crazy proposals such as a project to commission Socialist Realist writers to 'rewrite the world's books anew'. Stalin's apologies for late replies became ever more extreme: 'I'm as lazy as a pig on things marked "correspondence",' confessed Stalin to Gorky. 'How do you feel? Healthy? How's your work? Me and my friends are fine.' The NKVD actually printed false issues of *Pravda*, especially for Gorky, to conceal the persecution of his friend, Kamenev.* Gorky himself realized that he was now under house arrest: 'I'm surrounded,' he muttered, 'trapped.'

In the first week of June, Gorky slept much of the days as his condition worsened. He was supervised by the best doctors but he was failing.

'Let them come if they can get here in time,' said Gorky. Stalin, Molotov and Voroshilov were pleased to see that he had recovered – after a camphor injection. Stalin took control of the sickroom:

'Why are there so many people here?' he asked. 'Who's that sitting beside Alexei Maximovich dressed in black? A nun, is she? All she lacks is a candle in her hands.' This was Baroness Moura Budberg, the mistress Gorky shared with H. G. Wells. 'Get them all out of here except for that woman, the one in white, who's looking after him ... Why's there such a funereal mood here? A healthy person might die in such an atmosphere.' Stalin stopped Gorky discussing literature but called for wine and they toasted him and then embraced. Day later, Stalin arrived only to be told that Gorky was too ill to see him:

'Alexei Mikhailovich, we visited you at two in the morning,' he wrote. 'Your pulse was they say 82. The doctors did not allow us to come in to you. We submitted. Hello from all of us, a big hello. Stalin.' Molotov and Voroshilov signed underneath.

Gorky started to spit blood and died on 18 June, of TB,

---

* An old trick: Kuibyshev had suggested printing false issues of *Pravda* to disinform the dying Lenin.

pneumonia and heart failure. Later it was claimed that his doctors and Yagoda had murdered him deliberately: they certainly confessed to his murder. His death was convenient before Zinoviev's trial but his medical records in the NKVD archives suggest that he died naturally.

Yagoda was skulking in the dining room at Gorky's house but Stalin had already turned against him. 'And what's that creature hanging around here for? Get rid of him.'

* * *

Finally in July, Zinoviev asked to be able to talk to Kamenev on his own. Then they demanded to speak to the Politburo: if the Party would guarantee there would be no executions, they would confess. Voroshilov was itching to get at the 'scum': when he received some of the testimonies against them, he wrote to Stalin that 'these bad people ... all typical representatives of *petit bourgeois* with the face of Trotsky ... are finished people. There's no place for them in our country and no place among the millions ready to die for the Motherland. This scum must be liquidated absolutely ... we need to be sure the NKVD starts the purge properly ...' Here, then, was one leader who genuinely seemed to approve of a terror and the liquidation of the former oppositions. On 3 July, Stalin replied to 'dear Klim, did you read the testimonies ...? How do you like the bourgeois puppies of Trotsky ...? They wanted to wipe out all the members of the Politburo ... Isn't it weird? How low people can sink? J.St.'

Yagoda accompanied these two broken men on the short drive from the Lubianka to the Kremlin, where they had both once lived. When they arrived in the room where Kamenev had chaired so many Politburo meetings, they discovered that only Stalin, Voroshilov and Yezhov were present. Where was the rest of the Politburo?

Stalin replied that he and Voroshilov were a commission of the Politburo. Given Klim's venom, it is easy to see why he was there but where was Molotov? Perhaps the punctilious Iron-Arse was worried about the etiquette of lying to Old Bolsheviks: he certainly did not object to killing people.

Kamenev begged the Politburo for a guarantee of their lives.

'A guarantee?' replied Stalin, according to Orlov's version. 'What guarantee can there be? It's simply ridiculous! Maybe you want an official treaty certified by the League of Nations? Zinoviev and Kamenev forget they're not in a market-place haggling over a stolen horse but at the Politburo of the Bolshevik Communist Party. If an assurance by the Politburo is not enough, I don't see any point in talking further.'

'Zinoviev and Kamenev behave as if they're in a position to make conditions to the Politburo,' exclaimed Voroshilov. 'If they had any common sense, they'd fall to their knees before Stalin ...'

Stalin proposed three reasons why they would not be executed – it was really a trial of Trotsky; if he had not shot them when they were opposing the Party, then why shoot them when they were helping it; and finally, 'the comrades forget that we are Bolsheviks, disciples and followers of Lenin, and we don't want to shed the blood of Old Bolsheviks, no matter how grave their past sins ...'

Zinoviev and Kamenev wearily agreed to plead guilty, provided there were no shootings and their families were protected.

'That goes without saying,' Stalin finished the meeting.

Stalin set to work on the script for the Zinoviev trial, revelling in his hyperbolic talent as a hack playwright. The new archives reveal how he even dictated the words of the new Procurator-General, Andrei Vyshinsky, who kept notes of his leader's perorations.

Stalin issued a secret circular of 29 July which announced that a terrorist leviathan named the 'United Trotskyite-Zinovievite Centre' had attempted to assassinate Stalin, Voroshilov, Kaganovich, Kirov, Sergo, Zhdanov and others. These lists of purported targets became a bizarre honour since inclusion signified proximity to Stalin. One can imagine the leaders checking the list like schoolboys rushing to the noticeboard to make sure they are in the football team. Significantly, Molotov was not on the team, which was interpreted as a sign of opposition to the Terror but it seems he was indeed temporarily out of favour because of a different disagreement with Stalin. Molotov boasted, 'I'd always supported the measures taken,' but there is one intriguing hint in the archives that Molotov was under fire from Yezhov. The NKVD had arrested the German nurse of his daughter Svetlana Molotova* and her father had grumbled to Yagoda. A Chekist denounced Molotov for 'improper

---

* Many of the ruling families employed Volga Germans as housekeepers and nannies: Carolina Til managed Stalin's house; another Volga German ran Molotov's and the Berias employed Ella as their nanny-housekeeper. They would all prove vulnerable to the anti-German Terror of 1937.

behaviour ... Molotov behaved badly.' On 3 November, Yezhov sent Molotov the denunciation, perhaps a shot across his bows.

Yezhov was Stalin's closest associate in the days before the trial while Yagoda, now in disfavour for his resistance to it, was received only once. Stalin complained about his work: 'You work poorly. The NKVD suffers a serious disease.' Finally he called Yagoda, shouting that he would 'punch him in the nose' if he did not pull himself together. We have Stalin's notes from his 13 August meetings with Yezhov, which catch his mood. In one he considers sacking an official: 'Get him out? *Yes, get him out!* Talk with Yezhov.' Again and again: 'Ask Yezhov.'

* * *

The first of the famous show trials opened on 19 August in the October Hall upstairs in the House of Unions. The 350 spectators were mainly NKVD clerks in plain clothes, foreign journalists and diplomats. On a raised dais in the centre, the three judges, led by Ulrikh, sat on portentous throne-like chairs covered in red cloth. The real star of this theatrical show, the Procurator-General Andrei Vyshinsky, whose performance of foaming ire and articulate pedantry would make him a European figure, sat to the audience's left. The defendants, sixteen shabby husks, guarded by NKVD troopers with fixed bayonets, sat to the right. Behind them was a door that led to the suite that might be compared to the 'celebrity hospitality green room' in television studios. Here in a drawing room with sandwiches and refreshments sat Yagoda who could confer with Vyshinsky and the defendants during the trial.

Stalin was said to be lurking in a recessed gallery with darkened windows at the back where the orchestras once played for aristocratic quadrilles and whence puffs of pipe smoke were alleged to be emanating.

On the 13th, six days before the trial began, Stalin departed by train for Sochi, after a meeting with Yezhov. It is a mark of the impenetrable secrecy of the Soviet system that it has taken over sixty years for anyone to discover that Stalin was actually far away, though he followed the legal melodrama almost as closely as if he had been listening to it in his office. Eighty-seven NKVD packages of interrogations plus records of confrontations and the usual pile of newspapers, memos and telegrams arrived at the wicker table on the veranda.

Kaganovich and Yezhov checked every detail with Stalin. The protégé was now more powerful than his former patron – Yezhov signed his name ahead of Kaganovich in every telegram. While the will of the great actor-manager controlled all from afar, the two in Moscow doubled as PR-men and impresarios. On the 17th, Kaganovich and Yezhov reported to the *Khozyain* that 'we've fixed the press coverage … in the following manner: 1. *Pravda* and *Izvestiya* to publish a page-length account of the trial daily.' On the 18th Stalin ordered the trial to proceed next day.

The accused were indicted with a fantastical array of often bungled crimes ordered by the shadowy conspiracy led by Trotsky, Zinoviev and Kamenev ('The United Trotskyite-Zinovievite Centre') that had successfully killed Kirov but repeatedly failed to kill Stalin and the others (though never bothering with Molotov). For six days, they confessed to these crimes with a docility that amazed Western spectators.

The language of these trials was as obscure as hieroglyphics and could only be understood in the Aesopian imagery of the closed Bolshevik universe of conspiracies of evil against good in which 'terrorism' simply signified 'any doubt about the policies or character of Stalin'. All his political opponents were *per se* assassins. More than two 'terrorists' was a 'conspiracy' and, putting together such killers from different factions, created a 'Unified Centre' of astonishing global, indeed Blofeldian, reach, that reveals much about Stalin's internal melodrama as well as about Bolshevik paranoia, formed by decades of underground life.

While these crushed men delivered their lines, Procurator-General Vyshinsky brilliantly combined the indignant humbug of a Victorian preacher and the diabolical curses of a witch doctor. Small with 'bright black eyes' behind horn-rimmed spectacles, thinning reddish hair, pointed nose, and dapper in 'white collar, checked tie, well-cut suit, trimmed grey moustache', a Western witness thought he resembled 'a prosperous stockbroker accustomed to lunching at Simpson's and playing golf at Sunningdale'. Born into an affluent, noble Polish family in Odessa, Vyshinsky had once occupied a cell with Stalin with whom he shared hampers from his parents, an investment that may have saved his life. But as an ex-Menshevik, he was absolutely obedient and ravenously bloodthirsty: during the thirties, his notes to Stalin constantly propose shooting of defendants, usually 'Trotskyites preparing the death of Stalin', always ending with the words: 'I recommend VMN – death by shooting.'

Vyshinsky, fifty-three, was notoriously unpleasant to his

subordinates but cringingly sycophantic to his seniors: he used the word 'Illustrious' in his letters to Molotov and even Poskrebyshev (whom he cleverly cultivated). Even his subordinates found him a 'sinister figure' who, regardless of his 'excellent education', believed in the essential rule of Stalinist management: 'I believe in keeping people on edge' but he was always on the edge himself, suffering bouts of eczema, living in fear and helping to breed it. Alert, vigorous, vain and intelligent, he impressed Westerners as much as he chilled them with his forensic mannerisms and vicious wit: it was he who later described the Romanians as 'not a nation, but a profession'. He was very proud of his notoriety: presented to Princess Margaret in London in 1947, he whispered to the diplomat introducing them, 'Please add my former title as Procurator in the famous Moscow trials.'

Every day, Yezhov and Kaganovich, who must have been listening to the trial in the 'hospitality suite', reported to Stalin on the proceedings like this: 'Zinoviev declared that he confirms the depositions of Bakaiev on the fact that the latter had made a report to Zinoviev on the preparation of a terrorist act against Kirov ...' They revelled in reporting to the actor-manager-playwright the successful 'unfolding' of this theatrical piece.

However there was severe doubt among many of the journalists, exacerbated by the NKVD's comical blunders: the court heard how Trotsky's son, Sedov, ordered the assassinations in a meeting at the Hotel Bristol in Denmark – yet it emerged that the hotel had been demolished in 1917.

'What the devil did you need the hotel for?' Stalin is said to have shouted. 'You ought to have said "railway station". The station is always there.'

This show had a wider cast than the players actually on-stage because others were carefully implicated, raising the prospect of other famous 'terrorists' appearing in later trials. The defendants took great care to implicate a couple of military commanders and then both Leftists, such as Karl Radek, and Rightists, such as Bukharin, Rykov and Tomsky. Vyshinsky announced that he was opening new cases against these celebrated names.

The members of this off-stage cast performed their roles very differently: the gifted journalist, Karl Radek, a famous international revolutionary who cut an absurd figure with his round glasses, whiskers, pipe, leather boots and coats, had been close to Stalin during the early thirties, advising him on German politics.

Writers always imagine they can write their way out of danger. Now Stalin decreed that 'although not very convincing, I suggest to delay for the moment the question of Radek's arrest and to let him publish in *Izvestiya* a signed article ...' Opportunities, even temporary indulgence towards old friends, could change Stalin's meandering progress.*

On the 22nd, the accused refused to plead for their defence. The Politburo – Kaganovich, Sergo, Voroshilov and Chubar – along with Yezhov, asked for instructions: 'It's not convenient to authorize any appeal,' Stalin retorted, at 11.10 next night giving exact instructions on the press coverage of the sentences. Revealingly, the playwright thought the verdict required a little bit of 'stylistic polishing'. Half an hour later, he wrote again, worrying that the trial would be regarded as just a '*mise-en-scène*'.

Stalin's spin-doctors engineered public outrage against the terrorists. Khrushchev, rabid supporter of the trials and shootings, arrived one evening at the Central Committee to find Kaganovich and Sergo bullying the poet Demian Bedny to produce a blood-curdling ditty for *Pravda*. Bedny recited his effort. There was an awkward pause:

'Not what we had in mind, Comrade Bedny,' said Kaganovich. Sergo lost his temper and shouted at Bedny. Khrushchev glared at him.

'I can't!' protested Bedny, but he could. His 'No Mercy' was published the next day, while *Pravda* shrieked:

'Crush the Loathsome Creatures! The Mad Dogs Must Be Shot!'

In the court, Vyshinsky summed up:

'These mad dogs of capitalism tried to tear limb from limb the best of our Soviet land' – Kirov. 'I demand that these mad dogs should be shot – every one of them!' The dogs themselves now made their pathetic pleas and confessions. Even seventy years later, they are tragic to read. Kamenev finished his confession but then rose again, obviously off-message, to plead for his children whom he had no other means of addressing: 'No matter what my sentence will be, I in advance consider it just. Don't look back,' he

---

* Not all the off-stage cast behaved so conveniently. At 5.46 p.m. on 22 August, Stalin received the following telegram from Kaganovich, Yezhov and Ordzhonikidze: 'This morning Tomsky shot himself. He left a letter to you in which he tried to prove his innocence ... We have no doubt that Tomsky ... knowing that now it is no longer possible to hide his place in the Zinoviev-Trotskyite band had decided to dissimulate ... by suicide ...' As ever, the press release was the most important thing.

told his sons. 'Go forward ... Follow Stalin.' The judges withdrew to consider their pre-decided verdict, returning at two-thirty to sentence all to death, at which one defendant shouted:

'Long live the cause of Marx, Engels, Lenin and Stalin!'

Back in prison, the scared 'terrorists' shakily appealed for mercy, remembering Stalin's promise to spare them. As Zinoviev and Kamenev waited in their cells, Stalin, waiting in sunny Sochi, received a telegram at 8.48 p.m. from Kaganovich, Sergo, Voroshilov and Yezhov who informed him that the appeal of the defendants had been received. 'The Politburo proposed to reject the demands and execute the verdict tonight.'* Stalin did not answer, perhaps congratulating himself on his imminent revenge, perhaps having dinner, but surely aware that the murder of two of Lenin's closest comrades marked a giant step towards his next colossal gamble, an intense reign of terror against the Party itself, a slaughter that would consume even his own friends and family. Stalin waited for three long hours.

---

* Stalin had sent Mikoyan on a 12,000-mile tour of the American food industry. The shrewd Armenian made sure Stalin knew that he supported the verdict, writing to 'dear Lazar' Kaganovich from Chicago. 'Don't forget to write in your next letter to him that I send my warmest greetings to Our Master. How good that we have so quickly got rid of the Trotskyite gang of Zinoviev and Kamenev!' Mikoyan met Secretary of State Cordell Hull in DC, debated with Henry Ford – and inspected Maceys in New York. The trip had two effects: Mikoyan gave the Russians American hamburgers and ice-cream – and he lost his taste for wearing the Party tunic, sporting natty American-style suits for the rest of his career.

Part Four

Slaughter: Yezhov the Poison Dwarf,
1937–1938

17

The Executioner: Beria's Poison
and Bukharin's Dosage

Minutes before midnight, Stalin sent this laconic telegram: 'Okay.'1
During the first hour of 25 August, a number of limousines cruised
through the gates of the Lubianka prison, containing the officials
to witness the executions.

A dignified Kamenev and a feverish Zinoviev were led out of their
cells and down the steps. Yezhov and Yagoda were accompanied by
the ex-hairdresser, Pauker. Vyshinsky as Procurator-General was
meant to attend important executions but was said to be so squeamish
that he usually sent one of his chief investigators, Lev Sheinin.
Mikoyan supposedly said that Voroshilov represented the Politburo.

Stalin never attended torture or execution (though he witnessed
a hanging as a child and must have observed violent death in
Tsaritsyn) but he respected his executioners. Execution was
officially called the 'Highest Measure of Punishment', usually
shortened to the terrible letters 'VMN' or the acronym *Vishka*, but
Stalin called it 'black work', which he regarded as noble Party
service. The master of 'black work' under Stalin presided over this
sombre but brisk ritual: Blokhin, a pugnacious Chekist of forty-
one with a stalwart face and black hair pushed back, was one of
the most prolific executioners of the century, killing thousands
personally, sometimes wearing his own leather butcher's apron to
protect his uniform. Yet the name of this monster has slipped
through history's fingers.* In the theatre of Stalin's court, Blokhin
henceforth lurks in the background, but is rarely off-stage.

---

* There were many Chekists who sometimes doubled as executioners but Blokhin
himself, assisted by two murderous brothers, Vasily and Ivan Zhigarev, handled
important cases. V. M. Blokhin was a veteran of the Tsarist army in the First World
War and a Chekist since March 1921, who had risen to head the Kommandatura
Branch that was attached to the Administrative Executive Department. This meant
he was in charge of the internal prison at Lubianka; among other things, he was
responsible for executions. Major-General Blokhin was retired after Stalin's death
and praised for his 'irreproachable service' by Beria himself. After Beria's fall, he was
stripped of rank in November 1954 and died on 3 February 1955.

Zinoviev shouted that this was a 'Fascist coup' and begged the executioners:

'Please, comrade, for God's sake, call Joseph Vissarionovich! Joseph Vissarionovich promised to save our lives!' Some accounts have him actually hugging and licking the Chekist's boots. Kamenev reportedly answered:

'We deserve this because of our unworthy attitude at the trial' and told Zinoviev to be quiet and die with dignity. Zinoviev made such a noise that an NKVD lieutenant took him into a nearby cell and despatched him there and then. They were shot through the back of the head.

The bullets, with their noses crushed, were dug out of the skulls, wiped clean of blood and pearly brain matter, and handed to Yagoda, probably still warm. No wonder Vyshinsky found these events sickening. Yagoda labelled the bullets 'Zinoviev' and 'Kamenev' and treasured these macabre but sacred relics, taking them home to be kept proudly with his collection of erotica and ladies's stockings.* The bodies were cremated.

Stalin was always fascinated by the conduct of his enemies at the supreme moment, enjoying their humiliation and destruction: 'A man may be physically brave but a political coward,' he said. Weeks later, at a dinner to celebrate the founding of the Cheka, Pauker, Stalin's comedian, acted the death and pleadings of Zinoviev. To the raucous guffaws of the *Vozhd* and Yezhov, plump, corseted and shiny-pated Pauker was dragged back into the room by two friends playing the role of guards. There he performed Zinoviev's cries of 'For God's sake call Stalin' but improvised another ingredient. Pauker, a Jew himself, specialized in telling Stalin Jewish jokes in the appropriate accent with much rolling of 'R's and cringing. Now he combined the two, depicting Zinoviev raising his hands to the Heavens and weeping. 'Hear oh Israel the Lord is our God, the Lord is one',† Stalin laughed so much that Pauker repeated it. Stalin was almost sick with merriment and waved at Pauker to stop.

* * *

* When he was arrested they were found among his belongings and passed on to Yezhov who also kept them until his downfall.

† Zinoviev was unlikely to have recited the Shema prayer, the holiest in Jewish faith, since he, like all the Jews among these internationalist Bolsheviks, despised religion, but equally he would have remembered it from his childhood.

Bukharin was hill-climbing in the Pamirs when he read in the newspapers that he had been implicated in the Zinoviev trial. He frantically rushed back to Moscow. Bukharin had seemed forgiven for past sins. As the editor of *Izvestiya*, he had returned to prominence with frequent access to Stalin. In 1935, at a banquet, Stalin had even publicly toasted Bukharin: 'Let's drink to Nikolai Ivanovich Bukharin. We all love ... Bukharchik. May whoever remembers the past, lose an eye!' Whether to preserve Bukharin for his own trial (after Tomsky's suicide), because of a lingering fondness or just feline sadism, Stalin proceeded to play with beloved Bukharchik who waited anxiously in his Kremlin apartment.

On 8 September, the Central Committee summoned Bukharin to a meeting with Kaganovich, where, along with Yezhov and Vyshinsky, he was amazed to encounter his childhood friend, Grigory Sokolnikov, a venerable Old Bolshevik, who was delivered to the room by the NKVD. The 'confrontation' was one of Stalin's bizarre rituals in which, like an exorcism, Good was meant to confront and vanquish Evil. They were presumably designed to terrify the accused but also, and this may have been their main function, to convince the presiding Politburo members of the victim's guilt. Kaganovich played impartial observer while Sokolnikov declared there was a Left-Right Centre, involving Bukharin, which was planning the murder of Stalin.

'Can you have lost your reason and not be responsible for your own words?' Bukharin 'turned on the tears'. When the prisoner was led out, Kaganovich boomed: 'He's lying, the whore, from beginning to end! Go back to the newspaper, Nikolai Ivanovich, and work in peace.'

'But why is he lying, Lazar Moisevich?'

'We'll find out,' replied an unconvinced Kaganovich who still 'adored' Bukharin but told Stalin his 'role will yet be uncovered'. Stalin's antennae sensed that the time was not right: on 10 September, Vyshinsky announced that the investigation against Bukharin and Rykov had been closed due to lack of criminal culpability. Bukharin returned to work, safe again, while the investigators moved on to their next trial – but the cat did not stop caressing the mouse.

* * *

Stalin remained on holiday, directing a series of parallel tragedies in his escalating campaign to eliminate his enemies while devoting much of his energy to the Spanish Civil War. On 15 October, Soviet tanks, planes and 'advisers' started arriving in Spain to support the Republican Government against General Francisco Franco, backed by Hitler and Mussolini. Stalin treated this less as a rehearsal for World War 2 and more as a replay of his own Civil War. The internecine struggle with the Trotskyites on his own side, and the Fascists on the other, created a war fever in Moscow, stoking up the Terror. Stalin's real interest was to keep the war going as long as possible, embroiling Hitler without offending the Western powers, rather than helping the Republicans win. Furthermore, like an accomplished 'barrow boy', Stalin systematically swindled the Spanish of several hundred million dollars by rescuing their gold reserves and then tricking them into paying inflated prices for their arms.*

Gradually, instructing Voroshilov in military, Kaganovich in political, and Yezhov in security matters by telephone from Sochi, he presided over the effective NKVD takeover of the Republic itself, where he found himself in a genuine struggle with the Trotskyites. He set about the liquidation of Trotskyites along with his own men. The Soviet diplomats, journalists and soldiers serving in Spain spent as much time denouncing one another as fighting the Fascists.

After a short stay at the new little dacha built for him by Lakoba at Novy Afon (New Athos),† to the south in Abkhazia right beside Alexander III's monastery, Stalin returned to Sochi where he was joined by Zhdanov and President Kalinin. Yezhov was expanding the lists of suspects to include the whole of the old oppositions but also entire nationalities, particularly the Poles. Simultaneously he was pushing for the role of NKVD chief, attacking Yagoda for 'complacency, passivity, and bragging', in a letter that may have been sent to Stalin in a shameless job application: 'Without your intervention, things will come to no good.' Meanwhile Yagoda

* On the subject of Stalin's 'barrow boy' tendencies, he was always interested in discounts in his foreign dealings: 'How much was the purchase of the Italian warship?' he wrote to Voroshilov. 'If we buy two warships, what discount can they give us? Stalin.'

† Stalin had started to use this charmingly small house, a picturesque yellow bungalow on the hillside at Novy Afon, in 1935. There were walks up the hill to a summerhouse where Stalin held barbecues. Later he would build another house next to the first that would become one of his favourite residences in old age. Used by the President of Abkhazia, it is fully staffed. When the author visited in 2002, the manageress invited him to stay and offered to hold a banquet in his honour in Stalin's dining room.

bugged Yezhov's calls to Stalin, learning that Blackberry had been summoned to Sochi. Yagoda left immediately for Sochi but when he arrived, Pauker turned him back from the gates of Stalin's dacha.

On 25 September Stalin, backed by Zhdanov, decided to remove Yagoda and promote Yezhov:

'We consider it absolutely necessary and urgent to appoint Comrade Yezhov to the post of People's Commissar of Internal Affairs. Yagoda is not up to the task of exposing the Trotskyite-Zinovievite Bloc ... Stalin, Zhdanov.'

Sergo visited the dacha to discuss Yezhov's appointment and his own battles with the NKVD. Stalin felt he needed to win over Sergo to Yezhov's appointment, even though Blackberry and his wife were family friends of Sergo. 'This remarkably wise decision by our father suits the attitude of the Party and country,' Kaganovich wrote cheerfully to Sergo after he had sacked Yagoda and appointed him to Rykov's job as Communications Commissar.

There was relief at Yezhov's appointment: many, including Bukharin, regarded it as the end of the Terror, not the beginning, but Kaganovich knew his protégé better: he praised Yezhov's 'superb ... interrogations' to Stalin, suggesting his promotion to Commissar-General. 'Comrade Yezhov is handling things well,' Kaganovich told Sergo. 'He's dispensed with the bandits of the counter-revolutionary Trotskyites in Bolshevik style.' The dwarfish Blackberry was now the second most powerful man in the USSR.

Stalin was deeply dissatisfied with the 'sickness' inside the NKVD, which he rightly regarded as the ultimate Bolshevik old-boy network, filled with dubious Poles, Jews and Letts. He needed an outsider to get control of this self-satisfied élite and make it his own. There is evidence that during the thirties, he discussed appointing both Kaganovich and Mikoyan to run the NKVD and he had recently offered the job to Lakoba.*

Lakoba refused to move to Moscow from his paradisaical fiefdom. Loyal as he was to Stalin, Lakoba was better suited to

---

* Interestingly, none of these candidates are ethnic Russians but a Jew, an Armenian and an Abkhazian. Some historians believe there had always been a secret policy of placing Poles, Balts and Jews and other minorities to perform the unsavoury roles in the NKVD. This is credible but it is true that Stalin desperately needed NKVD officials he trusted: he was often closest to his fellow Caucasians. He had no interest in provoking Russian resentment of Georgians in high positions.

playing the magnanimious host in the resorts of Abkhazia than torturing innocents in the cellars of the Lubianka. But his refusal drew attention to the rule of Lakoba's clan in Abkhazia, known as 'Lakobistan', which he wanted to be made into a full Soviet republic, a dangerous idea in the fragile multinational USSR. There was no greater 'prince' than Lakoba. Stalin had already banned the use of Abkhazian names in Lakoba's fiefdom and foiled his plan to raise Abkhazia's constitutional status.

On 31 October, Stalin returned to Moscow where he dined with Lakoba. All seemed well. But it was not. When Lakoba returned to Abkhazia, Beria invited him to dinner in Tiflis. Lakoba refused until Beria's mother telephoned to insist. They dined on 27 December and then went to the theatre where Lakoba was overcome with nausea. Returning to his hotel, he sat by the window groaning,

'That snake Beria has killed me.' At 4.20 a.m., Lakoba died of a 'heart attack' aged forty-three. Beria saw off the coffin on its way back by train to Sukhumi. Lakoba's doctors were convinced he had been poisoned but Beria had the organs removed, later exhuming and destroying the cadaver. Lakoba's family were also killed. He was denounced as an Enemy of the People. Lakoba was the first of Stalin's circle to be killed. 'Poison, poison,' as Stalin wrote. He had given Beria *carte blanche* to settle scores in the Caucasus. In Armenia, Beria had earlier visited the First Secretary, Aghasi Khanchian, who had either killed himself or been murdered. Across the Imperium, the regions began to expose conspiracies of 'wreckers'* to justify the inefficiencies and corruption. The clock was ticking towards war with Hitler's Germany. But as tension was mounting with aggressive Japan in the Far East, and Soviet 'advisers' fought in Spain, the USSR was already at war.

* * *

Shortly before Lakoba's sinister death, Beria arrested Papulia Ordzhonikidze, Sergo's elder brother, a railway official. Beria knew that his former patron, Sergo, had warned Stalin that he was a 'scoundrel'. Sergo refused to shake hands with Beria and built a special fence between their dachas.

---

* In West Siberia, there was a regional show trial of 'wreckers' accused of trying to murder the local leader Eikhe – and of trying to assassinate Molotov during his earlier trip there. His driver testified that he planned to sacrifice himself and kill Molotov by driving over a precipice but he lost his nerve and only managed to capsize the car in a muddy rut. No doubt this cock-and-bull story consoled Molotov for being left off the list for the Zinoviev trial.

Beria's vengeance was just one of the ways in which Stalin began to turn the heat on to the emotional Sergo, the industrial *magnifico* who supported the regime's draconian policies but resisted the arrest of his own managers. The star of the next show trial was to be Sergo's Deputy Commissar, Yury Pyatakov, an ex-Trotskyite and skilled manager. The two men were fond of one another and enjoyed working together.

In July, Pyatakov's wife had been arrested for her links to Trotsky. Shortly before the Zinoviev trial, Yezhov summoned Pyatakov, read him all the affidavits implicating him in Trotskyite terrorism and informed him that he was relieved of his job as Deputy Commissar. Pyatakov offered to prove his innocence by asking to be 'personally allowed to shoot all those sentenced to death at the trial, including his former wife and to publish this in the press'. As a Bolshevik, he was willing even to execute his own wife.

'I pointed out to him the absurdity of his proposal,' Yezhov reported drily to Stalin. On 12 September, Pyatakov was arrested. Sergo, recuperating in Kislovodsk, voted for his expulsion from the Central Committee but he must have been deeply worried. A shadow of his former self, grey and exhausted, he was so ill that the Politburo restricted him to a three-day week. Now the NKVD began to arrest his specialist non-Bolshevik advisers and he appealed to Blackberry: 'Comrade Yezhov, please look into this.' He was not alone. Kaganovich and Sergo, those 'best friends', not only shared the same swaggering dynamism but both headed giant industrial commissariats. Kaganovich's railway experts were being arrested too. Meanwhile Stalin sent Sergo transcripts of Pyatakov's interrogations in which his deputy confessed to being a 'saboteur'. The destruction of 'experts' was a perennial Bolshevik sport but the arrest of Sergo's brother revealed Stalin's hand: 'This couldn't have been done without Stalin's consent. But Stalin's agreed to it without even calling me,' Sergo told Mikoyan. 'We were such close friends! And suddenly he lets them do such a thing!' He blamed Beria.

Sergo appealed to Stalin, doing all he could to save his brother. He did too much: the arrest of a man's clan was a test of loyalty. Stalin was not alone in taking a dim view of this bourgeois emotionalism: Molotov himself attacked Sergo for being 'guided only by emotions ... thinking only of himself.'

On 9 November, Sergo suffered another heart attack.

Meanwhile, the third Ordzhonikidze brother, Valiko, was sacked from his job in the Tiflis Soviet for claiming that Papulia was innocent. Sergo swallowed his pride and called Beria, who replied:

'Dear Comrade Sergo! After your call, I quickly summoned Valiko ... Today Valiko was restored to his job. Yours L. Beria.' This bears the pawprints of Stalin's cat-and-mouse game, his meandering path to open destruction, perhaps his moments of nostalgic fondness, his supersensitive testing of limits. But Stalin now regarded Sergo as an enemy: his biography had just been published for his fiftieth birthday and Stalin studied it carefully, scribbling sarcastically next to the passages that acclaimed Sergo's heroism:

'What about the CC? The Party?' Stalin and Sergo returned separately to Moscow where fifty-six of the latter's officials were in the toils of the NKVD. Sergo however remained a living restraint on Stalin, making brave little gestures towards the beleaguered Rightists. 'My dear kind warmly blessed Sergo,' encouraged Bukharin: 'Stand firm!' At the theatre, when Stalin and the Politburo filed into the front seats, Sergo spotted ex-Premier Rykov and his daughter Natalya (who tells the story), alone and ignored, twenty rows up the auditorium. Leaving Stalin, Sergo galloped up to kiss them. The Rykovs were moved to tears in gratitude.*

At the 7 November parade, Stalin, on the Mausoleum, spotted Bukharin in an ordinary seat and sent a Chekist to say, 'Comrade Stalin has invited you on to the Mausoleum.' Bukharin thought he was being arrested but then gratefully climbed the steps.

Bukharin, the enchanting but hysterical intellectual whom everyone adored, bombarded Stalin with increasingly frantic letters through which we can feel the screw tightening. When writers fear for their lives, they write and write: 'Big child!' Stalin scribbled across one letter; 'Crank!' on another. Bukharin could not stop appealing to Stalin, about whom he was having dreams:

'Everything connected with me is criticized,' he wrote on 19 October 1936. 'Even for the birthday of Sergo, they did not propose me to write an article ... Maybe I'm not honourable. To whom can I go, as a beloved person, without expecting a smash

---

* 'Men have gone to heaven for smaller things than that,' wrote Oscar Wilde in *De Profundis* about Robbie Ross waiting amongst the crowd at Reading Station and being the only one to step forward and raise his hat as the disgraced writer travelled to Reading Gaol. The stakes were even higher for Sergo.

Stalin's friendship was suffocating. After Nadya's death, Sergei Kirov, handsome, easy-going Leningrad boss, became Stalin's closest friend – here, he holidays with Stalin and Svetlana at Sochi. But there was tension when Kirov became dangerously popular. Did Stalin arrange his death?

Even before Kirov's assassination, Andrei Zhdanov, ebullient, burly yet frail, pretentious, self-important and ruthless, became Stalin's favourite – the only other magnate who qualified as his 'fellow intellectual'. Here, Zhdanov joins the family, probably at the Coldstream dacha (from left): Vasily, Zhdanov, Svetlana, Stalin and Yakov. *Right* On the same occasion, Stalin and Svetlana.

The Court of the Red Tsar in the mid-1930s. Stalin is surrounded by his male comrades and the circle of outspoken, bossy women who ultimately became over-familiar and paid the price. On 21 December 1934, still reeling from the assassination of Kirov, the courtiers, family and grandees gathered for Stalin's birthday at his Kuntsevo dacha and were photographed by General Vlasik. Lakoba and Beria arrived late. (Back row standing, from left): Stan Redens, Kaganovich, Molotov, Alyosha Svanidze, Anna Alliluyeva Redens; Vlas Chubar, Dora Khazan (married to Andreyev); Andrei Andreyev; Zinaida Ordzhonikidze; Pavel Alliluyev. (Middle Row): Maria Svanidze; Maria Kaganovich; Sashiko Svanidze; Stalin; Polina Molotova; Voroshilov. (Front row): unknown, possibly Shalva Eliava; Lakoba; possibly Lakoba's wife; Sergo Ordzhonikidze; Zhenya Alliluyeva; Bronislava Poskrebysheva; unknown; and at the bottom front Beria, Mikoyan and Poskrebyshev.

Stalin's women: his beaming mistress Zhenya Alliluyeva sits at his feet in her lace collar; she said what she liked to Stalin and it made her enemies. Pretty Bronislava Poskrebysheva, sits to the right of Zhenya. Bronislava's daughter claims she was also Stalin's mistress. Nonetheless she was liquidated.

Stalin micro-managed the theatre as he dominated cinema, literature and politics. The grandees ate in the avant-loge behind the box in between scenes. Here, in the former imperial box at the Bolshoi, sits (from left): Voroshilov, Kaganovich, Stalin, Sergo Ordzhonikidze, Mikoyan and their wives.

Stalin's mother Keke possessed the same sardonic and mocking wit as her son. They were not close but Stalin sent dutiful letters, leaving Beria to act as his surrogate son. Shortly before her death when he was on holiday in Georgia, Beria arranged for him to visit the ailing Keke. Former friends, now bitter rivals, Beria and Lakoba sit behind mother and son in her bedroom.

Left Like three boulevardiers in the sun, Beria, Caucasian viceroy (centre) hosts Voroshilov and Mikoyan (right) in Tiflis for the Rustaveli Festival at the height of the Terror, 1937.

Below A Jewish jeweller's son with a knowledge of poisons, and ruthless ambition, Genrikh Yagoda was the NKVD boss who had reservations about the Terror. Stalin threatened to punch him in the face. Yagoda enjoyed the good life: collecting wines, growing orchids, courting Gorky's daughter-in-law, amassing ladies underwear, and buying German pornographic films and obscene cigarette holders. Left to right: Yagoda in uniform, Kalinin, Stalin, Molotov, Vyshinsky, Beria.

Marshal Semyon Budyonny, swaggering Cossack horseman and hero of Tsaritsyn, famous for his handlebar moustaches, white teeth and equine level of intelligence, poses with Kaganovich on the left and Stalin amongst swooning females. Budyonny proved a better general than most of Stalin's cavalry cronies, but he was happiest breeding horses, which he believed were more useful than tanks.

The two most depraved monsters of Stalin's court. At the 17th Congress in 1934 when they joined the leadership (but before their rise to supreme power), Beria and Yezhov, a rising Central Committee official, hug for the camera. Yezhov was an ambitious fanatic, good-natured if prone to illness, a bisexual dwarf who was liked by everyone until he was promoted to NKVD boss in 1936 and became Stalin's frenzied killer. Beria was an unscrupulous but able and intelligent secret policeman. In 1938, he was brought to Moscow to destroy Yezhov whose execution he supervised.

Left Ascendant grandee Yezhov (hugging his adopted daughter Natasha) and his promiscuous literary wife Yevgenia, who slept with writers from Isaac Babel to Mikhail Sholokhov, entertain their powerful friend, Sergo Ordzhonikidze. Yezhov would soon help Stalin harass Sergo to his death. Yevgenia Yezhova became the 'black widow' of Stalin's circle: many of her lovers, including Babel, died because of their connections to her. She sacrificed herself to try to save their daughter Natasha. *Above right* Sergo and Yezhov

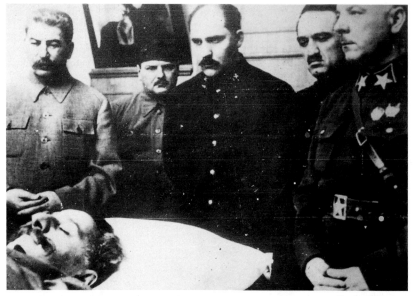

As the Terror gained pace, Sergo Ordzhonikidze clashed with Stalin. A shot rang out in Sergo's flat. His mysterious death solved a problem for Stalin who rushed to his Kremlin apartment where Sergo was lifted onto his table for this photograph. Stalin, Zhdanov (in a comical anti-headache bandage), Kaganovich, Mikoyan and Voroshilov pose with the body. Kaganovich and Mikoyan were especially close to Sergo and look particularly shocked.

In 1937, at the height of the Great Terror, two young magnates join the leadership: Yezhov, now NKVD boss in full uniform as Commissar-General of State Security (second from right) and (far right) his friend Nikita Khrushchev, newly appointed Moscow boss and later one of Stalin's successors, accompany Molotov, Kaganovich, Stalin, Mikoyan and Kalinin. Stalin trusted the ruthless bumpkin Khrushchev who described himself as the leader's 'pet'. He idolised Stalin.

Stalin regarded himself as an intellectual. He persuaded the famous novelist Gorky to return to become the regime's great writer, giving him a mansion in Moscow and two dachas outside. Gorky's house became the literary venue for the Politburo who visited regularly. There, Stalin told writers to become 'engineers of human souls'. Here, Stalin and Molotov (second from left) take tea with Gorky. When Stalin became disenchanted with Gorky, his death in 1936 proved convenient.

When she tipsily dropped a cream cake on his tunic, Poskrebyshev fell in love with a pretty, glamorous and well-connected young doctor Bronislava who became familiar with Stalin and his family. But her Jewish, Lithuanian origins, her friendship with Yezhov's wife and, worst of all, her distant connection to Trotsky led to her arrest by Beria and execution. Poskrebyshev wept when he heard her name, but remained working at Stalin's side, on good terms with Beria – and managed to remarry. Poskrebyshev with Bronislava (right) and her sister.

More powerful than many a magnate, Alexander Poskrebyshev (right) was Stalin's chef de cabinet for most of his reign. This former male nurse and master of detail ran the office and kept the secrets while at the leader's dinners, Stalin challenged him to drinking contests, nicknamed him the 'commander-in-chief' and laughed when he was dragged vomiting from the table.

Poskrebyshev ran the politics but General Nikolai Vlasik, Stalin's chief bodyguard and court photographer, ran his home life. This hard-drinking debauchee with a harem of 'concubines', also acted as Vasily Stalin's father figure. Here, just before the war, is Vlasik, on the left with Stalin's doomed son Yakov, probably at Kuntsevo.

Stalin remained close and affectionate with Svetlana but, by her early teens at the end of the 1930s, she was maturing early and this alarmed her father. When she sent him this photograph of her sporting her Young Pioneer's uniform, he sent it back scrawling, 'Your expression is not suitable for someone your age.' When she fell in love with an older man in the middle of the Second World War, Stalin was appalled and it destroyed their relationship for ever. Henceforth his fondest epithet to her was 'You little fool.'

in the teeth? I see your intention but I write to you as I wrote to Illich [Lenin] as a really beloved man whom I even see in dreams as I did Illich. Maybe it's strange but it's so. It's hard for me to live under suspicion and my nerves are already on edge.' Finally, on a sleepless night, he wrote a poem, an embarrassing hymn to 'Great Stalin!'

Bukharin's other old friend was Voroshilov. The two had been so close that Bukharin called him his 'honey seagull' and even wrote his speeches for him. Klim had presented him with a pistol engraved with his love and friendship. Voroshilov tried to avoid Bukharin's letters: 'Why do you hurt me so?' he asked Klim in one letter.

Now in real danger, Bukharin wrote a long plea to Klim in which he even announced that he was 'delighted the dogs [Zinoviev and Kamenev] were shot ... Forgive this confused letter: a thousand thoughts are rushing around inside my head like strong horses and I have no strong reins. I embrace you because I am clean. N Bukharin.' Voroshilov decided he had to end this ghost of a friendship so he ordered his adjutant to copy the letter to the Politburo and write: 'I enclose herewith, on Comrade Voroshilov's orders, Comrade Voroshilov's reply to Bukharin.' Voroshilov's reply was a study in amorality, cruelty, fear and cowardice:

To Comrade Bukharin, I return your letter in which you permit yourself to make vile attacks on the Party leadership. If you were hoping ... to convince me of your complete innocence, all you have convinced me of is that henceforth I should distance myself from you ... And if you do not repudiate in writing your foul epithets against the Party leadership, I shall even regard you as a scoundrel.
K Voroshilov 3 Sept 1936.

Bukharin was heartbroken by 'your appalling letter. My letter ended with "I embrace you". Your letter ends with "scoundrel".'

Yezhov was creating the case against the so-called Leftists Radek and Pyatakov, but by December, he had also managed to procure evidence against Bukharin and Rykov. The December Plenum was a sort of arraignment of these victims and, as always with Stalin, a test of the conditions necessary to destroy them. Stalin was the dominant will, but the Terror was not the work of one man. One can hear the evangelical enthusiasm of their blood-lust that sometimes totters on the edge of tragicomedy. Kaganovich even told a Stalinist shaggy-dog story.

Yezhov proudly listed the two hundred persons arrested in the Trotskyite Centre in the Azov–Black Sea organization, another three hundred in Georgia, four hundred in Leningrad. Molotov was not the only one who had avoided assassination: Kaganovich had just escaped death in the Urals. First Yezhov dealt with the Pyatakov–Radek trial that was about to begin. When he read out Pyatakov's description of the workers as a 'herd of sheep', these frightened fanatics reacted as if at a nightmarish revivalist meeting.

'The swine!' shouted Beria. There was a 'noise of indignation in the room'. Then the record reveals:

A voice: 'The brutes!'

'That's how low this vicious Fascist agent, this degenerate Communist has sunk, God knows what else! These swine must be strangled!'

'What about Bukharin?' a voice called.

'We need to talk about them,' agreed Stalin.

'There's a scoundrel for you,' snarled Beria.

'What swine!' exclaimed another comrade. Yezhov announced that Bukharin and Rykov were indeed members of the 'back-up Centre'. They were actually terrorists yet these assassins were sitting there with them. Bukharin was now meant to confess his sins and implicate his friends. He did not.

'So you think I too aspired to power? Are you serious?' he asked Yezhov. 'After all there are many old comrades who know me well … my very soul, my inner life.'

'It's hard to know someone's soul,' sneered Beria.

'There isn't a word of truth said against me … Kamenev stated at his trial that he met me every year up to 1936. I asked Yezhov to find out when and where so I could refute this lie. They told me Kamenev was not asked … and now it's impossible to ask him.'

'They shot him,' added Rykov sadly. Few of the old leaders kicked Bukharin but Kaganovich, Molotov and Beria hunted him zealously. Then, amidst deadly allegations, Kaganovich remembered Zinoviev's dog:

'In 1934, Zinoviev invited Tomsky to his *dacha* … After drinking tea, Tomsky and Zinoviev went in Tomsky's car to pick out a dog for Zinoviev. You see what friendship, what help they went together to pick out a dog.'

'What about this dog?' said Stalin. 'Was it a hunting dog or a guard dog?'

'It was not possible to establish this,' Kaganovich went on with gleeful, if chilling humour.

'Anyway, did they fetch the dog?' persisted Stalin.

'They got it,' boomed Kaganovich. 'They were searching for a four-legged companion not unlike themselves.'

'Was it a good dog or a bad dog?' asked Stalin. 'Anybody know?' There was 'laughter in the hall'.

'It was hard to establish this at the confrontation,' replied Kaganovich.

Finally, Stalin, sensing how many of the older members were not joining in against Bukharin, summed up more in sadness than anger:

'We believed in you and we were mistaken … We believed in you … we moved you up the ladder and we were mistaken. Isn't it true Comrade Bukharin?' Yet Stalin ended the Plenum without a vote in support of Yezhov; just an ominous decision to consider 'the matter of Bukharin and Rykov unfinished'. The regional 'princes' realized that even such a giant could be destroyed.

Stalin, assisted by Yezhov, shaped the febrile fears of war with Poland and Germany and the very real dangers of the Spanish Civil War, the inexplicable industrial failures caused by Soviet incompetence, and the resistance of the regional 'princes', into a web of conspiracies that dovetailed with the paranoic soul and glorious, nostalgic brutality of the Russian Civil War, and personal feuds of the Bolsheviks. Stalin was particularly suspicious of the infiltration of spies across the porous border with Poland, traditional enemy of Russia's western marches that had defeated Russia (and Stalin personally) in 1920.* At the Plenum, Khrushchev was denounced as a secret 'Pole'. Chatting in the corridor to his friend Yezhov, Stalin walked over, pushing a finger into Khrushchev's shoulder:

'What's your name?'

'Comrade Stalin, it's Khrushchev.'

'No you're not Khrushchev … So-and-so says you're not.'

'How can you believe that? My mother's still alive … Check.' Stalin cited Yezhov who denied it. Stalin let it pass but he was checking those around him.

* Stalin's political and personal obsessions often found a parallel in his favourite operas: he constantly attended performances of the opera *Ivan Susanin* by Glinka but only waited until the scene when the Poles are lured into a forest by a Russian and freeze to death there. He would then leave the theatre and go home.

Stalin was finally determined to bring the regional 'princes' to heel: Ukraine was a special case, the grain store, the second republic with a strong sense of its own culture. Kosior and Chubar had demonstrated their weakness during the famine while the Second Secretary, Postyshev, behaved like a 'prince' with his own entourage. On 13 January, Stalin struck with a telegram attacking Postyshev, for lacking the 'most basic Party vigilance'. Kaganovich, already the scourge of the Ukraine which he had governed in the late twenties, descended on Kiev, where he soon managed to find a 'little person' crushed by the local 'prince'. A half-mad crone and Party busybody named Polia Nikolaenko had criticized Postyshev and his wife, also a high official. Mrs Postyshev expelled the troublesome Nikolaenko from the Party. When Kaganovich informed Stalin of this 'heroic denunciatrix', he immediately grasped her usefulness.

On 21 December, the family and magnates danced until dawn at Stalin's birthday party. But the struggles and conspiracies took their toll on the actor-manager: Stalin often suffered from chronic tonsillitis when under pressure. Professor Valedinsky, the specialist from the Matsesta Baths, whom he had brought to Moscow, joined his personal physician, the distinguished Vladimir Vinogradov, who had been a fashionable doctor before the Revolution and still lived in an apartment filled with antiques and fine pictures. The patient lay on a sofa with a high temperature for five days, surrounded by professors and Politburo. The professors visited twice a day and kept vigil at night. By New Year's Eve, he was well enough to attend the party where the whole family danced together for the last time. When the doctors visited him on New Year's Day 1937, he reminisced about his first job as a meteorologist and his fishing exploits during his Siberian exiles. But Stalin's duel with Sergo again took a toll on him as he prepared for his most reckless gamble since collectivization: the massacre of Lenin's Party.

* * *

Stalin arranged a 'confrontation' between Bukharin and Pyatakov before the Politburo. Pyatakov, the abrasive industrial manager soon to star in his own show trial, testified to Bukharin's terrorism but was now a walking testament to the methods of the NKVD. 'Living remains,' Bukharin told his wife, 'not of Pyatakov but of his shadow, a skeleton with its teeth knocked out.' He spoke with his head lowered, trying to cover his eyes with his hands. Sergo stared intensely at his former deputy and friend:

'Is your testimony voluntary?' he asked.

'My testimony is voluntary,' retorted Pyatakov.

It seems absurd that Sergo even had to ask the question but to do more would be to go against the Politburo itself where men like Voroshilov were working themselves up into paroxyms of hatred:

'Your deputy turned out to be a swine of the first class,' Klim told him. 'You must know what he told us, the pig, the son of a bitch!' When Sergo read the signed pages of Pyatakov's interrogation, he 'believed it and came to hate him' but it was not a happy time for him.

Stalin was supervising Pyatakov's coming trial of the 'Parallel Anti-Soviet Trotskyite Centre' that was really an assault on Sergo's Commissariat of Heavy Industry where ten of the seventeen defendants worked. Stalin's intimate role in the famous trials has always been known but the archives reveal how he even dictated the words of Vyshinsky's summing-up. Recovering from his tonsillitis, Stalin must have seen Vyshinsky at Kuntsevo. One can imagine Stalin pacing up and down, smoking, as the cringing Procurator scribbled in his notebook: 'These villains don't even have any sense of being citizens ... they're afraid of the nation, afraid of the people ... Their agreements with Japan and Germany are the agreements of the hare with the wolf ...' Vyshinsky noted down Stalin's words: 'While Lenin was alive, they were against Lenin.' He used exactly the same words in court on 28 January. But Stalin's thoughts in 1937 reveal the broadest reason for the imminent murder of hundreds of thousands of people for little apparent reason: 'Maybe it can be explained by the fact that you lost faith,' Stalin addressed the Old Bolsheviks. Here was the essence of the religious frenzy of the coming slaughter.

Stalin's tonsillitis flared again. He lay on the dining-room table so the professors could examine his throat. Then the Politburo joined Stalin and the doctors for dinner. There were toasts and after dinner, the doctors were amazed to see the leaders dancing. But Stalin's mind was on the brutal tasks of that terrible year. He toasted Soviet medicine, then added that there were 'Enemies among the doctors – you'll find out soon!' He was ready to begin.

18

Sergo: Death of a 'Perfect Bolshevik'

The legal melodrama opened on 23 January and immediately expanded the Terror to thousands of new potential victims. Radek, who may have been coached personally by Stalin, revelled in his black humour, joking that he was not tortured under interrogation; on the contrary, he had tortured his investigators for months by refusing to co-operate. Then he delivered what were probably Stalin's own lines: 'But there are in our country semi-Trotskyites, quarter-Trotskyites, one-eighth Trotskyites, people who helped us [Trotskyites] not knowing of the terrorist organization but sympathizing with us.' The message was clear and when it is combined with Vyshinsky's own notes, the mystery of the crazy randomness of the Terror is solved. Those without blind faith were to die.

At 7.13 p.m. on 29 January, the judges retired to confer and at 3.00 next morning, they returned. Thirteen of the defendants, including Pyatakov, were sentenced to death but Radek received ten years. Blokhin again supervised the executions. Yezhov was rewarded with the rank of Commissar-General of State Security, and a Kremlin apartment.

In Moscow, 200,000 people, bedazzled by propaganda, massed in Red Square, despite temperatures of –27°C, bearing banners that read: 'The court's verdict is the people's verdict.' Khrushchev addressed them, denouncing the 'Judas-Trotsky', a line that strongly implied that Stalin was the metaphorical Jesus. (We know from Yury Zhdanov that he jokily compared himself to Jesus.) 'By raising their hand against Comrade Stalin,' Khrushchev told the crowds, 'they raised their hand against all the best that humanity has, because Stalin is hope ... Stalin is our banner. Stalin is our will, Stalin is our victory.' The country was swept by the 'emotional effervescence' of hatred, fear and blood-lust. Maria Svanidze wrote in her diary that Radek's 'human baseness ... exceeded all imagination: These moral monsters deserved their end .... How could we so blindly trust this band of scoundrels?'

Today it seems impossible that virtually every factory and railway line was being sabotaged by Trotskyite terrorists within their management but Soviet industry was riddled with mistakes and cursed with accidents thanks to poor management and the breakneck speed of the Five-Year Plans. There were thousands of accidents: for example in 1934 alone, there were 62,000 accidents on the railways! How could this happen in a perfect country? Enemies among the corrupt élite explained the failures. The arrest of saboteurs and wreckers in the industrial factories and railways spread. The staffs of Sergo and Kaganovich were again hit hard.

Stalin carefully prepared for the Plenum that would formally open the Terror against the Party itself. On 31 January, the Politburo appointed the two industrial kingpins to speak about wrecking in their departments. Stalin reviewed their speeches. Sergo accepted that wreckers had to be stopped but wanted to say that now they had been arrested, it was time to return to normality. Stalin angrily scribbled on Sergo's speech: 'State with facts which branches are affected by sabotage and exactly how they are affected.' When they met, Sergo seemed to agree but he quietly despatched trusted managers to the regions to investigate whether the NKVD was fabricating the cases: a direct challenge to Stalin.

An ailing Sergo realized that the gap between them was widening. He faced a rupture with the Party to which he had devoted his life.

'I don't understand why Stalin doesn't trust me,' he confided to Mikoyan probably walking round the snowy Kremlin at night. 'I'm completely loyal to him, don't want to fight with him. Beria's schemes play a large part in this – he gives Stalin the wrong information but Stalin trusts him.' Both were baffled, according to Mikoyan, 'about what was happening to Stalin, how they could put honest men in prison and then shoot them for sabotage'.

'Stalin's started a bad business,' said Sergo. 'I was always such a close friend of Stalin's. I trusted him and he trusted me. And now I can't work with him, I'll commit suicide.' Mikoyan told him suicide never solved anything but there were now frequent suicides. On 17 February, Sergo and Stalin argued for several hours. Sergo then went to his office before returning at 3 p.m. for a Politburo meeting.

Stalin approved Yezhov's report but criticized Sergo and

Kaganovich who retired to Poskrebyshev's study, like schoolboys to rewrite their essays. At seven, they too walked, talking, around the Kremlin: 'he was ill, his nerves broken,' said Kaganovich.

Stalin deliberately turned the screw: the NKVD searched Sergo's apartment. Only Stalin could have ordered such an outrage. Besides, the Ordzhonikidzes spent weekends with the Yezhovs, but friendship was dust compared to the orders of the Party. Sergo, as angry and humiliated as intended, telephoned Stalin:

'Sergo, why are you upset?' said Stalin. 'This Organ can search my place at any moment too.' Stalin summoned Sergo who rushed out so fast, he forgot his coat. His wife Zina hurried after him with the coat and fur hat but he was already in Stalin's apartment. Zina waited outside for an hour and a half. Stalin's provocations only confirmed Sergo's impotence, for he 'sprang out of Stalin's place in a very agitated state, did not put on his coat or hat, and ran home'. He started retyping his speech, then, according to his wife, rushed back to Stalin who taunted him more with his sneering marginalia: 'Ha-ha!'

Sergo told Zina that he could not cope with Koba whom he loved. The next morning, he remained in bed, refusing breakfast. 'I feel bad,' he said. He simply asked that no one should disturb him and worked in his room. At 5.30 p.m. Zinaida heard a dull sound and rushed into the bedroom.

Sergo lay bare-chested and dead on the bed. He had shot himself in the heart, his chest powder-burned. Zina kissed his hands, chest, lips fervently and called the doctor who certified he was dead. She then telephoned Stalin who was at Kuntsevo. The guards said he was taking a walk but she shouted:

'Tell Stalin it's Zina. Tell him to come to the phone right away. I'll wait on the line.'

'Why the big hurry?' Stalin asked. Zina ordered him to come urgently:

'Sergo's done the same as Nadya!' Stalin banged down the phone at this grievous insult.

It happened that Konstantin Ordzhonikidze, one of Sergo's brothers, arrived at the apartment at this moment. At the entrance, Sergo's chauffeur told him to hurry. When he reached the front door, one of Sergo's officials said simply:

'Our Sergo's no more.' Within half an hour, Stalin, Molotov and Zhdanov (for some reason wearing a black bandage on his forehead) arrived from the countryside to join Voroshilov,

Kaganovich and Yezhov. When Mikoyan heard, he exclaimed, 'I don't believe it' and rushed over. Again the Kremlin family mourned its own but suicide left as much anger as grief.

Zinaida sat on the edge of the bed beside Sergo's body. The leaders entered the room, looked at the corpse and sat down. Voroshilov, so soft-hearted in personal matters, consoled Zina:

'Why console me,' she snapped, 'when you couldn't save him for the Party?' Stalin caught Zina's eye and nodded at her to follow him into the study. They stood facing each other. Stalin seemed crushed and pitiful, betrayed again.

'What shall we say to people now?' she asked.

'This must be reported in the press,' Stalin replied. 'We'll say he died of a heart attack.'

'No one will believe that,' snapped the widow. 'Sergo loved the truth. The truth must be printed.'

'Why won't they believe it? Everyone knew he had a bad heart and everyone will believe it,' concluded Stalin. The door to the death-room was closed but Konstantin Ordzhonikidze peeped inside and observed Kaganovich and Yezhov in consultation, sitting at the foot of the body of their mutual friend. Suddenly Beria, in Moscow for the Plenum, appeared in the dining room. Zinaida charged at him, trying to slap him, and shrieked: 'Rat!' Beria 'disappeared right afterwards'.

They carried Sergo's bulky body from the bedroom and laid him on the table. Molotov's brother, a photographer, arrived with his camera. Stalin and the magnates posed with the body.

On the 19th, the newspapers announced the death of Sergo by heart attack. A list of doctors signed the mendacious bulletin: 'At 17.30, while he was having his afternoon rest, he suddenly felt ill and a few minutes later died of paralysis of the heart.' The Plenum was delayed by Sergo's funeral, but Stalin's obstacle had been removed. The death of 'the perfect Bolshevik' shocked Maria Svanidze who described the lying-in-state in the Hall of Columns among 'garlands, music, the scent of flowers, tears, honorary escorts. Thousands upon thousands passed' the open coffin. Sergo was sanctified by a cult. Some mourned him more than others. Bukharin penned a poem: 'He cracked like lightning in foamy waves' but also wrote another pathetic letter to Stalin:

'I wanted to write to Klim and Mikoyan. And if they hurt me too? Because the slanders have done their work. I am not me. I can't even cry on the body of an old comrade ... Koba, I can't live in such a situation ... I really love you passionately ... I wish you quick and resolute victories.' The suicide remained a tight secret. Stalin and others like the Voroshilovs* believed Sergo was a self-indulgent disappointment. At the Plenum, Stalin attacked that Bolshevik nobleman for behaving like a 'prince'.

Stalin was chief bearer of the urn of ashes that was buried near Kirov in the Kremlin Wall. But his antennae sensed other doubters who might follow Sergo's line. During the funeral, he reminded Mikoyan about his escape from the shooting of Twenty-Six Commissars during the Civil War: 'You were the only one to escape' in that 'obscure and murky story. Anastas, don't force us to try to clear it up.' Mikoyan must have decided not to rock the boat but he could hardly miss the warning and gathering darkness.

'I cannot live like this any more ...' wrote Bukharin to Stalin days later. 'I am in no physical or moral condition to come to the Plenum ... I will begin a hunger strike until the accusations of betrayal, wrecking and terrorism are dropped.' But Bukharin's agony was just starting: Anna his wife accompanied him to the first sitting during a snowstorm. It is striking that the main victims of the Plenum, Bukharin and Yagoda, both lived in the Kremlin just doors away from Stalin and the Politburo while simultaneously being accused of planning their murder. The Kremlin remained a village – but one of unsurpassed malevolence.

At 6 p.m. on 23 February, this febrile, cruel Plenum opened under the pall of Sergo's death, Pyatakov's execution, the spreading arrests and the bloodthirsty public effervescence whipped up by the media. If there was any moment when Stalin emerged as dictator with power over life and death, it was now. Yezhov opened with a savage indictment of Bukharin and his hunger strike.

'I won't shoot myself,' he replied, 'because people will say I killed myself to harm the Party. But if I die, as it were, from an illness, what will you lose from it?'

'Blackmailer!' shouted several voices.

---

* Ekaterina Voroshilova wrote twenty years later in her diaries: maybe Zinaida 'was right that Ordzhonikidze was a man of great soul but on this I have my own opinion.' Sergo's daughter Eteri recalled how Stalin called a couple of times to comfort the widow and then no one called them. Only Kaganovich still visited them. Years later, Khrushchev praised Sergo at Kuntsevo. Beria was insulting about him. Stalin said nothing. But when they left, Malenkov pulled Khrushchev aside: 'Listen, why did you speak so carelessly about Sergo? He shot himself ... Didn't you know? Didn't you notice how awkward it was after you said his name?' None the less the city of Vladikavkaz, in the Caucasus, was renamed Ordzhonikidze.

'You scoundrel,' shrieked Voroshilov at his ex-friend. 'Keep your trap shut! How vile! How dare you speak like that!'

'It's very hard for me to go on living.'

'And it's easy for us?' asked Stalin. 'You really babble a lot.'

'You abused the Party's trust!' declaimed Andreyev. This venom encouraged less senior officials to prove their loyalty:

'I'm not sure there's any reason for us to go on debating this matter,' declared I. P. Zhukov (no relation of the Marshal). 'These people ... must be shot just as the [other] scoundrels were shot!' This was so rabid that the leaders hooted with laughter: in the midst of the witch hunt, it was perhaps a relief to be able to laugh. But there were more jokes. Bukharin quipped that the testimonies against him were false:

'Demand produces supply – that means that those who give testimony know the nature of the general atmosphere!' More laughter. But it was all to no avail: a commission of magnates, chaired by Mikoyan, met to decide the fate of Bukharin and Rykov but when they returned after sleepless nights, no one would shake hands with them. Even before Yezhov came in for the kill, Stalin taunted Bukharin:

'Bukharin's on hunger strike. Who is your ultimatum aimed at, Nikolai, the Central Committee?'

'You're about to throw me out of the Party.'

'Ask the Central Committee for its forgiveness!'

'I'm not Zinoviev and Kamenev and I won't lie about myself.'

'If you won't confess,' replied Mikoyan, 'you're just proving you're a Fascist hireling.'

The 'hirelings' waited at home. In Stalin and Nadya's old apartment in the Poteshny Palace, Bukharin worked frantically on a letter to a future Central Commitee and Posterity, asking his beautiful wife Anna, just twenty-three, to memorize it. 'Again and again Nikolai Ivanovich read his letter in a whisper to me and I had to repeat it after him,' she wrote. 'Then I read and reread it myself, softly repeating the phrases aloud. Ah how he gripped [me] when I made a slip!'

Just across the river, in his apartment in the House on the Embankment, Rykov would only say: 'They'll send me to prison!' His wife suffered a stroke as the attacks on her husband became more deadly. His devoted 21-year-old daughter, Natalya, helped him dress each day for the Plenum – as her mother had done.

The commission voted on their fate. Many of Stalin's devotees such as Khrushchev wanted a trial but 'without application of the death penalty'. Yezhov, Budyonny and Postyshev, himself already under fire, voted for death. Molotov and Voroshilov slavishly supported 'the suggestion of Comrade Stalin' which was enigmatic because his vote originally suggested 'exile' but then was changed by hand to 'Transfer their case to NKVD'.

Bukharin and Rykov were summoned. Both faced the anguished panic and sad regrets of last goodbyes. Rykov asked his daughter to phone Poskrebyshev to find out his fate.

'When I need him,' replied Poskrebyshev, 'I'll send a car.' At dusk, this usher of doom called: 'I'm sending the car.' Natalya helped her beloved father dress in suit, tie, waistcoat and overcoat. He said nothing as they took the lift downstairs, walking out on to the Embankment. When they looked towards the Kremlin, they saw the black limousine. Father and daughter turned to one another on the pavement. They awkwardly shook hands then they kissed formally *à la russe*, three times on the cheek. Without a word, 'my father climbed into the car that sped off towards the Kremlin'. Natalya never forgot that moment: 'And I never saw him again – except in my dreams.'

When Poskrebyshev called Bukharin, Anna 'began to say farewell', in that heart-rending moment of eternal parting, which was to be shared by millions in the coming years. Poskrebyshev called again: the Plenum was waiting but Bukharin was in no hurry. He fell to his knees before his young Anna: 'With tears in his eyes, he begged forgiveness for my ruined life. But he begged me to raise our son as a Bolshevik – "A Bolshevik without fail," he said twice.' He swore her to deliver the memorized letter to the Party: 'You're young and you'll live to see it.' He then rose from the floor, hugged her, kissed her and said, 'See you don't get angry, Anyutka. There are irritating misprints in history but the truth will triumph.'

'We understood,' Anna wrote, 'we were parting for ever.' She could only say, 'See that you don't lie about yourself, but this was much to ask.' Pulling on his leather coat, he disappeared into the alleyways around the Great Kremlin Palace.

Moments later, Boris Berman, a fat, flashy old-fashioned Chekist in 'a stylish suit' with big rings on his fingers and one elongated fingernail, arrived with the NKVD to search the apartment. Meanwhile, at the Plenum, Stalin proposed that they be 'handed over to the NKVD'.

'Does anyone wish to speak?' Andreyev asked. 'No. Are there any other proposals besides the one made by Comrade Stalin? No. Let's vote ... All those against? None. Any abstentions? Two. So the resolution carries with two abstentions – Bukharin and Rykov.' The two, who had once ruled Russia alongside Stalin, were arrested as they left the Plenum. Bukharin took that one step that was like falling a thousand miles: one minute, he was living in the Kremlin, with cars, dachas and servants. The next minute, he was passing through the gates of the Lubianka, handing over his possessions, being stripped, having his rectum checked, his clothes returned though without belt or shoelaces, and then being locked in a cell with the usual stool pigeon to provoke him. But Bukharin was not tortured.

Bukharin's Anna and Rykov's half-paralysed wife and daughter Natalya were arrested soon afterwards, serving almost two decades of slave-labour.*

This ugly meeting dealt other blows too: Yezhov attacked Yagoda. Molotov, giving Sergo's report, cited 585 wreckers in Heavy Industry; Kaganovich ranted about the 'unmasking' of Enemies on the railways.

Stalin used the 'heroic denunciatrix' of Kiev, Polia Nikolaenko, against the Ukrainian potentate, Postyshev. Stalin hailed her as a 'simple member of the Party' treated by Postyshev like 'an annoying fly ... Sometimes the simple people are much closer to the truth than certain higher examples.' Postyshev was moved to another job, not arrested. The warning was clear: no Politburo 'Prince' and his 'family group' were safe. 'We old members of the Politburo, we're soon leaving the scene,' Stalin explained ominously. 'It's the law of nature. We would like to have some teams of replacements.'

Stalin, politician and man, was brilliantly equipped for the constant intensification of struggle which he formulated into his creed of Terror: 'The further we move forward, the more success we have, the more embittered will the remnants of the destroyed

---

* Natalya Rykova survived fifteen years of slave labour on the White Sea because 'of the beauty of nature that I saw every day in the forests and the kindness of people for there were more kind people than bad people'. The author thanks Natalya Rykova, aged eighty-five, indomitable and alive today in Moscow, who generously told her story without bitterness, but with tears running down her cheeks. Anna Larina was parted from her and Bukharin's baby son. But she too survived and wrote her memoirs.

exploiter classes become, the sooner they will resort to extreme forms of struggle.'

* * *

Blackberry set about converting the NKVD into a 'secret sect' of sacred executioners. Yezhov despatched Yagoda's officers to inspect the provinces and then arrested them on the train. Three thousand Chekists were to be executed. Security chief Pauker and Stalin's brother-in-law Redens remained in their posts. Between 19 and 21 March, Yezhov summoned the surviving Chekists to the Officers' Club. There, the diminutive Commissar-General announced that Yagoda had been a German spy since 1907 (when he joined the Party) and was also a corrupt thief. Yezhov referred absurdly to his own tininess: 'I may be small in stature but my hands are strong – Stalin's hands.' The killing would be deliberately random: 'There will be some innocent victims in this fight against Fascist agents,' Yezhov told them. 'We are launching a major attack on the Enemy; let there be no resentment if we bump someone with an elbow. Better that ten innocent people should suffer than one spy get away. When you chop wood, chips fly.'

19

The Massacre of Generals, Fall
of Yagoda, and Death of a Mother

Yezhov 'discovered' that Yagoda had tried to poison him by spraying mercury on to the curtains of his office. It later emerged that Yezhov had faked this outrage. None the less, Yagoda was arrested at his Kremlin apartment, even before the Politburo had formally given the order. The power of the Politburo was officially delegated to the so-called 'Five', Stalin, Molotov, Voroshilov, Kaganovich and Yezhov, even though the latter was not a member.

The search of Yagoda's residences – he had two apartments in central Moscow and the luxurious dacha – revealed the debauchery of NKVD élite in the list of his possessions. His pornographic collection contained 3,904 photographs plus eleven early pornographic movies. His career as a womanizer was amply illustrated by the female clothing he kept in his apartment which sounds as if he was running a lingerie store not a police force, but then the NKVD bosses could never resist exploiting their power. There were 9 foreign female coats, 4 squirrel coats, 3 sealskin cloaks, another in Astrakhan wool, 31 pairs of female shoes, 91 female berets, 22 female hats, 130 pairs of foreign silk stockings, 10 female belts, 13 bags, 11 female suits, 57 blouses, 69 nighties, 31 female jackets, another 70 pairs of silk tights, 4 silk shawls – plus a collection of 165 pornographic pipes and cigarette holders, and one rubber dildo.

Finally there was the macabre fetishism of the two labelled bullets that had been extracted from the brains of Zinoviev and Kamenev. Like holy relics in a depraved distortion of the apostolic succession, Yezhov inherited them, storing them in his office.

Yagoda, accused of diamond-dealing and corruption, complaisantly implicated the next generation of victims, guided by Yezhov, who ensured that his own protégés were left out, before the testimonies were sent over to Stalin. Within three weeks of his interrogation, starting on 2 April, Yezhov was reporting that Yagoda admitted encouraging Rykov to resist the

Party in the late twenties: 'You act. I won't touch you.' Then he denounced Pauker and confessed to the sprinkling of mercury around Blackberry's office. More importantly, Yagoda implicated Abel Yenukidze for planning a coup along with Marshal Tukhachevsky, Stalin's old enemy from the Civil War. By the time of his trial, along with Bukharin and Rykov, Yagoda had confessed to the medical murders of Gorky and his son and to the assassination of Kirov.

In his private hell, he knew his family and friends faced destruction with him: the rule in Stalin's world was that when a man fell, all those connected to him, whether friends, lovers or protégés, fell with him. His brother-in-law and father-in-law were soon shot, along with his salon of writers. Yagoda's sister and parents were exiled. Yagoda's father wrote to Stalin, disowning 'our only surviving son' for his 'grave crimes'. Two sons had given their lives for Bolshevism in earlier times. Now the 78-year-old jeweller of Nizhny Novgorod was losing the third. Both Yagoda's parents died in the camps.

Yagoda seemed to undergo a Damascene conversion. 'For the first time in my life, I'll have to tell the whole truth about myself,' the world-weary Chekist sighed as if it was a relief. Vladimir Kirshon, the writer whom Stalin had advised on his plays and who was to be shot soon afterwards, was placed as the stool pigeon in his cell. Yagoda asked what the town was saying about him, musing sadly:

'I simply want to ask you about Ida [his wife] and Timosha [his mistress, Gorky's daughter-in-law], the baby, my family, and to see some familiar faces before death.' He talked about death. 'If I was sure to be allowed to live, I'd bear the burden of admitting murdering' Gorky and his son. 'But it's intolerably hard to declare it historically in front of all, especially Timosha.' Yagoda told his interrogator, 'You can put down in your report to Yezhov that I said there must be a God after all. From Stalin I deserved nothing but gratitude for my faithful service; from God, I deserved the most severe punishment for having violated his commandments thousands of times. Now look where I am and judge for yourself: is there a God or not?'

Yagoda's belladonna bore fatal fruit: the Hungarian hairdresser and favourite of Kremlin children, Pauker, forty-four, was arrested on 15 April, guilty of knowing too much and living too well: Stalin no longer trusted the old-fashioned Chekists with foreign connections.

Pauker was shot quietly on 14 August 1937 – the first courtier to die. Yenukidze was arrested too and executed on 20 December. The NKVD now belonged to Stalin, who turned to the army.

* * *

On the evening of 1 May 1937, after the May Day Parade, there was the usual party at Voroshilov's but the mood was effervescent with blood-lust and tension. Budyonny* recorded how Stalin talked openly about the imminent slaughter with his inner circle: it was time, he said, 'to finish with our enemies because they are in the army, in the staff, even in the Kremlin'. It is often claimed, that Stalin planned the Terror alone with Yezhov and Molotov: this proves that, even socially, he was open with his entire circle, from his doctors to the Politburo, that they were about to 'finish with' their enemies across the whole regime. 'We must finish with them, not looking at their faces.' Budyonny guessed that this meant Marshal Tukhachevsky and senior commanders like Jonah Yakir and Jan Garmarnik, all of whom had been standing on the Mausoleum with them earlier that day. Budyonny claimed that he hoped this was not so. Yet the archives show how Voroshilov and Budyonny had been urging Stalin to 'destroy' Enemies within the Red Army for over a year. It is most likely that Voroshilov's guests not only backed Stalin but wildly encouraged him: a year earlier, Voroshilov, for example, sent Stalin an intelligence intercept of the German Embassy's reports to Berlin on how Tukhachevsky had suddenly ceased to be a 'Francophile' and now displayed 'big respect for the German Army'.

Tukhachevsky, Stalin's Civil War foe and probably his most talented general, was bound to be his main target. That 'refined nobleman, handsome, clever and able', as Kaganovich described him, did not suffer fools gladly which was why he was hated by Voroshilov and Budyonny. The dashing womanizer was so forceful and charismatic that Stalin nicknamed him 'Napoleonchik', while Kaganovich paraphrased Bonaparte's dictum: 'Tukhachevsky hid Napoleon's baton in his rucksack.'

He was as ruthless as any Bolshevik, using poison gas on peasant rebels. In the late twenties and early thirties, this 'entrepreneur of military ideas', as a recent historian calls him,

---

* Semyon Budyonny published his conventional, cautious memoirs long after Stalin's death but his personal notes, seventy-six mainly unpublished pages preserved by his daughter, provide fascinating glimpses of the time. I am grateful to Nina Budyonny for allowing me to use them.

advocated a huge expansion of the Red Army and the creation of mechanized forces to be deployed in so-called 'deep operations': he understood the era of Panzers and air power which brought him into conflict with Stalin's cronies, still living for cavalry charges and armoured trains. Stalin tried to indict Tukhachevsky for treason in 1930 but Sergo among others resisted and helped bring him back as Deputy Defence Commissar. But there was another row with the touchy, vindictive Voroshilov in May 1936. Voroshilov became so heated with Tukhachevsky's justified criticism that he shouted 'Fuck you!' They made up but it was just at that time that the first of the Red Army generals was arrested and interrogated to implicate Tukhachevsky. More generals were mentioned in the January trial. Yagoda, Yenukidze and the benighted generals delivered more kindling for this bonfire.

On 11 May, Tukhachevsky was sacked as Deputy Commissar and demoted to the Volga District. On the 13th, Stalin put his hand on Tukhachevsky's shoulder and promised he would soon be back in Moscow. He was as good as his word, for on the 22nd, Tukhachevsky was arrested and returned to Moscow. Yezhov and Voroshilov orchestrated the arrest of virtually the whole high command.

Yezhov took personal control of the interrogations. At a meeting with Stalin, Vyshinsky curried favour by recommending the use of torture.

'See for yourself,' Stalin ordered his Blackberry, who rushed back to the Lubianka to supervise the Marshal's agonies, 'but Tukhachevsky should be forced to tell everything ... It's impossible he acted alone.' Tukhachevsky was tortured.

Amidst this drama, Stalin's mother died on 13 May 1937, aged seventy-seven. Three professors and two doctors signed her death certificate, testifying to her cardiosclerosis. Poskrebyshev approved the official announcements.* Stalin himself wrote out his note for her wreath in Georgian, which read: 'Dear and beloved mother from her son Joseph Djugashvili', using his original name perhaps to signify the distance between Soso and Stalin. Embroiled in the Tukhachevsky plot, he did not attend the funeral: Beria, his wife and son Sergo presided in his stead but later Stalin asked about it as if guilty about not being there.

---

* Her apartment contained busts of Stalin and portraits of Lenin and Stalin. She owned 505 roubles in bonds but left 42 roubles and 20 kopeks in cash and 4,533 roubles to her lady friends plus lottery tickets worth 3 roubles. In her bedroom, there were a few packs of cigarettes, and more portraits of Stalin and, tellingly, Beria.

A few days later, as Yezhov buzzed in and out of Stalin's office, a broken Marshal Tukhachevsky confessed that Yenukidze had recruited him in 1928, that he was a German agent in cahoots with Bukharin to seize power. Tukhachevsky's confession, which survives in the archives, is dappled with a brown spray that was found to be blood spattered by a body in motion.

Stalin had to convince the Politburo of the soldiers' guilt. Yakir, one of the arrested commanders, was best friends with Kaganovich who was called into the Politburo and interrogated by Stalin about this friendship. Kaganovich reminded Stalin that it was he who had insisted on promoting Yakir, at which the *Vozhd* muttered, 'Right, I remember … The matter's closed.' Faced with the amazing confessions beaten out of the generals, Kaganovich believed 'that there was a conspiracy of officers'. Mikoyan too was friends with many arrested. Stalin read him extracts from Uborevich's confessions as a German spy:

'It's incredible,' admitted Stalin, 'but it's a fact, they admit it.' They even signed on each page to avoid 'falsification'.

'I know Uborevich very well,' said Mikoyan. 'A most honest man.' So Stalin reassured him that the military themselves would judge the generals: 'They know the case and they'll figure out what's true and what's not.'

Stalin tossed Deputy Premier Rudzutak into this broth perhaps *pour encourager les autres*, the first of the Politburo (a candidate member) to be arrested. 'He indulged too much in partying with Philistine friends,' recalled Molotov, which in Bolshevik doublespeak meant cultured friends. Becoming something of a bon viveur, 'he kept his distance from us'. Typical of Stalin's allies in the twenties, he was unreliable, even accusing Stalin of slandering him just after Kirov's assassination. 'You're wrong, Rudzutak,' Stalin had replied. He was arrested at dinner with some actors – it was said that the ladies were still wearing the rags of their ball gowns in the Lubianka weeks later. 'He was entangled … mixed up with devil knows what kind of people, with women …' said Molotov, and, added Kaganovich, 'young girls'. Perhaps he was shot for conviviality. Yet Molotov explained, 'I think consciously he was not a participant [in a conspiracy]', but he was guilty none the less: 'One must not act on personal impressions. After all we had materials incriminating him.' The NKVD now began to arrest many of the Old Bolsheviks, especially those obstinate Georgian 'old farts' who had crossed Stalin.

At first the leadership were actually canvassed on arrests, according to Party tradition: the signed votes in the archives capture the vile frenzy of this process. Usually the leaders just voted 'For' or 'Agreed' but sometimes in their desperation to show their bloodthirstiness, they added rabid exclamations:* 'Unconditionally yes,' wrote Budyonny on the arrests of Tukhachevsky and Rudzutak. 'It's necessary to finish off this scum.' Marshal Yegorov, whose actress wife (Stalin's flirtation at that dinner in November 1932) was already under investigation, wrote: 'All these traitors to be wiped off the face of the earth as the most hostile enemies and disgusting scum.'

On 1 June, Stalin, Voroshilov and Yezhov gathered over a hundred commanders in the Kremlin and broke the news that their high command overwhelmingly consisted of German agents. Voroshilov unveiled this 'counter-revolutionary conspiracy fascist organization', admitting he himself was close to the conspirators. He was guilty of not wanting to believe it! The next day, Stalin spoke, conjuring a miasma of mystery over the terrified meeting:

'I hope no one doubts that a military–political conspiracy existed,' he threatened, explaining that Tukhachevsky had been suborned by Trotsky, Bukharin, Rykov, Yenukidze, Yagoda and Rudzutak. As in any good spy novel, Stalin sought to *chercher la femme*, playing on Tukhachevsky and Yenukidze's womanizing. 'There's one experienced female spy in Germany, in Berlin … Josephine Heinze … she's a beautiful woman … She recruited Yenukidze. She helped recruit Tukhachevsky.' Officers were actually arrested during the meeting so it was hardly surprising the survivors supported Stalin.

Voroshilov revelled in his vengeance. 'I never trusted Tukhachevsky, I never particularly trusted Uborevich … They were scoundrels …' he declared to the Defence Commissariat, embroidering Stalin's tale of sexual depravity. 'Comrades,' he said, 'we have not purged everyone yet. I personally don't doubt there are people who thought they were only talking, that's all. They chattered: "It would be a good thing to kill Stalin and Voroshilov"

---

* Sometimes they realized they had not been vicious enough, hence Veinberg wrote: 'Today when I voted for the expulsion of Rudzutak and Tukhachevsky from the Central Committee, I remembered that in voting for the expulsion of … Eliava and Orakhelashvili, I accidentally forgot to add the words "and removal of their files to the NKVD" so I inform you I'm voting for the expulsion of all these traitors but also the removal of their files to the NKVD.'

... Our government will exterminate such people.'

'Right,' shouted his applauding audience.

'They were degenerates,' said Voroshilov. 'Filthy in their private lives!'

On 9 June, Vyshinsky interviewed the accused and reported to Stalin twice, arriving at the Little Corner at 10.45 p.m. The Politburo reviewed the officers' appeals, passing them round the table. On Yakir's plea, Stalin wrote:

'A scoundrel and a prostitute.'

'A completely precise description,' Voroshilov slavishly added. Molotov signed but Yakir's best friend, Kaganovich, almost had to dance on his grave:

'For this traitor, bastard and s—t, there is only one punishment – execution.'

On the 11th, the Supreme Court convened a special military tribunal to try the 'traitors'. The reptilian Ulrikh represented the Military Collegium but the key judges were the Marshals themselves. Budyonny was one of the most active, accusing them of 'wrecking' by urging the formation of armoured divisions.

'I feel I'm dreaming,' Tukhachevsky remarked of the accusations. There was no mention of Josephine, the gorgeous German spy. Ominously, many of the generals were accused of serving a 'second Motherland', Yakir being a Bessarabian Jew. Most of the judges were terrified: 'Tomorrow I'll be put in the same place,' one of them, Corps Commander Belov, told his friends afterwards. (He was right.) All were sentenced to death at 23.35 that day. Ulrikh rushed over to report to Stalin who, waiting with Molotov, Kaganovich and Yezhov, did not examine the sentences. He just said: 'Agreed.' Yezhov returned with Ulrikh to supervise the executions which took place within the hour early on the morning of 12 June. As ever, Stalin was sadistically curious.

'What were Tukhachevsky's last words?' Stalin asked Yezhov.

'The snake said he was dedicated to the Motherland and Comrade Stalin. He asked for clemency. But it was obvious he was not being straight, he hadn't laid down his arms.'

All the judges were later shot except Ulrikh, Budyonny and Shaposhnikov. If Budyonny had any doubts about supporting the Terror, the NKVD arrived to arrest him soon after the trial. He pulled out a pistol and threatened to kill the Chekists while he telephoned Stalin who cancelled the arrest. His wife was not so fortunate.

Voroshilov unleashed a massive purge of the army, personally demanding the arrests of three hundred officers in letters to the NKVD:* by 29 November 1938, Voroshilov boasted that 40,000 had been arrested and 100,000 new officers promoted. Three of the five marshals, fifteen of the sixteen commanders, sixty of the sixty-seven corps commanders, and all seventeen commissars were shot. Stalin earnestly encouraged the witchhunt at informal meetings with officers:

'We don't know up to now whether we can speak openly about Enemies of the People or not ...' naval commander Laukhin asked.

'To speak in public?' responded Stalin.

'No, here, internally?'

'We must – it's obligatory!' answered Stalin. The commanders discussed individual officers:

'Gorbatov is now worried,' reported Kulikov, a divisional commander in Ukraine.

'Why should he worry,' replied Stalin, 'if he is an honest man?'

'I wouldn't say he is pure. He was clearly connected,' said Kulikov.

'Is he scared?' asked Stalin.

The army had been the last force capable of stopping Stalin, reason enough for the destruction of its High Command. It is possible that the generals knew about Stalin's record as an Okhrana double agent and had considered action. The usual explanation is that German disinformation persuaded Stalin that they were plotting a coup. Hitler's spymaster, Heydrich, had concocted such evidence that was passed to Stalin by the well-meaning Czech President Beneš. But no German evidence was used at Tukhachevsky's trial – nor was it necessary. Stalin needed neither Nazi disinformation nor mysterious Okhrana files to persuade him to destroy Tukhachevsky. After all, he had played with the idea as early as 1930, three years before Hitler took power. Furthermore, Stalin and his cronies were convinced that officers were to be distrusted and physically exterminated at the slightest suspicion. He reminisced to Voroshilov, in an undated note, about the officers arrested in the summer of 1918. 'These

---

* A typically sinister note from Voroshilov to Yezhov read like this: 'N(ikolai) I(vanovich)! Nikolayev inquired whether Uritsky should be arrested. When can you take him in? You've already managed to take in Slavin and Bazenkov. It would be good if you could take in Todorovsky ... KV.' All named, except Todorovsky, were shot.

officers', he wrote, 'we wanted to shoot en masse.' Nothing had changed.

Voroshilov was assisted in this slaughter by one man who personified the tragedy that was to befall the Red Army. Stalin and Yezhov planned the publicity with the editor of *Pravda*, Lev Mekhlis, one of the most extraordinary of all his courtiers who now exploded on to the national stage, transformed from the scourge of the media to a military Mephistopheles, compared to a 'shark' and a 'gloomy demon'. Even Stalin called him a 'fanatic', found him hard to restrain, and enjoyed telling stories of his 'ludicrous zeal'.

With a nimbus-like plumage of black hair and a pointed, bird-like face, Mekhlis played a part as large in his way as Molotov or Beria. Born in Odessa in 1889 of Jewish parents, leaving school at fourteen, he only joined the Bolsheviks in 1918 after working with the Jewish Social Democratic Party but he served as a ruthless commissar in the Crimea during the Civil War, executing thousands. He first met Stalin during the Polish campaign, becoming one of his assistants, learning all the secrets. Devoted to 'my dear Comrade Stalin', for whom he worked in a neurotic, blood-curdling frenzy, he was too energetic and talented to remain hidden in the back rooms like Poskrebyshev. Married to a Jewish doctor, he placed Lenin's portrait with a red ribbon in his baby's cot and recorded the reactions of this New Man in a special diary. In 1930, Stalin appointed him *Pravda* editor where his management of writers was impressively brutal.*

---

* Just after the announcement of the shooting of the generals, Mekhlis discovered that the 'Proletarian Poet' Demian Bedny was resisting orders and secretly writing Dantean verses under the pseudonym Conrad Rotkehempfer. But Mekhlis immediately wrote to Stalin: 'What should I do? He explained it was his own literary method.' Stalin replied with dripping sarcasm: 'I'm answering with a letter you can read to Demian. To the new apparent Dante, alias Conrad, oh actually to Demian Bedny, the fable or poem 'Fight or Die' is mediocre. As a criticism of Fascism, it's unoriginal and faded. As a criticism of Soviet construction (not joking) it's silly but transparent. It's junk but since we [Soviet people] have a lot of junk around, we must increase the supply of other kinds of literature with another fable ... I understand that I must say sorry to Demian-Dante for my frankness.' Mekhlis locked Stalin's letters in his safe whence he extracted them to impress journalists whom he asked if they recognized the handwriting. 'In the middle of the night of 21 July,' he reported urgently to Stalin, 'I invited Bedny to criticize his poem' and to hear Stalin's damning letter. Bedny just said, 'I'm crazy ... maybe I'm too old. Maybe I should go to the country and grow cabbages.' Even this comment struck Mekhlis as suspicious and he floated the idea of arresting Bedny: 'Maybe he's implicated.' Stalin did not rise. Bedny was cut from Stalin's circle but remained free, dying in 1945.

Mekhlis, who left the Tsarist army as a bombardier, was now promoted to Deputy Defence Commissar, Head of its Political Department, descending on the army like a galloping horse of the Apocalypse. Stalin and his Five now devised an astonishing lottery of slaughter designed to kill a whole generation.

20

Blood Bath by Numbers

They did not even specify the names but simply assigned quotas of deaths by the thousands. On 2 July 1937, the Politburo ordered local Secretaries to arrest and shoot 'the most hostile anti-Soviet elements' who were to be sentenced by *troikas*, three-man tribunals that usually included the local Party Secretary, Procurator and NKVD chief.

The aim was 'to finish off once and for all' all Enemies and those impossible to educate in socialism, so as to accelerate the erasing of class barriers and therefore the bringing of paradise for the masses. This final solution was a slaughter that made sense in terms of the faith and idealism of Bolshevism which was a religion based on the systematic destruction of classes. The principle of ordering murder like industrial quotas in the Five-Year Plan was therefore natural. The details did not matter: if Hitler's destruction of the Jews was genocide, then this was democide, the class struggle spinning into cannibalism. On 30 July, Yezhov and his deputy Mikhail Frinovsky proposed Order No. 00447 to the Politburo: that between 5 and 15 August, the regions were to receive quotas for two categories: Category One – to be shot. Category Two – to be deported. They suggested that 72,950 should be shot and 259,450 arrested, though they missed some regions. The regions could submit further lists. The families of these people should be deported too. The Politburo confirmed this order the next day.

Soon this 'meat-grinder' achieved such a momentum, as the witch hunt approached its peak and as the local jealousies and ambitions spurred it on, that more and more were fed into the machine. The quotas were soon fulfilled by the regions who therefore asked for bigger numbers, so between 28 August and 15 December, the Politburo agreed to the shooting of another 22,500 and then another 48,000. In this, the Terror differed most from Hitler's crimes which systematically destroyed a limited target:

Jews and Gypsies. Here, on the contrary, death was sometimes random: the long-forgotten comment, the flirtation with an opposition, envy of another man's job, wife or house, vengeance or just plain coincidence brought the death and torture of entire families. This did not matter: 'Better too far than not far enough,' Yezhov told his men as the original arrest quota ballooned to 767,397 arrests and 386,798 executions, families destroyed, children orphaned, under Order No. 00447.*

Simultaneously, Yezhov attacked 'national contingents' – this was murder by nationality, against Poles and ethnic Germans among others. On 11 August, Yezhov signed Order No. 00485 to liquidate 'Polish diversionists and espionage groups' which was to consume most of the Polish Communist Party, most Poles within the Bolshevik leadership, anyone with social or 'consular contacts' – and of course their wives and children. A total of 350,000 (144,000 of them Poles) were arrested in this operation, with 247,157 shot (110,000 Poles) – a mini-genocide. As we will see, this hit Stalin's own circle with especial force.† Altogether, the latest estimates, combining the quotas and national contingents, are that 1.5 million were arrested in these operations and about 700,000 shot.

'Beat, destroy without sorting out,' Yezhov ordered his henchmen. Those who showed 'operational inertness' in the arrests of 'counter-revolutionary formations within and outside the Party ... Poles, Germans and kulaks' would themselves be destroyed, but most now 'tried to surpass each other with reports about gigantic numbers of people arrested'. Yezhov, clearly taking his cue from the 'Five', actually specified that 'if during this operation, an extra

* There has been a debate between those such as Robert Conquest who insisted that Stalin himself initiated and ran the Terror, and the so-called Revisionists who argued that the Terror was created by pressure from ambitious young bureaucrats and by the tensions between centre and regions. The archives have now proved Conquest right, though it is true that the regions outperformed their quotas, showing that the Revisionists were right, too, though missing the complete picture. The two views therefore are completely complementary.

† 170,000 Koreans were also deported. Bulgarians and Macedonians were soon added. Stalin was delighted by the Polish operation, writing on Yezhov's report: 'Very good! Dig up and purge this Polish espionage mud in the future as well. Destroy it in the interest of the USSR!' If Poles and Germans took the brunt of this operation, other nations deported included Kurds, Greeks, Finns, Estonians, Iranians, Latvians, Chinese, returnees from the Harbin railway and Romanians. Most exotically the NKVD shot 6,311 priests, lords and Communist officials, about 4 per cent of the population in the satellite state of Mongolia where the Mongoloid parody of Stalin, Marshal Choibalsang, also arrested and shot his own Tukhachevsky, Marshal Demid.

thousand people will be shot, that is not such a big deal.' Since Stalin and Yezhov constantly pushed up the quotas, an extra thousand here and there was inevitable but the point was that they deliberately destroyed an entire 'caste'. And, like Hitler's Holocaust, this was a colossal feat of management. Yezhov even specified what bushes should be planted to cover mass graves.

Once this massacre had started, Stalin almost disappeared from public view, appearing only to greet children and delegations. The rumour spread that he did not know what Yezhov was doing. Stalin spoke in public only twice in 1937 and once in 1938, cancelling all his holidays (he did not go southwards again until 1945). Molotov gave the 6 November addresses in both years. The writer Ilya Ehrenburg met Pasternak in the street: 'he waved his arms around as he stood between the snowdrifts: "If only someone would tell Stalin about it." ' The theatrical director Meyerhold told Ehrenburg, 'They conceal it from Stalin'. But their friend, Isaac Babel, lover of Yezhov's wife, learned the 'key to the puzzle': 'Of course Yezhov plays his part but he's not at the bottom of it.'

Stalin was the mastermind but he was far from alone. Indeed, it is neither accurate nor helpful to blame the Terror on one man because systematic murder started soon after Lenin took power in 1917 and never stopped until Stalin's death. This 'social system based on blood-letting', justified murder now with the prospect of happiness later. The Terror was not just a consequence of Stalin's monstrosity but it was certainly formed, expanded and accelerated by his uniquely overpowering character, reflecting his malice and vindictiveness. 'The greatest delight,' he told Kamenev, 'is to mark one's enemy, prepare everything, avenge oneself thoroughly and then go to sleep.' It would not have happened without Stalin. Yet it also reflected the village hatreds of the incestuous Bolshevik sect where jealousies had seethed from the years of exile and war. Stalin and his faction regarded the Civil War as their finest hour: 1937 was a Tsaritsyn reunion, as Stalin even reminisced to a group of officers:

'We were in Tsaritsyn with Voroshilov,' he began. 'We exposed [Enemies] within a week, even though we didn't know military affairs. We exposed them because we judged them by their work and if today's political workers judge men by their actual work, we would soon expose the Enemies in our army.' The anti-Bolshevik resurgence in Germany was real enough, the Spanish war setting new standards for betrayal and brutality. Economic disasters were glaring: Molotov's papers reveal there was still famine and cannibalism,* even in 1937.

The corruption of grandees was notorious: Yagoda seemed to be running palaces and diamond deals out of official funds, Yakir renting out dachas like a landlord. The wives of marshals, such as Olga Budyonny and her friend Galina Yegorova, Stalin's fancy at Nadya's last supper, blossomed at embassies and 'salons, reminiscent of glittering receptions ... in aristocratic Russia' with 'dazzling company, stylish clothes'.

'Why have the prices flown upwards 100% while nothing is in the shops,' Maria Svanidze asked her diary. 'Where is the cotton, flax and wool when medals were won for beating the Plan? And the construction of private dachas ... crazy money spent on magnificent houses and resthomes?'

The responsibility lies with the hundreds of thousands of officials who ordered, or perpetrated, the murders. Stalin and the magnates enthusiastically, recklessly, almost joyfully, killed, and they usually killed many more than they were asked to kill. None was ever tried for these crimes.

Stalin was surprisingly open with his circle about the aim to 'finish off' all their Enemies. He could tell his cronies this quite openly at Voroshilov's May Day party, as reported by Budyonny. He seems to have constantly compared his Terror to Ivan the Terrible's massacre of the *boyars*. 'Who's going to remember all this riffraff in ten or twenty years time? No one. Who remembers the names now of the *boyars* Ivan the Terrible got rid of?† No one ... The people had to know he was getting rid of all of his enemies. In the end, they all got what they deserved.'

'The people understand, Joseph Vissarionovich, they understand and they support you,' replied Molotov. Similarly, he told Mikoyan, 'Ivan killed too few *boyars*. He should have killed them all, to create a strong state.' The magnates were not as oblivious of Stalin's nature as they later claimed.

---

* On 14 April 1937, Procurator-General Vyshinsky wrote to the Premier to inform him of a cluster of cases of cannibalism in Cheliabinsk in the Urals in which one woman ate a four-month-old child, another ate an eight-year-old with her thirteen-year-old, while yet another consumed her three-month-old baby.
† This is eerily like Hitler's comment on the genocide of the Jews, referring to the Turkish slaughter of the Armenians in 1915: 'After all, who today speaks of the massacre of the Armenians?'

While the regions fulfilled their nameless quotas, Stalin was also killing thousands whom he knew well. Yezhov visited Stalin virtually every day. Within a year and a half, 5 of the 15 Politburo members, 98 of the 139 Central Committee members and 1,108 of the 1,966 delegates from the Seventeenth Congress had been arrested. Yezhov delivered 383 lists of names – which were known as 'albums' since they often contained photographs and potted biographies of the suggested victims – and proposed: 'I request sanction to condemn them all under the First Category.'

Most of the death-lists were signed by Stalin, Molotov, Kaganovich and Voroshilov but many were also signed by Zhdanov and Mikoyan. On some days, for example 12 November 1938, Stalin and Molotov signed 3,167 executions. Usually they simply wrote: 'For', VMN or *Viskha*. Molotov admitted: 'I signed most – in fact almost all – the arrest lists. We debated and made a decision. Haste ruled the day. Could one go into all the details? ... Innocent people were sometimes caught. Obviously one or two out of ten were wrongly caught, but the rest rightly.' As Stalin had put it, 'Better an innocent head less, than hesitations in the war.' They ordered the deaths of 39,000 on these lists of names. Stalin marked lists with notes to Yezhov: 'Comrade Yezhov, those whose names I've marked "arr" should be arrested if not already.' Sometimes Stalin simply wrote: 'Shoot all 138 of them.' When Molotov received regional death-lists, he simply underlined the numbers, never the names. Kaganovich remembered the frenzy of that time: 'What emotions.' They were 'all responsible' and perhaps 'guilty of going too far'.

Stalin declared that the son should not suffer for the sins of the father but then carefully targeted the families of Enemies: this may have reflected his Caucasian mentality or merely the incestuous labyrinth of Bolshevik connections. 'They had to be isolated,' explained Molotov, 'otherwise they'd have spread all kinds of complaints.' On 5 July 1937, the Politburo ordered the NKVD to 'confine all wives of condemned traitors ... in camps for 5–8 years' and to take under State protection children under fifteen: 18,000 wives and 25,000 children were taken away. But this was not enough: on 15 August, Yezhov decreed that children between one and three were to be confined in orphanages but 'socially dangerous' children between three and fifteen could be imprisoned 'depending on the degree of danger'. Almost a million of these children were raised in orphanages and often did not see their mothers for twenty years.*

Stalin was the engine of this murderous machine. 'Now everything will be fine,' he wrote on 7 May 1937 to one of his killers who complained that he had not 'lost his teeth' but had become somewhat dazed: 'The sharper the teeth the better. J.St.' This is just one of the many notes in the newly opened archives that show not merely Stalin's bureaucratic orders but his personal involvement in encouraging even junior officials to slaughter their comrades. The teeth were never sharp enough.

While all the leaders could save some of their friends – and not others – Stalin himself could protect whoever he wished: his whims only added to his mystique. When his old friend from Georgia, Sergo Kavtaradze, was arrested, Stalin did not approve his death but put a dash next to Kavtaradze's name. This tiny crayon line saved his life. Another old friend, Ambassador Troyanovsky, appeared on a list: 'Do not touch,' wrote Stalin.† However much someone was denounced, Stalin's favour could be well nigh impregnable but once his trust was shattered, damnation was final though it might take years to come. The best way to survive was to be invisible because sometimes ghastly coincidences brought people into fatal contact with Stalin: Polish Communist Kostyrzewa was tending her roses near Kuntsevo when she found Stalin looking over her fence: 'What beautiful roses,' he said. She was arrested that night – though this was at the time of the anti-Polish spy mania and perhaps she was on the lists anyway.

Stalin often forgot – or pretended to forget – what had happened to certain comrades and years later assumed an air of disappointment when he heard they had been shot. 'You used to have such nice people,' he later remarked to Polish comrades. 'Vera Kostyrzewa for example, do you know what's become of her?' Even his remarkable Rolodex of a memory could not remember all his victims.

---

* This reached its climax when sixty children aged between ten and twelve were accused of forming 'a terrorist counter-revolutionary group' in Leninsk-Kuznetsk and were imprisoned for eight months, until the NKVD themselves were arrested and the children released.

† Stalin's papers contain fascinating glimpses of his interventions: a father denounced his son to the police for having too many outrageous parties but the boy was arrested and embroiled in a case against Tomsky. The father appealed to Stalin who wrote on his note: 'It's necessary to change the punishment!' The father wrote to thank Stalin.

Stalin enjoyed rattling his colleagues: one such was Stetsky, formerly in Bukharin's kindergarten of young protégés who had successfully joined Stalin's CC Cultural Department. Now Bukharin, at one of his 'confrontations' with his accusers, gave Stalin an old letter Stetsky had written criticizing him: 'Comrade Bukharin,' Stalin wrote to Stetsky, 'gave me your letter to him [from 1926–7] with the hint that everything about Stetsky is not always clean. I have not read the letter. I'm giving it back to you. With Communist greetings, Stalin.' Imagine Stetsky's terror on receiving this handwritten note. He wrote back immediately:

'Comrade Stalin, I've received your letter and thank you for your trust. On my letter ... written when I was not clean ... I belonged to the Bukharin group. Now I'm ashamed to remember it ...' He was arrested and shot.

Stalin played games even with his closest comrades: Budyonny, for example, had performed well at the trial but when the arrests reached his own staff, he went to Voroshilov to complain with a list of innocent men under investigation. Voroshilov was terrified: 'Speak to Stalin yourself.' Budyonny confronted Stalin:

'If these are the Enemy, who made the Revolution? It means we must be jailed too!'

'What are you saying, Semyon Mikhailovich?' Stalin laughed. 'Are you crazy?' He called in Yezhov: 'Budyonny here claims it's time to arrest us.' Budyonny claimed that he gave his list to Yezhov who released some of the officers.

Stalin himself specialized in reassuring his victims and then arresting them. Early in the year, the wife of one of Ordzhonikidze's deputies at Heavy Industry was called by Stalin himself: 'I hear you're going about on foot. That's no good ... I'll send you a car.' Next morning the limousine was there. Two days later, her husband was arrested.

The generals, diplomats, spies and writers, who had served in the Spanish War, sunk in a quagmire of betrayals, assassinations, defeats, Trotskyite intrigues and denunciations, were decimated even when they had apparently done little wrong. Stalin's Ambassador to Madrid, Antonov-Ovseenko, an ex-Trotskyite, entangled himself by trying to prove his loyalty; he was recalled, affably promoted by Stalin, and arrested the next day. When Stalin received the journalist Mikhail Koltsov, he teased him about his adventures in the Spanish Civil War, calling him 'Don Miguel', but then asked: 'You don't intend to shoot yourself? So long, Don Miguel.' But Koltsov had played a deadly game in Spain, denouncing others to Stalin and Voroshilov. The 'Don' was arrested.

Stalin's office was bombarded with notes of execution from the regions: a typical one on 21 October 1937, listed eleven shot in Saratov, eight in Leningrad then another twelve, then six in Minsk then another five ... a total of 82. There are hundreds of such lists, addressed to Stalin and Molotov. On the other hand, Stalin received a stream of miserable cries for help. Bonch-Bruevich whose daughter was married into Yagoda's circle, insisted:

'Believe me, dear Joseph Vissarionovich, I'd bring a son or daughter to the NKVD myself if they were against the Party ...' Stalin's own secretary from the twenties, Kanner, who had been in charge of his dirty tricks against Trotsky and others, was arrested. 'Kanner cannot be a villain,' wrote a certain Makarova, perhaps his wife. 'He was friends with Yagoda but who could think the Narkom of Security could be such scum? Believe, Comrade Stalin, that Kanner deserved your trust!' Kanner was shot.

Often the appeals were from Old Bolsheviks who had been close friends, such as Vano Djaparidze whose tragic letter read: 'My daughter's been arrested. I cannot imagine what she could have done. I ask you dear Joseph Vissarionovich to ease the terrible destiny of my daughter ...'

Then he received letters from doomed leaders desperate to save themselves: 'I am unable to work, it's not a question of Partymindedness, but it's impossible for me not to act on the situation around me and to clear the air and understand the reason for it ... Please give me a moment of your time to receive me ...' wrote Nikolai Krylenko, the People's Commissar of Justice no less and signer of many a death sentence. He too was shot.

Yezhov was the chief organizer of the Terror, with Molotov, Kaganovich and Voroshilov as enthusiastic accomplices. But all the magnates had the power over life and death: years later Khrushchev remembered his power over a junior agronomist who crossed him:

'Well of course I could have done anything I wanted with him, I could have destroyed him, I could have arranged it so that, you know, he would disappear from the face of the earth.'

21

'The Blackberry' at Work and Play

Stalin received Yezhov 1,100 times during the Terror, second only to Molotov in frequency – and this only counted formal appointments in the Little Corner. There must have been many meetings at the dacha. The archives show how Stalin noted down those to be arrested in little lists to discuss with the 'Blackberry': on 2 April 1937, for example, he writes in his blue and red pencils to Yezhov a list of six points, many ominous, such as 'Purge State Bank'.* Sometimes Stalin gave him a lift home to his dacha.

Yezhov followed a punishing schedule of work, intensified by the terrible deeds he supervised and the pressure, from both above and below, to arrest and kill more: he lived the Stalinist nocturnal existence and was constantly exhausted, becoming paler and nervier. We now know how he worked: he tended to sleep in the morning, dine at home with his wife, meet his deputy Frinovsky for a drink at their dachas – and then drive to Butyrki or Lubianka to supervise the interrogations and tortures. Since Yezhov had been in the top echelons of the Party for about seven years, he often knew his victims personally. In June 1937, he signed off on the arrest of his 'godfather' Moskvin and his wife, whose house he had often visited. Both were shot. He could be brutal. When Bulatov, who had run a CC Department alongside Yezhov and had visited his home, was being interrogated for the fifth time, the Commissar-General appeared through a door in the wall:

'Well, is Bulatov testifying?'

'Not at all, Comrade Commissar-General!' replied the interrogator.

'Then lay it on him good!' he snapped and departed. But sometimes he clearly found his job difficult: when he had to witness the execution of a friend, he looked distressed. 'I see in

---

* Yezhov replied in black: 'In addition to the copy of Uzakovsky's report sent to you, I sent another one of 7th Division of GUGB [State Security] about the activities of Chinese-Trotskyites. Yezhov.'

your eyes that you feel sorry for me!' said the friend. Yezhov was
flustered but ordered the executioners to fire. When another old
buddy was arrested, Yezhov seemed moved but drunkenly ordered
his men 'to cut off his ears and nose, put out his eyes, cut him to
pieces', yet this was for show: he then chatted to his friend late
into the night but he too was shot. The Politburo greatly admired
Yezhov who, thought Molotov, 'wasn't spotless but he was a good
Party worker'.

Sometimes, amidst all the murder and thuggery, Yezhov showed
his old side. When he received Stalin's doctor, Vinogradov, who
had to testify in the upcoming Bukharin trial against his own
teacher, Yezhov tipsily advised him: 'You're a good person but you
talk too much. Bear in mind that every third person is my person
and informs me of everything. I recommend you talk less.'

The Commissar-General was at his peak. On holidays, Yezhov
was filmed strolling through the Kremlin, laughing with Stalin
while absurdly smoking what appears to be a very big cigarette.
During the long November 6th speeches at the Bolshoi Theatre,
US Ambassador Davies watched 'Stalin, Voroshilov and Yezhov
obviously whispering and joking among themselves'. *Pravda*
hailed him as 'an unyielding Bolshevik who without getting up
from his desk, night and day, is unravelling and cutting the
threads of the Fascist conspiracy'. Towns and stadiums were
named after him.* For the Kazakh 'bard' Dzhambul Dzhabaev, he
was 'a flame, burning the serpents' nests'.

He and Yevgenia now lived luxuriously in a dacha, with the
usual cinema, tennis court and staff, at Meshcherino near
Leninskie Gorki where many leaders had their homes. They had
adopted a daughter, Natasha, an orphan from a children's home.
Yezhov was tender, teaching her to play tennis, skate and bicycle.
In the photographs, he stands next to his friends, hugging
Natasha like any other father. He spoiled her with presents and
played with her on his return from work.

When Yezhov began to feed foreign Communists and returned
émigrés into the meat-grinder, he received an appeal from an
anxious, pretty and very pregnant Russian émigré named Vera

---

* His huge portraits were borne past the Mausoleum on all the State holidays. The
pun on the resemblance of his name to the 'steel gauntlet' had now spawned vast
posters showing his iron grip 'strangling the snakes' with the heads of Trotsky, Rykov
and Bukharin. The other Yezhovite slogan read: '*Yezhovy rukavitsy* – rule with an iron
rod!'

Trail, who was the daughter of Alexander Guchkov, the pre-revolutionary liberal. She received a call after midnight:

'Kremlin speaking. The Comrade Commissar will see you now.' A limousine took her into the Kremlin where she was led in to his long, dimly lit study with a green lampshade. The aphrodisiac of power working its wonders, she immediately admired his 'finely chiselled face', his 'brown wavy hair and blue eyes – the deepest blue I'd ever seen' and his 'small graceful slender hands'. She mentioned a list of friends, mainly writers, who had been arrested. He was acutely perceptive, 'a marvellous listener'. Blackberry dismissed his guards to receive her: 'I certainly don't make the habit of receiving total strangers unprotected.'

'I'm not even carrying a handbag,' she flirted back at him.

'No, only Belomor cigarettes. But you said you were pregnant.'

'Said? Can't you see?' Her belly was enormous.

'I see a bulge,' joked Yezhov, 'but how am I to know it's not a time-bomb cleverly wrapped in a pillow? You weren't searched ... were you?' Yezhov stood up and walked around the desk as if he was about to feel her belly but halfway he stopped and sat down, laughing:

'Of course you're pregnant. I was only joking.' Here was an authentic Yezhovian moment in which the Commissar displayed his clunkingly puerile humour (though thankfully, an improvement on the farting contests), the swagger of menace – and his paranoia. He promised to review her case and receive her again, kindly suggesting that she must go straight to bed. The next night, Yezhov's office called again:

'Leave for Paris at once.' She left on the train the next morning and was convinced that he had, for whatever reason, gone out of his way to save her life. Every one of the friends on her list were destroyed – but he saved her.

Yet personal attraction was rarely a reason to save the life of an Enemy: Blackberry had enjoyed a love affair with another Yevgenia, the wife of the Ambassador to Poland, throughout the thirties, offering to maintain her in Moscow. However Yevgenia Podoskaya refused, was arrested in November 1936 and shot on 10 March 1937.

Yezhov bombarded Molotov with reports of the conspiracies he had discovered. He and Kaganovich were enthusiasts: 'I've always considered that those chiefly responsible were Stalin and we who encouraged it, who were active. I was always active, I'd always supported the measures taken,' said Molotov. 'Stalin was right – "better an innocent head less ..."' Kaganovich agreed: 'Otherwise we'd never have won the war!' Molotov notoriously reviewed one list of arrests and personally wrote VMN next to a woman's name. It was Molotov who signed and apparently added names to the list of wives of Enemies such as Kosior and Postyshev, who were all shot. Of the twenty-eight Commissars under Premier Molotov in early 1938, twenty were killed. When he found the name of a Bolshevik named G. I. Lomov on a list Stalin asked: 'What about this?'

'In favour of immediate arrest of that bastard Lomov,' wrote Molotov. In the case of some unfortunate professor, Molotov asked Yezhov: 'Why is this professor still in the Foreign Ministry and not in the NKVD?' When some books by Stalin and Lenin were burned by mistake, Molotov ordered Yezhov to accelerate the case. When Molotov heard that a regional Procurator had grumbled about the Purge and joked, quite understandably, that it was amazing Stalin and Molotov were still alive when there were so many terrorists trying to kill them, he ordered the NKVD: 'Investigate, having agreed with Vyshinsky [the official's boss in Moscow]. Molotov.' Kaganovich boasted there was not one railway 'without Trotskyite/Japanese wreckers', writing at least thirty-two letters to the NKVD demanding eighty-three arrests – and signing death lists for 36,000. So many railwaymen were shot that an official telephoned Poskrebyshev to warn that one line was entirely unmanned.

Yet all the leaders also knew that they themselves were constantly being tested: both Molotov's secretaries were arrested.

'I sensed danger gathering around me,' he said as they collected testimony against him. 'My first assistant threw himself down the liftshaft at the NKVD.' No one was safe: they had their families to consider. Stalin had made it amply clear that the Enemies had to be destroyed 'without looking at their faces'. If they had hoped that their rank would protect them, the arrests of Politburo members like Rudzutak had corrected that impression. Testimonies were prepared against all, including Molotov, Voroshilov and Kaganovich. Their chauffeurs were arrested so frequently that Khrushchev grumbled to Stalin, who said: 'They're gathering evidence against me too.' All of them must have thought like Khrushchev who asked: 'Do you think I'm confident ... that tomorrow won't transfer me from this office to a prison cell?'

* * *

The case of Marshal Budyonny surely concentrated their minds: on 20 June 1937, soon after the execution of Tukhachevsky, Stalin told the cavalryman: 'Yezhov says your wife's conducting herself dishonourably and bear in mind we won't let anyone, even a wife, compromise you in the Party and the State. Talk to Yezhov about it and decide what to do if it's necessary. You missed an Enemy near you. Why do you feel sorry for her?'

'A bad wife is family, not political business, Comrade Stalin,' replied Budyonny. 'I'll look into it myself.'

'You must be brave,' said Stalin. 'Do you think I don't feel sorry when my closest circle turn out to be Enemies of the People?' Budyonny's wife, Olga, was a Bolshoi singer, who was best friends with the actress wife of Marshal Yegorov. It seems Olga was cuckolding Budyonny with a Bolshoi tenor and flirting with Polish diplomats. Budyonny went to Yezhov who told him that his wife 'along with Yegorova, visits foreign embassies ...' When he was inspecting the troops, his wife was arrested in the street, interrogated and sentenced to eight years and then another three. Budyonny sobbed, 'the tears pouring down his cheeks'. Olga went mad in solitary confinement. There used to be a legend that Stalin was more merciful to women: certainly female CC members were more likely to survive.* But Galina Yegorova, forty, was shot even before her Marshal husband. No chivalry there. Her flirtation with Stalin on the night of Nadya's suicide cannot have helped her case but he was always more pitiless if there was a hint of sexual debauchery.

The Terror was, among many more important things, the triumph of prissy Bolshevik morality over the sexual freedom of the twenties. The destruction of Yenukidze, Tukhachevsky and Rudzutak involved what Molotov called that 'weak spot ... women!' The scent of actresses, the whirl of diplomatic balls, and

---

* Alexandra Kollontai, now sixty-five and Ambassador to Sweden, was a beautiful Bolshevik noblewoman who wrote the manifesto of feminism and free love, her novel *Love of Worker Bees*. Her scandalous sex-life shocked and amused Stalin and Molotov. Several of her famous Bolshevik lovers were shot in the Great Terror. Yet she herself survived. Perhaps her letters to Stalin, always addressed to 'highly respected Joseph Vissarionovich' with 'friendly greetings from an open heart' with the flirtatious romanticism of a once beautiful woman, appealed to his chivalry. Similarly Stalin muttered to Dmitrov about the veteran Bolshevik Yelena Stasova that 'we shall probably arrest Stasova. Turned out she's scum.' Yet she was allowed to survive and continued to write Stalin warm letters of gratitude into honourable old age.

the glow of foreign decadence were sometimes enough to convince the lonely Stalin and the priggish Molotov, both reeking of Puritanical envy, that treason and duplicity lurked. But debauchery was never the real reason their victims were destroyed. That was always political. The accusations of sexual deviance were deployed to dehumanize them among their former colleagues. Yenukidze and Rudzutak were both said to seduce what Kaganovich called 'little girls'. Since it is unlikely that the Central Committee contained a cell of paedophiles, as well as a web of terrorists and spies, it seems more likely these hedonistic grandees just 'protected' ballerinas like millionaires past and present. None the less Stalin had tolerated (and probably enjoyed) Yenukidze's parties for years. Womanizers, such as Bulganin and Beria, continued to prosper, providing they were loyal and competent politically but no one could say this was mere tittle-tattle at Stalin's court.* People died of gossip.

Stalin was an awkward man of the nineteenth century: flirtatious with, and appreciative of, the well-dressed women of his circle, strictly prudish about his own daughter, shocked at the feminism and free love of the early twenties, yet crudely macho among his male friends. His prudishness was thoroughly 'Victorian': the appearance of Svetlana's knees, even her bold stare in a photograph, provoked absurd crises. Stalin disapproved of the 'first kiss' in Alexandrov's *Volga, Volga*, which was too passionate, with the result that not only was the kiss cut, but *all kissing* was almost banned from all Soviet films by over-zealous officials. In Eisenstein's *Ivan the Terrible, Part Two*, Stalin, who identified so closely with the Tsar, was embarrassed by Ivan's kiss which he said went on much too long and had to be cut. When Tatiana appeared in the opera *Onegin* wearing a sheer gown, Stalin exclaimed: 'How can a woman appear before a man dressed like that?' The director immediately restored 'Bolshevik modesty' to

* In their generation, the proud exception to this narrow-minded hypocrisy were those rare Bolsheviks who combined Party discipline with European Bohemianism, the Foreign Commissar Maxim Litvinov and his English wife Ivy. She sneered openly at humbugs like Molotov and flaunted her promiscuity with a parade of Germanic lovers: 'I don't care a pin what anyone says ... for I feel head and shoulders taller than anyone who can gloat on such outworn topics of scandal as who sleeps with whom.' Meanwhile Commissar Litvinov, the plump, rumpled and tough Jewish intellectual who had known Stalin a long time but was never close to him, started an affair with a 'very pretty, decidedly vulgar and very sexy indeed' girl who lodged with them. She even accompanied him to diplomatic receptions and arrived at the office in tight riding breeches.

Pushkin's worldliness. In old age, seeing a Georgian cigarette packet illustrated with a racy girl, Stalin furiously ordered the entire brand to be redesigned: 'Where would she learn to sit like that? Paris?'

He encouraged bourgeois morality among his magnates: Zhdanov's wife wanted to leave him for his alcoholism but just as Hitler insisted Goebbels return to his wife, so Stalin ordered, 'You must stay together.' It was the same with Pavel Alliluyev. When Stalin heard that Kuibyshev mistreated his wife, he exclaimed: 'If I'd known about it, I'd have put an end to such beastliness.'

However if an old friend needed help in an embarrassing situation, Stalin was amused to oblige, as a fascinating letter from his archives shows. Alexander Troyanovsky, probably the diplomat, asked for his help with a mistress (one F. M. Gratsanova) who worked for the NKVD and had been given a job by Yagoda. Now if they both left their jobs simultaneously, 'there'll be gossip. So can I leave earlier than her ... Please solve this for me as an old comrade,' he wrote to Stalin who helped with a snigger, writing:

'Comrade Yagoda, Arrange this business of Troyanovsky. He's entangled, the devil, and we are responsible [for helping him out]. Oh to God, or to the Devil, with him! Arrange this business and make him a calm bloke [*muzhik*]. Stalin.' In 1938, Troyanovsky again wrote to ask Stalin to get Yezhov to let the lady keep her apartment. Stalin helped again.

* * *

One of the mysteries of the Terror was Stalin's obsession with forcing his victims to sign elaborate confessions of unlikely crimes before they died. It was only with the slaughter of the NKVD and military brass between March and July 1937 that Stalin emerged as the absolute dictator. Even then, he still had to convince his magnates to do his bidding. How did he do it?

There was the character of Stalin himself: the cult of personality was so pervasive in the country that 'Stalin's word was law', said Khrushchev. 'He could do no wrong. Stalin could see it all clearly.' Mikoyan thought that the cult was the reason no one could challenge Stalin. But the Terror was not merely Stalin's will: he may have inspired much of it, and it may have reflected his own hatreds and complexes, but his magnates were constantly urging him to purge more Enemies. None the less when they knew the victim, they required proof. That was the reason Stalin paid such attention to the written words of confession, signed by the victims.

As soon as he received testimonies from Yezhov, Stalin distributed them to the Politburo who found this deluge of self-incrimination and denunciation hard to refute: in March 1937, Stalin typically sent a cover note to Molotov, Voroshilov, Kaganovich and Mikoyan:

'I ask you to recognize the testimony of Polish-German spies Alexandra (mother) and Tamara (daughter) Litzinskaya and Minervina, former secretary of A. Yenukidze.' All the magnates knew Yenukidze well so Stalin made sure they saw all the evidence. When Mikoyan doubted the confessions, Stalin accused him of weakness but then called him back and showed him the signed testimonies: 'He writes it himself ... signs every page.' These preposterous confessions were enough to convince Kaganovich: 'How could you not sign it [the death sentence] if according to the investigation ... this man was an Enemy?' Zhdanov, according to his son, 'did trust the denunciations from Yezhov ... For some time, my father did believe there were Tsarist agents among the Leningrad leadership.' But when his parents knew the victims personally as friends, then his mother would say, 'If he's an Enemy of the People, I am one too!' Again and again, in whispered conversations, the leaders and their wives used these same words to express their doubts about one or two of the arrests although they believed in the guilt of most of the victims.

The magnates were being disingenuous in their shock. When they knew the person, they naturally took a special interest in the proof, but all of them understood and accepted that the details of the accusations and confessions did not matter. So why were they all killed? Nadezhda Mandelstam wrote that they were killed 'for nothing' while Maya Kavtaradze, whose parents were arrested, simply says: 'Don't ask why!' They were killed not because of what they *had* done but because of what they *might* do. As Molotov explained, 'The main thing was, that at the decisive moment, they could not be depended on.' Indeed, some, such as Rudzutak, were not even 'consciously' disloyal. It was the *potential* nature of this betrayal which meant that Stalin could still admire the work or even personality of his victims: after Tukhachevsky and Uborevich's shootings, he could still lecture the Politburo about the talent of the former and encourage soldiers to 'Train your troops as Uborevich did.' But there was also a peculiarly religious aspect.

When Stalin briefed Vyshinsky on the January 1937 trial, he addressed the accused thus: 'You lost faith' – and they must die for losing it. He told Beria: 'An Enemy of the People is not only one who does sabotage but one who doubts the rightness of the Party line. And there are a lot of them and we must liquidate them.' Stalin himself implied this when he told a desperate comrade, who asked if he was still trusted, 'I trust you politically, but I'm not so positive in the sphere of the future perspectives of Party activities,' which seems to mean that he trusted him now but not necessarily in the coming war.

'There is something great and bold about the political idea of a general purge,' Bukharin, who understood Stalin so well, wrote to him from prison, because it would 'arouse an everlasting distrust ... In this way, the leadership is bringing about a full guarantee for itself.' The stronger the enemies of the State, the stronger the State (and Stalin) had to be. This circle of 'everlasting distrust' was his natural habitat. Did he believe every case? Not forensically, but this flint-hearted politician believed only in the sanctity of his own political necessity, sometimes fused with personal vengeance.

At the lunch after the 7 November parade, held as usual at Voroshilov's flat and attended by the magnates including Yezhov, Khrushchev and Redens, Mikoyan played the toastmaster proposing 'witty toasts for everyone in turn'. Then 'once more (a toast) to the great Stalin' who then stood up to explain and encourage the Terror: anyone who dared to weaken the power of the Soviet State 'in their thoughts, yes even their thoughts' would be considered an Enemy and 'we will destroy them as a clan'. Then he actually toasted this massacre: 'To the complete destruction of all Enemies, them and their kin!' at which the magnates gave 'approving exclamations: To the great Stalin!' This might have been a medieval Caucasian chieftain talking, 'a brilliant politician of the Italian Renaissance' – or Ivan. He explained that he, no great orator and an unimpressive fellow, had succeeded the 'eagle' Lenin because that was what the Party wanted. He and his men were driven by 'holy fear' of not justifying the trust of the masses. Thus, Stalin went on to explain, this was truly a holy terror that stemmed from Bolshevism's Messianic nature. No wonder Yezhov called the NKVD his 'secret sect'.

The squalidity of this sacred thuggery beggars belief: the distance from the torture chambers of the Lubianka to Stalin's Little Corner is about a mile, but it was much closer then.

22

Bloody Shirtsleeves:
the Intimate Circle of Murder

In the mornings, Blackberry visited the Politburo and attended meetings, coming straight from the torture chambers. Khrushchev one day noticed spots of clotted blood on the hem and cuffs of Yezhov's peasant blouse. Khrushchev, who himself was no angel, asked Yezhov what the spots were. Yezhov replied, with a flash of his blue eyes, that one should take pride in such specks because they were the blood of the Enemies of the revolution.

Stalin often wrote instructions beside the names. In December 1937, he added the order 'Beat, beat!' next to a name. 'Isn't it time to squeeze this gentleman and force him to report on his dirty little business,' Stalin wrote beside another. 'Where is he – in a prison or a hotel?' The Politburo specified that torture should be used officially in 1937. As Stalin later asserted, 'The NKVD practice of the use of physical pressure ... permitted by the Central Committee' was a 'totally correct and expedient method'.

Yezhov supervised his torturers who had their own jargon for their work: they called the process of destroying an innocent human 'French wrestling' – '*frantsuskaya borba*'. When some of them were interrogated themselves years later, they revealed how they used the *zhguti*, the special club, and the *dubinka*, the truncheon, as well as the more traditional prevention of sleep and constant interrogation that they called the 'conveyor belt'. The Cheka had long had a cult of torture: indeed Leonid Zakovsky, one of Yagoda's men, had written a guide to torture.

Frequently, the Politburo, such as Molotov and Mikoyan, would go over to interrogate their comrades in Yezhov's grand office at the Lubianka: 'Rudzutak had been badly beaten and tortured,' said Molotov about one such session. 'It was necessary to act mercilessly.' Kaganovich thought 'it was very difficult *not* to be cruel' but 'one must take into consideration that they were experienced Old Bolsheviks; how could they give testimonies voluntarily?' This may make it sound as if 'the Politburo was filled with gangsters', in Molotov's words. They may not have been Mafia hitmen – few except Yezhov and later Beria personally tortured or killed their victims, and no Mafia hitman would be foolish enough to spend so much time on tedious cod-ideology – but it is sometimes hard to tell the difference.

Stalin and his magnates often laughed about the NKVD's ability to get people to confess. Stalin told this joke to someone who had actually been tortured: 'They arrested a boy and accused him of writing *Eugene Onegin*,' Stalin joked. 'The boy tried to deny it … A few days later, the NKVD interrogator bumped into the boy's parents: "Congratulations!" he said. "Your son wrote *Eugene Onegin*." '* Many of the prisoners were beaten so hard that their eyes were literally popped out of their heads. They were routinely beaten to death, which was registered as a heart attack.

Yezhov himself devised the system of execution. Instead of using the cellars of the Lubianka or the other prisons, as his predecessors had done, he created a special abbatoir. Slightly behind and to the left of Lubianka, he used another NKVD building on Varsonofyevsky Lane. The prisoners were driven in Black Crows across the road from the Lubianka (there was no tunnel) and into the courtyard where a low squarish building had been specially constructed with a concrete floor sloping towards a far wall built of logs, to absorb the bullets, and hosing facilities to wash away the fluids. After a shot to the back of the head, the victims were placed in metal boxes and driven to one of the crematoria. in Moscow. The ashes were usually dumped into a mass grave such as the one at the Donskoi Cemetery.

The road that ended in the Donskoi often began in a note on Stalin's desk. Stalin received not only pleas for life but denunciations demanding death. Once the Terror was unleashed, denunciations worked like kerosene on a fire, keeping it flaring up. These denunciations were already a vital part of the Stalinist system: everyone was expected to denounce everyone else. In the Bolshevik universe, there were only two ways for mistakes to come to the notice of the leaders: accidents – and denunciations. Denunciations poured into Stalin's office: some were valid. 'If we lived in a capitalist state, they'd be

* The primitive interrogators tried to suit the crime to the criminal with often absurd results: on his arrest, the First Secretary of the Jewish Autonomous Oblast in Birobizhan was appropriately accused of poisoning Kaganovich's gefilte fish during his visit there. Presumably, throughout the many republics of the USSR, the poison was secreted in the national dishes – from the sausages of the Baltics to the spicy soups of the Buriats and the lamb stews of the Tajiks.

talking about us in the Parliament and newspapers,' said Voroshilov. Some denunciations were the Stalinist equivalent of awkward Parliamentary questions and investigative reporters:

'You probably find it unpleasant that such letters are written, but I'm glad,' Stalin explained. 'It would be a bad thing if no one complained. Don't be afraid of quarrelling ... This is better than friendship at the Government's expense.' But usually these poison letters were the result of witch-hunting mania, cannibalistic malice and amoral ambition.

Stalin relished the decision on how to treat the denunciations. If he did not like the person, the letters went to the NKVD with a note 'Check!' and death probably followed. If he wished to 'preserve' the person, he would file it and he might reactivate it years later. Hence his papers overflow with denunciations, some from ordinary people, others from top officials: a typical one, from a Comintern official, denounced Enemies in the Foreign Commissariat. One can only guess at the atmosphere of fear and intrigue within the Kremlin: Ordzhonikidze's ex-secretary, surely trying to save his skin, wrote to Stalin to denounce Sergo's widow, Zinaida, who had 'said several times she can't live without Sergo and I'm worried she'll do something silly ... She's often telephoned by the wives of traitors to our Party. These wives turn to her with requests (to give to Comrade Yezhov). It's not right and she must be told not to do it ... I ask for your instructions. Every order will be fulfilled to the last drop of blood. Devoted to you, Semyushkin.' Sometimes farce turned swiftly to tragedy, like the story of how Stalin's voice* was sabotaged by wreckers.

---

* At the end of 1936, when Stalin inaugurated the new Constitution, Shumiatsky, the film boss, asked Molotov if he could record Stalin's speech. On 20 November, Molotov gave permission. Maltsev, the chief of the All-Union Committee of Radiofication and Radiosound, reported joyfully to Stalin that the speech had been successfully recorded and approved. Now he wanted permission to make it into a gramophone record 'for you to hear it personally'. Stalin agreed. But on 29 April 1937, when the terrified officials of the Gramophone Plant Trust factory listened to the gramophone, something was wrong with Stalin's voice. They immediately reported to Poskrebyshev that there were: '1. Big noises. 2. Big intervals. 3. The absence of whole phrases. 4. Closed grooves. And 5. Jumps and lack of clarity.' The file also contained a nervous analysis of the sibilance of Stalin's voice and how hard it was to render on gramophone. Worse, a thousand of these gramophones had been manufactured. Some officials wanted to recall the discs but, typically for the period, the chief attacked this suggestion for its disrespect to Comrade Stalin's voice. He thought it more respectful to distribute them regardless of the gaps, noises, jumps. The file ends with a report from *Komsomolskaya Pravda* that suggested that something very sinister had happened to Comrade Stalin's voice at the Gramophone Factory where the insistence of Comrade Straik to 'distribute the discs more speedily' was a 'strange position'. He was obviously a wrecker and all the guilty wreckers at the factory 'must be harshly punished'. No doubt the NKVD came to listen to Comrade Straik's record collection.

A typical denunciation which Stalin read and marked, came from a certain Krylov in distant Saratov, who told his leader that 'Enemies have friends inside the NKVD and the Procuracy and are hiding enemies.' The military were as avid as anyone else: 'I ask you to dismiss Commander ... Osipov,' wrote an officer from Tiflis, 'who is a very suspicious person.' Stalin underlined 'suspicious' with his blue pen.

The lightning of this Muscovite Zeus struck the regions in different ways: in July 1937, Liushkov, a ruthless Chekist who had already ravaged Rostov, was summoned to the Kremlin and ordered to the Far East. Stalin talked about the lives of men as if they were old clothes – some we keep, some we throw away: the Far Eastern First Secretary Vareikis was 'not completely reliable', having his own clique, but 'it was necessary to keep' Marshal Blyukher. Liushkov obediently arrested Vareikis.

A less reliable way was to harness a local tool such as Polia Nikolaenko, the 'heroic denunciatrix of Kiev', championed by Stalin. The speciality of this terrifying crone, responsible for the deaths of as many as 8,000 people, was to stand up at meetings and shriek accusations: Khrushchev saw how she 'pointed her finger and said, "I don't know that man over there but I can tell by the look in his eyes that he's an Enemy of the People."' This talk of the 'look in the eyes' was another sign of the Terror's religious frenzy. The only way to rebut this was to answer quickly: 'I don't know this woman who's just denounced me but I can tell from the look in her eyes, she's a prostitute.' Now Polia Nikolaenko appealed to Stalin. Her cover note catches her simplicity:

'To the anteroom of Comrade Stalin. I ask you to give this declaration personally to Comrade Stalin. Comrade Stalin talked about me at the February Plenum.' Her letter did reach Stalin, with devastating consequences for her enemies: 'Dear Leader, Comrade Stalin,' she wrote on 17 September 1937, cunningly exposing how the local bosses were ignoring Stalin's orders. 'I ask for your intervention in Kiev matters ... Enemies here again gather unbeatable power ... sitting in their *apparat* doing bad deeds. Starting from the Plenum when you spoke about Kiev and my case as a "little person", they have actively organized my discrediting to destroy me politically.' Senior officials treated her as an 'Enemy' and once again used the language of witchcraft against the witch herself: 'One connected to Enemies of the People cried, "It's in her eyes, she's two-faced!"' Kosior, Ukrainian leader, and others ridiculed her 'amidst noisy laughter'. 'I was, am and will be devoted to the Party and the Great Leader. You helped me to find Truth. STALIN'S TRUTH IS STRONG! This time I again ask you to do all you can to the Kiev organization ...' Ten days later, Stalin swooped to her aid, telling the Ukrainian bosses:

'Pay attention to Comrade Nikolaenko (look at her letter). Can you protect her from this audience of hooligans! According to my information, Glaz and Timofeev really are not especially trust-worthy. Stalin.' Those two men were presumably arrested while Kosior survived for the moment.

The regions were soon killing too many, too quickly: Khrushchev,* Moscow leader, effectively ordered the shooting of 55,741 officials which more than fulfilled the original Politburo quota of 50,000. On 10 July 1937, Khrushchev wrote to Stalin to request shooting 2,000 ex-kulaks to fulfil the quota. The NKVD archives show him initialling many documents proposing arrests. By spring 1938, he had overseen the arrest of thirty-five of the thirty-eight provincial and city Secretaries, which gives some idea of this fever. Since he was based in Moscow, he brought death-lists directly to Stalin and Molotov.

'There can't be so many!' exclaimed Stalin.

'There are in fact more,' replied Khrushchev, according to Molotov. 'You can't imagine how many there are.' The city of Stalinabad (Askabad) was given a quota of 6,277 to shoot but actually executed 13,259.

But mostly, they were killing the wrong people. The regional bosses selected the victims, finding it irresistible to destroy their opponents and preserve their friends. Yet it was precisely these 'princes' with their entourages that Stalin wished to destroy. Thus the First Secretaries' initial blood-letting not only did not save them: it provided an excuse for their own eradication. It was only a matter of time before the centre unleashed a second wave of terror to eradicate the 'princes' themselves.

Only Stalin's personal viceroys, Zhdanov in Leningrad and Beria in Transcaucasia, did not require this 'help'. Zhdanov was another enthusiastic believer that Trotskyites had infiltrated Leningrad,

---

* Khrushchev was as fanatical a Stalinist terrorist as it was possible to be during the thirties yet his ability to destroy incriminating documents, and his memoirs, have shrouded his real conduct in mystery. A. N. Shelepin, ex-KGB boss, testified in 1988 that Khrushchev's death-lists had been removed by the secret policeman I. V. Serov. 261 pages of Khrushchev's papers were burned between 2 and 9 July 1954.

though he sometimes mused on cases: 'You know I never thought
Viktorov would turn out to be an Enemy of the People,' said
Zhdanov to Admiral Kuznetsov, who 'heard no doubt in his voice,
only surprise ... We spoke ... as of men who had passed beyond the
grave.' He oversaw the arrest of 68,000 in Leningrad. As for Beria,
this professional Chekist oversaw his initial quota of 268,950 arrests
and 75,950 executions. The quota was later raised. Ten per cent of
the Georgian Party, which was particularly well-known to Stalin,
were killed. Beria distinguished himself by personally performing
the torture of Lakoba's family, driving his widow mad by placing a
snake in her cell and beating his teenage children to death.

The solution was the despatch of Stalin's favourites to destroy the
'princes'; also a useful test of a magnate's loyalty. There was no better
blooding than a trip to the regions. Like the warlords of the Civil
War they set off riding shotgun with NKVD thugs in their own
armoured trains. Mikoyan, Foreign Trade and Food Supply
Commissar, enjoys the reputation of one of the more decent leaders:
he certainly helped the victims later and worked hard to undo
Stalin's rule after his death. In 1936, however, Mikoyan praised the
executions of Zinoviev and Kamenev – 'how just the verdict!' he
enthused to Kaganovich. In 1937, he too signed death-lists and
proposed the arrest of hundreds of his officials. Throughout Stalin's
reign, Mikoyan was shrewd enough to avoid intrigues, eschew
ambition for the highest offices, and with his sharp intelligence and
prodigious capacity for work, concentrate on his responsibilities: he
knew how to play the game and do just enough.

The magnates saved friends but they mainly saved them in 1939
in a different environment. Andreyev's anteroom, his daughter
claimed, 'was full of those he helped' but Kaganovich honestly
admitted that 'it was impossible to save friends and relatives'
because of 'the public mood'. They had to kill a lot to save a few.
Mikoyan probably did more than most, appealing to Stalin that
his friend Andreasian had been accused of being a French agent by
the moronic investigators because his first name was 'Napoleon'.

'He's as French as you!' joked Mikoyan. Stalin burst out laughing.*
Voroshilov, who was responsible for so many deaths, passed on the
appeal of a friend's arrested daughter to Stalin himself who wrote on

---

* Such absurdities abounded: in her terrible labour camp, Bukharin's widow
encountered this spirit when another prisoner informed on her because she owned
a book named *Dangerous Liaisons* that was presumed to be a deadly espionage guide.

it as usual: 'To Comrade Yezhov, check this out!' Her father was released and called to thank Voroshilov, who asked:

'Was it terrible?'

'Yes, very terrible.' The two friends never discussed it again.

Stalin was so besieged with requests that he passed a Politburo decree banning appeals. If a leader intervened to save a friend, the vital thing was to avoid him falling into the hands of another leader. Mikoyan managed to save one comrade and begged him to leave Moscow immediately but the Old Bolshevik, with all the punctiliousness of a knight who must have his sword returned, insisted on getting his Party card back. He called Andreyev who had him rearrested.

Perhaps Mikoyan's kindnesses reached Stalin's ears for he suddenly cooled towards him. In late 1937, he tested Mikoyan's commitment by despatching him to Armenia with a list of three hundred victims to be arrested. Mikoyan signed it but he crossed off one friend. The man was arrested anyway. Just as he was speaking to the Yerevan Party meeting, Beria arrived in the room, to watch him as much as to terrorize the locals. A thousand people were arrested, including seven out of nine Armenian Politburo members. When Mikoyan returned to Moscow, Stalin warmed to him again.

All the magnates set off on bloody tours of the country. Zhdanov purged the Urals and Middle Volga. Ukraine was unfortunate enough to welcome Kaganovich, Molotov and Yezhov. Kaganovich visited Kazakhstan, Cheliabinsk, Ivanovo and other places, spreading terror: 'First study ... shows the Obkom Secretary Epanchikev must be arrested at once ...' began his first telegram from Ivanovo in August 1937, which continued: 'Right-Trotskyite wrecking has assumed broad dimensions here, in industry, agriculture, supply, healthcare, trade, education and political work ... exceptionally infested.' But this was nothing compared to the killing frenzy of the two most prolific monsters on tour.

Andrei Andreyev, now forty-two, small, moustachioed and hangdog of countenance, had failed to rise to the challenge of the Soviet railways but he came into his own running the CC Secretariat with Yezhov. One of the rare proletarians among the leadership, this quiet Tchaikovsky addict, mountaineer and nature photographer, married to Dora Khazan, to whom he wrote loving postcards about their children, became the unchallengeable master of these murderous roadshows.

On 20 July, he arrived in Saratov to ravage the Volga German Republic:* 'All means are necessary to purge Saratov,' he told Stalin in the first of a stream of excited, fanatical telegrams. 'The Saratov organization meets all decisions of CC with great pleasure.' This was hard to believe. Everywhere he discovered how the local bosses 'did not want to discover the terrorist group' and had 'pardoned exposed Enemies'. By the next day, Andreyev was frantically arresting suspects: 'we had to arrest the Second Secretary ... On Freshier, we have evidence he was member of Rightist-Trotskyite organization. We ask permission to arrest.' One group consisted of 'twenty very obstructively working in the Machine Tractor Station. We decided to arrest and prosecute two of the directors' who turned out to be part of a '"Right-kulak organization" that had "wrecked tractors" or rather they had worked slowly since "only 14 out of 74 were ready".' At 11.38 that night, Stalin replied in his blue pencil: 'Central Committee agrees with your proposals about prosecution and shooting of former MTS workers.' Twenty were shot. Three days later, Andreyev boasted to Stalin that he had found 'a Fascist organization – we plan to arrest at once the first group of 50–60 people ... We had to arrest the Premier of the Republic, Luf, for proven membership of Right-Trotskyites.' He proceeded to Kuibyshev and then to Central Asia where he removed all the leaderships since Stalin had told him: 'Generally, you can act as you consider.' The result was that in Stalinabad, 'I have arrested 7 Narkoms, 55 CC chiefs, 3 CC Secretaries' and returning to Voronezh, he declared cheerfully: 'There is no Buro here. All arrested as Enemies. Off to Rostov now!'

Andreyev was accompanied on these manic trips by a plump young man of thirty-five, Georgi Malenkov, the killer bureaucrat whose career benefited the most from the Purges but who hailed from the provincial intelligentsia, a scion of Tsarist civil servants, and a nobleman.† He travelled with Mikoyan to Armenia and

* After interviewing Andreyev and Dora Khazan's daughter Natasha and hearing of his innocence of all crimes, the author came upon this damning file. Andreyev's notes and letters have survived because unlike his fellow criminals, such as Kaganovich, Malenkov and Khrushchev, he was out of power after Stalin's death when the others managed to destroy so many incriminating documents.

† Lenin, the founder of the Cheka Felix Dzerzhinsky, and the Foreign Commissar until 1930, Chicherin, were hereditary noblemen, as were Molotov, Zhdanov, Sergo and Tukhachevsky, according to Peter the Great's Table of Ranks which decreed rank until 1917. None were titled nobility.

Yezhov to Belorussia. One historian estimates that Malenkov was responsible for 150,000 deaths.

Small, flabby, pale and moon-faced with a hairless chin, freckles across his nose and dark, slightly Mongol eyes, his black hair hanging across his forehead, Malenkov had broad, female hips, a pear shape and a high voice. It is no wonder that Zhdanov nicknamed him 'Malanya' or Melanie. 'It seemed that under the layers and rolls of fat', a lean and hungry man was trying to get out. His great-great-grandfather had come from Macedonia during the reign of Nicholas I but as Beria joked, he was hardly Alexander the Great. Malenkov's ancestors had governed Orenburg for the Tsars. Descended from generals and admirals, he saw himself in the tradition of a *posadnik*, an elected administrator of old Novgorod, or a *chinovnik* like his forefathers. Unlike Stalinist bullies such as Kaganovich, who shouted and punched officials, Malenkov stood when subordinates entered his room and spoke quietly in fine Russian without swearing, though what he said was often chilling.

Malenkov's father had shocked the family by marrying a formidable blacksmith's daughter who had three sons. Georgi, who loved his dominant mother, was the youngest. He studied at the local classical *Gymnasium*, learning Latin and French. Malenkov, like Zhdanov, passed among cobblers and joiners for an educated man, qualifying as an electrical engineer. Like many other ambitious youngsters, he joined the Party during the Civil War: his family unconvincingly claim that he rode in the cavalry but he was soon on safer ground on the propaganda trains where he met his domineering wife, Valeria Golubtseva, who came from a similar background.

Happily married, Malenkov was known as a wonderful father to his highly educated children, teaching them himself and reading them poetry even when he was exhausted at the height of the war. His wife helped get him a job in the Central Committee where he was noticed by Molotov, joined Stalin's Secretariat and became Secretary of the Politburo during the early thirties, one of those keen young men like Yezhov who won first Kaganovich's, then Stalin's notice for their devotion and efficiency. Yet in company, he had a light sense of humour.

This cunning but 'eunuch-like' magnate never spoke unless necessary and always listened to Stalin, scribbling in a notebook headed 'Comrade Stalin's Instructions'. He succeeded Yezhov as head of the CC Personnel Registration department that selected cadres for jobs. In 1937, Mikoyan said, he played a 'special role'. He was the bureaucratic maestro of the Terror. One note in Stalin's papers laconically illustrates their relationship:

'Comrade Malenkov – Moskvin must be arrested. J.St.' The young stars Malenkov, Khrushchev and Yezhov were such close friends, they were called 'the Inseparables'. Yet in this paranoic lottery, even a Malenkov could be destroyed. In 1937, he was accused at a Moscow Party Conference of being an Enemy himself. He was talking about joining the Red Army in Orenburg during the Civil War when a voice cried out:

'Were there Whites in Orenburg at the time?'

'Yes –'

'That means you were with them.' Khrushchev intervened:

'The Whites may have been in Orenburg at the time but Comrade Malenkov was not one of them.' It was a time when hesitation could lead to arrest. Simultaneously, Khrushchev saved his own skin by going to Stalin personally and confessing a spell of Trotskyism during the early twenties.

The entourage rabidly encouraged the Terror. Even decades later, these 'fanatics' still defended their mass murder: 'I bear responsibility for the repression and consider it correct,' said Molotov. 'All Politburo members bear responsibility ... But 1937 was necessary.' Mikoyan agreed that 'everyone who worked with Stalin ... bears a share of responsibility'. It was bad enough to kill so many but their complete awareness that many were innocent even by their own arcane standards is the hardest to take: 'We're guilty of going too far,' said Kaganovich. 'We all made mistakes ... But we won WW2.' Those who knew these mass murderers later reflected that Malenkov or Khrushchev were 'not wicked by nature', not 'what they eventually became'. They were men of their time.

In October, another Plenum approved the arrest of yet more members of the Central Committee. 'It happened gradually,' said Molotov. 'Seventy expelled 1–15 people then sixty expelled another 15.' When the terrified local leaders appealed to Stalin 'to receive me for just ten minutes on personal matters – I'm accused in a terrible lie,' he scribbled in green to Poskrebyshev:

'Say I'm on holiday.'

23

Social Life in the Terror: the Wives
and Children of the Magnates

Yet all of this tragedy took place in a public atmosphere of jubilation, a never-ending fiesta of triumphs and anniversaries. Here is a scene from the years of the Terror that might have taken place anywhere and any time between a daughter, her best friend and her embarrassing papa. Stalin met his daughter Svetlana in his apartment for dinner daily. At the height of the Terror, Stalin dined with Svetlana, then eleven, and her best friend, Martha Peshkova, whose grandfather, Gorky, and father had both supposedly been murdered by Yagoda, her mother's lover. Stalin wanted Svetlana to be friends with Martha, introducing them especially. Now the girls were playing in Svetlana's room when the housekeeper came and told them Stalin was home and at table. Stalin was alone but in a very cheerful mood – he clearly adored coming home to see Svetlana for he would often appear shouting, 'Where's my *khozyaika*!' and then sit down and help her do her homework. Outsiders were amazed at how this harsh creature 'was so gentle with his daughter'. He sat her on his knee and told one visitor:

'Since her mother died, I always tell her she's the *khozyaika* but she so believed it herself that she tried to give orders in the kitchen but was made to leave immediately. She was in tears but I managed to calm her down.'

That night, he teased Martha, who was very pretty but with a tendency to blush like a beetroot:

'So Marfochka, I hear you are being chased by all the boys?' Martha was so embarrassed she could not swallow her soup or answer. 'So many boys are chasing you!' Stalin persisted. Svetlana came to her rescue:

'Come on, papa, leave her alone.' Stalin laughed and agreed, saying he always obeyed his darling *khozyaika*. Dinner, recalled Martha, 'was miserable for me', but she was not afraid of Stalin because she had known him since childhood. Yet nothing was quite what it seemed for these children: so many of Svetlana's parents' friends had disappeared. Martha had just seen* her mother's new lover arrested.

For the children of the leaders who were not arrested, there had never been a time of greater joy and energy. The jazz craze was still sweeping the country: Alexandrov's latest musical, *Volga, Volga*, came out in 1938 and its tunes were played over and over again in the dancehalls. At parties for the diplomatic corps, the killers danced to the jazz: Kaganovich hailed jazz as 'above all the friend of the jolly, the musical organizer of our high-spirited youth'. Kaganovich wrote a jazz guide leaflet with his friend Leonid Utesov, the jazz millionaire, entitled *How to Organize Railway Ensembles of Song and Dance and Jazz Orchestras* in which 'the Locomotive' commanded that there should be a '*dzhaz*' band at every Soviet station. They certainly needed cheering up.

'It was truly a time of huge hope and joy for the future,' remembers Stepan Mikoyan. 'We were perpetually excited and happy – the new Metro opened with its chandeliers, the giant Moskva Hotel, the new city of Magnitogorsk, and all sorts of other triumphs.' The propaganda machine sung of heroes of labour like the super-miner Stakhanov, of aviation, of exploration. Voroshilov and Yezhov were hailed as 'knights' in ballads. The movies had names like *Tales of Aviation Heroes*. 'Yes, it was an age of heroes!' reminisces Andreyev's daughter Natasha. 'We were not afraid then. Life was full – I remember smiling faces and climbing mountains, heroic pilots. Not everyone was living under oppression. We knew as children the first thing to be done was to make people strong, to make a New Man, and educate the people. At school, we learned how to use different tools, we went into the countryside to help with the harvest. No one paid us – it was our duty.'

The NKVD were heroes too: on 21 December, the 'Organs' celebrated their twentieth anniversary at a Bolshoi gala. Beneath flowers and banners of Stalin and Yezhov, Mikoyan in a Party tunic declared:

---

* Martha and her mother had been invited to Tiflis for the celebration of the poet Rustaveli's 750th anniversary by Timosha's new lover, Academician Lupel. There, through a slit in the door, she had seen him arrested at the dead of night: 'I saw five men take him away,' she remembered. Timosha's later affair with Stalin's court architect, Merzhanov, also ended in his arrest. 'I'm cursed,' Timosha Peshkova exclaimed. 'Everyone I touch is ruined.'

'Learn the Stalinist style of work from Comrade Yezhov just as he learned it from Comrade Stalin.' But the crux of his speech was: 'Every citizen of the USSR should be an NKVD agent.'

The country celebrated the anniversary of Pushkin's death as well as the anniversary of the Georgian poet Rustaveli which was organized by Beria and attended by Voroshilov and Mikoyan. Stalin was deliberately fusing traditional Russian culture with Bolshevism as Europe lurched closer to war. The Soviets were now fighting the Fascists by proxy in the Spanish Civil War, sparking a craze for Spanish songs and Spanish caps, 'blue with red edging on the visor', and big berets, 'tilted at a rakish angle'. Women wore Spanish blouses. 'If Tomorrow Brings War' was one of the most popular tunes. All the children of the leaders wanted to be pilots or soldiers:

'Even we children knew that war was coming,' recalls Stalin's adopted son Artyom, 'and we had to be strong not to be destroyed. One day, Uncle Stalin called we boys and said, "What would you like to do with your life?" Artyom wanted to be an engineer. 'No, we need men who understand the artillery.' Artyom and Yakov, already an engineer, both joined the artillery. 'This was the only privilege I ever received from my Uncle Stalin,' says Artyom. But aviators were the élite: more magnates' children joined 'Stalin's falcons' than any other service: Vasily trained as a pilot, alongside Stepan Mikoyan and Leonid Khrushchev.

Yet the families of the leaders endured a special experience during that time. For the parents, it was a daily torment of depression, uncertainty, exhilaration, anxiety as friends, colleagues and relatives were arrested. Yet to read Western histories and Soviet memoirs, one might believe that this new Bolshevik élite were convinced that all those arrested were innocent. This reflects the postdated guilt of those whose fathers took part in the slaughter. The truth was different: Zhdanov told his son Yury that Yezhov was right even in the most unlikely cases:

'The devil knows! I've known him many years but then there was Malinovsky!' he said, referring to the notorious Tsarist spy. Andreyev knew there were Enemies but thought they had to be 'thoroughly checked' before they were arrested. Mikoyan had his reservations on many arrests but his son Sergo knew his father was, in his words, a 'Communist fanatic'. The wives were if anything more fanatical than the husbands: Mikoyan recalled how his wife utterly believed in Stalin and was least likely to question his actions. 'My father,' says Natasha Andreyeva, 'believed wreckers and Fifth Columnists were destroying our State and had to be destroyed. My mother was utterly convinced. We prepared for war.'

The magnates never discussed the Terror before the children who lived in a world of lies and murder. The 'reluctance to reveal one's thoughts even to one's son was the most haunting sign of these times', remembered Andrei Sakharov the physicist. Yet the children naturally noticed when their uncles and family friends disappeared, leaving unspeakable and unaskable voids in their lives. The Mikoyan children heard their parents and uncles whispering about the arrests in Armenia, but their father sometimes could not stop himself exclaiming, 'I don't believe it!' Andreyev 'never mentioned it to us – it was our parents' business', recalls Natasha Andreyeva. 'But if someone important was arrested, my father would call to mama, "Dorochka, can you speak with me for a minute."' Indeed, Dora told her family she could identify Enemies by looking into their eyes. They whispered behind the kitchen door. Whenever his wife asked him something dangerous, Mikoyan replied: 'Shut up.' Before his death, Ordzhonikidze quietened his wife with a firm 'Not now!' Parents were constantly going for walks in the woods or round the Kremlin.

The inhabitants of the House on the Embankment, the hideous luxury building for younger leaders including the Khrushchevs, most of the People's Commissars and Stalin's cousinhood, like the Svanidzes and Redens, waited each night for the groan of the elevators, the knock on the doors, as the NKVD arrived to arrest their suspects.* As Trifonov relates in his novel *House on the Embankment*, every morning the uniformed doorman told the other inhabitants who had been arrested during the night. Soon the building was filled with empty apartments, doors ominously sealed by the NKVD. Khrushchev worried about the gossiping women in his family, furious when his peasant mother-in-law spent her time chattering downstairs, knowing well how loose talk cost lives.

Parents kept bags packed for prison and Mauser and Chagan

---

* Nadezhda Mandelstam wrote beautifully of how she and her husband had lain awake in the Writers' Union building until the lift had passed their floor.

pistols under their pillows, ready to commit suicide. The cleverer ones arranged a schedule for their children in case they were arrested: the mother of Zoya Zarubina, the stepdaughter of a Chekist, showed her how to gather warm clothes and take her little sister, aged eight, to a distant relative in the countryside.

The children noticed frequent house-moving because every execution created a vacant apartment and dacha which were eagerly occupied by survivors and their aspirational Party housewives, ambitious for grander accommodation. Stalin exploited this way of binding the leaders to the slaughter. Yezhov's family moved into Yagoda's apartments. Zhdanov received Rudzutak's dacha, Molotov acquired Yagoda's and later Rykov's. Vyshinsky was the most morbidly avaricious of all: he had always coveted the dacha of Leonid Serebryakov: 'I can't take my eyes off it ... You're a lucky man, Leonid,' he used to say. Days after Serebryakov's arrest on 17 August 1936, the Procurator demanded the dacha for himself, even managing to get reimbursed for his old house and then to receive 600,000 roubles to rebuild the new one. This vast sum was approved on 24 January 1937, the very day Vyshinsky cross-examined Serebryakov in the Radek trial.* Woe betide anyone who refused these ill-starred gifts: Marshal Yegorov unwisely rejected the dacha of a shot comrade. 'The souls of former owners,' wrote Svetlana Stalin, 'seemed to linger within those walls.'

'We were never afraid in 1937,' explains Natasha Andreyeva because she believed absolutely that the NKVD only arrested Enemies. Therefore she and their parents would never be arrested. Stepan Mikoyan 'wasn't worried but only later did I realize my parents lived in constant apprehension'. Furthermore, Politburo members were sent all the interrogation records. Stepan used to creep in and peep at the extraordinary revelations of their own family friends who turned out to be Enemies. Every household had its 'expunger': in the Mikoyan household, Sergei Shaumian, adopted son of a late Old Bolshevik, went through all the family photograph albums erasing the faces of Enemies as they were arrested and shot, a horrible distortion of the colouring-in books that most children so enjoy.

---

* After Stalin's death, the Serebryakovs managed to get half the property returned to them but the Vyshinskys kept the other half. Thus in 2002, sixty years after their father was shot by their neighbour, the Serebryakovs spend each weekend next to the Vyshinskys.

Even if they did not grasp the randomness of death, they were aware that it was ever present and they accepted that the coming of war meant Enemies had to be killed. The children talked about it among themselves: Vasily Stalin gleefully told Artyom Sergeev and his Redens cousins about arrests. Protected by whispers and mysteries at home, it was at school that the children learned more. Most of the leaders' children were at Schools No. 175 (or 110), driven there by their fathers' chauffeurs in their Packards and Buicks which could be as embarrassing as a Rolls-Royce at the school gates in the West. The Mikoyans insisted on the car dropping them off so they could walk the last half kilometre. At this élite school, the teachers (who included the English-teaching wife of Nikolai Bulganin, a rising leader) pretended nothing was happening, while the danger was just dawning on the children, who saw their friends being repressed: Stepan Mikoyan's best friend was Serezha Metalikov, son of the senior Kremlevka doctor and nephew of Poskrebyshev, who saw both of his parents arrested during 1937.

Svetlana was treated like a Tsarevna at school by the cringing teachers. A schoolgirl there recalled how her desk gleamed like a mirror, the only one to be polished. Whenever a parent was arrested, their children were removed mysteriously from Svetlana's class so this Tsarevna did not have to rub shoulders with the kin of Enemies.

Sometimes friends were actually arrested at teenage parties in front of all the others. Vasily Stalin and Stepan Mikoyan were carousing at a party given by one of their friends at the Military Academy when the doorbell rang. A man in plain clothes asked to speak to Vasily Stalin who came to the door where he was told, as a sign of almost feudal respect, that the NKVD had arrived to arrest a boy at the party. Vasily returned and told his friend to go to the door while whispering to Stepan that he was being arrested. They watched from the window as the Chekists put the boy into a black car as a 'member of a teenage anti-Soviet group'. He was never seen again.

Parents carefully vetted their children's friends: 'My stepfather was very cautious about my boyfriends,' remembered Zoya Zarubina. 'He always wanted to know who their parents were ...' and would check them out at the Lubianka. The Voroshilovs were stricter than the Mikoyans who were stricter than the Zhdanovs: when one of the Voroshilov children was phoned by a boy whose father had just been arrested, Ekaterina Voroshilova ordered him to break off relations. Zhdanov's son Yury claims that his parents let him bring the children of Enemies home. 'My parents made no objections.' But it was all a matter of timing: in the frenzy of 1937–8, this is hard to believe. After Stepan Mikoyan started going out with a girl called Katya, he found an NKVD report that mentioned her friendship with the son of an Enemy. 'I was waiting for my father to say something to me ... but he never did.' However, when some families close to Mikoyan fell under suspicion, he cut off all contact with them.

* * *

During early 1937, the arrival of Poskrebyshev and Yezhov's glamorous young wives meant that the entourage had never been more colourful and cosmopolitan. Out at Zubalovo, Stalin still took the family out for picnics, bringing chocolates for his daughter and Martha Peshkova. As the country shivered from the depredations of the NKVD, Stalin was solicitous to the children: once Leonid Redens, who was nine, got lost at Kuntsevo and finally galloped up to some adults who all laughed except Stalin. 'Have you got lost?' he asked. 'Come with me, I'll show you the way.' However, the old familiarity with Stalin was gradually freezing into fear.

Part Five

Slaughter: Beria Arrives,

1938–1939

24

Stalin's Jewesses and the Family in Danger

Once, when Stalin was resting at Zubalovo, Pavel and Zhenya Alliluyev's middle child Sergei kept crying and the parents worried that he would be disturbed. Pavel, who had a hysterical temper like his sister Nadya, slapped his daughter Kira for not keeping him quiet. Kira, now a teenager, was irrepressible and, having grown up around Stalin, could not understand the danger. When she refused to eat something Stalin offered her, Pavel kicked her under the table. Yet the children played around Stalin and his killers as obliviously as birds fluttering in and out of a crocodile's open mouth.

Stalin still visited his comrades' houses, often calling at Poskrebyshev's for dinner where there was dancing and he played charades. Poskrebyshev had recently married a sparky girl who had joined Stalin's circle. In 1934, this unlikely romantic hero went to a party at the house of the Kremlin doctor Mikhail Metalikov, whose wife Asya was indirectly related to Trotsky, her sister being married to his son, Sedov. Metalikov's real name was Masenkis, a family of Jewish Lithuanian sugar barons, a dangerous combination.

Metalikov's sister was Bronislava, dark and lithe, full of the energy and playfulness that was so often missing from Old Bolshevik women. The 24-year-old Bronka was married to a lawyer with whom she already had a daughter, while qualifying as an endocrinologist. Photographs show her slim, mischievous elegance in a polkadot dress. That day at the party, she was playing some sort of game, running round the table from which Poskrebyshev, Stalin's simian *chef de cabinet* of forty-three, watched her. When she started a food fight, she threw a cake that missed its target and landed right on Poskrebyshev's Party tunic: he fell in love with Bronka and married her soon afterwards. Family photographs show the worshipful devotion of Poskrebyshev, who appears in history as a Quasimodo but is seen here as the loving husband resting his head on his wife's lustrous shoulder, nuzzling her brown hair.

Beauty and the Beast caused much merriment in Stalin's entourage: Kira Alliluyeva heard 'Poskrebyshev's beautiful Polish wife joke that he was so ugly that she only went to bed with him in the dark'. But Poskrebyshev was proud of his ugliness: Stalin chose him for his hideous countenance. He cheerfully played court jester: Stalin dared Poskrebyshev to drink a glass of vodka in one gulp without a sip of water or to see how long he could hold up his hands with burning paper under each nail.

'Look!' Stalin would laugh. 'Sasha can drink a glass of vodka and not even wrinkle his nose!' Stalin liked Bronka, one of a new generation of lighthearted girls, secure in the heart of the élite, where she was accustomed to meet the magnates. She called Stalin the familiar *ty* and if she travelled abroad, she, like the Alliluyev women, always brought a present for Svetlana, calling Stalin to ask if she could give it. 'Will it suit her?' he asked about a Western pullover.

'Oh yes!'

'Then give it to her!'

Bronka's best friend was Yevgenia Yezhova, editor and irrepressible literary groupie. These two giggly and flighty glamour pusses of Jewish Polish or Lithuanian origins were so similar that Kira Alliluyeva thought they were sisters. They even shared the same patronymic Solomonova though they were no relation. Yezhov and Poskrebyshev were close friends too – they would go fishing together while their wives gossiped.

While Blackberry, now promoted to candidate Politburo member, massacred his victims, his wife was friends with all the artistic stars and slept with most of them. The enchanting Isaac Babel was Yezhova's chief lion: 'If you invited people "for Babel", they all came,' wrote Babel's wife, Pirozhkova. Solomon Mikhoels, the Yiddish actor who performed *King Lear* for Stalin, jazz-band leader Leonid Utesov, film director Eisenstein, novelist Mikhail Sholokhov and journalist Mikhail Koltsov attended the salon of this fascinating flibbertigibbet. At the Kremlin parties, Yezhova foxtrotted the most, not missing a dance. Her best friend, Zinaida Glikina, had also created a literary salon. When her marriage broke up, Yezhov invited her to live with them and seduced her. She was far from being his only mistress, while Yevgenia enthusiastically pursued literary affairs with Babel, Koltsov and

Sholokhov. Few refused an invitation from Yezhov's wife: 'Just think,' Babel said, 'our girl from Odessa has become the first lady of the kingdom!'

After Nadya's death, there was a rumour that Stalin fell in love with and married Lazar Kaganovich's sister, Rosa, his niece (also named Rosa) or his daughter Maya. This was repeated and widely believed: there were even photographs showing Rosa Kaganovich as a dark pretty woman. The Kaganoviches were a good-looking family – Lazar himself was handsome as a young man and his daughter Maya grew up to be compared to Elizabeth Taylor. The significance of the story was that Stalin had a Jewish wife, useful propaganda for the Nazis who had an interest in merging the Jewish and Bolshevik devils into Mr and Mrs Stalin. The Kaganoviches, father and daughter, were so emphatic in their denials that they perhaps protested too much but it seems this particular story is a myth.*

The story is doubly ironic since the Nazis had no need to invent such a character: Stalin was surrounded by Jewesses – from Polina Molotova and Maria Svanidze to Poskrebysheva and Yezhova. Beria's son, reliable on gossip, dubious on politics, recalled that his father gleefully listed Stalin's affairs with Jewesses.

These pretty young Jewesses fluttered around Stalin but they were all of 'dubious origins'. They were more interested in clothes, jokes and affairs than dialectical materialism. Along with Zhenya Alliluyeva and Maria Svanidze, they were surely the life and soul of this fatally interwoven society of Stalin's family and comrades. Stanislas Redens, chief of the Moscow NKVD, often took his family and the other Alliluyevs over to the Yezhovs. The children were fascinated by the NKVD boss: 'Yezhov pranced down the steps in the full dress uniform of Commissar-General in a rather scary way as if he was very full of himself,' recalls Leonid Redens. 'He was so sullen while my father was so open.' Kira Alliluyeva enjoyed the frothy banter of Yevgenia Yezhova and Bronka Poskrebysheva. Yezhov, who worked all night, was usually too tired to socialize so Kira and the other teenagers hid behind a curtain. When the minuscule Blackberry strode past in his boots, they started giggling. But their fathers, Pavel Alliluyev and

---

* There were two Rosa Kaganoviches: Lazar's sister Rosa died young in 1924 while his niece Rosa lived in Rostov and then moved to Moscow where she still lives. It is possible that they met Stalin but they did not marry him.

Stanislas Redens, who understood what was at stake, were furious with them – but how could they explain how dangerous a game it was? Now, the promiscuous horseplay of the women around Stalin made them suddenly vulnerable.

In the spring, Stalin began to distance himself from the family, whose gossipy arrogance suddenly seemed suspicious. When they gathered at his apartment for Svetlana's eleventh birthday on 28 February 1937, Yakov, Stalin's gentle Georgian son, brought Julia, his Jewish wife, for the first time. She had been married to a Chekist bodyguard when she met Yakov through the Redens, whom Stalin immediately blamed for making a match with 'that Jewish woman'. Maria Svanidze, always intriguing, called Julia 'an adventuress' and tried to persuade Stalin:

'Joseph, it's impossible. You must interfere!' This was enough to win Stalin's sympathy for his son.

'A man loves the woman he loves!' he retorted, whether she was a 'princess or a seamstress'. After they married and had their daughter Gulia, Stalin noticed how well Julia kept Yakov's clothes. She was a *baba* after all. 'Now I see your wife's a good thing,' Stalin finally told Yasha who lived with his little family in the grand apartment building on Granovsky Street. When Stalin finally met Julia, he liked her, made a fuss of her and even fed her with a fork like a loving Georgian father-in-law.

Stalin, losing patience with the family, did not attend the party. Maria Svanidze thought she could understand why: the Alliluyevs were useless: 'crazy Olga, idiot Fyodor, imbecilic Pavel and Niura [Anna Redens], narrow-minded Stan [Redens], lazy Vasya [Vasily Stalin], soppy Yasha [Djugashvili]. The only normal people are Alyosha, Zhenya and me and … Svetlana.' This was ironic since it was the Svanidzes who were the first to fall. Maria herself was ebulliently egotistical, tormenting her own husband with letters that boasted, 'I'm better looking than 70% of Bolshevik wives … Anyone who meets me remembers forever.' This was true but far from helpful at Stalin's court. One pities these haughty, decent women who found themselves in the quagmire of this place and time which they so little understood.

That spring, Stalin and Pavel played Svanidze and Redens at billiards. The losers traditionally had to crawl under the table as their penalty. When Stalin's side lost, Pavel diplomatically suggested that the children, Kira and Sergei, should crawl under the table for them. Sergei did not mind – he was only nine – but

Kira, who was eighteen, refused defiantly. As outspoken as her mother and fearless with it, she insisted that Stalin and her father had lost and under the table they should go. Pavel became hysterical and clipped her with the billiard cue.

Soon afterwards, Stalin and the blue-eyed, dandyish Svanidze suddenly ceased to be 'like brothers'. 'Alyosha was quite a liberal, a European,' explained Molotov. 'Stalin sensed this ...' Svanidze was Deputy Chairman of the State Bank, an institution filled with urbane cosmopolitans now under grave suspicion. On 2 April 1937, Stalin wrote an ominous note to Yezhov: 'Purge the staff of the State Bank.' Svanidze had also done secret and sensitive work for Stalin over the years. Maria Svanidze's diary stopped in the middle of the year: her access to Stalin had suddenly ended. By 21 December, they were under investigation and not invited for Stalin's birthday which must have been agony for Maria. Days later, the Svanidzes visited Zhenya and Pavel Alliluyev in the House on the Embankment (where they all lived). Maria showed off her low-cut velvet dress. After they left at midnight, Zhenya and Kira were doing the dishes when the bell rang. It was Maria's son from her first marriage: 'Mama and Alyosha have been arrested. She was taken away in her beautiful clothes.' A few months later, Zhenya received a letter from Maria who begged her to pass it on to Stalin: 'If I don't leave this camp, I'll die.' She took the letter to Stalin who warned her:

'Don't ever do this again!' Maria was moved to a harsher prison. Zhenya sensed the danger for her and her children of being so close to Stalin, although she adored him until the end of her days, despite her terrible misfortunes. She drew back from Stalin while nagging Pavel to speak to him about their arrested friends. Apparently he did so: 'They're my friends – so put me in jail too!' Some were released.

The other Alliluyevs also did their bit: grandmother Olga, living a *grande dame*'s life in the Kremlin, said little. While the others believed that Stalin did not know the details and was being tricked by the NKVD, she alone of this ship of fools understood: 'nothing happens that he does not know about.' But her estranged husband, the respected Sergei, appealed repeatedly to Stalin, waiting for him on the sofa in his apartment. Oftentimes he fell asleep there and awoke in the early hours to find Stalin arriving from dinner. There and then he begged for someone's life. Stalin teased his father-in-law by repeating his favourite expression: 'Exactly exactly':

'So you came to see me, "Exactly Exactly",' Stalin joked.

Just after Svanidze's arrest, Mikoyan arrived as normal at Kuntsevo for dinner with Stalin who, knowing how close he was to Alyosha, walked straight up to him and said:

'Did you hear we've arrested Svanidze?'

'Yes ... but how could it happen?'

'He's a German spy,' replied Stalin.

'How can it be?' replied Mikoyan. 'There's no evidence of his sabotage. What's the benefit of a spy who does nothing?'

Stalin explained that Svanidze was a 'special sort of spy', recruited when he was a German prisoner during the Great War, whose job was simply to provide information. Presumably, after this revelation, dinner at Stalin's continued as usual.

* * *

Once a leader was under attack, the Terror followed its own momentum. Just demoted, Postyshev, the tough, sallow-faced and arrogant 'prince' of the Ukraine, who had so entertained Stalin by slow-dancing with Molotov, frantically proved his ferocity by eliminating virtually the entire bureaucracy in the Volga town of Kuibyshev.* Now, at the Plenum in January 1938, he was to be destroyed for killing the wrong people.

'The Soviet and Party leaderships were in enemy hands,' claimed Postyshev.

'All of it? From top to bottom?' interrupted Mikoyan.

'Weren't there any honest people?' asked Bulganin.

'Aren't you exaggerating, Comrade Postyshev?' added Molotov.

'But there were errors,' Kaganovich declared, a cue to Postyshev to say:

'I shall talk about my personal errors.'

'I want you to tell the truth,' said Beria.

'Please permit me to finish and explain the whole business to the best of my ability,' Postyshev pleaded at which Kaganovich boomed: 'You're not very good at explaining it – that's the whole point.' Postyshev got up to defend himself but Andreyev snapped:

'Comrade Postyshev, take your seat. This is no place for strolling around.' Postyshev's strolling days were over: Malenkov attacked him. Stalin proposed his demotion from the Politburo: Khrushchev, who was soon appointed to run the Ukraine, replaced him as candidate member, stepping into the front rank. But the attacks

* The ancient city of Samara had been renamed after Kuibyshev on his death in 1935.

on Postyshev contained a warning for Yezhov whose arrests were increasingly frenzied. Meanwhile Stalin seemed undecided about Postyshev:* his high-handedness attracted enemies who perhaps persuaded Stalin to destroy him. His last hope was a personal appeal to Stalin, probably written after a confrontation with his accusers:

'Comrade Stalin, I ask you to receive me after the meeting.'

'I cannot receive you today,' Stalin wrote back. 'Talk to Comrade Molotov.' Within days, he had been arrested. Stalin signed another order for 48,000 executions by quota while Marshal Yegorov followed his 'beautiful' wife into the 'meat-grinder'. But Yezhov was already so exhausted that on 1 December 1937, Stalin was commissioned to supervise his week-long holiday.

In early February, a drunken Blackberry led an expedition to purge Kiev where, aided by the new Ukrainian viceroy Khrushchev,† another 30,000 were arrested. Arriving to find that virtually the whole Ukrainian Politburo had been purged under his predecessor Kosior, Khrushchev went on to arrest several commissars and their deputies. The Politburo approved 2,140 victims on Khrushchev's lists for shooting. Here again, he over-fulfilled his quota. In 1938, 106,119 people were arrested in Khrushchev's Ukrainian Terror. Yezhov's visit accelerated the bloodbath: 'After Nikolai Ivanovich Yezhov's trip to Ukraine ... the real destruction of hidden Enemies began,' announced Khrushchev, hailed as an 'unswerving Stalinist' for his 'merciless uprooting of Enemies'. The NKVD unveiled a conspiracy to poison horses and arrested two professors as Nazi agents. Khrushchev tested the so-called poison and discovered that it did not kill horses. Only after three different commissions had been appointed did he prove this particular conspiracy to be false – but one suspects that Khrushchev only questioned the NKVD's work when Stalin had signalled his displeasure.

In his cups in Kiev, Yezhov displayed alarming recklessness, boasting that the Politburo was 'in his hands'. He could arrest

---

* Did Stalin recall Postyshev's slight cheekiness in 1931? When Stalin wrote to him to complain about the list of those to receive the Order of Lenin: 'We give the Order of Lenin to any old shitters'. Postyshev replied cheerfully that the 'shitters' were all approved by Stalin himself.

† Khrushchev, like other regional bosses such as Beria and Zhdanov, became the object of an extravagant local cult: a 'Song of Khrushchev' soon joined the 'Song for Beria' and odes to Yezhov in the Soviet songbook.

anyone he wanted, even the leaders. One night he was literally carried home from a banquet. It could not be long before Stalin heard of his excesses, if not his dangerous boasting.

Yezhov returned in time for the third and last show trial of the 'Anti-Soviet Bloc of Rightists and Trotskyites' which opened on 2 March, starring Bukharin, Rykov and Yagoda, who admitted killing Kirov and Gorky among others. Bukharin scored his own private triumph in a confession of guilt, laced with oblique Aesopian mockery of Stalin and Yezhov's infantile plots. But this changed nothing. Yezhov attended the executions. He is said to have ordered Yagoda to be beaten:

'Come on, hit him for all of us.' But there was a hint of humanity when it came to the death of his old drinking companion, Yagoda's ex-secretary Bulanov: he had him given some brandy.

When it was over, Yezhov proposed a fourth super-trial against the Polish spies in the Comintern, which he had been preparing for months. But Stalin cancelled the trial. He rarely pursued one policy to the exclusion of all others: Stalin's antennae sensed that the massacre was exhausting his own lieutenants, especially the louche Blackberry himself.

25

Beria and the Weariness of Hangmen

On 4 April, Yezhov was appointed Commissar of Water Transport which made some sense since the building of canals was the task of the NKVD's slave labour. But there was a worrying symmetry because Yagoda had been appointed to a similar Commissariat on his dismissal. Meanwhile Yezhov ravaged even the Politburo: Postyshev was being interrogated; Eikhe of West Siberia was arrested. Stalin promoted Kosior from Kiev to Moscow as Soviet Deputy Premier. However, in April 1938, Kosior's brother was arrested. His one hope was to denounce his kin:

'I'm living under suspicion and distrust,' he wrote to Stalin. 'You can't imagine how that feels to an innocent man. The arrest of my brother casts a shadow over me too ... I swear on my life I've not only never suspected the real nature of Casimir Kosior, he was never close to me ... Why has he invented all this? I can't understand it but Comrade Stalin, it was all invented from start to finish ... I ask you Comrade Stalin and all the Politburo to let me explain myself. I am a victim of an enemy's lies. Sometimes I think this is a silly dream...' How often these victims compared their plight to a 'dream'. On 3 May he was arrested, followed by Chubar. Kaganovich claimed, 'I protected Kosior and Chubar' but faced with their handwritten confessions, 'I gave up.'

Yezhov, living a vampiric nocturnal existence of drinking and torture sessions, was being crushed under the weight of his work. Stalin noticed Blackberry's degeneration. 'You call the ministry,' Stalin complained, 'he's left for the Central Committee. You call the Central Committee, he's left for the ministry. You send a messenger to his apartment and there he's dead drunk.' The pressure on these slaughtermen was immense: just as Himmler later lectured his SS butchers on their special work, so now Stalin worked hard to reassure and encourage his men. But not all of them were strong enough to stand the pace.

The executioners survived by drinking. Even the sober purgers were dizzy with death. The official investigating the Belorussian Military District admitted to Stalin that 'I didn't lose my teeth but I must confess ... I became disorientated for a while.' Stalin reassured him. Even dread Mekhlis almost had a breakdown at the beginning of the Terror when he still ran *Pravda*, writing an extraordinary letter to Stalin that gives a fascinating window on to the pressures of being a Stalinist potentate in the whirlwind of terror:

> *Dear Comrade Stalin,*
> *My nerves did not stand up. I did not comport myself as a Bolshevik; especially I feel the pain of my words in our 'personal talk' when I personally owed my whole life and my* Partiinost *to you. I feel absolutely crushed. These years take away from us a lot of people ... I must run* Pravda *in a situation when there is no secretary and no editor, when we have not approved a theme, when I found myself finally in the role of 'persecuted editor'. This is organized bedlam which can eat up everybody. And it has eaten up people! In the last days, I've felt ill without sleep and only able to get to sleep at eleven or twelve in the morning ... I'm all the more frantic in my apartment after sleepless nights at the newspaper. It's time to relieve me [of this job]. I can't be chief of* Pravda *when I'm sick and sleepless, incapable of following what is happening in the country, economics, art and literature, never getting the chance to go to the theatre. I had to tell you this personally but it was silly, lying. Forgive me my dear Comrade Stalin for that unpleasant minute I gave you. For me it's very hard to experience such a trauma!*

The Procurator-General Vyshinsky also felt the pressure, finding this on his desk: 'Everyone knows you're a Menshevik. After using you, Stalin will sentence you to *Vishka* ... Run away ... Remember Yagoda. That's your destiny. The Moor has done his duty. The Moor can go.'

Constantly drunk, Yezhov sensed Stalin was, as he later wrote to his master, 'dissatisfied with the NKVD work which deteriorated my mood still further'. He made frantic attempts to prove his worth: he was said to have suggested renaming Moscow as 'Stalinodar'. This was laughed off. Instead Yezhov was called upon to kill his own NKVD appointees whom he had protected. In early 1938, Stalin and Yezhov decided to liquidate the veteran Chekist, Abram Slutsky, but since he headed the Foreign Department, they devised a plan so as not to scare their foreign agents. On 17 February, Frinovsky invited Slutsky to his office where another of Yezhov's deputies came up behind him and drew a mask of chloroform over his face. He was then injected with poison and died right there in the office. It was officially announced that he had died of a heart attack.* Soon the purge began to threaten those closer to Yezhov. When his protégé Liushkov was recalled from the Far East, Yezhov tipped him off. Liushkov defected to the Japanese. Yezhov was so rattled by this fiasco that he asked Frinovsky to go with him to tell Stalin: 'On my own I did not have the strength.' Yezhov 'literally went mad'. Stalin rightly suspected Yezhov of warning Liushkov.

Sensing his rising doubts, Stalin's magnates, who had proved their readiness to kill, began to denounce Yezhov's degeneracy and lies. Zhdanov in particular was said to oppose Yezhov's terror. His son Yury claims his father had wanted to talk to Stalin alone but Yezhov was always present: 'Father finally managed to see Stalin tête-à-tête and said, "Political provocation is going on ..."' This is convincing because Zhdanov was closest to Stalin personally but Malenkov's children tell a similar story. Molotov and Yezhov had a row in the Politburo in mid-1938. Stalin ordered the latter to apologize. When another NKVD agent, Alexander Orlov, the resident agent in Spain, defected, Yezhov was so scared of Stalin, that he tried to withhold this information.

On 29 July, Stalin signed another death-list that included more of Yezhov's protégés. Yezhov was so distraught with fear and foreboding that he started shooting prisoners who might incriminate him. Uspensky, the Ukrainian NKVD chief, was in Moscow and discovered that a thousand people were going to be shot in the next five days. 'The tracks should be covered,' Yezhov warned him. 'All investigation cases should be finished in an accelerated procedure so it'll be impossible to make sense of it.'

Stalin gently told Yezhov that he needed some help in running the NKVD and asked him to choose someone. Yezhov requested Malenkov but Stalin wanted to keep him in the Central Committee so someone, probably Kaganovich, proposed Beria. Stalin may have wanted a Caucasian, perhaps convinced that the cut-throat traditions of the mountains – blood feuds, vendettas and secret murders – suited the position. Beria was a natural, the only First Secretary who personally tortured his victims. The

---

* His splendid gravestone in the Novodevichy Cemetery not far from Nadya Stalin's grave gives no hint of his sinister end.

blackjack – the *zhguti* – and the truncheon – the *dubenka* – were his favourite toys. He was hated by many of the Old Bolsheviks and family members around the leader. With the whispering, plotting and vengeful Beria at his side, Stalin felt able to destroy his own polluted, intimate world.

Yezhov probably tried to arrest Beria, but it was too late. Stalin had already seen Beria during the Supreme Soviet on 10 August. Beria was coming to Moscow.

He had come a long way since 1931. Beria, now thirty-six, was complex and talented with a first-class brain. He was witty, a font of irreverent jokes, mischievous anecdotes and withering put-downs. He managed to be a sadistic torturer as well as a loving husband and warm father but he was already a Priapic womanizer whom power would distort into a sexual predator. A skilled manager, he was the only Soviet leader whom 'one could imagine becoming Chairman of General Motors', as his daughter-in-law put it later. He could run vast enterprises with a mixture of villainous threats – 'I'll grind you to powder' – and meticulous precision. 'Everything that depended on Beria had to function with the precision ... of a clock' while 'the two things he could not bear were wordiness and vagueness of expression.'* He was 'a good organizer, businesslike and capable', Stalin had told Kaganovich as early as 1932, possessing the 'bull nerves' and indefatigability that were necessary for survival at Stalin's court. He was a 'most clever man', admitted Molotov, 'inhumanly energetic – he could work a week without sleep'.

Beria had the 'singular ability to inspire both fear and enthusiasm'. 'Idolized' by his own henchmen even though he was often harsh and rude, he would shout: 'We'll arrest you and let you rot in the camps ... we'll turn you into camp dust.' A young man like Alyosha Mirtskhulava, whom Beria promoted in the Georgian Party, was still praising Beria for his 'humanity, strength, efficiency and patriotism' when he was interviewed for this book in 2002.† Yet he liked to boast about his victims: 'Let me have one night with him and I'll have him confessing he's the King of England.' His favourite movies were Westerns but he identified with the Mexican bandits. Well-educated for a Bolshevik

* He usually signed documents in tiny neat writing in a distinctive turquoise ink or on a turquoise typewriter that did not clash with Stalin's blue or red crayons.
† The author is grateful to Alyosha Mirtskhulava, Beria's Georgian Komsomol boss, and later Georgian First Secretary, for his interview in Tbilisi.

magnate, Stalin teased this architect *manqué* that his pince-nez were made of clear glass, worn to give an impression of intellectual gravitas.

This deft intriguer, coarse psychopath and sexual adventurer would also have cut throats, seduced ladies-in-waiting and poisoned goblets of wine at the courts of Genghis Khan, Suleiman the Magnificent or Lucrezia Borgia. But this 'zealot', as Svetlana called him, worshipped Stalin in these earlier years – theirs was the relationship of monarch and liege – treating him like a Tsar instead of the first comrade. The older magnates treated Stalin respectfully but familiarly, but even Kaganovich praised him in the Bolshevik lexicon. Beria however said, 'Oh yes, you are so right, absolutely true, how true' in an obsequious way, recalled Svetlana. 'He was always emphasizing that he was devoted to my father and it got through to Stalin that whatever he said, this man supported him.' Bearing a flavour of his steamy Abkhazia to Stalin's court, Beria was to become even more complex, powerful and depraved, yet less devoted to Marxism as time went on but in 1938, this 'colossal figure', as Artyom puts it, changed everything.

Beria, like many before him, tried to refuse his promotion. There is no reason to doubt his sincerity – Yagoda had just been shot and the writing was on the wall for Yezhov. His wife Nina did not want to move – but Beria was rapaciously ambitious. When Stalin proposed Beria as NKVD First Deputy, Yezhov pathetically suggested that the Georgian might be a good commissar in his own right. 'No, a good deputy,' Stalin reassured him.

Stalin sent Vlasik down to arrange the move. In August, after hurrying back to Georgia to anoint a successor to run Tiflis, Beria arrived in Moscow where, on 22 August 1938, he was appointed First Deputy Narkom of the NKVD. The family were assigned an apartment in the doom-laden House on the Embankment. Stalin arrived to inspect the flat and was not impressed. The bosses lived much better in the warm fertile Caucasus, with its traditions of luxury, wine and plentiful fruit, than elsewhere: Beria had resided in an elegant villa in Tiflis. Stalin suggested they move into the Kremlin but Beria's wife was unenthusiastic. So finally Stalin chose the Georgian new boy an aristocratic villa on Malaya Nikitskaya in the centre of the city, once the home of a Tsarist General Kuropatkin, where he lived splendidly by Politburo standards. Only Beria had his own mansion.

Stalin treated the newly arrived Berias like a long-lost family. He adored the statuesque blonde Nina Beria whom he always treated 'like a daughter': when the new Georgian leader Candide Charkviani was invited to dinner *chez* Beria, there was a phone call and a sudden flurry of activity.

'Stalin's coming!' Nina said, frantically preparing Georgian food. Moments later, Stalin swept in. At the Georgian *supra*, Stalin and Beria sang together. Even after the Terror, Stalin had not lost a certain spontaneity.

Beria and Yezhov ostensibly became friends: Beria called his boss 'dear Yozhik', even staying at his dacha. But it could not last in the jungle of Stalin's court. Beria attended most meetings with Yezhov and took over the intelligence departments. Beria waged a quiet campaign to destroy Blackberry: he invited Khrushchev for dinner where he warned him about Malenkov's closeness to Yezhov. Khrushchev realized that Beria was really warning him about his own friendship with Yezhov. No doubt Beria had the same chat with Malenkov. But the most telling evidence is the archives: Beria finagled Vyshinsky into complaining to Stalin about Yezhov's slowness.* Stalin did not react but Molotov ordered Yezhov:

'It is necessary to pay special attention to Comrade Beria and hurry up. Molotov.' That weather vane of Stalin's favour, Poskrebyshev, stopped calling Yezhov by the familiar *ty* and started visiting Beria instead.

Beria brought a new spirit to the NKVD: Yezhov's frenzy was replaced with a tight system of terror administration that became the Stalinist method of ruling Russia. But this new efficiency was no consolation to the victims. Beria worked with Yezhov on the interrogations of the fallen magnates, Kosior, Chubar and Eikhe, who were cruelly tortured. Chubar appealed to Stalin and Molotov, revealing his agonies.

Stalin, Blackberry and Beria now turned to the Far East where the army, under the gifted Marshal Blyukher, had largely escaped the Terror. In late June, the 'gloomy demon' Mekhlis descended on Blyukher's command with rabid blood-lust. Setting up his headquarters in his railway carriage like a Civil War chieftain, he was soon sending Stalin and Voroshilov telegrams like this:

---

* The case in question concerned an investigation to find the person who had mistakenly burned the books of Lenin, Stalin and Gorky in a furnace: another example of the absurdity and deadliness of the Terror.

'The Special Railway Corps leaves bits and pieces of dubious people all over the place ... There are 46 German Polish Lithuanian Latvian Galician commanders ... I have to go to Vladivostok to purge the corps.' Once there, he boasted to Stalin, 'I dismissed 215 political workers, most of them arrested. But the purge ... is not finished. I think it's impossible to leave Khabarovsk without even more harsh investigations ...' When Voroshilov and Budyonny tried to protect officers, Mekhlis sneaked on Voroshilov (they hated each other) to Stalin: 'I reported to CC and Narkom (Voroshilov) about the situation in the secret service department. There are a lot of dubious people and spies there ... Now C. Voroshilov orders the cancellation of the trial ... I can't agree with the situation.' Even Kaganovich thought Mekhlis 'was cruel, he sometimes overdid it!'

As Mekhlis headed east, the Japanese Kwangtung Army probed Soviet defences west of Lake Khasan, leading to a full-scale battle. Blyukher attacked the Japanese between 6 and 11 August and drove them back with heavy losses. Encouraged by Mekhlis, and alarmed by the losses and Blyukher's hesitations, Stalin berated the Marshal down the telephone:

'Tell me honestly, Comrade Blyukher, do you really want to fight the Japanese? If you don't, then tell me straight, like a good Communist.'

'The sharks have arrived,' Blyukher told his wife. 'They want to eat me. Either they eat me or I eat them, but the latter is unlikely.' The killer-shark sealed Blyukher's fate. Mekhlis arrested four of Blyukher's staff, requesting Stalin and Voroshilov to let him 'shoot all four without prosecution by my special order'. Blyukher was sacked, recalled and arrested on 22 October 1938.

'Now I am done for!' sobbed Yezhov in his office, as he went on executing any prisoners who 'may turn against us'. On 29 September, he lost much of his power when Beria was appointed to run the heart of the NKVD: State Security (GUGB). He now co-signed Yezhov's orders. Blackberry tried to strike back: he proposed to Stalin that Stanislas Redens, Beria's enemy married to Anna Alliluyeva, become his other deputy. There was no hope of this.

Yezhov sat boozing at his dacha with his depressed cronies, warning that they would soon be destroyed, and fantasizing about killing his enemies: 'Immediately remove all people posted in the Kremlin by Beria,' he loudly ordered the head of Kremlin security during one such bout, 'and replace them with reliable people.' Soon he said, in a slurred voice, that Stalin should be killed.

26

The Tragedy and Depravity of the Yezhovs

News of the lion-hunting literary sex-life of Yevgenia Yezhova suddenly reached Stalin. Sholokhov, one of his favourite novelists, had started an affair with her. Yezhov bugged his room at the National Hotel and was furious to read the blow-by-blow account of how 'they kissed each other' then 'lay down'. Yezhov was so intoxicated and jealous that he slapped Yevgenia in the presence of their lissom house-guest, Zinaida Glikina (with whom he was sleeping) but later forgave her. Sholokhov realized he was being followed and complained to Stalin and Beria. Stalin summoned Blackberry to the Politburo where he apologized to the novelist.

The magnates steered cautiously between Yezhov and Beria. When Yezhov arrested one commissar, Stalin sent Molotov and Mikoyan to investigate. Back at the Kremlin, Mikoyan acclaimed the man's innocence and Beria attacked Yezhov's case. 'Yezhov displayed an ambiguous smile,' wrote Mikoyan, 'Beria looked pleased' but 'Molotov's face was like a mask.' The Commissar* became what Mikoyan called a 'lucky stiff', back from the dead. Stalin released him.

When one NKVD officer needed the chief's signature, Yezhov was nowhere to be found. Beria told him to drive out to Yezhov's dacha and get his signature. There he found a man who was either 'fatally ill or had spent the night drinking heavily'. Regional NKVD bosses started to denounce Yezhov.

The darkness began to descend on Yezhov's family where his silly, sensual wife was unwittingly to play the terrible role of black widow spider: most of her lovers were to die. She herself was too

---

* Stalin backed Beria's dismissal of the case against Shipping Commissar Tevosian but told Mikoyan: 'Tell him the CC knows he was recruited by Krupp as a German agent. Everyone understands a person gets trapped ... If he confesses it honestly ... the CC will forgive him.' Mikoyan called Tevosian into his office to offer him Stalin's trick but the Commisssar refused to confess, which Stalin accepted. Tevosian was to be one of the major industrial managers of WW2.

sensitive a flower for Yezhov's world. Both she and Yezhov were promiscuous but then they lived in a world of high tension, dizzy power over life and death, and dynamic turmoil where men rose and fell around them. If there was justice in Yezhov's fall, it was a tragedy for Yevgenia and little Natasha, to whom he was a kind father. A pall fell on Yevgenia's literary salon. When a friend walked her home to the Kremlin after a party, she herself reflected that Babel was in danger because he had been friends with arrested Trotskyite generals: 'Only his European fame could save him ...' She herself was in greater peril.

Yezhov learned that Beria was going to use Yevgenia, an 'English spy' from her time in London, against him so he asked for a divorce in September. The divorce was sensible: in other cases, it actually saved the life of the divorcee. But the tension almost broke the nervy Yevgenia, who went on holiday to the Crimea with Zinaida to recover. It seems that Yezhov was trying to protect his wife from arrest, hence her loving and grateful letter to him.

'Kolyushenka!' she wrote to her beleaguered husband. 'I really ask you – I insist that I remain in control of my life. Kolya darling! I earnestly beg you to check up on my whole life, everything about me ... I cannot reconcile myself to the thought that I am under suspicion of committing crimes I never committed ...'

Their world was shrinking daily: Yezhov had managed to have her ex-husband Gladun shot before Beria took control of the NKVD, but another ex-lover, the publisher Uritsky, was being interrogated. He revealed her affair with Babel. Yezhov's secretary and friends were arrested too. Yezhov summoned Yevgenia back to Moscow.

Yevgenia waited at the dacha with her daughter Natasha and her friend Zinaida. She was desperately worried about the family – and who can blame her? Her nerves cracked. In hospital, they diagnosed an 'asthenic-depressive condition perhaps cyclothymia', sending her to a sanatorium near Moscow.

When Zinaida was arrested, Yevgenia wrote to Stalin: 'I beg you Comrade Stalin to read this letter ... I am treated by professors but what sense does it make if I am burned by the thought that you distrust me? ... You are dear and beloved to me.' Swearing on her daughter's life that she was honest, she admitted that 'in my personal life, there have been mistakes about which I could tell you, and all of it because of jealousy.' Stalin doubtless already knew all her Messalinian exploits. She made the sacrificial offer:

'Let them take away my freedom, my life … but I will not give up the right to love you as everybody does, who loves the country and the Party.' She signed off: 'I feel like a living corpse. What am I to do? Forgive my letter written in bed.' Stalin did not reply.

The trap was swinging shut on Yevgenia and her Kolyushenka. On 8 October, Kaganovich drafted a Politburo resolution on the NKVD. On 17 November, a Politburo commission denounced 'very serious faults in the work of the Organs of NKVD'. The deadly *troikas* were dissolved. Stalin and Molotov signed a report, disassociating themselves from the Terror.

At the 7 November parade, Yezhov appeared on the Mausoleum but lingered behind Stalin. Then he disappeared and was replaced by Beria in the blue cap and uniform of a Commissar First Class of State Security. When Stalin ordered the arrest of Yezhov's friend, Uspensky, Ukrainian NKVD chief, the dwarf forewarned him. Uspensky faked suicide and went on the run. Stalin (probably rightly) suspected that Yezhov was bugging his phones.

In her own way, Yevgenia loved Yezhov, despite all their infidelities, and adored their daughter Natasha, because she was willing to sacrifice herself to save them. Her friend Zinaida Ordzhonikidze, Sergo's widow, visited her in hospital, a heroic act of loyalty. Yevgenia gave her a letter for Yezhov in which she offered to commit suicide and asked for a sleeping draught. She suggested that he send a little statuette of a gnome when the time came. He sent Luminal, then, a little later, he ordered the maid to take his wife the statuette. Given Yezhov's dwarfish stature, this deadly gnome seems farcical: perhaps the statuette was an old keepsake representing 'darling Kolya' himself from the early days of their romance. When Glikina's arrest made her own inevitable, Yevgenia sent a note bidding Yezhov goodbye. On 19 November, she took the Luminal.

At 11 p.m., as she sank into unconsciousness, Yezhov arrived at the Little Corner, where he found the Politburo with Beria and Malenkov, who attacked him for five hours. Yevgenia died two days later. Yezhov himself reflected that he had been 'compelled to sacrifice her to save himself'. She had married a monster but died young to save their daughter which, in its way, was a maternal end to a life devoted to innocent fun. Babel heard that 'Stalin can't understand her death. His own nerves are made of steel so he just can't understand how, in other people, they give out.' The Yezhovs' adopted daughter* Natasha, nine, was taken in by his ex-wife's sister and then sent to one of those grim orphanages for the children of Enemies.

Two days after Yevgenia's death, on 23 November, Yezhov returned for another four hours of criticism from Stalin, Molotov and Voroshilov, after which he resigned from the NKVD. Stalin accepted it but he remained in limbo as CC Secretary, Commissar of Water Transport, and a candidate Politburo member, living in the Kremlin like a tiny ghost for a little longer, experiencing what his victims had known before him. His friends 'turned their back upon me as if I was plague-ridden ... I never realized the depth of meanness of all these people.' He blamed the Terror on the *Vozhd*, using a Russian idiom: 'God's will – the Tsar's trial' with himself as the Tsar and Stalin as God.

Yezhov consoled himself with a series of drunken bisexual orgies in his Kremlin apartment. Inviting two drinking buddies and homosexual lovers from his youth to stay, he enjoyed 'the most perverted forms of debauchery'. His nephews brought him girls but he also returned to homosexuality. When one crony, Konstantinov, brought his wife to the party, Yezhov danced the foxtrot with her, pulled out his member, and then slept with her. On the next night, when the long-suffering Konstantinov arrived, they drank and danced to the gramophone until the guest fell asleep only to be awoken: 'I felt something in my mouth. When I opened my eyes, I saw that Yezhov had shoved his member into my mouth.' Unzipped and undone, Yezhov awaited his fate.

Beria, whom Stalin nicknamed 'the Prosecutor', was triumphantly appointed Commissar on 25 November,† and summoned his Georgian henchmen to Moscow. Having destroyed the entourages of the Old Bolshevik 'princes', Stalin now had to import Beria's whole gang to destroy Yezhov's.

---

* Her name was changed to that of Yevgenia's first husband, Khayutin – but she remained loyal to her adoptive father into the next millennium. Natasha Yezhova survived after enduring terrible sufferings on her stepfather's behalf. Vasily Grossman, the author of the classic novel *Life and Fate*, who knew the family, attending the salons with Babel and others, wrote a short story about Natasha's tragic childhood. She became a musician in Penza and Magadan. In May 1998 she applied for Yezhov's rehabilitation. Ironically she had a case since he was certainly not guilty of the espionage for which he was executed. Her appeal was denied. At the time of writing, she is alive.

† The switch between the two secret police chiefs was seamless: on the 24th, Dmitrov, the Comintern leader, was still discussing arrests with Yezhov at his dacha but by nighttime on the 25th, he was working on the same cases with Beria at *his* house.

Ironically, Beria's courtiers were much more educated than Kaganovich or Voroshilov but education is no bar to barbarism. The grey-haired, charming and refined Merkulov, a Russified Armenian, who was to write plays under the pseudonym Vsevolod Rok that were performed on Moscow stages, had known Beria since they studied together at the Baku Polytechnic and had joined the Cheka in 1920. Beria, who, like Stalin, coined nicknames for everyone, called him 'the Theoretician'. Then there was the renegade Georgian prince (though aristocrats are as plentiful in Georgia as vines) Shalva Tsereteli, once a Tsarist officer and member of the anti-Bolshevik Georgian Legion, who had the air of an old-fashioned gentleman but was Beria's private assassin, among his other duties in the NKVD's Special Department. Then there was the bejewelled 300-pound giant – 'the worst man God put on the face of the Earth' – Bogdan Kobulov. 'A burly oversized Caucasian with muddy brown bullish eyes', the 'fat face of a man [who] likes good living ...hairy hands, short bow legs', and a dapper moustache, he was one of those hearty torturers who would have been as at home in the Gestapo as in the NKVD. He was so squat that Beria called him 'the Samovar'.

When Kobulov beat his victims, he used his fists, his elephantine weight and his favourite blackjack clubs. He arranged wiretaps of the magnates for Stalin but he also became a court jester, replacing the late Pauker, with his funny accents. He soon proved his usefulness: Beria was interrogating a victim in his office when the prisoner attacked him. Kobulov boasted about what happened next: 'I saw the boss [he used the Georgian slang – *khozeni*] on the floor and I jumped on the fellow and crushed his neck with my own bare hands.' Yet even this brute sensed that his work was not right for he used to visit his mother and sob to her like an overgrown Georgian child: 'Mama, mama, what are we doing? One day, I'll pay for this.'

The arrival of these exotic, strutting Georgians, some even convicted murderers, must have been like Pancho Villa and his *banditos* riding into a northern town in one of Beria's favourite movies. Stalin later made a great play of sending some of them home, replacing them with Russians, but he remained very much a Georgian himself. Beria's men gave Stalin's entourage a distinctly Caucasian flavour. On the official date of Beria's appointment, Stalin and Molotov signed off on the shooting of 3,176 people so they were busy.

Beria appeared nightly in Lefortovo prison to torture Marshal Blyukher, assisted by 'the Theoretician' Merkukov, 'the Samovar' Kobulov, and his top interrogator, Rodos, who worked on the Marshal with such relish that he called out: 'Stalin, can you hear what they're doing to me?' They tortured him so hard that they managed to knock out one of his eyes and he later died of his wounds. Beria drove over to tell Stalin who ordered the body's incineration. Meanwhile, Beria settled scores, personally arresting Alexander Kosarev, the Komsomol chief, who had once insulted him. Stalin later learned this was a personal vendetta: 'They told me Beria was very vindictive but there was no evidence of it,' he reflected years later. 'In Kosarev's case, Zhdanov and Andreyev checked the evidence.'

Beria revelled in the sport of power: Bukharin's lovely widow, Anna Larina, still only twenty-four, was shown into his Lubianka office by Kobulov who then brought in sandwiches like an infernal Jeeves.

'I should tell you that you look more beautiful than when I last saw you,' Beria told her. 'Execution is for one time only. And Yezhov would certainly have executed you.' When she would not betray anyone, Beria and Kobulov stopped flirting. 'Whom are you trying to save? After all, Nikolai Ivanovich [Bukharin] is no longer with us ... You want to live? ... If you don't shut up, here's what you'll get!' He put a finger to his temple. 'So will you promise me to shut up?' She saw that Beria wanted to save her and she promised. But she would not eat Kobulov's sandwiches.*

* * *

Stalin was careful not to place himself completely in the hands of Beria: the chief of State Security (First Branch), his personal security, was in a sensitive but dangerous position. Two had been shot since Pauker but now Stalin appointed his personal bodyguard, Vlasik, to the job, in charge of the leader's security as well as the dachas, food for the kitchens, the car pool and millions of roubles. Henceforth, explains Artyom, Stalin 'ruled through Poskrebyshev in political matters and Vlasik in personal ones'. Both were indefatigably industrious – and sleazy.

The two men lived similar lives: their daughters recall how they

---

* Anna Larina spent twenty years in the camps. Her son Yury was eleven months old when she was arrested in 1937 and she did not see him again until 1956, just one of many heart-breaking stories.

spent only Sunday at home. Otherwise they were always with Stalin, returning exhausted to sleep. No one knew Stalin better. At home they never discussed politics but chatted about their fishing expeditions. Vlasik, who lived in the elegant villa on Gogolevsky Boulevard, was doggedly loyal, uneducated and drunkenly dissolute: he was already an insatiable womanizer who held parties with Poskrebyshev. He had so many 'concubines', he kept lists of them, forgot their names, and sometimes managed to have a different one in each room at his orgies. He called Stalin *Khozyain*, but 'Comrade Stalin' to his face, rarely joining him at table.

Poskrebyshev's social status was higher, often joining the magnates at dinner and calling Stalin 'Joseph Vissarionovich'. He was the butt and perpetrator of jokes. He sat doggedly at his desk outside Stalin's office: the Little Corner was his domain. The magnates cultivated him, playing to his dog's vanity so that he would warn them if Stalin was in a bad mood. Poskrebyshev always called Vyshinsky to say that Stalin was on his way to Kuntsevo so the Procurator could go to bed, and he once protected Khrushchev. He was so powerful that he could even insult the Politburo. The 'faithful shield-bearer', in Khrushchev's words, played his role in Stalin's most mundane deeds and the most terrible, boasting later about their use of poison. He was a loving husband to Bronka, and an indulgent father to the two children, Galya by her first husband and his own Natalya. But when the *vertushka* rang on Sundays, no one else was allowed to answer it. He was proud of his position: when his daughter had an operation, he lectured her that she had to behave in a way that befitted their station. Poskrebyshev worked closely with Beria: they often visited each other's families but if there was business to conduct, they walked in the garden. But ultimately both Vlasik and Poskrebyshev were obstacles to Beria's power. The same could no longer be said of the Alliluyev family.

27

Death of the Stalin Family: a Strange Proposal and the Housekeeper

Letting Beria into the family was like locking a fox in a chicken coop but Stalin shares responsibility for their fates. 'All our family,' wrote Svetlana, 'was completely baffled as to why Stalin made Beria – a provincial secret policeman – so close to himself and the Government in Moscow.' This was precisely why Stalin had promoted him: no one was sacred to Beria.

The magnates and retainers all grumbled constantly about the self-importance of the 'aunties'. Impertinent with the greatness of his new power and burning with the inferiority complex of a scorned provincial, Beria was determined to prove himself by destroying these glamorous but snobbish members of the new nobility. In the early thirties, Beria had tried to flirt with Zhenya while her husband and Stalin were sitting near by. Zhenya strode up to Stalin:

'If this bastard doesn't leave me alone, I'll smash his pince-nez.' Everyone laughed. Beria was embarrassed. But when Beria began to appear more regularly at Kuntsevo, he still flirted with Zhenya who appealed to Stalin: 'Joseph! He's trying to squeeze my knee!' Stalin probably regarded Beria as something of a card. The family were typical of the élite he was trying to destroy. When Beria turned up in a turtleneck pullover for dinner, Zhenya, who was always dressed to the nines without a hint of Bolshevik modesty, said loudly, 'How dare you come to dinner like this?' Grandfather Alliluyev regularly described Beria as an 'Enemy'.

In November 1938, Stalin's family life really ended. Beria expanded the Terror to include anyone connected to Yezhov, who had not only appointed Stalin's brother-in-law, Stanislas Redens, to run the NKVD in Kazakhstan but had even requested him as his deputy: this was the kiss of death. Relations had certainly been warm when Stalin received the Redens family before they set off for Alma-Ata. We know little about Redens' role in the Terror but Moscow and Kazakhstan had been slaughtered on his watch. The arrival of Beria, his nemesis in Tiflis in 1931, was bad news but even without it, Stanislas would probably have been doomed.

Meanwhile Pavel Alliluyev's job, as a tank forces commissar, placed him in harm's way: close to the executed generals, he was also involved in spying on German tank production. When he saw the Soviet spy Orlov before his defection, Alliluyev warned him: 'Don't ever inquire about the Tukhachevsky affair. Knowing about it is like inhaling poison gas.' Then Pavel had been out in the Far East where the generals appealed to him and he had flown back, according to his daughter Kira, with evidence that proved their innocence. He clearly did not understand that evidence only existed to persuade others, not to prove guilt. Pavel is said to have put together a letter to Stalin, co-signed by three generals, suggesting the Terror be brought to a close. The generals' timing seemed fortuitous; the Terror was ebbing. Stalin did not openly punish them but he had clearly tired of Pavel's interference.*

After holidaying in Sochi, Pavel returned on 1 November. The next morning, Pavel ate breakfast and went to the office where he found that most of his department had been arrested, according to Svetlana: 'He attempted to save certain people, trying to get hold of my father, but it was no use.' At two in the afternoon, Zhenya was called: 'What did you give your husband to eat? He's feeling sick.' Zhenya wanted to rush over but they stopped her. He was sent to the Kremlevka clinic. In the words of the official medical report, 'When he was admitted, he was unconscious, cyanotic and apparently dying. The patient did not recover consciousness.' This was strange since the doctor who telephoned Zhenya to tell her this news said: 'Why did it take you so long? He had something to tell you. He kept asking why Zhenya didn't come. He's already dead.' So died the brother who had given Nadya her pistol. The inconsistencies in an already suspicious death, at a time when medical murder was almost routine, makes foul play possible. Stalin kept the death certificate. Zhenya was later accused of murdering Pavel. Stalin sometimes accused others of his own crimes. We will never know the truth.

'The next time I saw him,' Kira says, 'was lying in state at the Hall of Columns. He was only 44, and he was lying there all

---

* The three generals who signed the letter were said to be Stalin's Tsaritsyn crony, Grigory Kulik, commanders Meretskov and Pavlov plus commissar Savchenko. Savchenko was executed in October 1941; the fate of the others are told later in this book. All suffered grievously at Stalin's hands. Only Meretskov outlived him.

sunburnt, very handsome with his long eyelashes.' Looking into the casket, Sergei Alliluyev mused that there was no more tragic thing than to bury your own children.

Redens himself headed back to Moscow where he arrived on 18 November. At Kuntsevo, Vasily heard Beria demand that Stalin let him arrest Redens. 'But I trust Redens,' replied Stalin 'very decisively.' To Vasily's surprise, Malenkov supported Beria. This was the beginning of the alliance between these two who would not have pressed the arrest without knowing Stalin's instincts: these scenes of pretend argument resemble the mooting exercises practised by trainee lawyers. Yet Stalin was highly suggestible. Redens had the misfortune, like Pavel Alliluyev, to be in two or three overlapping circles of suspicion. Beria is always blamed for turning Stalin against his other brother-in-law but there was more to it than that. Stalin had removed Redens from the Ukraine in 1932. He was close to Yezhov. And he was a Pole. Stalin listened to Beria and Malenkov and then said: 'In that case, sort it out at the Central Committee.' As Svetlana put it, 'My father would not protect him.' On the 22nd, Redens was arrested on his way to work and was never seen again.

Anna Redens started phoning Stalin. She was no longer welcome at Zubalovo. She could not get through to Stalin. 'Then I'll call Voroshilov, Kaganovich and Molotov,' she sobbed. When the children arrived, they found their mother, hysterical at the disappearance of her beloved Stan, lying in bed reading Alexandre Dumas. She appealed to everyone until finally Stalin took her call. Stalin summoned her to the Little Corner. Redens 'would be brought and we shall make an inquiry about all this' but he made one condition: 'And bring Grandfather Sergei Yakovlevich with you.' Sergei, who had now lost two children, no longer waited for Stalin on the sofa every night but he agreed to come. At the last moment, he backed out. Beria either threatened him, or perhaps Sergei thought Redens was guilty of something in his unsavoury work at the Lubianka: Redens' son Leonid stressed that there were tensions between Old Bolsheviks like Sergei and the brash élite like Redens. Grandmother Olga went instead, a brave but foolish move since Stalin loathed interfering women:

'Why have you come? No one called you!' he snarled at her. Anna shouted at Stalin, who had her removed. Redens and the Svanidzes were in jail; Pavel Alliluyev dead. Stalin had allowed the Terror to ravage his own circle. When the Bulgarian Communist, Georgi Dmitrov, appealed for some arrested comrades, Stalin shrugged: 'What can I do for them, Georgi? All my own relatives are in prison too.' This is a revealing excuse. Certainly, with Pavel, Nadya's pistol must have always been on his mind but so were his military connections and intercession for 'Enemies'. Perhaps Stalin was settling private scores against his over-familiar, interfering family who reminded him of Nadya's rejection. But he did not regard the Terror as a private spree: he was cleansing his encircled country of spies to safeguard his vast achievements before war broke out. His family were among the casualties. He regarded them as *his own sacrifice* as the supreme pontiff of Bolshevism. But he was also asserting his own separation from private ties and, perhaps refreshingly, shaking off old obligations of family and friendship:* his vendettas were those of the Party because, as he told Vasily, 'I'm not Stalin ... Stalin IS Soviet power!' But they also provided a living excuse for demanding that his comrades sacrifice *their* own families. None the less, he could have saved anyone he wanted and he did not. The familial world of Stalin and his children was still shrinking.

Svetlana lost another part of her support system: Carolina Til, the dependable housekeeper, that cosy link to her mother, was sacked in the purge of Germans. Beria found her replacement in a niece of his wife Nina from Georgia – though as ever, his true motives are unclear. Svetlana's new governess was Alexandra Nakashidze, tall, slim, long-legged, with perfect pale skin and long thick blue-black hair. A naïve and poorly educated girl from a Georgian village, this NKVD lieutenant entered this increasingly monocoloured world like a purple-feathered peacock. The Alliluyevs and Mikoyan boys are still struck by her today.

Svetlana resented her so-called governess. Nakashidze's arrival shows Beria's special role in the family: could she be his spy in Stalin's household that was otherwise controlled by Vlasik? We know that the court encouraged Stalin to remarry: was she there for Stalin?† However, there was a more obvious candidate almost within the family.

---

* His old lover of 1913, 'my darling' Tatiana Slavotinskaya, is an example: Stalin had protected her well into the Thirties, promoting her in the Central Committee apparatus but now the protection stopped abruptly. Her family was repressed and she was expelled from the House on the Embankment. Slavotinskaya was the grandmother of Yury Trifonov, author of the novel, *House on the Embankment*.

† She remained a presence in the household until after the end of the war when she married an NKVD general and returned to Georgia where she had children. Her daughter still lives in Georgia.

Zhenya Alliluyeva was a widow but she was convinced her husband had been murdered by Beria. Was she guilty about her relationship with Stalin? There is no evidence of this. Her husband had surely known (or chosen not to know) what was going on, but the relationship with Stalin, such as it was, had already cooled by 1938. But now Stalin missed her and made a strange, indirect proposal to her. Beria came to see Zhenya and said: 'You're such a nice person, and you're so fine looking, do you want to move in and be housekeeper at Stalin's house?' Usually this is interpreted as a mysterious threat from Beria but it is surely unlikely that he would have made such a proposal without Stalin's permission, especially since she could have phoned him to discuss it. In Stalin's mind, a 'housekeeper' was his ideal *baba*, the *khozyaika*. This was surely a semi-marriage proposal, an awkward attempt to salvage the warmth of the old days from the destruction that he himself had unleashed. It was unforgivably clumsy to send Beria, whom Zhenya loathed, on this sensitive mission but that is typical of Stalin. If one has any doubt about this analysis, Stalin's reaction to Zhenya's next move may confirm it.

Zhenya was alarmed, fearing that Beria would frame her for trying to poison Stalin. She swiftly married an old friend, named N. V. Molochnikov, a Jewish engineer whom she had met in Germany, perhaps the lover who had almost broken up her marriage. Stalin was appalled, claiming that it was indecent so soon after Pavel's death. Beria's proposal puts Stalin's hurt in a slightly different light. Beria fanned the flames by suggesting that perhaps Zhenya had poisoned her husband, an idea with resonance in this poisoners' coven. Some say the body was dug up twice for tests. In spite of the poisoning allegations, Stalin retained his fascination with Zhenya, going out of his way just before the war to quiz her daughter Kira: 'How's your mother?' Zhenya and Anna Redens were banned from the Kremlin and Stalin looked elsewhere for his 'housekeeper'.

* * *

A young maid named Valentina Vasilevna Istomina had worked at Zubalovo since her late teens in the early thirties. In 1938, she came to work at Kuntsevo. Stalin was attracted to a specific ideal: the busty, blue-eyed, big-haired and retroussé-nosed Russian peasant woman, submissive and practical, a *baba* who could make a home without in any way becoming involved in his other life.

Zhenya had the looks but there was nothing submissive about her. He also found the same looks coupled with haughtiness in the top artistes of the time. Stalin was an avid attender of the theatre, opera and ballet, regularly visiting the Politburo (formerly imperial) *loge* in the Bolshoi or the Moscow Arts Theatre. His favourite singers were the soprano Natalya Schpiller, who was a blue-eyed Valkyrie, and the mezzo Vera Davydova. He liked to instruct them 'in a fatherly way' but he also played one off against the other. He acted being in love with Davydova who later boasted that he proposed marriage: if so, it was only a joke. He teased her by suggesting that she improve her singing by copying Schpiller. When Davydova appeared in a glittery belt, he told her, 'Look, Schpiller's a beguiling woman too but she dresses modestly for official receptions.'

These *divas* were much too glamorous for Stalin but there was no shortage of available admirers, as Vlasik told his daughter. There are many stories of women invited to Kuntsevo: Mirtskhulava, a young Georgian official, remembers Stalin at a Kremlin dinner in 1938 sending him to ask a girl in his Komsomol delegation if she was the daughter of some Old Bolshevik, then inviting her to the dacha. Stalin insisted Mirtskhulava asked her secretly, without either the knowledge of the magnates at his table or of the Georgians. The same happened with a beautiful Georgian pilot whom he met at the Tushino air show in 1938 and who regularly visited Stalin.

This was probably the pattern of his trivial dalliances but what happened at Kuntsevo is beyond our knowledge. Everyone who knew Stalin insists that he was no womanizer and he was famously inhibited about his body. We know nothing about his sexual tastes but Nadya's letters suggest they had a passionate relationship. A fascinating glimpse into his relations with women – perhaps connected to his views on sex – is provided by his attitude to dancing. He liked making Russian dance steps and kicks on his own but dancing *à deux* made him nervous. He told the tenor Kozlovsky at a party that he would not dance because he had damaged his arm in exile and so 'could not hold a woman by the waist'.

Stalin warned his son Vasily against 'women with ideas', whom he found uncomfortable: 'we've known that kind, herrings with ideas, skin and bones.' He was most at home with the women of the service staff. The maids, cooks and guards at his houses were all employed by Vlasik's department and all signed confidentiality contracts though these were hardly necessary in this kingdom of fear. Even when the USSR collapsed, very few of them ever spoke.* The Kremlin hairdresser, who so upset Nadya, was one of these and so was his maid Valentina Istomina, known as Valechka, who gradually became the mainstay of Stalin's home life.

'She laughed all the time and we really liked her,' said Svetlana, 'she was very young, with pink cheeks and she was liked by everyone. She was a pleasant figure, typically Russian.' She was Stalin's 'ideal' woman, buxom and neat, 'round-faced and pug-nosed', primitive, simple and unlettered; she 'served at table deftly, never joined in the conversation', yet she was always there when she was needed. 'She had light brown mousy hair – I remember her well from about 1936, nothing special, not fat not thin but very friendly and smiling,' says Artyom Sergeev. Out of Stalin's presence, she was fun in an unthreatening way, even shrewd: 'She was a clever one, talkative, a chatterbox,' recalled one of Stalin's bodyguards.

Valechka was promoted to housekeeper, taking care of Stalin's 'clothes, the food, the house and so on and she travelled with him wherever he went. She was a comfortable soul to be quiet with, yet he trusted her and she was devoted to him.' Stalin was farcically proud of the way she prepared his underwear: after the war, one Georgian official was amazed when he showed off the piles of gleaming white smalls in his wardrobe, surely a unique moment in the history of dictators.

At the Kremlin apartment, Valechka often served Svetlana and her friend Martha who recalls her 'in her white apron, like a kind woman from the villages, with her fair hair and shapeless figure, not fat though. Always smiling. Svetlana loved her too.' Artyom was one of the few who heard how Stalin spoke to her: 'he'd say about her birthday or something, "Of course I must give you a present."

'"I don't need anything, Comrade Stalin," she replied.

'"Well, if I forget, remind me."' At the end of the thirties, Valechka became Stalin's trusted companion and effectively his

---

* President Vladimir Putin's grandfather was a chef at one of Stalin's houses and revealed nothing to his grandson: 'My grandfather kept pretty quiet about his past life.' As a boy, he recalled bringing food to Rasputin. He then cooked for Lenin. He was clearly Russia's most world-historical chef since he served Lenin, Stalin and the Mad Monk.

secret wife, in a culture when most Bolshevik couples were not formally married. 'Valya looked after Father's creature comforts,' Svetlana said. The court understood that she was his companion and no more was said about it. 'Whether or not Istomina was Stalin's wife is nobody's business,' said the ageing Molotov. 'Engels lived with his housekeeper.' Budyonny and Kalinin 'married' their housekeepers.

'My father said she was very close to him,' asserts Nadezhda Vlasika. Kaganovich's daughter-in-law heard from 'Iron Lazar': 'I only know that Stalin had one common-law wife. Valechka, his waitress. She loved him.'*

Valechka appeared like a jolly, quiet and buxom hospital sister, always wearing a white apron at Stalin's dinners. No one noticed when she attended Yalta and Potsdam: this was as Stalin wished it. Henceforth Stalin's private life was frozen in about 1939: the dramas of Nadya and Zhenya that had caused him pain and anger were over. 'These matters,' recalled the Polish Communist Jakob Berman, who was often at Kuntsevo during the forties, 'were arranged with extreme discretion and never filtered out beyond his closest circle. Stalin was always very careful there shouldn't be any gossip about him ... Stalin understood the danger of gossip.' If other men could be betrayed by their wives, there at least he was safe. He sometimes asked Valechka's political opinions as an ordinary person. None the less, for this political man, she was no companion. He remained lonely.

* * *

Between 24 February and 16 March 1939, Beria presided over the executions of 413 important prisoners, including Marshal Yegorov and ex-Politburo members, Kosior, Postyshev and Chubar: he was already living in the dacha of the last of these. Now he suggested to Stalin that they call a halt, or there would be no one left to arrest. Poskrebyshev marked up the old Central Committee with VN – Enemy of the People – and the date of execution. The next day, Stalin reflected to Malenkov: 'I think

---

* Stalin's bodyguards, whose inaccurate but revealing memoirs were collected long after his death, were not sure about the Valechka relationship. When she became older, she married and, during Stalin's later years, she complained of her husband's jealous reproaches. After Stalin's death, Valechka never spoke of their relationship but when she was asked if the opera singer Davydova ever visited Kuntsevo, her answer perhaps displayed a proprietorial sting: 'I never saw her at the dacha ... She'd have been thrown out!' Valechka was not a Party member.

we're well and truly rid of the opposition millstone. We need new forces, new people ...' The message was sent down the *vertikal* of power: when Mekhlis demanded more arrests in the army for 'lack of revolutionary loyalty', Stalin replied:

'I propose to limit ourselves to an official reprimand ... (I don't see any ill-will in their actions – these aren't mistakes but misunderstandings).'* Blaming all excesses on Yezhov, Stalin protected his other grotesques. The 'denunciatrix' of Kiev, Nikolaenko, was discredited. But she once again appealed to Stalin and Khrushchev: 'I ask you to check everything, where I was mistaken, where I was lied to and where I was provoked, I'm ready to be punished,' she wrote to Khrushchev. But then, still playing high politics, she warned Stalin: 'I'm sure there are too many remnants of Enemies in Kiev ... Dear Joseph Vissarionovich, I've no words to tell you how to understand me but you understand us, your people, without words. I write to you with bitter tears.' Stalin protected her: 'Comrade Khrushchev, I ask you to take measures to let Nikolaenko find calm and fruitful work, J.St.'

The victims of his creatures could now appeal to Stalin. Khrulev, who was to be the outstanding Red Army quartermaster during the Second World War, complained to Stalin about the peripatetic, pompous Mekhlis. 'The lion is the king of the jungle,' Stalin laughed.

'Yes but Mekhlis's a dangerous animal,' said Khrulev, 'who told me he'd do all he could ... [to destroy me].' Stalin smiled genially:

'Well if me and you ... fight Mekhlis together, do you think we'll manage?' retorted the 'lion-king'.

Stalin had not forgotten his greatest enemy: Beria and one of the talented dirty tricks specialists in quiet and quick death, Pavel Sudoplatov, were received in the Little Corner where, pacing silently in soft Georgian boots, Stalin laconically ordered: 'Trotsky should be eliminated within a year.'

* * *

---

* Vyshinsky reported that the arrest of hundreds of teenagers in Novosibirsk had been faked by the NKVD: 'the children were innocent and have been released but three senior officials including the head of the NKVD and the town Procurator were guilty of "betraying revolutionary loyalty" and expelled from the Party'. What should be done with them? On 2 January 1939, Stalin scribbled: 'It's necessary to have a public trial of the guilty.'

On 10 March 1939, the 1,900 delegates of the Eighteenth Congress gathered* to declare the end of a slaughter that had been a success, if slightly marred by Yezhov's manic excesses. The survivors, from Molotov to Zhdanov, remained at the top but were challenged by the younger generation: Khrushchev joined the Politburo while Beria was elected candidate and 'Melanie' Malenkov became a CC Secretary. This leadership ruled the country for the next decade without a single casualty: contrary to his myth, Stalin, a master of divide and rule, could be surprisingly loyal to his protégés. But not to the Blackberry.

Yezhov was on ice yet he still attended the Politburo, sat next to Stalin at the Bolshoi and turned up for work at Water Transport, where he sat through meetings throwing paper darts. He caroused by day but appeared at Congress evening sessions, trying to get permission to speak. 'I strongly ask you to talk with me for only one minute,' he wrote to Stalin. 'Give me the opportunity.' Still a CC member, he attended the meeting of Party elders where the names for the new body were selected. No one objected to his name until Stalin called Yezhov forward:

'Well what do you think of yourself? Are you capable of being a member of the Central Committee?' Yezhov protested his devotion to the Party and Stalin – he could not imagine what he had done wrong. Since all the other murderers were being promoted, the dwarf's bafflement is understandable.

'Is that so?' Stalin started mentioning Enemies close to Yezhov.

'Joseph Vissarionovich!' Yezhov cried out. 'You know it was I – I myself – who disclosed their conspiracy! I came to you and reported it ...'

'Yes yes yes. When you felt you were about to be caught, then you came in a hurry. But what about before that? Were you organizing a conspiracy? Did you want to kill Stalin? Top officials of the NKVD are plotting but you are supposedly not involved. You think I don't see anything? Do you remember who you sent on a certain date for duty with Stalin? Who? With revolvers? Why revolvers near Stalin? Why? To kill Stalin? Well? Go on, get out of here! I don't know, comrades, is it possible to keep him as a member of the Central Committee? I doubt it. Of course think about it ... As you wish ... But I doubt it.'

* In the ugly wooden chamber that had been created by vandalizing the sumptuous Alexandrovsky Hall in the Great Kremlin Palace.

Yezhov was determined to spread the guilt and avenge his betrayal by destroying Malenkov, whom he now denounced. On 10 April, Stalin ordered Yezhov to attend a meeting to hear these accusations. Yezhov reported to Malenkov who ritualistically removed Yezhov's photograph from the array of leadership icons on his office wall like an angel removed from the heavens. Beria and his Georgian prince-executioner, Tsereteli, opened the door and arrested Blackberry, conveying 'Patient Number One' to the infirmary inside Sukhanov prison.

The search of Yezhov's apartment revealed bottles of vodka, empty, half-empty and full, lying around, 115 counter-revolutionary books, guns and those macabre relics: the flattened bullets, wrapped in paper, labelled Zinoviev and Kamenev. More importantly, the search revealed that Yezhov had collected materials about Stalin's pre-1917 police record: was this evidence that he was an Okhrana spy? There was also evidence against Malenkov.* The papers disappeared into Beria's safe.

Stalin was now so omnipotent that when he mispronounced a word from the podium, every subsequent speaker repeated the mistake. 'If I'd said it right,' Molotov reminisced, 'Stalin would have felt I was correcting him.' He was very 'touchy and proud'.† Europe was on the verge of war and Stalin turned his attention to the tightrope walk between Nazi Germany and the Western democracies. Meanwhile, Zhdanov heralded the end of Yezhov's slaughter, joking (in execrable taste) about 'big Enemies', 'little Enemies' and 'wee Enemies' while Stalin and Beria planned some of their most wanton acts of depravity.

---

* This blackmail against Malenkov, accusing him of noble connections, may have formed part of the basis of his alliance with Beria though Stalin knew of the evidence. 'Think yourself lucky these documents are in my hands,' Beria told him. When the latter was arrested in June 1953, after Stalin's death, these papers were given to Malenkov who destroyed them.

† On 5 February 1939, that shrewd observer of power, Svetlana Stalin, aged 13, listed the survivors of the Terror in a note: '1. To Stalin. 2. Voroshilov. 3. Zhdanov. 4. Molotov. 5. Kaganovich. 6. Khrushchev. Daily Order No. 8. I'm travelling to Zubalovo ... leaving you on your own. Hold onto your bellies with an iron hand! Setanka, mistress of the house.' The grandees each replied revealingly: 'I obey. Stalin, the poor peasant. L. Kaganovich. The obedient Voroshilov. The diligent escapee Ukrainian N. Khrushchev. V. Molotov.'

Part Six

'The Great Game': Hitler and Stalin,
1939–1941

28

The Carve-up of Europe: Molotov, Ribbentrop and Stalin's Jewish Question

When Stalin concentrated on diplomacy, he first aimed his guns at his own diplomats. On the night of 3 May 1939, NKVD troops surrounded the Foreign Commissariat, bringing home the urgency of the countdown to war and the coming revolution of alliances. Molotov, Beria and Malenkov arrived to inform Maxim 'Papasha' Litvinov, the worldly rambunctious champion of European peace through 'collective security', that he had been sacked. This was not a surprise to Litvinov: Stalin would pat his Foreign Commissar and say, 'You see, we can reach agreement.'

'Not for long,' Papasha Litvinov replied.

The new Foreign Commissar was Molotov, already the Premier. Stalin emerged from the Terror more paranoid and more confident, a state of mind that made him, if anything, less equipped to analyse the dangerous international situation. Mikoyan noticed this new Stalin 'was an utterly changed person – absolutely suspicious, ruthless and boundlessly self-confident, often speaking of himself in the third person. I think he went barmy.' Kaganovich recalled that he hardly ever called together the Politburo now, deciding most things informally. Stalin does not 'know the West', thought Litvinov. 'If our opponents were a bunch of shahs and sheikhs, he'd outwit them.' Nor were his two main advisers, Molotov and Zhdanov, any better qualified. Stalin educated himself by reading history, particularly Bismarck's memoirs, but he did not realize that the Iron Chancellor was a conventional statesman compared to Hitler. Henceforth Stalin quoted Talleyrand and Bismarck liberally.

Molotov always said that Bolshevik politics was the best training for diplomacy and regarded himself as a politician not a diplomat but he was proud of his new career: 'Everything was in Stalin's fist, in my fist,' he said. But he worked in his tireless, methodical way under immense pressure, arguing ideas through with Stalin, while terrorizing his staff in 'blind rages'. Yet in his letters to his wife Polina, he revealed the vainglory and passion within: 'We live under constant pressure not to miss something ... I so miss you and our daughter, I want to hold you in my arms, to my breast with all your sweetness and charm ...' More direct and less intellectual than Stalin, he told Polina that he was starting to read, not about Talleyrand, but about Hitler. Apart from the smouldering desire for Polina, the most amusing part of these letters was the unabashed delight Molotov took in his new fame. 'I can tell you, without boasting,' he boasted, 'that our opposite numbers feel ... they deal with people that know their stuff.'

Stalin and Molotov developed into an international double act of increasing subtlety, masters of the old 'good cop, bad cop' routine. Stalin was always more radical and reckless, Molotov the stolid analyst of the possible, but neither saw any contradiction between imperial expansionism and their Marxist crusade: on the contrary, the former was the best way to empower the latter.

Europe in early 1939 was, in Stalin's own words, a 'poker game' with three players, in which each hoped to persuade the other two to destroy one another and leave the third to take the winnings. The three players were the Fascists of Adolf Hitler's Nazi Germany, the Capitalists of Neville Chamberlain's Britain allied with Daladier's France – and the Bolsheviks. Though the Georgian admired the flamboyant brutality of the Austrian, he appreciated the danger of a resurgent Germany militarily, and the hostility of Fascism.

Stalin regarded the Western democracies as at least as dangerous as Germany. He had matured politically during their intervention during the Civil War. He instinctively felt he could work with Hitler. As soon as the 'Austrian corporal' took power, Stalin began probing gently, advised by Karl Radek, his German expert, and using as personal emissaries, Abel Yenukidze and David Kandelaki. The sensitivity of these discussions was absolute since Stalin was simultaneously shooting thousands as German agents, with the country in a frenzy of Prussophobic war preparations. The legates were shot.

Hitler kept Stalin at arm's length as long as the democracies continued to appease him. But the Munich agreement convinced Stalin that the West was not serious about stopping Hitler. On the contrary, Stalin was sure that they were willing to let Hitler destroy Soviet Russia. Munich rendered Litvinov's 'collective security' bankrupt. Stalin warned the West that the Soviet Union would not be left to 'pick their chestnuts out of the fire'. The way forward was a division of the world into 'spheres'. This was an oblique signal to Germany that he would deal with whoever would deal with him. Berlin noted the change. Afterwards, at the Plenum, Stalin attacked Litvinov:

'Does that mean you regard me as an Enemy of the People?' asked plucky Litvinov. Stalin hesitated as he left the hall: 'No, we don't consider Papasha an Enemy. Papasha's an honest revolutionary.'*

Meanwhile, Molotov and Beria were terrorizing a meeting of their worldly diplomats, many of them Jewish Bolsheviks at home in the great capitals of Europe. Beria glanced around at them:

'Nazarov,' he said. 'Why did they arrest your father?'

'Lavrenti Pavlovich, you no doubt know better than I.'

'You and I will talk about that later,' laughed Beria.

The Foreign Commissariat was almost next door to the Lubianka and the two ministries were nicknamed 'the Neighbours'. Molotov's deputy, Vladimir Dekanozov, forty-one, another of Beria's intelligent Caucasian henchmen, supervised the purge of diplomats. This red-haired midget, with a taste for English movies (he called his son Reginald) and teenage girls, was a failed medical student who had known Beria since university when they both joined the Cheka. He was a Russified Georgian. Molotov joked that he was an Armenian pretending to be Georgian to please Stalin, who nicknamed him 'Slow Kartvelian' after his region of origin. At Kuntsevo, Stalin mocked his ugliness. When he appeared at the door, Stalin said sarcastically to general laughter:

'Such a handsome man! Look at him! I've never seen anything like it!'

The press officer of the Foreign Commissariat, Yevgeni Gnedin, himself a piece of revolutionary history as the son of Parvus,

---

* This sort of courage counted for something with Stalin. Litvinov, who was three years older than Stalin, could never curb his tongue. That cosmopolitan curmudgeon complained to his friends of Stalin's 'narrow-mindedness, smugness, ambitions and rigidity' while he called Molotov 'a halfwit', Beria 'a careerist' and Malenkov 'short-sighted'. Molotov said that Litvinov remained 'amongst the living only by chance' yet Stalin always just preserved him, despite Molotov's hatred for a much more impressive diplomat, because he was so respected in the West that he might be useful again. There was a story that Litvinov had saved Stalin from being beaten up by dockers in London in 1907: 'I haven't forgotten that time in London,' Stalin used to say.

Lenin's financier and middle man with Kaiserine Germany, was
arrested by Dekanozov and taken to Beria's office where he was
ordered to confess to spying. When he refused, Beria ordered him
to lie on the floor while the Caucasian 'giant' Kobulov beat him
on the skull with blackjacks. Gnedin was a 'lucky stiff'. In July,
Beria ordered Prince Tsereteli to kill the Soviet Ambassador to
China, Bovkun-Luganets, and his wife, in cold blood in a faked
car accident (the method of killing those too eminent to just
disappear).*

Stalin's diplomatic Terror was designed to appeal to Hitler: 'Purge
the ministry of Jews,' he said. 'Clean out the "synagogue." ' 'Thank
God for these words,' Molotov (married to a Jewess) explained.
'Jews formed an absolute majority and many ambassadors …'

Stalin was an anti-Semite by most definitions but until after the
war, it was more a Russian mannerism than a dangerous
obsession. He was never a biological racist like the Nazis.
However, he disliked any nationality that threatened loyalty to
the multinational USSR. He embraced the Russian people not
because he rejected his own Georgian origins but for precisely the
same reason: the Russians were the foundations and cement of
the Soviet Union. But after the war, the creation of Israel, the
increased self-consciousness among Soviet Jews and the Cold War
with America combined with his old prejudice to turn Stalin into
a murderous anti-Semite.

Stalin and his Jewish comrades like Kaganovich were proudly
internationalist. Stalin, however, openly enjoyed jokes about
national stereotypes. He certainly carried all the traditional
Georgian prejudices against the Moslem peoples of the Caucasus
whom he was to deport. He also persecuted Germans. He enjoyed
the Jewish jokes told by Pauker (himself a Jew) and Kobulov, and
was amused when Beria called Kaganovich 'the Israelite'. But
he also enjoyed jokes about Armenians and Germans, and shared
the Russian loathing for Poles: until the forties, Stalin was as
Polonophobic as he was anti-Semitic.

He was always suspicious because the Jews lacked a homeland
which made them 'mystical, intangible, otherworldly'. Yet
Kaganovich insisted that Stalin's view was formed by the

---

* They planned to do the same to Litvinov but his English wife, Ivy, was terrified of
imminent arrest and when she confided this to some American friends, the letter
ended up on Stalin's desk. He phoned Papasha: 'You've an extremely courageous and
outspoken wife. You should tell her to calm herself. She's not threatened.'

Jewishness of his enemies – Trotsky, Zinoviev and Kamenev. On the other hand, most of the women around him and many of his closest collaborators, from Yagoda to Mekhlis, were Jewish. The difference is obvious: he hated the intellectual Trotsky but had no problem with the cobbler Kaganovich.

Stalin was aware that his regime had to stand against anti-Semitism and we find in his own notes a reminder to give a speech about it: he called it 'cannibalism', made it a criminal offence, and regularly criticized anti-Semites. Stalin founded a Jewish homeland, Birobizhan, on the inhospitable Chinese border but boasted, 'The Tsar gave the Jews no land, but we will.'

Yet nationality always mattered in Soviet politics, however internationalist the Party claimed to be. There were a high proportion of Jews, along with Georgians, Poles and Letts, in the Party because these were among the persecuted minorities of Tsarist Russia. In 1937, 5.7 per cent of the Party were Jews yet they formed a majority in the Government. Lenin himself (who was partly Jewish by ancestry) said that if the Commissar was Jewish, the deputy should be Russian: Stalin followed this rule.*

Yet Stalin was 'sensitive' about Kaganovich's Judaism. At Kuntsevo dinners, Beria tried to bully Kaganovich into drinking more but Stalin stopped him:

'Leave him alone ... Jews don't know how to drink.' Once, Stalin asked Kaganovich why he looked so miserable during Jewish jokes: 'Take Mikoyan – we laugh at Armenians and Mikoyan laughs too.'

'You see, Comrade Stalin, suffering has affected the Jewish character so we're like a mimosa flower. Touch it and it closes immediately.' It happened that the mimosa, that super-sensitive flower that flinches like an animal, was Stalin's favourite. He never again allowed such jokes in front of Kaganovich.

None the less, there was increasing anti-Semitism during the thirties: even in public, Stalin asked if a man was a '*natsmen*' – a euphemism for Jewish based on the fifth point on Soviet personnel forms which covered 'nationality'. When Molotov remembered Kamenev, he said he 'did not look like a Jew except when you looked into his eyes'.

---

* The first three Soviet Premiers were Russians. On Lenin's death, Rykov succeeded him as PredSovnarkom even though Kamenev, a Jew, usually chaired the meetings. In 1930, Rykov was succeeded by Molotov. But Stalin refused the Premiership as much for political as for racial reasons.

The Jews at Stalin's court felt they had to be more Russian than the Russians, more Bolshevik than the Bolsheviks. Kaganovich despised Yiddish culture, asking Solomon Mikhoels, the Yiddish actor: 'Why do you disparage the people?' When the Politburo debated whether to blow up the Temple of the Saviour, one of the acts of vandalism in the creation of Stalinist Moscow, Stalin, Kirov and the others supported it but Kaganovich said, 'The Black Hundreds [the anti-Semitic gangs of 1905] will blame it on me!' Similarly, Mehklis reacted to Stalin's swearing about Trotsky's 'Yids': 'I'm a Communist not a Jew.' More honestly, he explained his own rabidity: 'You should realize that there is only one way of fighting [anti-Semitism] – to be brave; if you're a Jew, to be the most honest, pure as crystal, a model person, especially in human dignity.'

Stalin realized that, while he had to be seen to oppose anti-Semitism, his Jews were one obstacle to rapprochement with Hitler, particularly Litvinov (Wallach). Many Jewish Bolsheviks used Russian pseudonyms. As early as 1936, Stalin ordered Mekhlis at *Pravda* to use these pseudonyms: 'No need to excite Hitler!' This atmosphere sharpened at the Plenum in early 1939 when Yakovlev attacked Khrushchev for promoting a cult of personality using his full name and patronymic, a sign of respect. Khrushchev, himself anti-Semitic, replied that perhaps Yakovlev should use his real name, Epstein. Mekhlis intervened to support Khrushchev, explaining that Yakovlev, being a Jew, could not understand this.

The removal of the Jews was a signal to Hitler – but Stalin always sent double messages: Molotov appointed Solomon Lozovsky, a Jew, as one of his deputies.

* * *

The European poker game was played out with swift moves, secret talks and cold hearts. The stakes were vast. The dictators proved much more adept at this fast-moving game than the democracies who had started to play in earnest much too late. As the fighting intensified against the Japanese, Hitler was raising the ante, having consumed Austria and Czechoslovakia, by turning his panzers towards Poland. Belatedly, the Western democracies realized he had to be stopped: on 31 March, Britain and France guaranteed the Polish borders. They needed Russia to join them but failed to place themselves in Stalin's seat and did not understand his sense of weakness and isolation. Ironically the

Polish guarantee increased Stalin's doubts about the depth of this British commitment: if Hitler invaded Poland, what was to stop 'perfidious Albion' from using the guarantee as a mere bargaining chip to negotiate another Munich-style deal, leaving Hitler on his borders?

Stalin therefore required a contractual military alliance with the West if he was not to turn to Hitler. On 29 June, Zhdanov backed the German option in a *Pravda* article in which he stated his 'personal opinion' that 'I permit myself to express ... although not all my friends share it ... They still think that in beginning negotiations with the USSR, the English and French Governments have serious intentions ... I believe the English and French Governments have no wish for a treaty of equality with the USSR ...' The vulnerability of Leningrad made a free hand in the Baltic States necessary: that was the price of what Zhdanov called 'equality'. Zhdanov's son Yury remembers Stalin and his father reading a specially translated *Mein Kampf* and endlessly discussing the pros and cons of a German alliance. Stalin read in D'Abernon's *Ambassador of the World* that if Germany and Russia were allies, 'the dangerous power of the east' would overshadow Britain. 'Yes!' Stalin noted approvingly in the margin.

Britain and France had despatched a hapless and ludicrously low-level delegation to Moscow by slow steamship to offer an alliance but no guarantee of Soviet frontiers and no freedom of action in the Baltics. When Admiral Sir Reginald Aylmer Ranfurly Plunkett-Ernle-Erle-Drax (author of a book called *Handbook on Solar Heating*) and General Joseph Doumenc, arrived in Leningrad on the night of 9–10 August, the German–Russian flirtation was getting serious. The Admiral and the General took the train to Moscow and were taken to meet Voroshilov and Molotov.

Stalin was unimpressed with the quadruple-barrelled Admiral when he discussed the delegations with Molotov and Beria: 'They're not being serious. These people can't have the proper authority. London and Paris are playing poker again ...'

'Still the talks should go ahead,' said Molotov.

'Well if they must, they must.' This was now turning into an auction for Stalin's favours but with only one serious bidder. In Germany, meanwhile, Hitler decided to invade Poland on 26 August: suddenly, the agreement with Stalin was desperately necessary. The meetings with the Western powers only got started on 12 August but the gap between what the West was willing to offer and the price Stalin demanded, was unbridgeable. That day, the Russians signalled to the Germans that they were ready to start negotiations, even on the dismemberment of Poland. On the 14th, Hitler decided to send Ribbentrop, his Foreign Minister, to Moscow. On the 15th, the German Ambassador Count Friedrich Werner von der Schulenburg requested a meeting with Molotov, who, rushing to check with Stalin, reported that Russia was ready. When this news reached Ribbentrop, he hurried to tell Hitler at the Bergdorf. On the 17th, Voroshilov proposed a treaty of mutual military assistance to the British and French but added that there was no point in continuing the discussion until they had persuaded the Poles and Romanians to allow the passage of Soviet troops in the event of a German attack. But Drax had not yet received orders from London.

'Enough of these games!' Stalin told Molotov. 'The English and French wanted us for farmhands and at no cost!' On the afternoon of Saturday the 19th, Molotov hurriedly summoned Schulenburg, handing him a draft non-aggression pact that was more formal than the German version but contained nothing objectionable. Having signed the trade treaty that Stalin had specified was necessary before the real business could begin, the Germans, whose deadline was fast approaching, waited with a gambler's anticipation. Hitler shrewdly decided to cut the Gordian knot of mutual trust and prestige by personally addressing Stalin in a telegram dated 20 August: 'Dear Mr Stalin.' Stalin, Molotov and Voroshilov agreed the reply:

> To Chancellor of Germany A. Hitler. Thank you for your letter. I hope the German–Soviet agreement of non-aggression will be a turning point towards serious improvement of political relations between our countries ... The Soviet government has instructed me to inform you that it agrees to Mr Ribbentrop visiting Moscow on 23 August.
> J. Stalin.

Far to the east, that Sunday the 20th, Georgi Zhukov, commander of the Soviet army on the Khalkin-Gol River, launched a formidable cannonade against the Japanese, then attacked across the front. By the 23rd, the Japanese were defeated with losses as high as 61,000 men, a bloody nose that was enough to dissuade them from attacking Russia again.

At 3 p.m. on Monday the 21st, Molotov received Schulenburg who passed on Hitler's request for a meeting on the 23rd. Two hours later, he and Stalin agreed to the historic visit of Ribbentrop. Suddenly the two dictators were no longer holding back but hurtling towards one another, arms outstretched. At 7 p.m. next day, Voroshilov dismissed the British and French: 'Let's wait until everything has been cleared up ...'*

Stalin's reply reached Hitler at eight-thirty that evening: 'Marvellous! I congratulate you' declaimed Hitler, adding, with the flashiness of the entertainer: 'I have the world in my pocket.'

That night, Voroshilov was leading a vital delegation of the Soviet leadership on a duck-shooting expedition into the countryside. Khrushchev had just arrived from Kiev. Before setting off to shoot duck, Khrushchev dined with Stalin at the dacha. It was then that Stalin, 'who smiled and watched me closely', informed him that Ribbentrop was arriving imminently. Khrushchev, who knew nothing about the negotiations, was 'dumbfounded. I stared back at him, thinking he was joking.'

'Why should Ribbentrop want to see us?' blurted out Khrushchev. 'Is he defecting?' Then he remembered that he was going hunting with Voroshilov on the great day. Should he cancel?

'Go right ahead. There'll be nothing for you to do ... Molotov and I will meet Ribbentrop. When you return, I'll let you know what Hitler has in mind ...' After dinner, Khrushchev and Malenkov set off to meet Voroshilov at his hunting reserve while Stalin remained at the dacha to consider tomorrow. Unless he was

---

* The comedy of these negotiations was neatly encapsulated in the question of the Order of the Bath. Drax had arrived without the relevant credentials, a mistake that told Stalin all he needed to know about Western commitment. At the very moment the credentials finally arrived, they had become utterly irrelevant. When Sir Reginald proudly read out his official titles and arrived at this noble order, the Soviet interpreter declaimed: 'Order of the Bath-tub.' Marshal Voroshilov, displaying both his overwhelming characteristics – childlike naïvety and heroic bungling capacity – interrupted to ask: 'Bathtub?' 'In the reign of our early kings,' Drax droned, 'our knights used to travel round Europe on horseback, slaying dragons and rescuing maidens in distress. They would return home travel-stained and grimy and report ... to the King [who] would sometimes offer a knight a luxury ... A bath in the royal bathroom.' The Western democracies could not deliver the 'price' of a Soviet alliance, namely to back up the Polish guarantee and deliver the Baltic States into Stalin's sphere of influence. Perhaps they were right since this would still not guarantee stopping Hitler, while there seemed little point in saving Poland from the Huns to deliver her to the Tatars.

in a very good mood, he thought 'hunting was a waste of time'.*
Perhaps it was that night that Stalin, reading Vipper's *History of Ancient Greece*, marked the passage about the benefits of dictators working closely together.

On Tuesday, 22 August, all the magnates visited the Little Corner some time during the day. If the details were secret, the policy was not. Its architects were Stalin assisted by Molotov and Zhdanov but there was no party against it. Even Khrushchev and Mikoyan, in their memoirs designed to blacken Stalin wherever possible, admitted that there was no choice. These Leninists, as Kaganovich put it, understood this was a Brest-Litovsk in reverse.

That evening, as the duck-shooters set off into the marshes of Zavidovo, seventy-miles north-west of Moscow, the tall, pompous, ex-champagne salesman Ribbentrop set off in Hitler's Condor aeroplane, Immelman III, with a delegation of thirty. At 1 p.m. on 23 August, Ribbentrop arrived and descended from the Condor in a leather coat, black jacket and striped trousers, impressed to find the airport emblazoned with swastikas. An orchestra played the German national anthem. Ribbentrop was then guided into a bullet-proof black ZiS (a Soviet Buick) by Vlasik. They sped into town for a short stop at the German Embassy for caviar and champagne. At three, Ribbentrop, due to meet Molotov, was driven through the Spassky Gate to the Little Corner. Ribbentrop was greeted by Poskrebyshev in military uniform and led up the stairs through anterooms, into a long rectangular room where they found Stalin, in Party tunic and baggy trousers tucked into boots, and Molotov in a dark suit, standing together.

When they sat down at the table, the Russians, with their interpreter V. N. Pavlov, on one side, the Germans on the other,

---

* Khrushchev's memoirs have left a confusing impression about the Politburo and the Pact. Molotov, Premier and Foreign Minister, was the front man in this diplomatic game and Stalin was clearly the engine behind it. It is usually stated that the Politburo, including Voroshilov, knew nothing about the negotiations until Ribbentrop's arrival was imminent but Politburo papers had always been confined to the 'Five' or the 'Seven' – and not distributed to regional leaders such as the Ukrainian First Secretary. The messages between Stalin and Hitler were discussed with Molotov, Voroshilov and Beria, who was in charge of intelligence and had to know. Zhdanov, with his Leningrad and Baltic viewpoint, his knowledge of German culture and his publicly stated suspicion of Western intentions, had been closely linked to this whole policy and may have been its co-architect with Stalin. The commercial aspects could not be negotiated without Mikoyan. Zhdanov was in and out of Stalin's office that week and he told his son that he was kept informed of the negotiations.

Ribbentrop declared: 'Germany demands nothing from Russia – only peace and trade.' Stalin offered Molotov the floor as Premier.

'No, no, Joseph Vissarionovich, you do the talking. I'm sure you'll do a better job than I.' They swiftly agreed to the terms of their pact which was designed to divide Poland and eastern Europe into spheres of influence – Stalin got Eastern Poland, Latvia, Estonia, Finland and Bessarabia in Romania, though Hitler kept Lithuania. But when Ribbentrop proposed a paean to German–Soviet friendship, Stalin snorted:

'Don't you think we have to pay a little more attention to public opinion in our two countries? For many years now, we have been pouring buckets of shit over each other's heads and our propaganda boys could not do enough in that direction. Now all of a sudden, are we to make our peoples believe all is forgotten and forgiven? Things don't work so fast.' With so much agreed so fast, Ribbentrop returned to the Embassy to telegraph Hitler.

At 10 p.m, he arrived back at the Little Corner, accompanied by a much larger delegation and two photographers. When Ribbentrop announced that Hitler approved the terms, 'a sudden tremor seemed to go through Stalin and he did not immediately grasp the hand proffered by his partner. It was as if he had first to overcome a moment of fear.' Stalin ordered vodka and toasted:

'I know how much the German nation loves its Führer. He's a good chap. I'd like to to drink his health.' Molotov then toasted Ribbentrop who toasted Stalin. One of the young Germans, a six-foot SS officer named Richard Schulze, noticed Stalin was drinking his vodka from a special flask and managed to fill his glass from it, only to discover it contained water. Stalin smiled faintly as Schulze drank it, not the last guest to sample this little secret.

By 2 a.m. on 24 August, the treaty was ready. The photographers – the Germans with up-to-date equipment, the Russians with ancient wooden tripod and wood-and-brass camera – were escorted into the room. The Red Army Chief of Staff, the ailing Shaposhnikov, respected by Stalin, took notes in a small notebook. When it came to the photograph, Stalin noticed the towering SS man who had sampled his flask and beckoned him into the picture where he positioned him between Ribbentrop and Shaposhnikov. Molotov signed.

A maid brought in champagne and snacks. When one of the German photographers flashed as Stalin and Ribbentrop raised their glasses, the former shook his finger and told him he did not want such a photograph published. The photographer offered to hand over his film but Stalin said he could trust the word of a German. At 3 a.m., as the excited leaders parted, Stalin told Ribbentrop: 'I can guarantee on my word of honour that the Soviet Union will not betray its partner.'

Stalin headed to Kuntsevo where the hunters awaited. Voroshilov, Khrushchev, Malenkov and Bulganin had already brought their ducks to be cooked in Stalin's kitchen. When Stalin and Molotov arrived jubilantly with a copy of their treaty, Khrushchev boasted about out-shooting Voroshilov, the vaunted 'First Marksman', before the laughing *Vozhd* told them how they had signed the world-shattering Molotov-Ribbentrop Pact: 'Stalin seemed very pleased with himself' but he was under no illusions about his new friendship. As they feasted on duck, Stalin boasted:

'Of course it's all a game to see who can fool whom. I know what Hitler's up to. He thinks he's outsmarted me but actually it's I who's tricked him.' War, he explained, 'would pass us by a little longer'.* Zhdanov mocked Ribbentrop's pear-shaped figure:

'He's got the biggest and broadest pair of hips in all of Europe,' he announced as the magnates laughed about Ribbentrop's preposterous girdle: 'Those hips! Those hips!'

The 'Great Game', as Molotov called the tournament of nerves between Stalin and Hitler, had begun.

* * *

At 2 a.m. on 1 September, Poskrebyshev handed Stalin a telegram from Berlin informing him that early that evening 'Polish' troops (in fact German security forces in disguise) had attacked the German radio station in Gleiwitz. Stalin left for the dacha and went to bed. A few hours later, Poskrebyshev called again: Germany had invaded Poland. Stalin monitored the campaign as Britain and France declared war on Germany, honouring their guarantees. 'We see nothing wrong in their having a good hard fight and weakening each other,' he told Molotov and Zhdanov. Stalin planned the Soviet invasion of Poland with Voroshilov,

---

* Across Europe at the Berghof, Hitler had heard the news at dinner, calling for silence and announcing it to his guests whom he then led out on to the balcony, whence they watched with awe as the northern lights illuminated the sky and the Unterberg mountains in an unnatural bath of blood-red light, dyeing the faces of the spectators incarnadine. 'Looks like a great deal of blood,' said Hitler to an adjutant. 'This time we won't bring it off without violence.'

Shaposhnikov and Kulik, who was to command the front along with Mekhlis, but waited until he had secured an end to the war with Japan first. At 2 a.m on 17 September, Stalin accompanied by Molotov and Voroshilov, told Schulenburg: 'At 6 a.m, four hours from now, the Red Army will cross into Poland.' Premier Molotov took to the radio to announce the 'sacred duty to proffer help to … Ukrainian and Belorussian brothers'. Mekhlis claimed to Stalin that the West Ukrainians welcomed the Soviet troops 'like true liberators' with 'apples, pies, drinking water … Many weep with joy.'

Khrushchev, Ukrainian First Secretary, donned a military uniform and, accompanied by his NKVD boss, Ivan Serov, joined the forces of Semyon Timoshenko, commander of the Kiev Military District. Timoshenko was a tough, shaven-headed veteran of the First Cavalry Army in Tsaritsyn; he was a competent officer, yet in the Terror, he had both denounced Budyonny and been denounced himself. Khrushchev claimed to have saved his life. Khrushchev's advance into Poland was an adventure for him, but even more so for his wife, Nina Petrovna who, also sporting military uniform and a pistol, liberated her own parents who had remained in Poland since 1920. Khrushchev, ensconced in Lvov, celebrated at the sight of her and her parents but lost his temper when he saw her pistol.*

If the invasion was joyous for the Khrushchevs, it unleashed depredations on the Polish population every bit as cruel and tragic as those of the Nazis. Khrushchev ruthlessly suppressed any sections of the population who might oppose Soviet power: priests, officers, noblemen, intellectuals were kidnapped, murdered and deported to eliminate the very existence of Poland. By November 1940, one tenth of the population or 1.17 million innocents had been deported. Thirty per cent of them were dead by 1941; 60,000 were arrested and 50,000 shot. The Soviets behaved like conquerors. When some soldiers were arrested for stealing treasures from a Prince Radziwill, Vyshinsky consulted Stalin.

'If there's no ill-will,' he wrote on the note, 'they can be pardoned. J.St.'

---

* There was a priceless moment when Nina's parents arrived in Khrushchev's apartment and marvelled at the running water: 'Hey Mother, look at this,' shouted the father. 'The water comes out of a pipe.' When the parents saw the impressive, lantern-jawed Timoshenko beside the small fat Khrushchev, they asked if the former was their son-in-law.

At 5 p.m. on Wednesday 27 September, Ribbentrop flew back to negotiate the notorious protocols, so secret that Molotov was still denying their existence thirty years later. By 10 p.m., he was at the Kremlin in talks with Stalin and Molotov around the green baize table. Stalin wanted Lithuania. Ribbentrop telegraphed Hitler for his permission so the talks were delayed until 3 p.m. the next day. But Hitler's message had not arrived by the time Ribbentrop returned to negotiate the cartological details.

That night, while Stalin held a gala dinner for the Germans to celebrate the carve-up of Europe, the Russians were meeting the unfortunate Estonian Foreign Minister to force him to allow Soviet troops into his country, the first step to outright annexation. The Nazis were greeted at the door of the Great Kremlin Palace, led through the dull wooden Congress Hall which looked like a giant schoolroom, and then dazzled by the scarlet and gold reception room where Stalin, Molotov and the Politburo, including Jewish Kaganovich, awaited them. Stalin's manner was 'simple and unpretentious', beaming with 'paternal benevolence' that could turn to 'icy coldness' as he 'rapped out orders', though he used a 'jocular and kind manner with his junior assistants'. The Germans noticed how respectful the Russians were to Stalin: Commissar Tevosian, the 'lucky stiff' who had narrowly avoided execution in 1938, rose 'like a schoolboy' whenever Stalin addressed him. The fear surrounding Stalin had become intense since 1937. But he was cordial with Voroshilov, friendly with Beria and Mikoyan, matter-of-fact with Kaganovich, chatty with Malenkov. Only Molotov 'would talk to his chief as one comrade to another'.

Their swagger was so raffish that Ribbentrop said he felt as at ease as he did among old Nazi comrades. While the guests were chatting, Stalin went into the sumptuous Andreevsky Hall to check the seating plan, which he enjoyed doing, even at Kuntsevo.* The twenty-two guests were dwarfed by the grandeur of the hall, the colossal flower arrangements, the imperial gold cutlery and, even more, by the twenty-four courses that included caviar, all manner of fishes and meats, and lashings of pepper vodka and Crimean champagne. The white-clad waiters were the

---

* Stalin was filmed checking places at Kuntsevo by Vlasik. Hitler too was a punctilious checker of dinner placement. Both men appreciated the importance of personal pride in matters of State.

same staff from the Metropol Hotel who would serve Churchill and Roosevelt at Yalta. Before anyone could eat, Molotov started to propose toasts to each guest. Stalin stalked over to clink glasses. It was an exhausting rigmarole that would become one of the diplomatic tribulations of the war. When Molotov had run through every guest, the Germans sighed with relief until he announced: 'Now we'll drink to all members of the delegations who couldn't attend this dinner.' Stalin took over, joking:

'Let us drink to the new anti-Comintern Stalin' and he winked at Molotov. Then he toasted Kaganovich, 'our People's Commissar of Railways'. Stalin could have toasted the Jewish magnate across the table but he deliberately rose and circled the table to clink glasses so that Ribbentrop had to follow suit and drink to a Jew, an irony that amused Stalin. Forty years on, Kaganovich was still telling the story to his grandchildren. When Molotov embarked on another toast to his *Vozhd*, Stalin chuckled:

'If Molotov really wants to drink, no one objects but he really shouldn't use me as an excuse.' Stalin himself drank almost nothing and when Ribbentrop noticed how well he was bearing the toasts, he cheerfully revealed that he was drinking white wine. But Beria, who had transformed the Georgian tradition of forced hospitality into a despotic trial of submission, delighted in making his guests drink. The German diplomat Hilger, who wrote vivid memoirs of the evening, refused another vodka. Beria insisted, drawing the attention of Stalin himself who was sitting opposite them.

'What's the argument about?' he asked, adding, 'Well if you don't want to drink, no one can force you.'

'Not even the chief of the NKVD himself?' smiled the German.

'Here at this table,' replied Stalin, 'even the NKVD chief has no more say than anyone else.' At the end of the dinner, Stalin and Molotov excused themselves as the Germans were despatched off to the Bolshoi to watch *Swan Lake*. As he left, Stalin whispered to Kaganovich, 'We must win time.' They then walked upstairs where the Estonian Foreign Minister miserably waited for Stalin to emasculate his little Baltic nation. Molotov demanded a Soviet garrison of 35,000 troops, more than the entire Estonian army.

'Come on, Molotov, you're rather harsh on our friends,' said Stalin, suggesting 25,000 but the effect was much the same. Having swallowed a country during the first act of *Swan Lake*, Stalin returned to the Germans at midnight for a final session during which Hitler telephoned his agreement to the Lithuanian concession.

'Hitler knows his business,' muttered Stalin. Ribbentrop was so excited that he declared the two countries must never fight again:

'This ought to be the case,' replied Stalin, shocking Ribbentrop who asked for it to be retranslated. When the German suggested Russia join a military alliance against the West, Stalin just said,

'I shall never allow Germany to become weak.' He obviously believed that Germany would be restrained in the West by Britain and France. When the maps were finally ready in the early hours, Stalin signed them in blue crayon, with a massive signature ten inches long, an inch high, and a tail eighteen inches long. 'Is my signature clear enough for you?'

By 3 October, all three Baltic States had agreed to Soviet garrisons. Stalin and Molotov turned their guns and threats on the fourth Baltic country in their sphere of influence, Finland, which they expected to buckle like the others.

29

The Murder of the Wives

As the world watched Stalin and Hitler carve up the East, the *Vozhd* was probing the submission of his comrades by investigating and sometimes killing their wives. His fragile trust in women was irreparably undermined by Nadya's suicide but this had been exacerbated by his own destruction of the wives of Enemies. As Khrushchev said, he became interested in other men's wives for the unusual reason that they were possible spies rather than mistresses.

Stalin had always shown a minute interest in the wives. When he received the 1939 census, he ticked the names of some magnates' wives and children in red pen. The meaning of the ticks was a mystery but it is tempting to regard everything about him as sinister. Maybe he was just working out how many cars the family needed. Wives now sat apart from their husbands at Kremlin dinners. Stalin's attitude to old favourites, Polina and Dora, had become malicious and suspicious, partly reflecting their relationship with Nadya. But he had always been obsessed with wives knowing too much. As early as 1930, he suggested to Molotov that some comrade's wife 'should be checked ... she could not help but know about the outrageous goings-on at their house.' This burning suspicion of uxoriousness partly derived from Stalin's dislike of anything that interfered with blind devotion to the Party and himself. 'Stalin did not recognize personal relations,' said Kaganovich. 'The love of one person for another did not exist.' He saw the wives as hostages for his comrades' good behaviour and punishment for bad: 'No one who contradicts Stalin,' Beria told Nina, 'keeps his wife.' But the slaughter of wives coincided with Beria's arrival.

Polina Molotova, the First Lady, was in danger. She was now Commissar of Fishing, a CC candidate member and mistress of her perfume empire. Yet Beria now started investigating her, discovering 'vandals' and 'saboteurs' secreted in her staff. She had 'unknowingly facilitated their espionage'.* Stalin may have been sending another anti-Semitic signal to Hitler.

On 10 August, when Stalin and Molotov were plotting their diplomatic somersaults, the Politburo indicted Polina. Stalin proposed her expulsion from the Central Committee. Molotov bravely abstained, showing his ability to disagree with Stalin, confidence – and love of Polina. On 24 October, she was relieved of her Commissariat, reprimanded for 'levity and hastiness' but declared innocent of 'calumnies'. Promoted to run Soviet haberdashery, she returned to her accustomed magnificence: her daughter Svetlana was already notorious as the ultimate Soviet 'princess' in her furs and French fashions but the family was constantly watched.† Stalin forgot neither Molotov's defiance nor Polina's sins, which would return to haunt her. Stalin and Beria had considered kidnapping and murdering her. She was lucky to be alive.

On 25 October 1938, Beria arrested President Kalinin's wife. In a land where the Head of State's wife was in prison, no one was safe from the Party. The ineffectual Kalinin, who had not dared resist Stalin since the warnings of 1930 and balletomanic romantic entanglements, though he seethed about his ill treatment, actually lived with another woman, his aristocratic housekeeper, Alexandra Gorchakova. His wife, a snub-nosed Estonian, Ekaterina Ivanovna, set off with a lady friend to arrange an anti-illiteracy campaign in the Far East. When she and this possibly Sapphic lady-friend returned to Kalinin's apartment, they were bugged grumbling about Stalin's blood lust. The lady friend was executed, Kalinina sent into exile, like Budyonny's wife before her. When petitioners asked for the President's help, Kalinin used the same excuse as Stalin himself: 'My dear chap, I'm in the same position! I can't even help my own wife – there's no way I can help yours!' Not everyone was as lucky as Molotova and Kalinina.

---

*Polina had an Achilles heel: not only was she Jewish but her brother Karp was a successful businessman in the USA. Indeed, in the mid-thirties, Stalin had even encouraged the US Ambassador Davies to do business in Moscow using Karp, a rare example of his nepotism.
†Take the case of Molotov's fitness instructor, a role that reveals a whole new side of the Foreign Commissar. A few months later, Vlasik, who did nothing without Stalin's knowledge, wrote to Molotov to inform him that Olga Rostovtseva, the fitness lady, was boasting about her closeness to the family: 'We know of cases not only where she talks about her sports instruction ... but also about your family and apartments ...'

In April 1937, Dr Bronka Poskrebysheva, twenty-seven, pretty wife of the *chef de cabinet*, rang Stalin and asked to see him alone at Kuntsevo, putting on her best dress, perhaps the polkadot which appears in all her family photographs. Her husband did not know about this appointment and would have been furious if he had. Vlasik alone knew of this secret meeting. She came to ask for the release of her arrested brother Metalikov, the Kremlin doctor, indirectly related through his wife to Trotsky. After Stalin's death, Vlasik revealed it to the family and hinted, according to Poskrebyshev and Bronka's daughter Natalya, that the two started an affair. This is unlikely since Stalin hated women pleading for relatives though one of the tragedies of Soviet life at this time was that women did beg potentates for the lives of their loved ones, offering anything they could, even their bodies. Bronka's mission failed.* She was terrified of being tarred with the Trotskyite brush.

Before his promotion to Moscow, Beria had groped Bronka at Kuntsevo and she slapped him. 'I won't forget it,' he said. But Bronka did not give up. On 27 April 1939, she called Beria and asked if she could come to discuss her brother. She was never seen again.

Poskrebyshev waited until midnight, then called Beria at home, who revealed that she was in custody but would not discuss it. In the morning, without having slept at all, Poskrebyshev complained to Stalin who said,

'It doesn't depend on me. I can do nothing. Only the NKVD can sort it out,' a line that could not have convinced Poskrebyshev. Stalin phoned Beria who reminded him of Bronka's Trotskyite connections. The three met, possibly around midnight on 3 May, when Beria was next in the Little Corner. Beria produced a confession implicating Bronka. Poskrebyshev begged Stalin to release her, using the most unBolshevik argument which would have moved anyone but these flinthearts: 'What am I to do with my girls? What will happen to them?' and then thinking of his wife's child by her first marriage: 'Will Galia go to an orphanage?'

---

*In a story that is criss-crossed with emotional distortions, perhaps the strangest cut of all is that Natalya Poskrebysheva, who was born nine months after her mother's visit to Stalin, believes she may be Stalin's daughter not only because of Vlasik's story but also because she once met the daughter of Mikhail Suslov, the ideological boss for most of Brezhnev's reign, who said: 'Everyone knows your real father is lying in the Mausoleum next to Lenin.' This was when Stalin still rested in the Mausoleum. 'Do I look like somebody?' Miss Poskrebysheva asked the author. 'Like Svetlana Stalin?' It is ironic that she believes her mother's murderer, Stalin, was her father because she in fact looks the image of Poskrebyshev.

'Don't worry, we'll find you another wife,' Stalin supposedly replied. This was typical Stalin, the man who had threatened Krupskaya that if she did not obey the Party, they would appoint someone else as Lenin's widow. By the standards of the time, Poskrebyshev made a fuss but he could do no more. After two years, Bronka was shot aged just thirty-one as the Germans approached Moscow.*

Her daughter Natalya was told she had died naturally. Poskrebyshev brought up the girls himself with loving devotion. He kept photographs of Bronka around the house. When Natalya pointed at one of the photos and said 'Mama,' Poskrebyshev burst into tears and ran out of the room. It was typical of the tragedies of the time that Natalya only discovered her mother had been shot when she was told at school by the daughter of Kozlovsky the singer. She sobbed in the lavatories. Poskrebyshev remarried.

Bronka's destruction did not affect Poskrebyshev's relationship with Stalin or Beria: the Party was just. Stalin took a solicitious interest in Bronka's daughter:

'How's Natasha?' he often asked his *chef de cabinet*. 'Is she plump and sweet?' Years later when she could not do her homework, she called her father to ask his help. Someone else answered.

'Can I speak to my father?' she asked.

'He's not here,' replied Stalin. 'What's the problem?' – and he solved her mathematical questions. The only awkwardness in Poskrebyshev's apparent friendship with Beria was when the latter hugged little Natalya and sighed:

'You're going to be as beautiful as your mother.' Poskrebyshev 'turned green', struggled to control his emotions, and rasped:

'Natalya, go and play.'

* * *

Before he turned to wantonly kill another of his friend's wives, Stalin capriciously saved two old friends from death. Sergo Kavtaradze was an Old Bolshevik Leftist, who had known Stalin since the turn of the century. He was an intelligent cosmopolitan Georgian married to Princess Sofia Vachnadze, whose godmother had been Empress Maria Fyodorovna, Nicholas II's mother. They

---

* Her body was buried in a mass grave near Moscow while her brother is in one of the pits at the Donskoi Cemetery along with many others. Dr Metalikov's daughter raised a monument to them in the Novodevichy Cemetery.

were an unusual couple. Kavtaradze consistently joined the oppositions yet Stalin always forgave him. Arrested in the late twenties, Stalin brought him back and ordered Kaganovich to help him. He was arrested again in late 1936, appearing on Yezhov's death-lists. His wife was also arrested. His daughter Maya, then eleven, thought both parents were already dead but she courageously wrote to Stalin to beg for their lives, signing her letters: 'Pioneer Maya Kavtaradze'. Both Kavtaradzes were tortured but because Stalin had put a dash next to his old friend's name on the death-list, their lives were spared. Now, in late 1939, 'Pioneer Kavtaradze's' letters reminded Stalin to ask Beria if his old friend was still alive.

In the Lubianka, Kavtaradze was suddenly shaved by a barber, given a comfortable room, and a menu from which he could order any food he liked. Delivered to the Hotel Lux, he found his wife was there, a frail shadow of her former self – but alive. Their daughter arrived from Tiflis. Soon afterwards, Kavtaradze was called: 'Comrade Stalin is waiting for you. If you're ready, a car will pick you up in half an hour.' He was taken to Kuntsevo where Koba greeted him in the study: 'Hello Sergo,' he said as if Kavtaradze had not been found guilty of involvement in a plot to kill him. 'Where've you been?'

'Sitting [in prison].'

'Oh you found time to sit?' The Russian slang for being in prison is *sidet* – to sit – hence Stalin's joke, a line he used frequently. After dinner, Stalin turned to him anxiously: 'Nevertheless, you all wanted to kill me?'

'Do you really think so?' Kavtaradze replied. Stalin just grinned. Afterwards, when he got home, Kavtaradze whispered to his wife: 'Stalin's sick.' A few weeks later, the family received a bizarre and revealing visitation.*

The Kavtaradzes had some friends to dinner when the telephone rang at 11 p.m. Kavtaradze said he had to rush out and

---

* This is often mentioned in Stalin biographies but never with the testimony of any of the five people present. The following is based on the author's interview with Maya Kavtaradze, the last of those five still alive whose story has never before been published. Now seventy-six and living in her father's huge, antique-filled apartment in Tbilisi, she has generously allowed the author to use her father's unpublished memoirs which are an invaluable source. In 1940, Kavtaradze was appointed to the State Publishing House and then as Deputy Foreign Commissar in charge of the Near East for the whole war. Since the Foreign Commissariat was just next door to the Lubianka, Kavtaradze used to joke: 'I crossed the road.' Kavtaradze was Soviet Ambassador to Romania after the war and died in 1971.

left without an explanation. His wife and their daughter Maya, fourteen, went to bed. At 6 a.m. Kavtaradze staggered into their three-room apartment on Gorky Street, still dizzy from drinking. 'Where've you been?' his wife scolded him.

'We've guests,' he announced.

'You're drunk!' Then she heard footsteps: Stalin and Beria tipsily walked in and sat down at the kitchen table. Vlasik stood guard at the front-door. While Kavtaradze poured out drinks, his wife rushed into Maya's room:

'Wake up!' she whispered.

'What's wrong?' asked the schoolgirl. 'They've come to arrest us at night?'

'No, Stalin's come.'

'I won't meet him,' retorted Maya who understandably hated him.

'You must,' replied her mother. 'He's a historical personage.' So Maya got dressed and came into the kitchen. As soon as she appeared, Stalin beamed:

'Ah, it's you – "Pioneer Kavtaradze."' He recalled her letters appealing for her parents. 'Sit on my lap.' She sat on Stalin's knee. 'Do you spoil her?'

Maya was charmed: 'He was so kind, so gentle – he kissed me on the cheek and I looked into his honey-coloured, hazel, gleaming eyes,' she recalls, 'but I was so anxious.'

'We've no food!' the little girl exclaimed.

'Don't worry,' said Beria. Ten minutes later, Georgian food was delivered from the famous Aragvi restaurant. Stalin looked closely at Kavtaradze's wife, the princess born at the imperial court. Her hair was white:

'We tortured you too much,' Stalin said.

'Whoever mentions the past, let him lose his eyes,' she answered shrewdly, using the proverb Stalin had used to Bukharin. He asked Beria about Kavtaradze's brother, also arrested, but they were too late: he had already died, like so many others, en route to Magadan.

Kavtaradze started singing a Georgian song but he was out of tune.

'Don't, Tojo', said Stalin, who nicknamed Kavtaradze, with his Oriental eyes, after the Japanese General Tojo. He started to sing himself 'in a sweet tenor'. Maya was 'shocked – there he was short and pock-marked. Now he was singing!' Then he announced: 'I want to see the apartment,' and inspected it carefully. The feast continued until 10 a.m. and Maya missed school that day.

Stalin appointed Kavtaradze to a publishing job that involved another prisoner, Shalva Nutsibidze, a celebrated Georgian philosopher. As a young man, Nutsibidze had once met Stalin. While in jail, Nutsibidze started translating the Georgian epic poem by Rustaveli, *The Knight in the Panther Skin*, into Russian. Every day, his work was taken from him and returned marked with the pen of an anonymous editor. Kobulov tortured him, tearing off his fingernails. Then he suddenly became friendly, telling the prisoner that during a recent meeting, Stalin had asked Beria if he knew what kind of bird the thrush was:

'Ever heard of a thrush singing in his cage?' Beria shook his head. 'It's the same with poets,' Stalin explained. 'A poet can't sing in a cell. If we wish to have Rustaveli perfectly translated, free the thrush.' Nutsibidze was released and, on 20 October 1940, Kavtaradze picked him up in a limousine and the two 'lucky stiffs' drove to the Little Corner to report to Poskrebyshev on the Rustaveli translation. When they were shown into the office, Stalin was smiling at them:

'You're Professor Nutsibidze?' he said. 'You've been offended a bit but let's not rake up the past,' and then he started to rave about the 'magnificent translation of Rustaveli'. Sitting the two men down, Stalin handed the astounded professor a leather-bound draft of the translation, adding, 'I've translated one couplet. Let's see how you like it.' Stalin recited it. 'If you really do like it, I give it to you as a present. Use it in your translation, but don't mention my name. I take great pleasure in being your editor.' He then invited the two to dinner where they reminisced about the old days in Georgia. After many horns of wine, Nutsibidze recalled the political meeting where he had first met Stalin, declaiming his speech from memory. Stalin was delighted:

'Extraordinary talent goes hand in hand with extraordinary memory!'* He came round the table and kissed Nutsibidze on the forehead.

* * *

They were particularly fortunate 'stiffs' because after the Ribbentrop Pact, Stalin liquidated the backlog of Yezhov cases,

---

* For the rest of his career, whenever Nutsibidze was challenged, he would point to his forehead and say, 'Stalin kissed me here.' The Rustaveli edition was expensively published and Stalin's name was never mentioned. Stalin ensured that Nutsibidze was allowed to live for the rest of his life in a large mansion in Tiflis still owned by the family. The author is most grateful to the Professor's stepson Zakro Megrelishvili for the extracts from his mother's autobiography.

including Blackberry himself who confessed to being an English, Japanese and Polish spy. But he also denounced his wife's literary lovers. Thus the indelible mark of Yevgenia's kisses proved fatal long after her own exit. Sholokhov was protected by the penumbra of Stalin himself but Isaac Babel was arrested, telling his young wife: 'Please see our girl grows up happy.'

On 16 January 1940, Stalin signed 346 death sentences, a list of the tragic flotsam of Terror that combined monsters with innocents, including some of the outstanding talents of the arts, such as Babel, theatre director Meyerhold, and Yezhova's lover, the journalist Koltsov (on whom Karpov in Hemingway's *For Whom the Bell Tolls* is based), as well as Yezhov himself with his innocent brother, nephews and socialite mistress, Glikina, and the fallen magnate Eikhe. Most (though not Yezhov) were mercilessly tortured with the relish that Beria and Kobulov brought to their work at Sukhanov prison, Beria's special realm which, ironically, had once been the St Catherine's Nunnery.

'The investigators began to use force on me, a sick sixty-five-year-old man,' Meyerhold wrote to Molotov. 'I was made to lie face down and then beaten on the soles of my feet and my spine with a rubber strap. They sat me on a chair and beat my feet from above ... For the next few days when those parts of my legs were covered with extensive internal haemorrhaging, they again beat the red, blue and yellow bruises and the pain was so intense it felt as if boiling water was poured on ... I howled and wept from pain. They beat my back ... punched my face, swinging their fists from a great height ... The intolerable physical and emotional pain caused my eyes to weep unending streams of tears ...'

Over the next few days, Stalin's hanging judge Ulrikh sentenced all to 'the highest measure of punishment' in perfunctory trials at Lefortovo prison before attending a Kremlin gala, starring the tenor Kozlovsky and the ballerina Lepeshinskaya. Babel was condemned as an 'agent of French and Austrian intelligence ... linked to the wife of Enemy of the People Yezhov'. At 1.30 a.m. on 27 January 1940, Babel was shot and cremated.

Eikhe was subjected to one last session of 'French wrestling' at Sukhanov prison. Beria and Rodos 'brutally beat Eikhe with rubber rods; he fell but they picked him up and went on beating him. Beria kept asking him, 'Will you confess to being a spy?' Eikhe refused. 'One of Eikhe's eyes had been gouged out and blood was streaming out of it but he went on repeating "I won't confess." When Beria had convinced himself he could not get a confession ... he ordered them to lead him away to be shot.'

It was now Yezhov's turn. On 1 February, Beria called his predecessor to his office at Sukhanovka to propose that if he confessed at his trial, Stalin would spare him. To his meagre credit, Yezhov refused: 'It's better to leave this earth as an honourable man.'

On 2 February, Ulrikh tried him in Beria's office. Yezhov read out his last statement to Stalin, dedicated to the sacred order of Bolshevik chivalry. He denied all charges of spying for what he called 'Polish landowners ... English lords and Japanese samurai' but 'I do not deny I drank heavily but I worked like a horse. My fate is obvious,' but he asked 'one thing: shoot me quietly, without putting me through any agony.' Then he requested that his mother be looked after, 'my daughter taken care of' and his innocent nephews spared. He finished with the sort of flourish that one might expect to find from a knight to his king at the time of the Round Table: 'Tell Stalin that I shall die with his name on my lips.'

He faced the *Vishka* less courageously than many of his victims. When Ulrikh pronounced the sentence, Yezhov toppled over but was caught by his guards, loaded into a Black Crow in the early hours of 3 February and driven to his special execution yard with the sloping floor and hosing facilities at Varsonofyevsky Lane. There Beria, the Deputy Procurator (N. P. Afanasev) and executioner, Blokhin, awaited him. Yezhov, according to Afanasev, hiccuped and wept. Finally his legs collapsed and they dragged him by the hands. That day, Stalin met Beria and Mikoyan for three hours, probably discussing economic matters, but there is no doubt that he would have wished to know the details of Blackberry's conduct at the supreme moment.

The ashes of these men, Yezhov the criminal, Babel the genius, were dumped into a pit marked 'Common Grave Number One – unclaimed ashes 1930–42 inclusive' at old Donskoi Cemetery. Just twenty paces away there is a gravestone that reads: 'Khayutina, Yevgenia Solomonovna 1904–1938'. Yezhov, Yevgenia and Babel lie close.*

---

* In the nineties, a monument was raised there that reads: 'Here lie buried the remains of the innocent, tortured and executed victims of political repressions. May they never be forgotten.' Antonina Babel did not find out that her husband had been executed until 1954 when he was rehabilitated. She spent many years living in America. Her heart-rending memoirs stand with those of Nadezhda Mandelstam and Anna Larina as classics.

Yezhov's eminence was eradicated from the memories of the time. Henceforth he was portrayed as a blood-crazed renegade killing innocents against Stalin's wishes. The era was named the *Yezhovshchina*, Yezhov's time, a word that Stalin probably coined for he was soon using it himself. Yagoda and Yezhov were both 'scum', thought Stalin. Yezhov was 'a rat who killed many innocent people', Stalin told Yakovlev, the aircraft designer. 'We had to shoot him,' he confided to Kavtaradze. But after the war, Stalin admitted: 'One can't believe a lot of the evidence from 1937. Yezhov couldn't run the NKVD properly and anti-Soviet elements penetrated it. They destroyed some honest people, our best cadres.'

Looking back, he also questioned Beria's Terror: 'Beria runs too many cases and everyone confesses.' But Stalin was always aware that the NKVD invented evidence: he jested and grumbled about it but often he chose to believe it because he had already decided who was an Enemy. More often, he had created it himself. 'Meyerhold was a huge talent,' Stalin reflected in 1950, but 'our Chekists don't understand artists who all have faults. The Chekists collect them and then destroy good people. I doubt Meyerhold was an Enemy of the People.' He protested too much. Stalin had carefully followed their careers. He disapproved of 'frivolous' Babel and his *Red Cavalry* 'of which he knows nothing' – and he signed the death-lists: no ruler has supervised his secret police as intimately as he.

Now Beria, cleaning the Augean stables of Yezhov's detritus, brought Stalin the death sentence for Blokhin the executioner himself. Stalin refused Beria's request, saying that this '*chernaya rabota*' – black work – was a difficult job but very important for the Party. Blokhin was spared to kill thousands more. Stalin's brother-in-law Stanislas Redens (implicated by Yezhov), was shot on 12 February, 1940.* His wife Anna was still convinced he would return and often called Stalin and Beria to inquire. Finally Beria told her to forget her marriage. After all, it had never been registered ...

---

* There was one strange mercy: Redens's widow and children did not share the tragedy of the families of other Enemies though they later suffered too. For the moment, they spent their weekends at Zubalovo with Svetlana and their life carried on as if nothing had happened. Indeed, Anna continued to ring Stalin and berate him about Svetlana's clothes or Vasily's drinking. Soon they were even reconciled.

30

Molotov Cocktails:
The Winter War and Kulik's Wife

Stalin was in high spirits after the Ribbentrop Pact but he remained dangerously paranoid, especially to the wives of his friends. In November 1939, the phone rang at the dacha of Kulik, the bungling Deputy Defence Commissar who had commanded the Polish invasion. He and his long-legged, green-eyed wife, Kira Simonich, said to be the finest looking in Stalin's circle, were holding his birthday party attended by an *Almanac de Gotha* of the élite, from Voroshilov and the worker-peasant-Count Alexei Tolstoy, to the omnipresent court singer, Kozlovsky, and a flurry of ballerinas. Kulik answered it:

'Quiet!' he hissed. 'It's Stalin!' He listened. 'What am I doing? I'm celebrating my birthday with friends.'

'Wait for me,' replied Stalin who soon arrived with Vlasik and a case of wine. He greeted everyone and then sat at the table, where he drank his own wine while Kozlovsky sang Stalin's favourite songs, particularly the Duke's aria from *Rigoletto*.

Kira Kulik approached Stalin, chatting to him like an old friend. The most unlikely member of Stalin's circle was born Kira Simonich, the daughter of a count of Serbian origins who had run Tsarist intelligence in Finland then been shot by the Cheka in 1919. After the Revolution she had married a Jewish merchant exiled to Siberia: she went with him and they then managed to settle in the south where she met Grigory Kulik, the stocky, 'always half-drunk' *bon vivant* who had commanded Stalin's artillery at Tsaritsyn, but whose knowledge of military technology was frozen in 1918. The Countess was his second wife: they fell in love on the spot, leaving their respective spouses – but she was trebly tainted, for she was an aristocrat with links to Tsarist intelligence and the ex-wife of an arrested Jewish merchant. Like Bronka, Kira Kulik chatted to Stalin informally and 'shone at Kremlin parties', recalled one lady who was often there herself. 'She was very beautiful. Tukhachevsky, Voroshilov, Zhdanov,

Yagoda, Yezhov, Beria all paid court to her.' Naturally there were rumours that Stalin himself had made her his mistress.

Now, by the piano at the party, Kulik and other young women surrounded him: 'We drink your health, Joseph Vissarionovich,' said a famous ballerina, 'and let me kiss you in the name of all women.' He kissed her in return, and toasted her. But then Kira Kulik made a mistake.

When she was alone by the piano with just Stalin, she asked him to free her brother, a former Tsarist officer, from the camps. Stalin listened affably, then put on the gramophone, playing his favourites. Everyone danced except Stalin.* Stalin gave Kulik a book inscribed 'To my old friend. J Stalin' but Kira's approach, presuming on her familiarity and prettiness, set a mantrap in his suspicious mind.

* * *

Days later, Kulik ordered the artillery barrage that commenced the Soviet invasion of Finland, the fourth country in their sphere of influence, which like the Baltic States had been part of the Russian Empire until 1918 and which now threatened Leningrad.

On 12 October, a Finnish delegation met Stalin and Molotov in the Kremlin to hear the Soviet demands for the cession of a naval base at Hango. The Finns refused the Soviet demands, much to Stalin's surprise. 'This cannot continue for long without the danger of accidents,' he said. The Finns replied that they needed a five-sixths majority in their Parliament. Stalin laughed: 'You're sure to get 99 per cent!'

'And our votes into the bargain,' joked Molotov. Their last meeting ended with less humour: 'We civilians,' threatened Molotov, 'can see no further ... Now it's the turn of the military ...'

During dinner with Beria and Khrushchev at his flat, Stalin sent Finland his ultimatum. Molotov and Zhdanov, who was in charge of Baltic policy, the navy, and the defence of Leningrad, backed him. Mikoyan told a German diplomat that he had warned the Finns: 'You should be careful not to push the Russians too far. They have deep feelings in regard to this part of the world and ... I can only tell you that we Caucasians in the Politburo are having a great deal of difficulty restraining the Russians.' When the

---

* Kozlovsky always sang the same songs at all Kremlin receptions. When he put some other songs into the repertoire, he arrived at the Kremlin to find the same programme as usual. 'Comrade Stalin likes this repertoire. He likes to hear the same things as usual.'

ultimatum ran out, they were still drinking in the Kremlin. 'Let's get started today,' said Stalin, sending Kulik to command the bombardment. The very presence of Kulik at any military engagement seemed to guarantee disaster.

On 30 November, five Soviet armies attacked along the 800-mile border. Their frontal assaults on the Mannerheim Line were foiled by the ingenious Finns, who, dressed like ghosts in white suits, were slaughtering the Russians. The forests were decorated with frozen pyramids of Soviet corpses. The Finns used 70,000 empty bottles, filled with gasoline, against the Russian tanks – the first 'Molotov cocktails', one part of his cult of personality that the vain Premier surely did not appreciate. By mid-December, Stalin had lost about 25,000 men. He amateurishly planned the Winter War like a local exercise, ignoring the Chief of Staff Shaposhnikov's professional plan. When Kulik's artillery deputy, Voronov, later a famous marshal, asked how much time was allotted for this operation, he was told, 'Between ten and twelve days.' Voronov thought it would take two or three months. Kulik greeted this with 'derisive gibes' and ordered him to work on a maximum of twelve days. Stalin and Zhdanov were so confident they created a crude puppet government of Finnish Communists. After 9 December, the Ninth Army was decimated around the destroyed village of Suomussalmi.

Stalin's military amateurs reacted with spasms of executions and recriminations. 'I regard a radical purge … as essential,' Voroshilov warned the 44th Division. The need for the reform of the Red Army was plain to the cabinets of Europe. Yet Stalin's first solution was to despatch the 'gloomy demon' Mekhlis, now at the height of his power, to the front:

'I'm so absorbed in the work that I don't even notice the days pass. I sleep only 2–3 hours,' he told his wife. 'Yesterday it was minus 35 degrees below freezing … I feel very well … I have only one dream – to destroy the White Guards of Finland. We'll do it. Victory's not far off.'* On the 26th, Stalin finally appointed Timoshenko to command the North-Western Front and restore

* Bowing before the imperial status of his leader, Mekhlis was obsessed too with delivering a victory for Stalin on his birthday on 21 December 1939: 'I want to celebrate it with full defeat of Finnish White Guards!' When the great day arrived Mekhlis told his family: 'I'm saluting you. 60th birthday of JV. Celebrate it in the family!' Back at the Kremlin that night, Stalin celebrated his birthday with his courtiers, partying until 8 a.m. in the morning: 'An unforgettable night!' Dmitrov recorded in his diary.

order to his frayed forces who were now dying of hunger. Even
Beria took a more humane stand, reporting to Voroshilov the lack
of provisions: '139th Division's in difficulties ... no fodder at all
... no fuel ... Troops scattering.' Stalin sensed the army was
concealing the scale of the disaster. Trusting only Mekhlis, he
wrote:

'The White Finns published their operations report that claims
"the annihilation of the 44th Division ... 1,000 Red Army soldiers
as prisoners, 102 guns, 1,170 horses and 43 tanks." Tell me first –
is this true? Second – where is the Military Council and Chief of
Staff of the 44th Division? How do they explain their shameful
conduct? Why did they desert their division? Third, why does the
Military Council of the 9th Army not inform us ...? We expect an
answer. Stalin.'

Mekhlis arrived in Suomussalmi to find chaotic scenes which he
made worse. He confirmed the losses and shot the whole
command: 'the trial of Vinogradov, Volkov and chief of Political
Department took place in the open air in the presence of the
division ... The sentence of shooting was performed publicly ...
The exposure of traitors and cowards continues.' On 10
December, Mekhlis himself was almost killed when his car was
ambushed, as he proudly recounted to Stalin: unlike many of
Stalin's commissars, Mekhlis was personally courageous, if not
suicidally reckless, under fire, partly because, as a Jew, he wanted
to be 'purer than crystal'. Indeed, he took command of fleeing
companies and led them at the enemy. Mekhlis and Kulik did not
conceal the mess: 'We lack bread in the army,' Mekhlis reported.
Kulik agreed: 'rigidity and bureaucracy are everywhere.' When
Kulik rushed into a Politburo meeting to report yet more defeats,
Stalin lectured him: 'You're lapsing into panic ... The pagan Greek
priests were intelligent ... When they got disturbing reports,
they'd adjourn to their bathhouses, take baths, wash themselves
clean and only afterwards assess events and take decisions ...'

Stalin was saddened by these disasters: 'The snows are deep. Our
troops are on the march ... full of spirit ... Suddenly there's a burst
of automatic fire and our men fall to the ground.' At times, he
looked helplessly depressed. Khrushchev saw him lying on a
couch, despondent, a rehearsal of his collapse in the early days of
the Nazi invasion. The pressure made Stalin ill with his usual
streptococcus and staphylococcus, a temperature of 38°C and an
agonizing sore throat. On 1 February, his health improved as

Timoshenko probed Finnish defences, launching his great offensive on the 11th. Soviet superiority finally took its toll on the plucky Finns. When the doctors re-examined Stalin, he showed them the maps: 'We'll take Vyborg today.' The Finns sued for peace. On 12 March, Zhdanov signed a treaty in which Finland ceded Hango, the Karelian Isthmus, and the north-eastern shore of Ladoga, 22,000 square miles, to insulate Leningrad. Finland lost around 48,000 soldiers, Stalin over 125,000.

'The Red Army was good for nothing,' Stalin later told Churchill and Roosevelt. Stalin was incandescent and he was not alone: Khrushchev later blamed Voroshilov's 'criminal negligence', sneering that he spent more time in the studio of Gerasimov, the court painter, than in the Defence Commissariat. At Kuntsevo, Stalin's anger boiled over. He started shouting at Voroshilov, who gave as good as he got. Turning red as a turkeycock, Voroshilov shrieked at Stalin,

'You have yourself to blame for all of this. You're the one who annihilated the old guard of our army, you had our best generals killed.' Stalin rebuffed him, at which Voroshilov 'picked up a platter of roast suckling pig and smashed it on the table'. Khrushchev admitted, 'It was the only time in my life I witnessed such an outburst.' Voroshilov alone could have got away with it.

On 28 March 1940, Voroshilov, who became Stalin's 'whipping boy' for the Finnish disasters, confessed, at the Central Committee, 'I have to say neither I nor General Staff ... had any idea of the peculiarities and difficulties involved in this war.' Mekhlis, who hated Voroshilov and coveted his job, declared: he 'cannot simply leave his post – he must be severely punished.' But Stalin could not afford to destroy Voroshilov.

'Mekhlis made a hysterical speech,' he said, restraining his creature. Instead he held a uniquely frank, sometimes comical, Supreme Military Council in mid-April. One commander admitted that the army had been surprised to find forests in Finland, at which Stalin sneered: 'It's time our army knew there were forests there ... In Peter's time, there were forests. Elizabeth ... Catherine ... Alexander found forests! And now! That's four times!' (Laughter) He was even more indignant when Mekhlis revealed that the Finns often attacked during the Red Army's afternoon nap. 'Afternoon nap?!' spat Stalin.

'An hour's nap,' confirmed Kulik.

'People have afternoon naps in rest homes!' growled Stalin, who went on to defend the campaign itself: 'Could we have avoided the war? I think the war was inevitable ... A delay of a couple of months would have meant a delay of twenty years.' He won more territory there than Peter the Great but he warned against the 'cult of the traditions of the Civil War. It brings to mind the Red Indians who fought with clubs against rifles ... and were all killed.' On 6 May, Voroshilov was sacked as Defence Commissar and succeeded by Timoshenko.* Shaposhnikov was sacked as Chief of Staff even though Stalin admitted he had been right in the first place, 'but only we know that!' He raised military morale, restoring the rank of General and the single command by soldiers, whose tasks had been made incomparably harder by sharing control with interfering commissars. He freed 11,178 purged officers who officially returned 'from a long and dangerous mission'. Stalin asked one of them, Konstantin Rokossovsky, perhaps noticing his lack of fingernails, 'Were you tortured in prison?'

'Yes, Comrade Stalin.'

'There're too many yesmen in this country,' sighed Stalin. But some did not come back: 'Where's your Serdich?' Stalin asked Budyonny about a mutual friend.

'Executed!' reported the Marshal.

'Pity! I wanted to make him Ambassador to Yugoslavia ...'

Stalin attacked his military 'Red Indians' but then turned to his own tribe of primitive braves who remained obsessed with cavalry and oblivious to modern warfare. Budyonny and Kulik believed tanks could never replace horses. 'You won't convince me,' Budyonny had recently declared. 'As soon as war comes, everyone will shout, "Send for the cavalry!"' Stalin and Voroshilov had abolished special tank corps. Fortunately, Timoshenko now persuaded the *Vozhd* to reverse his folly.

None the less, Mikoyan called the dominance of these incompetents 'the triumph of the First Cavalry Army' since they were veterans of Stalin's favoured Civil War unit. Despite the

---

* A muscular paragon of peasant masculinity, typical of Stalin's cavalrymen, Timoshenko had been a divisional commander in the Polish War of 1920: he appears as the 'captivating Savitsky' in the *Red Cavalry* stories of Isaac Babel who praises the 'beauty of his giant's body', the power of his decorated chest 'cleaving the hut as a standard cleaves the sky' and his long cavalryman's legs which were 'like girls sheathed to the neck of shining jackboots'. The less poetical Mikoyan simply calls him a 'brave peasant'.

tossing of the suckling pig, Voroshilov was promoted to Deputy Premier for 'cultural matters' which Mikoyan regarded as a joke, given the Marshal's love of being painted.

Mekhlis, who also became Deputy Premier, fancied himself a great captain: he harassed Timoshenko to ask Stalin to reappoint him as Deputy Defence Commissar. Stalin mocked Timoshenko's naïvety: 'We want to help him but he doesn't understand. He wants us to leave him Mekhlis. But after three months, Mekhlis will chuck him out. Mekhlis wants to be Defence Commissar himself.' Mekhlis enjoyed Stalin's 'unbounded confidence'. Kulik, the buffoonish artillery chief, who encouraged his subordinates by shrieking 'Prison or medal', was an ignorant Blimp. He despised anti-tank artillery: 'What rubbish – no rumble, no shell-holes ...' He denounced the invaluable new Katyusha rockets: 'What the hell do we need rocket artillery for? The main thing is the horse-drawn gun.' He delayed the production of the outstanding T-34 tank. Khrushchev, whom Stalin liked for his cheek, questioned Kulik's credentials.

'You don't even know Kulik,' roared Stalin. 'I know him from the Civil War when he commanded the artillery in Tsaritsyn. He understands artillery.'

'But how many cannons did you have there? Two or three? And now he's in charge of all the artillery in the land?' Stalin told Khrushchev to mind his own business. Higher than all of them, Zhdanov was now Stalin's artillery and naval expert. 'There were competent people,' wrote Mikoyan, 'but Stalin was increasingly distrustful of people so trust was more important than anything.' Stalin wavered, meandered and reversed his own decisions. It is remarkable any correct decisions were made at all.

* * *

In May, Stalin ordered the kidnapping of Kulik's wife, Kira at whose house he had been a guest in November. In the name of the *Instantsiya*, Beria commissioned 'the Theoretician' Merkulov to arrange it. On 5 May, Kobulov, the prince-assassin Tsereteli and a favoured torturer Vladzimirsky trailed Kira on her way to the dentist, then bundled the beauty into a car and took her to the Lubianka. Stalin and Beria evidently shared a playful sadism and perverse taste for these depraved games. The reason for the kidnapping is a mystery because no charges were made against her, but Mekhlis built a file against the Kuliks which catalogues Kira's nobility as well as Grigory's drunken indiscretions, incompetence, anti-Semitism, Social Revolutionary past, complaints about the Terror, and connections with Trotskyites. Was she kidnapped for appealing to Stalin or was she denounced by her latest lover, another victim of prudery? The most suspicious mark against her in Stalin's eyes, may have been Kulik's dangerous tendency to give 'orders in front of' his various wives.*

Two days after Kira's kidnapping, on 7 May, Stalin promoted her husband to Marshal, along with Timoshenko and Shaposhnikov, in what can only be called a stroke of ironical sadism. Next day, Kulik's delight at his Marshalate was tempered by worry about his wife. He called Beria, who invited him to the Lubianka. While Kulik sipped tea in his office, Beria called Stalin:

'Marshal Kulik's sitting in front of me. No, he doesn't know any details. She left and that's all. Certainly, Comrade Stalin, we'll announce an all-Union search and do everything possible to find her.' They both knew that Kira was in the cells beneath Beria's office. A month later, Countess Simonich-Kulik, mother of an eight-year-old daughter, was moved to Beria's special prison, the Sukhanovka, where Blokhin murdered her in cold blood with a shot to the head. Kobulov complained that Blokhin killed her before he arrived. Stalin perhaps took comfort or pleasure in the promotion of cronies such as Kulik while knowing, as they did not, the fate of their beloveds.

The public search for Kira Kulik continued for twelve years but the Marshal himself had long since realized that her dubious connections had destroyed her. He soon married again.

* * *

Meanwhile Stalin and his magnates debated the fate of the Polish officers, arrested or captured in September 1939 and held in three camps, one of which was close to Katyn Forest. When Stalin was undecided about an issue, there was surprisingly frank discussion. Kulik, commander of the Polish front, proposed freeing all the Poles. Voroshilov agreed but Mekhlis was adamant there were Enemies among them. Stalin stopped the release but Kulik persisted. Stalin compromised. The Poles were released – except for about 26,000 officers whose destiny was finally decided at the Politburo on 5 March 1940.

---

* No papers of formal charges were ever filed so the kidnapping was illegal even by Bolshevik standards. When Beria was arrested after Stalin's death, this kidnapping and murder was one of the crimes on the indictment.

Beria's son claimed that his father argued against a massacre, not out of philanthropy, but because the Poles might be useful later. There is no evidence for this, except that Beria often took a practical rather than ideological approach. If so, Beria lost the argument. He dutifully reported that the 14,700 officers, landowners and policemen and 11,000 'counter-Revolutionary' landowners, were 'spies and saboteurs ... hardened ... enemies of Soviet power' who should be 'tried by ... Comrades Merkulov, Kobulov and Bashtakov'. Stalin scrawled his signature first and underlined it, followed by Voroshilov, Molotov and Mikoyan. Kalinin and Kaganovich were canvassed by phone and voted 'For'.

This massacre was a chunk of 'black work' for the NKVD who were accustomed to the *Vishka* of a few victims at a time, but there was a man for the task: Blokhin travelled down to the Ostachkov camp where he and two other Chekists outfitted a hut with padded, soundproofed walls and decided on a Stakhanovite quota of 250 shootings a night. He brought a butcher's leather apron and cap which he put on when he began one of the most prolific acts of mass murder by one individual, killing 7,000 in precisely twenty-eight nights, using a German Walther pistol to prevent future exposure. The bodies were buried in various places – but the 4,500 in the Kozelsk camp were interred in Katyn Forest.*

* * *

That June, the *Führer* unleashed his *Blitzkrieg* against the Low Countries and France. Stalin still had a profound respect for the power of France and Britain, whom he counted on holding up Hitler in the West. On 17 June 1940, France sued for peace, a shock that should have made Stalin reassess his alliance with Hitler though it was also now the only game in town. Molotov congratulated Schulenburg 'warmly' but through gritted teeth, 'on the splendid success of the German *Wehrmacht*'. A rattled Stalin 'cursed' the Allies:

'Couldn't they put up any resistance at all?' he asked Khrushchev. 'Now Hitler's going to beat our brains in!'

* In November 1941, the Polish Ambassador Stanislaw Kot quizzed Stalin on the whereabouts of these men. Stalin made a show of setting up a phone call to Beria and changed the subject. In December 1941, he told General Anders they had escaped to Mongolia. As we have seen, these sort of sniggering acts of concern were part of his game with Beria. Mikoyan's son Stepan wrote graciously that his father's signature on this order was 'the heaviest burden for our family'.

Stalin rushed to consume the Baltic States and Bessarabia, part of Romania. As troops moved across the borders, Soviet bombers flew Stalin's proconsuls to their fiefdoms: Dekanozov to Lithuania, Deputy Premier (the former 'shoot the mad dogs' Procurator) Vyshinsky to Latvia, and Zhdanov to Estonia. Zhdanov drove through the Estonian capital, Tallinn, in an armoured car flanked by two tanks and then nominated a puppet 'Prime Minister', lecturing the Estonians 'that everything will be done in accordance with democratic parliamentary rules ... We're not Germans!' For some Baltic citizens, they were worse. A total of 34,250 Latvians, almost 60,000 Estonians and 75,000 Lithuanians were murdered or deported. 'Comrade Beria,' said Stalin, 'will take care of the accommodation of our Baltic guests.' The NKVD put icing on Stalin's cake on 20 August, when Beria's agent Ramon Mercader shattered Trotsky's skull with an icepick. Trotsky might have undermined Stalin's foreign policy but really his death simply closed the chapter of the Great Terror. Vengeance was Stalin's.

Stalin had seized a buffer zone from the Baltic to the Black Sea but he now started to receive intelligence of Hitler's intention to attack the USSR. He redoubled his attentions to the Germans. Yet he also laughed at the Nazis with Zhdanov by putting on Wagner's *Flight of the Valkyries* directed by the Jewish Eisenstein.

'And who's singing Wotan?' Zhdanov joked with Stalin. 'A Jewish singer.' These Hebraic Wagnerians did not restrain Hitler from gradually moving troops eastwards. Stalin instinctively distrusted the intelligence from the new chief of GRU, military intelligence, General Filip Golikov, an untried mediocrity, and from the NKVD under Beria and Merkulov. He regarded Golikov as 'inexperienced, naïve. A spy should be like the devil; no one should trust him not even himself.' Merkulov, head of the NKVD Foreign Department, was 'dextrous' but still scared in case 'someone will be offended'. It was understandable they were afraid of offending 'someone'. All their predecessors had been murdered.*

Stalin and Molotov's suspicions of their own spies reflected their origins in the murky Bolshevik underground where many

---

* At the Eighteenth Party Conference in February 1941, Stalin divided Beria's NKVD into two commissariats. Beria retained the NKVD while State Security (NKGB) was hived off under his protégé Merkulov. This was not yet a direct demotion for Beria: he was promoted to Deputy Premier and remained overlord or *curator* of both 'Organs'.

comrades (including the *Vozhd* himself) were double or treble agents. They evaluated the motives of others by the standards of their own paranoid criminality: 'I think one can never trust intelligence,' Molotov admitted years later. 'One has to listen ... but check on them ... There are endless provocateurs on both sides.' This was ironic because Stalin possessed the world's best intelligence network: his spies worked for Marx not Mammon. Yet the more he knew, the less he trusted: 'his knowledge', writes one historian, 'only added to his sorrow and isolation.' However insistent the facts of the German military build-up, the Soviet spymasters were under pressure to provide the information that Stalin wanted: 'We never went out looking for information at random,' recalled one spy. 'Orders to look for specific things would come from above.'

Stalin reacted to this uneasiness by aggressively pushing the traditional Russian interests in the Balkans which in itself alarmed Hitler, who was weighing up whether to attack his ally. He decided to invite Molotov to Berlin to sidetrack the Soviets into a push for the Indian Ocean. The night before Molotov left, he sat up late with Stalin and Beria, debating how to maintain the Pact. In his handwritten directive, Stalin instructed Molotov to insist on explanations for the presence of German troops in Romania and Finland, discover Hitler's real interests and assert Russian interests in the Balkans and Dardanelles. Molotov meanwhile told his wife, 'my pleasure honey', that he was studying Hitler: 'I've been reading Rauschning's *Hitler Spoke to Me* ... Rauschning explains much that H is carrying out now ... and in the future.'

31

Molotov Meets Hitler:
Brinkmanship and Delusion

Molotov set off late on 10 November 1940 from the Belorussia Station with a pistol in his pocket and a delegation of sixty which included Beria's two protégés, Dekanozov, Deputy Foreign Commissar, and Merkulov, sixteen secret policemen, three servants and a doctor. This was Molotov's second trip to Europe. In 1922, he and Polina had visited Italy in the early days of Fascism. Now he was to observe Fascism at its apogee.

At 11.05 a.m., Molotov's train pulled into Berlin's Anhalter Station, which was festooned with flowers sinisterly illuminated with searchlights and Soviet flags hidden behind swastikas. Molotov dismounted in a dark coat with his grey Homburg hat and was greeted by Ribbentrop and Field Marshal Keitel. He spent longest shaking hands with Reichsführer-SS Himmler. The band deliberately played the *Internationale* at double time in case any ex-Communist passers-by joined in.

Molotov sped off in an open Mercedes with outriders to his luxurious hotel, the Schloss Bellevue, once an imperial palace, on the Tiergarten where the Soviets were dazzled by the 'tapestries and paintings', the 'finest porcelain standing round exquisitely carved cabinets' and, above all, the 'gold-braided livery' of the staff. Molotov's entire delegation wore identical dark blue suits, grey ties, and cheap felt hats, obviously ordered in bulk. Since some wore the hats like berets, some on the back of their heads like cowboys and some low over the eyes like Mafiosi, it was clear that many had never worn Western headgear before. The tepidity of the visit became obvious when Molotov met Ribbentrop in Bismarck's old office and gave little away. 'A rather frosty smile glided over his intelligent, chess-player's face,' noticed a German diplomat who was amused that, in the gilded Bismarckian chairs, little Dekanozov's feet barely touched the floor. When Ribbentrop encouraged Russia to seek an outlet for her energies in warm oceans, Molotov asked: 'Which sea are you talking about?'

After lunch at the Bellevue, the open Mercedes drove Molotov to the Chancellery, where he was led through bronze doors, guarded by heel-clicking SS men, into Hitler's magnificent study. Two blond SS giants threw open the doors and formed an archway with impeccable Nazi salutes through which this plain, stalwart Russian marched towards Hitler's gargantuan desk at the far end. Hitler hesitated, then walked jerkily to greet the Russians with 'small, rapid steps'. He stopped and made a Nazi salute before shaking hands with Molotov and the others with a 'cold and moist' palm, while his 'feverish eyes' burned into them 'like gimlets'. Hitler's theatrical rigmarole to terrorize and impress his guests did not affect Molotov, who regarded himself as a Marxist-Leninist and therefore superior to everyone else, particularly Fascists: 'There was nothing remarkable in his appearance.' Molotov and Hitler were exactly the same height – 'medium' as the small Russian put it. But Hitler 'was very smug … and vain. He was clever but narrow-minded and obtuse because of his egotism and the absurdity of his primordial idea.'

Hitler showed Molotov to a lounge area where he, Dekanozov and the interpreters sat on the sofa while Hitler occupied his usual armchair, whence he treated them to a long soliloquy about his defeat of Britain, generosity to Stalin, and disinterest in the Balkans, none of which was true. Molotov retorted with a series of polite, but awkward questions on the relationship between the two powers, pinpointing precisely Finland, Romania, Bulgaria. 'I kept pushing him for greater detail. "You've got to have a warm-water port. Iran, India – that's your future." And I said, "Why that's an interesting idea, how do you see it?"' Hitler ended the meeting without providing the answer.

That night, Ribbentrop hosted a reception for Molotov at the Kaiserhof Hotel attended by Reichsmarschall Göring, sporting a preposterous sartorial creation of silver thread and jewels, and Deputy Führer Hess. The Russian interpreter Berezhkov, observing Molotov talking to Göring, could not imagine two more different men. A telegram from Stalin awaited him, insisting again on the Balkans and Straits. The next morning, Molotov sent Stalin a telegram: 'I'm leaving for lunch and talk with Hitler. I will press him on the Black Sea, the Straits and Bulgaria.' First he called on Göring at the Air Ministry where he asked Hitler's 'paladin' more embarrassing questions which the Reichsmarschall simply doused with his pinguid heartiness. He then visited Hess.

'Do you have a Party programme?' he asked the Deputy Führer, knowing the Nazis did not. 'Do you have Party rules? And do you have a Constitution?' The Bolshevik ideologue was contemptuous: 'How could it be a Party without a programme?'

At 2 p.m., Hitler received Molotov, Merkulov and Dekanozov for a dinner with Goebbels and Ribbentrop. The Russians were disappointed by Hitler's austere menu that read simply: '*Kraftbruhe, Fasan, Obstsalat*' – beef tea, pheasant and fruit salad.

'The war is on so I don't drink coffee,' Hitler explained, 'because my people don't drink coffee either. I don't smoke, I don't drink liquor.' Molotov added later: 'It goes without saying that I was abstaining from nothing.'

Their second meeting, after the meal, lasted for a 'bad-tempered' three hours. Molotov pressed Hitler for answers. Hitler accused Russia of greed. Nothing dented the stolid persistence of 'Iron-Arse'. Molotov obeyed Stalin's telegraphed instructions to explain that 'all events from the Crimean War ... to the landing of foreign troops during the Intervention [Civil War] mean Soviet security cannot be settled without ... the Straits.'

Hitler almost lost his temper about his troops in Finland and Romania: 'That's a trifle!'

Molotov tartly commented that there was no need to speak roughly. But how could they agree on big issues when they failed to do so on small ones? Molotov noticed that Hitler 'became agitated. I persisted. I wore him down.'

Hitler drew out his handkerchief, wiped the sweat off his upper lip and saw his guest to the door.

'I'm sure history will remember Stalin's name forever,' he said.

'I don't doubt it,' replied Molotov.

'So we should meet ...' suggested Hitler vaguely, a meeting that never happened. 'But I hope it will remember me too,' he added with mock-modesty, for he had just two days earlier signed his Directive No. 18 that moved the Soviet invasion to the top of his agenda, an enterprise that would guarantee his place in history.

'I don't doubt it.'

Göring, Hess and Ribbentrop were the star guests at Molotov's banquet, with caviar and vodka at the grand but faded Soviet Embassy, which was interrupted by the RAF.

'Our British friends are complaining they have not been invited to the party,' joked Ribbentrop as Göring stampeded like a bejewelled, scented bison through the crowd, out to his Mercedes.

There was no air-raid shelter at the Embassy so most of the Russians were driven back to the hotel. Several got lost and Molotov was shepherded to Ribbentrop's private bunker. Here, to the music of the RAF bombs, and the cackle of AA-guns, the stuttering Russian sliced through the German's florid promises. If, as Hitler said, Germany was waging a life-and-death struggle against England, Molotov suggested this must mean that Germany was fighting 'for life' and England 'for death'. Britain was 'finished', answered Ribbentrop.

'If that's so, then why are we in this shelter and whose bombs are those falling?' Molotov responded.

Molotov departed next morning, having, as he told Stalin, achieved 'nothing to boast of but ... it does clarify the present mood of Hitler.'

* * *

Stalin congratulated Molotov on his defiance of Hitler: 'How,' he asked, 'did he put up with you telling him all this?' The answer was that Hitler did not: Molotov's obstinate Balkan ambitions convinced Hitler that Stalin would soon challenge his European hegemony. Having wavered over attacking Russia, he now accelerated his plans. On 4 December, Operation Barbarossa was set for May 1941.

A few days later, Yakovlev, the aircraft designer, who had been with Molotov in Berlin, bumped into the Foreign Commissar in Stalin's anteroom:

'Ah, here is the German!' joked Molotov. 'We'll both have to repent!'

'For what?' asked Yakovlev nervously.

'Well, did we dine with Hitler? We did. Did we shake hands with Goebbels? We did. We shall have to repent.' The Bolsheviks lived in a world of sin and repentance. When Stalin received Yakovlev, he ordered him to study Nazi planes:

'Learn how to beat them.'

On 29 December 1940, eleven days after Hitler signed Directive No. 21 on Operation Barbarossa, Stalin's spies alerted him to its existence. Stalin knew the USSR would not be ready for war until 1943 and hoped to delay it by frantic rearming and aggressive brinkmanship in the Balkans – but without provoking Hitler. The Führer, on the other hand, realized the urgency of his enterprise and that he had to secure the Balkans before he could attack Russia.

Stalin's panic to produce the best weapons and create the best strategy created a new Terror around him. The countdown to war redoubled the unreal miasma of fear and ignorance at the heart of the Soviet power. At a Kremlin lunch attended by all the magnates, they were just standing to leave when Stalin suddenly tore into them, complaining of the symptoms of his own dictatorship. 'I am the ONLY one dealing with all these problems. None of you could be bothered with them. I am out there by MYSELF. Look at me: I am capable of learning ... every day.' Kalinin alone dared reply:

'Somehow there's never enough time!' at which Stalin retorted furiously:

'People are thoughtless ... THEY'LL HEAR ME OUT AND GO ON JUST AS BEFORE. But I'll show you, if ever I lose my patience. You know very well I can do that. I'll hit the fatsos so hard you'll hear the crack for miles around!' He addressed himself especially to Kaganovich and Beria, who knew 'very well' how hard Stalin could hit 'the fatsos'. By the end, there were 'tears in Voroshilov's eyes'. The more Stalin realized the parlous condition of his military, the more he floundered, both convinced of his own infallibility and oblivious of his technical ignorance. He supervised every detail of every weapon. His meetings became ever more disturbing, his conduct, thought Mikoyan, ever more 'unhinged'.

There was a clear etiquette: it was deadly to disagree too much but, amazingly, his managers and generals stubbornly defended their expertise. 'I would have been more afraid if I'd known more,' said one commissar later. Silence was often a virtue and veterans advised neophytes on how to behave and survive.

When Stalin sent the Naval Commissar, Nikolai Kuznetsov, to inspect the Far East, the Admiral complained to Zhdanov, the naval overlord, that he was too busy with his new job.

'The papers can wait,' replied Zhdanov. 'I advise you not to say a word about them to Comrade Stalin.'*

When a new official arrived who had never attended a Stalin meeting, he called out 'Joseph Vissarionovich' when he wanted to speak. 'Stalin looked in my direction and again I saw ... an

---

* When Admiral Kuznetsov got to know him on their trip to the Far East, Zhdanov chatted about how much he enjoyed working with the navy. 'I'd love to go [on a cruiser]. But it's not always so easy to get away,' he said, adding with a smile, 'I am more a river man than a seaman. A freshwater sailor as they say. But I love ships.' Kuznetsov admired Zhdanov who 'did a great deal for the Navy'. But he was less helpful to other services.

unfriendly expression on his face. Suddenly a whisper from the man sitting behind me explained everything: "Never call him by his name and patronymic. He only allows a very narrow circle of intimates to do that. To all of us, he is Stalin. Comrade Stalin." ' It was shrewder to keep silent. Kuznetsov was about to object to building a fleet of heavy cruisers when another official whispered kindly:

'Watch your step! Don't insist!'

* * *

On 23 December 1940 Stalin called meetings of the high command which might have been a good idea had they not been paralysed with fear. Marshal Timoshenko and his most dynamic general, Georgi Zhukov, who commanded the Kiev Military District, criticized the glaring weaknesses of Soviet strategy and proposed a return to the forbidden 'deep operations' devised by the gifted Tukhachevsky. The powerful Zhdanov, Stalin's chief adviser on everything from howitzers to ships, Finland to culture, sat in on the meetings and reported back to Stalin, who next day summoned the generals. The insomniac Stalin, who was so accustomed to nocturnal life that he could only sleep after 4 a.m., confessed that he had not slept at all the night before. Timoshenko replied nervously that Stalin had approved his speech:

'You don't really think I have time to read every paper which is tossed at me,' replied Stalin, who at least ordered new plans and urgent war games. However, these merely exposed Soviet weakness, which rattled Stalin so much that on 13 January 1941 he summoned the generals without giving them time to prepare. The Chief of Staff, Meretskov, stumbled as he tried to report until Stalin interrupted:

'Well, who finally won?' Meretskov was afraid to speak, which only enraged Stalin even more. 'Here among ourselves ... we have to talk in terms of our real capabilities.' Finally Stalin exploded: 'The trouble is we don't have a proper Chief of Staff.' He there and then dismissed Meretskov. The meeting deteriorated further when Kulik declared that tanks were overrated; horse-drawn guns were the future. It was staggering that after two Panzer *Blitzkrieg* and only six months before the Nazi invasion, the Soviets were even debating such a thing. It was Stalin's fault that Kulik had been over-promoted but, typically, he blamed someone else:

'Comrade Timoshenko, as long as there's such confusion ... no mechanization of the army can take place at all.' Timoshenko retorted that only Kulik was confused. Stalin turned on his friend:

'Kulik comes out against the engine. It's as if he had come out against the tractor and supported the wooden plough ... Modern warfare will be a war of engines.'

The next afternoon, General Zhukov, forty-five, was rushed to the Little Corner, where Stalin appointed him Chief of Staff. Zhukov tried to refuse. Stalin, impressed by Zhukov's victory over the Japanese at Khalkin-Gol, insisted. The quintessential fighting general who would become the greatest captain of the Second World War was another Civil War cavalryman and a protégé of Budyonny since the late twenties. The son of an impoverished shoemaker, this convinced Communist had just managed to survive the Terror with Budyonny's help. Short, squat, indefatigable, with blunt features and a prehensile jaw, Georgi Zhukov shared Stalin's ruthless brutality, combining savage reprisals and Roman discipline with carelessness about losses. However, he lacked Stalin's deviousness and sadism. He was emotional and brave, often daring to disagree with Stalin who, sensing his gifts, indulged him.

A few days later, at Kuntsevo, Timoshenko and Zhukov tried to persuade Stalin to mobilize, convinced that Hitler would invade. Timoshenko advised him on handling Stalin: 'He won't listen to a long lecture ... just ten minutes.' Stalin was dining with Molotov, Zhdanov and Voroshilov, along with Mekhlis and Kulik. Zhukov spoke up: should not they bolster defences along the Western frontier?

'Are you eager to fight the Germans?' Molotov asked harshly.

'Wait a minute,' Stalin calmed the stuttering Premier. He lectured Zhukov on the Germans: 'They fear us. In secret, I will tell you that our ambassador had a serious conversation with Hitler personally and Hitler said to him, 'Please don't worry about the concentration of our forces in Poland. Our forces are re-training ...' The generals then joined the magnates for Ukrainian *borscht* soup, buckwheat porridge, then stewed meat, with stewed and fresh fruit for pudding, washed down with brandy and Georgian *Khvanchkara* wine.

* * *

Kulik's imbecilic advice unleashed another paroxysm of terror that would bring death to a Politburo family. On hearing that the Germans were increasing the thickness of their armour, he demanded stopping all production of conventional guns and switching to 107mm howitzers from World War I. The Armaments Commissar, Boris Vannikov, a formidable Jewish super-manager, who had studied at Baku Polytechnic with Beria, sensibly opposed Kulik but lacked his access to Stalin. Kulik won Zhdanov's backing. On 1 March, Stalin summoned Vannikov: 'What objections do you have? Comrade Kulik said you don't agree with him.' Vannikov explained that it was unlikely the Germans had updated their armour as swiftly as Kulik suggested: the 76mm remained the best. Then Zhdanov entered the office.

'Look here,' Stalin said to him, 'Vannikov doesn't want to make the 107mm gun ... But these guns are very good. I know them from the Civil War.'

'Vannikov,' replied Zhdanov, 'always opposes everything. That's his style of working.'

'You're the main artillery expert we have,' Stalin commissioned Zhdanov to settle the question, 'and the 107mm is a good gun.' Zhdanov called the meeting where Vannikov defied Kulik. Zhdanov accused him of 'sabotage'. 'The dead hold back the living,' he added ominously. Vannikov shouted back:

'You're tolerating disarmament in the face of an approaching war.' Zhdanov stiffly 'declared he was going to complain about me to Stalin'. Stalin accepted Kulik's solution, which had to be reversed when the war began. Vannikov was arrested.* Only in Stalin's realm could the country's greatest armaments expert be imprisoned just weeks before a war. But Kulik's motto, 'Prison or a medal,' had triumphed again. As the poison spread, it reached Kaganovich's brother. In the almost biblical sacrifice of a beloved sibling, Lazar's steeliness was grievously tested.

* * *

Vannikov was cruelly tortured about his recent post as deputy to Mikhail Kaganovich, Lazar's eldest brother and Commissar for Aircraft Production. The air force was always the most accident-prone service. Not only did the planes crash with alarming regularity, reflecting the haste and sloppiness of Soviet manu-facturing, but someone had to pay for these accidents. In one year four Heroes of the Soviet Union were lost in crashes and Stalin himself questioned the air-force generals even down to the

---

* This was far from the only such madness: on other occasions, Stalin commissioned a tank based on a crazy principle that 'in being destroyed, it protects'.

engineers working on each plane. 'What kind of man is he?' Stalin asked about one technician. 'Maybe he's a bastard, a *svoloch*.' The crashes had to be the fault of 'bastards'. Vannikov was forced to implicate Mikhail Kaganovich as the 'bastard' in this case.

Meanwhile, Vasily Stalin, now a pilot avid to win paternal love, usually by denouncing his superiors to his father, played some part in this tragedy. He remained so nervous that, Svetlana recalled, when his father addressed him at dinner, he jumped and often could not even reply, stammering, 'I didn't hear what you said, Father ... What?' In 1940, he fell in love with a pretty trumpet-playing blonde from an NKVD family, Galina Bourdonovskaya, and married her. Yet he was truculent, arrogant, drunken and, while often bighearted, more often, dangerous. In this peculiar world, the 'Crown Prince' became, according to Svetlana, 'a menace'.

'Hello dear Father,' he wrote on 4 March 1941. 'How's your health? Recently I was in Moscow on the orders of Rychagov [the Chief of the Main Directorate of the Air Force], I wanted to see you so much but they said you were busy ... They won't let me fly ... Rychagov called me and abused me very much saying that instead of studying theory, I was starting to visit commanders proving to them I had to fly. He ordered me to inform you of this conversation.' Vasily had to fly in old planes 'that are terrible to see' and even future officers could not train in the new planes: 'Father, write me just a couple of words, if you have time, it's the biggest joy for me because I miss you so much. Your Vasya.'

This subtle denunciation cannot have helped Pavel Rychagov, thirty-nine, a dashing pilot just promoted to the high command. He arrived drunk at a meeting to discuss the planes. When Stalin criticized the air force, Rychagov shouted that the death rate was so high 'because you're making us fly in coffins!' Silence fell but Stalin continued to walk around the room, the only sounds being the puffing of the pipe and the pad of soft boots.

'You shouldn't have said that.' He walked round the deathly quiet table one more time and repeated: 'You shouldn't have said that.' Rychagov was arrested within the week along with several air-force top brass, and General Shtern, Far Eastern commander, all later shot. They, like Vannikov, implicated Mikhail Kaganovich.

'We received testimonies,' Stalin told Kaganovich. 'Your brother's implicated in the conspiracy.' The brother was accused of building the aircraft factories close to the Russian border to help Berlin. Stalin explained that Mikhail, a Jew, had been designated head of Hitler's puppet Government-in-waiting, an idea so preposterous that it was either the moronic solecism of a NKGB simpleton or, more likely, a joke between Stalin and Beria. Did they remember Ordzhonikidze's fury on the arrest of his brother? Ordzhonikidze had been Kaganovich's closest friend.

'It's a lie,' Kaganovich claimed to have replied. 'I know my brother. He's a Bolshevik since 1905, devoted to the Central Committee.'

'How can it be a lie?' retorted Stalin. 'I've got the testimonies.'

'It's a lie. I demand a confrontation.' Decades later, Kaganovich denied that he had betrayed his own brother: 'If my brother had been an Enemy I'd have been against him ... I was sure he was right. I protected him. I protected him!' Kaganovich could afford to give an opinion but he also had to make clear that if the Party needed to destroy his brother, his brother must die. 'Well, so what?' he added. 'If necessary, arrest him.'

Stalin ordered Mikoyan and that sinister duo Beria and Malenkov to arrange a confrontation between Mikhail Kaganovich and his accuser, Vannikov, but 'Iron Lazar' was not invited to attend.

'Don't make him anxious, don't bother him,' said Stalin.

Mikoyan held the 'confrontation' in his office in the same building as the Little Corner where Mikhail defended himself 'passionately' against Vannikov.

'Are you insane?' he asked his former deputy who had spent nights at his home during the Terror, afraid of arrest.

'No, you were part of the same organization with me,' replied Vannikov.

Beria and Malenkov told Mikhail to wait in the corridor while they interrogated Vannikov some more. Mikhail went into Mikoyan's private lavatory (one of the perks of power). There was a shot. The three of them found Kaganovich's brother dead. By killing himself before his arrest, he saved his family. Lazar passed the test. A scapegoat for the aircraft blunders had been found.*

* * *

As these commissars travelled from Kremlin to torture chamber and back, the Germans surreptitiously deployed their legions along the Soviet frontier while Stalin channelled much of his

---

* Kaganovich was despised for not saving his brother but he buried him with honour as a Central Committee member in the Novodevichy Cemetery, not far from Nadya Stalin. Vannikov survived but remained in prison.

energy into reasserting Russian influence in the Balkans. But by March, Hitler had managed to lure Bulgaria, Romania and Yugoslavia into his camp. Then, on 26 March, the pro-German Government in Yugoslavia was overthrown, probably with the help of the NKGB and the British secret service. Hitler could not afford such a sore on his flank so the Germans prepared to invade Yugoslavia, which delayed Operation Barbarossa by a month.

On 4 April, Stalin threw himself into negotiations with the new Yugoslav Government, hoping this glitch in Hitler's plan would either drive Hitler back to the negotiating table or, at the very least, delay the invasion until 1942. When he signed a treaty with the Yugoslavs just as the Wehrmacht began to bombard Belgrade, Stalin cheerfully dismissed the threat: 'Let them come. We've strong nerves.' But Yugoslavia was Hitler's most successful *Blitzkrieg* of all: ten days later, Belgrade surrendered. Events were moving faster than the erosion of Stalin's illusions.

That same day, Yosuke Matsuoka, the Japanese Foreign Minister, arrived in Moscow on his way back from Berlin. As the *Wehrmacht* crushed the Yugoslavs, Stalin realized that he required a fresh path back to Hitler. But he was also aware of the priceless benefit of a quiet Far Eastern front if Hitler invaded. Zhukov's victory in the Far East had persuaded Tokyo that their destiny lay southwards in the juicier tidbits of the British Empire. On 14 April 1941, when Matsuoka signed a non-aggression pact with the Soviet Union, Stalin and Molotov reacted with almost febrile excitement, as if they had single-handedly changed the shape of Europe and saved Russia. Stalin exclaimed how rare it was 'to find a diplomat who speaks openly what is on his mind. What Talleyrand told Napoleon was well known, "the tongue was given the diplomat so that he could conceal his thoughts". We Russians and Bolsheviks are different ...' For once, Stalin unwound at the resulting Bacchanal, while Molotov tossed back the champagne until both were as drunk as Matsuoka.

'Stalin and I made him drink a lot,' boasted Molotov later. By 6 a.m., Matsuoka 'almost had to be carried to the train. We could barely stand up.' Stalin, Molotov and Matsuoka burst into song, rendering that Russian favourite, 'Shoumel Kamysh' that went: 'The reeds were rustling, the trees are crackling in the wind, the night was very dark ... And the lovers stayed awake all night', to guffaws. At Yaroslavsky Station, the assembled diplomats were amazed to see an intoxicated Stalin, in his greatcoat, brownvizored cap and boots, accompanied by Matsuoka and Molotov who kept saluting and shouting: 'I'm a Pioneer! I'm ready!' – the Soviet equivalent of the Boy Scout's 'Dib! Dib! Be prepared!' The Bulgarian Ambassador judged Molotov 'the least drunk'. Stalin, who had never before seen any visitor off at the station, hugged the staggering Japanese but since neither could speak the other's language, their new intimacy was expressed in embraces and grunts of 'Ah! Ah!'

Stalin was so excited that he jovially punched the minuscule bald Japanese Ambassador-General on the shoulder so hard that he 'staggered back three or four steps which caused Matsuoka to laugh in glee'. Then Stalin noticed the tall attaché Colonel Hans Krebs and, abandoning the Japanese, tapped him on the chest:

'German?' he asked. Krebs stiffened to attention, towering over Stalin who slapped him on the back, wrung his hand and said loudly, 'We've been friends with you and we'll remain friends with you.'

'I'm sure of that,' replied Krebs, though the Swedish Ambassador thought he 'did not seem so convinced of it'.* Finally lumbering back to the Japanese, Stalin again embraced the much-hugged Matsuoka, exclaiming, 'We'll organize Europe and Asia!' Arm in arm, he led Matsuoka into his carriage and waited until the train departed. Japanese diplomats escorted Stalin to his armoured Packard while their Ambassador, 'standing on a bench, waved his handkerchief and cried in a strident voice, "Thank you thank you!"'

* * *

The celebration was not over for Stalin and Molotov. As he got into the car, Stalin ordered Vlasik to call the dacha at Zubalovo and tell Svetlana, now fifteen, that she was to assemble the family for a party:

'Stalin's arriving any minute.' Svetlana ran to tell her aunt, Anna Redens, who was there with her children and Gulia Djugashvili, aged three, Yakov's daughter:

'Father's coming!' Anna Redens had not seen Stalin since the row about her husband's arrest and certainly not since his execution. All of them gathered on the steps. Minutes later, the tipsy, unusually cheerful Stalin arrived. Throwing open the car door, he hailed the twelve-year-old Leonid Redens:

* Krebs was Chief of Staff of the Wehrmacht during the last hours of the Third Reich in April 1945.

'Get in – let's go for a drive!' The driver sped them round the flower-bed. Then Stalin got out and hugged the apprehensive Anna Redens, who was holding her younger son Vladimir, now six. Stalin admired this angelic nephew: 'For the sake of such a wonderful son, let's make peace. I forgive you.' Little Gulia, Stalin's first grandchild, was brought out to be admired but she waved her arms and screamed and was swiftly taken to her room. Stalin sat at the table where he had once presided with Nadya over their young family. Cakes and chocolates were brought. Stalin took Vladimir on to his lap and started opening the chocolates: the little boy noticed his 'very beautiful long fingers'.

'You're spoiling the children by buying them presents they don't even want,' Stalin reprimanded the staff but, Vladimir says, 'in his gentle way that made him very loved by them'.

After tea, Stalin went upstairs for a catnap. He had not slept the previous night. Then Molotov, Beria and Mikoyan arrived for dinner* at which 'Stalin threw orange peel at everyone's plates. Then he threw a cork right into the ice-cream' which delighted Vladimir Alliluyev. The family could not know that Hitler's imminent invasion, and Stalin's exhaustion and paranoia, would make this the end of an era.

* * *

This was an oasis of exhilaration in a darkening sky. Torn between the wishful thinking of his powerful will – and the mounting evidence – Stalin persisted in believing that a diplomatic breakthrough with Hitler was just round the corner, even though he now knew the date of Operation Barbarossa from his spy-masters. When Stafford Cripps, the British Ambassador delivered a letter from Winston Churchill warning of the invasion, it backfired, convincing Stalin that Britain was trying to entrap Russia: 'We're being threatened with the Germans, and the Germans with the Soviet Union,' Stalin told Zhukov. 'They're playing us off against each other.'

Yet he was not completely oblivious: in the contest that Molotov called 'the great game', Stalin thought Russia might

---

* On 13 March 1941, Svetlana wrote to her father: 'My dear little Secretary! Why have you recently been coming home so late? ... Never mind, I wouldn't make my respected Secretaries miserable with my strictness. Eat as much as you like. You can drink too. I only ask you not to put vegetables or other food on the chairs in the hope that someone will sit on it. It will damage the chairs ...' This was an early hint of the brutish games that characterized Stalin's dinners after the war. 'We obey,' replied Stalin. 'Kisses to my little sparrow. Your little Secretary, Stalin.'

manage to stay out of the war until 1942. 'Only by 1943 could we meet the Germans on an equal footing,' he told Molotov. As ever Stalin was trying to read himself out of the problem, carefully studying a history of the German–French war of 1870. He and Zhdanov repeatedly quoted Bismarck's sensible dictum that Germany should never face war on two fronts: Britain remained undefeated hence Hitler would not attack. 'Hitler's not such a fool,' Stalin said, 'that he's unable to understand the difference between the USSR and Poland or France, or even England, indeed all of them put together.' Yet his entire career was a triumph of will over reality.

He persisted in believing that Hitler, the reckless gambler and world-historical 'sleepwalker', was a rational Bismarckian Great Power statesman, like himself. After the war, talking to a small group that included Dekanozov, his Ambassador to Berlin in 1941, Stalin, thinking aloud about this time, obliquely explained his behaviour: 'When you're trying to make a decision, NEVER put yourself into the mind of the other person because if you do, you can make a terrible mistake.'*

Military measures were agonizingly slow. Zhdanov and Kulik proposed removing the old armaments from the Fortified Areas and putting them in the unfinished new ones. Zhukov objected: there was no time. Stalin backed his cronies, so the fortifications were unfinished when the onslaught came.

On 20 April, Ilya Ehrenburg, the Jewish novelist whom Stalin admired, learned that his anti-German novel, *The Fall of Paris*, had been refused by the censors who were still following Stalin's orders not to offend Hitler. Four days later, Poskrebyshev called, telling him to dial a number: 'Comrade Stalin wants to talk to you.' As soon as he got through, his dogs started barking; his wife had to drive them out of the room. Stalin told him he liked the book: did Ehrenburg intend to denounce Fascism? The novelist replied that it was hard to attack the Fascists since he was not allowed to use the word. 'Just go on writing,' said Stalin jocularly, 'you and I will try to push the third part through.' It was typical of this strangely literary dictator to think this would alarm the Germans: Hitler was beyond literary nuances.

* Dekanozov repeatedly told this story to his young son, Reginald, who recorded it in his Notes before his own recent death. It has never been published. The author is most grateful to Nadya Dekanozova of Tbilisi, Georgia, for making this source available.

Even Stalin's inner circle could smell war now. It was so pervasive that Zhdanov suggested they cancel the May Day Parade in case it was too 'provocative'. Stalin did not cancel it but he placed Dekanozov, the Ambassador to Germany, right next to him on the Mausoleum to signal his warmth towards Berlin.

On 4 May, he sent another signal to Hitler that he was ready to talk: Stalin replaced Molotov as Premier, promoting Zhdanov's protégé, Nikolai Voznesensky, the brash economic maestro, as his deputy on the inner Buro. At thirty-eight, Voznesensky's rise had been meteoric and this angered the others: Mikoyan, who was particularly sore, thought he was 'economically educated but a professor-type without practical experience'. This good-looking, intelligent but arrogant Leningrader was 'naïvely happy with his appointment', but Beria and Malenkov already resented the acerbic technocrat: Stalin's 'promoting a teacher to give us lessons', Malenkov whispered to Beria. Henceforth, Stalin ruled as Premier through his deputies as Lenin had, balancing the rivalry between Beria and Malenkov, on the one hand, and Zhdanov and Voznesensky, on the other. Stalin expressed his emergence on the world stage sartorially, discarding his baggy trousers and boots. He 'started wearing well ironed, untucked ones with lace-up bootkins'.

Finally, Stalin prepared the military for the possibility of war. On 5 May, he saw only one visitor: Zhdanov, just promoted to Stalin's Party Deputy, visited him for twenty-five minutes. At 6 p.m. the two men walked from the Little Corner to the Great Kremlin Palace where two thousand officers awaited them: Stalin entered with Zhdanov, Timoshenko and Zhukov. President Kalinin introduced a 'severe' Stalin who praised the modern mechanization of his 'new army'. Then he eccentrically attributed the French defeat to amorous disappointment: the French were 'so dizzy with self-satisfaction' that they disdained their own warriors to the extent that 'girls wouldn't even marry soldiers'. Was the German army unbeatable? 'There are no invincible armies in the world' but war was coming. 'If VM Molotov … can delay the start of war for 2–3 months, this'll be our good fortune.' At the dinner, he toasted: 'Long live the dynamic offensive policy of the Soviet State,' adding, 'anyone who doesn't recognize this is a Philistine and a fool.' This was a relief to the military: Stalin was not living in cloud cuckoo land. The State was ready to fight, or was it? The State was not sure.*

The magnates tried to steer a path between Stalin's infallibility and Hitler's reality: the absurdity of explaining how the army had to be ready to fight an offensive war which was definitely not going to happen, while claiming this was not a change of policy, was so ridiculous that they tied themselves in knots of Stalinist sophistry and Neroesque folly. 'We need a new type of propaganda,' declared Zhdanov at the Supreme Military Council. 'There is only one step between war and peace. So our propaganda can't be peaceful.'

'We ourselves designed the propaganda this way,' Budyonny exploded, so they had to explain why it was changing.

'We're only altering the slogan,' claimed Zhdanov.

'As if we were going to war tomorrow!' sneered the pusillanimous Malenkov, eighteen days before the invasion.

On 7 May, Schulenburg, secretly opposed to Hitler's invasion, breakfasted with the Soviet Ambassador to Berlin, Dekanozov, whom he ambiguously tried to warn. They met thrice but 'he did not warn,' said Molotov later, 'he hinted and pushed for diplomatic negotiations.' Dekanozov informed Stalin who was becoming ever more bad-tempered and nervous. 'So, disinformation has now reached ambassadorial level,' he growled. Dekanozov disagreed.

'How could you allow yourself to argue with Comrade Stalin! He knows more and can see further than all of us!' Voroshilov threatened Dekanozov during a recess.

On 10 May, Stalin learned of Deputy Führer Hess's quixotic peace flight to Scotland. His magnates, remembered Khrushchev who was in the office that day, were all understandably convinced that Hess's mission was aimed at Moscow. But Stalin was finally willing to prepare for war, admittedly in a manner so timid that it was barely effective. On 12 May, Stalin allowed the generals to

---

* But the speeches have spawned a grand debate about whether Stalin was planning a pre-emptive strike against Hitler: the so-called Suvorov Debate following Victor Suvorov's article in June 1985. Suvorov argued that Stalin was about to attack Hitler because of the partial mobilization and build-up on Western borders, the proximity of airfields, and because General Zhukov produced such a plan of attack. His view is now discredited. It now seems that the real view of the General Staff, including General Vasilevsky, was that they would have to retreat much deeper into their territory – hence Vasilevsky's proposal to move airfields and infrastructure back to the Volga, a proposal attacked as 'defeatist' by Kulik and Mekhlis. However, Stalin always kept an offensive war as a real possibility as well as an ideological necessity. As for the speeches, they were designed purely to raise the morale of the army and display a measure of realism about the Soviet situation.

strengthen the borders, calling up 500,000 reserves, but was terrified of offending the Germans. When Timoshenko reported German reconnaissance flights, Stalin mused, 'I'm not sure Hitler knows about those flights.' On the 24th, he refused to take any further measures.

The paralysis struck again. Stalin never apologized but he very indirectly acknowledged his mistakes when he later thanked the Russian people for their 'patience'. But he blamed most of his blunders on others, admitting that he 'trusted too much in cavalrymen'. Zhukov confessed his own failures: 'Possibly I did not have enough influence.' This was not the real reason for his quiescence. If he had demanded mobilization, Stalin would have asked: 'On what basis? Well, Beria, take him to your dungeons!' Kulik caught the attitude of most soldiers: 'This is high politics. It's not our business.'

The intelligence was now flooding in. Earlier it had been presented in an ambiguous way but now it was surely clear that something ominous was darkening the Western border. Merkulov daily reported to Stalin who was now defying an avalanche of information from all manner of sources. On 9 June, when Timoshenko and Zhukov mentioned the array of intelligence, Stalin tossed their papers at them and snarled, 'And I have different documents.' He mocked Richard Sorge, the masterspy in Tokyo who used his amorous and sybaritic appetites to conceal his peerless intelligence-gathering: 'There's this bastard who's set up factories and brothels in Japan and even deigned to report the date of the German attack as 22 June. Are you suggesting I should believe him too?'

32

The Countdown: 22 June 1941

On 13 June, Timoshenko and Zhukov, themselves depressed and baffled, alerted Stalin to further border activities. 'We'll think it over,' snapped Stalin who next day lost his temper with Zhukov's proposal of mobilization: 'That means war. Do you two understand that or not?' Then he asked how many divisions there were in the border areas:

Zhukov told him there were 149.

'Well, isn't that enough? The Germans don't have so many ...' But the Germans were on a war footing, replied Zhukov. 'You can't believe everything in intelligence reports,' said Stalin.

On the 16th, Merkulov confirmed the final decision to attack, which came from agent 'Starshina' in Luftwaffe headquarters.* 'Tell the "source" in the Staff of the German Air Force to fuck his mother!' he scrawled to Merkulov. 'This is no source but a disinformer. J.St.' Even Molotov struggled to convince himself: 'They'd be fools to attack us,' he told Admiral Kuznetsov.

Two days later, at a three-hour meeting described by Timoshenko, he and Zhukov beseeched Stalin for a full alert, with the *Vozhd* fidgeting and tapping his pipe on the table, and the magnates agreeing with Stalin's maniacal delusions or else brooding in sullen silence, the only way of protesting they possessed. Stalin suddenly leapt to his feet and shouted at Zhukov:

'Have you come to scare us with war, or do you want a war because you're not sufficiently decorated or your rank isn't high enough?'

Zhukov paled and sat down but Timoshenko warned Stalin again, which aroused a frenzy:

'It's all Timoshenko's work, he's preparing everyone for war. He

---

* On 14 June, Hitler held his last military conference before the beginning of Barbarossa, with the generals arriving at the Chancellery at different times so as not to raise suspicion. On the 16th, he summoned Goebbels to brief him.

ought to have been shot, but I've known him as a good soldier since the Civil War.'

Timoshenko replied he was only repeating Stalin's own speech that war was inevitable.

'So you see,' Stalin retorted to the Politburo. 'Timoshenko's a fine man with a big head but apparently a small brain,' and he held up his thumb. 'I said it for the people, we have to raise their alertness, while you have to realize that Germany will never fight Russia on her own. You must understand this.' Stalin stormed out leaving an excruciating silence but then he 'opened the door and stuck his pock-marked face round it and uttered in a loud voice: "If you're going to provoke the Germans on the frontier by moving troops there without our permission, then heads will roll, mark my words" – and he slammed the door.'

Stalin summoned Khrushchev, who should have been monitoring the Ukrainian border, to Moscow and would not let him leave: 'Stalin kept ordering me to postpone my departure: "Wait," he said, "Don't be in such a hurry. There's no need to rush back."' Khrushchev held a special place in Stalin's affections: perhaps his irrepressible optimism, sycophantic devotion and practical cunning made him a useful companion at such a moment. Stalin was in a 'state of confusion, anxiety, demoralization, even paralysis', according to Khrushchev, soothing his anxiety with sleepless nights and heavy drinking at endless Kuntsevo dinners. 'You could feel the static,' said Khrushchev, 'the discharge of tension.' On Friday the 20th, Khrushchev finally said,

'I have to go. The war is about to break out. It may catch me here in Moscow or on the way back to the Ukraine.'

'Right,' said Stalin. 'Just go.'

On the 19th, Zhdanov, who was running the country with Stalin and Molotov, left for one and a half months' holiday. Suffering from asthma, and Stalin's boa-constrictor-like friendship, he was exhausted. 'But I have a bad foreboding the Germans could invade,' Zhdanov told Stalin.

'The Germans have already missed the best moment,' replied Stalin. 'Apparently they'll attack in 1942. Go on holiday.'* Mikoyan thought he was naïve to go but Molotov shrugged:

---

* Perhaps Stalin had encouraged Zhdanov to bolster his own wavering confidence: when Dmitrov passed on an Austrian warning, Stalin replied that there could not be anything to worry about if Zhdanov, who ran the Leningrad Military District and the navy, had gone on holiday.

'A sick man has to rest.' So 'we went on holiday', remembers Zhdanov's son Yury. 'We arrived in Sochi on Saturday 21 June.'

On 20 June, Dekanozov, back in Berlin, warned Beria firmly that the attack was imminent. Beria threatened his protégé while Stalin muttered that 'Slow Kartvelian' 'wasn't clever enough to work it out'. Beria forwarded the 'disinformation' to Stalin with the sycophantic but slightly mocking note:

'My people and I, Joseph Vissarionovich, firmly remember your wise prediction: Hitler will not attack us in 1941!'

At about 7.30 p.m., Mikoyan, the Deputy Premier in charge of the merchant navy, was called by the harbourmaster of Riga: twenty-five German ships were setting sail, even though many had not yet unloaded. He rushed along to Stalin's office where some of the leaders were gathered.

'That'll be a provocation,' Stalin angrily told Mikoyan. 'Let them leave.' The Politburo were alarmed – but of course said nothing. Molotov was deeply worried: 'The situation is unclear, a great game is being played,' he confided to the Bulgarian Communist Dmitrov, on Saturday 21 June. 'Not everything depends on us.' General Golikov brought Stalin further evidence: 'This information,' Stalin wrote on it, 'is an English provocation. Find out who the author is and punish him.' The fire brigade reported that the German Embassy was burning documents. The British Government and even Mao Tse-tung (a surprising source, via the Comintern) sent warnings. Stalin telephoned Khrushchev to warn him the war might begin the next day and asked Tiulenev, the commander of Moscow:

'How do things stand with the anti-aircraft defence of Moscow? Note the situation's tense ... Bring the troops of Moscow's anti-aircraft defence to 75 per cent of combat readiness.'

Saturday the 21st was a warm and uneasy day in Moscow. The schools had broken up for the holidays. Dynamo Moscow, the football team, lost its game. The theatres were showing *Rigoletto*, *La Traviata* and Chekhov's *Three Sisters*. Stalin and the Politburo sat all day, coming and going. By early evening, Stalin was deeply disturbed by the persistently ominous reports that even his Terror could not disperse. Molotov joined him again around 6.30.

Outside the Little Corner, Poskrebyshev sat by the open window, sipping Narzan water: he called Chadaev, the young Sovnarkom assistant. 'Something important?' whispered Chadaev.

'I'd say so,' replied Poskrebyshev. 'The Boss talked to Timoshenko, he was very agitated ... They're waiting for ... you know ... the German attack ...'

At about seven, Stalin ordered Molotov to summon Schulenburg to protest about the German reconnaissance flights – and find out what he could. The Count sped into the Kremlin. Molotov hurried along to his office in the same building. Meanwhile* Timoshenko telephoned to report that a German deserter had revealed the German invasion plan for dawn. Stalin swung between the force of reality and the self-delusion of his infallibility.

In Molotov's office, Schulenburg was relieved to see that the Foreign Commissar was still oblivious to the enormity of his country's plight. The Russian asked him why Germany seemed dissatisfied with their Soviet allies. And why had the women and children of the German Embassy left Moscow?

'Not ALL the women,' said Schulenburg. 'My wife is still in town.' Molotov gave what the Ambassador's aide, Hilger, called a 'resigned shrug of the shoulders' and returned to Stalin's office.

Timoshenko then arrived, along with most of the magnates: Voroshilov, Beria, Malenkov and the powerful young Deputy Premier Voznesensky. At 8.15 p.m., Timoshenko returned to the Defence Commissariat whence he informed Stalin that a second deserter had warned that war would begin at 4 a.m. Stalin called him back. Timoshenko arrived at 8.50 with Zhukov and Budyonny, Deputy Defence Commissar, who knew Stalin much better than they did and was less frightened of the *Vozhd*. Budyonny admitted that he did not know what was happening at the frontier since he was only in command of the home front. The outspoken Budyonny had played an ambiguous role in the Terror but even then he was willing to speak his mind, a rare quality in those circles. Stalin appointed him commander of the Reserve Army. Then Mekhlis, newly restored to his old job – head of the army's Political Department, Stalin's military enforcer, joined this funereal vigil.

* This account is based on the memoirs of Molotov, Mikoyan, Zhukov, Timoshenko, Hilger and others but the times are based on the Kremlin Logbook which is clearly incomplete but since the fear, uncertainty and chaos of that night ensured that everyone gave different times for their meetings, it at least provides a framework. Zhukov is not shown as attending the first meeting at 7.05 and Vatutin, who was deputy Chief of Staff and appears in Zhukov's account, is not mentioned at all. Nor is Mikoyan. That does not mean they were not there: in the manic comings and goings, even Poskrebyshev could be forgiven a few mistakes.

'Well what now?' the pacing Stalin asked them. There was silence. The Politburo sat like dummies. Timoshenko raised his voice: 'All troops in frontier districts' must be placed on 'full battle alert!'

'Didn't they send the deserter on purpose to provoke us?' said Stalin but then he ordered Zhukov: 'Read this out.' When Zhukov reached his order of High Alert, Stalin interrupted, 'It would be premature to issue that order now. It might still be possible to settle the situation by peaceful means.' They had to avoid any provocations. Zhukov obeyed his instructions exactly – he knew the alternative: 'Beria's dungeon!'

The magnates now spoke up diffidently, agreeing with the generals that the troops had to be put on alert 'just in case'. Stalin nodded at the generals who hurried next door to Poskrebyshev's office to redraft the order. When they returned, the obsessive editor watered it down even more. The generals rushed back to the Defence Commissariat to transmit the order to the military districts: 'A surprise attack by the Germans is possible during 22–23 June ... The task of our forces is to refrain from any kind of provocative action ...' This was only completed just after midnight on Sunday 22 June.

Stalin told Budyonny that the war would probably start tomorrow. Budyonny left at ten, while Timoshenko, Zhukov and Mekhlis left later. Stalin kept pacing. Beria left, presumably to check the latest intelligence reports, and reported back at ten-forty. At eleven, the leaders moved upstairs to Stalin's apartment where they sat in the dining room. 'Stalin kept reassuring us that Hitler would not begin the war,' claimed Mikoyan.

'I think Hitler's trying to provoke us,' said Stalin, according to Mikoyan. 'He surely hasn't decided to make war?'

Zhukov phoned again at twelve-thirty: a third deserter, a Communist labourer from Berlin named Alfred Liskov, had swum the Pruth to report that the order to invade had been read to his unit. Stalin checked that the High Alert order was being transmitted, then commanded that Liskov should be shot 'for his disinformation'. Even on such a night, it was impossible to break the Stalinist routine of brutality – and entertainment: the Politburo headed out through the Borovitsky Gate to Kuntsevo in a convoy of limousines, speeding through the empty streets with their NKGB escorts. The generals, watched by Mekhlis, remained tensely in the Defence Commissariat. But elsewhere in the city, the weary commissars, guards and typists who waited every night (even Saturdays) until Stalin left the Kremlin, could stagger home to sleep. By Stalin's standards, it was early.

Molotov drove to the Foreign Commissariat to send a final telegram to Dekanozov in Berlin, who was already trying to get through to Ribbentrop, to put the questions Schulenburg had failed to answer. Molotov then joined the others at Kuntsevo: 'we might even have watched a film,' he said. At around 2 a.m., after an hour or so of dining, drinking and talking (the memories of Zhukov, Molotov and Mikoyan are confused about that night), they headed back to their Kremlin apartments.*

Far away, all along the Soviet border, *Luftwaffe* bombers were heading for their targets. On the same day that Napoleon's Grand Army had invaded Russia 129 years earlier, Hitler's over three million soldiers – Germans, Croats, Finns, Romanians, Hungarians, Italians and even Spaniards backed by 3,600 tanks, 600,000 motorized vehicles, 7,000 artillery pieces, 2,500 aircraft and about 625,000 horses, were crossing the border to engage the Soviet forces of almost equal strength, as many as 14,000 tanks (2,000 of them modern), 34,000 guns and over 8,000 planes. The greatest war of all time was about to begin in the duel between those two brutal and reckless egomaniacs. And both were probably still asleep.

---

* At roughly the same time, Hitler decided to snatch an hour's sleep before the invasion started: 'The fortune of war must now decide.' Earlier, an overtired and anxious Hitler had been pacing up and down the office with Goebbels working out the proclamation to be read to the German people the next day. 'This cancerous growth has to be burned out,' Hitler told Goebbels, 'Stalin will fall.' Liskov, the German defector, was still being interrogated two and a half hours later when the invasion began: he was not shot. The events of that night were so dramatic that the participants all recall different times: Molotov thought he had left Stalin at midnight, Mikoyan at 3 a.m. Molotov claimed Zhukov, who is used as a source by most historians, placed events later to amplify his own role. At least some of the confusion is due to the hour difference between German and Russian times: this account is based on Russian time. But it is easier to pace events according to the Teutonic efficiency of the German invasion that started at 3.30 a.m. German summertime (4.30 a.m. Russian time) and the arrival of Schulenberg's instructions from Berlin. It is clear from the three memoirs that the group moved from Stalin's office, to the apartment and then to Kuntsevo in the course of the hours between 9 p.m. and 3 a.m.

Part Seven

War: The Bungling Genius,
1941–1942

33

Optimism and Breakdown

Stalin had retired when Zhukov called Kuntsevo.

'Who's calling?' the sleepy voice of the NKGB general answered.

'Zhukov. Chief of Staff. Please connect me to Comrade Stalin. It's urgent.'

'What, right now? Comrade Stalin's sleeping.'

'Wake him immediately,' Zhukov told the duty officer. 'The Germans are bombing our cities.'

There was a silence. Zhukov waited for what seemed like an eternity. He was not the only one trying to report the invasion to Stalin, but the generals remained as petrified of their own leader as they were of the Germans. At 4.17 a.m. (Russian time) the Black Sea command called Zhukov at the Defence Commissariat to report a swarm of bombers. At 4.30 a.m. the Western Front was on the line, at 4.40, the Baltic was under attack. Around the same time, Admiral Kuznetsov was telephoned by his Sebastopol commander: the German bombing had started. Kuznetsov immediately phoned the Kremlin where he encountered the bureaucratic narrow-mindedness that is so characteristic of tyrannies. It was meant to be a secret that Stalin lived at Kuntsevo, so the officer replied:

'Comrade Stalin is not here and I don't know where he is.'

'I have an exceedingly important message which I must immediately relay to Comrade Stalin personally ...'

'I can't help you in any way,' he replied and hung up, so Kuznetsov called Timoshenko who, deluged with such calls, was afraid to inform Stalin. Kuznetsov tried all the numbers he had for Stalin but to no avail, so he called the Kremlin again:

'I request you to inform Comrade Stalin that German planes are bombing Sebastopol. This is war!'

'I shall report it to the proper person.' A few minutes later the Admiral discovered who 'the proper person' was: flabby, quiet-spoken Malenkov called, asking in 'a dissatisfied, irritated voice':

'Do you understand what you're reporting?' Even as German bombers strafed Kiev and Sebastopol and as their troops crossed the borders, Stalin's courtiers were still trying to bully away reality. Malenkov rang off and called Sebastopol to check the story.

Timoshenko was not alone in his office: Mekhlis, 'the Shark', spent the night with the generals. Like Malenkov, he was determined that there would be no invasion that night. When the head of anti-aircraft artillery, Voronov, hurried in to report, Timoshenko was so nervous that he handed him a notebook and absurdly 'told me to present my report in writing' so that if they were all arrested for treason, he would be responsible for his crimes. Mekhlis sidled up behind him and read over his shoulder to check that he was writing exactly what he had said. Then Mekhlis made him sign it. Timoshenko ordered anti-aircraft forces not to respond: Voronov realized 'he did not believe the war had begun'.

Timoshenko was called by the Deputy Commander of the Western Special Military District, Boldin, who frantically reported that the Germans were advancing. Timoshenko ordered him not to react.

'What do you mean?' shouted Boldin. 'Our troops are retreating, towns are in flames, people are dying ...'

'Joseph Vissarionovich believes this could be a provocation by some German generals.' Timoshenko's instinct was to persuade someone else to break the news to Stalin. He asked Budyonny: 'The Germans are bombing Sebastopol. Should I or shouldn't I tell Stalin?'

'Inform him immediately!'

'You call him,' beseeched Timoshenko. 'I'm afraid.'

'No, you call him,' retorted Budyonny. 'You're Defence Commissar!' Finally, Budyonny agreed and started calling Kuntsevo. Timoshenko, who could not spread this task widely enough, ordered Zhukov to telephone Stalin too.

Zhukov was still waiting on the line to Kuntsevo as Stalin was roused. Three minutes later, he came to the phone. Zhukov reported and asked permission to counter-attack. There was silence. He could just hear Stalin breathing.

'Did you understand me?' asked Zhukov. 'Comrade Stalin?' He could still only hear heavy breathing. Then Stalin spoke: 'Bring Timoshenko to the Kremlin. Tell Poskrebyshev to summon the Politburo.' Mikoyan and the Politburo were already being rung:

'It's war!' Now Budyonny reached Stalin at the dacha and added that Riga was being bombed as well. Stalin called Poskrebyshev, who was sleeping in his study: 'The bombing's started.'*

Stalin sped into town: he had banned the Politburo from staying in their dachas so they were already there. Stalin rode up in the lift to the second floor, hurried along the red-carpeted corridors with their wooden panelling and snapped at Poskrebyshev as he walked into his office: 'Get the others here now.' Zhukov claimed the Politburo assembled at 4.30 a.m. but Molotov thought it was earlier. However, Stalin's office logbook shows the meeting started at 5.45 a.m., just over an hour after the full German attack. Molotov, who lived in the same building, not far from Stalin's flat, arrived first, swiftly joined by Beria, Timoshenko, Zhukov and Mekhlis.

Stalin did not collapse: Mikoyan thought he was 'subdued'. Zhukov noticed he was 'pale' and 'bewildered' sitting at the green baize table, 'a pipe in his hand'. Voronov thought him 'depressed and nervy', but he was in command of his office at least. Outside the fronts were in anarchy. But here, Chadaev, the Sovnarkom assistant, remembered that Stalin 'spoke slowly, choosing his words carefully, occasionally his voice broke down. When he had finished, everybody was silent for some time and so was he.' But amazingly, he still persisted in the idea that the war might be 'a provocation by the German officers', convinced that Hitler might have a Tukhachevsky among the high command of the *Wehrmacht*. 'Hitler simply does not know about it.' Stalin would not order resistance until he had heard from Berlin.

'That scoundrel Ribbentrop tricked us,' he said to Mikoyan several times, still not blaming Hitler. It was now almost five: Stalin ordered Molotov: 'We have to call the German Embassy immediately.' Molotov called from Stalin's desk, laden with telephones, and stammered, 'Tell him to come.' Schulenburg had already contacted Molotov's office, asking to see the Foreign Commissar. 'I started from Stalin's office upstairs to my own office' which took about three minutes. Schulenburg, accompanied by Hilger, arrived in the office overlooking Ivan the Terrible's church for the second time that night – and the last time in his career. The

---

* The telephone was ringing in Zhdanov's dacha in Sochi that morning too: 'My mother came into my room first thing,' recalled Yury Zhdanov, 'and she said, "It's war!" and we headed back to Moscow with my father.'

summery Kremlin was bathed in the first light and fragrant with the acacias and roses of the Alexandrovsky Gardens.*

Schulenburg read out the telegram that had arrived at 3 a.m. Berlin time: the concentrations of Soviet forces had forced the Reich to take military 'counter measures'. He finished. Molotov's face twitched with disbelief and anger. Finally, he stammered:

'Is this supposed to be a declaration of war?' Schulenburg could not speak either: he shrugged sadly. Molotov's anger overcame his shock: 'The message I have just been given couldn't mean anything but a declaration of war since German troops have already crossed the border and Soviet cities like Odessa, Kiev and Minsk have been bombed by German aircraft for an hour and a half.' Molotov was shouting now. This was 'a breach of confidence unprecedented in history'. Now Germany had unleashed a terrible war. 'Surely we haven't deserved that.' There was nothing more to say: Count von der Schulenburg, who would be executed by Hitler for his part in the July 1944 plot, shook hands and departed, passing limousines rolling into the Kremlin bearing generals. Molotov rushed to Stalin's office where he announced: 'Germany's declared war on us.'

Stalin subsided into his chair, 'lost in thought'. The silence was 'long and pregnant'. Stalin 'looked tired, worn out', recalled Chadaev. 'His pock-marked face was drawn and haggard.' This, recalled Zhukov, 'was the only time I saw Stalin depressed'. Then he roused himself with a wildly optimistic slogan: 'The enemy will be beaten all along the line' – and he turned to the generals: 'What do you recommend?'

Zhukov suggested that the frontier districts must 'hold up' the Germans –

'Annihilate,' interrupted Timoshenko, 'not "hold up".'

'Issue a directive,' said Stalin, still under the spell of his grand delusion. 'Do not cross the border.' Timoshenko, not Stalin,

---

* Simultaneously, in Berlin, Soviet Ambassador Dekanozov was summoned to the Foreign Ministry. As he arrived, he noticed that the German press was present to record the moment. Adopting his most 'freezing manner', Ribbentrop received him in the office of Prince Bismarck, the statesman who had warned Germany against a war on two fronts and who had been quoted to this effect so often by Stalin and Zhdanov. Apparently drunk, 'purple-faced' and 'swaying a little', Ribbentrop read his statement. 'I deeply regret this ...' replied Dekanozov. He departed without shaking hands. But as he was leaving, Ribbentrop trotted after him, whispering that he had tried to stop Hitler from launching this war but he would not listen to anyone. 'Tell Moscow I was against the attack,' he hissed. Ribbentrop sensed the Soviet Pact had been the climax of his career.

signed the series of directives that were issued throughout the morning. Chadaev noticed the mood improve: 'on that first day of war, everyone was ... quite optimistic.'

Yet despite everything, Stalin persisted in clinging on to shards of his shattered illusion: he said he hoped to settle things diplomatically. No one dared contradict this absurdity except Molotov, his comrade since 1912 who was one of the last who could openly argue with him.

'No!' replied Molotov emphatically. It was war and 'nothing could be done about it'. The scale of the invasion and Molotov's stark insistence managed to shake the reality into Stalin. When Dmitrov, the Comintern leader, arrived, the outer office was a hive of activity with Poskrebyshev, Mekhlis (in uniform again), Marshal Timoshenko, Admiral Kuznetsov at work – and Beria 'giving orders on the phone'. Inside, he noticed Stalin's 'striking calmness, resoluteness, confidence ...'

'They fell on us, without making any claims, making a vile attack like bandits,' he told Dmitrov. The 'bandits' had the advantage of total surprise. The Soviet front line had been overwhelmed. Stalin's armies were strongest in the south. However, while the Germans thrust towards Leningrad and the Ukraine, Hitler's strongest army group was meant to take Moscow. Army Group Centre's two pincers shattered the Soviet Western Front, under Colonel-General Pavlov whose counter-attack was tossed aside as the Panzers charged towards Minsk and the road to Moscow.

Stalin reacted with a steady stream of orders that admittedly bore little relation to the disaster at the front: none the less, Beria, Malenkov, Mikoyan, Kaganovich and Voroshilov came, went and returned to the Little Corner throughout the morning so that by midday, all of them had been there at least twice, Beria thrice. Mekhlis was one of the first to arrive, Kulik came later. The *Vozhd* ordered Kaganovich to prepare the trains to remove factories and 20 million people from the front – nothing was to fall into German hands. Mikoyan was to supply the armies.

Stalin retained minute control over everything, from the size and shape of bayonets to the *Pravda* headlines and who wrote the articles, losing neither his jealousy of others' glory nor his flawless instinct for self-preservation. When General Koniev received several mentions in the newspapers during the first week, Stalin found the time to telephone the editor and snap: 'You've printed enough on Koniev.' When the same editor asked if he would publish one writer whom Stalin had savagely denounced before the war, he replied: 'You may print. Comrade Adveenko has atoned.' Meanwhile he himself deliberately disappeared from the public eye. His appearances on the front page of *Pravda* fell dramatically. Amazingly, the USSR possessed no Supreme Command: at nine that morning, Stalin created an early version, the *Stavka*. Naturally, the decree named Stalin as Commander-in-Chief but he crossed it out and put Timoshenko's name instead.

Everyone agreed that the Government had to announce the war. Mikoyan and the others proposed Stalin should do it but he refused: 'Let Molotov speak.' After all, Molotov had signed the treaty with Ribbentrop. The entourage disagreed – surely the people would not understand why they were not hearing from the Premier. Stalin insisted that he would speak another time. 'He didn't want to be first to speak,' said Molotov. 'He needed a clear picture ... He couldn't respond like an automaton to everything ... He was a human being after all.'

Molotov, who still regarded himself as a political journalist, immediately set to work on the announcement but Stalin dominated the drafting for he possessed the gift of distilling complex ideas into the simple and stirring phrases that henceforth characterized his war speeches. At midday, Molotov drove to the Central Telegraph Office on Gorky Street, just up from the Kremlin. He mastered his stammer and delivered the famous speech in his flat but quavering voice:

'Our cause is just. The enemy will be crushed. Victory will be ours.'

When Molotov returned, Stalin walked up to his office to congratulate him: 'Well, you sounded a bit flustered but the speech went well.' Molotov needed praise: he was much vainer than he looked. Just then the *vertushka* rang: it was Timoshenko reporting on the chaos of the frontier where the commanders, especially Pavlov on the vital Western Front that covered Minsk and the road to Moscow, had lost contact with their troops. Stalin fulminated about how 'unexpected attack is very important in war. It gives the initiative to the attackers ... You must strictly prevent ... any panic. Call the commanders, clear the situation and report ... How long will you need? Two hours, well not more ... How is the situation with Pavlov?' But Pavlov, bearing the brunt of the German attack, 'has no connection with the staff of his armies ...'

Attended by Molotov, Malenkov and Beria, the threesome who were to spend most of the war in the Little Corner, Stalin gradually learned of the startling German successes and the Soviet collapse. During that first week, Beria, master of the Special Department, the *Osobyi Otdel*, the secret police in every military unit responsible for hunting down traitors, met Stalin fifteen times while Mekhlis, political boss of the army, virtually resided in the Little Corner: terror was Stalin's solution to defeat. But these two, along with Civil War cronies like Voroshilov and Kulik, were little comfort when Timoshenko reported that almost a thousand planes had been eliminated on the ground by the end of the day.

'Surely the German air force didn't manage to reach every single airfield?' Stalin asked pathetically.

'Unfortunately it did.' But it was the disaster of Pavlov's Western Front that reduced Stalin to wild, if impotent, fury:

'This is a monstrous crime. Those responsible must lose their heads.' Stalin abruptly ordered his most trusted cronies to travel to the fronts and find out what was happening. When they hesistated, Stalin shouted:

'Immediately.' Chief of Staff Zhukov headed for the South-Western Front but asked who would run things in his absence.

'Don't waste time,' scoffed Stalin. 'We'll manage somehow.' Malenkov and Budyonny, a strange coupling, the bloodless bureaucrat and the swashbuckling Cossack, flew to Briansk; Kulik to the Western Front.

The whirlwind almost consumed them: in a series of semi-farcical fiascos, all were lucky to escape with their lives. Meanwhile, in the Little Corner, Stalin's hours were as inconsistent as the performance of his armies. Stalin and Beria were the last two to leave at 4.45 that afternoon, having been up since dawn. They still believed their counter-offensives would throw the battle on to enemy territory. They must have grabbed some sleep but Stalin was back in the office at 3.20 on the morning of 23 June to meet Molotov, Mekhlis and Beria until the early hours. By the 25th, faced with the free fall of the fronts, Stalin was spending the whole night, from 1.00 to 5.50 a.m., in the office in a state of rising outrage as one by one his special envoys disappeared into the cataclysm.

'That good-for-nothing Kulik needs a kick in the arse,' he said.

Only Zhukov, brutal, courageous and energetic, managed to

counter-attack on the South-Western Front, brandishing the
Stalinist ruthlessness that distinguished him throughout the war:
'Arrest immediately', reads one of his typical orders to the Special
Departments about retreating officers. 'And bring them to trial
urgently as traitors and cowards.'

The boozy buffoon Marshal Kulik, whose war was to be a
chronicle of tragicomical blunders, outfitted himself in a pilot's
fetching leathers, cap and goggles and arrived on the Western
Front like a Stalinist Biggles on the evening of 23 June. Bewildered
by the rout of the Tenth Army, he was cut off, surrounded and
almost captured. He had to escape in fancy dress. 'The behaviour
of Marshal Kulik was incomprehensible,' the regimental
Commissar denounced Kulik to Mekhlis. 'He ordered everyone to
take off their regalia, throw out documents and then change into
peasant garb,' a disguise he was more than capable of carrying off.
Burning his marshal's uniform (and his Biggles outfit), 'he
proposed to throw away our arms and he told me personally
to throw away my medals and documents ... Kulik rode on
a horse-drawn cart along the very road just taken by German
tanks ...' The Western Front itself was disintegrating. Ailing
Marshal Shaposhnikov collapsed from the strain. Headquarters
lost him too.

Like a game of hide-and-seek, in which more and more children
are sent to find the ones hiding, Stalin sent Voroshilov to find
Kulik and Shaposhnikov. On 26 June, the 'First Marshal' arrived
in Mogilev on a special train but was unable to find either the
Western Front or the two marshals. Eventually his adjutant came
upon a pitiful sight that looked more like a 'gypsy encampment'
than a headquarters and espied Shaposhnikov on the ground
covered by a coat, looking very dead. Then he saw Pavlov, the
commander, lying alone beneath a tree eating *kasha* out of a mess-
tin in the pouring rain which he did not seem to have noticed.
Shaposhnikov stirred. The adjutant realized he was alive and
introduced himself. Shaposhnikov, wincing with pain, thanked
God that Voroshilov had come and started to shave. Pavlov, who
had now finished his *kasha*, was dazed and desperate:

'I'm done for!' Voroshilov descended on the camp with an
explosion of threats, while sending his adjutant to hunt for Kulik.
Then the two marshals retired to the special train to decide what
to do about poor Pavlov. Voroshilov ordered dinner: a cook brought
in ham, bread and tea, a repast that evidently disappointed the

Marshal because he became furious, screaming for his cook, Comrade Franz, who emerged and stood to attention. Voroshilov demanded to know how he dared serve such a meal for two marshals.

'Why've you sliced the ham? Do people cut ham this way? In a goddamn inn, they serve better ham!' Voroshilov summoned Pavlov, berating him for his failures. In another of those moments that reveal the importance of personal vendetta, he reminded Pavlov that he had once complained to Stalin about him. Pavlov fell to his knees, begged for forgiveness and kissed the Marshal's boots. Voroshilov returned to Moscow.

At dawn on 4 July, Mekhlis arrested Pavlov for treason:

'We ask you to confirm arrest and prosecution,' Mekhlis reported. Stalin welcomed it 'as one of the true ways to improve the health of the Front'. Under torture, Pavlov implicated General Meretskov who was immediately arrested too. Before Pavlov's 'trial', Poskrebyshev brought Stalin the '[Draft] Sentence'. Seeing that it contained the traditional inventions, Stalin told Poskrebyshev: 'I approve the sentence but tell Ulrikh to get rid of all that rubbish about "conspiratorial activity". The case shouldn't drag out. No appeal. And then inform the fronts so that they know that defeatists will be punished without mercy.' Mikoyan (and presumably the rest of the Politburo) approved of the sentence and still did so thirty years later when he wrote his memoirs: 'It was a pity to lose him but it was justified.' On 22 July, the four commanding officers of the Western Front were shot. So many telegrams flooded in asking permission to shoot traitors, they blocked up the wires in Mekhlis's office. That day, he told them to sentence and shoot their own traitors.

Stalin was absorbing the scale of the catastrophe. The fronts were out of control: the Nazis were approaching Minsk, the air force decimated, thirty divisions shattered. On the 26th Stalin urgently recalled Zhukov from the South-Western Front: the Chief of Staff found Timoshenko and General Vatutin standing to attention before Stalin, their 'eyes red from lack of sleep'. Stalin ordered: 'Put your heads together and tell me what can be done.'* He gave them forty minutes to propose new lines of defence.

* * *

* Some time that day, the Politburo secretly ordered Lenin's body to be removed from the Mausoleum and despatched to Tyumen in Siberia.

Yet even in these frantic times, Stalin remembered his own family. On 25 June, Stalin was meeting with Timoshenko to discuss a 'situation that was extremely serious on all fronts' when the Defence Commissar plucked up the courage to ask if Yakov Djugashvili, the leader's oldest son by his first marriage who had always disappointed him and whom he had treated callously, should be sent to the front, as he requested. Stifling his anger, Stalin replied,

'Some, to put it mildly, inordinately zealous officials are always trying too hard to please their superiors. I don't include you in that number but I advise you never to ask me questions like that again.' Stalin said nothing else about it but later, he checked that the elder boys, Yakov and Artyom, both artillerymen, were to be sent to the front line. After Vasily threw a goodbye party, Yakov's wife, Julia, saw off her beloved Yasha in her red dress, which she later believed was cursed.

One night during the first ten days of the war, Stalin called Zhenya Alliluyeva whom he had cut ever since her remarriage. Visiting Kuntsevo, she had 'never seen Joseph so crushed'. He asked her to take Svetlana and the children to the dacha in Sochi and then gave her a stunningly honest précis of the war situation that shocked her since the propaganda was still claiming that the heroic Red Army was about to crush the Fascist invader: 'The war will be long. Lots of blood will be shed ... Please take Svetlana southwards.' It was a mark of Zhenya's force of personality, the very thing that made her so attractive and irritating, that she refused. She must accompany her husband. Stalin was 'upset and angry'. He never saw Zhenya again.

Instead Anna Redens shepherded Svetlana, Alexandra Nakashidze, Vasily's wife Galina, Yakov's daughter Gulia as well as her own sons to the dacha in Sochi where they remained until the front approached there.

* * *

On 28 June, the Germans, who had penetrated three hundred miles into Soviet territory, closed the net on the encirclement of 400,000 troops – and took the capital of Belorussia, Minsk. As scraps of this information reached the Little Corner during a long session from mid-afternoon until 2.40 a.m., Stalin was beside himself. After a few hours' sleep, he visited the Defence Commissariat to find out more, probably accompanied by Molotov, Malenkov and Budyonny. The fall of Minsk would open the road to Smolensk and Moscow, but such was the rout that Timoshenko again lost contact with the armies. This infuriated Stalin who arrived back at the Little Corner at 7.35 p.m. While Timoshenko and Zhukov came and went with worsening news, Beria and Mikoyan arrived to join their comrades in an emergency Politburo. After midnight, Stalin called Timoshenko for some concrete news from Belorussia: there was none. This was the final straw.* Stalin stormed out of the office. Poskrebyshev and Chadaev watched Stalin, Molotov and Beria getting into their Packard outside.

'The Germans have obviously taken Minsk,' said Poskrebyshev.

Minutes later, the 'Five' pulled up at the Defence Commissariat. Stalin led his men into Timoshenko's office and announced that he wanted to acquaint himself personally with the reports from the front. Zhukov was about to leave but Timoshenko gestured for him to stay. The 'Five' gathered around the operations map.

'What's happening at Minsk?' asked Stalin.

'I'm not yet able to report on that,' replied Timoshenko.

'It's your duty to have the facts clearly before you at all times and keep us up to date,' said Stalin. 'At present, you're simply afraid to tell us the truth.' At this, the fearless Zhukov interjected rudely:

'Comrade Stalin, have we permission to get on with our work?'

'Are we perhaps in your way?' sneered Beria, who must have been shocked to see Stalin addressed in such a way. The meeting now degenerated into a row between Zhukov and Beria, with a bristling Stalin standing in the middle.

'You know that the situation on all fronts is critical. The front commanders await instructions and it's better if we do it ourselves,' replied Zhukov.

'We too are capable of giving orders,' shouted Beria.

'If you think you can, do it!' retorted Zhukov.

'If the Party tells us to, we will.'

---

* Now that we have access to so many different sources on this remarkable episode, from Molotov and Mikoyan's memoirs to those of Chadaev, the Sovnarkom assistant, who recorded Deputy Chief of Staff Vatutin's account, we can reconstruct this heretofore obscure story. Mikoyan dates the scene at the Defence Commissariat 29 and Chadaev 27 June, an indication of the chaos of those days. In fact, it was the 28th since we know from his logbook that Stalin was in his office throughout the 28th but did not appear on the 29th or 30th. Zhukov says that Stalin visited the Commissariat twice that day but it is likely that the showdown was in the evening, as Mikoyan recalled it.

'So wait until it tells you to. As things are, we've been told to do the job.' Zhukov appealed to Stalin: 'Excuse my outspokenness, Comrade Stalin, we shall certainly get it worked out. Then we'll come to the Kremlin and report.' Zhukov was implying that the generals might be more competent than the Politburo. Stalin, who had been quiet up to this point, could no longer contain his fury:

'You're making a crass mistake trying to draw a line between yourselves and us ... We must all be thinking how to help the fronts.' Stalin, in Mikoyan's words, now 'erupted': 'What is General Headquarters? What sort of Chief of Staff is it who since the first day of the war has no connection with his troops, represents nobody, and commands nobody?'

The granite-faced Zhukov collapsed under this barrage and burst into tears, 'sobbing like a woman' and 'ran out into another room'. Molotov followed him. One of the harshest Bolsheviks comforted one of the most severe soldiers of that bloody century: did Molotov offer a handkerchief or put a hand on Zhukov's shoulder? Five minutes later, that incongruous duo returned. Zhukov was 'quiet but his eyes were moist'.

'We were all depressed,' admitted Mikoyan. Stalin suggested that Voroshilov or someone else be despatched to make contact with the Belorussian front. 'Stalin was very depressed.' Then he looked at his comrades.

'There we are then,' said Stalin. 'Let them get it sorted out themselves first. Let's go, comrades.' Stalin led the way out of the office. As they climbed into the cars outside, Stalin uttered his first words of truth since the war began: 'Everything's lost. I give up. Lenin founded our state and we've fucked it up.' Stalin cursed all the way to Kuntsevo. 'Lenin left us a great heritage and we his successors have shitted it all up ...' Even when they had arrived at the house, Molotov remembered him swearing, '"We fucked it up!" The "we" was meant to include all of us!' Stalin said he could no longer be the leader. He resigned. At Kuntsevo, Molotov 'tried to cheer him up'. They left the broken Stalin sulking at the dacha.*

* The versions used here are Molotov's: 'We've fucked it up'; Mikoyan's: 'Lenin left us a great heritage and we his successors have shitted it up'; Beria's (via Khrushchev who was himself not in Moscow): 'Everything is lost. I give up. Lenin left us a proletarian state and now we've been caught with our pants down and let the whole thing go to shit'; and Chadaev's: 'Lenin founded our state and we've fucked it up.'

Mikoyan was not impressed with this performance. On the way home, he discussed it with Molotov, whom he disliked but trusted: they knew Stalin as well as anyone. 'We were struck by this statement of Stalin's. What now, is everything irrevocably lost? We thought he said it for effect.' They were right that Stalin was partly performing but 'he was a human being too', in Molotov's words. The fall of Minsk jolted Stalin, who lost face in front of his comrades and generals. This was the gravest crisis of his career.

The next day they discovered it was not merely 'for effect'. At midday, when Stalin usually arrived at the Kremlin, he did not come. He did not appear later in the day. The vacuum of power was palpable: the titan who, in fourteen-hour marathons, decided every tiny detail left a gaping hole. When Stalin's phone rang, Poskrebyshev responded.

'Comrade Stalin's not here and I don't know when he will be.' When Mekhlis tried to ring Stalin at Kuntsevo, there was no reply. 'I don't understand it,' sighed Poskrebyshev. By the end of the day, Stalin's *chef de cabinet* was saying: 'Comrade Stalin is not here and is unlikely to be here.'

'Has he gone to the front?' asked young Chadaev.

'Why do you keep bothering me? I've told you he isn't here and won't be here.'

Stalin 'had shut himself away from everybody, was receiving nobody and was not answering the phone'. Molotov told Mikoyan and the others that 'Stalin had been in such a state of prostration for the last two days that he was not interested in anything, didn't show any initiative and was in a bad way.' Stalin could not sleep. He did not even bother to undress but simply wandered around the dacha. At one point, he opened the door of the guardhouse where Vlasik's deputy, Major-General Rumiantsev, leapt to attention, but Stalin did not say a word and just returned to his room. He later told Poskrebyshev, he had the taste of wormwood in his mouth. Yet Stalin had read his history: he knew that Ivan the Terrible, his 'teacher', had also withdrawn from power to test the loyalty of his *boyars*.

The Soviet *boyars* were alarmed but the experienced ones sensed danger. Molotov was careful not to sign any documents. As the Germans advanced, the Government was paralysed for two long days.

'You've no idea what it's like here,' Malenkov told Khrushchev.

On the evening of the 30th, Chadaev returned to the office to get Stalin's signature as Premier but there was still no sign of him: 'He wasn't here yesterday either.'

'No, he wasn't here yesterday either,' Poskrebyshev replied, without a trace of sarcasm. But something had to be done. The new boy, Voznesensky, appeared at Poskrebyshev's desk like all the others. When Chadaev asked him to sign the documents, he refused and called Stalin himself but 'No reply from the dacha.' So he called upstairs to Molotov who suggested meeting later but gave no clue that he was already closeted with Beria, Malenkov and Voroshilov, arranging what to do. Now the dynamic Beria devised a new super-war cabinet, an ultra-Politburo with a tiny membership and sweeping powers, chaired by Stalin, if he would accept it, and containing Molotov, Voroshilov, Malenkov and himself: three Old Bolsheviks and two ascendant meteors. The exclusion of many of the magnates was a triumph for Beria and Malenkov, who were not even full Politburo members.

Once this was fixed, Molotov called Mikoyan, who was talking to Voznesensky, and the Politburo gathered. The magnates had never been so powerful: these manoeuvres most resembled the intrigues just after Stalin's stroke twelve years later, for this was the only real opportunity they had to overthrow Stalin since the revelation of Lenin's damning Testament almost twenty years earlier. Molotov told them about Stalin's breakdown but Mikoyan replied that, even if the *Vozhd* was incapacitated, 'the very name Stalin was a great force for rousing the morale of the people.' But bumptious Voznesensky made what ultimately proved to be a fatal mistake:

'Vyacheslav!' he hailed Molotov. 'You go ahead and we'll follow you!' Molotov must have blanched at this deadly suggestion and turned to Beria* who proposed his State Defence Committee. They decided to go out to Kuntsevo.

When they arrived, they cautiously stepped into the gloomy, dark-green house, shrouded in pinewoods, and were shown into the little dining room. There, sitting nervously in an armchair, was a 'thinner ... haggard ... gloomy' Stalin. When he saw the

---

* Beria's son Sergo, whose memoirs are reliable on personal anecdotes and unreliable on political matters, claims it was Alexander Shcherbakov, the Moscow Party leader, who made this mistake and used to ask Beria if he would ever betray him to Stalin. Mikoyan, who was actually there, is much more trustworthy but Shcherbakov may have lost his nerve on another occasion, the threat to Moscow in October.

seven or so Politburo members entering, Stalin 'turned to stone'. In one account, Stalin greeted them with more depressed ramblings: 'great Lenin's no more ... If only he could see us now. See those to whom he entrusted the fate of his country ... I am inundated with letters from Soviet people, rightly rebuking us ... Maybe some among you wouldn't mind putting the blame on me.' Then, he looked at them searchingly and asked: 'Why've you come?'

Stalin 'looked alert, somewhat strange', recalled Mikoyan, 'and his question was no less strange. Actually he should have summoned us himself. I had no doubt: he decided we had arrived to arrest him.' Beria watched Stalin's face carefully. 'It was obvious,' he later told his wife, 'Stalin expected anything could happen, even the worst.'

The magnates were frightened too: Beria later teased Mikoyan for hiding behind the others. Molotov, who was the most senior and therefore the most exposed to Stalin's vengeance, stepped forward:

'Thank you for your frankness,' said Molotov, according to a possibly secondary source, 'but I tell you here and now that if some idiot tried to turn me against you, I'd see him damned. We're asking you to come back to work ...'

'Yes but think about it,' answered Stalin. 'Can I live up to people's hopes any more? Can I lead the country to final victory? There may be more deserving candidates.'

'I believe I shall be voicing the unanimous opinion,' interjected Voroshilov. 'There's none more worthy.'

'*Pravilno!* Right!' repeated the magnates. Molotov told Stalin that Malenkov and Beria proposed to form a State Defence Committee.

'With whom at its head?' Stalin asked.

'You, Comrade Stalin.' Stalin's relief was palpable: 'the tension left his face' – but he did not say anything for a while, then:

'Well ...' Beria stepped forward and said:

'You Comrade Stalin will be the head' and he listed the members.

Stalin noticed Mikoyan and Voznesensky had been excluded but Beria suggested they should run the Government. The pragmatic Mikoyan, knowing that his responsibilities for army supply were relevant, asked to be a special representative. Stalin assigned industries – Malenkov took over aeroplanes; Molotov, tanks; Voznesensky, armaments. Stalin was back in power.

So had Stalin really suffered a nervous breakdown or was this simply a performance? Nothing was ever straightforward with this adept political actor. The breakdown was real enough: he was depressed and exhausted. It was not out of character: he had suffered similar moments on Nadya's death and during the Finnish war. His collapse was an understandable reaction to his failure to read Hitler, a mistake which could not be hidden from his courtiers who had repeatedly heard him insist there would be no invasion in 1941. But that was only the first part of this disaster: the military collapse had revealed the damage that Stalin had done and his ineptitude as commander. The Emperor had no clothes. Only a dictator who had killed any possible challengers could have survived it. In any other system, this would have brought about a change of government but no such change was available here.

Yet Molotov and Mikoyan were right: it was also 'for effect'. The withdrawal from power was a well-tried pose, successfully employed from Achilles and Alexander the Great to Ivan. Stalin's retreat allowed him to be effectively re-elected by the Politburo, with the added benefit of drawing a line under the bungles up to that point. These had been forgiven: 'Stalin enjoyed our support again,' Mikoyan wrote pointedly. So it was both a breakdown and a political restoration.

'We were witnesses to Stalin's moments of weakness,' said Beria afterwards. 'Joseph Vissarionovich will never forgive that move of ours.' Mikoyan had been right to hide.

* * *

Next afternoon, Stalin reappeared in the office, 'a new man' committed to play the role of warlord for which he believed himself specially qualified. On 1 July, the newspapers announced that Stalin was the Chairman of the State Defence Committee, the GKO. Soon afterwards he sent Timoshenko to command the Western Front defending Moscow: on 19 July, Stalin became Commissar of Defence and, on 8 August, Supreme Commander-in-Chief: henceforth, the generals called him *Verkhovnyi*, Supremo. On 16 July, he restored the dual command of political commissars that the army so hated, abolished after Finland: the commissars, led by Mekhlis, were to conduct 'ceaseless struggles against cowards, panic-mongers and deserters' but these overweening amateurs often took actual command, like their master. 'The Defence Commissariat,' said Khrushchev, 'was like a kennel of mad dogs with Kulik and Mekhlis.'* Meanwhile Stalin reunited the security forces, the NKVD and NKGB, under Beria. On 3 July, Stalin spoke to the people in a new voice, as a Russian national leader:

'Comrades, citizens,' he began conventionally, his voice low, his breathing audible across the radio waves of the Imperium, along with his sips of water and the clink of his glass. 'Brothers and sisters! Warriors of the army and the fleet! I call upon you, my friends.' This was a patriotic war but patriotism stiffened by terror: 'Cowards, deserters, panic-mongers' would be crushed in a 'merciless struggle'. A couple of nights later, Stalin and Kalinin walked out of the Kremlin at 2 a.m. under heavy guard, commanded by Vlasik, and entered Lenin's Mausoleum to bid goodbye to the mummy of their late leader before it set off by secret sealed train to Siberia.

Stalin's new resolve hardly improved the plight of the fronts. Within three weeks of war, Russia had lost around 2,000,000 men, 3,500 tanks, and over 6,000 aircraft. On 10 July, the Germans Panzers renewed their advance on the gateway to Moscow, Smolensk, which fell six days later. The Germans broke through to take another 300,000 Red Army prisoners and capture 3,000 guns and 3,000 tanks – but Timoshenko's hard fighting temporarily sapped their momentum. Hitler ordered Army Group Centre to regroup at the end of July. As he pressed his advance, in the south towards Kiev, and in the north towards Leningrad, Hitler had won astounding victories yet none of Barbarossa's objectives – Moscow, Leningrad and the Donets Basin – had fallen. The Soviet army had not been obliterated. While German generals begged him to throw their Panzers against Moscow, Hitler, perhaps recalling Napoleon's empty conquest, wanted to seize the oil and grain of the south. Instead he compromised with a new strategy, 'Moscow and Ukraine'.

The new Stalin even took some lip from the Politburo. Just after the fall of Smolensk, Stalin summoned Zhukov and Timoshenko to the dacha, where they found him wearing an old tunic, pacing, pipe unlit, always a sign of trouble, accompanied by some of the

---

* The see-saw between traditional 'single command' by a general, and 'dual command' by generals and Party Commissars, charted the progress of the Party: the Commissars were introduced three times – in 1918, 1937 and 1941 – and abolished three times when the prestige of the soldiers needed to be raised – in 1925, 1940 and 1942.

Politburo. 'The Politburo has discussed dismissing Timoshenko ... What do you think of that?' Timoshenko said nothing but Zhukov objected.

'I rather think he's right,' said old Kalinin who had barely disagreed with Stalin since 1930. Stalin 'unhurriedly lit the pipe and eyed the Politburo'.

'What if we agree with Comrade Zhukov?' he asked.

'You're right, Comrade Stalin,' they replied in one voice. But Zhukov did not always get his way.

Faced with the threat of more giant encirclements in the south, Stalin devised draconian measures to terrorize his men into fighting. In the first week, he approved NKGB Order No. 246 that stipulated the destruction of the families of men who were captured, and now he made this public in his notorious Order No. 270. He ordered it to be signed by Molotov, Budyonny, Voroshilov and Zhukov, even though some of them were not present, but it was, after all, a traditional method of Bolshevik rule. These measures ruined the lives of millions of innocent soldiers and their families, including Stalin's own.*

* * *

On 16 July, in one of the encirclements, this one at Vitebsk, an artillery lieutenant of 14th Howitzer Regiment of the 14th Armoured Division, found himself overrun by German forces. Feeling himself special, he did not withdraw: 'I am Stalin's son and I won't allow my battery to retreat,' but nor did he honourably commit suicide. On 19 July, Berlin announced that, amongst the teeming mass of Soviet prisoners, was Yakov Djugashvili. Zhdanov sent Stalin a sealed package that contained a photograph of Yakov that his father examined closely, tormented by the thought of his weak son breaking and betraying him. For the second time in Yakov's life, Stalin cursed that his own son could not kill himself:

'The fool – he couldn't even shoot himself!' he muttered to Vasily. Stalin was immediately suspicious of Yakov's wife Julia. 'Don't say anything to Yasha's wife for the time being,' Stalin told

---

* Order No. 270 is written very much in Stalin's personal style: 'I order that (1) anyone who removes his insignia ... and surrenders should be regarded as a malicious deserter whose family is to be arrested as a family of a breaker of the oath and betrayer of the Motherland. Such deserters are to be shot on the spot. (2) Those falling into encirclement are to fight to the last ... those who prefer to surrender are to be destroyed by any available means while their families are to be deprived of all assistance.'

Svetlana. Soon afterwards, under Order No. 270, Julia was arrested. Her three-year-old daughter Gulia did not see her mother for two years. Yet we now know how Stalin fretted about Yakov's fate and how he mulled over it for the rest of his life.

He quickly banned Vasily from flying on active missions: 'One prisoner's more than enough for me!' But he was irritated when the 'Crown Prince' phoned to ask for more pocket money for a new uniform and more food:

'1. As far as I know [wrote Stalin] the rations in the air force are quite sufficient. 2. A special uniform for Stalin's son is not on the agenda.'

Around the time of Yakov's capture, Stalin made his first approach to Hitler. He and Molotov ordered Beria to sound out the Bulgarian Ambassador, Ivan Stamenov. Beria gave the job to the assassination/ intelligence specialist Sudoplatov, who told the story in his semi-reliable memoirs: his instructions were to ask why Germany had violated the Pact, on what conditions Hitler would end the war, and whether he would be satisfied with the Ukraine, Belorussia, Moldova and the Baltics, a second Brest-Litovsk? Beria told Sudoplatov this was to win time. Sudoplatov met Stamenov at Beria's favourite Georgian restaurant, Aragvi, on 25 July but the Bulgarian never passed on the message to Berlin, saying:

'Even if you retreat to the Urals, you'll still win in the end.'

* * *

Meanwhile the German advance in the south was inexorable: the Panzer pincers of Army Group South, under Guderian and Kleist, swung round Kiev to encircle General Kirponos's South-Western Front with hundreds of thousands more men. It was obvious that Kiev would have to be abandoned but on 29 July, Stalin summoned Zhukov to discuss all fronts. Poskrebyshev ominously said the meeting would not begin until Mekhlis had arrived. When 'the gloomy demon' appeared with Beria and Malenkov, the Chief of Staff predicted, under the Medusan glare of this grim trio, that the Germans would crush the South-Western Front before turning back to Moscow. Mekhlis interrupted to ask, threateningly, how Zhukov knew so much about the German plans.

'What about Kiev?' asked Stalin. Zhukov proposed abandoning it.

'Why talk nonsense?' bawled Stalin.

'If you think the Chief of Staff talks nonsense, then I request you relieve me of my post and send me to the front,' Zhukov shouted back.

'Who gave you the right to speak to Comrade Stalin like that?' snarled Mekhlis.

'Don't get heated,' said Stalin to Zhukov, but 'since you mentioned it, we'll get by without you.' Zhukov gathered his maps and left the room, only to be summoned back forty minutes later to be told that he was relieved as Chief of Staff, a blessing in disguise, which allowed this fighting general to return to his natural habitat. Stalin soothed him: 'Calm down, calm down.' Shaposhnikov was recalled as Chief of Staff. Stalin knew he was ailing but 'we'll help him'. Zhukov asked to leave but Stalin invited him for tea: Stalin was drawn to Zhukov. The unfolding disaster around Kiev soon proved the wisdom of his 'nonsense'.

The Panzer claws were closing around the South-Western Axis, commanded by Marshal Budyonny and Khrushchev who begged to be allowed to withdraw. Stalin was informed by the NKVD that Khrushchev was going to surrender Kiev and rang to threaten him: 'You should be ashamed of yourself! ... What's the matter with you? [You have] given up half of Ukraine. You're ready to give up the other half too ... Do whatever it takes. If not ... we'll make short work of you!' In the alternation of roaring panic and becalmed anxiety that are the moods of a rout, Khrushchev found Budyonny drinking brandy with the front's Operations chief, Bagramian, and affectionately telling him he should be shot.

On 11 September, with time running out, Budyonny, who was both braver and more competent than most of the 'cavalrymen', knew he might be dismissed or even arrested but he now insisted to Stalin that 'delay [will] lead to losses in men and a huge quantity of equipment'. Stalin dismissed him next day. Appointing Timoshenko to the front, Stalin gave him a quaint gift of two pipes marked with a deer to symbolize his transfer from north to south, a rare gesture.

'You take command,' Budyonny told Timoshenko at the front. 'But let's call Stalin together and tell him to retreat from Kiev. We're real Marshals and they'll believe us.'

'I don't want to put my head in the noose,' replied Timoshenko. Two days later, Kleist and Guderian's Panzer Groups One and Two linked up at 18.20 hours a hundred miles east of Kiev, sealing five entire Soviet armies in a giant encirclement, the rotten fruit of

Stalin's obstinacy: 452,720 men were captured. By the 18th, Kiev had fallen. Stalin's nerves held: 'Plug the hole,' he ordered Shaposhnikov. 'Quickly!'

Stalin and Beria stepped up both the repression and the redemption. More 'lucky stiffs' were released to help the war effort. 'There aren't any people on whom one can rely,' Stalin murmured during one meeting on air defence at which the aircraft designer Yakovlev spoke up:

'Comrade Stalin, it's already more than a month since Balandin, our Deputy People's Commissar, was arrested. We don't know what he was arrested for but we can't conceive he was an Enemy. He is needed ... We ask you to examine his case.'

'Yes,' replied Stalin, 'he's already been in prison for forty days but he's confessed nothing. Perhaps he's not guilty of anything.' The next day, Balandin, 'with hollow cheeks and shaven head' appeared for work 'as though nothing had happened'. Beria and Mikoyan requested the freeing of Vannikov, arrested for arguing about artillery with Kulik. He was brought straight from his cell to Stalin who apologized, admitting that Vannikov had been right, and then promoted him to high office.

There was a certain awkwardness when the 'lucky stiffs' met their torturers. Broad-faced, fair-haired General Meretskov, arrested during the first weeks of the war, had been horribly tortured by the debonair Merkulov, 'the Theoretician', with whom he had been friends before his arrest. As one of his interrogators later testified: 'Brutal continuous torture was applied to Meretskov by high-ranking officials ... he was beaten with rubber rods' until he was covered in blood. Now he was cleaned up and brought to Merkulov but Meretskov told his torturer that they could no longer be friends, a conversation unique to this strange time:

'Vsevolod Nikolaievich, we used to meet on informal terms but I'm afraid of you now.' Merkulov smiled. Minutes later, in full uniform, General Meretskov reported for his next assignment to Stalin:

'Hello, Comrade Meretskov? How are you feeling?'

Beria also redoubled the Terror. As the NKVD retreated, the prisoners were not all released – even though Stalin had every opportunity to do so. Those 'German spies' who had been so close to Stalin, Maria and Alyosha Svanidze, had been in prison since December 1937. Stalin remembered Alyosha who, as he himself told Mikoyan, 'was sentenced to death. I ordered Merkulov to tell him before execution that if he asks the Central Committee for forgiveness, he will be pardoned.' But Svanidze proudly replied that he was innocent so 'I can't ask for pardon.' He spat in Merkulov's face:

'That's my answer to him,' he cried. On 20 August 1941, he was shot. A few days later, at Kuntsevo, Stalin turned to Mikoyan:

'Want to hear about Alyosha?'

'What?' Mikoyan, who had adored Svanidze, hoped he would be released. But Stalin matter-of-factly announced his death.

'He wouldn't apologize. Such noble pride!' mused Stalin.

'When was this?' asked Mikoyan.

'He was shot just recently.' Maria Svanidze, who had so worshipped Stalin, was, with Aloysha's sister, Mariko, shot the following year.

34

'Ferocious as a Dog': Zhdanov and the
Siege of Leningrad

While Molotov sat beside Stalin in the Little Corner, Zhdanov ruled beleaguered Leningrad like a mini-Stalin. But Stalin now turned his fury on to the commanders of the city of Lenin.* By 21 August 1941, a German north-easterly thrust almost cut off Leningrad's link with the rest of Russia. Voroshilov, now sixty, took command alongside Zhdanov. Both men had much to prove but as Leningrad was gradually enveloped, they struggled to keep Stalin's confidence.

Day by day, the Germans tightened their grip and Stalin smelt defeatism. In a stream of dictated anxiety, he accused them of failing to grasp 'this fatal danger. Stavka cannot agree with the mood of doom, and impossibility of taking strong measures and conversations about how everything possible has been done and it's impossible to do any more ...' Then Stalin heard that Voroshilov, replaying his glory days of Tsaritsyn in 1918, was planning to raise morale by electing officers – but this time the outraged War Commissar was not Trotsky.

'Immediately stop the elections because it will paralyse the army and elect impotent leaders,' ordered Stalin, together with Molotov and Mikoyan. 'We need all-powerful leaders. It will spread like a disease. This isn't Vologda – this is the second city of the country!' He added: 'We ask Voroshilov and Zhdanov to inform us about operations. They have not done so yet. That's a pity.'

'All's clear,' replied Leningrad. 'Goodbye Comrade Stalin. That helps. Great gratitude!'

Zhdanov took control of every facet of Leningrad life, declaring famously: 'the enemy is at the gates.' Now plump, asthmatic and exhausted, always chain smoking his Belomor cigarettes, clad in

---

* The opening of Stalin's and Zhdanov's papers allows us for the first time to listen in on their frantic efforts to save Leningrad.

an olive-green belted tunic, pistol in holster, Zhdanov ran the front from the third floor of the right wing of the Smolny Institute from an office hung with pictures of Stalin, Marx and Engels. His long table was covered in red baize just as Stalin's was in green. His desk was set with Urals stone, a present from some Leningrad factory. He drank tea, like Stalin, from a glass held in a silver holder, chewing sugar lumps and, like him, slept on his office divan. He wrote the newspaper editorials, personally allocated every volt of electricity, threatened 'panic-mongers' with instant death, and shared command of the front.

Voroshilov meanwhile displayed the admirable courage that he had shown at Tsaritsyn. When he appeared at the front at Ivanovskoye, the soldiers watched as the First Marshal pranced around under heavy shellfire:

'That's him! Voroshilov! Klim!' gasped the soldiers. 'Look how he stands as if he grew out of the earth!' A few miles away, the Marshal came upon some troops who had broken under a German attack. He stopped his staff car, pulled out his pistol and led the troops against the Germans to the shout of 'Hurrah!' The old cavalryman could buckle his swash but was unable to stabilize the front.

Stalin was unmoved by the heroic ineptitude of this *beau sabreur*. His warmth towards Zhdanov was cooling fast. When the Leningraders referred respectfully to their boss as 'Andrei Alexandrovich', Stalin answered icily: 'Andrei Alexandrovich? Now which Andrei Alexandrovich do you mean?' The terrified agreement to his own orders did not help matters: 'If you don't agree,' he told Zhdanov, 'say it straight.' But he also showed his sarcastic irritation, scribbling in his red pencil: 'You didn't answer the proposal. You didn't answer? Why not? ... Is it understood? When do you begin the attack? We demand an immediate answer in two words: "Yes" will mean a positive answer and swift implementation and "No" will mean a negative. Answer yes or no. Stalin.' None the less he resisted any attempt to dismiss Zhdanov even though he was staggering under the burden of Leningrad's plight.

On the 21st Stalin, realizing the desperate situation, ordered Molotov and Malenkov, armed with his full authority, to descend on Leningrad and designate a scapegoat, marking Zhdanov's fall from grace. 'To Voroshilov, Malenkov, Zhdanov ... Leningrad Front thinks of only one thing: any way to retreat ... Isn't it time you got rid of these heroes of retreat?' But they also had a bigger unspoken mission: should Leningrad be abandoned?

Their journey itself was an adventure: they flew to Cherepovets where they took a special train westward but suddenly the train could go no further and stopped at the little station of Mga, twenty-five miles east of the city. The magnates could see a German bombing raid up ahead but they did not realize this was the beginning of the German advance that would encircle Leningrad only two days later: Mga had been the last way in. Molotov and Malenkov were unsure what to do. They walked along the tracks towards Leningrad until they found a suburban trolleybus which they boarded like commuters. They were met further up the line by an armoured train.

They found Zhdanov just about holding things together, but comforting himself with drink and struggling against his asthma. Zhdanov was never the strongest of Stalin's men: 'a bit spineless', thought Molotov. Alcohol became the one flaw in this perfect Stalinist. He was now close to collapse, admitting openly to Stalin that he had at one point lost his nerve, panicked during the bombardment and hidden, drinking, in the Smolny bunker. But the very confession helped keep Stalin's favour. He worked like a man possessed but his health never recovered.

Malenkov enjoying spreading the story of Zhdanov's alcoholic cowardice while boasting that he never reported it to Stalin, which is hard to believe. Zhdanov got on well with Molotov but had despised Malenkov since the late thirties. It was he who had coined the nickname for that fat, eunuch-like bureaucrat: 'Malanya.' The mutual hatred of these two noble scions of the provincial intelligentsia would seethe until it ended in a massacre. Malenkov probably proposed Zhdanov's arrest but Beria, knowing Stalin's fondness for 'the Pianist', said this was no time for court-martialling Politburo members. Molotov agreed: 'Zhdanov was a good comrade' but he was 'very dejected'.

Apart from hunting scapegoats, Stalin's plenipotentiaries hardly improved matters: 'I fear,' Stalin wrote hysterically to Molotov and Malenkov, 'Leningrad will be lost through imbecilic folly, and all Leningrad risks encirclement. What are Popov [front commander] and Voroshilov doing? They don't even tell us of the measures they're taking against the danger. They're busy looking for new lines of retreat. As far as I can see, this is their only purpose ... This is pure peasant fatalism ... What people! I can't understand anything. Don't you think someone's opening the road to the Germans in this important direction? On purpose? What's this man Popov? What's Voroshilov doing? How's he helping Leningrad? I write about this because I'm disturbed by the lack of activity of Leningrad's commander ... return to Moscow. Don't be late. Stalin.'

On their return, the emissaries advised Stalin to scrap Voroshilov's North-Western Axis and sack the First Marshal who spent 'all his time in the trenches'. Meanwhile Schlüsselberg, the fortress on the Neva, and Mga, fell. Voroshilov did not tell Moscow, and when Stalin discovered these prevarications, he was outraged.

'We're so indignant about your conduct,' he told Voroshilov and Zhdanov. 'You tell us only of losses but no word of measures to save towns ... and the loss of Schlüsselberg? What'll be the end of our losses? Have you decided to surrender Leningrad?'

On 8 September, Stalin summoned Zhukov to his flat where he was dining with his usual companions – Molotov, Malenkov and the Moscow boss, Alexander Shcherbakov.*

'Where will you be off to now?' Stalin asked casually.

'Back to the front,' replied Zhukov.

'Which front?'

'The one you consider most necessary.'

'Then go to Leningrad at once ... The situation is almost hopeless there ...' and he handed Zhukov a note to Voroshilov that read: 'Hand over command to Zhukov and fly to Moscow immediately.' Stalin scrawled to Zhdanov: 'Today Voroshilov's recalled!'

Zhukov took command at Leningrad's Smolny headquarters, combining professionalism with draconian ruthlessness, shouting at the staff: 'Don't you understand that if Antonov's division doesn't occupy the line ... the Germans'll break into the city? And then I'll have you shot in front of the Smolny as a traitor.' Zhdanov, standing beside his new partner in command, frowned: he disapproved of swearing.

---

* Shcherbakov was one of those New Men who had risen over the bodies of the dead of the thirties. 'With his impassive Buddha face, with thick horn-rimmed glasses resting on the tiny turned-up button of a nose', Shcherbakov, who was Zhdanov's brother-in-law, another example of the intermarriage of the élite, had made his name managing cultural questions, then succeeded Khrushchev as Moscow First Secretary, becoming a candidate member of the Politburo in 1941 with Malenkov and Voznesensky. A coarse alcoholic anti-Semite, Khrushchev called him: 'a snake ... one of the worst.'

The crestfallen Voroshilov addressed his staff: 'Goodbye comrades,' he said. 'Stavka's recalled me back.' He paused. 'That's what an old man like me deserves. This isn't the Civil War. Now we have to fight differently ... But don't doubt for a minute that we'll smash the Fascist scum!'

Back in Moscow, Stalin admitted, 'We might have to abandon "Peter".' But Zhukov stiffened resistance to the German attack and then counter-attacked. Zhdanov, working closely with Zhukov, now showed his steel, complaining that his 'tribunals are being inactive against spreaders of false and provocative rumours ... The Special Departments should arrange trials of provocateurs and rumour-mongers. The public should know how we regard these bastards.' Whatever Stalin suggested was put into action.*
On 13 November, Stalin told him that the Germans were constructing strongholds in the cellars of ordinary homes: 'People's Commissar of Defence Comrade Stalin gives the following instructions,' wrote Zhdanov. 'When moving forward don't try to capture one or other point but ... burn to ashes these populated areas. So the German staffs and units will be buried ... Toss away any sentiment and destroy all populated areas you meet on your way!'

Zhukov and Zhdanov succeeded in making the storming of Leningrad very costly for the Germans. Hitler hesitated, cancelled the assault and ordered instead that Leningrad be starved into submission and then razed to the ground: the 900-day siege of the city had begun. Zhdanov had not lost the habit of writing Stalin personal letters with a fine ink pen: 'The main cause of our failure was the weak performance of our infantry ... We remembered what you told us during the Finnish War' but 'our people have a bad habit of not finishing things and analysing them – and then running in different directions ... Today we're working strongly to change our style of attack ... The worst is that the hunger is spreading.'

There were 2.2 million people trapped in Leningrad. That December alone, 53,000 died and there would be many more to follow. People dropped dead in the streets, in their beds, whole

---

* When, on 31 October, Stalin heard that the Nazis were using 'delegations' of Russian men and women as human shields, he ordered Zhdanov: 'It's said that amongst the Leningrad Bolsheviks there are those who thought it impossible to use arms against these "delegates". If there are such people ... they must be liquidated first of all because they are more dangerous than German soldiers. My advice – no sentiment ... Destroy the Germans and their delegates!'

families died one by one. There were too many bodies and everyone was too weak to bury them. Cannibalism flourished: it was not rare to find a body lying in the hall of an apartment block with thighs and breasts carved off. Between now and July 1942, it is estimated that a million people died in Leningrad.

Zhdanov, assisted by his respected Second Secretary, Alexei Kuznetsov, won back Stalin's respect and that of the Leningraders. They gradually became heroes as they shared the plight of their citizens, personally living on a full military ration of a pound of bread a day plus a bowl of meat or fish soup and some *kasha*. While hundreds of thousands were dying in the streets, the leaders worked day and night. Kuznetsov, a tall, gangly young man with a long handsome face, kept Leningrad together during Zhdanov's moments of weakness, touring the trenches accompanied by his little son. Stalin himself praised Kuznetsov: 'The Motherland won't forget you!' he wrote.

In November, they ordered the building of the 'Road of Life' across the ice of Lake Ladoga which became the city's only channel for the supply of food. During the famine, Zhdanov assigned food supplies in such detail that, at one point, he was the only man allowed to replace a lost ration card. He sometimes displayed flashes of human decency: when dysentery broke out in a school, he suspected the staff of stealing the children's food and sent in a general who reported that the children were taking the food in jars to their families – but he did not stop them.

'I'd have done the same thing,' Zhdanov admitted and ordered the evacuation of the children. After the war, Zhdanov was quoted as saying that 'people died like flies' but 'history would have never have forgiven me had I given up Leningrad'.

Still Stalin became furious when Zhdanov showed dangerous independence: 'Do you imagine Leningrad under Zhdanov is not situated in the USSR but is somewhere on an island in the middle of the Pacific?'

'We admit our mistake,' replied Zhdanov, who then reported a problem with the operations on Lake Lagoda which he blamed on the 'cowardice and betrayal' of the commanders of the 80th Division. 'We send a demand to let us ... shoot the chief of 80th Frolov and his commissar Ivanov ... The Council needs to fight panic and cowardice even among officers.'

'Frolov and Ivanov should be shot and tell the media,' replied Stalin.

'Understood. All will be done.'

'Don't waste time,' said Stalin. 'Every moment's dear. The enemy concentrates power against Moscow. All other fronts have the chance to counter-attack. Seize the moment!'

Zhdanov ended his handwritten reply: 'We're waiting the start of the German defeat outside Moscow. Be healthy!' Then he added this: 'PS: I've become as ferocious as a dog!'*

* * *

Hitler switched his Panzers to Operation Typhoon, the grand offensive against Moscow, designed to deliver the knockout blow to Soviet Russia. Guderian's Panzers surprised and then outflanked the Briansk Front just as Stalin welcomed Lord Beaverbrook, the puckish Canadian press baron and member of the British War Cabinet, and Averell Harriman, the handsome lantern-jawed railway heir and American envoy, who had come to negotiate military aid to keep Russia in the war.

The two plutocrats observed Stalin play the gracious host while facing catastrophe. 'Stalin was very restless, walking about and smoking continuously and appeared to both of us to be under an intense strain,' recalled Beaverbrook. As always, Stalin swung between rudeness and charm, sketching wolves on his notepad one moment, and then tossing aside an unopened letter from Churchill to exclaim:

'The paucity of your offers clearly shows you want to see the Soviet Union defeated.' He was 'sallow, tired, pock-marked ... almost emaciated'. By 1 October, the Moscow front was collapsing just as Stalin laid on a lavish banquet in the Great Kremlin Palace. At 7.30 p.m., the hundred guests chattered loudly in the eighteenth-century Catherine Hall, with its chairs and divans covered in the monograms of Catherine the Great, green silk wallpaper, and the old portraits in their golden frames. Just before eight, the Russian guests began to glance anxiously at the high, gilded door and on the hour, silence fell as Stalin, in a tunic that 'seemed to hang off his wasted frame', walked slowly down the line.

At dinner, he placed himself between the tycoons, with Molotov in his accustomed seat opposite him and, down the table, Voroshilov and Mikoyan, who henceforth negotiated the

---

* Perhaps as a reward for his ferocity, on 11 December, Zhdanov, who had not seen Stalin since 24 June, flew to Moscow and began to climb back to the top.

Western aid.* As the waiters unleashed upon the guests a barrage of hors d'oeuvres, caviar, soup, and fish, suckling pig, chicken and game, ice-cream and cakes, washed down with champagne, vodka, wine and Armenian brandy, Stalin toasted victory before Molotov took up the baton. There were thirty-two toasts before the night was done. When Stalin enjoyed a toast, he would clap his hands before drinking to it but he happily talked on while others were speaking. He 'drank continuously from a small glass (liqueur),' wrote Beaverbrook, who recorded everything with the avidity of one of his *Daily Express* columnists. 'He ate well and even heartily', nibbling caviar off his knife, without bread and butter. Stalin and Beaverbrook, two mercurial rogues, jousted mischievously. Pointing at President Kalinin, Beaverbrook, who had heard about his taste for ballerinas, asked if the old man had a mistress. 'He's too old,' chuckled Stalin. 'Do you?'

Stalin then led the way, with hands behind his back, to the cinema where he intently watched two movies, drinking champagne and laughing. Even though it was already 1.30 a.m., the omnipotent insomniac suggested a third movie but Beaverbrook was too tired. As the Westerners departed, the Germans broke through towards Moscow.

On 3 October, Guderian took Orel, 125 miles behind the supposed Russian front line. Yeremenko's Briansk and Budyonny's Reserve Fronts were smashed: 665,000 Russians surrounded. On the 4th Stalin lost contact with the shattered Western Front under Koniev, leaving a twelve-mile hole in Moscow's defences. Early on the 5th, the Moscow air commander, Sbytov, reported the almost incredible news that a long column of German tanks was heading for Moscow along the Ukhnovo highway, 100 kilometres from the Kremlin. A second reconnaissance plane confirmed the same sight. 'Very well,' Stalin told the Moscow Commissar Telegin. 'Act decisively and energetically ... mobilize every available resource to hold the enemy ...'

Simultaneously, Stalin's entourage tried to crush this news as they had tried to deny the German invasion. 'Look,' Beria threatened Telegin, 'do you take every bit of nonsense as the truth? You've evidently received information from panic-mongers

---

* Even Stalin admitted how this Western assistance decisively aided his war effort. Mikoyan reported to him in detail as the aid arrived, whether trucks via Persia or weapons via Archangel. Such was the urgency that in November 1941, Stalin totted up the number of planes (432) in his red pen on Mikoyan's notes.

and provocateurs!' Minutes later, poor Colonel Sbytov ran into Telegin's office, 'pale and trembling'. Beria had ordered him to report at once to the feared chief of the Special Department, Victor Abakumov who threatened Sbytov and his pilots with arrest for 'cowardice and panic-mongering'. When a third plane confirmed that all three fronts had collapsed, the hyenas were called off.

Stalin telephoned Zhukov in Leningrad: 'I've only got one request. Can you get on a plane and come to Moscow?'

'I request to fly at dawn.'

'We await you in Moscow.'

'I'll be there.'

'All the best,' said Stalin. Meanwhile he sent Voroshilov to find the fronts and learn what he could.

At dusk on 7 October, Vlasik sped Zhukov straight to the Kremlin flat where Stalin, suffering from flu, was chatting to Beria. Probably 'unaware of my arrival', in Zhukov's words, Stalin was ordering Beria to 'use his "Organ" to sound out the possibilities of making a separate peace with Germany, given the critical situation ...' Stalin was probing German resolve but there was no moment when Hitler was less likely to make peace than when Moscow seemed to be falling.* Beria is said to have arranged a second probe, either using a Bulgarian 'banker' or the Ambassador again but with no results.

Without a wisp of small talk, Stalin ordered Zhukov to fly to Koniev's and Budyonny's fronts. Stalin needed a scapegoat, wondering if Koniev was a 'traitor'. Heading into the whirlwind, Zhukov found the dazed commanders of the Western Front, the tough, shaven-headed Koniev and the Commissar, Bulganin, in a desolate room barely lit by candles. Bulganin had just spoken to Stalin but could not tell him anything 'because we ourselves don't know'. At 2.30 a.m. on the 8th, Zhukov called Stalin, who was still ill: 'The main danger now is that the roads into Moscow are virtually undefended.' And the reserves? Stalin asked:

'Encircled.'

'What do you intend to do?'

'I will go to Budyonny ...'

'And do you know where his headquarters are?' Stalin inquired.

* In 1966, when Zhukov's memoirs were published in Moscow, this was regarded as too dangerous to be included. It was only in 1990, when the full version was published, that this account appeared.

'No ... I'll look for him ...'

Stalin despatched Molotov and Malenkov into this cauldron to take control – and assign blame. Such was the havoc that Zhukov could not find Budyonny. At Maloyaroslavets, he found a small town completely deserted except for a chauffeur asleep in a jeep who turned out to be Budyonny's driver. The Marshal was inside the district Soviet, trying to find his own armies on his map. The two cavalrymen embraced warmly. Budyonny had saved Zhukov from arrest during the Terror, but now he was confused and exhausted. The next morning, Stalin ordered Zhukov to return to the Western Front headquarters north of Mozhaisk and take command.

There he found Molotov, Malenkov, Voroshilov and Bulganin indulging in an ugly hunt for the scapegoat: a stand-up row broke out between Koniev and Voroshilov about who had ordered what withdrawal. Koniev's life hung in the balance when Voroshilov shrieked that he was 'a traitor'. He was supported by Nikolai Bulganin, that blond and goatee-bearded ex-Chekist who had been Mayor of Moscow and boss of the State Bank. This apparently affable womanizer, who cultivated an aristocratic elegance but was nicknamed 'the Plumber' by Beria because of his work on the Moscow sewers, was deftly ambitious and suavely ruthless: he wanted Koniev shot, perhaps to save his own skin.

Stalin phoned to order Koniev's arrest but Zhukov persuaded the Supremo that he needed Koniev as his deputy: 'If Moscow falls,' Stalin threatened, 'both your heads'll roll ... Organize the Western Front quickly and act!' Two days later, Molotov telephoned and threatened to shoot Zhukov if he did not stop the retreat. If Molotov could do any better, he was welcome to try, retorted Zhukov. Molotov hung up.

Zhukov stiffened the resistance though he possessed only 90,000 men to defend Moscow. He fought for time, with the fray reaching unprecedented frenzies of savagery. By the 18th, Kalinin had fallen to the north and Kaluga to the south and there were Panzers on the battlefield of Borodino. Snow fell, then thawed, stirring up a boggy quagmire which temporarily halted the Germans. Both sides fought heroically, tank helm to tank helm, like two giants wrestling in a sea of mud.

35

'Can You Hold Moscow?'

Stalin controlled every aspect of the battle, keeping a list of men and tanks in his little leather notebook. 'Are they hiding guns from me again?' he asked Voronov. As early as 3 August, he had secretly ordered the creation of a special tank reserve for Moscow: these tanks were 'to be given to nobody', he specified. But visitors were amazed 'by Zhukov's tone': he spoke to Stalin 'in sharp commanding tones as if he was the superior officer and Stalin accepted this'.

Again and again, he raised the intensity of cruelty. It was perhaps now that he marked the passage in d'Abernon that claimed that the Germans were more afraid of their officers than of the enemy. First he unleashed his 'scorched earth' policy 'to destroy and burn to ashes all populated areas in the German rear to a depth of 40–60 kms from the front line'. Beria, Mekhlis and the rising head of the Special Departments, Abakumov, reported every week on the arrests and shootings of Soviet troops: for example, Beria wrote to Mekhlis during the Battle of Moscow to report that 638,112 men had been detained in the rear since the start of the war, with 82,865 arrested, while Abakumov reported to Stalin that in one week, his Special Departments arrested 1,189 and shot 505 deserters. Now on the front near Moscow, Bulganin's 'interceptor battalions', set up to terrorize cowards, arrested 23,064 'deserters' in just three days. There is a myth that the only time Stalin ceased the war against his own people was during 1941 and 1942; but during that period, 994,000 servicemen were condemned, and 157,000 shot, more than fifteen divisions.

Beria was also liquidating old prisoners: on 13 October, Poskrebyshev's wife, the once effervescent Bronka was shot, an event, like the murder of the Svanidzes, that could only have happened on Stalin's order. As they moved back, the NKVD tossed grenades into their own prisons or transferred prisoners to the interior. On 3 October, Beria liquidated 157 'celebrity' prisoners such as Kameneva, Trotsky's sister and Kamenev's widow, in Medvedev Forest near Orel. On the 28th, Beria ordered the shooting of another twenty-five, including the ex-Air Force commander, Rychagov, who had answered back to Stalin about the 'flying coffins'. The 4,905 unfortunates on death row were despatched within eight days.

On the streets of Moscow, the chains of Stalinist control were snapped by the fear of the German armies. Law broke down. By 14 October, food shops were being looted; empty apartments burgled. Refugees clogged the streets, harassed by gangs of desperadoes. The smoke of bonfires hung over the city as officials burned papers. At Kursk Station, 'a crush of women, children and old people filled the square. The cold was piercing. Children were weeping' but the masses waited 'patiently and submissively'. A hundred soldiers joined arms to hold back the mob. Some commissariats and the families of most officials were evacuated to Kuibyshev. AA guns illuminated the sky while the half-deserted Kremlin was blacked out and weirdly camouflaged: a huge canvas painted with the façades of a row of houses, a veritable Potemkin village, had been hoisted up over the walls facing the river.

Beria, Malenkov and Kaganovich, according to Stalin's bodyguards, 'lost their self-control', encouraging the popular flight. 'We shall be shot down like partridges,' Beria told one meeting, advocating the swift abandonment of Moscow. These magnates advised Stalin to evacuate to Kuibyshev. Beria summoned Sudoplatov, his expert on 'Special Tasks', to his Lubianka office where he was sitting with Malenkov, and ordered him to dynamite all the main buildings, from the Kaganovich Metro to the football stadium. On the night of the 15th, Beria made things worse, calling a meeting of the local Party leaders in his office in the bomb-proof basement at 2 Dzerzhinsky Street, and announcing: 'The connection with the front is broken.' He ordered them to 'evacuate everyone who's unable to defend Moscow. Distribute food to the inhabitants.' There were riots at factories because the workers could not get in since the buildings were mined. Molotov told ambassadors that they would be immediately evacuated.

Stalin himself presented an air of solitary inscrutability, revealing his plans to no one, while the magnates prepared for evacuation. As the air raids on Moscow intensified, Stalin climbed up on to the sunroof at Kuntsevo and watched the dogfights.

Once some shrapnel fell near him as he watched from his garden and Vlasik handed him the warm fragments. Vasily Stalin arrived one night to visit his father. When a German plane passed over the house, the guards did not open fire since they did not want to draw attention to Stalin's residence.

'Cowards!' shouted Vasily, firing the guns himself.

Stalin came out: 'Did he hit anything?' he asked.

'No, he didn't.'

'Winner of the Voroshilov Marksman Prize,' he said drily. But the stress was telling on him: no one could believe how much he had aged. Stalin was now a 'short man with a tired haggard face ... his eyes had lost their old steadiness, his voice lacked assurance.' Khrushchev was appalled to see this 'bag of bones'. When Andreyev and his daughter Natasha walked around the freezing Kremlin, they saw Stalin strolling up and down beside the battlements, quite alone and, as usual, under-dressed, with no gloves on and his face blue with the chill. In his spare moments, he kept reading history: it was now that he scribbled on a new biography of Ivan the Terrible: 'teacher teacher' and then: 'We shall overcome!' His moods swung between Spartan grit and hysterical rantings. Koniev was amazed to receive a call in which Stalin cried:

'Comrade Stalin's not a traitor. Comrade Stalin's an honourable man; his only mistake was that he trusted too much in cavalrymen.' He was harassed by constant 'sightings' of Nazi parachutists landing in the middle of Moscow: 'Parachutist? How many? A company?' Stalin was barking into the phone when one general arrived to report. 'And who saw them? Did you see them? And where did they land? You're insane ... I tell you I don't believe it. The next thing you'll be telling me is that they have already landed on your office!' He slammed down the phone. 'For several hours now they've been tormenting me with wails about German parachutists. They won't let me work. Blabbermouths!'

Stalin's staff prepared for his departure, without actually checking with him. The dachas were dynamited. A special train was prepared, standing in a hidden siding, packed with belongings from his houses such as his beloved library. Four American Douglas DC-3 aeroplanes stood ready.

At the end of 15 October, Stalin ordered his guards to drive him out to Kuntsevo, which had been closed down and mined. The commandant told him he could not go in but Stalin ordered:

'Clear the mines in two or three hours, stoke the stove in the little house and I'll work there.'

The next morning he headed into the Kremlin earlier than usual. On the way, this worshipper of order was amazed to see mobs looting the shops along his route. His guards claimed that he ordered the car to stop on Smolensk Square, where he was surrounded by a crowd who asked rather pertinent questions such as: 'When will the Soviet Army stop the enemy?'

'That day's near,' he replied before driving on to the Kremlin.

At 8 a.m., Mikoyan, who had been working as usual until six in the morning, was woken up and summoned. At nine, the magnates gathered in Stalin's flat to debate the great decision of the war. Stalin proposed to evacuate the whole Government to Kuibyshev, to order the army to defend the capital and keep the Germans fighting until he could throw in his reserves. Molotov and Mikoyan were ordered to manage the evacuation, with Kaganovich providing the trains. Stalin proposed that all the Politburo leave that day and, he added sensationally, 'I will leave tomorrow morning.'

'Why do we have to leave today if you're leaving tomorrow?' Mikoyan indignantly asked Stalin. 'We can also go tomorrow. Shcherbakov and Beria shouldn't leave until they've organized the underground resistance. I'm staying and I'll go tomorrow with you.' Stalin agreed. Molotov and Mikoyan began to brief the commissars: the Foreign Commissariat was called at 11 a.m. and ordered to report to Kazan Station at once. In the lift from Stalin's office, Kaganovich said to Mikoyan:

'Listen, when you leave, please tell me so I don't get left behind.' As the leaders rushed in and out of Stalin's office, their families were given just an hour's notice to evacuate the city.* At 7 p.m. the next day, Ashken Mikoyan and the three younger Mikoyanchiks, along with President Kalinin and other top

---

* In distant Kuibyshev, the ancient city of Samara on the Volga that had been chosen as the new capital should Moscow have to be abandoned, several buildings, including the local Party headquarters and a mansion in a narrow gully beside the steep banks of the Volga, surrounded by paved walks overlooking the river, were prepared for Stalin. A special air-raid shelter, reached by a lift, was constructed whence he could rule what was left of Russia. Svetlana Stalin was set up in a small town house with a courtyard along with her housekeeper Alexandra Nakashidze, and Galina, Vasily's pregnant wife and Yakov's daughter, Gulia (without her arrested mother), Kalinin and his mistress shared a small house with the Mikoyans, the Khrushchevs shared with the Malenkovs. The Poskrebyshevs, Litvinovs and others lived in the local sanatorium.

families, boarded the CC train. In the heavily guarded station, women in fur coats stood chatting with their well-dressed children amidst the steam of the trains while soldiers carefully loaded crates marked 'handle with care – crystal'. Poskrebyshev sobbed as he put three-year-old Natasha on the train with her nanny, unaware that her mother, Bronka, had been executed three days earlier. He promised to visit his daughter as soon as possible – and hurried back to Stalin. As he waited, Valentin Berezhkov, Molotov's interpreter, noticed that the puddles of melted snow were freezing. The German Panzers could advance again.

Zhukov resolved to hold the line. But he could sense the panic at the top. He was convinced he could save Moscow, he told a visiting editor, 'but are THEY, there?' he asked, meaning Stalin in the Kremlin.

That evening, the leaders arrived in an eerily deserted Kremlin. As one commissar entered his apartment, Stalin appeared from his bedroom, smoking and pacing, in his old tunic and baggy, booted trousers. They noticed that the bookcases were empty, books all loaded on to the train. No one sat down. Then Stalin stopped pacing:

'What's the situation like in Moscow?' The magnates remained silent but a junior commissar spoke up: the Metro was not running, the bakeries were closed. The factories thought the Government had fled. Half of them had not been paid. Workers believed the boss of the State Bank had run off with the money.

'Well, it's not so bad. I thought it would be worse.' Stalin ordered the money be flown back from Gorky. Shcherbakov and Pronin, Moscow's Party chief and Mayor, must restore order and broadcast the fact that Moscow would be held to the last drop of blood: Stalin remained in the Kremlin. The leaders headed out into the town: Mikoyan appeared before five thousand restless, unpaid workers at the Stalin Automobile Works. But the panic continued: stragglers and thieves patrolled the streets. Even the British Embassy across the Moskva from the Kremlin was looted, its guards having fled. Demolition units mined Moscow's sixteen bridges.

* * *

Stalin hesitated for two long days. No one knows his exact movements but he no longer appeared in his office. At the height of the legendary struggle for Moscow the Supremo actually dossed down in his greatcoat on a mattress in the subterranean halls of the Metro, not unlike an omnipotent tramp. Stalin's working arrangements reveal the dire lack of preparation for war. There were frequent air raids but there were no bunkers at either the Kremlin or Kuntsevo. While Kaganovich supervised the urgent construction of bunkers precisely modelled on Stalin's study, the Supremo moved to work in the only proper command post available, the air defence HQ in the town house at 33 Kirov Street (Myasnitskaya Street), where he had a bedroom. During air raids, he descended by elevator to work in the Kirov Metro Station (now Chistye Prudy) until, on 28 October, a bomb fell in the courtyard of the house. Then Stalin started to work permanently in the station, where he also slept.

In the Metro, he bunked in a specially constructed compartment that was sealed off from the running trains by plywood panels. Many of his staff slept on ordinary subway trains parked in the station, while the General Staff worked in the Belorusski Metro Station. Offices, desks and sleeping compartments divided up this subterranean headquarters deep under Kirov Street. Passing trains caused pages to fly so they were pinned to desks. After working all day in his subterranean offices, Stalin would finally stagger over to his sleeping compartment in the early hours. Vlasik and his bodyguards stood on guard around this flimsy refuge and probably slept across the doors like squires guarding a medieval king. A staff colonel, Sergei Shtemenko, an efficient, charismatic Cossack of thirty-four, with a lush black moustache, worked closely with Stalin and sometimes they simply 'bunked together', sleeping in their greatcoats on mattresses in the office. It is hard to imagine any of the other warlords living in such a way but Stalin was accustomed to dossing down like the young revolutionary he once was.

* * *

On 17 October Shcherbakov made his radio broadcast to restore morale in Moscow. It had little effect as the streets were clogged with gangs of deserters and refugees piling their belongings on to carts. Stalin was still debating whether to leave Moscow but the moment finally arrived, probably late on the evening of the 18th, when he had to make this decision. Air Force General Golovanov remembered seeing Stalin depressed and undecided. 'What shall we do?' he kept repeating. 'What shall we do?'

At the most world-shattering moment of his career, Stalin

discussed the decision with generals and commissars, bodyguards and servants, and of course he read his history. He was reading the biography, published in 1941, of Kutuzov – who had abandoned Moscow. 'Until the last minute,' he underlined heavily, 'no one knew what Kutuzov intended to do.' Back in his apartment, Valechka in her white apron was cheerfully serving Stalin and the magnates their dinner. When some of them seemed to lean towards evacuation, Stalin's eyes fell on his 'ever-smiling' mistress.

'Valentina Vasilevna,' Stalin asked her suddenly. 'Are you preparing to leave Moscow?'

'Comrade Stalin,' she replied in peasant idiom, 'Moscow is our Mother, our home. It should be defended.'

'That's how how Muscovites talk!' Stalin told the Politburo.

Svetlana also seemed to discourage the abandonment of Moscow when she wrote from Kuibyshev: 'Dear Papa, my precious joy, hello ... Papa, why do the Germans keep creeping nearer all the time? When are they going to get it in the neck as they deserve? After all, we can't go on surrendering all our industrial towns to them.'

Stalin called Zhukov and asked him: 'Are we certain we can hold Moscow? I ask you this with pain in my heart. Speak the truth, like a Bolshevik?'* Zhukov replied that it could be held. 'It's encouraging you're so certain.'

Stalin ordered the guards to take him out to his 'faraway' dacha at Semyonovskoe, which was further from the fighting than Kuntsevo. Beria replied in Georgian that this too was dynamited. But Stalin angrily insisted on going. Once he was there, he found the commandant packing up the last belongings.

'What sort of removals are going on here?' he asked gruffly.

'We're preparing, Comrade Stalin, for the evacuation to Kuibyshev.' Stalin may also have ordered his driver to take him to the special train that was parked under close guard at the Abelmanovsky junction, normally used for storing wooden sleepers. One source in Stalin's office recounted how he walked alongside the train. Mikoyan and Molotov do not mention it, and even a hint of Stalin near a train would have caused panic, but it was the sort of melodramatic scene that Stalin would have

* Zhukov recalled him asking this again in mid-November but V. P. Pronin, Chairman of the Moscow Soviet (Mayor), remembered the question being asked on '16 or 17 October'. He surely asked it several times.

relished. If it happened, the image of this tiny, thin figure 'with his tired haggard face' in its tattered army greatcoat and boots, strolling along the almost deserted but heavily guarded siding through the steam of the ever-ready locomotive is as emotionally potent as it was to be historically decisive. For Stalin ordered the commandants of his dacha to stop loading: 'No evacuation. We'll stay here until victory,' he ordered 'calmly but firmly.'

When he got back to the Kremlin, he gathered his guards and told them: 'I'm not leaving Moscow. You'll stay here with me.' He ordered Kaganovich to cancel the special train. The Stalinist system allowed the magnates, who swung between defeatism and defiance, to pursue their own policies until Stalin himself spoke. Then his word was law. On the 'damp dank' evening of the 18 October, the team in charge of defending the city were gathered at Beria's office where the Georgian 'tried to convince us that Moscow must be abandoned. He considered,' wrote one of those present, 'that we have to withdraw behind the Volga. With what are we going to defend Moscow? We have nothing ... They'll smother us all here.' Malenkov agreed with him. Molotov, to his credit, 'muttered objections'. The others 'remained silent'. Beria was said to be the main advocate of withdrawal though he became the scapegoat for everything unsavoury that happened under Stalin. The alcoholic Moscow boss Shcherbakov wanted to withdraw too and it seems that he lost his composure: afterwards, 'in a state of terror', he asked Beria what would happen if Stalin found out.

On the 19th at 3.40 in the afternoon, Stalin summoned his magnates and generals to the the Little Corner. Stalin 'stepped up to the table and said:

"The situation is known to all of you. Should we defend Moscow?"' No one answered. The silence was 'gloomy'. Stalin waited, then said: 'If you don't want to speak, I shall ask each of you to give his opinion.' He started with Molotov, who stuck to his opinion:

'We must defend Moscow.' Everyone, including Beria and Malenkov, gave the same answer. Beria had converted to Stalin's view, as his son admitted: 'My father would never have acted as he did if he had not known ... [and] anticipated [Stalin's] reactions.'

'If you go, Moscow will be lost,' Beria declared. Shcherbakov was one of those who sounded doubtful.

'Your attitude can be explained in two ways,' said Stalin. 'Either you're good-for-nothings and traitors or idiots. I prefer to regard you as idiots.' Then he expressed his opinion and asked Poskrebyshev to bring in the generals. When Telegin and the commander of Moscow, NKVD General Artemev, arrived, Stalin was pacing tensely up and down the narrow carpet, smoking his pipe. 'The faces of those present,' recalled Commissar Telegin, 'revealed that a stormy discussion had just taken place and that feeling was still running high. Turning to us without a greeting, Stalin asked:

'What's the situation in Moscow?'

'Alarming,' reported Artemev.

'What do you suggest?' snapped Stalin.

'A state of siege' should be declared in Moscow, answered Artemev.

'Correct!' and Stalin ordered his 'best clerk', Malenkov, to draft it. When Malenkov read out his verbose decree, Stalin became so irritated that he rushed up and 'literally snatched the sheets of paper from him'. Then he briskly dictated his decree to Shcherbakov, ordering 'the shooting on the spot' of suspected offenders.

Stalin brought up the divisions to defend Moscow, naming many of them from memory, then calling their commanders directly. The NKVD was unleashed on to the streets, executing deserters and even concierges who had tried to leave. The decision to stay and fight had been made. The presence of Stalin in Moscow, said the Comintern leader Dmitrov, was 'worth a good-sized army'. Stalin was refreshed by the end of the uncertainty: when a commissar phoned in from the front to discuss evacuation eastwards, Stalin interrupted him:

'Find out, do your comrades have spades?'

'What, Comrade Stalin?'

'Do they have spades?' The Commissar asked in the background if they had spades.

'What kind of spades, Comrade Stalin – ordinary ones or digging tools?'

'It doesn't matter.'

'Yes, we've got spades! What shall we do with them?'

'Tell your comrades,' replied Stalin calmly, 'to take their spades and dig their own graves. We won't leave Moscow. They won't leave either ...'

Even now Stalin's courtiers bickered among themselves: Stalin ordered Molotov to travel down to Kuibyshev to check on Voznesensky, who was running the Government there.

'Let Mikoyan come with me,' said Molotov.

'I'm not your tail,' Mikoyan shouted, 'am I?'

'Why don't you go too?' suggested Stalin. Five days later Stalin recalled them.

The Panzers were still advancing on the frozen snow and threatening to encircle Moscow. Zhukov had no reserves left. Having lost three million of his soldiers since June, Stalin's notebook was virtually empty. Like a despotic shopkeeper, assisted by his fat accountant son, Stalin jealously guarded his secret reserves while Malenkov sat beside him, keeping tally. When Stalin asked one general what would save the capital, he replied, 'Reserves.'

'Any idiot,' snapped Stalin, 'could defend the city with reserves.' Stalin generously gave him fifteen tanks, at which Malenkov observed that this was all they had left. Amazingly, in just a few months, the vast military resources of this endless empire had been reduced to fifteen tanks in a notebook. In Berlin, the Reich Press Office declared that 'Russia was finished' but Stalin's iron husbandry of his reserves, coupled with Zhukov's brilliant and brutal fighting, was telling on the Germans whose machines were beginning to suffer from the mud and ice while their men were freezing and exhausted. They again halted to prepare for a final push, convinced that Stalin's resources were exhausted. But there was a page in the notebook that they had forgotten.

Stalin's Far Eastern Army, 700,000 strong, guarded against Japan but in late September, Richard Sorge, the spy Stalin called a brothel-keeper, reported that Japan would not attack Russia. On 12 October, Stalin discussed this with his Far Eastern satraps who then confirmed Tokyo's lack of hostile intentions from local intelligence. Kaganovich arranged non-stop trains that, within days and hours, rushed 400,000 fresh troops, 1,000 tanks and 1,000 planes across the Eurasian wastes, in one of most decisive logistical miracles of the war. The last train left on the 17th and these secret legions began to mass behind Moscow.

* * *

Stalin moved into his new Kremlin bunker, an exact replica of the Little Corner, even down to the wood panelling, though its long corridors resembled nothing so much as a 'railway sleeping car. To the right was a row of doors' with 'a heavy security guard'. The officers waited in 'one of the sleeping compartments to the left' until Poskrebyshev appeared and led them into a 'spacious brightly lit room with a big desk in the corner' where they came upon the pacing Stalin, usually accompanied by his Chief of Staff, the ailing gentleman officer, Marshal Shaposhnikov.

Just younger than Stalin, with his thinning hair centre-parted and a tired, yellow face with Tartar cheekbones, Shaposhnikov seemed 'propelled by some special act of Voodooism as he looked quite dead (at least 3 months gone) and must, even when alive, have been very very old', according to a British diplomat. Shaposhnikov called everyone *golubchik*, dear fellow, and Stalin was charmed by the gentility of this Tsarist colonel. When some generals had not reported one day, Stalin angrily asked Shaposhnikov if he had punished them. Oh yes, retorted Shaposhnikov: he had given them a 'severe reprimand'. This did not impress Stalin:

'For a soldier that's no punishment!' But Shaposhnikov patiently explained 'the old military tradition that if the Chief of Staff reprimands [an officer], the guilty party must offer his resignation'. Stalin could only chuckle at this old-worldliness. But Shaposhnikov was a survivor: he had attacked Tukhachevsky in the twenties, served as his judge in 1937 and even denounced a cook saboteur for over-salting the meat. He never signed anything without checking first. In Stalin's presence, he was 'without an opinion'. While he never renounced his views, he never objected to being overruled. He was the only general Stalin called by his name and patronymic, the only one allowed to smoke* in his office.

The war had truly reached the Kremlin, which was now peppered by bomb craters. Mikoyan was knocked down by a bomb. On 28 October, Malenkov was working at Old Square when Stalin called him to the Kremlin: he had no sooner left than a German bomb destroyed the building. 'I saved your life,' Stalin told him.

One day, Stalin insisted that he wanted to witness an artillery barrage against German positions. Beria, in attendance, was very

---

* No one else was ever invited to join Stalin in his constant smoking. This honour to Shaposhnikov resembles Queen Victoria graciously permitting the old Disraeli to sit during their audiences, the only Prime Minister to receive such a privilege.

anxious that he would be blamed if something went wrong. Stalin's car and bodyguards set off down the Volokolamsk highway towards the front but as they were approaching the fighting, Vlasik refused to let them proceed any further. Stalin had to watch the explosions from a distance. Then a tank splashed his limousine, which sent his bodyguards into palpitations. Beria forced Stalin to change cars and go home. Yet Stalin had regained some spirit: he even let Svetlana visit him for a couple of days but then gruffly ignored her in the bunker, cursing the privileges of the 'damned caste' of the élite in Kuibyshev. More importantly, the great actor-manager now devised a scene of reckless but inspired showmanship.

* * *

On 30 October, Stalin suddenly asked General Artemev: 'How are we going to have the military parade?'

There could be no parade, answered Artemev. The Germans were less than fifty miles away. Molotov and Beria thought he was joking. But Stalin calmly ignored them:

'A parade will be held on 7th November ... I'll see to it personally. If there's an air raid during the parade and there are dead and wounded, they must be quickly removed and the parade allowed to go on. A newsreel should be made and distributed throughout the country. I'll make a speech ... What do you think?'

'But what about the risk?' mused Molotov. 'Though I admit the political response ... would be enormous.'

'So it's decided!'

Artemev asked when the parade should begin. 'See to it that no one knows, not even I,' said Stalin, 'until the last hour.' A week later, German spies might have glimpsed the odd sight of Muscovites, supervised by Chekists, collecting chairs from the Bolshoi Theatre and carrying them down the stairs to the Mayakovsky Metro. That evening, the magnates caught the elevator down into Mayakovsky Station where they found a train parked on one side, with its doors open. There were tables inside with sandwiches and soft drinks. After these refreshments, they took their seats on those theatrical chairs. Then, in a slightly vaudeville touch, Stalin, accompanied by Molotov, Mikoyan, Beria, Kaganovich and Malenkov, assembled at the next station, and caught the subway to Mayakovsky. They took their places on the Politburo rostrum to wild applause. Levitan the newsreader broadcast the programme from a radio-station-carriage. The

NKVD Ensemble played the songs of Dunaevsky and Alexandrov. Kozlovsky sang. Stalin spoke for half an hour in a tone of inspiring calm, warning:

'If they want a war of extermination, they shall have one.' Afterwards, General Artemev approached Stalin: the parade was set for 8 a.m. Even the officers involved were not to know the full details until 2 a.m.

Just before eight o'clock, in a snowstorm and with biting winds that preserved them from German air attack, Stalin led the Politburo up the steps to the Mausoleum, just like old times – except it was earlier and everyone was extremely nervous. Beria and Malenkov ordered their wizard of Special Tasks, Sudoplatov, to report to them on the Mausoleum if the Germans attacked. The public favourite at parades, Budyonny, sabre drawn on a white stallion, rode out from the Spassky Gates, saluted and then mounted to review the parade. The tanks, including the T34s, the outstanding machine of the war, and troops paraded in columns, U-turned at St Basil's, then headed up Gorky Street to the front.

There was a tense moment when a heavy Kliment Voroshilov tank stopped abruptly and turned in the wrong direction, followed by another. Since they were all fully armed, and since Stalin was watching this blunder carefully, Artemev ordered his subordinates to investigate at once. Having caught up with the tanks, their crews were interrogated and innocently revealed that the first tank had simply received a message that another tank was in trouble; following their training the other tanks had gone to its aid. When Artemev reported this on the Mausoleum, the potentates were so relieved that they laughed: no one was punished. Stalin spoke shortly about the patriotic struggle of the Russia of Suvorov, Kutuzov and Alexander Nevsky. The Motherland was in peril but defiant. Appropriately, that very night, the Russian freeze really set in.

On 13 November, Stalin called Zhukov to plan the counter-attacks to put the German attacks off balance. Zhukov and Commissar Bulganin felt that their resources were so low they could not attack but Stalin insisted. 'What forces are we to use?' asked Zhukov.

'Consider it settled!' Stalin rang off but immediately telephoned Bulganin:

'You and Zhukov're giving yourselves airs. But we'll put a stop to that.'

Afterwards Bulganin ran into Zhukov's office: 'Well, I got it really hard this time!' he said.

The counter-attacks were subsumed in the grinding German offensive of 15 November, the last push to take Moscow. The Germans broke through. Again Stalin asked Zhukov: could he hold Moscow?

'We'll hold Moscow without doubt. But we've got to have at least two more armies and no fewer than two hundred tanks.' Stalin delivered the armies 'but for the time being, we don't have any tanks'. Zhukov fought the Germans to a standstill on 5 December, having lost 155,000 men in twenty days. Effectively, Hitler's *Blitzkrieg* had failed. On 6 December, Stalin delivered three new armies to Zhukov and ordered a grand counter-offensive on the four nearest fronts. The next day, Japan attacked America at Pearl Harbor.

Zhukov drove the Germans back two hundred miles. Yet even in such a desperate battle, the generals never forgot Stalin's imperial vanity: just as Mekhlis had tried to win victory on Stalin's birthday in Finland, so now Zhukov and Bulganin ordered Golubev, commander of the Tenth Army: 'Tomorrow will be the birthday of Stalin. Try to mark this day by the capture of Balabanovo. To include this message in our report to Stalin, inform us of its fulfilment not later than 7 p.m. 21 December.' The Battle of Moscow was Stalin's first victory, but a limited one. However, he was immediately dangerously over-optimistic, telling the visiting British Foreign Secretary, Anthony Eden: 'The Russians have already been in Berlin twice and will be a third time.'* It would take millions more dead and almost four years to reach Berlin. Zhukov was so exhausted that, even when Stalin telephoned, his adjutants had to tell him:

'Zhukov is asleep and we can't wake him.'

'Don't wake him up until he wakes himself,' answered the Supremo benevolently. 'Let him sleep.'

* * *

On 5 January, the over-confident Supremo gathered Zhukov and the generals to hear the plan for a massive offensive from Leningrad to the Black Sea to capitalize on the German defeat before Moscow.

---

* In 1760, during the Seven Years War, Empress Elizabeth's General Todtleben took Berlin. Alexander I took the Prussian capital in 1813.

'Who wishes to speak?' asked Stalin. Zhukov criticized the offensive, saying the army needed more men and tanks. Voznesensky was against it too, saying he could not supply the necessary tanks. Stalin insisted on the offensive, at which Malenkov and Beria attacked Voznesensky for 'always finding insuperable and unforeseen' objections. 'On that,' said Stalin, 'we'll conclude the meeting.' In Stalin's anteroom, old Shaposhnikov tried to console Zhukov:

'You argued in vain. These issues had been decided beforehand by the Supremo ...'

'Then why was our opinion solicited?'

'I don't know, dear fellow.'

The intelligent and indefatigable Beria, now forty-three, proved a voracious empire-builder in running the war, but he delivered the tanks and guns Stalin needed. Beria was keen to win points off Voznesensky, whom he loathed, and he soon outstripped Molotov and the older generation. No industry was too complex or too vast for Beria to master: he was in many ways not only the Himmler of Stalin's entourage but also the Speer, another architect. He used the most colourful threats he could muster, asking his subordinates: 'Do you care about seeing the sun rise and fall every day? Be careful!'

In early January 1942, at his flat, Stalin consulted this top industrial *troika*, Beria, Malenkov and Mikoyan, about the armaments shortage.

'What's the problem?' exclaimed Stalin. Beria produced a diagram that showed how Voznesensky was failing to produce enough guns. 'And what should be done?'

'I don't know, Comrade Stalin,' replied Beria artfully. Stalin immediately gave him control of this vital industry.

'Comrade Stalin, I don't know whether I can manage it ... I'm inexperienced in this sort of thing ...'

'It's not experience that's needed here but a strong organizer ... Use prisoners for labour.'

The railways remained impossible to run, even by the energetic and bellowing Kaganovich. When one commissar, Baibakov, reported to Kaganovich, 'the Locomotive' jumped up and shook him by the lapels. Beria reported Kaganovich's table-thumping tempers to Stalin:

'The railways deteriorate because [Kaganovich] won't listen to advice ... he just answers with hysterics.' Kaganovich was criticized for mismanaging the evacuations of industry and, twice, sacked 'for being unable to cope with work under wartime conditions' but he was soon back. Molotov fared no better at running tank production:

'How's [Molotov] managing?' Stalin asked Beria, again accompanied by Malenkov and Mikoyan.

'He has no communication with the factories, doesn't manage them properly ... and holds endless meetings ...' replied Beria, who added tanks to his empire. Molotov lost the tanks but gained the world.

36

Molotov in London, Mekhlis in the
Crimea, Khrushchev in Collapse

On 8 May, the Foreign Commissar took off in a four-engine bomber for London. Stalin instructed him to win a promise of a Second Front – and to clinch recognition of the Soviet borders of 1941, including the Baltics.

He personally charged his favourite air-force general, Golovanov, to plan the route. 'Stalin was a great conspirator,' recalled Golovanov. 'The journey was planned in total secrecy. I had to hide a map of the route in my desk even when my assistant entered my office. Stalin ... told me "Only the three of us know about this – you, Molotov and me." '

'Mr Brown', Molotov's codename, landed in Scotland and was greeted by Eden with whom he took a train from Glasgow to London. When he learned the Second Front was out of the question, Molotov refused to discuss Eden's proposal of a treaty that did not mention the Soviet borders. Molotov immediately reported this to Stalin: 'We consider the treaty unacceptable ... an empty declaration,' but the Supremo changed his mind:

'1. We don't consider it an empty declaration but regard it as important ... Not bad perhaps. It gives us a free hand. The question of borders will be decided by force. 2. It is desirable to sign the treaty as soon as possible and fly to America.'

Meanwhile Molotov also got a taste of English country-house life: he had requested to be lodged outside London, perhaps for security reasons, so Churchill handed over Chequers, his official country mansion. 'Mr Brown' was unimpressed by its Tudor elegance. 'Not a fancy old building,' he mused. 'Some sort of small garden. Apparently some nobleman* had given it to the Government.' Stalin and Molotov were infinitely snobbish about the superiority of Russian grandeur: after all, they lived and

---

* This description certainly complimented Arthur Lee, the colourful adventurer and Conservative MP who bought the house with the fortune of his American heiress wife. He was ennobled as Baron (later Viscount) Lee of Fareham by Lloyd George.

worked in Catherine the Great's palaces. However Molotov had an eye for bathrooms: he remembered the lavatories long after he had forgotten the negotiations. 'There was a bathroom,' he complained, 'but no shower.' As soon as he arrived, his guards asked 'for the keys to all the bedrooms' and he locked himself in every night. 'When the staff at Chequers succeeded in getting in to make the beds,' wrote Churchill, 'they were disturbed to find pistols under the pillows. At night, a revolver was laid out beside his dressing-gown and his despatch cases.' When Molotov was out, his 'maids' guarded his bedroom like Cerberus.

After signing the treaty on 26 May, Molotov flew to Washington to meet President Roosevelt who presented him with a signed photograph, framed in green silk, that read: 'To my friend Vyacheslav Molotov from Franklin Roosevelt 30 May 1942.' Finding FDR 'sociable and pleasant', he was more impressed by the White House than Chequers, especially in the bathroom department: 'Everything there was as it should be,' he said. 'It had a bathroom with a shower too.'

On 9 June, he stopped in London on his way home. Before he left on his dangerous return journey, there was a moment of sentiment when Churchill stood talking with the iron-arsed Russian at the garden gate of 10 Downing Street: 'I gripped his arm,' wrote Churchill, 'and we looked each other in the face. Suddenly he appeared deeply moved. Inside the image, there appeared the man. He responded with equal pressure. Silently we wrung each other's hands ... We were all together and it was life or death for the lot.' Molotov admitted to getting on well with Churchill:

'Yes, we drank a glass or two,' he reminisced. 'We talked the whole night long.' But he could never forget that Churchill was 'an Imperialist, the strongest, the cleverest among them ... 100% Imperialist. So I came to be friends with the bourgeoisie.' He returned with the vague promise of a Second Front, an invaluable Lend-Lease treaty with America, and an alliance with Britain: 'My journey and its results were a great victory for us.' On the flight back to Moscow, Molotov's plane was attacked by enemy fighters and then by Russian ones.

* * *

As Molotov set off for the West, Stalin was launching a wave of counter-attacks along the entire front. He quite reasonably presumed that Hitler would again attack Moscow but the *Führer* actually planned a powerful summer offensive to seize the grain of the Ukraine and, more importantly, the oil of the Caucasus. But Stalin's real fault lay in his raging over-confidence: he lacked the resources for this vast enterprise which, instead of capitalizing on his Moscow victory, handed Hitler the constellation of stunning victories that led to the ultimate crisis of Stalingrad.

He certainly did not help matters by granting draconian powers to his crew of military amateurs. Apart from Stalin himself, no one contributed more to these defeats than the brave, indefatigable and blood-thirsty Mekhlis, now at the height of his power. 'The Shark' could never resist showing off his privileged access: 'When he arrived in the anteroom to Stalin's office,' remembered one commissar, Mekhlis 'didn't even wait for an invitation to go in, he crossed the waiting-room and went straight in.' But 'he never hid anything from Stalin ... who knew this and trusted him.' This gave him the power to get things done: 'If Mekhlis wrote to the Supremo, the measures were very quick.' Yet his antics were always uneasily suspended between the farcical and the diabolical: once when Stalin asked which front needed supplies, the generals were silent except for Mekhlis who piped up to criticize the quartermaster Khrulev. Stalin angrily looked up and asked who was complaining.

'Mekhlis most likely,' replied Khrulev to peals of laughter. Stalin asked Mekhlis to list his needs. 'We lack vinegar, pepper and mustard,' retorted Mekhlis. Even Stalin laughed.

When Mekhlis learned that an arsenal of German pornography had been captured, he immediately launched a new front against Nazi erotica, writing a leaflet called 'How Hitler Corrupts His Army'. His advisers suggested that pornography was natural in a bourgeois army and their nocturnal reading habits were not dictated by Hitler personally, but Mekhlis ignored them and printed eleven million copies of this much mocked document.

He started the year with a visit to the Volkhov Front which had been ordered to relieve the Siege of Leningrad. It was in no shape to launch an offensive which predictably ended in disaster. Mekhlis arrived to investigate, arrest and shoot the culprits. Stalin then offered the front to Voroshilov who courageously, having finally realized his limits, refused it. This outraged Stalin who dictated a sarcastic denunciation of Klim's 'bankruptcy of leadership'. The conclusion was humiliating but not fatal: 'That

Comrade Voroshilov be posted ... to the rear.'* By the end of June, none of these murderous amateurs could save the Volkhov Front: the army was lost along with its talented young General Vlasov. Exhausted and sickened by Stalin's blunders, he turned traitor. Stalin raged about the betrayal to Beria and Molotov, who asked revealingly:

'How did we miss him before the war?' Stalin tried to blame Khrushchev for Vlasov but the Ukrainian boss argued back 'that Stalin had put him in charge of the Moscow counter-offensive'. Stalin, who reacted well to courageous defiance, let the matter drop.

Voroshilov had finally been discredited but Mekhlis and Kulik, despite the latter's string of disasters, still rode high. In October 1941, Kulik had failed to relieve Leningrad; in November at the opposite end of the front, he had been sent to save the city of Kerch in the Crimea. Kulik arrived late and Kerch was temporarily lost to Manstein, one of Hitler's finest captains. Now Stalin considered shooting Kulik and scribbled a note: 'Today. Kulik to Siberia?' but finally settled for demoting him to Major-General and sending Mekhlis to investigate Kulik's late arrival in his DC-3 plane.

'The Gloomy Demon' exposed Kulik's hedonistic junket involving barrels of wine and vodka, a missing 85,898 roubles and the Marshal's new teenage wife. Kulik had soon recovered from the disappearance of his last wife and swiftly romanced this friend of his daughter, a misalliance that Stalin mocked as cradle-snatching. He sacked Kulik as Deputy Commissar yet Zhukov interceded for him. This primitive but popular martinet was reprieved again and, amazingly, promoted. However, his old friendship with Stalin would not end well.

That March, Stalin ordered an assault from Kerch towards the centre of the Crimea to relieve the besieged Sebastopol. Mekhlis, who like his amateur Supremo believed himself a true soldier, gleefully took over the command of these 250,000 men, terrorizing their general, Kozlov, and ignoring the front commander, Budyonny. In this sensitive and complicated battle, Stalin had exchanged an inept and corrupt drunkard for an inept and incorruptible maniac. As Stalin pressured Mekhlis to launch the

---

* Stalin's nephew, Leonid Redens, met the crestfallen Marshal bathing affably with children in the Volga at Kuibyshev.

offensive on time, 'the Shark' replied that his ammunition was low but 'I'll arrest [the officer] if he doesn't straighten out the situation in two days ... We're organizing the big music for the Germans!'

On 2 March, Mekhlis launched his 'big music' in a fiasco that proved to be the insane apogee of terror applied to military science. He banned the digging of trenches 'so that the offensive spirit of the soldiers would not be undermined' and insisted that anyone who took 'elementary security measures' was a 'panic-monger'. All were 'mashed into a bloody porridge'. He bombarded Stalin with demands for more terror: 'Comrade Beria,' Stalin wrote on one of Mekhlis's notes. 'Right! In Novorossisk, make sure that not one scum, not one scoundrel is breathing.'

Mekhlis himself, speeding around the front in his jeep waving a pistol trying to stop the retreat, displayed 'irreproachable personal courage and did nothing for his own glory' yet the 'stupid tyranny and wildly arbitrary ways of this military illiterate', in the words of the poet Konstantin Simonov, a witness, proved disastrous.

On 7 May, Manstein's counter-attack drove Mekhlis off the Crimea altogether, capturing an awesome bag of 176,000 men, 400 planes and 347 tanks. Mekhlis lashed about him, blaming Kozlov and begging Stalin for a great general, a Hindenburg. Stalin was beside himself:

'You take the strange attitude of an outside observer not responsible for the Crimean Front,' he castigated Mekhlis. 'It's a very comfortable position – but it absolutely stinks! You're not an outsider but the representative of Stavka ... You demand the replacement of Kozlov by someone like Hindenburg. But ... we don't have any Hindenburgs ... If you had used aviation against tanks and enemy soldiers and not for sideshows, the enemy would not have broken the front ... You don't have to be Hindenburg to understand this simple thing ...' It was a mark of the obsolete standards of Stalin's court that Hindenburg, the German hero of 1914, was still their paragon in 1942: they needed Guderians not Hindenburgs.

On 28 May, a haggard Mekhlis was waiting in Stalin's anteroom where one could always see the Supremo reflected in the attitudes of his assistants. Poskrebyshev ignored him, then said: 'The Boss's very busy today. Dammit, there are many troubles.'

'Probably something's gone wrong at the front?' asked Mekhlis disingenuously.

'You'd know,' replied Poskrebyshev.

'Yes, I want to report our unfortunate business to Comrade Stalin.'

'Apparently,' said Poskrebyshev, 'the running of the operation wasn't equal to the task. Comrade Stalin's very unhappy ...'

Mekhlis blushed. Young Chadaev joined in:

'I suppose you think the defeat was caused by circumstances?'

'What did you say?' Mekhlis turned on the whippersnapper. 'You're not a soldier! I'm a real soldier. How dare you ...' Then Stalin emerged from his office.

'Hello Comrade Stalin, may I report ...' said Mekhlis.

'Go to hell!' snarled Stalin, slamming his door. Mekhlis, according to Poskrebyshev, later 'almost threw himself at Stalin's feet'. He was courtmartialled, demoted, sacked as Deputy Defence Commissar.

'It's all over!' sobbed Mekhlis but Stalin remained amazingly loyal: twenty-four days later, he was appointed a Front Commissar and later promoted to Colonel-General.

* * *

As if Stalin, Kulik and Mekhlis had not wrought enough defeat, the worst was befalling the South-Western Front where Timoshenko and Khrushchev were launching their offensive from a Soviet salient to retake Kharkov, oblivious of Hitler's imminent attack. Zhukov and Shaposhnikov wisely warned against it but Timoshenko, Stalin's favourite fighting general, insisted on proceeding and the Supremo agreed.

On 12 May, Timoshenko and Khrushchev, both uneducated, crude and energetic, successfully attacked and pushed back the Germans. If Stalin was delighted, Hitler could not believe his luck. Five days later, his Panzers smashed through Timoshenko's flanks, enveloping Soviet forces in steel pincers so that the Russians were no longer advancing but simply burrowing deeper into a trap. The Staff begged Stalin to call off the operation and he warned Timoshenko of the German forces on his flank, but the Marshal jovially reassured him that all was well. By the 18th, 250,000 men were almost encircled when Timoshenko and Khrushchev finally realized their plight.

Around midnight, Timoshenko, the 'brave peasant' terrified of Stalin, persuaded Khrushchev to beg the Supremo to cancel their offensive. At Kuntsevo, Stalin asked Malenkov to answer the phone. Khrushchev asked to speak to Stalin.

'Tell ME!' said Malenkov.

'Who's calling?' Stalin called out.

'Khrushchev,' replied Malenkov.

'Ask him what he wants!'

'Comrade Stalin repeats that you should tell me,' said Malenkov. Then, 'He says the advance on Kharkov should be called off ...'

'Put down the receiver,' yelled Stalin. 'As if he knows what he's talking about! Military orders must be obeyed ... Khrushchev's poking his nose into other people's business ... My military advisers know better.' Mikoyan was shocked that Khrushchev 'was calling him from the front line in battle with people dying around him' and Stalin 'would not walk ten steps across the room'.

The trap snapped shut on a quarter of a million men and 1,200 tanks. The next day, Stalin called off the offensive but it was too late. The exhilarated Germans pushed on towards the Volga and the Caucasus: the road to Stalingrad was open.

* * *

Timoshenko and Khrushchev feared they would be shot. The two friends soon fell out in the scramble to save their careers and lives. There is a story that Khrushchev suffered a nervous breakdown after the encirclement, flying to Baku where he stayed with Bagirov, Beria's ally, who naturally reported Khrushchev's arrival. An unstable Khrushchev started vehemently denouncing Timoshenko, who repaid him in kind:

'Comrade Stalin,' wrote Timoshenko by hand, 'I must add something to our report. The increasingly nervous state of Comrade Khrushchev influences our work. Comrade Khrushchev has no faith in anything – one can't make decisions in doubt ... The whole Council think this is the reason for our fall!' He seems to confirm that Khrushchev did have a mental breakdown: 'It's difficult to discuss – Comrade Khrushchev is very ill ... We gave our report without saying who was guilty. Comrade Khrushchev wants to blame only me.'

Stalin played with the idea of appointing Bulganin to investigate the situation. Bulganin, sensing Stalin's reluctance and, perhaps, guilt, begged to be excused for the un-Bolshevik reason that he and Khrushchev were such friends. Stalin did not insist but reflected mildly on Khrushchev's simplicity: 'He doesn't understand statistics,' said Stalin, 'but we have to put up with him' since only he, Kalinin and Andreyev were 'real proletarians'.

Instead Stalin summoned Khrushchev for a threatening history lesson: 'You know in World War One, after our army fell into German encirclement, the general was court-martialled by the Tsar – hanged.' But Stalin forgave him and sent him back to the front. Khrushchev was still terrified since 'I knew of many cases when Stalin reassured people by letting them leave his office with good news and then had them picked up.'

Stalin was also astonishingly tolerant when Timoshenko asked for more men, having squandered so many: 'Maybe the time has come for you to wage war by losing less blood, as the Germans are doing? Wage war not by quantity but by skill. If you won't learn how to fight better, all the armaments produced in our whole country won't be enough for you ...' This was highly ironic from the most wasteful Supremo in history. Even as they retreated, Stalin remained sarcastically mild to Timoshenko: 'Don't be afraid of Germans – Hitler's not as bad as they say.'

Khrushchev thought they were spared because Mikoyan and Malenkov had witnessed his call to Kuntsevo but it was perhaps simpler: life and death was Stalin's prerogative, and he liked* Khrushchev and Timoshenko. Either way, this was Khrushchev's greatest crisis until, as Stalin's successor, he blundered into the Cuban Missile Crisis twenty years later. Later, Stalin humiliatingly emptied his pipe on Khrushchev's head: 'That's in accordance with Roman tradition,' he said. 'When a Roman commander lost a battle, he poured ashes on his own head ... the greatest disgrace a commander could endure.'

* * *

On 19 June, a *Luftwaffe* aircraft crashed beyond German lines, containing a briefcase bearing the plans for Hitler's summer offensive to exploit the Kharkov disaster and push towards Stalingrad and the North Caucasus. But Stalin decided that the information was either incomplete or a plant. A week later, the Germans attacked exactly as the plans warned, smashing a hole between the Briansk and South-Western Fronts, heading towards Voronezh and then Stalingrad. But it was the oilfields that Hitler really coveted. When he flew in to headquarters at Poltava, he told Field Marshal von Bock: 'If we don't take Maikop and Grozny, then I must put an end to the war.'

---

* Timoshenko's letters to Stalin, scribbled on pages torn out of a notebook, which are in the newly opened Stalin archive, shed light on the Kharkov offensive and Khrushchev's near breakdown.

Timoshenko and Khrushchev fell back towards Stalingrad. When Timoshenko asked for more divisions, Stalin replied sharply:

'If they sold divisions in the market, I'd buy you one or two but unfortunately they don't.' Once again, Timoshenko's front was in free fall. On 4 July, Stalin sarcastically quizzed the Marshal: 'So is it a fact that the 301st and 227th Divisions are now encircled and you're surrendering to the enemy?'

'The 227th is retreating,' replied Timoshenko pathetically, 'but the 301st – we can't find it …'

'Your guesses sound like lies. If you continue to lose divisions like this, you'll soon be commander of nothing. Divisions aren't needles and it's a very complicated matter to lose them.'

Dizzy with over-confidence, Hitler divided his forces into two: one to push across the Don to Stalingrad while the other headed southwards towards those Caucasian oilfields. When Rostov-on-Don fell, Stalin drafted another savage order: 'Not One Step Backwards', decreeing that 'panic-mongers and cowards must be liquidated on the spot' and 'blocking units' must be formed behind the lines to kill waverers. None the less, Hitler's southern Army Group A broke into the Caucasus. On 4 and 5 August, Stalin, Beria and Molotov spent most of the nights in the office as the Germans took Voroshilovsk (Stravropol), racing towards Grozny and Ordzhonikidze (Vladikavkaz), in the Caucasus and, on the Volga, approached Stalingrad. Von Paulus's Sixth Army was poised to take the city and split Russia in two.

* * *

On 12 August, amidst the calamitous stirrings of the decisive battle of the entire war, Winston Churchill arrived in Moscow to tell Stalin that there would be no Second Front soon, a mission he compared to 'carrying a lump of ice to the North Pole'. Molotov met him at the airport and then escorted him to the residence he had been assigned. On the way, Churchill noticed that the Packard's windows were over two inches thick:

'It's more prudent,' said Molotov. Stalin and Beria took Churchill's visit very seriously, assigning him a bodyguard of 120. The defences around the Kremlin were redoubled. Stalin gave up his own house, Kuntsevo, dacha No. 7. It is a mark of Soviet obscurity that the British were never told and it has taken sixty years to emerge. Perhaps Stalin was repaying Churchill in kind for lending *his* dacha, Chequers, to Molotov.

37

Churchill Visits Stalin:
Marlborough vs Wellington

A strapping aide-de-camp of a princely family, according to Churchill, acted as his host at Kuntsevo. Churchill was shown into Stalin's dining room, where the long table was laden with 'every delicacy and stimulant that supreme power can command'. The British curiously explored.* Without realizing it, Churchill described Stalin's home: surrounded by a stockade, fifteen feet high, guarded on both sides, it was a 'fine large house standing in its own extensive lawns and gardens in a fir wood of about twenty acres. There were agreeable walks ... fountains ... and a large glass tank with ... goldfish. I was conducted through a spacious reception room to a bedroom and bathroom† of almost equal size. Blazing almost dazzling electric lights displayed the spotless cleanliness.'

Within three hours, Churchill, Harriman, and the British Ambassador Sir Archibald Clark Kerr, were driven into the Kremlin to meet with Stalin, Molotov and Voroshilov who, banned from front-line commands, now became the *Vozhd*'s diplomatic gimp, a comedic sideshow to Stalin's diplomatic double act with Molotov. Churchill decided to declare the bad news first: no Second Front that year. Stalin, faced with a fight for his life on the Volga, reacted sarcastically:

'You can't win wars without taking risks,' he said and later: 'You mustn't be so afraid of the Germans.' Churchill growled that

---

* Kuntsevo's furniture was 'stylish "Utility", sumptuous and brightly coloured', thought a young British diplomat, John Reed, 'vulgarly furnished and possessed of every convenience a Soviet commissar's heart could desire. Even the lavatories were modern and ... clean.' A hundred yards from the house was Stalin's new air-raid shelter of the 'latest and most luxurious type', with lifts descending ninety feet into the ground where there were eight or ten rooms inside a concrete box of massive thickness, divided by sliding doors. 'The whole airconditioned and execrably furnished ... like some monstrous ... Lyons Corner House,' wrote Reed.

† The bathrooms in all Stalin's dachas were capacious with the baths specially constructed to fit his precise height.

Britain had fought alone in 1940. Having got the worst bit out of the way, Churchill revealed that the British and Americans were about to launch Operation Torch to seize North Africa, which he illustrated with the drawing of a soft-bellied crocodile and the big globe that stood in the room adjacent to Stalin's office. In an impressive demonstration of his geopolitical instincts, Stalin immediately rattled off the reasons that this operation made sense. This, wrote Churchill, 'showed the Russian Dictator's swift and complete mastery' of military strategy. Then Stalin surprised them more: 'Let God help the success of this enterprise!'

The next morning, Churchill met that 'urbane, rigid diplomatist' Molotov alone to warn him: 'Stalin will make a great mistake to treat us roughly when we have come so far.'

'Stalin's a very wise man,' Molotov replied. 'You may be sure that, however he argues, he understands all.'

At eleven, Stalin and Molotov, accompanied by the usual interpreter Pavlov, received Churchill in the Little Corner where the *Vozhd* handed his guest a memorandum attacking the West for not launching a Second Front, and again mocked British cowardice.

'I pardon that remark only on account of the bravery of Russian troops,' replied the Prime Minister, who then launched into a magnificent Churchillian soliloquy on the Western commitment to the war. When Churchill poked his unsatisfactory interpreter Dunlop: 'Did you tell him this? Did you tell him that?', Stalin finally smiled:

'Your words are of no importance. What's important is your spirit.' But the conviviality was ice-thin: Stalin's insults infuriated Churchill, who afterwards stalked Kuntsevo, no stranger to gloom and malice, threatening to go home.

Still angry and sullen, Churchill had to appear at the Catherine Hall for the Bacchanalian banquet Stalin held in his honour. Stalin sat in the centre with Churchill on his right, Harriman on his left, then an interpreter followed by General Alan Brooke, Chief of Imperial General Staff, and Voroshilov. Molotov kept the toasts coming for over three hours as nineteen courses were piled on to the table, which was 'groaning with every description of hors d'oeuvre and fish etc.,' wrote Brooke, 'a complete orgy ... Among the many fish dishes was a small suckling pig ... He was never eaten and, as the evening slipped by, his black eye remained fixed on me, and the orange peel mouth developed a sardonic smile!'

Stalin was at his most charming, making it clear that 'he wanted to make amends', thought Clark Kerr, 'but the PM ... cold-shouldered him'. Stalin tried backhanded flattery:

'Some years ago, we had a visit from Lady Astor,' Stalin recounted mischievously. When she suggested inviting Lloyd George to Russia, Stalin had replied: 'Why should we invite ... the head of the Intervention?' Lady Astor corrected him: 'That's not true ... It was Churchill.' Stalin told Astor: 'If a great crisis comes, the English ... might turn to the old warhorse.' Besides, he added, 'we like a downright enemy better than a false friend.'

'Have you forgiven me?' asked Churchill.

'All that is in the past,' replied the ex-seminarian, 'and the past belongs to God. History will judge us.' There was then a crash as Churchill's bodyguard, Commander Thompson, slumped backwards knocking the ice-cream out of a waiter's hand, which then narrowly missed Stalin himself.

'Then,' recorded the Soviet interpeter Pavlov portentously in his notes, 'Stalin spoke.' During the Supremo's toasts, Voroshilov, whom Brooke thought 'a fine hearty old soul, willing to talk about anything with great vivacity' though with the military expertise of a 'child', spotted the Ulsterman was drinking water instead of vodka. Voroshilov ordered yellow pepper vodka, with an ominous chilli floating in it, with which he filled both their glasses:

'No heel taps,' he said – but Brooke managed to sip his glass. Voroshilov then downed two glasses of this firewater: 'The result did not take long to show itself. His forehead broke out in beads of perspiration which soon started to flow down his face. He became sullen and quiet sitting with a fixed stare straight to his front and I wondered whether the moment had arrived for him to slip under the table. No, he retained his seat ...' But just as this cherubic inebriate subsided into peppery oblivion, Stalin, who noticed everything, 'descended straight on him' with a toast the irony of which was missed by the Westerners.

'One of the main organizers of the Red Army was Marshal Voroshilov and he, Stalin, would like to raise a toast to Marshal Voroshilov.' Stalin grinned roguishly like a wicked old satyr because, as Molotov and the others knew well, it was only three months since he had denounced Voroshilov's 'bankruptcy'. Voroshilov struggled to his feet, holding on tightly to the table with both hands, 'swaying gently backwards and forwards with a distant and vacant look in his eyes'. When Stalin raised his toast, Voroshilov tried to focus and then lurched forward, just managing to clink glasses. As Stalin swaggered off to toast Shaposhnikov, 'Voroshilov, with a deep sigh, sank back on to his chair.'

After dinner, Stalin invited Churchill to watch a film – *The German Rout before Moscow* – but Churchill was too angry and tired. He said goodbye and was halfway across the crowded room before Stalin hurried after him and accompanied him to his car.

Churchill awoke as sulky as 'a spoilt child' according to Clark Kerr who arrived at the dacha to discover that 'the PM had decided to pack up and go'. Sporting 'a preposterous ten-gallon hat', surely the most bizarre headgear ever seen at Kuntsevo, Churchill stomped into the garden and turned his back on Clark Kerr who found himself addressing 'a pink and swollen neck'. The Ambassador explained that Churchill 'was an aristocrat and a man of the world and he expected these people to be like him. They weren't. They were straight from the plough or the lathe.'

'This man has insulted me,' retorted Churchill. 'From now on, he can fight his battles alone.' Finally he stopped: 'Well, and what do you want me to do?'

Within the hour, Churchill's entourage was calling the Kremlin to ask for a tête-à-tête with Stalin. The only response was that 'Stalin was out walking', surely a diplomatic promenade since Churchill's tantrum coincided with momentous events that would lead directly to the Battle of Stalingrad: at 4.30 that morning, the German Sixth Army had attacked and smashed the Fourth Tank Army in the loop of the Don River, a more immediate crisis than a pinguid Englishman fulminating in a 'ten-gallon hat'.

At 6 p.m., Stalin agreed to meet. Churchill bade Stalin goodbye in the Little Corner. When he was about to leave, Stalin 'seemed embarrassed' and then asked when they would meet again: 'Why don't you come to my house and have a little drink?'

'I replied,' wrote Churchill, 'that I was in principle always in favour of such a policy.' So Stalin led Churchill and his interpreter, Major Birse, 'through many passages and rooms till we came out into a still roadway within the Kremlin and in a couple of hundred yards gained the apartment where he lived.' Stalin showed the Englishman round his 'simple, dignified' four-room apartment with its empty bookshelves: the library was in Kuibyshev. A housekeeper, not Valechka, since Churchill described her as 'ancient', started to lay up dinner in the dining room. Stalin had planned this dinner: that afternoon, Alexandra Nakashidze called Zubalovo and announced that Stalin had ordered Svetlana to be ready that evening 'to be shown off to Churchill'. Stalin brought the conversation round to daughters. Churchill said his daughter Sarah was a redhead. So is mine, said Stalin who had his cue: he asked the housekeeper to get Svetlana.

A 'handsome red-haired girl' arrived and kissed her father, who rather ostentatiously presented her with a little present. He patted her on the head: 'She's a redhead,' he smiled. Churchill said he had been a redhead as a young man.

'My father,' wrote Svetlana, 'was in one of those amiable and hospitable moods when he could charm anyone.' She helped lay the table while Stalin uncorked the wine. Svetlana hoped to stay for dinner but when the conversation returned to 'guns and howitzers', Stalin kissed her and 'told me to go about my business'. She was disappointed but dutifully disappeared.

'Why shouldn't we have Molotov?' Stalin asked. 'He's worrying about the communiqué. We could settle it here. There's one thing about Molotov – he can drink.' When Molotov joined them, followed by a parade of heavy dishes, culminating in the inevitable suckling pig, Stalin started to tease his Foreign Commissar 'unmercifully'. Churchill joined in:

'Was Mr Stalin aware that his Foreign Secretary on his recent visit to Washington had said he was determined to pay a visit to New York entirely by himself and that the delay in his return was not due to any defect in the aeroplane but because he was off on his own?'

Molotov frowned, Churchill noticed, not realizing he may have been sowing the seeds of mistrust that almost cost Molotov his life. But Stalin's face lit with merriment: 'It was not to New York he went. He went to Chicago where the other gangsters live.'

'Have the stresses of this war been as bad to you personally as carrying through the policy of collective farms,' Churchill asked.

'Oh no,' replied Stalin revealingly. That had been 'a terrible struggle'.

Churchill invited Stalin to London and the *Vozhd* recalled his visit in 1907 with Lenin, Gorky and Trotsky. On the subject of great historical figures, Churchill praised his ancestor the Duke of Marlborough as an inspiration for he, 'in his time, put an end to the danger to European freedom during the War of Spanish

Succession'. Churchill got 'carried away' praising Marlborough's military brilliance. But a roguish 'smile loomed on Stalin's face':

'I think Britain had a more talented military leader,' teased Stalin, 'in the person of Wellington who crushed Napoleon who presented the greatest danger in History.' By 1.30 a.m., they had not yet started eating but Stalin popped out, probably to hear the latest dire news from the Caucasus. When Sir Alexander Cadogan, Permanent Under-Secretary at the Foreign Office, arrived with a draft of the press release, Stalin offered him the suckling pig. 'When my friend excused himself,' wrote Churchill, 'our host fell upon the victim single-handedly.' The dinner finally ended around 3 a.m. Churchill begged Molotov not to see him off at dawn for he 'was clearly tired out'.

'Do you really think I would fail to be there?' replied Molotov urbanely.

Back at Kuntsevo, Churchill lay full length on Stalin's sofa, 'started to chuckle and to stick a pair of gay legs in the air: Stalin had been splendid ... What a pleasure it was to work with "that great man".' As before Churchill, undressed to reveal a 'skimpy crumpled vest' whence 'a pair of wrinkled creamy buttocks protruded', he continued to rave as he finally climbed into a bath, 'Stalin this, Stalin that.' It was already dawn; the alliance was saved; Molotov arrived to take him to the airport.

38

Stalingrad and the Caucasus:
Beria and Kaganovich at War

Stalin recuperated from his Churchillian carousal at home but at 11.30 p.m., he arrived at the office to face the deteriorating crisis in the North Caucasus where the Germans were approaching Ordzhonikidze and Grozny. Budyonny, commander of the North Caucasus Front, had just been joined by Kaganovich who had demanded the right to redeem himself at the front after being sacked as railway boss. Stalin agreed, saying he 'knows the North Caucasus well and got on well with Budyonny in the Civil War'. The bow-legged Cossack and the Jewish Iron Commissar struggled to stop the Germans. Budyonny lost none of 'his dash and sense of irony', refusing to go into his shelter during raids: 'Never mind: let them bomb!' but 'the Locomotive' at war was not a pretty sight.

Surrounded by a 'suite of officers from his personal bodyguard and consultants from Moscow ... toadies, wranglers and intriguers', working all night in a permanent state of bellowing hysteria, always playing with his trademark worry-beads or a key chain, Kaganovich fancied himself 'a great strategist ... issuing orders all on his own' and insisted on interfering in every military plan, setting impossible deadlines, shouting, 'Report personally ... on the fulfilment of the order – or else!' When some trucks blocked the path of his limousine, 'Lazarus,' as his officers nicknamed him, went berserk, bellowing: 'Demote! Arrest! Court martial! Shoot!' But these bawlings did not stop the Germans:

'What's the good of a defence ridge if it isn't defended?' Stalin reprimanded Kaganovich. 'And it seems you have not managed to turn the situation around even where there is no panic and the troops fight quite well.'

Kaganovich however came closer to war than many others. He was hit by shrapnel in the hand, a badge of honour of which he was deeply proud. He was the only Politburo member to be wounded.* When Kaganovich flew back to Moscow for meetings, Stalin, whom he regarded as 'our father', tenderly inquired about his health and then toasted his wound. However, he was also incensed that one of his closest comrades had risked his life in this way.

As the Germans pushed southwards, Stalin feared the Transcaucasus Front would collapse, yielding the oilfields, possibly bringing Turkey into the war, and tempting the restless Caucasian peoples to rebel. Four days after Churchill's departure, Stalin turned to Beria:

'Lavrenti Pavlovich,' he respectfully addressed him. 'Take with you whoever you like and all the armaments you think necessary, but please stop the Germans.' As the Germans took Mount Elbrus, Beria and Merkulov recruited Stalin's staff officer, Shtemenko, ordered Sudoplatov to bring 150 Georgian Alpinists, assembled his flashy entourage, as well as his son Sergo, aged eighteen – and all flew down in a fleet of American C-47s stopping in Tiflis on the way. The generals were contemplating a strategic abandonment of Ordzhonikidze but on the 22nd, Beria, accompanied by his posse, arrived there to terrorize the Transcaucasus commanders. Charkviani, the Georgian boss, was in the room when Beria 'peered coldly round the table with a piercing stare' and told them:

'I'll break your back if you mention a word of this retreat again. You will defend the town!' When one general suggested placing 20,000 NKVD troops in the front line, Beria exploded into 'foul abuse and threatened to break my back if I ever mentioned it again'. Though Charkviani (no great admirer of Beria) thought the NKVD chief saved the day, the generals, all writing after his downfall, complained that his progress along the front was simply 'showiness and noise' which seriously disrupted their work.

Beria also had to destroy any oil that might fall into Nazi hands. Back in Moscow, Stalin summoned Nikolai Baibakov, thirty, Deputy Commissar of Oil Production, to his office. He was alone:

'Comrade Baibakov, you know Hitler wants the oil of the Caucasus. That's why I'm sending you there – you're responsible on the pain of losing your head for ensuring no oil is left behind.' But he would also 'lose his head' if he DID destroy the oil too early.

---

* He received an engraved clock from the Front to show its gratitude: it is now in the Kaganovich archive at RGASPI. Interestingly, both Leonid Brezhnev and Mikhail Suslov, who together ruled the Soviet Union for almost two decades after 1964, got to know Kaganovich on this front.

As he left, with his head spinning, Stalin added: 'Do you know that Hitler has declared that without oil, he'll lose the war?'

Beria added more gruesome threats. 'I was just weighed down by the great responsibility,' says Baibakov who was not afraid but perhaps should have been. 'I underestimated the danger of my personal position.' The correct oilfields were dynamited with minutes to spare. Baibakov kept his head.*

Beria's other mission was to stamp out the embers of treason among the ethnic groups in the North Caucasus. Hence he set up his own NKVD command. As a Georgian Mingrel brought up among non-Georgian Abkhazians, Beria possessed all the prejudices of one tiny Caucasian people for another. The Georgians had always been particularly suspicious of Moslem peoples like the Chechens: in Grozny, Beria investigated the reports that some Chechens had greeted the Germans with open arms. Sergo Beria, who accompanied his father, wrote that they sent delegations to show their support for Moscow, promising to fight like their national hero, Shamyl. Since Shamyl had defied Russia for thirty years, this analogy did their cause no good at all. Beria's cheerfulness with the Chechens concealed his distrust.

Beria descended on Kaganovich and Budyonny in Novorossisk but was not impressed by their demeanour: 'These two idiots disorganized everything,' wrote Sergo Beria, exaggerating somewhat. They found Budyonny 'dead drunk' and in 'a deep torpor' while Kaganovich was 'sober' but 'trembled like a leaf and crawled on his knees before my father'.

'Don't make such an exhibition of yourself,' Beria told Kaganovich.

The German advance ebbed outside Ordzhonikidze and Grozny, undermined by the Soviet resistance at Stalingrad. Beria returned triumphant to Moscow where Stalin, who was viciously jealous of anyone else's military glory, overheard him boasting to Malenkov of his exploits.

---

* Baibakov's interview for this book has been invaluable as he is one of the last of Stalin's Ministers still living. Baibakov became a perennial member of the Soviet Government: Stalin appointed him Commissar for Oil in 1944 and later he ran Gosplan, the main economic agency, except for a short interval, until being sacked by Gorbachev in the eighties. It is a mark of the obsolescence of Soviet economics that the young men Stalin appointed were still running it forty years later. At the time of writing, this tireless nonagenerian is working in the oil industry, taking conference calls with Stalinist dynamism while wearing his medals, beneath a portrait of Lenin.

'Now Beria's going to imagine he's a military leader,' Stalin growled to Shaposhnikov. Beria recommended the sacking of Budyonny, who returned to Moscow from his last active command to be placed in charge of the cavalry. But he appealed to Stalin:

'My soul longs to be in battle. Let me go to Stalingrad!' Stalingrad was indeed about to become the battle of battles, the focus of the world.

* * *

The Germans attacked by land and devastated Stalin's city from the sky, destroying that industrial leviathan in an infernal bombardment that converted its stark Stalinist factories into a primeval landscape of caves and canyons. Stalin, in the office in the early hours, was beside himself, berating his envoys to Stalingrad, Malenkov and Chief of Staff Vasilevsky: 'The enemy broke through ... with small forces. You have enough forces to annihilate the enemy ... Mobilize armoured trains ... Use smoke-screens ... Fight day and night ... The most important thing now is – don't panic, don't fear the impudent enemy and keep up your confidence in our success.'

The gravity of Stalingrad finally concentrated Stalin's mind and brought about a revolution in his conduct of the war. Now he realized that the road to survival and glory lay with professional generals instead of his own impatient amateurism and his bungling cavalrymen. On 27 August, he ordered Zhukov to rush to Stalingrad and promoted him to Deputy Supreme Commander. Zhukov refused the promotion:

'My character wouldn't let us work together.'

'Disaster threatens the country,' replied Stalin. 'We must save the Motherland by every possible means, no matter the sacrifice. What of our characters? Let's subordinate them to the interests of the Motherland. When will you leave?'

'I need a day.'

'Well, that's fine. But aren't you hungry? It wouldn't hurt to have a little refreshment.' Tea and cakes were brought in to celebrate the beginning of the war's most successful partnership.

Zhukov met up with Vasilevsky in Stalingrad where he found the Germans creeping into the city. Stalin demanded counter-attacks but his forces were not yet up to it. Stalin was so anxious that he now slept on a couch in his office with Poskrebyshev waking him every two hours. He was so pale, tired and skinny that Poskrebyshev let him sleep an extra half-hour because he had not the heart to wake him: 'A philanthropist all of a sudden. Get Vasilevsky on the line. Quick! The bald philanthropist!'

Stalin yelled at Vasilevsky: 'What's the matter with them? Don't they understand if we surrender Stalingrad, the south of the country'll be cut off from the centre and we'll probably not be able to defend it? Don't they realize that this isn't only a catastrophe for Stalingrad? We'd lose our main waterway and soon our oil too!' But its importance was no longer merely strategic: Stalingrad bore his name because it had played a formative part in his life. There, at Tsaritsyn in 1918, he had gained his confidence as a man of action, learned how to govern by terror, won Lenin's trust and Trotsky's hatred. At the 'Red Verdun', he had met his cronies, from Voroshilov to Budyonny, and embarked on his marriage with Nadya.

'I think there's still a chance we won't lose the city,' replied Vasilevsky carefully. Stalin rang Zhukov and ordered the attack: 'Delay's equivalent to a crime.' When Zhukov reported that there would be a delay, Stalin sneered: 'Do you think the enemy's going to wait until you bestir yourselves?'

At dawn the Russians attacked again – but made limited gains. The Germans had almost taken the city but one force stood in their way: the 62nd Army under General Vasily Chuikov, spiky-haired, snub-nosed, gold-fanged, clung on to the Volga's west bank, commanding from dugouts and fighting in the skeletal ruins of an apocalyptic industrial landscape, supplied only by ferryboats that crossed the burning Volga in which the destiny of Russia was reflected. The valour, nobility, despair and brutality is best described in Vasily Grossman's epic *Life and Fate*. They fought with modern weapons and ancient ones, sniper rifles and grenades, spades, pipes and fingers, dying to win time:

'Blood,' said Chuikov, 'is time.'

The attention of virtually every minute of Stalin's day was concentrated on one of the most intense battles ever fought: Chuikov's direct commanders were General Andrei Yeremenko and Commissar Khrushchev, now back in favour, but it was much too important to be left to them. Stalin himself supervised the front with Zhukov and Vasilevsky in active command while Malenkov acted as his personal spy. They would appear in Yeremenko's dugout. 'I'd notice Vasilevsky and Malenkov whispering,' said Khrushchev, 'preparing to denounce someone.'

Malenkov summoned officers to be dressed down. They arrived in the dugout to find a 'short man with a soft puffy face in a tunic' alongside ruffians like Zhukov and Yeremenko. During one dressing-down, Malenkov found himself addressing Vasily Stalin who, though banned from flying active missions himself, was commanding a division:

'Colonel Stalin!' Malenkov said. 'The combat performance of your flyers is revolting …' Then he turned to another officer: 'And you, the general in the skull-cap? Did you intend to fight or simply play around?' After Malenkov had gone, Khrushchev and Yeremenko would be left alone again in their dugout 'in an eerie silence … like a forest after a storm'. It was Khrushchev's finest hour,* living in his dugout building the friendships with generals that were to be so useful after Stalin's death.

On 12 September, the rival commanders of Stalingrad flew simultaneously to see their respective Supremos with a neat dictatorial symmetry. As von Paulus met the *Führer* at his *Werwolf* headquarters, a stockade of wooden cabins and bunkers at Vinnitsa, Zhukov and Vasilevsky were on their way to see their *Vozhd*. As Hitler ordered von Paulus to 'capture as quickly as possible the whole of Stalingrad', Zhukov and Malenkov, the rough-hewn soldier and the silky-palmed courtier, presented a report for Stalin proposing further offensives 'to grind down the enemy … and simultaneously to prepare … a more powerful blow'. But what? Stalin looked at his own map and studied it quietly, ignoring the soldiers for a long moment, lost in his thoughts.

Zhukov and Vasilevsky retreated from the green baize table, talking to one another in low voices. There might be 'some other solution'.

'And what does "another solution" mean?' asked Stalin, suddenly raising his head. 'I never thought he had such a keen ear,' noted Zhukov. Before the generals could answer, Stalin added: 'Go over to the General Staff and think over carefully what must be done . . We'll meet here at nine tomorrow night.' Victory has many fathers and many claimed paternity for Stalingrad but it was really the child of the unique collaboration between Stalin, Vasilevsky and Zhukov, all gifted in their own ways.

---

* When Khrushchev was in power, he ordered his cronies like Yeremenko to inflate his heroic role at Stalingrad, just like Stalin himself.

At 10 p.m. on 13 September, Stalin welcomed Zhukov and Vasilevsky to his study with an unusual gesture – a handshake: 'Well, what are your views? What have you come up with? Who's making the report?'

'Either of us,' Vasilevsky replied. They handed over their map which showed their basic plan to launch a massive offensive against the German flanks, held by the weaker Romanian forces, smashing into their rear and linking up to encircle them: Operation Uranus. Just at this moment, the German attack, ordered by Hitler at Vinnitsa earlier that day, descended on the embattled 62nd Army. Poskrebyshev entered the room – Yeremenko was on the line from Stalingrad. Chuikov was just maintaining his bare-knuckle grip on the west bank of the Volga while Stavka prepared the operation. Sending both generals straight back to Stalingrad to reconnoitre Uranus, Stalin said portentously:

'No one else knows what we three have discussed here. No one beyond the three of us is to know about it for the time being.'

On 9 October, Stalin restored the unitary command of the armies to the generals. He again celebrated by shaking hands with Zhukov and Vasilevsky, whom he used as special representatives at the fronts: he did not like them 'sitting around' in Moscow. Chief of Staff since May, Alexander Vasilevsky, aged forty-seven, was the third of the extraordinary Stalingrad team. In many ways, he was closer to Stalin even than Zhukov.

* * *

Broad-shouldered and barrel-chested but with a sensitive expression and a gentle, courtly charm, Vasilevsky had been groomed by Shaposhnikov. This outstanding staff officer was his successor not only professionally but also as the sole gentleman among cut-throats, and as Stalin's special confidant. His decency puzzled, impressed and amused Stalin who so lacked it himself:

'You command so many armies,' he reflected, 'yet you wouldn't hurt a fly.' Vasilevsky also hailed from a vanished world that fascinated Stalin: his father had been a prosperous village priest on the Volga and he was educated for the priesthood but became a captain in the Tsar's army. When he joined the Red Army, he had had to forsake his priest-father and cut off relations. After meetings, Stalin frequently asked Vasilevsky to stay behind to discuss whether he was tempted by the priesthood: 'Well, well, I didn't want you to be,' laughed Stalin. 'That's clear. But Mikoyan and I wanted to be priests but were rejected. Until now, I can't understand why!' Then: 'Did your religious education do anything for you?'

'No knowledge is entirely wasted,' Vasilevsky replied cautiously: 'Some of it turned out to be useful in military life.'

'The thing priests teach best, is how to understand people,' mused Stalin, who once said his father was a priest. Perhaps he sometimes thought about his own paternity for around this time, he told Vasilevsky: 'One shouldn't forget one's parents.' On a later occasion he asked him: 'When did you last see your parents?'

'I've forsaken them,' replied the General, worried that this was a test. 'My father's a priest, Comrade Stalin.'

'But is he a counter-revolutionary?'

'No, Comrade Stalin, he believes in God as a priest but he's not a counter-revolutionary.'

'When the war's quieter, I think you should take a plane, visit your parents and ask for their forgiveness.' Stalin did not forget Vasilevsky's father:

'Did you ever fly and see your parents and ask their blessing?' he asked later.

'Yes, Comrade Stalin,' replied Vasilevsky.

'It'll be a long time before you pay off your debt to me.' Stalin then opened his safe and showed him some papers. They were money orders in Stalin's own name that had been sent to Vasilevsky's father throughout the war. The son, amazed and somewhat moved, thanked Stalin profusely. Now, Vasilevsky's special responsibility was Stalingrad.

* * *

The two messianic tyrants almost simultaneously prepared their peoples for victory. 'There will be a holiday on our street too,' Stalin hinted in his 7 November speech. The next day, Hitler boasted to his people:

'I wanted to reach the Volga ... at a particular city. By chance it bore the name of Stalin himself ... I wanted to capture it and ... we have as good as got it!'

The Little Corner was now a-quiver with tension. Stalin agonized that the Germans would guess what was afoot. On the 11th he was worrying that he did not have enough aircraft. On the 13th, as von Paulus launched a last attempt to dislodge Chuikov, now holding a ruined splinter of territory only fifty yards deep, Zhukov and Vasilevsky flew into Moscow for a final briefing. 'By the way Stalin smoked his pipe, smoothed his moustache and never interrupted once, we could see he was pleased,' wrote Zhukov. Afterwards, Vasilevsky returned to Stalingrad.

On the 18th, Stalin, accompanied by Beria, Molotov, Malenkov, and Zhukov, who remained to command Operation Mars* before Moscow, worked in the Little Corner until 11.50 p.m. Three hours before the attack, the three fronts facing Stalingrad, under Generals Yeremenko, Rokossovsky and Vatutin, were informed they were to attack imminently. Presumably Stalin and his comrades then went to dinner or watched a movie to pass the time. Stalin rarely slept before 4 a.m. – 'the need just passed', he later told Churchill – so he surely stayed up to hear that the troops had gone in. At 7.20 on the misty morning of 19 November, the 3,500 guns on the northern sector opened up. When this Jupiterian thunderclap was unleashed, the earth shook thirty miles away. A million men, 13,541 guns, 1,400 tanks and 1,115 planes, smashed into Hitler's forces.

---

* Simultaneously with Stalingrad's Operation Uranus, Zhukov launched the forgotten Operation Mars against the Rzhev salient facing Moscow, probably his greatest defeat: hundreds of thousands of men were lost in just two days of an operation that illustrated his bold but crude style.

Part Eight

War: The Triumphant Genius, 1942–1945

39

The Supremo of Stalingrad

During Stalingrad, the Supremo usually fell asleep wearing all his clothes on the metal campbed that stood under the stairs that led to the second floor at Kuntsevo. If there was an emergency, the 'bald philanthropist' Poskrebyshev, who slept in his office, would call. He awoke around eleven when Shtemenko called from the Operations Department to give him his first report of the day. The Politburo and Staff had already been working for hours since they not only had to share Stalin's insomnia but also had their own onerous empires to run: Mikoyan worked from 10 a.m. until almost 5 a.m., napping in his office.

At noon, Stalin ate a light breakfast, served by Valechka, often remaining at home, whether at Kuntsevo or the Kremlin, to work in the early afternoon. But wherever he was, the Supremo, now sixty-three, would spend the next sixteen hours running the war. He now received bulletins from all his roving Stavka plenipotentiaries, who had to report twice a day, noon and 9 p.m.: Vasilevsky in Stalingrad was the most eagerly awaited that day. Stalin turned very nasty if his envoys neglected to report. When Vasilevsky once failed to do so, Stalin wrote:

> It's already 3.30 ... and you have not yet deigned to report ... You cannot use the excuse that you have no time as Zhukov is doing just as much at the front as you yet he sends his report every day. The difference between you and Zhukov is that he is disciplined ... whereas you lack discipline ... I am warning you for the last time that if you allow yourself to forget your duty ... once more, you will be removed as Chief of General Staff and sent to the front.

Malenkov was always punctilious in his reports but even the meticulous Zhdanov was sometimes distracted by battle, provoking another reprimand: 'It's extremely strange that Comrade Zhdanov feels no need to come to the phone or to ask us for mutual advice at this dangerous time for Leningrad.' Independence was dangerous in Stalin's eyes.

At 4 p.m., General Alexei Antonov, 'young, very handsome, dark and lithe', who became his trusted Chief of Operations, after Vasilevsky's promotion, and after trying a series of officers all of whom were swiftly sacked, arrived with the next report. Antonov was a 'peerlessly able general and a man of great culture and charm', wrote Zhukov. Stalin was a stickler for accurate reporting and would, recalled Shtemenko, 'not tolerate the slightest ... embellishment'. Antonov handled him deftly: always calm, 'a master at assessing the situation', he graded the urgency of his files by colour and 'knew when to say, "Give me the green folder".' Then Stalin smilingly replied: 'Well now, let's look at your "green file".'

In the early evening, Stalin arrived in the Kremlin in his convoy of speeding Packards or else walked downstairs from his flat to the Little Corner where the 'cosy' anteroom, with its comfortable armchairs, strictly policed by Poskrebyshev, was already full. Visitors found themselves in a world of control, sparseness and cleanliness. There was nothing unnecessary anywhere. Everyone had shown their papers repeatedly and been searched for weapons. Even Zhukov had to surrender his pistol. 'The inspection was repeated over and over again.' Poskrebyshev, now in NKVD General's uniform, greeted them at his desk. They waited in silence though regulars greeted one another before falling quiet. It was tense. Those who had never met Stalin before were full of anticipation but as one colonel recalled, 'I noticed that those ... *not* here for the first time, were considerably more perturbed than those ... here for the first time.'

At around 8 p.m., when Stalin arrived, a murmur passed through the room. He said nothing, but nodded at some. The colonel noticed 'my neighbour wiped drops of sweat from his brow and dried his hands on a handkerchief'. A small room, a cubbyhole, contained the last bodyguards at a desk before the office. Stalin entered that 'bright spacious room', with its long green table. At the other end of the room was his desk, on which there was always a heap of documents in their *papki*, a broad-frequency telephone, a line of different-coloured telephones, a pile of sharpened pencils. Behind the desk, there was a door that led to Stalin's own lavatory and the signal room which contained easy chairs, all the Baudot and telegraph equipment to connect

Stalin to the fronts, and the famous globe at which he had discussed Operation Torch with Churchill.

* * *

That night, Molotov, Beria and Malenkov, the perennial three-some, were waiting with Voroshilov and Kaganovich. Stalin nodded and opened the GKO with no chit-chat; its sessions continued until he left many hours later. Stalin sat at his desk and then paced up and down, returning to get his Herzogovina Flor cigarettes which he broke into pieces to fill his pipe. The civilians, as always, sat with their backs against the wall, looking up at the new portraits of Suvorov and Kutuzov while the generals sat on the other side of the table, looking up at Marx and Lenin, a deployment that reflected the constant war between them. The generals immediately spread their maps on the table and Stalin continued his pacing, waddling somewhat. 'He would stop in front of the person he was addressing and look straight into his face' with what Zhukov called a 'clear tenacious gaze that seemed to envelop and pierce through the visitor'.

Poskrebyshev began calling in the experts from the anteroom: 'soon my neighbour also rose ... the receptionist called him by name, he went livid, wiped his trembling hands on his handker-chief, picked up his file ... and went with hesitant steps.' As he showed them in, Poskrebyshev advised:

'Don't get excited. Don't think about disagreeing with anything. Comrade Stalin knows everything.' The visitor must report quickly, no small talk, then leave. Inside the room, the grim *troika* of Molotov, Beria and Malenkov swivelled to peer coolly at the newcomer.

Stalin exuded power and energy. 'One felt oppressed by Stalin's power,' wrote his new Railways Commissar who reported to him hundreds of times, 'but also by his phenomenal memory and the fact he knew so much. He made one feel even less important than one was.' Stalin drove the pace, restless, fidgeting, never far from an eruption. Most of the time he was laconic, tireless and icily cold. If he was displeased, wrote Zhukov, 'he lost his temper and objectivity failed him'.

The visitors could always sense the danger, yet they were also surprised by the genuinely collegiate argument at these sessions. Mikoyan looked back on the 'wonderfully friendly atmosphere' among the magnates during the first three years of the war. The country was run in the form of the GKO through Stalin's meetings with key leaders in the presence of whoever was in his office – usually the GKO with Mikoyan, and, later, Zhdanov, Kaganovich and Voznesensky.

'Sharp arguments arose,' recalled Zhukov, with 'views expressed in definite and sharp terms' as Stalin paced up and down. Stalin would ask the generals' opinions: 'Stalin listened more' when 'they disagreed. I suspect', thought Admiral Kuznetsov, 'he even liked people who had their own point of view and weren't afraid to stand up for it.' Having created an environment of boot-licking idolatry, Stalin was irritated by it.

'What's the point of talking to you?' he would shout. 'Whatever I say, you reply, "Yes Comrade Stalin; of course, Comrade Stalin … wise decision, Comrade Stalin."' The generals noticed how 'his associates always agreed with him', while the generals could argue, though they had to be very careful. But Molotov and the brash newcomer Voznesensky did argue with him: 'The discussions were frank,' recalled Mikoyan. When Stalin, reading one of Churchill's letters, said the Englishman thought 'he had saddled the horse and now he can enjoy a free ride … Am I right, Vyacheslav?', Molotov replied:

'I don't think so.' Zhukov 'witnessed arguments and … stubborn resistance … especially from Molotov when the situation got to the point where Stalin had to raise his voice and was even beside himself, while Molotov merely stood up with a smile and stuck to his point of view.' When Stalin asked Khrulev to take over the railways, he tolerated his refusal: 'I don't think you respect me, refusing my proposal,' he said, indulging the quartermaster, one of his favourites. Amidst rows, Stalin insisted 'Come to the point' or 'Make yourself clear!'

Once Stalin had formed his opinion and argument had ceased, he appointed a man to do the job with the usual death threat as an added incentive. 'This very severe man controlled the fulfilment of every order,' recalls Baibakov, the oil engineer, 'When he gave the command, he always helped you to carry it out so you received every possible means necessary to do it. Hence I wasn't scared of Stalin – we were direct with one another. I fulfilled my tasks.' But Stalin had a 'knack for detecting weak spots in reports'. Woe betide anyone who appeared before him without mastery of their front. 'He would at once drop his voice ominously and say, "Don't you know? What are you doing then?"'

Operation Uranus seemed to refresh Stalin who, observed Khrushchev, started to act 'like a real soldier', considering himself 'a great military strategist'. He was never a general let alone a military genius but, according to Zhukov, who knew better than anyone, this 'outstanding organizer ... displayed his ability as Supremo starting with Stalingrad'. He 'mastered the technique of organizing front operations ... and guided them with skill, thoroughly understanding complicated strategic questions', always displaying his 'natural intelligence ... professional intuition' and a 'tenacious memory'. He was 'many-sided and gifted' but had 'no knowledge of all the details'. Mikoyan was probably right when he summed up in his practical way that Stalin 'knew as much about military matters as a statesman should – but no more'.

* * *

At about 10 p.m., Antonov made his second report. There were limits to the friendly spirit that Mikoyan described. War was the natural state of the Bolsheviks and they were good at it. Terror and struggle, the ruling Bolshevik passions, pervaded these meetings. Stalin liberally used fear but he himself lived on his nerves: when the new Railways Commissar arrived, Stalin simply said, 'Transport is a matter of life and death ... Remember, failure to carry out ... orders means the Military Tribunal', at which the young man felt 'a chill run down my spine'. When a train was lost in the spaghetti of fronts and railways, Stalin threatened, 'If you don't find it as general, you'll be going to the front as a private.' Seconds later the Commissar, 'white as a sheet', was being shown out by Poskrebyshev who added,

'See you don't slip up. The Boss's at the end of his tether.' Stalin was always pacing up and down. There were various warning signals of a black temper: if the pipe was unlit, it was a bad omen. If Stalin put it down, an explosion was imminent. Yet if he stroked his moustache with the mouthpiece of the pipe, this meant he was pleased. The pipe was both a prop and a weather vane.* His tempers were terrifying: 'he virtually changed before one's eyes,' wrote Zhukov, 'turning pale, a bitter expression in his eyes, his

---

* As the war went on, it became a symbol of his avuncular image in the West – Uncle Joe – and statesmen tended to send him pipes as presents. Maisky, Ambassador to London, for example, wrote to Stalin: 'After Mr Kerr [British Ambassador] gave you a pipe and it was reported in the press, I was presented with pipes for you from two firms ... and I send herewith an example for you ...'

gaze heavy and spiteful.' When some armies complained that they had not received their supplies, Stalin berated Khrulev:

'You're worse than the Enemy: you work for Hitler.'

The three guard dogs of the Little Corner, Molotov, Malenkov and Beria, 'never asked questions, just sat there and listened, sometimes jotting a note ... and looking at either Stalin or whoever came in. It was as if Stalin needed them either to deal with anything that came up or as witnesses to history.' Their purpose was to preserve the illusion of collective rule and terrorize the generals. Stalin and the magnates all regarded themselves as amateur commanders and shared their Civil War suspicion of 'military experts'.

'Look at an old coachman,' Mekhlis explained. 'They love and pity the animals but the whip is always ready. The horse sees it and draws its own conclusions.' There in a nutshell, from one of Stalin's mini-dictators, was the essence of the Supremo's style of command. 'We could all remember 1937,' said Zhukov. If anything went wrong, they knew 'you'd end up in Beria's hands and Beria was always present during my meetings with Stalin'. The generals' sins were recorded: Mekhlis had accused Koniev of having kulak parents in 1938. Rokossovsky and Meretskov were naturally keen not to return to Beria's torture chambers. Stalin received information, complaints and denunciations from the secret police and from his generals.

When they wrote their memoirs in the sixties, the generals presented themselves as Beria's innocent victims. They were certainly under the constant threat of arrest but were themselves avid denouncers. Timoshenko had denounced Budyonny and Khrushchev. Even now Operation Uranus was launched in a fever of denunciations: Golikov (the hapless pre-war spymaster), denounced the commander Yeremenko. Stalin simultaneously used Malenkov to watch Khrushchev and Yeremenko. When Stalin accused Khrushchev of wanting to surrender Stalingrad, the Commissar started to distrust his own staff. But Khrushchev himself was no slouch at denouncing generals, having blamed Kharkov on Timoshenko. Simultaneously at Stalingrad, a member of the rising General Malinovsky's staff had committed suicide, leaving a note emblazoned 'Long Live Lenin' but not mentioning Stalin: perhaps Malinovsky, who had served in the Russian Legion in France during WW1, was an Enemy?

'You'd better keep an eye on Malinovsky,' Stalin ordered Khrushchev, who protected the general.

The magnates fought ferociously for power and resources with one another and with the generals. When Beria requested 50,000 extra rifles for the NKVD, General Voronov showed the request to Stalin.

'Who made this request?' he snapped.

'Comrade Beria.'

'Send for Beria.' Beria arrived and started trying to persuade Stalin, speaking in Georgian. Stalin interrupted him angrily and told him to speak Russian.

'Half'll be enough,' ruled Stalin but Beria argued back. Stalin, 'irritated to his limit', reduced the numbers again. Afterwards, Beria caught up with Voronov outside.

'Just you wait,' he hissed, 'we'll fix your guts.' Voronov hoped this was an 'Oriental joke'. It was not.

Stalin frequently acted as a conciliator in rows over resources: when he ordered that the artillery be given 900 trucks, Beria and Malenkov, who worked as a gruesome duo, caught up with Voronov. 'Take 400 trucks.'

'I'll go back and report to the Supremo,' threatened the general. Malenkov delivered the full quota of trucks.

Living in this environment of fear and competition, the magnates themselves were tormented by mutual jealousies: 'Molotov was always with Stalin,' wrote Mikoyan disdainfully, 'just sitting in the office, looking important, but really discharged from actual business.' Stalin only needed him 'as the second man, being a Russian' but kept him 'isolated'. Molotov assisted on foreign policy but lacked the responsibilities of the others. Mikoyan was one of the chief workhorses, overseeing the rear, rations, medical supplies, ammunition, the merchant navy, food, fuel, clothing for the people and armies, while also as Commissar of Foreign Trade negotiating Lend-Lease with the Allies, a stupendous portfolio. 'Only Molotov saw Stalin as often as I did,' he boasted, forgetting the tireless, omnipresent Beria.

The 'terror of the Party', Beria, who behaved like a villain in a *film noir*, blossomed in wartime,* using the Gulag's 1.7 million slave labourers to build Stalin's weapons and railways. It is

---

* His commissars included Boris Vannikov and I. F. Tevosian, both arrested and released, and D. F. Ustinov who was just thirty-three and would rise to be the ultimate master of the Soviet military-industrial complex, becoming a CC Secretary, Marshal – and the Defence Minister who would order the Soviet invasion of Afghanistan in 1979.

estimated that around 930,000 of these labourers perished during the war. But his NKVD was the pillar of Stalin's regime, representing the supremacy of the Party over the military. After General Voronov had twice defied him in front of Stalin, Beria was finally allowed to arrest him. When Voronov did not appear at a meeting, Stalin casually asked Beria:

'Is Voronov at your place?' Beria replied that he would be back in two days. The generals are said to have coined a euphemism for these terrifying interludes: 'Going to have coffee with Beria.' His minions watched the soldiers on every front, their reports pouring in to Beria and often to Stalin himself. In 1942, Stalin raised the surveillance another step by ordering Kobulov to bug Voroshilov, Budyonny – and Zhukov himself whose officers were harassed and arrested.

Yet Stalin was wary of Beria's empire-building. When Beria got Kaganovich dismissed from the railways, he tried to nominate his successor.

'Do you think I'd agree to the candidate … Beria imposes on me? I'll never agree to it …' But the railways were a constant headache and only Kaganovich, that 'real man of iron' in Stalin's admiring words, could perform the necessary miracles.

* * *

For sixteen hours, Stalin never ceased 'issuing instructions, talking on the phone, signing papers, calling in Poskrebyshev and giving him orders'. When he heard from Mikoyan and Khrulev that the soldiers were short of cigarettes, he made time during the battle of Stalingrad to telephone Akaki Mgeladze, Party boss of Abkhazia, where the tobacco was grown: 'Our soldiers have nothing to smoke! Tobacco's absolutely necessary at the front!' He personally drafted every press release, a master of succinct yet rousing phrases such as 'Blood for blood!', inserting quotations from Suvorov. Yet while jealously checking the kudos of his generals, he was punctilious in giving them credit for their victories.

Stalin's hours of pressure and work were awesome but his commissars and generals had invariably been up since dawn, a life that demanded 'enormous physical and moral resources' with 'nervous exhaustion' a real danger. Stalin legislated the lives of his generals, personally decreeing their rota of work and rest. Vasilevsky had to sleep from 4 a.m to 10 a.m. without fail. Stalin sometimes rang Vasilevsky like a strict nanny to check he was asleep. If he answered the phone, Stalin cursed him. Yet Vasilevsky found it impossible to attend Stalin's nocturnal dinners and films and then do all his work, so he had to break the rules, stationing his adjutant at the telephone to reply: 'Comrade Vasilevsky's resting until ten.' Stalin's other workhorses, Beria and Mikoyan, were expected to spend most nights with him while achieving a Herculean workload, yet they managed it, running sprawling and sleepless administrative empires on the adrenalin of war and patriotism, Bolshevik threats and the talent to survive.

Stalin drank little and expected others to be sober. Artillery general Yakovlev once arrived to report, fortified with cognac. Without raising his head from his desk, Stalin said: 'Come closer, Comrade Yakovlev.' Yakovlev stepped forward. 'Come closer.' Then: 'You're a little drunk, aren't you?'

'Yes slightly, Comrade Stalin.' Stalin said no more about it.

* * *

At midnight, Vasilevsky reported jubilantly from Stalingrad: Hitler's Romanian allies were crumbling. As he listened, Stalin called Poskrebyshev and ordered tea. When the tea arrived in a glass in a silver ornamental holder, the commissar or general, usually Antonov, fell silent. All watched Stalin's ritual as he squeezed his lemon into the tea, then slowly got up, opened the door behind his desk into the restroom, opened the cupboard, built into the wall and took out a bottle of Armenian brandy. Then he returned, poured a half a teaspoon of this into the tea, replaced the brandy, sat, stirred it and said: 'Carry on.'

In high spirits at this instant success, Stalin and his companions left the Little Corner and probably headed over to Kuntsevo for dinner and then a film, but these dinners were not the drunken carousals of later years. When the exhausted Berias and Molotovs staggered home with only a few hours until they had to start work again, Stalin read his history books on his divan until he fell asleep in the early hours.

* * *

Within four days of the launch of Operation Uranus, the German Sixth Army, 330,000 men, was encircled in what Stalin called the 'decisive moment of the war'. As the Russians tightened their grip, von Manstein's counter-attack failed to break through. The *Luftwaffe* proved incapable of supplying from the air. The encircled Germans suffered a cruel slow death from starvation, ice and dynamite. On 16 December, the Russians counter-attacked into Manstein's rear, threatening to cut off Army Group Don and break through towards Rostov. In the Little Corner, the impatient Stalin chose General Rokossovsky, not the Stalingrad commander Yeremenko, to oversee Operation Ring, the liquidation of the Sixth Army.

'Why don't you say anything?' he asked Zhukov, who had frowned.

'Yeremenko will be very hurt,' replied Zhukov.

'It's no time for feeling hurt,' said Stalin. 'We're not schoolgirls. We're Bolsheviks!'

On 10 January, Rokossovsky attacked the benighted Germans, slicing their pocket in half. The Sixth Army diminished daily. The military defeat became a human struggle for survival, as the Germans ate horsemeat, cats, rats, each other, and finally nothing. On 31 January, Field Marshal Paulus surrendered and 92,000 starving, frostbitten scarecrows, barely recognizable as men let alone soldiers, became prisoners. Stalin himself wrote out this newsflash: 'Today our armies trapped the commander of the Sixth Army near Stalingrad with all his staff ...'

* * *

Now a confident, preening Stalin and a gold-braided, bemedalled, imperial Bolshevik Russia emerged, blood-spattered but swaggering with pride, from behind the iron mask of Soviet austerity, to fight their way into Europe.*

On 6 January 1943 Stalin, having consulted two old comrades Kalinin and Budyonny, overturned the Bolshevik slogan 'Down with the golden shoulderboards!' and restored the auric epaulettes and braid of Tsarist officers. He teased Khrulev 'for suggesting we restore the old regime' but personally instructed the media how to spin it: the gold braid was not 'just decoration but also about order and discipline: tell about this.'

Two weeks later, he promoted Zhukov to Marshal. On 23 February, the omniscient military amateur himself joined the Marshalate: during the next two years, Stalin rarely appeared out of its uniform.

---

* This confidence was immediately reflected in Stalin's ungrateful treatment of his Western allies despite their gallantry in risking their lives to deliver aid to Russia: Mikoyan reported that the British had brought radio equipment on their Naval Mission in Murmansk 'without documentation. Either we should ask them to take it back or give it to us. I ask directions.' Molotov simply wrote 'Agreed.' But Stalin grumpily scribbled in his blue crayon: 'Comrade Molotov agreed – while Mikoyan suggested nothing!' As for the Royal Navy's radio: 'I propose confiscate the equipment as contraband!'

Simultaneously, he slightly clipped Beria's powerful wings: in April,* he brought military counter-intelligence, with its dreaded Special Departments, under his own aegis as Defence Commissar. He renamed it *Smersh*, an acronym for 'Death to Spies' that he coined himself, but kept Abakumov in charge. This slick but vicious secret policeman of thirty-five had worked closely with Beria but Stalin, the ultimate patron, now took him under his wing.

Yet Stalin's world-historical triumphs were always embittered by private disappointments. Soon after Stalingrad, Stalin received two disturbing messages: a letter that denounced the debauchery of his son Vasily and revealed the seduction of his adored Svetlana, and a German offer to exchange his prisoner son, Yakov.

---

* On 16 April 1943, Stalin once again split the huge NKVD into two separate agencies – the NKGB under Merkulov, containing the State Security police, and the NKVD under Beria that controlled the normal police and the huge slave labour camps. However, Beria remained *curator* or overlord of both 'Organs'.

40

Sons and Daughters: Stalin and the
Politburo's Children at War

The unprecedented surrender of a German Field Marshal humiliated Hitler just as acutely as Yakov's capture exposed Stalin: both
dictators expected these embarrassments to fall on their swords.
Now Count Bernadotte of the Red Cross approached Molotov
with an offer to swap Yakov for von Paulus. Molotov mentioned
the offer but Stalin refused to swap a marshal for a soldier:

'All of them are my sons,' Stalin replied like a good Tsar, telling
Svetlana, 'War is war!'

The refusal to swap Yakov has been treated as evidence of
Stalin's loveless cruelty but this is unfair. Stalin was a mass
murderer but in this case, it is hard to imagine that either
Churchill or Roosevelt could have swapped their sons if they had
been captured – when thousands of ordinary men were being
killed or captured.* After the war, a Georgian confidant plucked
up the courage to ask Stalin if the Paulus offer was a myth. He
'hung his head', answering 'in a sad, piercing voice':

'Not a myth ... Just think how many sons ended in camps! Who
would swap them for Paulus? Were they worse than Yakov? I had
to refuse ... What would they have said of me, our millions of
Party fathers, if having forgotten about them, I had agreed to
swapping Yakov? No, I had no right ...' Then he again showed the
struggle between the nervy, angry, tormented man within and the
persona he had become: 'Otherwise, I'd no longer be "Stalin".' He
added: 'I so pitied Yasha!'

---

* Yakov's daughter Gulia believes Stalin 'did the right thing'. Svetlana Stalin
compares his behaviour to Margaret Thatcher's refusal to negotiate with the terrorists
holding Terry Waite: 'We don't talk to those people.' Yakov was not the only one of
Stalin's family in encirclements: Artyom Sergeev was caught too – but he broke out
and made it back to Moscow where he told his story to Mikoyan. He was sent to a
Deputy Defence Commissar who told him: 'You're a Lieutenant and I'm Deputy
Commissar. You mustn't repeat this to anyone more senior. Forget it all There are
those who might not understand and this could ruin your life so write and sign here:
"I was not there and I saw nothing."'

A few weeks later, on 14 April in a POW camp near Lübeck, Yakov, who courageously refused to co-operate with the Germans, committed suicide by throwing himself on to the camp wire. At the Little Corner that night, oblivious to Yasha's heroism, Stalin worked with Molotov and Beria before heading off to dinner at about 1 a.m. He did not find out the truth for some time but when he did, he regarded his son with pride. Once at Kuntsevo, he left his own dinner and was found looking at Yasha's photograph.

'Did you ever see Yasha?' he asked the Georgian after the war, drawing out the photograph. 'Look! He's a real man eh! A noble man right to the end! Fate treated him unjustly ...' He ordered the release of Yakov's wife Julia (though she returned damaged by the trauma). Like Nadya, Yakov for ever troubled him.

* * *

Stalin now received a letter from the leading documentary film-maker Roman Karmen that denounced Colonel Vasily Stalin for the seduction of his wife and flaunting his debauchery. This letter opened a can of worms that ruined Stalin's relationships with both drunken Vasily and treasured Svetlana. Stalin started to look into their lives and what he found, shocked him profoundly.

By the climax of Stalingrad, Vasily was back in Moscow, living a life that was a caricature of the decadent wassails of aristocratic swells in Pushkin's *Onegin*. Spoiled by the sycophancy of his own Tsarevich's court, scarred by a mother's loss and a father's irritation, over-promoted and arrogant yet also terrified of his eminence and wildly generous to friends, Vasily took over Zubalovo, once the home of his ascetic mother and severe father, and turned this mansion (rebuilt after its dynamiting) into a pleasure dome of drinking, dancing and womanizing. The Tsarevich's set were glamorous film stars, screenwriters, pilots, ballerinas and free-loaders, a sort of Stalinist 'Ratpack': Karmen and his beautiful actress wife, Nina, were the centre of it along with the dashing poet Konstantin Simonov and his film-star wife, Valentina Serova. Stalin knew them all personally and liked Simonov's best-selling collection of love poems *With You and Without You*.

'How many copies are you printing?' Stalin asked Merkulov.

'Two hundred thousand,' replied the secret policeman.

'I read it,' joked Stalin, 'and I think it would have been enough to print just two: one for her and one for him.' Stalin was so pleased with this joke that he repeated it throughout the war.

The fun at Vasily's orgies was often rather desperate. He was 'permanently drunk' and often hit his wife Galina who had recently given birth to their son, Alexander. He was always drawing his revolver and firing at the chandeliers with his daredevil friends. Frustrated by Stalin's ban on his active missions, reckless of his own safety and that of his companions, Vasily enjoyed flying planes drunk, an aerodynamic version of Russian roulette. When he wanted to show off to his sister's pretty friend Martha Peshkova, he arrived drunk in Tashkent and insisted on flying her to see Svetlana in Kuibyshev. 'He flew me, legless, and with a drunk crew,' she recalls. 'Even though there was ice on the wings, they drank the spirit instead of using it for de-icing so the plane would not keep its height. Finally we had to crash-land and glided into a haystack in a clearing.' Martha was terrified. Vasily hiked to the nearest collective farm from where he despatched a rescue mission and was fêted in the local Party Chairman's house. He was so drunk that the Chairman's wife locked Martha in her room to protect her. Even his friend Vladimir Mikoyan, killed at Stalingrad, complained of Vasily's 'drinking, wilfulness and outbursts of rudeness: what a cretin!'

Yet for the young heroes and artistic stars during the war, Zubalovo was 'like Heaven', says Vasily's cousin Leonid Redens, 'because it was piled high with all that food and drink and far away from the fighting!' The Crown Prince had his pick of the girls at Zubalovo but when he began an affair with Nina Karmen, he fell in love with her and moved her into the mansion. Even though his wife Galina and baby had long since returned from Kuibyshev, along with Svetlana, and were meant to be living at Zubalovo, he flaunted the affair which, says Redens, 'went beyond all bounds'. No one could stop the Tsarevich except the Tsar himself, so the aggrieved husband wrote to Stalin who was outraged. When he ordered the NKGB to investigate Vasily's set, he discovered something that was enough to provoke any Georgian father to reach for his shotgun.

* * *

Svetlana, sixteen, living between the sterile austerity of the Kremlin apartment and the vapid degeneracy of Zubalovo, felt 'lonely' and unappreciated both by her busy father and her 'unpleasant' brother but this freckled redhead had matured early into a curvaceous, intelligent and sensitive girl who resembled Stalin's mother and possessed much of her father's obstinacy and toughness. Indeed her Redens cousins thought Vasily, for all his faults, was 'much softer and gentler'. A voracious reader and with fluent English, Svetlana found a copy of the *Illustrated London News*, perhaps at Beria's house, which she often visited, with the revelation about her mother's suicide: 'Something in me was destroyed,' she wrote. 'I was no longer able to obey the word and will of my father … without question.'

At one of Vasily's parties during Stalingrad, a handsome, worldly and famous screenwriter named Alexei Kapler arrived at Zubalovo. Kapler, nicknamed Lyusia, was a suave and mesmerizing raconteur and Casanova, though married: 'Oh he could talk and had the gift of communication with any age group, he was like a child himself,' wrote Svetlana. Stalin himself was his patron, supervising his own portrayal in Kapler's scripts for the films *Lenin in October* and *Lenin in 1918*. Kapler brought a reel of film of Greta Garbo in *Queen Christina*. He was immediately charmed by Svetlana, imagining their situation resembled the movie. 'She was the great lady and I was poor Don Alphonso. She was bold and unpretentious. I was forty and someone of importance in cinema' yet 'she was surrounded and oppressed in an atmosphere worthy of a god'. To the clever but brooding Svetlana, he was like a character out of one of her Dumas novels.

'Can you do the foxtrot?' he asked. Svetlana felt awkward in her flat shoes – but 'Kapler assured me I was a good dancer … I was wearing my first good dress from a dressmaker' with 'an old garnet brooch of my mother's'. She trusted him.

'Why are you so unhappy today?' he asked. Svetlana explained that 'it was ten years to the day since my mother's death yet no one seemed to remember'. The two were 'irresistibly drawn to one another' – it was wartime 'and we reached out to each other'. He lent her 'adult' books and poetry about love which helped overcome her fear of the vulgarity of sex about which Vasily constantly told her: 'I was afraid of this part of life presented to me in an ugly way by Vasily's dirty talk.'

Their relationship was passionate but never fully sexual: 'A kiss, that's all,' remembered Kapler. Yet it was thrilling for Svetlana: 'Romantic and pure. I was brought up that sex was only for marriage,' she revealed later. 'Father would not think to permit me anything outside of marriage.' But the war had changed everything: at any other time, Kapler might have thought the better of seducing Stalin's only daughter but 'I thought she really needed me.'

'To me,' said Svetlana, 'Kapler was the cleverest, kindest, most wonderful person on earth. He radiated knowledge and all its fascination,' introducing the schoolgirl to the exciting wartime freedoms: he took her to the theatre, lent her an illegal translation of Hemingway's *For Whom the Bell Tolls*. Vasily held wild parties at the Aragvi restaurant where they foxtrotted to a jazz orchestra. Svetlana breathlessly recounted her romance to Martha Peshkova at school every day: Kapler gave her an expensive brooch – a leaf with an insect on it.

This charismatic womanizer was moved by Svetlana's plight but he also revelled in his new adventure, boasting to movie director Mikhail Romm that he was now close to Stalin. He was despatched to cover Stalingrad for *Pravda*, filing his 'Letters of Lieutenant L from Stalingrad' in which he daringly paraded his affair with the words: 'It's probably snowing in Moscow. You can see the crenellated wall of the Kremlin from your window.' The *cognoscenti* were amazed at the folly of taunting a vindictive Georgian father on the front page of *Pravda* but to Svetlana, this was 'staggering in its chivalry and recklessness. The moment I saw it, I froze' but 'I sensed the whole thing might come to a terrible end.' At school, Svetlana showed Martha the article under the desk.

When Kapler returned, Svetlana begged him not to see her but, as he said, 'I don't remember who suggested the risk of that heart-rending farewell.' They met in an empty apartment near Kursk Station where Vasily's pals had assignations. Her bodyguard Klimov sat anxiously next door.

Beria had already informed Stalin, who warned Svetlana 'in a tone of extreme displeasure that I was behaving in a manner that could not be tolerated' but he blamed Vasily for corrupting her. Seething about Vasily's debauchery, Stalin dismissed his son as Air-force Inspector for conduct unbecoming, and ordered him to be locked up in the guardhouse for ten days, then posted to the North-West Front. Vlasik, Stalin's domestic panjandrum, suggested Kapler leave Moscow. Kapler told him to 'go to hell' but arranged an assignment away from the city.

Meanwhile Merkulov handed Stalin the phone intercepts of Svetlana and Kapler's conversations, a tool not usually available to the irate fathers of errant daughters. Stalin was enraged. On 2 March, Kapler was bundled into a car which was followed by a sinister black Packard 'in which General Vlasik sat, looking very important'. At the Lubianka, Vlasik and Kobulov supervised his sentencing for 'anti-Soviet opinions' to five years in Vorkuta.

The next day, already under pressure as Manstein's counter-offensive retook Kharkov and threatened the success of Stalingrad, Stalin was so angry he got up hours earlier than usual. Svetlana was getting dressed for school with her nanny when Stalin 'strode briskly into my bedroom, something he had never done before'. The look in his eyes was 'enough to rivet my nurse to the floor'. Svetlana had 'never seen my father look that way before'. Stalin, in a blazing Georgian temper, was 'choking with anger and nearly speechless'.

'Where, where are they all?' he spluttered. 'Where are all these letters from your "writer"? I know the whole story! I've got all your telephone conversations right here!' He tapped his tunic pocket. 'All right! Hand them over! Your Kapler's a British spy. He's under arrest!' Svetlana surrendered Kapler's letters and screenplays, but shouted: 'But I love him!'

'Love!' shrieked Stalin 'with hatred of the very word', and, 'for the first time in my life', slapped her twice across the face. Then he turned to the nanny: 'Just think, nurse, how low she's sunk. Such a war going on and she's busy fucking!'

'No, no, no,' the nanny tried to explain, fat hands flapping.

'What do you mean "no",' Stalin asked more calmly, 'when I know the whole story?' Then to Svetlana: 'Take a look at yourself! Who'd want you? You fool! He's got women all around him!' Stalin gathered up the letters and took them into the dining room where he sat at the table where Churchill had dined – and, ignoring the war altogether, started to read them. He did not appear at the Little Corner that day.

That afternoon, when Svetlana returned from school, Stalin was waiting for her in the dining room, tearing up Kapler's letters and photographs. 'Writer!' he sneered. 'He can't even write decent Russian! She couldn't even find herself a Russian!' Kapler's Jewishness especially riled him. She left the room and they did not speak again for many months: their loving relationship was shattered for ever.

This is often presented as the height of Stalin's brutality yet, even today, no parents would be delighted by the seduction (as he thought) of their schoolgirl daughters, especially by a married middle-aged playboy. Yet Stalin was a traditional Georgian steeped in nineteenth-century prudery and to this day, Georgian fathers are liable to resort to their shotguns at the least provocation. 'Being a Georgian, he SHOULD have shot that ladies' man,' says Vladimir Redens. Long after she wrote her memoirs, Svetlana understood that 'my father over-reacted': he thought he was 'protecting his daughter from a dirty older man'.*

Days later, Vasily and his retinue flew up to the North-Western Front where he finally flew one or two combat missions, but his outrages continued. In May, he set off on a drunken fishing expedition in which the pilots caught fish by tossing aircraft rockets into a pond with delayed fuses. One of the rockets exploded, killing a Hero of the Soviet Union.

On 26 May, Stalin ordered Air-force Commander Novikov to '1. dismiss Colonel VJ Stalin immediately from ... command of air regiment; 2. announce to the regimental officers and VJ Stalin that Colonel Stalin is dismissed for hard drinking, debauchery and corrupting the regiment.' But it was impossible to keep a dictator's son down: by the end of the year, the scapegrace had once again been promoted and he was soon driving his Rolls-Royce along the front, borrowing official planes whenever it suited him. One of his boon companions was alarmed when he insisted on trying to overtake an army lorry on the crowded roads of the Baltic front. When the lorry refused to give way, Vasily simply shot out the tyres.

As for Svetlana, she was soon in love with someone whose name was so dreaded that, in two published memoirs and many interviews over fifty years, she has still never revealed his identity.

* * *

Not until March 1943, shortly after the Kapler affair, did Stalin finally contain Manstein's counter-attack, leaving a swollen Soviet salient bulging into the German lines around Kursk. Hitler approved Operation Citadel to cut off the bulge while Stalin and his generals debated what to do. His instincts were always to attack, but Zhukov and Vasilevsky managed to persuade him to wait and break the Germans in a defensive position. This made Stalin even more agitated and nervous, but he had learned the great lesson of Stalingrad: he took their advice on what would become the world's greatest tank battle, Kursk.

---

* Their age difference was twenty-four years, not much more than that between Stalin and Nadya in 1918 but this was a parallel that may have intensified his anger. The two slaps are not Stalin's greatest crimes. Kapler's five years were cruel but he was fortunate not to be quietly shot. On his release in 1948, he returned against his parole to Moscow, was rearrested and sentenced to another five years in the mines. He returned after Stalin's death, remarried and was then reunited with Svetlana with whom he finally enjoyed a passionate affair. He died in 1979.

After a dinner with Stalin that lasted from 3 to 7 a.m., Zhukov and Vasilevsky rushed to the front to plan the battle. Malenkov supervised the generals, Mikoyan amassed the reserves, Beria provided 300,000 slave labourers to dig an unbreachable 3,000 miles of trenches. Over a million men and, including reserves, around 6,000 tanks waited.

The waiting was agony for the jittery Supremo who let off steam in a volcanic tantrum with his aircraft designer. Yakovlev arrived in the study to find Stalin and Vasilevsky examining fragments of the wing of his Yak-9 fighter. Stalin pointed to the pieces ... and asked:

'Do you know anything about this?' He then exploded in a frenzied rant: 'I had never seen Stalin in such a rage,' remembered Yakovlev. Stalin demanded to know when this fault had been discovered. When he heard that it had only been noticed 'in the face of the enemy', he 'lost his composure even more'.

'Do you know that only the most cunning enemy could do such a thing – turn out planes in such a way that they would seem good at the plant and no good at the front. This is working for Hitler! Do you know what a service you've rendered Hitler? You Hitlerites!'

'It was difficult to imagine our condition at that moment ... I was shivering,' admitted Yakovlev. The silence was 'tomb-like' as Stalin paced the room until he asked:

'What are we going to do?'

At dawn on 5 July, the Germans threw 900,000 men and 2,700 tanks into this colossal battle of machines in which fleets of metallic giants clashed, helm to helm, barrel to barrel. By the 9th, the Germans had reached their limit. On the 12th, Zhukov unleashed the costly but highly successful counter-attack. The Battle of Kursk was the climax of the Panzer era, the 'mechanized equivalent of hand-to-hand combat', which left a graveyard of 700 tanks and burnt flesh. Agreeing to cancel Citadel, Hitler had lost his last chance to win the war.

On the afternoon of 24 July, Stalin welcomed Antonov and Shtemenko to the Little Corner in a 'joyously jubilant mood'. Stalin did not even want to hear their report – just tinkered cheerfully with the victory communiqué, adding the words: 'Eternal glory to the heroes who fell on the battlefield in the struggle for the liberty and honour of our Motherland!'

* * *

Stalin was not alone in finding it difficult to control his own
children during wartime: Khrushchev and Mikoyan played stellar
roles in the Kursk triumph, the former as Front Commissar, the
latter as Supply maestro, but simultaneously they both found
their children embroiled in dangerous crises. Stalin was both
sympathetic and heartless in dealing with the tragedies of the
Politburo families.

Leonid Khrushchev, Nikita's eldest son from his first marriage,
was already notorious as a ne'er-do-well. Now he became a Stalinist
William Tell. Reprimanded by Komsomol for 'drunkenness', he had
settled down, married Lyubov Kutuzova, with whom he had a little
girl, Julia, and shown courage as a bomber pilot, though he
remained a drunken brawler.* Leonid boasted boozily of his
marksmanship and was challenged to balance a bottle on a pilot's
head. He shot off the neck of the bottle. This did not satisfy these
daredevils. Leonid shot again, fatally wounding the officer in the
forehead. He was court-martialled.

Khrushchev may have appealed to Stalin for clemency, citing
the boy's bravery. But Stalin, who would not save Yakov, 'did not
want to pardon Khrushchev's son', as Molotov recalled. However,
he was not sentenced but allowed to retrain as a fighter pilot. On
11 March 1943, he was shot down during a dogfight with two
FockeWulf 190s near Smolensk. He was never found. Rumours
spread that he had turned traitor – which, in Stalin's system, cast
doubt on his widow, Lyubov, who had visited the theatre in
Kuibyshev with an 'amazingly attractive' French military attaché.
Lyubov was probably denounced by Khrushchev's chief bodyguard. She was arrested and interrogated by Abakumov himself,
and condemned.

In another of those tragedies of Stalinist family life, little Julia
was told her mother was dead. The memory of her parents was
obliterated and she was adopted by her grandfather, Khrushchev
himself, whom she called '*Papa*'.† The Khrushchevs were cold
parents. Nikita himself seemed to believe the charges against
Lyubov. 'Stalin played this game,' recalls Julia, 'and Khrushchev

---

* In 1941, Leonid had shouted that Stalin was far from being 'the greatest one and
father of peoples' – he was a 'damned scoundrel' and Kirov's murderer!
† Her mother served five years in a Mordovia labour camp, followed by five years in
exile. When she returned in 1954, Khrushchev refused to meet her. Julia only met
her mother again in 1956. They were strangers – and remain so: the mother is still
alive, living in Kiev. In 1995, a plane was discovered near Smolensk containing the
skeleton of a pilot still in his goggles and helmet: it was probably Leonid.

was playing for his life' but 'Nikita never spoke about it and even as a pensioner, he spoke only in general terms. This was very humiliating and painful for him.' Perhaps, says Julia Khrushcheva, it contributed to his later decision to denounce Stalin.

* * *

That summer, it was Mikoyan's turn. Two of his sons were pilots. Stepan was wounded, then during Stalingrad, 18-year-old Vladimir was killed. So Stalin 'expressly ordered' his son Vasily to take Stepan into his own division and 'make sure not to lose any more Mikoyans'. On Vasily's orders, Stepan's engineer claimed the plane was not ready for him to fly whenever possible. This indulgence did not last.

Among all the other children in Kuibyshev, Mikoyan's younger boys Vano, fifteen, and Sergo, fourteen, were friends with the unhinged son of Shakhurin, the Aircraft Production Commissar. Volodya Shakhurin played a silly but risky game in which he pretended to 'appoint' a mock government with the teenage Mikoyans as ministers, all recorded in his exercise book. When they returned to Moscow, this Volodya Shakhurin fell in love with Nina, daughter of Ambassador Umansky who was just leaving for his next posting.

'I won't let you go,' young Shakhurin told Nina. The schoolchildren were walking across the Kamennyi Most, close to the Kremlin, when Shakhurin borrowed Vano Mikoyan's pistol which he had been lent by his father's bodyguards. The boy ran ahead with Nina then, on the bridge, shot her dead and killed himself. A horrified Vano Mikoyan ran back to the Kremlin to tell his mother. The NKGB discovered the gun belonged to the young Mikoyans who were also 'ministers' in the schoolboy 'government', which was obviously a conspiracy. Vano was arrested.

'Vano just disappeared,' remembers Sergo. 'My mother was frantic and they called the police stations.' Mikoyan, working down the corridor from Stalin himself, rang Beria, then called his wife Ashken:

'Don't worry. Vano's in the Lubianka.' Mikoyan knew that this could only happen with Stalin's permission. The shrewd Armenian decided not to appeal to Stalin 'so as not to make things worse'. Ten days later, Sergo was also arrested at Zubalovo and taken to the Lubianka in his pyjamas:

'I must tell mama.'

'It'll only take an hour,' they replied. Twenty-six schoolboys were arrested and imprisoned, including Stalin's nephew, Leonid Redens, whose father had been shot in 1940. The secret police reported the children's innocence but Stalin replied:

'They must be punished.' This was so vague that no one was quite sure what to do with the young prisoners. The boys were interrogated by Lieut.-Gen. Vlodzirmirsky, one of Beria's cruellest torturers, 'tall and handsome in his uniform', who was, says Sergo, 'very nasty. He shouted at us.' Sergo was placed in solitary for a week. In December, after six months in the Lubianka, the interrogations ceased and the children became really frightened. Sergo's interrogator showed him a confession that he had been 'a participant in an organization ... to overthrow the existing government'.

'Just sign and you can see your mother again!'

'I won't sign, it's not true,' said Sergo.

'It doesn't make any difference,' bellowed the general. 'Sign – you go home. If not, back to your cell. Listen!' He could hear his mother's voice in the next room. All the children signed their confessions. 'Of course this could have been used against my father.' Sergo and Vano were driven with their mother back to the Kremlin. 'I was very glad my father wasn't there – I was afraid of his anger,' says Sergo.

Mikoyan told the elder boy:

'If you're guilty, I'd strangle you with my own hands. Go and rest.' He never mentioned it to the youngest. But the matter was not closed: after three days at home, the children had to go into exile. The Mikoyans spent a year in Stalinabad, cared for by their housemaid. Stalin never forgot the case and later considered using it against Mikoyan.

41

Stalin's Song Contest

At about 11 p.m. on 1 August 1943, Stalin and Beria arrived at Kuntsevo Station and boarded a special train, camouflaged with birch branches, armed with howitzers and packed with specially tested provisions. The train, which, with its theatrical shrubbery poking out of its guns, must have resembled a locomotive Birnam Wood, puffed westwards. The Kursk counter-attacks, Operations Rumiantsev, to the north, and Kutuzov, to the south, both named after Tsarist heroes, were so successful that Stalin felt safe to embark on this preposterously staged visit to the front.

Stalin slept at Gzhatsk, then headed towards Rzhev on the Kalinin Front. Transferring into his Packard, he set up his headquarters in a self-consciously humble wooden cottage with a picturesque veranda (still a museum today) in the hamlet of Khoroshevo where he received his generals. Knowing from Zhukov that Orel and Belgorod would fall imminently, Stalin ate 'a cheerful supper' with his entourage.

The old lady who lived there was on hand to provide a touch of folksy authenticity until Stalin, who prided himself on his popular touch, unexpectedly insisted that he must pay her for his stay. He was unable to work out a sensible sum because he had not handled money since 1917 but, in any case, he had no cash on him. Stalin asked his flunkies for the money. Here was a classic moment in the farce of the workers' State when, with much tapping of tunic pockets, jiggling of medals and rustling of gold braid, not one of the boozy, paunchy commissars could find a single kopeck to pay her. Stalin cursed the 'spongers'. Since he could not pay in cash, he compensated the crone with his own provisions.

Then Stalin peered grumpily out at the village which he immediately noticed was teeming with ill-concealed Chekists: he asked how many there were, but the NKVD tried to conceal the real number. When Stalin exploded, they admitted there was an entire division. Indeed, the generals noticed that the village itself had been completely emptied: there was no one except the NKVD for miles around.

He slept on the old lady's bed in his greatcoat. Yeremenko briefed him. Voronov was summoned, covering miles to make it to the mysterious meeting. 'Finally we came to a beautiful grove where small wooden structures nestled among the trees.' Led into the cottage, Stalin stood in front of a 'wretched wooden table that had been hastily dashed together' and two crude benches. A special telephone had been fixed to link Stalin to the fronts, with the wires going out of the window. Waiting to report to the Supremo, the generals were unimpressed with this *mise-en-scène*.

'Well, this is some situation!' whispered one general to Voronov who suddenly realized: 'It's intentional – to resemble the front.' Stalin cut off the briefing, contenting himself with giving some orders, then dismissed the generals who had to slog back to the real fray. Stalin asked if he could go further towards the fighting but Beria forbade him. He visited the hospital at Yukono, according to his bodyguards, and was depressed by so many amputees. Afterwards, he felt ill and his arthritis played up.* Stalin returned by road in his armoured Packard and a convoy of security cars.

Suddenly the cars stopped. 'He needed to defecate,' wrote Mikoyan, who heard the story from someone who was there. Stalin got out of the car and asked 'whether the bushes along the roadside were mined. Of course no one could give such a guarantee ... Then the Supreme Commander-in-Chief pulled down his trousers in everyone's presence.' In a metaphorical commentary on his treatment of the Soviet people, and his performance as military commander, he 'shamed himself in front of his generals and officers ... and did his business right there on the road.'

On his return, Stalin was immediately able to deploy his heroic journey in a letter to President Franklin D. Roosevelt, with whom he was discussing the venue for the first meeting of the three leaders of the Grand Alliance: 'Having just returned from the front, I am only now able to reply to your letter ...' He could not meet FDR and Churchill at Scapa Flow in Orkney – 'I have to

---

* This scene resembles the moment when Hitler, in his train, found himself looking into a hospital train on its way back from the Eastern Front: he and the wounded stared at each other for a second before he ordered the blinds to be closed.

make personal visits to ... the front more and more often.' He proposed they meet in a more convenient place – Teheran, the capital of Iran, occupied by British-Soviet forces.

Stalin's courtiers knew the significance of this visit to the front. A month later, Yeremenko, his host, prodded by Beria and Malenkov, proposed that Stalin receive the Order of Suvorov First Class for Stalingrad, and for giving 'such valuable orders that guaranteed victory on the Kalinin Front, ... inspired by the visit to the front of the Supreme Commander-in-Chief...'

On 5 August, when Orel and Belgorod fell, Stalin jovially asked Antonov and Shtemenko: 'Do you read military history?' Shtemenko admitted he was 'confused, not knowing how to answer'. Stalin, who had been rereading Vipper's *History of Ancient Greece*, went on: 'In ancient times, when troops won victories, all the bells would be rung in honour of the commanders and their troops. It wouldn't be a bad idea for us to signify victories more impressively ... We' – and he nodded at his comrades, 'we're thinking of giving artillery salutes and arranging some kind of fireworks ...' That day, the guns of the Kremlin fired the first victory salvo. Henceforth, Stalin punctiliously worked out the salutes to be given for each victory and the staff had to get every detail correct. Just before 11 p.m. the messages were rushed to the stentorian newsreader Levitan who telephoned Poskrebyshev for Stalin's approval. Then the salvoes resounded across the Motherland.

'Let's listen to it,' Stalin often suggested in the Little Corner. The generals now competed to be the first to give Stalin good news. On the 28th, Koniev phoned to announce he had taken Kharkov but was told that Stalin always slept in in the mornings. Koniev daringly phoned Kuntsevo directly. A delighted Stalin answered it himself. But when there was a mistake in the victory announcements, Stalin yelled: 'Why did Levitan omit Koniev's name? Let me see the message!' Shtemenko had left it out. Stalin was 'dreadfully furious'. 'What kind of anonymous message is this? What have you got on your shoulders? Stop that broadcast and read everything over again. You may go!'

The next time, he asked Shtemenko to bring the communiqué on his own, asking, 'You didn't leave out the name?' Shtemenko was forgiven.

As he massed fifty-eight armies, from Finland to the Black Sea, to embark on a colossal wave of offensives, an elated Stalin, having closed down the Comintern and enlisted the support of the Church by appointing a Patriarch, decided to create a new national anthem to replace the *Internationale*. It was to catch Russia's new euphoric confidence. Stalin decided the quickest way to find the tune and words was to hold a competition that resembled a dictatorial Eurovision Song Contest, with Molotov and Voroshilov contributing to the lyrics, and Shostakovich and Prokofiev to the music.

* * *

In one week in late October, while the Allied Foreign Ministers were in Moscow preparing for the Big Three meeting, the anthem was forged in the white-hot frenzy of musical Stakhanovitism to be ready for the 7 November celebrations. In late September, Stalin invited composers from all over the Soviet Union to put forward their offerings. In mid-October, fifty-four composers, including Uzbeks, Georgians and some singing Jews, in traditional costume, arrived in Moscow to perform round one in the Stalin song contest. Before the music was even decided, Stalin appointed the lyricists, Sergei Mikhalkov and El-Registan, whose notes in the archives tell this story. They handed in their first draft. At lunchtime on the 23rd, the lyricists were summoned from the Moskva Hotel, that colossal Stalinist pile, across to the Kremlin where Molotov and Voroshilov received them. 'Come in,' they said. 'He is reading the lyrics.' They did not need to ask who 'he' was. Two minutes later, Stalin called. Voroshilov, who was 'cheerful and smiling', took El-Registan's hands: 'Comrade Stalin,' he announced, 'has made some corrections.' These were words they would hear often during the next two weeks. Meanwhile the dour Molotov was suggesting changes of his own.

'You must add some thoughts about peace, I don't know where, but it must be done.'

'We'll give you a room,' said Voroshilov. 'It has to be warm. Give 'em tea or they'll start drinking! And don't let them out until they've finished.' They worked for four hours.

'We need to think about this overnight,' said Mikhalkov.

'Think all you like,' snapped Molotov, 'but we can't wait.' As they left, they heard him order: 'Send it to Stalin!'

At a quarter to midnight, Stalin tinkered with the new draft in his red pencil, changing the words of the verses, sending it to Molotov and Voroshilov: 'Look at this. Do you agree?' On 26 October, Voroshilov, the Marshal demoted to song judge, was diligently listening to another thirty anthems in the Bolshoi's Beethoven Hall, when suddenly 'Stalin arrived and all was done very fast.' It was now a remarkable gathering, with Stalin, Voroshilov and Beria sitting down with Shostakovich and Prokofiev to discuss the composition. When the lyricists arrived, they found Stalin, 'very grey and very energetic' in his new Marshal's uniform. Walking around as he listened to the melodies, Stalin asked Shostakovich and Prokofiev which orchestra was best – should it be an ecclesiastical one? It was hard to choose without an orchestra. Stalin gave them five days to prepare some more anthems, said goodbye and left the hall.

At three the following morning, Poskrebyshev called the lyricists, putting through the Supreme Songwriter who said that he now liked the text, but it was too 'thin' and short. They must add one verse, one rousing verse about the Red Army, power, 'the defeat of the Fascist hordes'.*

Stalin celebrated the Allied conference with a banquet on 30 October and then returned to music. At 9 a.m. on 1 November, flanked by Molotov, Beria and Voroshilov, he arrived at the Beethoven Hall and listened to forty anthems in four hours. Over dinner afterwards, the magnates finally came to a decision: Voroshilov telephoned the two lyricists in the middle of the night to announce that they liked the anthem of A. V. Alexandrov. He then handed the phone to Stalin who was still tinkering:

'You can leave the verses,' he said, 'but rewrite the refrains. "Country of Soviets" – if it's not a problem, change it to "country of socialism". Status: secret!' The lyricists worked all night, now with Alexandrov's music. Voroshilov sent it to Stalin and invited the composers to his dacha where he presided like 'a very funny and cheerful uncle' over a sumptuous feast.

At nine the next evening, Stalin was ready. The composers

---

* When they sang 'the Fascist hordes were beaten, are beaten and will be beaten', they started laughing because the words 'are beaten' in Russian sounded like 'are fucking us' when sung. Laughing, they quickly changed the words to 'We'll beat them to death and we'll beat them.' Marshal Voroshilov returned from his meetings and 'liked it very very much' so they told him about the problem with the 'fucking' and the 'defeating'. This of course greatly appealed to Voroshilov's earthy cavalryman's humour: 'Wonderful for a village song but not so good for a national anthem!' he laughed and then they started remembering all the hilarities of the song contest. What about those four Jewish singers in traditional dress who sang their Jewish song looking right into the eyes of Voroshilov! The Marshal guffawed heartily: 'Bring me some vodka! We must drink. From us in your honour! I present it to you!' In the late afternoon, they left the Kremlin exhausted.

arrived. Beria, Voroshilov and Malenkov sat round the table. Stalin formally shook their hands, that special sign of battles won and songs written:

'How's everything?' he asked warmly, but had not yet finished his tinkering. He wanted to emphasize the role of 'the Motherland! Motherland's good!' The writers rushed off to type in the changes. Stalin wanted Shostakovich involved in the orchestration.

'All right. Done!' snapped Beria. Then Malenkov sensibly piped up that they should listen once to the entire anthem. Stalin assigned this to Voroshilov who, demonstrating his rambunctious disrespect that belonged in another era, retorted:

'Let someone else do it – I've heard it a hundred times until I'm foaming at the mouth!' The new Soviet national anthem, Stalin raved, 'parts the sky and heaven like a boundless wave'. At its first playing at the Bolshoi Theatre, Stalin arrived to toast the composers who were invited up to the box and then to a dinner in the *avant-loge*. When Mikhalkov* and El-Registan downed their vodkas, Stalin bantered:

'Why drain your glasses? You won't be interesting to chat to!'

* * *

The elation spread from the top down. As the national anthem was unveiled, Molotov presided over a 7 November party that few would ever forget. The élite emerged that night from the grimness of the thirties and the austerity of years of defeat. 'The whole party,' noted the journalist Alexander Werth, 'sparkled with jewels, furs, gold braid and celebrities ... The party had something of that wild and irresponsible extravagance which one usually associates with pre-Revolution Moscow.' The dress was white tie and tails, which made Shostakovich look 'like a college boy who had put it on for the first time'. Henceforth, Stalin's court began to behave more like the rulers of an empire than dour Bolsheviks. Molotov sported the new diplomatic uniform that, like the gold braid, marked the new imperial era: it was 'black, trimmed in

---

* Sergei Mikhalkov remained a favoured Stalinist wordsmith: the archives contain his note to Stalin, 'At the Bolshoi Theatre on 30 December 1943, I promised you and Comrade Molotov to write a poem for children. I'm sending you "A Fable for Children".' Stalin liked it: 'It's a very good poem,' he scrawled to Molotov. 'It must be published today in *Pravda* and some other edition for children ...' Mikhalkov's son Nikita is today Russia's greatest film director, *auteur* of *Burnt by the Sun* and *Barber of Siberia*.

gold, with a small dagger at the belt ... much like Hitler's élite SS', thought the US diplomat Chip Bohlen.

Molotov, Vyshinsky and Stalin's old friend Sergo 'Tojo' Kavtaradze greeted the guests in a receiving line. Kavtaradze's companion was his beautiful daughter Maya, now eighteen and wearing the long flowing ball gown of the era. She caught the eye of Vyshinsky who 'oiled his way across the floor' to ask her to open the dancing with him.

A 'jovial' Molotov proceeded to become uproariously drunk, tottering up to Averell Harriman's daughter Kathleen and slurringly asking why she alone had failed to compliment him on his gorgeous uniform. Didn't she like it? She thought the Russians were as excited about their regalia 'as a little boy all dressed up in his new Christmas-present fireman's suit'. When he spotted the Swedish Ambassador, Molotov staggered up to him and declared that he did not like neutrals.

The Politburo members then each hit on a Western ambassador whom they tried to get as drunk as they were: Mikoyan, 'famous for his ability to put any guy under the table' according to Kathleen Harriman, worked on her father along with Shcherbakov, himself in the later stages of alcoholism. Molotov, who 'carried his liquor better than others', managed to remain on his feet while Clark Kerr, the British Ambassador 'fell flat on his face on to a table covered with bottles and wineglasses', cutting his face. Maya Kavtaradze saw an American general arrive accompanied by two prostitutes. Later in the evening, she noticed that all the potentates had disappeared and went to look for her father. She found him in a red hall, the Bolshevik equivalent of the 'VIP room', with the dashing and exuberant Mikoyan who was serenading the hussies on one knee.

The next day, Roosevelt finally agreed to meet at Teheran twenty days later: 'The whole world is watching for this meeting of the three of us ...'

42

Teheran: Roosevelt and Stalin

On 26 November 1943, Colonel-General Golovanov, the bomber commander who was to be Stalin's pilot, drove out to Kuntsevo to begin their long voyage to Persia. When he arrived, he heard shouting and found Stalin 'giving Beria a good dressing-down' while Molotov watched, perched on the window-sill. Beria sat in a chair 'with his ears all red' as Stalin sneered at him:

'Look at him Comrade Golovanov! He's got snake's eyes!' Molotov had jokingly complained that he could not read Beria's spidery handwriting. 'Our Vyacheslav Mikhailovich can't see very well. Beria keeps sending him messages and he insists on wearing his pince-nez with blank glasses!' This marked Stalin's growing disdain for the dynamic Georgian.

Afterwards, they boarded their train that arrived in Baku at 8 a.m., driving straight to the aerodrome where four SI-47s were gathered under the command of Air Marshal Novikov. Stalin had never flown before – and did not like the sound of it. But there was no other way from Baku. As he approached his plane with Golovanov, he glanced at Beria's plane standing next door with his pilot, Colonel Grachev, and decided to switch planes.

'Colonel-Generals don't often pilot aircraft,' he said, 'we'd better go with the Colonel,' reassuring Golovanov: 'Don't take it badly' – and he climbed into Beria's own plane. Guarded by twenty-seven fighters, Stalin was terrified when the plane hit an air pocket.

A few hours later, Stalin arrived in warm, dusty Teheran ('very dirty place, great poverty,' wrote Roosevelt) where he was speeded the five miles to the Soviet Embassy which was separated from the British Legation by two walls and a narrow road. Only the American Legation was out of town.

Teheran was the cosiest of the Big Three meetings: Stalin himself travelled with a tiny delegation. There were only Molotov and Voroshilov, his official deputies in the negotiations, Beria as security overlord, Vlasik as head of personal security and his physician Professor Vinogradov. Stalin's bodyguard of twelve Georgians was led by Tsereteli, whom Westerners found 'good-looking, highly intelligent and courteous'. None the less there was something appropriate about the master of this Eastern Empire being protected by a guard of his fellow countrymen led by a cut-throat Prince. Perhaps Churchill thought the same way for his bodyguard there was made up of turbaned Sikhs with tommy-guns.

The Soviet Embassy was an elegant estate, built for some Persian magnate, surrounded by a high wall. There were several cottages and villas in the grounds: Stalin lived in one house while Molotov and Voroshilov shared the two-storey Ambassador's residence. The advance guard of the NKVD had been frantically preparing the Embassy for two weeks. 'No one dared disobey' Beria, wrote Zoya Zarubina, a young NKGB officer in Teheran.*

As soon as Roosevelt arrived, Stalin invited him to move into the Soviet compound. The drive from the Soviet complex to the US Legation along narrow Oriental streets was impossible to guard – and no doubt Beria was more concerned about Stalin's security than Roosevelt's. Soviet intelligence had allegedly uncovered a Nazi plot to assassinate the leaders. Stalin was also determined to separate the Westerners, whom he expected to gang up on him. It happened that this also suited Roosevelt's strategy to engage Stalin directly, without the British, to prove his suspicions groundless. Harriman hurried over. Molotov explained their security worries. Molotov later ordered Zarubina to call and find out when FDR would be moving in. Admiral William Leahy, White House Chief of Staff, replied: 'We'll come tomorrow.'

When Zarubina reported this back to Molotov, he exploded: 'What do you think you're doing? Who the hell are you anyway? Who commanded you to do this job? Are you sure? What am I going to say to Stalin?'

Meanwhile, in one of those forgotten meetings between

---

* Beria personally ordered one of the Chekists, the young Zoya Zarubina, the step-daughter of NKGB General Leonid Eitingon (who had arranged Trotsky's assassination), to choose the furniture for the conference. There was no round table so it had to be made. Since the conference was a closely guarded secret, Beria told Zarubina to go into Teheran city and pretend to order a table to seat twenty-two 'for a wedding'.

potentates who seem to belong to different epochs, Stalin called on the proud Mohammed Pahlavi, the 21-year-old Shah of an occupied Iran, whose father Reza Shah, a former Cossack officer and founder of the dynasty, had been deposed for pro-German leanings in 1941. Stalin believed he could charm this imperial boy, whose Empire had once embraced Georgia, into granting him an Iranian foothold. Molotov, already a master of the diplomatically possible, was sceptical. Beria advised against this excursion for security reasons. Stalin insisted. The King of Kings was pleasantly 'surprised' by the feline Stalin who was 'particularly polite and well-mannered and he seemed intent on making a good impression on me'. His offer of 'a regiment of T-34 tanks and one of our fighter planes' impressed the Shah too. 'I was most tempted,' he later wrote, but he sensed danger in this Georgian bearing gifts. Molotov grumbled that Stalin 'did not understand the Shah and got into a bit of an awkward situation. Stalin thought he could impress him but it didn't work.' The gifts were to come with Soviet officers. 'I declined with thanks,' wrote the Shah.

Next morning, Beria personally patrolled the gates, waiting for Roosevelt who finally arrived at the Soviet Embassy with the Secret Service riding on the running-boards and brandishing tommy-guns in a gangsterish manner that the NKVD thought unprofessional. A jeep-load of Roosevelt's Filipino mess-boys confused the NKVD but they finally admitted them too.

Stalin sent word that he would call on the President, a meeting he had prepared for carefully. Naturally Beria bugged the presidential suite. Beria's handsome scientist son, Sergo, whom Stalin knew well, was among the Soviet eavesdroppers. Stalin summoned him: 'How's your mother?' he asked, Nina Beria being a favourite. Small talk out of the way, he ordered Sergo to undertake the 'morally reprehensible and delicate' mission of briefing him every morning at 8 a.m. Stalin always quizzed him, even on Roosevelt's tone: 'Did he say that with conviction or without enthusiasm? How did Roosevelt react?' He was surprised at the naïvety of the Americans: 'Do they know we are listening to them?'* Stalin rehearsed strategies with Molotov and Beria,

---

* Roosevelt presumed he was being bugged but hoped the results might fortify Stalin's confidence in his honesty. Sergo Beria's account suggests this worked.

even down to where he would sit.* He did the same for his meetings with Churchill, according to Beria's son, saying, 'You can expect absolutely anything from him.'

Just before three, on this 'beautiful Iranian Sunday afternoon, gold and blue, mild and sunny', Stalin, accompanied by Vlasik and Pavlov, his interpreter, and surrounded by his Georgian bodyguards, who walked ten metres ahead and behind, as they did in the Kremlin, strode 'clumsily like a small bear' out of his residence in his Marshal's mustard-coloured summer tunic, with the Order of Lenin on his chest, and across the compound, to call on Roosevelt in the mansion. A young US officer met Stalin with a salute and led him into the President's room but then found himself inside the meeting-room with just the two leaders and their interpreters. He was about to panic until Bohlen, acting as interpreter, whispered that he should leave.

'Hello Marshal Stalin,' said Roosevelt as the men shook hands. His 'round tubby figure', with swarthy pock-marked face, grey hair, broken stained teeth and yellow Oriental eyes, was worlds away from the aristocratic blue-suited President sitting erect in his wheelchair: 'If he'd dressed in Chinese robes,' wrote Bohlen, 'he would be the perfect subject for a Chinese ancestor portrait.'

Stalin stressed his need for the Second Front before Roosevelt established a rapport by undermining the British Empire. India was ripe for a revolution 'from the bottom', like Russia, said FDR, who was as ill-informed about Leninism as he was about the untouchables. Stalin showed that he knew more about India, replying that the question of castes was more complicated. This short *tour d'horizon* established the unlikely partnership between the crippled New York Brahmin and the Georgian Bolshevik. Both of legendary charm when they wished to be, Stalin's fondness for Roosevelt was as genuine a diplomatic friendship as he ever managed with any imperialist. Stalin left Roosevelt to rest.

At 4 p.m., the Big Three gathered around the specially constructed 'wedding feast table' in a big hall decorated in heavy

* In a piece of interpreter mountebankism, the second Soviet interpreter Valentin Berezhkov described how Stalin rehearsed the meeting and how Roosevelt came to Stalin's residence without an interpreter. In fact, Stalin went to Roosevelt's rooms where Chip Bohlen interpreted for the Americans and Pavlov for the Soviets. Pavlov was Stalin and Molotov's interpreter in English and German; Berezhkov occasionally worked for Molotov. The only part of this incident that holds together is Stalin rehearsing positions, which was typical of him. Perhaps Berezhkov did witness this scene.

imperial style with striped silk armchairs and armrests: Stalin sat next to Molotov and Pavlov. Voroshilov often sat in a chair in the second row. Stalin and Churchill agreed that Roosevelt was to chair the meeting: 'As the youngest!' joked the President.

'In our hands,' declaimed Churchill, 'we have the future of mankind.' Stalin completed this declamatory triumvirate:

'History has spoiled us,' he said. 'She's given us very great power and very great opportunities ... Let's begin our work.' When they turned to the question of Operation Overlord, the invasion of France, Stalin complained that he had not expected to discuss military issues so he had no military staff. 'But I've only got Marshal Voroshilov,' he said rudely. 'I hope he'll do.' He then ignored Voroshilov and handled all military matters himself. A young British interpreter, Hugh Lunghi,* was shocked to see that Stalin treated Voroshilov 'like a dog'. Stalin insisted on the earliest preference for Overlord, the cross-Channel invasion – and then quietly filled his pipe. Churchill was still unconvinced, preferring a preliminary Mediterranean operation, using troops already in the area. However FDR was already committed to the Channel. As a flustered Churchill realized he was outvoted, Roosevelt winked at Stalin, the start of his gauche flirtation that greatly enhanced the Marshal's position as arbiter of the Grand Alliance. Churchill handled Stalin much better by being himself.

Stalin was expansively charming to the foreigners but grumpy with his own delegates. When Bohlen approached him from behind, mid-session, Stalin snapped without turning, 'For God's sake, allow us to finish this work.' He was embarrassed when he found it was the young American. That night, Roosevelt held a dinner at his residence. His mess-boys prepared steaks and baked potatoes while the President shook up his cocktails of vermouth, gin and ice. Stalin sipped and winced: 'Well, it's all right but cold on the stomach.' Roosevelt suddenly turned 'green and great drops of sweat began to bead off his face'. He was wheeled to his room. When Churchill said God was on the side of the Allies, Stalin chaffed, 'And the Devil's on my side. The Devil's a Communist and God's a good Conservative!'

On the 29th, Stalin and Roosevelt met again: the Supremo knew from his briefing from Sergo Beria that his charm had worked.

---

* Major Hugh Lunghi, whose interview has greatly helped with this account, is probably the last man living to attend all the Plenary Big Three meetings at Teheran, Yalta and Potsdam.

'Roosevelt always expressed a high opinion of Stalin', recalled Sergo, which allowed him to put pressure on Churchill. That morning, the President proposed the creation of an international organization that became the United Nations. Meanwhile the generals were meeting with Voroshilov who, according to Lunghi, absolutely refused to understand the amphibious challenge of an invasion of France, thinking it was like crossing a Russian river on a raft.

Before the next session, Churchill, the only British Prime Minister to sport military uniforms in office, arrived in a blue RAF uniform with pilot's wings, to open a solemn ceremony to celebrate Stalingrad. At 3.30 p.m., all the delegations assembled in the hall of the Embassy. Then the Big Three arrived. A guard of honour formed up of British infantry with bayonets and NKVD troops in blue uniforms, red tabs and slung tommy-guns. An orchestra played their national anthems, in the Soviet case, the old one. The music stopped. There was silence. Then the officer of the British guard approached the large black box on the table and opened it. A gleaming sword lay on a bed of 'claret-coloured velvet'. He handed it to Churchill, who, laying the sword across his hands, turned to Stalin:

'I've been commanded by His Majesty King George VI to present to you ... this sword of honour ... The blade of the sword bears the inscription: "To the steel-hearted citizens of Stalingrad, a gift from King George VI as a token of the homage of the British People." ' Churchill stepped forward and presented the sword to Stalin who held it reverently in his hands for a long moment and then, with tears in his eyes, raised it to his lips and kissed it. Stalin was moved.

'On behalf of the citizens of Stalingrad,' he answered in 'a low husky voice', 'I wish to express my appreciation ...' He walked round to Roosevelt to show him the sword. The American read out the inscription: 'Truly they had hearts of steel.' Stalin handed the sword to Voroshilov. There was a crash as Voroshilov let the scabbard slip off the sword and on to his toes. The bungling cavalryman, who had charged waving his sabre many a time, had managed to introduce comedy in the most solemn moment of Stalin's international career. His cherubic cheeks blushing a bright scarlet, Klim remastered the sword. The Supremo, noticed Lunghi, frowned with irritation then gave 'a frosty, grim, forced-looking smile'. The NKVD lieutenant held the sword aloft and carried it away. Stalin must have snarled that Voroshilov should apologize because when he returned, he chased after Churchill, recruiting Lunghi to interpret. Flushed, he 'stammered his apologies' but then suddenly wished Churchill 'a happy birthday' for the following day. A special birthday banquet was being planned at the British Legation. 'I wish you a hundred more years of life,' said the Marshal, 'with the same spirit and vigour'. Churchill thanked him but whispered to Lunghi:

'Isn't he a bit premature? Must be angling for an invitation.'* Then the Big Three went outside for the famous photograph of the conference.

After a short interval, the delegations moved back to the round table for the next session. As ever, Stalin made sure that he always arrived last. When everyone was ready the Chekist Zoya Zarubina, on duty outside, was sent on an errand. She ran headlong down the steps and 'hit someone on the shoulder'. To her horror, it was Stalin. 'I stood frozen, stiff at attention ...' she wrote. 'I thought they'd surely shoot me on the spot.' Stalin did not react and walked on, followed by Molotov. But Voroshilov, always kind to the young and with more reason than most to indulge bunglers, 'patted me on the hand and said, "It's all right, kid, it's all right."'

Stalin, 'always smoking and doodling wolf-heads on a pad with his red pencil', was never agitated, rarely gestured and seldom consulted Molotov and Voroshilov. But he kept up the pressure on Churchill for the Second Front:

'Do the British really believe in Overlord or are you only saying so to reassure the Russians?' When he heard that the Allies had not yet agreed on a commander, he growled: 'Then nothing will come of these operations.' The Soviet Union had tried committee rule and found it had not worked. One man had to make the decisions. Finally, when Churchill would not give a date, Stalin suddenly got to his feet and turning to Molotov and Voroshilov, said,

'Let's not waste our time here. We've got plenty to do at the front.' Roosevelt managed to pour unction on troubled waters.

That night, it was Stalin's turn to host a banquet in the usual Soviet style with an 'unbelievable quantity of food'. A huge Russian 'waiter' in a white coat stood behind the Supremo's chair

---

* Hugh Lunghi typed up this farcical exchange and asked Churchill to sign it for him the next day. As interpreter for the British Chiefs of Staff, he also deputized for Churchill's principal interpreter, Major Arthur Birse.

throughout the meal.* Stalin 'drank little' but got his kicks by needling Churchill, exchanges in which Roosevelt seemed to take an undignified pleasure. Stalin sneered that he was glad Churchill was not a 'liberal', that most loathsome of creatures in the Bolshevik lexicon, but he then tested his severity by joking that 50,000 or perhaps 100,000 German officers should be executed. Churchill was furious: pushing his glass forward, knocking it over so brandy spread across the table, he growled:

'Such an attitude is contrary to the British sense of justice. The British Parliament and public would never support the execution of honest men who had fought for their country.' Roosevelt quipped that he would like to compromise: only 49,000 should be shot. Elliott Roosevelt, the President's ne'er-do-well son who was also present, jumped tipsily to his feet to josh: wouldn't the 50,000 fall in battle anyway?

'To your health, Elliott!' Stalin clinked glasses with him. But Churchill snarled at Roosevelt *fils*:

'Are you interested in damaging relations between the Allies ... How dare you!'† He headed for the door but as he reached it, 'hands were clapped on my shoulders from behind, and there was Stalin, with Molotov at his side, both grinning broadly and eagerly declaring that they were only playing ... Stalin has a very captivating manner when he chooses to use it.' Roosevelt's deference to Stalin and shabbiness to Churchill were both unseemly and counterproductive but the heartiness was restored by Stalin tormenting Molotov:

'Come here, Molotov, and tell us about your pact with Hitler.'

The finale was Churchill's sixty-ninth birthday held in the dining-hall of the British Legation which, Alan Brooke wrote in his diary, resembled 'a Persian temple', with the walls 'covered in a mosaic of small pieces of looking glass' and 'heavy deep red curtains. The Persian waiters were in blue and red livery' with

---

* The Americans thought he was the *maitre d'* and at the end of the conference were going to present him with some cigarettes when they found him resplendent in the uniform of an NKVD Major-General.

† Stalin had specially invited Elliott to the dinner. Perhaps he sensed the similarity with his own scapegrace son, Vasily. Both were pilots, inadequate yet arrogant drunks who were intimidated and dominated by brilliant fathers. Both exploited the family name and embarrassed their fathers. Both failed in multiple marriages and abandoned their wives. Perhaps there is no sadder curse than the gift of a titanic father.

oversized 'white cotton gloves, the tips of the fingers of which hung limply and flapped about'. Sikhs guarded the doorways.

Beria, who was there *incognito*, insisted that the NKVD search the British Legation, which was supervised by him personally with that glossy ruffian Tsereteli. 'There simply cannot be any doubt,' wrote a British security officer, Beria 'was an extremely intelligent and shrewd man with tremendous willpower and ability to impress, command and lead other men.' He disdained anyone else's opinion, becoming 'very angry if anyone ... opposed his proposals'. The other Russians 'behaved like slaves in his presence'.

Once Beria had signed off, Stalin arrived, but when a valet tried to take his coat, a bodyguard overreacted by reaching for his pistol. Calm was quickly restored. A cake with sixty-nine candles stood on the main table. Stalin toasted 'Churchill my fighting friend, if it is possible to consider Mr Churchill my friend' and then walked round to clink glasses with the Englishman, putting his arm around his shoulders. Churchill answered: 'To Stalin the Great!' When Churchill joked that Britain was 'becoming pinker', Stalin joked: 'A sign of good health.'

At the climax, the chef of the Legation cuisine produced a creation that came closer to assassinating Stalin than all the German agents in all the *souks* of Persia. Stalin was making a toast when two mountainous ice-cream pyramids were wheeled in with 'a base of ice one foot square and four inches deep', a religious nightlight inside it and a tube rising ten inches out of the middle on which a plate supporting a 'a vast ice-cream' had been secured with icing sugar. But as these creations approached Stalin, Brooke noticed that the lamp was melting the ice and 'now looked more like the Tower of Pisa'. Suddenly the tilt assumed a more dangerous angle and the British Chief of Staff shouted to his neighbours to duck. 'With the noise of an avalanche the whole wonderful construction slid over our heads and exploded in a clatter of plates.' Lunghi saw the nervous Persian waiter 'stagger sideways at the last moment'. Pavlov in his new diplomatic uniform 'came in for the full blast! ... splashed from head to foot' but Brooke guessed 'it was more than his life was worth to stop interpreting'. Stalin was unblemished.

'Missed the target,' whispered Air Marshal Sir Charles Portal.

At the final meetings next day, Roosevelt explained privately to Stalin that, since he had a Presidential election coming up, he

1941–1945

Stalin was shocked and bewildered by Hitler's attack, but after a crisis Stalin assumed the role he believed was made for him: supreme warlord. Initially, Stalin worked with his magnates and generals in an almost collegiate atmosphere before success allowed him to play the military genius. Here, Stalin runs the war assisted by (standing, from left): Bulganin (in uniform), Mikoyan, Khrushchev, Andreyev, Voznesensky, Voroshilov (in uniform) and Kaganovich; (seated, from left): Shvernik, Molotov, Beria and Malenkov.

The outstanding military partnership of the war: in late 1942, after his bungles had caused a series of unnecessary disasters, Stalin appointed Georgi Zhukov his deputy. He admired his military gifts, energy and brutal drive. Zhukov played a decisive role in the victories of Moscow, Leningrad, Stalingrad and Berlin. At the victory parade, Stalin allowed Zhukov to take the salute, but afterwards jealousy and paranoia led him to demote and humiliate his greatest general. Here in 1945, Stalin places Zhukov on his right, but is flanked on the other side by his 'political' Marshals, Voroshilov, who proved brave but inept, and Bulganin, who rose ruthlessly but without trace to become heir apparent.

Stalin as the arbiter of the Grand Alliance, playing Roosevelt against Churchill: here at Teheran in 1943, a grinning Voroshilov stands behind his master while General Alan Brooke (behind Churchill and Roosevelt) glances sardonically at their unsavoury ally.

Churchill and Stalin at Yalta, followed by General Vlasik.

At the Potsdam Conference, Stalin, resplendent in his white Generalissimo's uniform, poses with Churchill, who was about to be thrown out by the British electorate, and the new US President Harry Truman who informed him that America had the Bomb. Stalin despised Truman, missed Roosevelt, and thought Churchill the strongest of the capitalists.

10, Downing Street,
Whitehall.

WORDS EXCHANGED BETWEEN THE PRIME MINISTER OF GREAT
BRITAIN THE RT.HON.WINSTON CHURCHILL M.P. AND MARSHAL
OF THE SOVIET UNION K.E.VOROSHILOV AT THE CONCLUSION
OF THE THIRD PLENARY CONFERENCE OF THE THREE POWER
CONFERENCES (GREAT BRITAIN, U.S.S.R. and U.S.A) HELD
AT TEHRAN, IRAN, 28th.NOVEMBER TO 1st.DECEMBER 1943.
        (Interpreted by Captain H.A.Lunghi,R.A.).
                  ----

29 Nov. 1943

Marshal Voroshilov: I congratulate you heartily.

The Prime Minister: Thank you.

Marshal Voroshilov: I wish you a hundred more
        years of life displaying the same
        fine spirit and vigour as
        now.

The Prime Minister: Thank you very much.

30 Nov. 1943
The Prime Minister's
        Birthday.

Winston. Churchill

At Teheran, Churchill presented the Sword of Stalingrad to an emotional Stalin who passed
it to Voroshilov who dropped it. Stalin sent Voroshilov to apologise to Churchill. A blushing
Voroshilov grabbed Hugh Lunghi, a young English diplomat, to interpret. Voroshilov
apologised, then wished Churchill a happy birthday. The British Prime Minister thought the
Marshal was angling for a party invitation.

At Potsdam, Stalin placed Beria in charge of the race to get the Bomb, the greatest challenge of his career – he could not afford to fail. Here, Beria and Molotov visit the sights in the ruins of Hitler's Berlin, flanked by secret policemen Kruglov (left) and Serov, the expert on deportations.

Beria and family around 1946. Beria was a rapist and sadist – but a delightful father-in-law and grandfather. His blonde, clever and long-suffering wife, Nina (second from left) was the most beautiful of all the grandees' spouses – Stalin treated her like a daughter. Svetlana Stalin was in love with his handsome, dashing son Sergo (far left) whom Stalin also liked. But Sergo married Gorky's lissom granddaughter Martha Peshkova (far right), much to Svetlana's ire.

In 1938, when he promoted him to NKVD boss and brought him to Moscow, Stalin chose Beria's house himself. Only Beria was allowed this sumptuous nobleman's mansion (now the Tunisian Embassy). His wife and son lived in one wing; his own rooms and offices were in another: here many of his female victims were raped. When one refused him and was presented by a guard with the usual bouquet, Beria allegedly snarled: 'It's not a bouquet, it's a wreath.'

Just across from the Kremlin, the hideous colossus, the House on the Embankment, with its own cinema, built for the government in the early 1930s, was decimated during the 1937 Terror when many of its inhabitants were shot. In the morning the doorman told the survivors who had been arrested overnight. Here Natalya Rykova saw off her father for the last time. Stalin's family, such as Pavel and Zhenya Alliluyev, lived here; after the war Svetlana and Vasily had flats here.

In 1949, death stalked the elegant, pink Granovsky apartment block close to the Kremlin where the younger magnates lived in palatial apartments: Khrushchev and Bulganin on the fifth floor, Malenkov on the fourth. Beria was often to be seen waiting at the gates in a black limousine for his friends Khrushchev and Malenkov.

STALIN'S RESIDENCES.

Left His main Moscow house, Kuntsevo, from 1932, the place where he died. Like most of his residences, it was painted a gloomy khaki green.

Middle His favourite holiday house before the war: Sochi (viewed from outside the security gate), and (inset) inside the courtyard.

Bottom The centre of all his houses was always the vaulted dining room where he enjoyed long Georgian feasts with his henchmen, this one at Sochi. On the left his specially built paddling pool since he did not like swimming.

Opposite page STALIN'S FAVOURITE SOUTHERN HOUSES. From top: his post-war holiday headquarters, Coldstream; the millionaire's mansion in Sukhumi; and Museri.

Over-promoted, alcoholic, unstable, cruel and terrified, General Vasily Stalin abandoned two wives whom he treated abysmally and tried to win his father's favour by denouncing air force officers, often with fatal results. Stalin, ashamed of his wartime debauchery and hi-jinks, demoted him. Vasily feared that after his father's death, Bulganin and Khrushchev would kill him: he preferred the bottle or suicide. Girls flocked to the 'Crown Prince'.

After the war, General Vasily Stalin persuaded General Vlasik to give him his exquisite townhouse not far from the Kremlin.

Power and family: the heir apparent Zhdanov. At the end of the war, a tired but cheerful Stalin sits between the two rivals: the flabby, vicious and pusillanimous 'clerk', Malenkov – who was nicknamed 'Melanie' for his broad hips – and (right) smiling, alcoholic Zhdanov. Kaganovich sits on the left. (Back row, left to right): unknown, Vasily Stalin, Svetlana, Poskrebyshev. Stalin pushed Svetlana to marry Zhdanov's son. But the struggle between Zhdanov and Malenkov ended in a massacre.

could not discuss Poland at this meeting. The subordination of the fate of the country for which the war was fought to American machine politics can only have encouraged Stalin's plans for a tame Poland. At the last plenary meeting, it was a sign of the amateurism and immediacy of this intimate conference that Churchill and Stalin discussed Polish borders using a map torn out of *The Times*. The dangers of these meetings for Stalin's entourage were underestimated by the Westerners until Churchill's interpreter Birse presented his opposite number Pavlov with a set of Charles Dickens. Pavlov uneasily accepted the present.

'You're getting VERY close to our Western friends,' smiled Stalin to Pavlov's anxious discomfort.

On 2 December, Stalin, 'satisfied' that the Allies had finally promised to launch Overlord in the spring, flew out of Teheran and changed out of his Marshal's togs at Baku aerodrome, re-emerging in his old greatcoat, cap and boots. His train conveyed him to Stalingrad, his only post-battle visit to the city that had played such a decisive role in his life. He visited Paulus's headquarters but his limousine drove too fast down the narrow streets strewn with heaps of German equipment. It collided with a woman driver who almost expired when she realized with whom she had crashed. She started crying:

'It's my fault.' Stalin got out and calmed her:

'Don't cry. It's not your fault. Blame the war. Our car's armoured and didn't suffer. You can repair yours.' Afterwards he headed back to Moscow.

* * *

Stalingrad, Kursk and Teheran restored Stalin's zealous faith in his own infallible greatness. 'When victory became obvious,' wrote Mikoyan, 'Stalin got too big for his boots and became capricious.' The long boozy dinners started again: Stalin began to drink again, playing the ringmaster of a circus of uncouth hijinks, but in the mass of information he received from Beria, there was always much to worry him.

Beria arrested 931,544 persons in the liberated territory in 1943. As many as 250,000 people in Moscow attended Easter church services. He delivered the phone intercepts and informer reports to Stalin who read them carefully. Here the Supremo learned how Eisenstein was cutting his new movie, *Ivan the Terrible, Part Two*, because the Tsar's murders reminded him of Yezhov's Terror 'which he couldn't recall without shuddering ...' The message was clear: liberalism and ill-discipline threatened the State. The cost of Stalin's victories were vast: almost 26 million were dead, another 26 million homeless. There was a raging famine, treason among the Caucasian peoples, a Ukrainian nationalist civil war, and dangerous liberalism among the Russians themselves. All these had to be solved with the traditional Bolshevik solution, Terror.

Before they turned to terrorizing Russia proper, Beria and the local boss, Khrushchev, were running a new war in the Ukraine where three nationalist armies were fighting Soviet forces. Then there was the the dubious loyalty of the Caucasus and Crimea.

In February 1944, Beria proposed the deportation of the Moslem Chechen and Ingush. There had been cases of treason but most had been loyal. None the less Stalin and the GKO agreed – though Mikoyan claimed that he objected to it. On 20 February, Beria, Kobulov and the deportations expert, Serov, arrived in Grozny along with 19,000 Chekists and 100,000 NKVD troops. On 23 February, the locals were ordered to gather in their squares, then suddenly arrested and piled into trains bound for the East. By 7 March, Beria reported to Stalin that 500,000 innocents were on their way.

Other peoples, the Karachai and Kalmyks, joined the Volga Germans who had been deported in 1941. Beria constantly expanded the net: 'The Balkars are bandits and ... attacked the Red Army,' he wrote to Stalin on 25 February. 'If you agree, before my return to Moscow, I can take necessary measures to resettle the Balkars. I ask your orders.' Over 300,000 of these people were deported, but where to dump them all? Like the Nazis with their Jews, Stalin's men had to distribute this unwanted human flotsam throughout their Empire. Molotov suggested 40,000 in Kazakhstan, 14,000 somewhere else. Kaganovich found the trains. Andreyev, now running Agriculture, dealt with their farming equipment. Everyone was involved. When an official noticed that there were 1,300 Kalmyks still living in Rostov, Molotov replied that they must be deported at once. Mikoyan may have disapproved but the capital of the Karachais, Karachaevsk, was now renamed after him. In the dry language of these bureaucratic notes, we can only glimpse the tragedy and suffering of this monumental crime.

Then Beria reported the treason of Tatars in the Crimea and soon 160,000 were on their way eastwards in forty-five trains: he listed their food allowance to Stalin but given the thousands who died, it is unlikely that they received most of it. Throughout the year, Beria kept finding more pockets of these poor people: on 20 May, there were 'still German supporters in the Kabardin republic after resettlement of Balkars' and he asked if he could 'remove' another 2,467 people: 'Agreed. J. Stalin' is written at the bottom. By the time he had finished, a triumphant Beria had removed 1.5 million people. Stalin approved 413 medals for Beria's Chekists. More than a quarter of the deportees died, according to the NKVD, but as many as 530,000 perished en route or on arrival at the camps. For each of these peoples, this was an apocalypse that approached the Holocaust.

While these cattle cars of human cargo trundled eastwards, famine was raging in Russia, Central Asia and the Ukraine. In a replay of collectivization, Stalin sensed weakness in his Politburo. There are hints of disturbing things in the archives: in November 1943, Andreyev reported to Malenkov from Saratov that 'things are very bad here ... Yesterday driving from Stalingrad ... I saw terrible sights ...' On 22 November 1944, Beria reported to Stalin another case of cannibalism in the Urals when two women kidnapped and ate four children. Mikoyan and Andreyev suggested giving the peasants seeds:

'To Molotov and Mikoyan,' Stalin scrawled on their note, 'I vote against. Mikoyan's behaviour is anti-state ... he has absolutely corrupted Andreyev. Patronage over Narkomzag [Commissariat of Supply] should be taken away from Mikoyan and given to Malenkov ...' This was the beginning of a growing iciness between Stalin and Mikoyan that was to become increasingly dangerous.

* * *

On 20 May 1944, Stalin met his generals to co-ordinate the vast summer offensive that would finally toss the Germans off Soviet territory. Much of the Ukraine was already liberated and the Leningrad siege finally lifted. Stalin proposed a single thrust towards Bobruisk to Rokossovsky, who knew two thrusts were required to avoid senseless casualties. But Stalin was set on just one. Rokossovsky, the tall and graceful half-Polish general who was favoured by Stalin yet had been tortured just before the war, was brave enough to insist on his own view.

'Go out and think it over again,' said Stalin, who later summoned him back: 'Have you thought it through, General?' asked Stalin again.

'Yes sir, Comrade Stalin.'

'Well then ... a single thrust?' – and Stalin marked it on the map. There was silence until Rokossovsky replied:

'Two thrusts are more advisable, Comrade Stalin.' Again silence fell.

'Go out and think it over again. Don't be stubborn, Rokossovsky.' The general again sat next door until he realized he was not alone: Molotov and Malenkov loomed over him. Rokossovsky stood up.

'Don't forget where you are and with whom you're talking, General,' Malenkov threatened him. 'You're disagreeing with Comrade Stalin.'

'You'll have to agree, Rokossovsky,' added Molotov. 'Agree – that's all there is to it!' The general was summoned back into the study:

'So which is better?' asked Stalin.

'Two,' answered Rokossovsky. Silence descended until Stalin asked:

'Can it be that two blows are really better?' Stalin accepted Rokossovsky's plan. On 23 June, the offensive shattered the German forces. Minsk and then Lvov were recaptured. On 8 July, Zhukov found Stalin at Kuntsevo in 'great gaiety'. As he ordered the advance on the Vistula, Stalin was determined to impose his own government on Poland so that it would never again threaten Russia: on 22 July, he established a Polish Committee under Boleslaw Bierut to form the new government.

'Hitler's like a gambler staking his last coin!' exulted Stalin.

'Germany will try to make peace with Churchill and Roosevelt,' said Molotov.

'Right,' said Stalin, 'but Roosevelt and Churchill won't agree.' Then the Poles threw a spanner into the works of the Grand Alliance.

* * *

The Red Army offensive ground to an exhausted halt on the Vistula just east of Warsaw when, on 1 August, General Tadeusz Bor-Komorowski and the 20,000 patriots of the Polish Home Army rose against the Germans in the Warsaw Rising. But the patriots, in the words of one distinguished historian, aimed 'not to help the Soviet advance but to forestall it'. Hitler ordered that Warsaw be razed, deploying a ghoulish crew of SS fanatics, convicts and Russian renegades to slaughter 225,000 civilians in one merciless inferno.

The extermination of the Home Army completed the 'black work' of Katyn Forest for Stalin who had no interest in coming to their rescue. Yet the rising and, more particularly, the Western sympathy for it, sent Stalin into a spin. If its success threatened his Polish plans, then Anglo-American fury about its failure threatened the Grand Alliance.

On 1 August, Zhukov and Rokossovsky arrived to find Stalin 'agitated', pacing up to the maps and then striding off again, even putting down his unlit pipe, always a storm petrel. Stalin pressured the generals – could their armies advance? Zhukov and Rokossovsky said they must rest. Stalin seemed angry. Beria and Molotov threatened them. Stalin sent the generals into the library next door where they nervously discussed their plight. Rokossovsky thought Beria was inciting Stalin. Things could end badly: 'I know very well what Beria is capable of,' whispered Rokossovsky, ultra-cautious as the son of a Polish officer. 'I've been in his prisons.' Twenty minutes later, Malenkov appeared and claimed he was supporting the generals. There would be no rescue of Warsaw.

Zhukov suspected the Supremo had set up this charade as an alibi. But Soviet forces were exhausted: as Rokossovsky told a Western journalist, 'The rising would have made sense only if we were on the point of taking Warsaw. That point had not been reached at any stage ... We were pushed back.' Meanwhile, as Churchill and Roosevelt exerted intense pressure on their ally to aid the Poles, Stalin coolly claimed that their account of the rising was 'greatly exaggerated'. By the time his armies pushed into Poland, Hungary and Romania, it was much too late for the patriots of Warsaw.

* * *

Seven days after the surrender of the Home Army, Churchill arrived in Moscow to divide up the spoils of Eastern Europe. Stalin had stated his real view to Molotov in 1942: 'The question of borders will be decided by force.' At Stalin's Kremlin flat, Churchill, who was this time staying in a town house, proposed a 'naughty document' to list their interests in the small countries by percentage. The Soviet record in Stalin's own archives showed that, just as Roosevelt had undermined Churchill at Teheran, so now the Englishman opened this conversation by saying that the 'Americans including the President would be shocked by the division of Europe into spheres of influence'. In Romania, Russia had 90 per cent, Britain 10 per cent; in Greece, Britain had 90 per cent, Russia 10 per cent. Stalin ticked it.

'Might it not be thought cynical if it seemed we'd disposed of these issues, so fateful to millions of people, in such an offhand manner?' said Churchill, half guilty at, and half-revelling in, the arrogance of the Great Powers.

'No, you keep it,' replied Stalin. The document was taken seriously enough for Eden and Molotov to negotiate for two more days about the percentage of Soviet influence in Bulgaria and Hungary, both raised to 80 per cent, and Stalin did stick to his part of the deal on Greece but that was because it suited him. The percentages agreement was, from Stalin's point of view, surely a bemusing attempt to negotiate what was already a *fait accompli*.

The climax of the visit was Stalin's first public appearance at the Bolshoi since the war began, accompanied by Churchill, Molotov, Harriman and his daughter Kathleen. When they arrived at the theatre, the lights were already dimmed – Stalin usually slipped in after the play had started. When the lights went up and the audience saw Stalin and Churchill, there were 'thunderous cheers and clapping'. Stalin withdrew modestly but Churchill sent Vyshinsky to bring him back. The two stood there together, beaming amidst cheering so loud it was 'like a cloudburst on a tin roof'. Stalin and Molotov then shepherded their guests into the *avant-loge* where a dinner for twelve was laid out. Quaffing champagne, Stalin performed like a roguish old satyr, charming and chilling his guests in equal parts. When Molotov raised his glass to the 'great leader', Stalin quipped:

'I thought he was going to say something new about me.' Someone joked that the Big Three were like the Trinity.

'If that's so,' said Stalin, 'Churchill must be the Holy Ghost. He flies about so much.'* When Churchill finally left on 19 October, having made little progress over Poland, Stalin personally came to the airport to see him off, waving his handkerchief.

Stalin was now enjoying the power of victory – and the bullying showman who emerged was not a pretty sight. His respectful

---

* Stalin made one joke about Maisky, the ex-embassador to London, who was present, that was not translated. The Russians though laughed uproariously at it so Brooke asked him what was so funny. Maisky glumly explained, 'The Marshal has referred to me as the Poet-Diplomat because I have written a few verses at times but our last poet-diplomat was liquidated – that is the joke.' The original Poet-Diplomat was the Russian Ambassador to Persia, Griboyedov, who was torn to pieces by the Teheran mob in 1829. Maisky was later arrested and tortured.

gaiety with Churchill metamorphosed into threatening drunken-ness with the less powerful such as Charles de Gaulle. In December, the Frenchman visited Moscow to sign a treaty of alliance and mutual assistance. In return, Stalin wanted French recognition of Bierut's Polish Government which de Gaulle refused to give. By the time of the banquet, the negotiations were stuck. This did not stop Stalin getting swaggeringly drunk, to the horror of the gloomy de Gaulle. Stalin complained to Harriman that de Gaulle was 'an awkward and clumsy man', but that did not matter because they 'must drink more wine and then everything will straighten out'.

Stalin, swigging champagne, took over the toasts from Molotov. After praising Roosevelt and Churchill, while pointedly ignoring de Gaulle, Stalin embarked on a terrifying gallows tour of his entourage: he toasted Kaganovich, 'a brave man. He knows that if the trains do not arrive on time' – he paused – 'we shall shoot him!' Then: 'Come here!' Kaganovich rose and they clinked glasses jovially. Then Stalin lauded Air Force Commander Novikov, this 'good Marshal, let's drink to him. And if he doesn't do his job properly, we'll hang him.' (Novikov would soon be arrested and tortured.) Then he spotted Khrulev: 'He'd better do his best, or he'll be hanged for it, that's the custom in our country!' Again: 'Come here!' Noticing the distaste on de Gaulle's face, Stalin chuckled: 'People call me a monster, but as you see, I make a joke of it. Maybe I'm not horrible after all.'

Molotov collared his French opposite number, Bidault, with whom he began arguing over the treaty. Stalin gestured at them, calling out to Bulganin: 'Bring the machine guns. Let's liquidate the diplomats.' Leading his guests out for coffee and movies, Stalin 'kept hugging the French and lurching around', noticed Khrushchev who was also present but had avoided a threatening toast. He was 'completely drunk'. While the diplomats negotiated, Stalin drank more champagne. Finally in the early hours, when de Gaulle had gone to bed, the Russians suddenly agreed to sign the treaty without recognition of Bierut. De Gaulle was rushed back into the Kremlin where Stalin first asked him to sign the original treaty. When de Gaulle angrily retorted: 'France has been insulted', Stalin cheerfully called for the new draft which was then signed at 6.30 a.m.

As the fastidious Frenchman left, Stalin called for his interpreter and laughed: 'You know too much. I'd better send you to Siberia!'

De Gaulle looked back one last time: 'I saw Stalin sitting alone at a table. He had started eating again.'

The same exuberant victor presided over a series of dinners and banquets for the visiting Yugoslavs that winter. Stalin was outraged that the Yugoslav Politburo member Milovan Djilas had complained about the rape and pillage of the Red Army. Stalin regarded any criticism of the army as an attack on himself. He drunkenly lectured the Yugoslavs about his army 'which pushed its way across thousands of miles' only to be attacked 'by none other than Djilas! Djilas whom I received so well!' In the absence of the man himself, Djilas's wife, Mitra Mitrovic, one of the delegates, caught his eye and he 'proposed toasts, joked, teased, wept' before kissing her repeatedly, jesting salaciously: 'I'll kiss you even if the Yugoslavs and Djilas accuse me of having raped you!'

When Stalin invited some American officials to the Kremlin cinema, he moved to sit between the leading Westerners but then he turned round to Kavtaradze:

'Come on, boy, sit next to me!'

'How can I?' answered Kavtaradze. 'You've guests.' Stalin waved his hand, adding in Georgian:

'Fuck them!'

That New Year's Eve, Stalin and his magnates, along with General Khrulev, saw in 1945 with an all-night, singing and dancing Bacchanal.

43

The Swaggering Conqueror:
Yalta and Berlin

When Stalin eyed the great prize of Berlin, he decided to change the way he ran the war: there would be no more Stavka representatives in charge of fronts. Henceforth, the Supremo would command directly.

Zhukov was to command the First Belorussian Front that was to fight the five hundred miles to Berlin. Six million Soviet soldiers were massed for the Vistula–Oder offensive. Two weeks later, Koniev was plunging into the 'gold' of industrial Silesia, Zhukov had expelled the Germans from central Poland, and Malinovsky was fighting frenziedly for Budapest. The Second and Third Belorussian Fronts broke into East Prussia, Germany itself, in a fiesta of vengeance: two million German women were to be raped in the coming months. Russian soldiers even raped Russian women newly liberated from Nazi camps. Stalin cared little about this, telling Djilas: 'You have of course read Dostoevsky? Do you see what a complicated thing is man's soul ...? Well then, imagine a man who has fought from Stalingrad to Belgrade – over thousands of kilometres of his own devastated land, across the dead bodies of his comrades and dearest ones? How can such a man react normally? And what is so awful about his having fun with a woman after such horrors?'

Roosevelt and Churchill had been discussing the next Big Three meeting ever since July 1944. Stalin was reluctant: when, in September, Harriman suggested a meeting in the Mediterranean, Stalin retorted that his doctors had told him 'any change of climate would have a bad effect', this from a man who distrusted doctors intensely. Molotov could go instead. Molotov politely insisted that he could never replace Marshal Stalin.

'You're too modest,' said Stalin drily. They agreed on Yalta. By 29 January, Zhukov was on the Oder. As German forces counter-attacked the Soviet bridgeheads, Roosevelt and Churchill were being greeted on 3 February at Saki airforce base in the Crimea by

Molotov, in stiff white collar, black coat and fur hat, and Vyshinsky, resplendent in his diplomatic uniform, who hosted a 'magnificent luncheon' on their way to Yalta.

* * *

Stalin himself had not yet left Moscow but he had approved Beria's arrangements in a memorandum so secret that key names were left out and only filled in by hand. The conference would be guarded by four NKVD regiments and defended by arrays of AA guns and 160 fighter planes. Stalin's security was described thus: 'For the guarding of the chief of the Soviet delegation, besides the bodyguards under Comrade Vlasik, there are additionally 100 operative workers and a special detachment of 500 from NKVD regiments.' In other words, Stalin himself had a bodyguard of about 620 men but in addition, there were two circles of guards by day, three circles by night, and guard dogs. Five districts spanning twenty kilometres had been 'purged of suspicious elements' – 74,000 people had been checked and 835 arrested. With its towns deserted and ruined after the depredations of the Nazis and the deportation of the Tartars, it was no wonder Churchill dubbed Yalta 'The Riviera of Hades'.

On Sunday morning, 4 February, Stalin boarded his green railway car, accompanied by Poskrebyshev and Vlasik, travelling south via Kharkov. His residence, the Yusupov Palace, once the home of the Croesian transvestite prince who had assassinated Rasputin, was ready for the Soviet delegation with its twenty rooms and its 77-square-foot hall. Everything had been brought down from Moscow including plates, cutlery and the trusty waiters of the Metropol and National hotels. Special bakeries made bread and special fisherman delivered fresh fish. 'A special "*Vch*" high frequency telephone and Baudot telegraph as well as an automatic telephone station of 20 numbers ... possible to increase to 50' had been set up so that Stalin could 'call Moscow, the fronts, and all towns'. He could avail himself of a bomb shelter that could withstand 500kg bombs.

Stalin immediately received his delegates in the study, Beria's room being almost next door, while the younger diplomats stayed in the adjoining wing. Sudoplatov delivered psychological portraits of the Western leaders, Molotov evaluated intelligence and again, Sergo Beria claimed he was on bugging duty. This time, they even used positional directional microphones to listen to FDR as he was wheeled outside.

At 3 p.m., Stalin* called on Churchill at his residence, the fantastical palace of Prince Michael Vorontsov, an Anglophile who had created a unique architectural pot-pourri of Scottish baronial, neo-Gothic and Moorish Arabesque. He then drove to Roosevelt's white granite Livadia Palace, built in 1911 as the summer home of the last Tsar.† At dinner that night, Roosevelt misjudged Stalin's prickly self-image when he confided that his nickname was 'Uncle Joe'. Stalin was offended, muttering,

'When can I leave this table?' He was assured it was a joke. At 4 p.m. next day, the conference opened in the Livadia's ballroom. Sitting between Molotov and Maisky, chain-smoking cigarettes, Stalin greatly impressed the young Andrei Gromyko, his Ambassador to America who later became Brezhnev's perennial Foreign Minister: he 'missed nothing' and worked 'with no papers, no notes', using a 'memory like a computer'. It was during these plenary meetings that Stalin delivered his most famous one-liner. As always with his jokes, he repeated it frequently and it entered the political vernacular as an expression of force over sentiment. They were discussing the Pope:

'Let's make him our ally,' proposed Churchill.

'All right,' smiled Stalin, 'but as you know, gentlemen, war is waged with soldiers, guns, tanks. How many divisions has the Pope? If he tells us ... let him become our ally.'‡

In the evenings, Stalin held little parties to meet his entourage, where Gromyko noticed how he 'exchanged a few words with each member', and moved from group to group, making jokes, remembering all fifty-three delegates by name. There were meetings every morning and evening: he was often crushing to his advisers if they did not do their job. Hugh Lunghi, once again

---

*A month later, the editor of *Izvestiya* prepared a special photographic album which he sent to Poskrebyshev: 'Esteemed Alexander Nikolaievich, I send you the photographs of the Crimean conference for JV Stalin.' Its front was embossed in big letters to him. Stalin was a shabby sight next to the dapper Molotov: his Yalta photo album shows the poorly darned pockets of his beloved but rumpled old greatcoat. The porcine Vlasik was always just a step behind him, beaming affably, but Stalin's security was as tight as ever. Once when Bohlen noticed Stalin visit the lavatory, two Soviet bodyguards ran around, yelling, 'Where's Stalin! Where's he gone?' Bohlen pointed to the W.C.

† The President was exhausted and ailing. His suite had a living room, a dining room (the Tsar's billiard room), bedroom and bathroom. His closest adviser Harry Hopkins was so ill that he spent most of the time in bed. According to Alan Brooke, General Marshall 'is in the Tsarina's bedroom' and Admiral King 'in her boudoir with the special staircase for Rasputin to visit her!'

‡ Stalin told his version to Enver Hoxha, the Albanian leader.

interpreting at the conference, heard him saying, 'I don't trust Vyshinsky but with him all things are possible. He'll jump whichever way we tell him.' Vyshinsky reacted to Stalin 'like a frightened hound'.

When Roosevelt was ill, Stalin, Molotov and Gromyko visited him for twenty minutes. Afterwards, coming down the stairs, 'Stalin suddenly stopped, took the pipe out of his pocket, filled it unhurriedly and as if to himself said quietly, "Why did nature have to punish him so? Is he any worse than other people?"' He had always distrusted Churchill but Roosevelt seemed to fascinate him:

'Tell me,' he asked Gromyko, 'what do you think of Roosevelt? Is he clever?' Stalin did not hide his fondness for FDR from Gromyko which amazed the young diplomat because his character was so harsh that he 'rarely bestowed his sympathy on anyone from another social system'. Only occasionally did he 'give way to positive human emotions'.

The next day, 6 February, they met to discuss the painful subject of Poland and the world organization that would become the UN. Russia would take eastern slices of Poland in exchange for grants of German territory in the west. Stalin assented only to include a few Polish nationalists in his Communist-dominated government. When FDR said the Polish elections had to be 'beyond question like Caesar's wife', Stalin quipped,

'They said that about her but she had her sins.' Stalin explained the Russian obsession with Poland: 'Throughout history, Poland has served as a corridor for enemies coming to attack Russia' – hence he wanted a strong Poland. If Beria's son can be believed, his father came into his room that day saying, 'Joseph Vissarionovich has not moved an inch on Poland.' They approved the three zones of occupation in a demilitarized and de-Nazified Germany. The Americans were pleased by Stalin's repeated promise to intervene against Japan, agreeing to his demands for Sakhalin and the Kurile Islands.

On the 8th, after another meeting, they dined with Stalin at the Yusupov Palace where their opening speeches became more and more emotional as the Big Three, all aged by the war, contemplated their victory. Stalin rose to the occasion, toasting Churchill, 'a man who is born once in a hundred years, and who bravely held up the banner of Great Britain. I've said what I feel, what I have in my heart, and of what I'm conscious.' Stalin was 'in the very best of form', wrote Brooke, 'and was full of fun and good humour.' Stalin, who fooled no one when he described himself as a 'naïve ... garrulous old man', ominously toasted the generals 'who are recognized only during a war and whose services after the war are quickly forgotten. After the war, their prestige goes down and the ladies turn their back on them.' The generals did not yet realize he meant to forget them himself.

This epic dinner boasted one unusual guest: Stalin invited a delighted Beria, who was beginning to find his secret role constricting. Roosevelt noticed him and asked Stalin:

'Who's that in the pince-nez opposite Ambassador Gromyko?'

'Ah, that one. That's our Himmler,' replied Stalin with deliberate malice. 'That's Beria.' The secret policeman 'said nothing, just smiled, showing his yellow teeth' but 'it must have cut him to the quick', wrote his son, who knew how he longed to step on to the world stage. Roosevelt was upset by this, observed Gromyko, especially since Beria heard it too. The Americans examined this mysterious figure with fascination: 'He's little and fat with thick lenses which give him a sinister look but quite genial,' said Kathleen Harriman while Bohlen thought him 'plump, pale with pince-nez like a schoolmaster'. The sex-obsessed Beria was soon discussing the sex-life of fishes with the boozy, womanizing Sir Archibald Clark Kerr. When he was thoroughly drunk, Sir Archibald stood up and toasted Beria – 'the man who looks after our bodies', a compliment that was not only inappropriate but bungled. Churchill considered Beria the wrong sort of friend for HM Ambassador:

'No, Archie, none of that. Be careful,' he waved his finger.

On 10 February, at Churchill's dinner, Stalin proposed George VI's health with a proviso that he had always been against kings because he was on the side of the people. Churchill, somewhat irritated, suggested to Molotov that in future he should just propose a toast to the 'three Heads of State'. With only twelve or so at dinner, they discussed the upcoming British elections, which Stalin was sure Churchill would win:

'Who could be a better leader than he who won the victory?' Churchill explained there were two parties.

'One party is much better,' Stalin said. When they talked about Germany, Stalin regaled them with a story about the country's 'unreasonable sense of discipline' which he had told repeatedly to his own circle. When he arrived in Leipzig for a Communist conference, the Germans had arrived at the station but found no ticket collector so they waited for two hours on the platform until he arrived.

After a final dinner in the Tsar's billiard room at Livadia, Molotov escorted Roosevelt back to Saki, getting on to the presidential plane, the *Sacred Cow*, to say goodbye.

Churchill spent the night on the *Franconia* in Sebastopol harbour, flying out next day. Stalin was already on his train to Moscow. Budapest fell two days later.*

Stalin had won virtually all he wanted from the Allies and this is usually blamed on Roosevelt's illness and susceptibility to Stalinist charm. Both Westerners stand accused of 'selling out Eastern Europe to Stalin'.† Roosevelt's courtship of Stalin and discourtesy to Churchill were misguided. FDR was certainly ill and exhausted. But Stalin always believed that force would decide who ruled Eastern Europe which was occupied by 10 million Soviet soldiers. He himself told an anecdote after the war which reveals his view of Yalta. 'Churchill, Roosevelt and Stalin went hunting,' Stalin said. 'They finally killed their bear. Churchill said, "I'll take the bearskin. Let Roosevelt and Stalin divide the meat." Roosevelt said, "No, I'll take the skin. Let Churchill and Stalin divide the meat." Stalin remained silent so Churchill and Roosevelt ask him: "Mister Stalin, what do you say?" Stalin simply replied, "The bear belongs to me – after all, I killed it."' The bear is Hitler, the bearskin is Eastern Europe.

On 8 March, amidst operations to clean up Pomerania, Stalin summoned Zhukov to Kuntsevo for a strange meeting that marked the apotheosis of their close, touchy partnership. The Supremo was ill and 'greatly over-exhausted'. He seemed depressed. 'He had worked too much and slept too little,' thought Zhukov. The Battle for Berlin was his last great effort. Afterwards,

---

* There is an intriguing note in the archives concerning Churchill: a General Gorbatov reports to Beria on 5 May that orders had been sent to the NKVD with Marshal Malinovsky's army in Hungary to find a relative of Winston Churchill named Betsy Pongrantz and she had been found. The meaning is not precisely clear but none of the Churchills have heard of this 'relative'. Sir Winston's surviving daughter Lady Soames is unaware of the existence of this possibly Hungarian kinswoman: 'Perhaps Mr Beria and the NKVD had just got it wrong!' she suggests.
† If there was a sell-out, it had probably occurred much earlier at the Moscow Foreign Minister's Conference in October 1943. None the less, Stalin was surely delighted to leave Yalta with Foreign Secretary Eden's signature on the agreement to return all 'Soviet' ex-POWs, many of them White Cossack émigrés from the Civil War who had fought for the Nazis. Many were either shot or perished in Stalin's Gulags.

he could no longer sustain that tempo of work. He was not alone: Roosevelt was dying; Hitler almost senile; Churchill often ill. Total war took a total toll on its warlords. The Stalin who emerged from the war was both more sentimental and also more deadly.

'Let's stretch our legs a little, I feel sort of limp,' said Stalin. As they walked, Stalin talked about his childhood for an hour. 'Let's get back and have tea. I want to talk something over with you.' Encouraged by this surprising intimacy, Zhukov asked about Yakov:

'Have you heard about his fate?'

Stalin did not answer. His son Yakov tormented him. After about a hundred steps in silence, he answered in a 'subdued voice':

'Yakov won't be able to get out of captivity. They'll shoot him, the killers. From what we know, they're keeping him separately … and persuading him to betray his country.' Stalin was silent again, then he said, 'No, Yakov would prefer any kind of death to betraying the Motherland.' He was proud of his son at last but did not know he had been dead for almost two years. Stalin did not eat but sat at table: 'What a terrible war. How many lives of our people borne away. There'll probably be few families who haven't lost someone dear to them.' He talked about how he liked Roosevelt. Yalta had been a success. Just then Poskrebyshev arrived with his bag of papers and Stalin turned to Berlin:

'Go to Stavka and look at the calculations for the Berlin operation …' Three weeks later, on the morning of 1 April, Stalin held a conference with his two most aggressive marshals, Zhukov of the 1st Belorussian Front and Koniev of the 1st Ukrainian, at the Little Corner. 'Well. Who's going to take Berlin: we or the Allies?'

'It's we who'll take Berlin!' barked Koniev before Zhukov could even answer.

'So that's the sort of man you are,' Stalin grinned approvingly. Zhukov was to assault Berlin from the Oder bridgeheads over the Seelow Heights; Koniev to push towards Leipzig and Dresden, with his northern flank thrusting towards southern Berlin parallel to Zhukov. The Supremo of ambiguity allowed them both to believe that they could take Berlin: 'without saying a word', Stalin drew the demarcation line between the fronts into Berlin – then stopped and erased the line to the south of Berlin. Koniev understood this allowed him to join in the storming of

Berlin – if he could. 'Whoever breaks in first,' Stalin teased them, 'let him take Berlin.' That very day, in what one historian has described as 'the greatest April Fool in modern history', Stalin reassured Eisenhower that 'Berlin has lost its former strategic importance.' Two days later, the two marshals actually raced to the airport, their planes taking off within two minutes of each other. Such, Koniev admitted, was 'their passionate desire' to take the prize.

As they were marshalling their forces, Roosevelt died, the end of an era for Stalin. Their *entente* had won his paltry trust and roused his meagre human sympathy. Molotov 'seemed deeply moved and disturbed'. Harriman had 'never heard Molotov talk so earnestly'. Stalin, 'deeply distressed', received Harriman, holding his hand for thirty seconds. Years later, Stalin, on holiday at his New Athos dacha, judged 'Roosevelt was a great statesman, a clever, educated, far-sighted and liberal leader who prolonged the life of capitalism ...'

At 5 a.m. on 16 April, Zhukov unleashed a barrage of 14,600 guns against the Seelow Heights. The two marshals wielded 2.5 million men, 41,600 guns, 6,250 tanks and 7,500 aircraft, 'the largest concentration of firepower ever assembled'. But the Heights were a well-defended obstacle. Zhukov's losses were punishing. At midnight, he telephoned Stalin who taunted him:

'So you've underestimated the enemy on the Berlin axis? Things have started more successfully for Koniev.' The Supremo then phoned Koniev: 'Things are pretty hard with Zhukov. He's still hammering at the defences.' Stalin stopped. Koniev, who understood the workings of the Supremo, kept silent until Stalin asked: 'Is it possible to transfer Zhukov's tank forces and send them to Berlin through the gap on your front?' Koniev replied excitedly that his own tank forces could turn on Berlin. Stalin checked the map. 'I agree. Turn your tank armies on Berlin.' Zhukov was determined to take Berlin himself: ignoring tank lore, he stormed the Heights with tanks which became stuck in a churning swamp of pulverized earth and corpses. He lost 30,000 men. Stalin did not call him for three days.

On 20 April, Zhukov reached Berlin's eastern suburbs. Both marshals fought, house by house, street by street, towards Hitler's Chancellery. On the 25th, Koniev ordered an assault towards the Reichstag. Three hundred yards from the Reichstag building, Chuikov, who was leading Zhukov's thrust, encountered Russian forces – Koniev's tanks. Zhukov himself sped up and shouted at Rybalko, Koniev's tank commander:

'Why have you appeared here?' Koniev, disappointed, swerved west, leaving the Reichstag to Zhukov, but Stalin offered another prize:

'Who's going to take Prague?'

Stalin waited at Kuntsevo, only appearing in the office for a couple of hours around midnight each day. On 28 April, in the *Führerbunker*, Hitler married Eva Braun, dictated his testament, and they drank champagne.* Two days later, as Zhukov pushed closer, Hitler tested cyanide ampoules on his Alsatian, Blondi. Around 3.15 p.m., to the distant buzz of partying upstairs, Hitler committed suicide, shooting himself in the head. Eva took poison. Goebbels and Bormann made a final Hitler salute before the pyre of Hitler's body in the Chancellery garden. At 7.30 p.m., an unknowing Stalin arrived at the office to meet Malenkov and Vyshinsky for forty-five minutes before returning to Kuntsevo.

In the early hours of May Day, the German Chief of Staff visited Chuikov, announcing Hitler's death and requesting a ceasefire. Ironically, this was Hans Krebs, the tall German officer whom Stalin, seeing off the Japanese in April 1941, had told: 'We shall remain friends.' Chuikov refused a ceasefire. Krebs left and committed suicide. In a reverse of 22 June 1941, Zhukov, eager to break this world-historical news, telephoned Kuntsevo. Once again, the security refused to help.

'Comrade Stalin's just gone to bed,' replied General Vlasik.

'Please wake him,' retorted Zhukov. 'The matter's urgent and cannot wait until morning.'

Stalin picked up the phone and heard that Hitler was dead.

'So that's the end of the bastard.'

---

* In the higher levels of the Bunker, Hitler's secretary discovered 'an erotic fever seemed to take possession of everybody. Everywhere even on the dentist's chair, I saw bodies interlocked in lascivious embraces. The women had discarded all modesty and were freely exposing their private parts.'

Part Nine

The Dangerous Game of Succession,
1945–1949

44

The Bomb

'Too bad we couldn't take him alive,' Stalin told Zhukov. 'Where's Hitler's body?'

'According to General Krebs, his body was burned.' Stalin banned negotiations, except for unconditional surrender. 'And don't ring me until the morning if there's nothing urgent. I want some rest before tomorrow's parade.'

At 10.15 a.m., Zhukov's artillery bombarded the city centre. By dawn on the 2nd, Berlin was his. On 4 May, a Smersh colonel discovered the wizened, charred remains of Hitler and Eva. The bodies were spirited away. Zhukov was not told. Indeed, Stalin enjoyed humiliating the Marshal by asking if he had heard anything about Hitler's body.* Meanwhile Stalin was fascinated by the Nazi leadership: 'I'm sending you ... the correspondence of the top Germans ... found in Berlin,' Beria wrote to him, listing Himmler's letters to Ribbentrop.

After the war, during a late dinner on the Black Sea coast, Stalin was asked whether Hitler was a lunatic or an adventurer:

'I agree that he was an adventurer but I can't agree he was mad. Hitler was a gifted man. Only a gifted man could unite the German people. Like it or not ... the Soviet Army fought their way into the German land ... and reached Berlin without the German working-class ever striking against ... the Fascist regime. Could a madman so unite his nation?'

On 9 May, Moscow celebrated Victory Day but the curmudgeonly conqueror was wearily impatient with the jubilation. Stalin was furious when a junior general signed the German surrender at Reims and, pacing the floor, ordered Zhukov to sign a proper surrender in Berlin, 'whence German aggression sprang'. But the

---

* The jawbone and a portion of skull were kept in Moscow; the rest of his cadaver was tested by Smersh and then buried beside a garage at a Soviet army base in Magdeburg where it remained until KGB Chairman Yury Andropov ordered it cremated and the ashes scattered in April 1970.

glory days of the generals were over: Vyshinsky arrived to 'handle political matters' and spent the entire ceremony, 'bobbing up to whisper instructions in Zhukov's ear'. Stalin closely watched Zhukov and his supposed delusions of grandeur. Later in the year, he summoned him to the Kremlin to warn him that Beria and Abakumov were gathering evidence against him:

'I don't believe all this nonsense but stay out of Moscow.' That was not a problem since Zhukov was Stalin's proconsul in Berlin. Stalin despatched his satraps to rule his new Empire. Mikoyan flew in to feed the Germans. Malenkov and Voznesensky arrived to fight about whether to loot German industry or preserve it to build a Soviet satellite regime. Zhdanov held court in Finland, Voroshilov in Hungary, Bulganin in Poland, Vyshinsky in Romania. When Khrushchev called to congratulate him, Stalin cut him off for 'wasting his time'.

A call from Svetlana cheered Stalin:

'Congratulations on victory, papa!'

'Yes we've won,' he laughed. 'Congratulations to you too!'

At 8 p.m. on 24 May, Stalin hosted a banquet for the Politburo and marshals, singers, actors and even Polish miners, in the Georgevsky Hall. There was a traffic jam of limousines all the way to the Borovitsky Gate. The guests found their seats and waited eagerly. When Stalin appeared, 'ovations and shouts of "Hurrah" shook the vaulted halls ... with a deafening roar.' Molotov toasted the marshals who clinked glasses with the Politburo. When Admiral Isakov, who had lost his leg in 1942, was toasted, Stalin, still a master of the personal touch, walked all the way over to his distant table to clink glasses. Then Stalin praised the Russian people and referred to his own mistakes: 'Another people could have said to the government: you have not justified our expectations, go away and we will install another government which will conclude peace with Germany and guarantee us a quiet life.'

Later, Stalin asked Zhukov and the marshals:

'Don't you think we should celebrate the defeat of Fascist Germany with a victory parade?' Stalin decided to take the review on horseback. He could not ride but his hunger for glory still burned and he started secretly training to ride a white Arabian stallion, chosen by Budyonny. Around 15 June, a week before the parade, a spurred and booted Stalin in jodhpurs, apparently accompanied by his son Vasily, mounted the steed. He jerked his spurs. The horse reared. Stalin grabbed the mane and tried to stay in the saddle but was thrown, bruising his shoulder. Pulling himself to his feet, he spat:

'Let Zhukov take the parade. He's a cavalryman.' At Kuntsevo, he asked Zhukov if he had forgotten how to ride.

'I haven't,' replied Zhukov. 'I still ride sometimes.'

'Good ... You take the parade.'

'Thanks for the honour. But ... you're the Supremo and by right you should take it.'

'I'm too old ... You do it. You're younger.' Zhukov would ride a white Arabian stallion which Budyonny would show him. The next day, Zhukov was reviewing the rehearsals at the central airfield when Vasily Stalin buttonholed him:

'I'm telling you this as a big secret. Father had himself been preparing to take the parade but ... three days ago, the horse bolted ...'

'And which horse was your father riding?'

'A white Arab stallion, the one on which you're taking the parade. But I beg you not to mention a word of this.' Zhukov mastered the Arabian.

At 9.57 a.m. on 24 June, Zhukov mounted the stallion at the Spassky Gate. It was pouring with rain. The clocks struck ten: 'Parade-shun!'

'My heart beat faster,' wrote Zhukov. Simultaneously, Marshal Rokossovsky was waiting on Budyonny's own black charger, appropriately named Polus – the Pole – at the Nikolsky Gate. Stalin, in his greatcoat, showing no expression, walked clumsily, slowly, out on his own then lightly bounded up the steps to the Mausoleum, with Beria and Malenkov sweating breathlessly in their efforts to keep up. When the crowds saw him, hurrahs resounded across the Square. The rain poured, the water running down his vizor. He never wiped his face. As the chimes rang out, Zhukov and Rokossovsky rode out, both soaked, the bands played Glinka's *'Slavsya!'* – Glory to You – and tanks and Katyushas rumbled over the cobblestones. Silence fell on Red Square. 'Then a menacing staccato beat of hundreds of drums could be heard,' wrote Yakovlev. 'Marching in precise formation and beating out an iron cadence, a column of Soviet soldiers drew nigh.' Two hundred veterans each held a Nazi banner. At the Mausoleum they did a right turn and flung the banners, emblazoned with black and scarlet swastikas, at Stalin's feet where the downpour soaked them. Here was the climax of Stalin's life.

As soon as it was over, Stalin and the top brass poured into the room behind the Mausoleum for a buffet and drinks. It was here, according to Admiral Kuznetsov, that one of the marshals, probably Koniev, first proposed promoting Stalin to Generalissimo. He waved this away but then declared that he was now sixty-seven and weary:

'I'll work another two or three years, then I'll have to retire.' The Politburo and the marshals cried out on cue that he would live to rule the country for a long time yet. During the hard-drinking festivities, Stalin laughed as Poskrebyshev slipped the ceremonial dagger out of Vyshinsky's diplomatic uniform and replaced it with a pickle. Much to Stalin's amusement, the pompous ex-Procurator strutted around for the rest of the day oblivious of the vegetable in his scabbard, and smirks of the magnates.

That night, at a banquet for 2,500 officers, Stalin, who was already thinking about how to tighten discipline and bind the Union together, toasted the 'Russian people ...' and the 'screws', the ordinary people, 'without whom all of us, marshals and commanders of fronts and armies ... would not be worth a damn.'

In these carefully phrased toasts, Stalin set down a marker for his courtiers. The marshals were 'not worth a damn' compared to the Russian people whom only the Party (Stalin) could represent. His talk of retirement unleashed a brutal struggle among ruthless men to succeed a twentieth-century emperor who had no intention of ever retiring. Within five years, three of the contenders would be dead.

Koniev's proposal to Molotov and Malenkov that they promote Stalin to Generalissimo to differentiate him from the marshals was not completely Ruritanian – Suvorov had been Generalissimo – but there was now something of the South American *junta* about it. Stalin was against the idea. He was endowed with all the prestige of a world conqueror, a 'deity ... an ungainly dwarf of a man who passed through gilded and marble Imperial halls', but the magnates were determined to honour him with Hero of the Soviet Union, another Order of Victory, and the rank of Generalissimo.

'Comrade Stalin doesn't need it,' he replied to Koniev. 'Comrade Stalin has the authority without it. Some title you've thought up! Chiang Kai-shek's a Generalissimo. Franco's a Generalissimo – fine company I find myself in!' Kaganovich, proud inventor of 'Stalinism', also suggested renaming Moscow as Stalinodar, an idea that had first been suggested by Yezhov in 1938. Beria seconded him. This simply 'outraged' Stalin: 'What do I need this for?'

The wise courtier senses when his master secretly wants him to disobey. Malenkov and Beria had Kalinin sign the decree. Three days after the parade, *Pravda* announced Stalin's new rank and the Hero of the Soviet Union gold star. He was furious and summoned Molotov, Malenkov, Beria, Zhdanov and old Kalinin, who was already extremely ill with stomach cancer. 'I haven't led regiments in the field ... I'm refusing the star as undeserved.' They argued but he insisted. 'Say what you like. I won't accept the decorations.' But they noticed that he had taken care to accept the Generalissimo.

Since the marshals now resembled Christmas trees of braid and clanking medals, the Generalissimo's uniform had to be completely over-the-top: the tailor of the élite, Lerner, created a gilded Ruritanian extravaganza with a golden cape. Khrulev dressed three strapping officers in these Göringesque outfits. When Stalin wandered out of his office to see Poskrebyshev, he snarled:

'Who are they? What's this peacock doing here?'

'Three samples of the Generalissimo's uniform.'

'They're not right for me. I need something more modest ... Do you want me to look like a doorman?' Stalin finally accepted a white gilded high-collared tunic with black and red-striped trousers which made him look like a bandmaster, if not a Park Avenue doorman. When he put it on, he regretted it, muttering to Molotov: 'Why did I agree?'

Malenkov and Beria were left with the star of Hero of the Soviet Union: how to get him to accept it? Here Stalin's court dissolves into an *opéra bouffe* farce in which the cantankerous Generalissimo was virtually pursued around Moscow by courtiers trying to pin the medal on him. First Malenkov agreed to try but Stalin would not listen. Next he recruited Poskrebyshev who accepted the mission but gave up when Stalin resisted energetically. Beria and Malenkov tried Vlasik but he too failed. They decided it was best to ambush Stalin when he was gardening because he loved his roses and lemon-trees so they persuaded

Orlov, the Kuntsevo commandant, to present it. When Stalin asked for the secateurs to prune his beloved roses, Orlov brought the secateurs but kept the star behind his back, wondering what to do with it.

'What are you hiding?' asked Stalin. 'Let me see.' Orlov gingerly brought out the star. Stalin cursed him:

'Give it back to those who thought up this nonsense!' Finally, he accepted the medal: 'You're indulging an old man. Won't do anything for my health!' Stalin did not just accept the rank of Generalissimo in order to join Franco. Vanity merged with politics: it helped diminish the dangerously prestigious marshalate. On 9 July, he further watered down their honours by promoting Beria, their scourge, to Marshal, equal to Zhukov or Vasilevsky.

The victor's good humour, though, could be chilling. Whenever he saw the Shipbuilding Commissar Nosenko, he joked 'Haven't they arrested you yet?' The next time he saw him, he chuckled: 'Nosenko, have you still not been shot?' Nosenko each time smiled anxiously. Finally at a celebratory Sovnarkom meeting, Stalin declared, 'We believed in victory and ... never lost our sense of humour. Isn't that true, Comrade Nosenko?'

* * *

A week later, Stalin, who, according to Gromyko, now 'always looked tired', mounted his eleven-coach armoured train for the journey to Potsdam: he travelled in four green carriages that had been taken from the Tsar's train in some museum, along a route of exactly 1,923 kilometres, according to Beria, who organized perhaps the tightest security ever for a travelling potentate. 'To provide proper security,' he wrote to Stalin on 2 July, '1,515 NKVD/GB men of operative staff and 17,409 NKVD forces are placed in the following order: on USSR territories, 6 men per kilometre; on territory of Poland, 10 men per kilometre; on German territory, 15 men per kilometre. Besides this on the route of the special train, 8 armoured trains will patrol – 2 in USSR, 2 in Poland and 4 in Germany.' 'To provide security for the chief of the Soviet delegation', there were seven NKVD regiments and 900 bodyguards. The inner security 'will be carried out by the operative staff of the 6th Department of the NKGB' arranged 'in three concentric circles of security, totalling 2,041 NKVD men'. Sixteen companies of NKVD forces alone were responsible for guarding his phone-lines while eleven aeroplanes provided quick links to Moscow. In case of urgent need, Stalin's own three planes, including a Dakota, stood ready. The secret police were 'to guarantee proper order and purges of anti-Soviet elements' at all stations and airports.*

The night before he arrived in Potsdam, Stalin called Zhukov:

'Don't get it into your head to meet us with an honour guard and band. Come to the station yourself and bring anyone you consider necessary.'

At 5.30 a.m. on 16 July, the day of Stalin's arrival, the United States tested a nuclear bomb in New Mexico that would change everything and, in many ways, spoil Stalin's triumph. The news was telegraphed to Harry S. Truman, who had succeeded Roosevelt as President, with the understatement of the century:

'Babies satisfactorily born.'

Stalin and Molotov, attended by Poskrebyshev, Vlasik and Valechka, found the platform virtually empty except for Zhukov, Vyshinsky and a table bearing three telephones connected to the Kremlin and the armies. 'In good spirits', Stalin raised his hat and climbed into the waiting ZiS 101 armoured limousine but then he opened the door and invited Zhukov to ride with him to his Babelsberg residence, 'a stone villa of two floors' with 'fifteen rooms and an open veranda', Beria informed him, 'supplied with all necessary electricity, heating and organized telephone stations with *VCh* for 100 numbers'. It had been Ludendorff's home. Stalin hated the extravagant furniture and ordered much of it to be removed – as he once had done in his Kremlin flat.

Stalin was late for the conference but it mattered little: the great decisions had been made at Yalta. The other leaders had arrived on the 15th and gone sightseeing to Hitler's Chancellery. Beria, who was already in Berlin to oversee the arrangements, accompanied by his son Sergo, longed to visit the ruins but obediently waited to ask Stalin's permission. Stalin refused to go himself, no tourist he. So Beria, in a baggy suit and open-necked shirt, went with the immaculate Molotov.

At midday on Tuesday the 17th, Stalin, resplendent in a fawn Generalissimo's uniform, arrived at Truman's 'Little White House'

---

* The NKVD had mended all the electrical systems of Babelsberg and, as at Yalta, they even brought their own fire brigade. More than that, Stalin had his own 'organized store of economic supplies with 20 refrigerators ... and 3 farms – a cattle farm, a poultry farm and a vegetable farm' plus '2 special bakeries, manned by trusted staff and able to produce 850 kg of bread a day'.

for their first meeting. The new President said nothing about the topic that dominated the conference. Sergo Beria wrote that his father, informed by spies in the American nuclear project, gave Stalin the news during this week: 'I didn't know then, at least not from the Americans,' was how Stalin put it. Beria had first informed him of the Manhattan Project in March 1942: 'We need to get started,' said Stalin, placing Molotov in charge. But, under Iron Arse, it advanced with excruciating, ponderous slowness. Finally in September 1944, the leading Russian nuclear scientist, Professor Igor Kurchatov, wrote to Stalin to denounce plodding Molotov and begged Beria to take it over. Stalin had little conception of nuclear fission's world-shattering importance nor of the vast resources it would require. He and Beria distrusted their own scientists and spies. None the less, they were aware of the urgency in procuring uranium, and twice during the Conference, Stalin and Beria debated how to react to the Americans.* They had agreed that Stalin should 'pretend not to understand', when the subject was mentioned. But so far, Truman said nothing. They discussed Russia's entry into the war against Japan. Truman asked Stalin to stay for lunch but he refused:

'You could if you wanted,' said Truman. Stalin stayed, unimpressed by the Missouri haberdasher who was no substitute for FDR: 'They couldn't be compared,' he said later. 'Truman's neither educated nor clever.' (Truman was none the less charmed: 'I like Stalin!' but, revealingly, he reminded the President of his patron, T. J. Pendergast, the machine politician boss of Kansas City.)

Stalin, ever more sartorially aware, changed into his white, gilded Generalissimo's magnificence with the single Hero of the Soviet Union gold star, and arrived last for the first session at the Cecilienhof Palace, built in 1917 for the last Crown Prince, mocking its Kaiserine grandeur: 'Hmm. Nothing much,' he told Gromyko. 'Modest. The Russian Tsars built themselves something much more solid.' At the Conference, Stalin sat between Molotov and his interpreter Pavlov, flanked by Vyshinsky and Gromyko. Champagne glasses were brought to toast the Conference.

---

* Beria had also secured as much uranium as possible in a special operation in the ruins of Berlin: he and Malenkov reported to Stalin they had found '250 kgs of metallic uranium, 2 tons of uranium oxide and 20 litres of heavy water' at the Kaiser Wilhelm Institute, rounded up key German physicists, and spirited all this treasure back to the USSR. Roy Medvedev in his *Neizvestnyi Stalin* claims Beria did not tell Stalin about the American test until 20 or 21 August but we do not know the precise date.

Churchill, puffing at a cigar, approached Stalin who was himself smoking a Churchillian cigar. If anyone were to photograph the Generalissimo with a cigar, it would 'create an immense sensation', Churchill beamed, 'everyone will say it is my influence'. Actually British influence was greatly diminished in the new world order of the superpowers in which they could agree on the deNazification of Germany but not on reparations or Poland. Now Hitler was gone, the differences were mountainous.

When Stalin decided he wanted a stroll in the gardens after a session, a British delegate was amazed to see 'a platoon of Russian tommy-gunners in skirmishing order, then a number of guards and units of the NKVD army. Finally appeared Uncle Joe on foot with his usual thugs surrounding him, followed by another screen of skirmishers. The enormous officer who always sits behind Uncle at meetings was apparently in charge of operations and was running around directing tommy-gunners to cover all the alleys.' After a few hundred yards, Stalin was picked up by his car.

At 8.30 p.m. on the 18th, Churchill dined at Ludendorff's villa, noticing that Stalin was ill, 'physically oppressed'. Smoking cigars together, they discussed power and death. Stalin admitted that the monarchy held together the British Empire, perhaps considering how to hold together his own.* No psephologist, he predicted that Churchill would win the election by eighty seats. Then he reflected that people in the West wondered what would happen when he died but it had 'all been arranged'. He had promoted 'good people, ready to step' into his shoes.

Finally, on 24 July, two monumental moments symbolized the imminent end of the Grand Alliance. First Churchill attacked Stalin for closing off Eastern Europe, citing the problems of the British mission in Bucharest:

'An iron fence has come down around them,' he said, trying out the phrase that would become 'the iron curtain'.

'Fairy tales!' snapped Stalin. The meeting ended at 7.30 p.m. Stalin headed out of the room but Truman seemed to hurry after him. Interpreter Pavlov deftly appeared beside Stalin. Churchill, who had discussed this moment with the President, watched in

---

* Stalin was a regicide who constantly compared himself to monarchs: he even joked with his Yugoslav visitors, 'Maybe Molotov and I should marry princesses,' a prospect that no doubt sent a shiver through the Almanac de Gotha. He was happy to use monarchies when necessary, urging Tito to restore the young Yugoslav King: 'You can always stick a knife in his back when no one's looking.'

fascination as Truman approached the Generalissimo 'as if by chance', in Stalin's words:

'The USA,' said Truman, 'tested a new bomb of extraordinary destructive power.' Pavlov watched Stalin closely: 'no muscle moved in his face.' He simply said he was glad to hear it:

'A new bomb! Of extraordinary power! Probably decisive on the Japanese! What a bit of luck!' Stalin followed the plan he had agreed with Beria to give the Americans no satisfaction but he still thought the Americans were playing games: 'An A-bomb is a completely new weapon and Truman didn't exactly say that.' He noticed Churchill's glee too: Truman spoke 'not without Churchill's knowledge'.

Back at Ludendorff's villa, Stalin, accompanied by Zhukov and Gromyko, immediately told Molotov about the conversation. But Stalin knew that, as yet, the Americans only possessed one or two Bombs – there was just time to catch up.

'They're raising their price,' said Molotov, who was in charge of the nuclear project.

'Let them,' said Stalin. 'We'll have to talk it over with Kurchatov and get him to speed things up.' Professor Kurchatov told Stalin that he lacked electrical power and had not enough tractors. Stalin immediately ordered power to be switched off in several populated areas and gave him two tank divisions to act as tractors. The Bomb's revolutionary importance was still percolating when the first device was dropped on Hiroshima. The scale of resources needed was just dawning on Stalin.

He then convened a meeting with Molotov and Gromyko at which he announced:

'Our Allies have told us that the USA has a new weapon. I spoke with our physicist Kurchatov as soon as Truman told me. The real question is should countries which have the Bomb simply compete with one another or ... should they seek a solution that would mean prohibition of its production and use?' He realized that America and Britain 'are hoping we won't be able to develop the Bomb ourselves for some time ...' and 'want to force us to accept their plans. Well that's not going to happen.' He cursed them in what Gromyko called 'ripe language', then asked the diplomat if the Allies were satisfied with all the agreements.

'Churchill's so riveted by our women traffic police in their marvellous uniforms that he dropped his cigar ash all over his suit,' replied Gromyko. Stalin smiled.

Next morning, Churchill and the Labour leader Clement Attlee flew back to London where they discovered that the warlord had been roundly defeated in the general election, thereby ending the triumvirate of Teheran and Yalta. Stalin preferred Roosevelt but he most admired Churchill: 'A powerful and cunning politician,' he remembered him in 1950. 'In the war years, he behaved as a gentleman and achieved a lot. He was the strongest personality in the capitalist world.'

During this interval, Stalin met up with his son Vasily, now stationed in Germany, who reported that Soviet aeroplanes were still inferior to the Americans', and dangerous to boot. Vasily's denunciations may have been well-meaning but Stalin always found a deadly use for them. At lunchtime on the 25th, Stalin met Queen Victoria's great-grandson, a cousin of Nicholas II, and Allied Supreme Commander, Southeast Asia, the ebullient Admiral Lord Louis Mountbatten who flattered him that he had diverted his trip from India to Britain 'specially to meet the Generalissimo', having long been 'an admirer of the Generalissimo's achievements not only in war but in peace as well'.

Stalin replied that he had done his best. 'Not everything' had been 'done well' but it was the Russian people 'who achieved these things'. Mountbatten's real motive was to wangle an invitation to visit Russia where he was convinced his Romanov connections would be appreciated, explaining that he had frequently visited the Tsar as a child for 'three or four weeks at a time'.

Stalin inquired drily, with a patronizing smile, whether 'it was some time ago that he had been there'. Mountbatten 'would find things had changed very considerably'. Mountbatten repeatedly asked for an invitation and returned to his imperial connections which he expected to impress Stalin. 'On the contrary,' says Lunghi, Mountbatten's interpreter, 'the meeting was embarrassing because Stalin was so unimpressed. He offered no invitation. Mountbatten left with his tail between his legs.'*

Potsdam ended with an affable but increasingly chilly impasse: Stalin possessed Eastern Europe but Truman had the Bomb. Before he left on 2 August, he realized the Bomb would require a colossal

---

* This may be the reason this story appears in none of Mountbatten's biographies and is told here for the first time. I am grateful to Hugh Lunghi for both his interview on the episode and his generous gift of his unpublished official minutes.

effort and his most dynamic manager. He removed Molotov and commissioned Beria to create the Soviet Bomb. Sergo Beria noticed his father 'making notes on a sheet of paper ... organizing the future commission and selecting its members.' Beria included Malenkov and others in the list.

'What need have you to include these people?' Sergo asked Beria.

'I prefer that they should belong. If they stay outside they'll put spokes in the wheels.' It was the climax of Beria's career.

45

Beria: Potentate, Husband,
Father, Lover, Killer, Rapist

On 6 August 1945, America dropped its bomb on Hiroshima. Stalin did not wish to miss out on the spoils, sending his armies against Japan, but the destruction of Hiroshima made a far greater impact than Truman's warning. Svetlana visited Kuntsevo that day: 'Everyone was busy and paid no attention to me,' she grumbled. 'War is barbaric,' reflected Stalin, 'but using the A-bomb is a superbarbarity. And there was no need to use it. Japan was already doomed!' He had no doubt that Hiroshima was aimed at himself: 'A-bomb blackmail is American policy.'

Next day, Stalin held a series of meetings at Kuntsevo with Beria and the scientists:

'Hiroshima has shaken the whole world. The balance has been destroyed,' he told them. 'That cannot be.' Now Stalin understood that the project was the most important in his world; codenamed 'Task Number One', it was to be run 'on a Russian-scale' by Beria's 'Special Committee' that functioned like an 'Atomic Politburo'. The scientists had to be coaxed and threatened. Prizes and luxuries were vital: 'Surely it's possible to ensure that several thousand people can live very well ... and better than well.' Stalin was 'bored' by the science but treated Kurchatov kindly: 'If a child doesn't cry, the mother does not know what she needs. Ask for whatever you like. You won't be refused.'

Beria threw himself into Task Number One as if his life depended on it – which it did. The project was on a truly Soviet scale, with Beria managing between 330,000 and 460,000 people and 10,000 technicians. Beria was the pre-eminent Terror entrepreneur, telling one of his managers, 'You're a good worker but if you'd served six years in the camps, you'd work even better.' He controlled his scientists in the *sharashki*, special prisons for technical experts, described by Solzhenitsyn in *The First Circle*: when one expert suggested he might work better if he was free,

Beria scoffed, 'Certainly. But it would be risky. The traffic in the streets is crazy and you might get run over.'

Yet he could also be 'ingratiating', asking the physicist Andrei Sakharov charmingly, 'Is there anything you want to ask me?' His handshake, 'plump, moist and deathly cold,' reminded Sakharov of death itself: 'Don't forget we've plenty of room in our prisons!' His name was enough to terrify most people: 'Just one remark like "Beria has ordered" worked absolutely without fail,' remembered Mikoyan. When he called Vyshinsky, he 'leapt out of his chair respectfully' and 'cringed like a servant before a master'.

Task Number One, like all Beria's projects, functioned 'as smoothly and reliably as a Swiss clock'. Kurchatov thought Beria himself 'unusually energetic'. But he also won the scientists' loyalty by protecting them, appealing to Stalin who agreed:

'Leave them in peace. We can always shoot them later.' Mephistophelian brutality, Swiss precision and indefatigable energy were the hallmarks of Beria who was 'incredibly clever ... an unusual man and also a great criminal.'

Beria was one of the few Stalinists who instinctively understood American dynamism: when Sakharov asked why their projects so 'lag behind the USA', only Beria would have answered like an IBM manager: 'we lack R and D.' But the scientific complexities completely foxed Beria himself and his chief manager, Vannikov, the ex-Armaments boss. 'They're speaking while I blink,' admitted Vannikov. 'The words sound Russian but I'm hearing them for the first time.' As for Beria, one scientist joked to Sakharov: 'Even Lavrenti Pavlovich knows what mesons are.' His solution was high-handed arrogance and the threat: 'If this is misinformation, I'll put you in the dungeon!'

This fusion of Beria's bludgeon and Kurchatov's mesons led to some bombastic rows. In November 1945, Pyotr Kapitsa, one of the most brilliant Soviet scientists, complained to Stalin that Beria and the others behaved 'like supermen'. Kapitsa reported his argument with Beria: 'I told him straight, "You don't understand physics."' Beria 'replied that I knew nothing about people'. Beria had 'the conductor's baton' but the conductor 'ought not only to wave the baton but also understand the score'. Beria did not understand the science. Kapitsa suggested that he should study physics and shrewdly ended his letter: 'I wish Comrade Beria to be acquainted with this letter for it is not a denunciation but useful criticism. I would have told him all this myself but it's a great deal of trouble to get to see him.' Stalin told Beria that he had to get on with the scientists. Beria summoned Kapitsa who amazingly refused him:

'If you want to speak to me, then come to the Institute.' Beria ate humble pie and took a hunting rifle as a peace offering. But Kapitsa refused to help any more. Stalin meanwhile wrote him a note:

'I have received all your letters ... There is much that is instructive and I'm thinking of meeting you some time ...' But he never did.

* * *

Beria was at the centre not only of Stalin's political world but also of his private one. Now their families almost merged in a Georgian dynastic alliance. Svetlana, still suffering from the end of her first love affair with Kapler, spent much time at Beria's houses with his wife, Nina, blonde, beautiful (though with stocky legs), and a qualified scientist from an aristocratic family who also managed to be a traditional Georgian housewife. Stalin still treated her paternally even as he began to loathe Beria himself. 'Stalin asked Nina to look after Svetlana because she had no mother,' said Beria's daughter-in-law.

Beria always craved athletic women, haunting the locker-rooms of Soviet swimmers and basketball players. Nina herself was something of an Amazon, always exercising, playing tennis with bodyguards, cycling on a tandem. Beria was, like many a womanizer, a very jealous husband and the bodyguards were the only men allowed close to her. Beria lived in some style: he divided his grand town mansion into offices and private rooms on one side, and apartments for his wife and family on the other. His wife and son mainly lived at his 'sumptuous, immense' white dacha at Sosnovka near Barvikha, which 'was in Jugend style, lots of glass and stone, like art deco with a terrace and lots of guards around,' as well as pet bear cubs and foxes.* Yet Nina kept it 'cosy' and it was always littered with English and German magazines and books. On holidays in the south, Beria, who was a trained architect, designed his own dacha at Gagra close to Stalin's. The Master often invited over the Berias who brought along their son Sergo.

---

* Many of the Soviet leaders had their own zoos or menageries: Bukharin had collected bear cubs and foxes. Khrushchev had foxcubs and deer; Budyonny, Mikoyan and Kaganovich kept horses.

By the end of the war, the balding broad-faced Beria with his swollen, moist lips and the cloudy brown eyes, was 'ugly, flabby and unhealthy-looking with a greyish-yellow complexion'. The life of a Stalinist magnate was not a healthy one. No one worked harder than the 'inhumanly energetic' Beria, but he still played volleyball every weekend with Nina and his team of bodyguards: 'Even though he was so unfit, he was amazingly fast on his feet.' In common with other human predators, Beria became a vegetarian, eating 'grass' and Georgian dishes but only rarely meat. He came home at weekends, practised shooting his pistol in the garden, watched a movie in his cinema and then drove off again.

Dressing like a southern winegrower, Beria hated uniforms, only sporting his Marshal's uniform during 1945: usually he wore a polo-neck sweater, a light jacket, baggy trousers and a floppy hat. Beria was cleverer, brasher and more ambitious than the other magnates and he could not resist letting them know it. He teased Khrushchev about his looks and his womanizing, saying, 'Look at Nikita, he's nothing much to look at but what a ladykiller!', tormented Andreyev about his illnesses, Voroshilov about his stupidity, Malenkov about his flabbiness and he told Kobulov that he dressed like Göring. No one ever forgot any of Beria's wisecracks. Nina begged him to be more circumspect: 'she hated his way of wounding people,' wrote their son. His own courtiers, who 'idealized him,' met like modern corporate directors at his box at the Dynamo football stadium. The major organizations had their own football teams – Beria's MVD had Dynamo, the trade unions had Spartak. The competition was so vicious in 1942 that Beria had the successful manager of the Spartak team, Nikolai Starostin, arrested and sent into exile. An invitation to watch a game in Beria's box for a young Chekist meant entering his circle.

An inventory of his desk after his later arrest revealed his interests: power, terror and sex. In his office, Beria kept blackjack clubs for torturing people and the array of female underwear, sex toys and pornography that seemed to be obligatory for secret-police chiefs. He was found to be keeping eleven pairs of silk stockings, eleven silk corsets, seven silk nighties, female sports outfits, the equivalent of Soviet cheerleaders' costumes, blouses, silk scarves, countless obscene love letters and a 'large quantity of items of male debauchery'.

Despite his mountainous workload, Beria found time for a Draculean sex-life that combined love, rape and perversity in almost equal measure. The war had given him the opportunity to engage in a life of sexual brigandage even more intense and reckless than that enjoyed by his predecessors in the job. The secret-police chiefs always had the greatest sexual licence: only Smersh watched Beria; otherwise he could do whatever he wanted. It was once thought Beria's seductions and rapes were exaggerated but the opening of the archives of his own interrogation, as well as the evidence of witnesses and even those who were raped by him, reveals a sexual predator who used his power to indulge himself in obsessive depravity. It is often impossible to differentiate between women he seduced who went to him to plead for loved ones – and those women he simply kidnapped and raped. Yet mothers often pimped their daughters in return for limousines and privileges. Beria himself could also be a gentleman, treating some mistresses so kindly that they never criticized him even when he had been exposed as a Soviet Bluebeard.* He combined seduction with espionage: he seduced a willing female friend of Kira Alliluyeva's by saying 'What lovely cherry lips you have! A figure like Venus!' Afterwards, he quizzed her on her circle, recruiting her to spy on the Alliluyevs.

He was a familiar sight in Moscow as he cruised the streets in his armoured Packard and sent his Caucasian bodyguards Colonels Sarkisov and Nadaraia to procure women for him. The colonels were not always happy with their role – indeed, Sarkisov kept a record of Beria's perversions with which to denounce him to Stalin. The girls were usually taken to the town house where a Georgian feast and wine awaited them in a caricature of Caucasian chivalry. One of the colonels always proffered a bouquet of flowers on the way home. If they resisted, they were likely to get arrested. The film star Zoya Fyodorovna was picked up by these Chekists at a time when she was still breastfeeding her baby. Taken to a party where there were no other guests, she was

---

* In December 2003, the fiftieth anniversary of Beria's death, the Tunisian Ambassador to Moscow revealed that human remains had been discovered in the cellars of his embassy, Beria's home: presumably Beria's victims. We may never know whether they were rape victims or executed Enemies. On 17 January 2003, the Russian Prosecutor confirmed the existence of forty-seven volumes of files on Beria's criminal activities which were gathered on his arrest after Stalin's death. Even though the case against him was entirely political, with trumped-up charges, the files confirm the dozens of women who accused him of raping them. The State television network RTR was allowed to film the handwritten list of their names and telephone numbers. The files will not be opened for another twenty-five years.

joined by Beria whom she begged to let her go as her breasts were painful. 'Beria was furious.' The officer who was taking her home mistakenly handed her a bouquet at the door. When Beria saw, he shouted: 'It's a wreath not a bouquet. May they rot on your grave!' She was arrested afterwards.

The film actress Tatiana Okunevskaya was even less lucky: at the end of the war, Beria invited her to perform for the Politburo. Instead they went to a dacha. Beria plied her with drink, 'virtually pouring the wine into my lap. He ate greedily, tearing at the food with his hands, chattering away.' Then 'he undresses, rolls around, eyes ogling, an ugly, shapeless toad. "Scream or not, doesn't matter," he said. "Think and behave accordingly." ' Beria softened her up by promising to release her beloved father and grandfather from prison and then raped her. He knew very well both had already been executed. She too was arrested soon afterwards and sentenced to solitary confinement. Felling trees in the Siberian *taiga*, she was saved, like so many others, by the kindness of ordinary people.

These women were just the tip of a degenerate iceberg. Beria's priapic energy was as frenzied and indefatigable as his bureaucratic drive. 'I caught syphilis during the war, in 1943 I think, and I had treatment,' he later confessed. After the war, it was Vlasik and Poskrebyshev, who, remembering Bronka, told Stalin about the syphilis. Lists were already a Stalinist obsession so this sex addict felt compelled to keep a record of his conquests. His colonels kept the score; some say the list numbered thirty-nine, others seventy-nine: 'Most of those women were my mistresses,' he admitted. Beria ordered Sarkisov to destroy the list which he did but being a Chekist, the bodyguard kept a copy, later used against his master ...

Some mistresses, like 'Sophia' and 'Maya', a student at the Institute of Foreign Relations, inconveniently became pregnant. Once again, Colonels Sarkisov and Nadaraia were called upon to arrange abortions at the MVD's Medical Department – and when a child was born, the colonels placed it in an orphanage.*

---

* To this day, Beria's illegitimate children are well known among Moscow and Tbilisi society: they include a highly respected Georgian Member of Parliament and a Soviet matron who married the son of a member of Brezhnev's Politburo. After the war, Stalin changed the People's Commissariats to Ministries so that the NKVD and NKGB became the MVD and MGB. The State Defence Committee, the GKO, was abolished on 4 September 1945. The Politburo once again became the highest Party body though Stalin ruled as Premier, leaving the Party Secretariat to Malenkov.

Beria was also notorious among the magnates themselves: Stalin himself tolerated the peccadilloes of his potentates as long as they were politically reliable. During the war, when Beria was running half the economy and he was informed of his priapism, Stalin answered indulgently, 'Comrade Beria is tired and over-worked.' But the less he trusted Beria, the less tolerant he became. Once, hearing that Svetlana was at Beria's house, Stalin panicked, rang and told her to leave at once. 'I don't trust Beria.' Whether this referred to his sexuality or to his politics is not clear. When Beria told Poskrebyshev that his daughter was as pretty as her mother, the *chef de cabinet* told her, 'Never accept a lift from Beria.' Voroshilov's daughter-in-law was followed by Beria's car all the way back to the Kremlin. Voroshilov's wife was terrified:

'It's Beria! Say nothing! Don't tell a soul!' The leaders' wives hated Beria:

'How can you work with such a man?' Ashken Mikoyan asked her husband.

'Be quiet,' Mikoyan would reply, but Ashken would not go to functions if Beria was likely to be present:

'Say I've a headache!'

Beria's wife Nina told Svetlana and other friends that she 'was terribly unhappy. Lavrenti's never home. I'm always alone.' But her daughter-in-law remembers that 'she never stopped loving Beria'. She knew that he had other women 'but she took a tolerant Georgian view of this'. When he came home for the weekend, 'she spent hours having manicures and putting on makeup. She lived downstairs in her own room but when he came home, she moved upstairs to share his bed.' They 'sat cosily by the fire, watching Western films, usually about cowboys and Mexican banditos. His favourite was *Viva Villa!* about Pancho Villa. They chatted lovingly in Mingrelian.' Nina never believed the scale of his exploits: 'When would Lavrenti have found time to make these hordes of women his mistresses? He spent all day and night at work' so she presumed these women must have been his 'secret agents'.

* * *

Sergo Beria, now twenty-one, named after Ordzhonikidze, had been at School No. 175 with Svetlana Stalin, Martha Peshkova and most of the élite children. As a father, Beria was absent much of the time but he was enormously proud of Sergo. Theirs was a typically formal relationship between a Bolshevik and his son. 'If Sergo wanted to talk to his father,' recalled his wife, 'Lavrenti would say, "Come and see me in the office."' Like Malenkov and most of the other leaders, Beria was determined that his son should not go into politics.

Like all Politburo parents, he encouraged him to become a scientist: Colonel Beria rose to prominence in military technology as head of the sprawling missile Design Bureau Number One. Sergo had grown up around Stalin, and Beria therefore could not prevent the Generalissimo inviting him to the wartime conferences.

Sergo was intelligent, cultured and, according to Martha Peshkova, Svetlana Stalin's best friend, 'so beautifully handsome that he was like a dream – all the girls were in love with him'. In 1944, Svetlana fell for him too, a fact that she leaves out of both her memoirs and her interviews. When Sergo wrote his own memoirs and claimed this was so, many historians disbelieved it. Yet Svetlana wanted to marry him, an ambition she never gave up even when he himself married someone else. When he was in Sverdlovsk during the war, Svetlana got her brother to fly her there. After the Kapler affair, this crush worried the Berias:

'Don't you realize what you're doing?' Nina Beria told Svetlana. 'If your father finds out about this, he'll skin Sergo alive.'

Stalin wanted her to marry one of his potentate's sons, specifying to Svetlana that she should marry either Yury Zhdanov, Sergo Beria or Stepan Mikoyan. But this honour appalled Beria.

'That would be terrible,' he said to Mikoyan. Even though Stalin had shown interest in the idea, both knew that he would actually 'interpret this as an attempt to worm your way into his family', as Beria told Sergo. Svetlana was determined to marry Sergo but the Berias put a firm stop to it. As she obliquely admitted:

'I wanted to marry someone when I was a young girl ... But his parents would not accept me because of who I am. It was a very painful blow.'

Worse was to follow: Martha Peshkova was now 'as pretty and plump as a quail' and seemed to exist in a 'warm scented cloud of strange attraction': it was, recalled Gulia Djugashvili, 'difficult to have Martha as a friend.' Martha's boyfriend was Rem Merkulov, the son of the NKGB boss. Perhaps, having grown up around Yagoda, she had a taste for Cheka princelings because she now fell in love with Sergo Beria whom she married soon afterwards. The Berias did not have a big wedding: 'it was not the style of the time,' says Martha. Beria told Sergo that Stalin would not approve of 'your getting connected with that family' – the Gorkys. Sure enough, Stalin invited Sergo to Kuntsevo:

'Gorky himself wasn't bad but what a lot of anti-Soviet people he had around him. Don't fall under your wife's influence,' warned Stalin, always suspicious of wives.

'But she's quite non-political,' answered Sergo.

'I know. But I regard this marriage as a disloyal act on your part ... not to me, but to the Soviet State. Was it ... forced on you by your father?' He accused Beria of making connections with the 'oppositionist intelligentsia'. Instead Sergo blamed Svetlana for introducing him to Martha.

'You never breathed a word of it to Svetlana,' Stalin replied. 'She told me herself.' Then he smiled at Sergo: 'Don't take any notice, old people are always peevish ... As for Marfochka, I saw her grow up.'

Martha moved into the Berias' dacha where she got to know, and love, the most infamous man of his time.* Beria could not have been kinder to her: 'I was very fond of him. He was very cheerful and very funny, always singing the Mexican song, "*La Paloma*", and telling comical anecdotes of his life' such as how he lost his virginity in Romania, getting entangled in the woman's voluminous pantaloons. He claimed that as a Herculean baby, he was found crawling in the garden holding a snake in his hands. On Sundays, his only rest day, he and Nina slept late and then played Martha and Sergo at volleyball, each assisted by the bodyguards. When Martha gave Beria his first grandchild, 'he couldn't have been sweeter, spending hours sitting by the cradle just looking at her. In the morning, he'd have the baby brought into his and Nina's room where he'd sit her between them and just smile at her.' He was so indulgent of the child that 'he let her put her whole hands into her birthday cakes'.

Martha was less keen on Nina. Her mother-in-law turned out to be as despotic in the house as her father-in-law was out. Nina was lonely and Martha soon found she was seeing more of her mother-in-law than her husband. She wanted them to set up their

* I am fortunate that Martha Peshkova, Gorky's granddaughter, Svetlana's best friend and Beria's daughter-in-law, helped with her unique memories and introduced me to the Gorky/Beria family including Beria's granddaughters (see Postscript). As a wedding present, Stalin gave Sergo and Martha a copy of Rustaveli's *The Knight in the Panther Skin*, which he had edited himself with Professor Nutsibidze, inscribing it teasingly: 'You'd do better to form bonds with the Georgian intelligentsia!'

own home but Nina told her, 'If you mention that again, you'll find yourself very far from your children.'

Beria, says Martha, was 'the cleverest person around Stalin. In a way, I'm sorry for him because it was his fate to be there at that time. In another era, he would have been so different. If he'd been born in America, he would have risen to something like Chairman of General Motors.' She was sure he was never a real Communist: he once amazed her when he was playing with his granddaughter. 'This girl,' he said, 'will be tutored at home and then she's going to Oxford University!' No other Politburo member would have said such a thing.

* * *

Svetlana Stalin rebounded from Sergo into an unsuitable marriage. At Vasily's apartment in the House on the Embankment, Svetlana met Grisha Morozov, who served in the war in the traffic police. 'A friendship developed,' recalls Svetlana, but 'I wasn't in love with him.' However he was in love with her. Stalin was dubious about Morozov, another Jew: after Kapler, he began to feel these Jews were worming their way into his family. But Svetlana was attracted to their warmth and culture, so Stalin said,

'It's spring ... You want to get married. To hell with you. Do what you like.'

'I just wanted to get over the rejection,' explained Svetlana years later, 'so we married but under other circumstances, it wasn't my choice. My first husband was a very good person who always loved me.' There was no ceremony: they just went to the register office where the official looked at her passport and asked:

'Does your papa know?' Marrying into Stalin's family, Morozov 'instantly became rather grand', says Leonid Redens. They quickly had their first baby – a son named Joseph, of course. Svetlana found herself unprepared for marriage: 'I had a son when I was nineteen ... My young husband was a student too. We had people to look after the baby. I had three abortions and then a very bad miscarriage.' Meanwhile Stalin refused to meet Morozov.

Svetlana was still in love with Sergo Beria. 'She never forgave me for marrying him,' says Martha. Svetlana reminded Sergo that Stalin 'was furious' about the marriage. She still visited Nina, her surrogate mother. Once Svetlana suggested that they remove Martha, who could take the elder daughter and then she would move in with Sergo and raise the younger one. 'She's just like her father,' Mikoyan said. 'She always gets what she wants!'

However, she could also be very kind. When Yakov's heroism in German captivity had been proven, his widow Julia was released but found that her seven-year-old daughter, Gulia, hardly knew her. Svetlana agreed to look after Gulia and one day she announced, 'Today we're going to meet Mama.' But the child was afraid of the stranger, so daily, with the most touching sensitivity, Svetlana took her to see her mother until gradually the two bonded. This had to be done surreptitiously because, while Gulia was brought up by nannies, her mother remained outside the family. Finally, she wrote to Stalin: 'Joseph Vissarionovich, I ask you very much not to refuse my request because it's hard to see Gulia. We live in the hope of seeing you and talking about things not put in this letter. We would like you to meet Gulia ...' Later, thanks to Svetlana, Stalin did meet his first granddaughter.

46

A Night in the Nocturnal Life of Joseph Vissarionovich: Tyranny by Movies and Dinners

The true victor of the war, Stalin enjoyed the prestige of a world conqueror yet the disparity between his political power and his personal exhaustion made him feel vulnerable.

The Generalissimo and Molotov were satisfied, though never satiated, by their prizes. At a southern dinner, Stalin sent Poskrebyshev to bring the new map. They spread it on the table. Using his pipe as a baton, Stalin reviewed his Empire: 'Let's see what we've got then: in the north, everything's all right, Finland greatly wronged us, so we've moved the frontier farther from Leningrad. The Baltic States, which were Russian territory from ancient times, are ours again, all the Belorussians are ours now, Ukrainians too, and the Moldavians are back with us. So to the west everything's okay.' But he turned to the east: 'What have we got here? The Kurile Islands are ours and all of Sakhalin ... China, Mongolia, all as it should be.' The Dunhill pipe trailed round to the south: 'Now this frontier I don't like at all. The Dardanelles ... We also have claims to Turkish territory and to Libya.' This could have been the speech of a Russian Tsar – it was hardly that of a Georgian Bolshevik. Molotov shared this mission: 'My task as Foreign Minister was to expand the borders of our Motherland. And it seems Stalin and I coped ... quite well. Yes I wouldn't mind getting Alaska back,' he joked. But Molotov understood that there was no contradiction between Bolshevism and empire-building: 'It's good the Russian Tsars took so much land for us in war. This makes our struggle with capitalism easier.'

But Stalin's courtiers noticed that his triumph had turned his head. 'He became conceited,' said Molotov, 'not a good feature in a statesman.' His prestige was so great that he was absolute in all matters: his mere words were taken as 'Party orders and instantly obeyed'. Yet he now ruled in a very different way: he 'stepped aside from direct ruling', said one of his officials, and assumed the Olympian mantle of a paramount leader, like the old Chairman

Mao, who liked to guide his men with anecdotes, signs and hints. He used secrecy, caprice and obscurity to maintain his mastery over his younger, stronger, ambitious magnates. He dominated his entourage by mystery.

'He never gave direct orders,' wrote his Georgian boss, Charkviani, 'so you had to make your own conclusions.' Stalin understood that 'it doesn't matter what part of the pool you throw a stone, the ripples will spread'. He once showed his Abkhazian leader, Mgeladze, his beloved lemon trees again and again until the *apparatchik* finally understood and declared that Abkhazia would produce lemons for the whole USSR.

'Now you've got it!' smiled Stalin. Unless he was in a temper, he usually ended his orders: 'Do as you wish' but no one mistook his meaning. If, on the other hand, he gave a direct order, writing 'I don't think my reasons need to be discussed, they are perfectly clear,' or simply shouted his wishes, he was instantly obeyed. In the MGB, the mere mention of the *Instantsiya* justified any act of barbarism.

However, the Generalissimo was also weaker and older than before. Shortly before the victory parade, Stalin had experienced some sort of heart attack or what Svetlana called 'a minor stroke', hardly surprising given the strain of warlordism on his remarkably durable metabolism. 'Certainly overexhausted,' observed Molotov, Stalin already suffered from arthritis but it was the hardening of his arteries, arteriosclerosis, that reduced the flow of blood to the brain and could only impair his mental faculties. After returning from Potsdam, he fell ill again, making him feel weaker at the very moment when his position was strongest. They brought him under the power of doctors, a profession he despised and which he had corrupted (making his own physician Vinogradov testify at the show trials during the thirties). Poskrebyshev, the ex-nurse, became his secret doctor, prescribing pills and remedies.

These contradictions gave Stalin a deadly unpredictability, lashing out at those around him. The hopes and freedoms of the war made no difference to his belief that the problems of the USSR were best solved by the elimination of individuals. The poverty of his Empire compared to the surging wealth of America dovetailed with his own feeling that his powers were failing, and the inferiority complexes of a lifetime.

Usually 'calm, reserved and patient', he often 'exploded instantly and made irrelevant and wrong decisions'. Khrushchev said, 'after the war, he wasn't quite right in the head'. He remained a supreme manipulator though it is likely that the arteriosclerosis exacerbated his existing tempers, depression and paranoia. He was never mad: indeed, his strangest obsessions always had a basis in real politics. Yet mortality made him realize the sterility he had created inside himself: 'I'm a most unfortunate person,' he told Zhukov, 'I'm afraid of my own shadow.' But it was this super-sensitivity that made him such a frightening but masterful politician. His fear of losing control of his Empire was based on reality: even in his own Politburo, Mikoyan felt the war was a 'great school of freedom' with no need to 'return to terror'.

Stalin despised this laxity. He even joked about it when he sent some writers to tour conquered Japan and asked Molotov if they had departed. It turned out they had put off the trip: 'Why didn't they go?' he asked. 'It was a Politburo decision. Maybe they didn't approve of it and wanted to appeal to the Party Congress?' The writers left quickly. But he sensed this lax attitude all around him.

'He was very jittery,' said Molotov. 'His last years were the most dangerous. He swung to extremes.' He was jealous of Molotov and Zhukov's prestige, suspicious of Beria's power, and disgusted by the soft smugness of his magnates: even when he was ill and old, he was never happier than when he was orchestrating a struggle. It was his gift, his natural state. Some backs would have to be broken. Stalin ruled 'through a small group close to him at all times' and formal 'government ceased to function'. Even on long holidays away from Moscow, he maintained his paramount power by directing each portfolio through his direct relationship with the official in question, and no one else. His interventions were almost deliberately capricious and out of the blue.

More than ever, his courtiers had to know how to handle him but first, they had to survive his nocturnal routine. It is no exaggeration to say that henceforth Stalin ruled, from Berlin to the Kurile Islands, from the dinner-table and the cinema. The defiance of time itself is the ultimate measure of tyranny: the lights in his capitals – from Warsaw to Ulan Bator, from Budapest to Sofia – shone throughout the night.

* * *

The magnates met at the Little Corner after which the Generalissimo always proposed a movie. He led his guests along the red-and-blue-carpeted corridors to the cinema which had been luxuriously built in the old winter garden on the second floor of the Great Kremlin Palace. Beria, Molotov, Mikoyan and Malenkov remained his constant companions but his proconsuls in Finland and Ukraine, Zhdanov and Khrushchev, often visited too.

Then there was the whole new court of European vassals: his favourites were the Polish leader Boleslaw Bierut, 'polite, well-dressed, well-mannered', a 'perfect gentleman with women' but a ruthless Stalinist with 'a fanatical faith in the dogma', his deputy Jakob Berman, the Czech President Clement Gottwald, Hungary's Matyas Rakosi. The prouder Yugoslavs, Marshal Tito and Milovan Djilas, were less liked. Each of them was honoured to come to Moscow to pay homage and receive Stalin's sacerdotal wisdom and imperial commands. They too had to learn how to behave in the cinema and at dinner.

The sight of the Generalissimo and his guards approaching was a terrifying one for any young official who happened to be walking along these corridors. The plain-clothed guards walked twenty-five steps in front and two metres behind Stalin, while the uniformed guards followed him with their eyes. Amidst this phalanx of myrmidons, walking noiselessly but quickly and jauntily, with a heavy, pigeon-toed step, came the potbellied emperor with his fine mountain man's head, his sloping shoulders, the tigerish creases of his roguish smile. Anyone who saw him approaching had to stand back against the wall and show their hands. Anatoly Dobrynin, a young diplomat, once found himself in this dilemma: 'I pressed my back against the wall.' Stalin 'did not fail to notice my confusion' and asked 'who I was and where I worked'. Then 'stressing his words by a slow moving of the finger of his right hand' before Dobrynin's face, he declared,

'Youth must not fear Comrade Stalin. He is its friend.' Dobyrnin shuddered.

The walk to the cinema took a few minutes. Decorated in blue, there were rows of soft upholstered armchairs set in pairs, with tables between each seat with mineral water, wine, cigarettes, boxes of chocolates. The carpet was grey with rugs on it. Before Stalin arrived, the Politburo took their seats, leaving the front row empty. They were met by the Minister of Cinema, Ivan Bolshakov, who had run the film industry since 1939 and became a vital but comical presence in the entourage. Bolshakov was terrified of Stalin since his two cinematic predecessors had been shot. As Stalin got older, the cinema became an obsessive ritual, as well as an aid, and venue, for governing.

Bolshakov's big decision was which film to show. This he judged by trying to guess Stalin's mood. He observed the leader's gait, intonation of voice and sometimes, if he was lucky, Vlasik or Poskrebyshev gave him a clue. If Stalin was in a bad mood, Bolshakov knew it was not a good idea to show a new movie. Stalin was a creature of habit: he loved his old favourites from the thirties like *Volga! Volga!* or foreign films such as *In Old Chicago*, *Mission to Moscow*, the comedy *It Happened One Night*, or any Charlie Chaplin.

Stalin now possessed a new library of American, English and German films that had until recently been the property of Goebbels. If Stalin was in a bad mood, one of the Goebbels films would please him. He liked detective films, Westerns, gangster films – and he enjoyed fights. He banned any hint of sexuality. When Bolshakov once showed him a slightly risqué scene involving a naked girl, he banged the table and said:

'Are you making a brothel here, Bolshakov?' Then he walked out, followed by the Politburo, leaving poor Bolshakov awaiting arrest. From then on, he cut even the slightest glimpse of nudity.

Stalin ordered Bolshakov to interpret the foreign films. Yet Bolshakov spoke only pidgin English. He therefore spent much of his time preparing for these midnight sessions by having interpreters go over the film for him and then learning the script. This was a challenge because at any time, he had hundreds of films to show Stalin. Thus his interpretation was usually absurdly obvious and very late, long after it was clear what the character had already said. The Politburo laughed and teased the flustered Bolshakov on his translations. Beria pointed at the screen and called out:

'Look he's started running ...' All laughed – but Stalin, who evidently enjoyed this farce, never demanded a proper interpreter. In 1951, Bolshakov asked Stalin to approve the *Tarzan* film: one imagines his translation of Tarzan's jungle-swinging shriek and courting grunts with Jane thoroughly entertained his audience. If Bolshakov showed the old favourite, *Volga! Volga!*, Stalin liked to show off how well he knew it and would perform every part just before the actor.

If Stalin was in a good mood, Bolshakov had the chance to choose a new Soviet movie. Stalin remained the censor of the entire industry: no movie could be shown without his personal approval. When he was in the south for months, no decision

After victory, Stalin fell ill with a series of minor strokes or heart attacks. Here, the clearly ailing Generalissimo arrives to rest, accompanied by the porcine Vlasik.

On 12 August 1945 Generalissimo Stalin cheerfully leads his magnates for the parade – Mikoyan, Ukrainian viceroy Khrushchev, Malenkov, Beria in Marshal's uniform, Molotov (with Vlasik behind him).

Zhdanov, in Colonel-General's uniform, was Stalin's heir apparent and cultural supremo who attacked the arts after the war. Stalin promoted his son Yury and wanted him as his own son-in-law. But the charlatan geneticist Trofim Lysenko (far left) proved the nemesis of the Zhdanovs.

Opposite page The exhausted Stalin gloomily leads Beria, Mikoyan and Malenkov through the Kremlin to the Mausoleum for the 1946 May Day parade. In this nest of vipers, they walked arm in arm, but their friendships were masks: each would liquidate the others. Stalin now loathed Beria and mocked Malenkov for being so fat he had lost his human appearance. When Beria tormented dapper Mikoyan at Stalin's dinners by hiding tomatoes in his well-cut suits and squashing them, Mikoyan started bringing a spare suit.

Top As the struggle for the succession builds up, Stalin leads the mourning at Kalinin's funeral in 1946. (Front row, from left): Beria, Malenkov, Stalin and Molotov. Behind Molotov stands the ill and frail Zhdanov at the height of his power. Zhdanov's two protégés, Voznesensky and Kuznetsov, are both to the right behind Malenkov's shoulder. Kaganovich is behind Molotov.

Bottom The death of Zhdanov, Stalin's friend and favourite, here in an open coffin, unleashes the vengeance of Beria and Malenkov against his faction. Stalin, Voroshilov and Kaganovich follow the coffin. That night, at the funeral supper, Stalin became drunk: with Zhdanov gone, he had lost his only intellectual equal.

Here, in late 1948, Stalin sits with the older generation, Kaganovich, Molotov and Voroshilov, while an intrigue is being prepared behind them amongst the younger. After ten years without a single top leader being shot, Beria (second row, far left) and Malenkov (second row, second from left) helped Stalin murder his two appointed successors, Kuznetsov (second row between Molotov and Stalin) and Voznesensky (second row between Stalin and Voroshilov) in the 'Leningrad Case'.

Left Summertime chez Stalin: natty Mikoyan in whites with 'young handsome' and doomed Kuznetsov, Molotov and Poskrebyshev in uniform.

Bottom At his seventieth birthday gala on stage at the Bolshoi, Stalin stands between Mao Tse-tung and Khrushchev, whom Stalin summoned from Ukraine to offset Malenkov and Beria.

He effectively ruled Russia for months on end from his new house at New Athos in the late forties – this was his favourite *(top)*. He also returned to a house where he had enjoyed a happy holiday with Nadya after Vasily's birth in 1921 – the Likani Palace, which once belonged to Tsar Nicholas II's brother Grand Duke Michael *(middle)*. When Khrushchev and Mikoyan visited, they had to share a room. He spent weeks in this remote house at Lake Ritsa *(bottom)*. He was now so frail that his guards built these green metal boxes (inset) containing special phones so that Stalin could call for help if he was taken ill on his daily strolls.

All his life, Stalin slept on the big divans that were placed in virtually every room of all his houses. This is the sofa at Kuntsevo on which he died on 5 March 1953.

Left Plotting the destruction of Molotov and Mikoyan, the aging but determined Stalin watches Malenkov give the chief report at his last public appearance at the Nineteenth Congress in 1952. While organising the anti-semitic Doctors' Plot, he ordered his secret police to torture the doctors: 'Beat, beat and beat again!' he shouted. But he still found time to play with his grandchildren...

The fight for power began over the deathbed. On the right Khrushchev and Bulganin (alongside Kaganovich and Mikoyan) face Beria and Malenkov (alongside Molotov and Voroshilov) across Stalin's body. Beria seemed to have won the struggle for succession, but he fatally underestimated Khrushchev.

Stalin at the 1927 Congress: unshaven, pockmarked, sardonic, sarcastic and utterly vigilant, the supreme politician, the messianic egotist, fanatical Marxist, and superlative mass-murderer, in his prime.

could be made so he had to see all the new films when he returned.

As Stalin approached, Bolshakov took up position outside the cinema. He once frightened Stalin by lurking in the shadows: 'Who are you? What are you doing?' Stalin barked. 'Why are you hiding?' Stalin scowled at Bolshakov for weeks afterwards. Taking his seat in the front row with his guests around him, usually mixing a spritzer of Georgian wine and mineral water, he always asked:

'What will Comrade Bolshakov show us today?' Bolshakov announced the movie, sat down at the back and ordered the projectionists to begin. Once, one of them dropped and broke part of the projector, which spread mercury on the floor. They were accused of attempting to assassinate the Generalissimo.*

Stalin talked throughout the film. He enjoyed cowboy films, especially those directed by John Ford and admired Spencer Tracy and Clark Gable but he also 'cursed them, giving them an ideological evaluation', recalled Khrushchev, 'and then ordering new ones'.†

Stalin admired the actors, frequently asking 'Where've we seen this actor before?' After the war, actors and directors often joined Stalin's dinners, particularly the Georgian director of films featuring the heroic leader, Mikhail Chiaureli, and the actors who often played him, Mikhail Gelovani (who did Stalin with a Georgian accent) and Alexei Diky (increasingly after the war, with a Russian accent). 'You're observing me thoroughly,' Stalin told Gelovani. 'You don't waste time do you?' He once asked Diky how he would 'play Stalin'.

'As the people see him,' replied the actor.

'The right answer,' said Stalin, giving him a bottle of brandy.

When the film was over, Stalin always asked his fellow intellectual:

'What will Comrade Zhdanov tell us?' Zhdanov gave his

---

* Mercury poisoning had a special pedigree at Stalin's court: Yezhov had sprayed his own office with mercury and claimed that Yagoda was trying to poison him.
† A recent biography of John Wayne claims the film star's symbolism as an American hero and enemy of Communism infuriated Stalin who suggested that 'Duke' should be assassinated. When Khrushchev visited Holywood in 1958, he is said to have explained to Wayne: 'That was the decision of Stalin in his last mad years. When Stalin died, I rescinded the order.' The story is based on rumour; it sounds like the sort of grim joke Stalin favoured in his cups. If true, it is hard to image why Wayne survived – and why Khrushchev did not use the tale against Stalin in his memoirs.

pompous verdict followed by Molotov's laconic judgement and Beria's sarcastic jokes. Stalin enjoyed joking about the *auteurs*:

'If Comrade [director or screenwriter]'s no good, Comrade Ulrikh'll sign his death sentence.' Bolshakov once called Beria and Molotov to ask if *Zhukovsky*, a film about the aviator, could be launched on Air-force Day, but Stalin, on holiday, had still not seen it. It was his decision not theirs, they replied, so Bolshakov launched the film. When Stalin returned, he watched *Zhukovsky* and then said:

'We know you decided to put it on the screens of the USSR! They want to trick me but it's impossible.' Bolshakov froze. On whose authority, asked Stalin? Bolshakov replied that he had 'consulted and decided'.

'You consulted and decided,' repeated Stalin quietly. He got up and walked to the door, opened it and repeated: 'You decided.' He went out, leaving a doom-laden silence. Then he opened the door again, smiling: 'You decided correctly.' If Stalin hated the film, he would simply walk out but not before teasing Bolshakov.

Bolshakov made notes of all these august critiques. In the morning, he called the directors or scriptwriters and passed on the comments without specifying their source but no doubt his quivering voice and breathless awe made it obvious.*

Stalin imposed politics on film but also film on reality. Djilas noticed how he seemed to mix up what was going on 'in the manner of an uneducated man who mistakes artistic reality for actuality'. He revelled in films about murdering friends and associates. Khrushchev and Mikoyan repeatedly sat through a British film, no doubt one of the Goebbels collection, about a pirate who stole some gold and then, 'one by one', killed his accomplices to keep the swag.

'What a fellow, look how he did it!' exclaimed Stalin. This was 'depressing' for his comrades who could not forget that, as Khrushchev put it, 'we were temporary people'. Stalin's isolated position made these films increasingly powerful. After the war, Stalin wanted to impose taxes on the peasants even though the countryside was stricken with famine. The whole Politburo sensibly opposed this, which angered Stalin. He was convinced the peasants could afford it: he pointed to the plenty shown in his

---

* Bolshakov survived Stalin to serve Khrushchev as Deputy Trade Minister. He died in 1980.

propaganda movies, allowing him to ignore the starvation. After seeing the movie on Catherine the Great's admiral, *Ushakov*, Stalin became obsessed with building a powerful fleet, quoting a character in the film who says: 'Land forces are a sword in one hand, sea forces a sword in the other.'

He often insisted on seeing two movies in a row and afterwards, around 2 a.m., would say:

'Let's go and get something to eat,' adding 'if you have time' as if there was any choice in the matter.

'If that's an invitation,' replied Molotov, 'with the greatest satisfaction.' Then Stalin turned to his guests, often Tito or Bierut:

'What are your plans for tonight?' as if they would have any at that hour. Stalin laughed. 'Hmm, a government without a state plan. We'll take a bite.' The average 'bite' lasted the interminable six hours until dawn.

* * *

Stalin ordered the omnipresent Poskrebyshev to summon the cars but when they were delayed, he trembled 'with rage, shouted, his features distorted, sharply motioned and poured invective into the face of his secretary who was ... paling as if he had heart failure.' Poskrebyshev rounded up other guests. The guests had to prepare for the dinners, resting in the afternoon because 'those sleeping at Stalin's table came to a bad end', said Khrushchev.* Sometimes he invited his Georgian film directors and actors to liven up the party: 'Do you know if Chiaureli and Gelovani are in Moscow now?'

Foreign guests rode with Stalin who always sat in the fold-up seat right behind the driver and sometimes turned on a light above him to read. Molotov usually took the other folding seat with the favourite, Zhdanov, and any other guests in the back seats. Beria and Malenkov, 'that pair of scoundrels' as Stalin called them, always shared a car.† As the cars sped out of the city at the speed that Stalin relished, he planned the route, taking 'strange detours' to confuse terrorists.

---

* The magnates' families recognized their tense waiting for the call to the cinema or dacha from Stalin's secretaries. At weekends, the only chance they got to see their families, the leaders were especially tense whenever the phone rang. They did not eat during the day to leave room for the endless procession of dishes. But when the call came, Sergei Khrushchev noticed how hastily his father departed.

† The chauffeurs of the leaders were very pleased when their bosses were invited to Stalin's place. Voroshilov was now invited less often than before the war. 'My old man ain't invited there very much any more,' his veteran chauffeur would complain.

After driving ten miles up the Government Highway, they reached a barrier, turned left and approached a clump of young fir trees. After another checkpoint, they entered the gates of Kuntsevo. Once inside, they passed a big map in the hall where Stalin, Zhdanov and Molotov stopped to make grand geopolitical statements and capricious decisions. Zhdanov, his rival Malenkov and Voznesensky always had their notebooks ready to record Stalin's orders while Molotov and Mikoyan, Old Bolsheviks, regarded themselves as above such sycophancy.

The lavatories were in the basement and when the guests washed before dinner, Molotov joked at the urinals: 'We call this unloading before loading!' This lavatory was one of the only rooms in Moscow where the magnates could indulge in honest discussion: Beria and the others whispered to each other about the tedium of Stalin's tales of his Siberian exile. When he claimed to have skied twelve kilometres to shoot twelve partridges, Beria, already coming to loathe Stalin, insisted, 'He's just lying!'

They entered the roomy dining room with a long table with about fourteen covered chairs along each side; there were comfortable chairs alongside it, high windows with long drapes, and two chandeliers and lights set in the walls. As in all Stalin's houses, the walls, floors and ceilings were made of light Karelian pine panelling. It was so clean, so 'dead quiet' and so 'isolated from the other world', that visitors imagined they were 'in a hospital'.

Stalin always sat to the left of the head of the table with Beria at the end, often as *tamada*, and the guest of honour on Stalin's left. As soon as they sat down, the drinking started. At first it was civilized, with a few bottles of wine, sometimes weak Georgian 'juice' and some champagne, which Stalin greatly enjoyed. Mikoyan and Beria used to bring wine.

'Being Caucasian, you understand wine better than the others, try it …' Stalin would say: it was soon clear that he was testing the wines for poison so they stopped bringing it. Stalin provided his own wine and genially opened the bottles himself. As the evening went on, the toasts of vodka, pepper vodka and brandy became more insistent until even these iron-bellied drinkers were blind drunk. Stalin liked to blame Beria for the excessive drinking. At Georgian dinners, hosts customarily play at forcing their guests to drink, and then taking umbrage if they resist. But by now, this hospitality was grossly distorted and represented nothing but power and fear. After Stalin's binges in 1944–5, Professor Vinogradov warned him to cut down on the drinking and he started to water down his drinks to wine with mineral water. None the less he occasionally over-imbibed and Svetlana saw him singing a duet with the legless but proud Health Minister. Forcing his tough comrades to lose control of themselves became his sport and a measure of dominance.

The drinking started with Stalin not Beria: he 'forced us to drink to loosen our tongues,' wrote Mikoyan. Stalin liked the old drinking game of guessing the temperature. When Djilas was there, Beria was three degrees out and had to drink three vodkas. Beria, whom Svetlana called 'a magnificent modern specimen of the artful courtier', played up to Stalin's longing to see his courtiers humiliate themselves, and policed the drinking, ensuring that no one missed a bumper.

'Come on, drink like everyone else does,' Beria tormented Molotov because he 'always wanted to make a show in front of Stalin – he would never lag behind if Stalin said something'. Sometimes Stalin defended foreign visitors and he spared Kaganovich because 'Jews weren't great drinkers.' Even during these sessions, Beria's mind throbbed with sexual imagery: after forcing Djilas to down a pepper vodka, he sneered that it was 'bad for the sexual glands'. Stalin gazed at his guest to see if he was shocked, 'ready to burst out laughing'.

Secretly, Beria hated these drinking sessions – he complained bitterly about them to Nina, Khrushchev and Molotov. Nina asked why he did it: 'You have to put yourself on the same level as the people you're with,' he replied, but there was more to it than that. Beria relished his power: in this, as in many other things, 'I couldn't resist it.' Khrushchev agreed that the dinners were 'frightful'.

Sometimes the drinking at these Bacchanals was so intense that the potentates, like ageing, bloated students, staggered out to vomit, soiled themselves or simply had to be borne home by their guards. Stalin praised Molotov's capacity but sometimes even he became drunk. Poskrebyshev was the most prolific vomiter. Khrushchev was a prodigious drinker, as eager to please Stalin as Beria. He sometimes became so inebriated that Beria took him home and put him to bed, which he promptly wet. Zhdanov and Shcherbakov could not control their drinking and became alcoholics: the latter died of the disease in May 1945 but Zhdanov tried to fight it. Bulganin was 'practically an alcoholic'. Malenkov just became more bloated.

Beria, Malenkov and Mikoyan managed to suborn a waitress to serve them 'coloured water' but they were betrayed to Stalin by Shcherbakov. After swallowing some colossal brandies, Mikoyan staggered out of the dining-room and found a little room next door with a sofa and a basin. He splashed his face with water, lay down and managed to sleep for a few minutes, which became a secret habit. But Beria sneaked to Stalin who was already turning against the Armenian: 'Want to be smarter than the rest, don't you!' Stalin said slowly. 'See you don't regret it later!' This was always the threat *chez* Stalin.

Stalin's *Mitteleuropean* vassals coped no better. Gottwald was so inebriated that he requested that Czechoslovakia join the USSR. His wife, who came with him, heroically volunteered: 'Allow me, Comrade Stalin, to drink in my husband's place. I'll drink for us both.' Rakosi foolishly told Beria that the Soviets were 'drunkards'.

'We'll see about that!' scoffed Stalin who joined Beria in 'pumping' the Hungarian with drink.

* * *

In summertime, the guests staggered outside on to the verandas. Stalin asked Beria or Khrushchev's advice on his roses (which he lovingly clipped), lemons and kitchen garden. Stalin supervised the planting of a vegetable garden where he devised new varieties such as crossing pumpkins with water melons. He fed the birds every day. Once Beria built a greenhouse as a present to Stalin:

'What fool ordered this?' Stalin asked. 'How much electricity do you spend on floodlights?' He had it destroyed.

The standard of drunken horseplay was not much better than a university fraternity house. Khrushchev and Poskrebyshev drunkenly pushed Kulik into the pond – they knew Stalin had lost respect for the buffoon. Kulik, famously strong, jumped out soaking and chased Poskrebyshev who hid in the bushes. Beria warned: 'If anyone tried something like that on me, I'd make mincemeat of them.' Poskrebyshev was regularly pushed in until the guards became so worried that a drunken magnate would drown, that they discreetly drained the pond. The infantilism delighted Stalin: 'You're like little children!'

One evening, Beria suggested that they do some shooting in the garden. There were quails in a cage. 'If we don't shoot them,' said

Beria, 'the guards'll eat them!' The leader, who was probably already drunk, staggered out and called for guns. Stalin, old, weak and tipsy, not to mention his frail left arm, first felt 'giddy' and fired his gun at the ground, only just missing Mikoyan. He then fired it in the air and managed to pepper his bodyguards, Colonels Tukov and Khrustalev, with shot. Afterwards Stalin apologized to them but blamed Beria.*

* * *

In the dining room, the maids, plump peasant women wearing white pinafores, like Victorian nurses, emerged with an array of Georgian dishes which they laid on the sideboard or the other end of the long table, then disappeared. When one of them was serving tea to Stalin and the Poles, she stopped and hesitated. Stalin noticed immediately: 'What's she listening to?' If there were no foreign eminences, dinner was served by one of the housekeepers, usually Valechka, and a bodyguard. The guests helped themselves, then joined Stalin at the table.

'Gradually Stalin began to take a great interest in his food,' recalled Mikoyan. The weary Generalissimo was fuelling his failing energy with 'enormous quantities of food suitable for a much larger man'. 'He ate at least twice as much as I did,' wrote Mikoyan. 'He took a deep plate, mixed two soups in it, then in a country custom that I knew from my own village, crumbled bread into the hot soup and covered it all by another plate – and then ate it all up to the end. Then there would be entreés, the main course and lots of meat.' He liked fish, especially herring, but 'he also liked game – guinea-fowl, ducks, chickens' and boiled quails. He even invented a new dish which he called *Aragvi*, made of mutton with aubergines, tomatoes, potatoes and black pepper, all in a spicy sauce, which he ordered frequently. Yet he was so suspicious that he usually tried to persuade Khrushchev, the greediest of the magnates, to try his lamb or herring before he did.

The dinners were a sort of culinary imperialism, designed to impress with their simplicity yet awe with their power – and they worked. While the independent Yugoslavs were appalled by the coarseness of the company, the pliant Poles were impressed by the 'delicious roast bear' and regarded their host as 'a charming man' who treated them with paternal warmth, always asking if their

* This resembles the blinding in one eye of Marshal Masséna by the Emperor Napoleon on a shooting expedition. The incident convinced Beria and Khrushchev even more that Stalin's shooting tales were lies and that he could not shoot at all.

families enjoyed their Crimean holidays. With outsiders, Stalin retained his earlier gift of being a masterful practitioner of 'the human touch'. This charm had its limits. Bierut persisted in asking Stalin what had happened to the Polish Communists who had disappeared in 1937.

'Lavrenti, where are they?' Stalin asked Beria. 'I told you to look for them, why haven't you found them?' Stalin and Beria shared a relish for these sinister games. Beria promised to look for the vanished Poles but when Stalin was not listening, he turned on Bierut:

'Why fuck around with Joseph Vissarionovich? Fuck off and leave him alone. Or you'll regret it.' Bierut did not mention his lost friends again.

Stalin suffered from bad teeth which affected his court since he would only eat the softest lamb or the ripest fruit. His dentures, when they were fitted, unleashed yet another vicious competition. This gourmand also insisted on Bolshevik austerity, two instincts that were hard to match as his courtiers competed to procure the choicest cuts for him. Once he enjoyed a delicious lamb but asked a bodyguard:

'Where did you get the lamb?'

'The Caucasus,' replied the guard.

'How did you fuel the plane? With water? This is one of Vlasik's pranks!'* Stalin ordered a farm to be built at Kuntsevo where cows, sheep and chickens could be kept and the lake stocked with fish, and this was managed by a special staff of three agricultural experts. When Beria delivered thirty turbots, Stalin teased his guards: '*You* couldn't find turbot but Beria could.' The guards sent them for laboratory analysis and revealed that Beria's fish were rotten.

'That trickster can't be trusted,' said Stalin. Despite his swelling paunch, Stalin criticized the spreading flab of 'Malanya'

---

* Vlasik and Lieut.-Gen. Sasha Egnatashvili, the trusted son of the Gori innkeeper and Keke's protector, were probably responsible for Stalin's food which was prepared at an MGB laboratory named 'The Base' and then marked 'No poisonous elements found'. A recent book claims that Egnatashvili was Stalin's food taster, which is apparently a myth. Stalin however often did get his entourage to try food and wine before he did. When he arrived at a party, he brought his own box of wine and his own cigarettes which he opened himself. He would only eat or drink if he had broken the seal himself, leaving the food, unfinished wine and cigarettes to be divided up by Vlasik. The waste was vast; the temptation for venality irresistible but dangerous. Vlasik could never resist such goodies.

Malenkov, ordering him to take exercise in order to 'recover the look of a human being'. Beria joined in teasing his ally:

'So, that human-being look, where is it? Have you lost any weight?' But Khrushchev's gluttony entertained Stalin who whispered to the guards: 'He needed more than two fish and some pheasants, the glutton!' Yet he encouraged the spherical Khrushchev to eat more: 'Look! The giblets, Nikita. Have you tried them yet?' The potentates tried to control their diets by living on fruit and juices one day a week to 'unload', but it did not seem to work. Beria insisted on eating vegetables as his diet, for he was already as fat as Malenkov.

'Well Comrade Beria, here's your grass,' announced Stalin's housekeeper.

* * *

Stalin believed his dinners resembled a 'political dining society' but his 'fellow intellectual' Zhdanov persuaded him their wide-ranging discussions were the equivalent of the *symposia* of the ancient Greeks. None the less these vomit-flecked routs were the closest he came to cabinet government. The Imperium was truly being 'governed from the dining table', Molotov said. The leadership was like 'a patriarchal family with a crotchety head whose foibles caused the home folks to be apprehensive' but 'unofficially and in actual fact,' wrote Djilas, 'a significant part of Soviet policy was shaped at these dinners. It was here that the destiny of the vast Russian land, of the newly acquired territories and ... the human race was decided.' The conversation meandered from jokes and literature on to 'the most serious political subjects'. The Politburo exchanged news from their fiefdoms but the informality was illusory: 'The uninstructed visitor might hardly have detected any difference between Stalin and the others but it existed.'

At dinner, Zhdanov, 'the Pianist', was the most loquacious, showing off about his latest cultural campaign or grumbling that Molotov should have let him annex Finland, while his chief rival, the obese super-clerk, Malenkov, was usually silent – 'extreme caution with Stalin' was his policy. Beria, the most sycophantic yet the most irreverent, was artful at provoking and manipulating Stalin or, as his wife put it, 'playing with the tiger': he could shoot down anyone else's proposal if they had not first checked it with him. Beria was 'very powerful' because he could 'pick the exact moment to ... turn Stalin's goodwill or ill will to his advantage'.

When foreigners were absent, the fate of men was often decided. Yet Stalin talked about their acquaintances murdered during the thirties 'with the calm detachment of a historian, showing neither sorrow nor rage, just a light humour'. Once he wandered up to one of his marshals who had been arrested and released: 'I heard you were recently in confinement?'

'Yes, Comrade Stalin, I was, but they figured out my case and released me. But how many good and remarkable people perished there.'

'Yes,' mused Stalin thoughtfully, 'we've lost a lot of good and remarkable people.' Then he walked out of the room into the garden. The courtiers turned on the Marshal:

'What did you say to Comrade Stalin?' demanded Malenkov who always behaved like the school prefect. 'Why?' Then Stalin reappeared holding a bouquet of roses which he presented to the Marshal as a weird sort of apology.

* * *

Supreme power is often the supreme power to bore: nothing beats the obligatory tedium and inebriated verbosity of the absolute monarch in decline. The old Generalissimo had become repetitive, irritable and forgetful. Beria and Khrushchev knew by heart Stalin's exaggerated exploits in exile, his trips to London and Vienna, his childhood beatings at the hands of his father. Stalin dwelt more and more on the curious happiness of his exile, perhaps the only true happiness he had known. He now received an appeal for help from a friend from his Turukhansk exile during the First World War: 'I am daring to trouble you from the village of Kureika,' wrote an old teacher named Vasily Solomin who lived on a pension of 150 roubles. 'I remember when … you caught a sturgeon. How much happiness it gave me!'

'I got your letter,' replied Stalin. 'I haven't forgotten you and my friends from Turukhansk and be sure I'll never forget you. I send you 6,000 roubles from my deputy's salary. The sum isn't very large but it'll be useful. Good health, Stalin.'

Each magnate policed the others, constantly vigilant to protect their interests and avoid provoking the old tiger. It became increasingly difficult to discuss real politics. When Mikoyan told Stalin there was a food shortage, Stalin became anxious and, while feasting on the myriad dishes, kept asking 'Why's there no food?'

'Ask Malenkov, he's in charge of Agriculture,' replied Mikoyan.

At that moment, the heels of both Beria and Malenkov landed hard on Mikoyan's foot under the table.

'What's the use of it?' Beria and Malenkov attacked Mikoyan afterwards. 'It just irritates Stalin. He begins to attack one or other of us. He should be told only what he likes to hear to create a nice atmosphere, not to spoil the dinner!'

* * *

They studied Stalin like zoologists to read his moods, win his favour and survive. The key was to understand Stalin's unique blend of supersensitive discomfiture and world-historical arrogance, his longing to be liked and his heartless cruelty: it was vital not to make him anxious. When Mikoyan's aircraft designer brother was in trouble, he 'advised Artyom how to handle Stalin'. Khrushchev noticed how the Pole, Bierut, 'managed to avoid disaster because he knew how to handle Stalin'.

There were certain key rules which resemble the advice given to a tourist on how to behave if he is unlucky enough to encounter a wild animal on his camping holiday. The first rule was to look him straight in the eyes. Otherwise he asked: 'Why don't you look me in the eye today?' But it was dangerous to look into his eyes too much: Gomulka, one of the Polish leaders, took notes and showed respect but his intensity made Stalin nervous: 'What kind of fellow's Gomulka? He sits there all the time looking into my eyes as though searching for something.' Perhaps he was an agent?

The visitor had to maintain calm at all times: panic alarmed Stalin. Bierut 'never made Stalin nervous and self-conscious'. Visitors must show respect by taking notes, like Malenkov, but not too frantically like Gomulka: 'Why does he bring a notepad with him?' Stalin wondered. If the guards were over-formal in clicking their heels, Stalin became flighty: 'Who are you? Soldier Svejk?' he snapped. Yet firmness and humour with Stalin usually worked well: he admired and protected Zhukov and appreciated Khrushchev for their strong views.

He knew Beria and Malenkov tried to prefix decisions so he appreciated Voznesensky's honesty. But he no longer appreciated the bluntness of old comrades. Voroshilov, 'the most illustrious of the Soviet grandees' whom he now distrusted for his taste for splendour and Bohemian circle, tried to remind him of their long friendship: 'I don't remember,' Stalin replied. Mikoyan was one of the frankest and often contradicted Stalin, which had been acceptable during the war, but no longer: once when they were discussing the Kharkov offensive, Mikoyan courageously blurted out that the disaster was Stalin's fault. The military genius was furious, becoming ever more suspicious of Molotov and Mikoyan.

The potentates could never meet in private: 'Danger lurked in friends and friendship,' wrote Sergei Khrushchev. 'An innocent meeting could end tragically.' Although Khrushchev, Malenkov, Mekhlis, Budyonny and others lived on Granovsky Street, they virtually never visited their neighbours. Stalin relished their mutual hatreds: Beria and Malenkov loathed Zhdanov and Voznesensky; Mikoyan hated Beria; Bulganin hated Malenkov. Their homes were all now bugged. ('I've been bugged all my life,' Molotov admitted when his bodyguard confided that his own house was wired.) But Beria claimed that he deliberately criticized policy at home because otherwise Stalin would become suspicious. Their importance depended, not on seniority, but purely on their relationships with Stalin. Thus Poskrebyshev, a factotum, if CC member, openly insulted Mikoyan, a Politburo member, when the latter was under a cloud.

Stalin had to be consulted about everything, however small, yet he did not want to be harassed for decisions because this too made him nervous. Beria boasted that while Yezhov rushed to Stalin with every detail, he himself only consulted him on major questions. If Stalin was on holiday, the safest option was to make no decisions at all, a strategy perfected by Bulganin who rose without trace as a result. If in doubt, appeal to Stalin's sagacity: 'Without you no one will solve this question,' read one such note. Stalin liked to hear everyone else's opinion before giving his own but Mikoyan preferred 'waiting to hear what Stalin would say'.

Beria said the only way to survive was 'always to strike first'. It was sensible to denounce your fellow bosses at all times or, as Vyshinsky put it, 'keep people on edge'. When Molotov made a mistake, Vyshinsky revelled in it. But the denouncers were on edge too: Manuilsky wrote a ten-page denunciation of Vyshinsky: 'Dear Comrade Stalin, I'm turning to you about the case of Vyshinsky ... Abroad without the control of the CC, he is a person of petit bourgeois and boundless self-importance, for whom his own interests take precedence.' Stalin decided to do nothing with this but, as always, he informed the victim: later that day, Vyshinsky was found staring into oblivion: 'I'm only theoretically alive. I just got through the day. Well at least that's something, thank God!'

The overriding rule was to conceal nothing from Stalin: Zhdanov neutralized his crisis in Leningrad, Khrushchev, his youthful Trotskyism, by submissive confession to Stalin. Stalin's eye for any weakness was aquiline: when Vyshinsky felt ill and walked out of a diplomatic meeting, Stalin heard about it instantly and phoned his subordinate, Gromyko: 'What happened to Vyshinsky? Was he drunk?' Gromyko denied it. 'But the doctors say he's an alcoholic ... Oh well all right!'

* * *

After dinner, Stalin solemnly toasted Lenin whose illuminated bust flickered on the wall: 'To Vladimir Illich, our leader, our teacher, our all!' But this sacerdotal blessing ended any remaining decorum. When foreigners were not present, Stalin criticized Lenin, the hero who had turned against him: he even told young Sergo Beria stories about Lenin's affairs with his secretaries. 'At the end of his life', Khrushchev thought he 'lost control over what he was saying.' It was probably after 4 a.m.; the guests were desperately drunk, tired and nauseous but the omnipotent insomniac was awake, vigilant and almost sober.

There was a short rest to wash their hands, another opportunity to roll their eyes at Stalin's latest peccadillo: the magnates chuckled at the ever-increasing number of locks on the doors and whispered about another of Stalin's boasts of his drinking exploits: 'You see, even in youth, he'd drink too much!' Then it was back to the dinner which now sank to the level of a Neanderthal stag night.

Sometimes Stalin himself 'got so drunk he took such liberties,' said Khrushchev. 'He'd throw a tomato at you.' Beria was the master of practical jokes along with Poskrebyshev. The two most dignified guests, Molotov and Mikoyan, became the victims as Stalin's distrust of them became more malicious. Beria targeted the sartorial splendour of the 'dashing' Mikoyan. Stalin teased him about his 'fancy airs' while Beria delighted in tossing Mikoyan's hat into the pine trees where it remained. He slipped old tomatoes into Mikoyan's suits and then 'pressed him against the wall' so they exploded in his pocket. Mikoyan started to bring spare pairs of trousers to dinner. At home, Ashken found chicken bones in his pockets. Stalin smiled as Molotov sat on a tomato or Poskrebyshev downed a vodka full of salt that would make him vomit. Poskrebyshev often collapsed and had to be dragged out. Beria once wrote 'PRICK' on a piece of paper and stuck it on to Khrushchev's back. When Khrushchev did not notice, everyone guffawed. Khrushchev never forgot the humiliation.

Sometimes Svetlana popped in during dinner but could not hide her embarrassment and distaste. She thought the magnates resembled 'Peter the Great's *boyars*' who had almost killed themselves with drink to entertain the Tsar at his drunken 'Synod'.

After dinner, 'Stalin played the gramophone, considering it his duty as a citizen. He never left it,' said Berman. He relished his comic records, including one of the 'warbling of a singer accompanied by the yowling and barking of dogs' which always made him laugh with mirth. 'Well, it's still clever, devilishly clever!' He marked the records with his comments: 'Very good!'

Stalin urged his grandees to dance but this was no longer the exhilarating whirligig of Voroshilov and Mikoyan tripping the light fantastic. This too had become a test of power and strength. Stalin himself 'shuffled around with his arms spread out' in Georgian style, though he had 'a sense of rhythm'.

'Comrade Joseph Vissarionovich, how strong you are!' chirped the Politburo. Then he stopped and became gloomy:

'Oh no, I won't live long. The physiological laws are having their way.'

'No no!' Molotov chorused. 'Comrade Joseph Vissiaronovich we need you, you still have a long life ahead of you!'

'Age has crept up on me and I'm already an old man!'

'Nonsense. You look fine. You're holding up marvellously ...'

When Tito was present, Stalin waved away these reassurances and looked at his guest whose assassination he would later order: 'Tito should take care of himself in case anything happens to him. Because I won't live long.' He turned to Molotov: 'But Vyacheslav Mikhailovich will remain here.' Molotov squirmed. Then, in a bizarre demonstration of his virility, Stalin declared: 'There's still strength in me!' He slipped both arms around Tito's arms and thrice lifted him off the floor in time to the Russian folk song on the gramophone, a *pas-de-deux* that was the tyrannical equivalent of Nureyev and Fonteyn.

'When Stalin says dance,' Khrushchev told Mikoyan, 'a wise man dances.' He made the sweating Khrushchev drop to his haunches and do the *gopak* that made him look like 'a cow

dancing on ice'. Bulganin 'stomped'. Mikoyan, the 'acknowledged dancer', still managed his wild *lezginka*, and 'our city
dancer' Molotov immaculately waltzed, displaying his unlikely
terpsichorean talent. Ever since the thirties, Molotov's party trick
had been gravely slow-dancing with other men to the guffaws
of Stalin: his last male partner, Postyshev, had been shot long
ago.

Polish security boss Berman was amazed when the Soviet
Foreign Minister asked him to slow-dance to a waltz. 'I just moved
my feet in rhythm like the woman,' said Berman. 'Molotov led.
He wasn't a bad dancer. I tried to keep in step but what I did
resembled clowning more than dancing. It was pleasant but with
an inner tension.' Stalin watched from the gramophone, grinning
roguishly as Molotov and Berman glided across the floor. It was
Stalin who 'really had fun. For us,' said Berman, 'these dancing
sessions were a good opportunity to whisper to each other things
that couldn't be said out loud.' Molotov warned Berman 'about
being infiltrated by various hostile organizations', a warning
prearranged with Stalin.*

There were rarely women at these dinners but they were
sometimes invited for New Year's Eve or on Stalin's birthday.
When Nina Beria was at Kuntsevo with her husband, Stalin asked
her why she was not dancing. She said she was not in the mood
so Stalin went over to a young actor and ordered him to ask Nina
to dance. This was to tease the jealous Beria who was furious.
Svetlana hated her visits to these orgies. Stalin insisted she dance
too: 'Well go on, Svetlana, dance! You're the hostess so dance!'

'I've already danced, Papa. I'm tired.' Stalin pulled her hair,
expressing his 'perverse affection in its brutish form'. When she
tried to flee, he called: 'Comrade Hostess, why have you left us
poor unenlightened creatures without ... direction? Lead us! Show
us the way!'

When Zhdanov moved to the piano, they sang religious hymns,
White anthems and Georgian folk songs like 'Suliko'. When
Georgian actors and directors such as Chiaureli were present, the
entertainment was more elevated. Chiaureli's 'imitations, songs,

---

* This male slow-dancing symbolizes the sinister degeneracy of Stalin's dictatorship
but it was not unique. In November 1943, at President Roosevelt's Thanksgiving
party in Cairo, just before their departure to meet Stalin in Teheran, there was a
shortage of female dancers. So Churchill happily danced with FDR's military
assistant General Edwin 'Pa' Watson.

anecdotes made Stalin laugh'. Stalin loved singing and was very good at it. The two choirboys, Stalin and Voroshilov, joined Mikoyan, Beria and Zhdanov at the piano.*

It was almost dawn but the haunting nostalgia of these songs from those lost worlds of seminaries and church choirs was instantly shattered by Stalin's explosions of anger and contempt. 'A reasonable interrogator,' said Khrushchev, 'would not behave with a hardened criminal the way Stalin behaved with friends at his table.' When Mikoyan disagreed with Stalin, he flared up: 'You've all got old. I'll replace you all.'

At about 5 a.m., Stalin dismissed his exhausted comrades who were often so drunk they could hardly move. The guards ordered the cars round to the front and the chauffeurs 'dragged away their charges'. On the way home, Khrushchev and Bulganin lay back, relieved to have survived: 'one never knows,' whispered Bulganin, 'if one's going home or to prison.'

The guards locked the doors of the dacha and retired to their guardhouse. Stalin lay on one of his divans and started to read. Finally, drink and exhaustion soothed this obsessional dynamo. He slept. His bodyguards noted the light go out in Stalin's quarters: 'no movement.'

---

* They were so pleased with these sessions that they made a record of this murderous boy band with Voroshilov on lead vocals, backed up by Zhdanov on piano. There one can actually hear the fine voices and tinkling piano of a night at Kuntsevo. This remarkable recording is in the possession of the Zhdanov family.

47

Molotov's Chance:
'You'll Do Anything When You're Drunk!'

'The war,' Stalin admitted, 'broke me.' By October 1945, he was ill again. Suddenly at dinner, he declared: 'Let Vyacheslav go to work now. He's younger.' Kaganovich, sobbing, begged Stalin not to retire. There is no less enviable honour than to be appointed the heir of a murderous tyrant. But now Molotov, the first of a deadly line of potential successors, got his chance to act as proxy leader.

On 9 October, Stalin, Molotov and Malenkov voted 'to give Comrade Stalin a holiday of a month and a half' – and the Generalissimo set off in his special train for Sochi and then Gagra on the Black Sea. Some time between 9 and 15 October, Stalin suffered a serious heart attack. A photograph in the Vlasik family archive shows a clearly ailing Stalin, followed by an anxious Vlasik, probably arriving at Sochi, now a sizeable green two-storey mansion built around a courtyard. Then he headed south to Coldstream near Gagra. This was Stalin's impregnable eyrie, cut out of the rock, high on a cliff over the sea. Rebuilt, by Merzhanov, into a green southern house that closely resembled Kuntsevo, this became his main southern residence for the rest of his life, a sort of secret Camp David. Its studded wooden gates could only be reached by a 'narrow and sharply serpentine road'. It was completely surrounded by a Georgian veranda and there was a large sunroof. A rickety wooden summerhouse perched on the edge of the mountain.*

In this beautiful isolation, Stalin recuperated in a restful and hermetic holiday rhythm, sleeping all morning, walking during the day, breakfasting on the terrace, reading late, receiving a

---

* There was a little villa down the steps on the cliffside for Svetlana. When Stalin saw it, he muttered, 'What is she? A member of the Politburo?' Vasily's cottage adjoined the guardhouse: visitors drove through a long tunnel within the guardhouse to reach Stalin's house.

stream of paperwork, including the two files he never missed: NKGB reports and translations of the foreign press. Perhaps because he so closely supervised the Soviet press, he had surprising faith in foreign journalists.

During his absence, Molotov ran the government with Beria, Mikoyan and Malenkov, the Politburo Four. But Molotov's moment in the sun was soon overshadowed by unsettling rumours that Stalin was dying, or already dead. On 10 October, *TASS*, the Soviet press agency, announced that 'Comrade Stalin has left for a rest.' But this only awakened curiosity and aroused Stalin's vigilance. The *Chicago Tribune* reported that Stalin was incapacitated. His successors would surely be Molotov and Marshal Zhukov – a report sent southwards as 'Rumours in Foreign Press on the State of Health of Comrade Stalin.' Stalin's suspicions deepened when he read an interview with Zhukov in which the Marshal took the credit for victory in the war, only deigning to praise Stalin rather late in the proceedings. Stalin focused on why these rumours had appeared. Who had spread them, and why had Soviet honour, in his person, been desecrated?

Perhaps 'our Vyascheslav' was so thrilled at last to have the responsibility that he did not notice the brooding in Abkhazia. Molotov was at the height of his prestige as an international statesman. He had only just returned from a series of international meetings. There had been tension between them when Stalin had demanded that his Minister put pressure on Turkey to surrender some territory: Molotov argued against it, but Stalin insisted – Soviet demands were rebuffed. In April, Molotov had visited New York, Washington and San Francisco to meet President Truman and attend the opening of the UN. In an unpleasant meeting, Truman confronted Molotov on Soviet perfidy in Poland. 'We live under constant pressure, not to miss anything,' Molotov wrote to 'Polinka my love' but as ever he gloried in his eminence: 'Here among the bourgeois public,' he boasted, 'I was the focus of attention, with barely any interest in the other ministers!' As ever, 'I miss you and our daughter. I shan't conceal sometimes I am overcome with impatient desire for your closeness and caresses.' But the essential thing was that 'Moscow [i.e. Stalin] really supports our work and encourages it.'

In September, Molotov was in London for the Council of Foreign Ministers where he pushed for a Soviet trusteeship in

Italian Libya, joking drily about the Soviet talent for colonial administration. Unlike Stalin who restlessly pushed for radical leaps, Molotov was a realistic gradualist in foreign policy and he knew the West would never agree to a Soviet Libya. He made some gaffes but Stalin forgave him for the conference's failure, blaming it on American intransigence. Molotov again complained to Polina of the 'pressure not to fail'. He hardly left the Soviet Embassy, watching movies like *An Ideal Husband* by Wilde, but 'Once, only once I went to Karl Marx's tomb.' In typically Soviet style, he congratulated Polina on her 'performance of the annual [textiles] plan' but 'I want to hold you close and unburden my heart.'

Now, with Stalin recuperating and Molotov acting slightly more independently, the temperature was rising. Molotov felt the time was right for a deal with the West. Stalin overruled him: it was time to 'tear off the veil of amity'. When Molotov continued to behave too softly towards the Allies, Stalin, using the formal *vy*, attacked him harshly. 'Molotov's manner of separating himself from the Government to portray himself as more liberal ... is good for nothing.' Molotov climbed down with a ritualistic apology: 'I admit that I committed a grave oversight.' It was a telling moment for the magnates: even Stalin and Molotov ceased to address each other informally: no more 'Koba', just 'Comrade Stalin.'

On 9 November, Molotov ordered *Pravda* to publish a speech of Churchill's praising Stalin as 'this truly great man, the father of his nation'. Molotov had not grasped Stalin's new view of the West. He cabled a furious message: 'I consider the publication of Churchill's speech with his praise of Russia and Stalin a mistake,' attacking this 'infantile ecstasy' which 'spawns ... servility before foreign figures. Against this servility, we must fight tooth and nail ... Needless to say, Soviet leaders are not in need of praise from foreign leaders. Speaking personally, this praise only jars on me. Stalin.'

Just as the foreign media was trumpeting Stalin's illness and Molotov's succession, Molotov got tipsy at the 7 November reception and proposed the easing of censorship for foreign media. Stalin called Molotov who suggested treating 'foreign correspondents more liberally'. The valetudinarian turned vicious:

'You blurt out anything when you're drunk!'

Stalin devoted the next three days of his holiday to the crushing of Molotov. By the time the *New York Times* had written about Stalin's illness 'in a ruder way even than has taken place in the French yellow press', he decided to teach Molotov a lesson, ordering the Four to investigate – was it Molotov's mistake? The other three tried to protect Molotov by blaming a minor diplomat but they admitted he was following Molotov's instructions. On 6 December, Stalin cabled Malenkov, Beria and Mikoyan, ignoring Molotov, and attacking their 'naïvety' in trying to 'paper over the affair' while covering up 'the sleight of hand of the fourth'. Stalin was burning at this 'outrage' against the 'prestige' of the Soviet Government. 'You probably tried to hush up the case to slap the scapegoat ... in the face and stop there. But you made a mistake.' Hypocritically referring to the pretence of Politburo government, Stalin declared: 'None of us has the right to act single-handedly ... But Molotov appropriated this right. Why? ... Because these calumnies were part of his plan?' A reprimand was no longer sufficient because Molotov 'cares more about winning popularity among certain foreign circles. I cannot consider such a comrade as my First Deputy.' He ended that he was not sending this to Molotov 'because I do not trust some people in his circle'. (This was an early reference to the Jewish Polina.)

Beria, Malenkov and Mikoyan, who sympathized with poor Molotov, summoned him like judges, read him Stalin's cable and attacked him for his blunders. Molotov admitted his mistakes but thought it was unfair to mistrust him. The three reported to Stalin that Molotov had even 'shed some tears' which must have satisfied the Generalissimo a little. Molotov then wrote an apology to Stalin which, one historian writes, was 'perhaps the most emotional document of his life in politics'.

'Your ciphered cable is imbued with a profound mistrust of me, as a Bolshevik and a human being,' wrote the lachrymose Molotov, 'and I accept this as a most serious warning from the Party for all my subsequent work, whatever job I may have. I will seek to excel in deeds to restore your trust in which every honest Bolshevik sees not merely personal trust but the Party's trust – something I value more than life itself.'

Stalin let Molotov stew for two days, then at 1.15 a.m. on 8 December replied to the Four again, restoring his errant deputy to his former place as First Deputy Premier. But Stalin never spoke of

Molotov as his successor again and stored up these mistakes to use against him.*

* * *

This was only the beginning. Stalin was feeling better but he had mulled angrily over the challenges from abroad, indiscipline at home, disloyalty in his circle, impertinence among his marshals. He was bored and depressed by stillness and solitude but his angry energy and zest for life were stimulated by struggle. He revelled in the excitement of personal puppeteering and ideological conflict. Returning in December with a glint in his yellow eyes and a spring in his step, he resolved to reinvigorate Bolshevism and to diminish his over-mighty *boyars* in a deft sweep of arrests and demotions.

Having shaken Molotov, Stalin turned on Beria and Malenkov. He did not need to invent the scandal. When Vasily Stalin had visited him at Potsdam, he reported the disastrous safety record of Soviet planes: of 80,300 planes lost in the war, 47 per cent were due to accidents, not enemy fire or pilot error. Stalin had mused over this on holiday, even inviting the Aircraft Production Minister, Shakhurin,† to Sochi. Then he ordered the investigation of an 'Aviators' Case' against Shakhurin and the Air Force Commander, Air Marshal Novikov, one of the heroes of the war, whom he had jokingly threatened at de Gaulle's banquet.

On 2 March, Vasily Stalin was promoted to Major-General. On 18 March, Beria and Malenkov, the two wartime potentates, were promoted to full Politburo membership – just as the Aviators' Case nipped at their heels. Then Shakhurin and Air Marshal Novikov were arrested and tortured. Their agonies were carefully directed to kill two birds with one stone: the overlord of aircraft production was Malenkov.

Abakumov, the Smersh boss and Stalin's protégé, arranged the Aviators' Case which was also aimed at Beria. Stalin's old fondness for the Mingrelian had long since turned to a surly disdain. Beria's

---

* Mikoyan too felt his icy disapproval. He sensed his two old comrades were closet Rightists, absurd in Molotov's case. But during the complex arguments about whether to strip Germany of its industry or build the eastern sector as a satellite, and the endless crises of famine and grain, Mikoyan had become a moderating voice. When Mikoyan did not report properly from the Far East, he received another sharp note from Stalin: 'We sent you to the Far East not so you could fill your mouth with water [say nothing], and not send information to Moscow.'

† It was Shakhurin whose son had killed his girlfriend and then himself on Kamenny Most in 1943.

theatrical sycophancy and murderous creativity disgusted Stalin as much as his administrative genius impressed him. Stalin no longer trusted 'Snake Eyes'. His first rule was to maintain personal control over the secret police. 'He knows too much,' Stalin told Mikoyan. Stalin's resentment burned slowly. They were strolling in the Kuntsevo gardens with Kavtaradze when Stalin hissed venomously at Beria in the Mingrelian dialect (which no one except Georgians understood): 'You traitor, Lavrenti Beria!' Then he added 'with an ironic smile': 'Traitor!' When he dined at Beria's house, he was charming to Nina but dismissive of Lavrenti: in his toasts, he damned Beria with the faintest of praise. Beria reminisced about his first meeting with Stalin in 1926:

'I don't remember,' Stalin replied crushingly. Beria's attempt to speak Georgian to him at meetings now irritated Stalin: 'I keep no secrets from these comrades. What kind of provocation is this! Talk the language everyone understands!'

Stalin sensed, correctly, that Beria, the industrial and nuclear magnifico, wanted to be a statesman. 'He's ambitious on a global scale,' he confided in a Georgian protégé, 'but his ammunition isn't worth a penny!' Stalin decided something was rotten in the Organs. During his holiday, he asked Vlasik about the conduct of Beria. Vlasik, delighted to destroy Beria, denounced his corruption, incompetence and possibly his VD. At a dinner in the south, Stalin told a joke about Beria:

'Stalin loses his favourite pipe. In a few days, Lavrenti calls Stalin: "Have you found your pipe?" "Yes," replies Stalin. "I found it under the sofa." "This is impossible!" exclaims Beria. "Three people have already confessed to this crime!"' Stalin relished stories about the power of the Cheka to make innocent people confess. But he became serious: 'Everyone laughs at the story. But it's not funny. The law-breakers haven't been rooted out of the MVD!'

Stalin moved swiftly against him: Beria was retired as MVD Minister in January, but remained *curator* of the Organs with Merkulov as MGB boss. Then Merkulov was denounced by his secretary. Beria washed his hands of him. On 4 May, Stalin, backed by Zhdanov, engineered the promotion of Abakumov to Minister of State Security: his qualifications for the job were his blind obedience and independence from Beria. When Abakumov modestly refused, Stalin jokingly asked if he would 'prefer the Tea Trust'.

Abakumov remains the most shadowy of Stalin's secret-police bosses just as the post-war years remain the murkiest of Stalin's reign, although we now know much more about them. The coming atrocities were Abakumov's doing, not Beria's, even though most histories blame the latter. Beria, who, as Deputy Premier in charge of the Bomb and the missile industry, now moved his office from the Lubianka to the Kremlin, was henceforth 'sacked' from the Organs. He bitterly resented it.

'Beria was scared to death of Abakumov and tried at all costs to have good relations ...' recalled Merkulov. 'Beria met his match in Abakumov.' Like a rat on a sinking ship, Beria's pimp Colonel Sarkisov denounced the sexual degeneracy of the Bolshevik 'Bluebeard' to Abakumov who eagerly took it to Stalin: 'Bring me everything this arsehole will write down!' snapped Stalin.

48

Zhdanov the Heir and
Abakumov's Bloody Carpet

Abakumov, tall with a heart-shaped, fleshy face, colourless eyes, blue-black hair worn *broussant*, pouting lips and heavy eyebrows, was another colourful, swaggering torturer, amoral *condottiere* and 'zoological careerist' who possessed all Beria's sadism but less of his intelligence.* Abakumov unrolled a bloodstained carpet on his office floor before embarking on the torture of his victims in order not to stain his expensive Persian rugs. 'You see,' he told his spy Leopold Trepper, 'there are only two ways to thank an agent: cover his chest with medals or cut off his head.' He was hardly alone in this Bolshevik view.

Until Stalin swooped down to make him his own Chekist, Victor Abakumov was a typical secret policeman who had won his spurs purging Rostov in 1938. Born in 1908 to a Moscow worker, he was a *bon viveur* and womanizer. During the war, he stashed his mistresses in the Moskva Hotel and imported trainloads of plunder from Berlin. His splendid apartment had belonged to a soprano whom he had arrested and he regularly used MGB safehouses for amorous assignations. He loved jazz. The bandleader, Eddie Rosner, played at his parties until jazz was banned.

Abakumov dealt directly with Stalin, seeing him weekly, but never joined the dining circle: 'I did nothing on my own,' he claimed after Stalin's death. 'Stalin gave orders and I carried them out.' There is no reason to disbelieve him. He cultivated Stalin's children. At one Kremlin dinner, 'he suddenly started, jumped up and obsequiously inclined his head before a short and reddish-haired girl' – Svetlana Stalin. Stalin's grandeur was such that people now bowed to his daughter. Abakumov went drinking

---

* Abakumov appears as the consummate cunning courtier, utterly submissive to Stalin's mysterious whims, in Solzhenitsyn's novel of the post-war Terror, *The First Circle*, and as a shrewd and debauched secret-police careerist in Rybakov's *Fire and Ashes*, the last volume of his *Children of the Arbat* trilogy.

with Vasily Stalin. Together, they fanned the Aviators' Case. Vasily purloined Novikov's dacha while the 'father of the Soviet air force' was tortured. Stalin asked for Abakumov's recommendations:

'They should be shot.'

'It's easy to shoot people,' replied Stalin. 'It's more difficult to make them work. Make them work.' Shakhurin received seven years' hard labour, Novikov ten years – but their confessions implicated bigger fish.

On 4 May, Malenkov was abruptly removed from the Secretariat. His family remembered that they had to move out of their dacha. Their mother took them on a long holiday to the Baltic. Malenkov was despatched to check the harvest in Central Asia for several months, but never arrested. Beria tried to persuade Stalin to bring him back, which amused the Generalissimo: 'Why are you taking such trouble with that imbecile? You'll be the first to be betrayed by him.'

* * *

Beria had lost his Organs and his ally, Malenkov, so the success of the Bomb was paramount. Later in the year, he rushed to Elektrostal at Noginsk, near Moscow, to see Professor Kurchatov's experimental nuclear reactor go critical, creating the first Soviet self-sustaining nuclear reaction. Beria watched Kurchatov raise the control rod at the panel and listened to the clicks that registered the neutrons rise to a wail.

'It's started!' they said.

'Is that all?' barked Beria, afraid of being tricked by these eggheads. 'Nothing more? Can I go to the reactor?' This would have been a delicious prospect for millions of Beria's victims but they dutifully restrained him, so helping to preserve the diminished Beria.

* * *

The reversal of fortunes of Beria and Malenkov marked the resurrection of their enemy, Andrei Zhdanov, Stalin's special friend, that hearty, pretentious intellectual who, after the stress of Leningrad, was a plump alcoholic with watery eyes and a livid complexion. Stalin openly talked about Zhdanov as his successor. Meanwhile, Beria could hardly conceal his loathing for Zhdanov's pretensions: 'He can just manage to play the piano with two fingers and to distinguish between a man and a bull in a picture, yet he holds forth on abstract painting!'

'The Pianist' had become a hero in Leningrad where he was apt to boast that the siege had been more important than the battle for Stalingrad. Sent as Stalin's proconsul in Finland in 1945, he mastered Finnish history, displayed an encyclopaedic knowledge of Helsinki politics and even charmed the British representative there. When he pushed to annex Finland (a Russian duchy until 1917), Molotov reprimanded him: 'You've gone too far ... You're too emotional!' But none of this harmed his standing with Stalin who recalled him from Leningrad and promoted him to Party Deputy in charge of both Agitprop and relations with foreign Parties, making him even more powerful than he had been before the war. His family, particularly his son Yury, became close to Stalin again. Indeed, they wrote to him *en famille*: 'Dear Joseph Vissarionovich, we cordially congratulate you on ... the anniversary of Bolshevism's victory and ask you to accept our warmest greetings, Zinaida, Andrei, Anna and Yury Zhdanov.'

Zhdanov had played his cards cleverly since returning in January 1945. He consolidated his triumph over Malenkov and Beria by persuading Stalin to promote his own camarilla of Leningraders to power in Moscow: Alexei Kuznetsov, the haggard, long-faced and soft-spoken hero of the siege, received Malenkov's Secretaryship. Zhdanov understood that Stalin did not wish Beria to control the MGB so he suggested Kuznetsov to replace him as *curator* of the Organs. It was 'naive' of Kuznetsov to accept this poisoned chalice; 'he should have refused,' said Mikoyan, but he was 'unworldly'. Kuznetsov's promotions earned him the undying hatred of the two most vindictive predators in the Stalinist jungle: Beria and Malenkov.

By February 1946, with Stalin in semi-retirement, Zhdanov seemed to have control of the Party as well as cultural and foreign policy matters, and to have neutralized the Organs and the military.* Zhdanov was hailed as the 'second man in the Party', its 'greatest worker', and his staff whispered about 'our Crown Prince'. Stalin toyed with appointing him General Secretary. During 1946, Zhdanov signed decrees as 'Secretary' alongside Stalin as Premier: 'the Pianist' was so important that the Yugoslav

---

* Stalin himself soon retired as Armed Forces Minister, handing this to Bulganin, another ally of Zhdanov who hated Malenkov because he had removed him from the Western Front in 1943. The ruling inner circle of Five (Stalin, Molotov, Mikoyan, Malenkov and Beria) gradually expanded to embrace Zhdanov, Voznesensky, Bulganin and Kuznetsov, regardless of whether they were yet formally Politburo members.

Ambassador noticed how, when a bureaucrat entered his office, he bowed 'to Zhdanov as he was approaching' and then retreated backwards, managing to cover 'six or seven yards and in bowing himself out, he backed into the door, nervously trying to find the doorknob with his hand'. At the November parade, Zhdanov, in Stalin's absence, took the salute with his Leningrad camarilla filling the Mausoleum.

Yet his health was weak.* Zhdanov never wanted to be the successor. During Stalin's serious illnesses, he was terrified at the prospect, telling his son, 'God forbid I outlive Stalin!'

* * *

Stalin and Zhdanov picked up where they had left off before the war, debating how to merge the patriotic Russianness of the war with the Bolshevism of the Revolution in order to eradicate foreign influence and restore morality, pride and discipline. Like two crabby professors, obsessed with the greatness of nineteenth-century culture and repulsed by the degeneracy of modern art and morals, the old seminarist and the scion of provincial intelligentsia reached back to their youths, devising a savage attack on modernism ('formalism') and foreign influence on Russian culture ('cosmopolitanism'). Poring over poetry and literary journals late into the night, these two meticulous, ever-tinkering 'intellectuals', who shared that ravenous Bolshevik appetite for education, cooked up the crackdown on the cultural freedom of wartime.

Steeped in the classics, despising new-fangled art, Zhdanov embarked on a policy that would have been familiar to Tsars Alexander I and Nicholas I. Victory had blessed the marriage of Russianness and Bolshevism: Stalin saw the Russians as the binding element of the USSR, the 'elder brother' of the Soviet peoples, his own new brand of Russian nationalism very different from its nineteenth-century ancestor. There would be no new freedoms, no foreign influences, but these impulses would be suppressed in an enforced celebration of Russianness.

The Leningrad journals were the natural place to start because they published the works of the satirist Mikhail Zoshchenko, whom Stalin had once read to his children, and the poetess Anna

---

* In late 1946, Zhdanov suffered heart trouble and had to rest in Sochi, reporting to Stalin on 5 January 1947, 'Now I feel much better ... I don't want to end the course of treatment ... I ask you to add 10 days to my holiday ... Let me return 25th ... For which I'll be enormously grateful. Greetings! Your Andrei Zhdanov.'

Akhmatova, whose passionate verses symbolized the indestructible dignity and sensitivity of humanity in terror and war. Zhdanov's papers reveal in his own words what Stalin wanted: 'I ask you to look this through,' Zhdanov asked the master, 'is it good for the media and what needs to be improved?'

'I read your report. I think it's perfect,' Stalin replied in crayon. 'You must hurry to publish it and then as a book. Greetings!' But 'there are some corrections' – which expressed Stalin's thinking: 'if our youth had read Akhmatova and been educated in such an atmosphere, what would have happened in the Great Patriotic War? Our youth [has been] educated in the cheerful spirit able to win victory over Germany and Japan ... This journal helps our enemies to destroy our youth.'*

On 18 April, Zhdanov launched his cultural terror, known as the *Zhdanovshchina*, with an attack on the Leningrad journals. In August, the literary inquisitor travelled to Leningrad to demand: 'How weak was the vigilance of those citizens in Leningrad, in the leadership of the journal *Zvezda*, for it to publish, in this journal, works ... poisoned with the venom of zoological hostility to the Soviet leadership.' He castigated Akhmatova as this 'half-nun, half-harlot or rather harlot-nun whose sin is mixed with prayer', a grotesque distortion of her own verses. He followed this up with attacks on film-makers and musicians. At a notorious meeting with Shostakovich and others, 'the Pianist' tinkled on the piano to demonstrate easily-hummed people's tunes, a vision as absurd as Joseph II admonishing Mozart for writing 'too many notes'. Yury Zhdanov went to the theatre with his father and Stalin. When they talked to the actors afterwards, the cast boasted that their show had been acclaimed in Paris:

'Those French aren't worth the soles of your shoes,' replied Stalin. 'There's nothing more important than Russian theatre.'

Bantering playfully, the omnipotent double-act, Stalin and Zhdanov, held *conversazione* to guide writers and film directors. On the night of 14 May 1947, they received Stalin's two favoured literary bureaucrats, the poet Simonov and the hack novelist,

---

* Zhdanov discussed the campaign with his son Yury, who had studied chemistry, taken a master's degree in philosophy – and remained Stalin's ideal young man and his dream son-in-law. Zhdanov explained that 'after the war, with millions dead and the economy destroyed, we have to form a new concept of spiritual values to give a foundation to a devastated country, based on classical culture ...' Zhdanov, raised on nineteenth-century 'authors from Pushkin to Tolstoy, composers like Haydn and Mozart', sought 'an ideological basis in the classics'.

Fadeev, the head of the Writers' Union. Stalin first set the pay for writers:

'They write one good book, build their dacha and stop working. We don't begrudge them the money,' laughed Stalin, 'but this can't happen.' So he suggested setting up a commission:

'I'll join!' declared Zhdanov, showing his independence.

'Very modest!' Stalin chuckled. As they discussed the commission, Zhdanov opposed Stalin thrice before being overruled, another example of how his favourite could still argue with him. Stalin teased Zhdanov fondly. When 'the Pianist' said he had received a pitiful letter from some writer, Stalin joked:

'Don't believe pitiful letters, Comrade Zhdanov!' Stalin asked the writers: 'If that's all, I've a question for you: what kind of themes are writers working on?' He launched into a lecture about 'Soviet patriotism'. The people were proud but 'our middle intelligentsia, doctors and professors don't have patriotic education. They have unjustified admiration for foreign culture ... This tradition comes from Peter ... admiration of Germans, French, of foreigners, of assholes –' he laughed. 'The spirit of self-abasement must be destroyed. You should write a novel on this theme.'

Stalin had a recent scandal in mind. A pair of medical professors specializing in cancer treatment had published their work in an American journal. Stalin and Zhdanov created 'courts of honour', another throwback to the Tsarist officer class, to try the professors. (Zhdanov chaired the court.) Stalin set Simonov to write a play about the case. Zhdanov spent an entire hour giving literary criticism to Simonov before Stalin himself rewrote the play's ending.*

In August, Bolshakov, the cinematic impresario, showed Stalin a new movie, *Ivan the Terrible, Part Two*. Knowing from MGB reports that Eisenstein compared The Terrible with Yezhov, Stalin rejected this 'nightmare', hating its lack of Russian pride, its portrayal of Ivan (and the length of his kisses, and beard). Eisenstein shrewdly appealed to Stalin. At 11 p.m. on 25 February 1947, Eisenstein and his scriptwriter arrived in the Little Corner where Stalin and Zhdanov gave them a master-class on national Bolshevism, a most revealing *tour d'horizon* of history, terror and

---

* 'I have fulfilled the orders according to Comrade Stalin's instructions which I wrote down about the play,' Simonov wrote to Poskrebyshev on 9 February 1949, delivering the work for inspection.

even sex. Stalin attacked the film for making the Tsar's MGB, the *Oprichnina*, resemble the Ku Klux Klan. As for Ivan himself, 'Your Tsar is indecisive – he resembles Hamlet,' said Stalin. 'Tsar Ivan was a great wise ruler ... wise ... not to let foreigners into the country. Peter the Great's also a great Tsar but treated foreigners too liberally ... Catherine, more so. Was Alexander I's Court Russian? ... No, it was German ...' Then Zhdanov gave his own view, with its interesting reflection on Stalin's own nature:

'Ivan the Terrible seems a hysteric in the Eisenstein version!'

'Historical figures,' added Stalin, 'must be shown correctly ... Ivan the Terrible kissed his wife too long.' Kisses, again. 'It wasn't permitted at that time.' Then came the crux: 'Ivan the Terrible was very cruel,' said Stalin. 'You can show he was cruel. But you must show why he *needed to be cruel*.' Then Zhdanov raised the crucial question of Ivan's beard. Eisenstein promised to shorten it. Eisenstein asked if he could smoke.

'It seems to me there's no ban on smoking. Maybe we'll vote on it.' Stalin smiled at Eisenstein. 'I don't give you instructions, I merely give you the comments of a viewer.'*

Zhdanov's campaign to promote Russian patriotism was soon so absurd that Sakharov remembered how people would joke about 'Russia, homeland of the elephant'. More ominously, the unleashing of Russian nationalism and the attacks on 'cosmopolitans' turned against the Jews.

* Eisenstein died before he could shorten the beard, cut the kiss and show why The Terrible 'needed to be cruel'. This was a mercy since it seems unlikely he would have survived the anti-Semitic purge of 1951–3.

49

The Eclipse of Zhukov and the Looters
of Europe: the Imperial Elite

Early in the war, Stalin realized the usefulness of Soviet Jewry in appealing for American help but even then the project was stained with blood.* Stalin then ordered Beria to set up the Jewish Anti-Fascist Committee, controlled by the NKVD but officially led by the famous Yiddish actor, Solomon Mikhoels, 'short, with the face of a puckish intellectual, with a prominent forehead and a pouting lower lip', whom Kaganovich had perform *King Lear* for Stalin. When Mikhoels toured America to raise support for Russia in April 1943, Molotov briefed him and Stalin emerged from his office to wave goodbye. The JAFC was supervised by Solomon Lozovsky, a grizzled Old Bolshevik with a biblical beard who was the token Jew in the highest echelons of Molotov's Foreign Commmissariat.

The ghastly revelations of the Nazi Holocaust, the Mikhoels tour and the attractions of Zionism to give the Jewish people a safe haven, softened the stern internationalism of even the highest Bolsheviks. Stalin tolerated this but encouraged a traditional anti-Semitic reaction. When casting *Ivan the Terrible, Part Two*, Bolshakov openly rejected one actress because 'her Semitic features are clearly visible'. Anyone too Jewish-looking was sacked.

When the advancing Soviet Army exposed Hitler's unique Jewish genocide, Khrushchev, the Ukrainian boss, resisted any special treatment for Jews staggering home from the death camps. He even refused to return their homes, which had meanwhile been occupied by Ukrainians. This habitual anti-Semite grumbled that 'Abramoviches' were preying on his fiefdom 'like crows'.

This sparked a genuine debate around Stalin. Mikhoels complained to Molotov that 'after the Jewish catastrophe, the local authorities pay no attention'. Molotov forwarded this to Beria who, to his credit, was sympathetic. Beria demanded that Khrushchev

---

* The first two candidates to lead this wartime PR campaign, Polish leaders of the Bund (Jewish Socialist Party), V. Alter and G. Ehlich, demanded too much and were arrested, respectively being shot and committing suicide in prison.

help the Jews who 'were more repressed than any others by the Germans'. In this he was taking a risk since Stalin had decreed that *all* Soviet citizens suffered *equally*. Stalin later suspected Beria of being too close to the Jews, perhaps the origin of the rumour that Beria himself was a 'secret' Jew. Molotov forwarded Beria's order. Khrushchev agreed to help his 'Abramoviches'.

Encouraged by this growing sympathy, Mikhoels and his colleague Fefer, a poet* and MGB plant, suggested a Jewish republic in the Crimea (now empty of Tartars), or in Saratov (now empty of the Volga Germans) to Molotov and his deputy in charge of the JAFC, Lozovsky. Molotov thought the Volga German idea ridiculous, 'it's impossible to see a Jew on a tractor', but preferred the Crimea: 'Why don't you write a memorandum to me and Comrade Stalin, and we'll see.'

'Everyone,' recalls Vladimir Redens, 'believed Jewish Crimea would happen.' Molotov, showing more independence than before, may have discussed this with Beria but his judgement almost cost him his life. Most of those involved were dead within five years.

On 2 February 1944 Mikhoels delivered his letter to Molotov, copied to Stalin who now decided that the actor had moved from Soviet to Jewish propaganda. Stalin, with his acute awareness of anti-Semitism, sent Kaganovich to pour cold water on the idea of this 'Jewish California': 'Only actors and poets could come up with such a scheme,' he said, that was 'worth nothing in practice!' Zhdanov supervised the making of lists of Jews in different departments and recommended closing down the JAFC.† Like Molotov in 1939, Zhdanov loosed his hounds against Jews in the *apparat* which, he said, had become 'some kind of synagogue'.

Stalin's anti-Semitism remained a mixture of old-fashioned prejudice, suspicion of a people without a land, and distrust, since his enemies were often Jewish. He was so unabashed that he openly told Roosevelt at Yalta that the Jews were 'middlemen, profiteers and parasites'. But after 1945, there was a change: Stalin emerged as a vicious and obsessional anti-Semite.

---

* Fefer was the author of an absurd poem during WW2 called 'I a Jew' in which he praised the great Jewish Bolsheviks from King Solomon to Marx, Sverdlov and 'Stalin's friend Kaganovich' which no doubt enormously embarrassed the latter.

† Zhdanov's chief ideological anti-Semite was the tall, thin and ascetic CC Secretary Mikhail Suslov, who had played a key role in the Caucasian deportations and then served as Stalin's proconsul in the Baltics which he brutally purged after the war. Working alternately under both Zhdanov and Malenkov, he became one of Stalin's youngish protégés.

Always supremely political, this was partly a pragmatic judgement: it matched his new Russian nationalism. The supremacy of America with its powerful Jewish community made his own Jews, with their US connections restored during the war, appear a disloyal Fifth Column. His suspicion of the Jews was another facet of his inferiority complex towards America as well as a symptom of his fear of the new self-assertive confidence of his own victorious people. It was also a way to control his old comrades whose Jewish connections symbolized their new cosmopolitan confidence after victory. Equally, he loathed any people with mixed loyalties: he noticed the Holocaust had touched and awakened Soviet Jewry even among the magnates. His new anti-Semitism flowed from his own seething paranoia, exacerbated when Fate entangled the Jews in his family.

Yet he still played the internationalist, often attacking people for anti-Semitism and rewarding Jews in public, from Mekhlis to the novelist Ehrenburg. Soon this malevolent whirlpool threatened to consume Molotov, Beria and his own clan.

* * *

'As soon as hostilities end,' Stalin said at Yalta, 'the soldiers are forgotten and lapse into oblivion.' He wished this was so but the prestige of Marshal Zhukov had never been higher. The Western press even acclaimed him as Stalin's successor. Stalin liked Zhukov but 'didn't recognize personal ties' and he probed to see if this idea had any support.

'I'm getting old,' he casually told Budyonny, his old pal and Zhukov's friend. 'What do you think of Zhukov succeeding me?'

'I approve of Zhukov,' he replied, 'but he's a complicated character.'

'You managed to govern him,' said Stalin, 'and I can manage him too.'

Stalin 'managed' Zhukov by using the 'Aviators' Case' against him, torturing Air Marshal Novikov to implicate him.* 'Broken morally, brought to desperation, sleepless nights, I signed,'

---

* Churchill himself had bouts of jealousy of his generals: 'Monty wants to fill the Mall when he gets his baton! And he will not fill the Mall,' Churchill told Sir Alan Brooke on his way back from Moscow in October 1944. 'He will fill the Mall because he is Monty and I will not have him filling the Mall!' It was, wrote Brooke, 'a strange streak of almost unbelievable petty jealousy on his part ... Those that got between him and the sun did not meet his approval.' There was a great tradition of rulers jealous of, and threatened by, brilliant but overmighty generals: Emperor Justinian humiliated Belisarius; Emperor Paul did the same to Suvorov.

admitted Novikov later. Abakumov tortured seventy other generals to get the necessary evidence. In March, Zhukov was recalled to Moscow. Instead of reporting directly to the Generalissimo, he was summoned by Stalin's deputy as Armed Forces Minister, Bulganin, 'the Plumber' (as Beria called him) who was in high favour. Zhukov grumbled at Bulganin's arrogance and Bulganin grumbled that Zhukov had pulled rank on him, resisting orders from the Party. Stalin ordered 'the Plumber' to prepare a kangaroo court against Zhukov. Abakumov searched Zhukov's homes which turned out to be an Aladdin's cave of booty:

'We can simply say,' Abakumov reportedly gleefully to Stalin, 'that Zhukov's dacha is a museum', filled with gold, 323 furs, 400 metres of velvet and silk. There were so many paintings, some even hung in the kitchen. Zhukov even went so far as to hang over his bed a huge canvas depicting two naked women ... we did not find a single Soviet book.' Then there were 'twenty unique shotguns from Holland & Holland'. They left the trophies (returning for them in 1948) but for now they bizarrely confiscated a doll of one of the Marshal's daughters, and his memoirs:

'Leave history writing to the historians,' Stalin warned Zhukov.

In early June, Zhukov was summoned to the Supreme Military Council. Stalin strode in 'as gloomy as a black cloud'. Without a word, he tossed a note to Shtemenko.

'Read it,' he snapped. Shtemenko read out Novikov's testimony that Zhukov had claimed credit for the Soviet victory, criticized Stalin and created his own clique. He had even awarded a medal to the starlet Lydia Ruslanova, with whom he may have been having an affair.

This was 'intolerable', declared Stalin, turning to the generals. Budyonny (who had been coached by Bulganin) vaguely criticized his friend but not damningly. Zhukov's rival, Koniev, called him difficult but honest. Only Golikov, whom Zhukov had removed from the Voronezh Front in 1943, really denounced him. But Molotov, Beria and Bulganin attacked the Marshal for 'Bonapartism', demanding that Zhukov 'be put in his place'. Zhukov defended himself but admitted to having inflated his importance.

'What shall we do with Zhukov?' asked Stalin who, typically, had expressed no opinion. The potentates wanted him repressed, the soldiers did not. Stalin, seeing this was not 1937, suggested demoting Zhukov to the Odessa Military District. The Terror against the victors was a deliberate policy, with Admiral Kuznetsov, among others, arrested (though also only demoted). Ex-Marshal Kulik was bugged grumbling on his telephone that politicians were stealing the credit from the soldiers. This was heresy: he was quietly shot in 1950. Zhukov himself was expelled from the CC, his trophies confiscated, friends tortured, and then further demoted to the Urals. He suffered a heart attack but Stalin never let Abakumov arrest him for planning a Bonapartist coup:

'I don't trust anyone who says Zhukov could do this. I know him very well. He's a straightforward, sharp person able to speak plainly to anyone but he'll never go against the CC.'

Finally Stalin demonstrated the subordination of the generals by writing this note to the Politburo:

'I propose Comrade Bulganin be promoted to Marshal for his distinction in the Patriotic War.' In case anyone wished to query 'the Plumber's' utterly undistinguished war – and civilian – record, Stalin added: 'I think my reason requires no discussion – it's absolutely clear.'

* * *

Zhukov was not alone in his 'museum' of gold and paintings. Corruption is the untold story of Stalin's post-war Terror: the magnates and marshals plundered Europe with the avarice of Göring, though with much more justification after what the Germans had done to Russia. This imperial élite cast aside much of their old 'Bolshevik modesty'. Yet 'Comrade Stalin', foreign visitors were told, 'cannot endure immorality' though he had always believed that conquerors could help themselves to some booty and local girls. He laughed about the luxuries of his generals with their courtesans and batmen yet his archives overflow with denunciations of corruption which he usually filed away for later.

The marshals benefited from the feudal etiquette of plundering whereby officers stole their booty and then paid a sort of tribute to their superiors. Some needed no such help: Air Marshal Golovanov, one of Stalin's favourites, dismantled Goebbels' country house and flew it back to Moscow, an exploit that ruined his career.

The soldiers reached the treasures first but it was the Chekists who enjoyed the best swag. At Gagra, Beria pursued and impressed female athletes in a fleet of plundered speedboats. Abakumov drove around Moscow in Italian sports cars, looted Germany with Göringesque extravagance, sent planes to Berlin to commandeer

Potemkinesque quantities of underwear, assembling an antique treasure-trove like a department store. He flew in the German film star and international woman of mystery, Olga Chekhova, for an affair. When actress Tatiana Okunevskaya (already raped by Beria) refused him, she got seven years in the Gulags. Stalin's staff were mired in corruption. Vlasik, the *vizier* who ran a luxurious empire of food, drink and mansions, entertained his courtesans at official rest homes with a crew of raffish painters, thuggish Chekists and sybaritic bureaucrats. Limousines delivered the 'concubines' who received apartments, caviar, tickets to Red Square parades and football games. Vlasik seduced his friends' wives by showing them his photographs of Stalin and maps of Potsdam. He even pilfered Stalin's own houses, stripping his villa at Potsdam, stealing 100 pieces of porcelain, pianos, clocks, cars, three bulls and two horses, transported home in MGB trains and planes. He spent much of the Potsdam Conference drinking, fornicating, or stealing.

Then there was the massive wastage of food at Stalin's dachas. Vlasik was soon denounced for selling off the extra caviar, probably by Beria whom he had denounced in turn. In 1947, he was almost arrested but, instead, Stalin let him explain his sins: 'Every time, the mealtime was changed by [Stalin], part of the dishes were not used. They were distributed among the staff.' Stalin forgave him – and ordered less food than before. Vlasik kept his job.

Yet Vlasik's mistresses, like Beria's pimps, informed on him to Abakumov who in turn was denounced by his MGB rival, General Serov, who wrote to Stalin about the Minister's corruption and debauchery. Stalin stored the letters for later use. Serov himself was said to have stolen the crown of the King of Belgium. By now courtesans, procurers and MGB generals were informing on each other in a merry-go-round of sexual favours and betrayals.

*　*　*

Stalin's potentates now existed in a hothouse of rarefied privilege, their offices bedecked with fine Persian carpets and broad oil paintings.* Their houses were palatial: the Moscow boss now occupied the whole of Grand Duke Sergei Alexandrovich's palace.

---

* The size and quality of their Stalin portrait was as much a mark of rank as the stars on an officer's shoulder-boards: a life-size oil original by a court artist like Gerasimov was the sign of a potentate. Budyonny and Voroshilov also boasted life-size portraits of themselves in military splendour on horseback with sabre by Gerasimov. These 'grandees' were now so pompous, recalled Svetlana, that they made 'authoritative speeches' on 'any pretext', even at lunch in their own homes while their families 'sighed with boredom'.

Stalin himself fostered this new imperial era when, after Yalta, he took a fancy to Nicholas II's Livadia and Prince Vorontsov's Alupka Palaces: 'Put these palaces in order,' Stalin wrote to Beria on 27 February 1945. 'Prepare for responsible workers.' He so liked Alexander III's Palace at Sosnovka in the Crimea that he had a dacha built there which he only visited once. Henceforth, the magnates and their children booked these palaces through the MGB 9th Department: Stepan Mikoyan honeymooned at Vorontsov's palace; Stalin himself holidayed at Livadia. The families flew south on a special section of the state airline – Sergo Mikoyan remembers flying home on this with Poskrebyshev. The children enjoyed their privileges but had to set an example and follow Party dictums: when Zhdanov denounced jazz, Khrushchev broke his son's beloved jazz records in a temper.

Svetlana Stalin noticed how the dachas of the Mikoyans, Molotovs and Voroshilovs were 'crammed with gifts from workers … rugs, gold Caucasian weapons, porcelain' which they received like 'the medieval custom of vassals paying tribute'. The magnates travelled in armoured ZiS limousines, based on the American Packards, on Stalin's orders, followed by another 'tail' of Chekists, with sirens blaring. Muscovites called this procession 'a dog's wedding'.

An entire detachment, commanded by a colonel or a general, was assigned to each leader, actually living at their dachas, half an extended family, half MGB informers. There were so many of them that each Politburo member was able to form a volleyball team, with the Berias playing the Kaganoviches. But Kaganovich refused to play on his own team: 'Beria always wins and I want to be on the winning side,' he said. In MGB vernacular, the magnate was called 'the subject', their house 'the object' and the guards 'attachments to the subject', so the children used to laugh when they heard them say, 'The subject's on his way to the object.' Malenkov often walked to the Kremlin from Granovsky Street surrounded by a phalanx of 'attachments'.

The Politburo ladies now had their own haute couture designer. All the 'top ten families' went to the *atelier* on Kutuzovsky Prospekt, controlled by an MGB department where Abram (Donjat Ignatovich according to Nina Khrushcheva) Lerner and Nina Adzhubei designed the men's suits and the women's dresses. Lerner was a traditional Jewish tailor who designed uniforms including Stalin's Generalissimo extravaganza. If he was the

Politburo's Dior, Nina Adzhubei, 'short, round, pug-nosed and very strong', trained by 'monks in a monastery', was its Chanel. Heaps of *Harper's Bazaar* and *Vogue* lay around. She would either copy fashions from Dior, from *Vogue* or *Harper's* or design her own, 'but she was as good as Chanel', says her client Martha Peshkova, Beria's daughter-in-law. 'You didn't have to pay if you didn't ask the price,' explains Sergo Mikoyan. 'My mother always paid but Polina Molotova didn't.' This practice was finally denounced, like everything else, to Stalin who reprimanded the Politburo: Ashken Mikoyan threw the bills in Anastas's face, proving she always paid. Adzhubei 'made Svetlana Stalin's first dress'.*

The dressmaker was discovered by Nina Beria but Polina Molotova, the grand 'first lady', was her best client. Once the grandees of Victorian Europe had taken the waters at the Bohemian resort of Carlsbad. Now Zinaida Zhdanova and Nina Beria held court there. 'Lavishly dressed and covered in furs', with her daughter in a 'mink stole', Polina often arrived at the same spa in an official plane with an entourage of fifty. Her daughter Svetlana, a 'real Bolshevik princess', was chauffered daily to the Institute of Foreign Relations, where many of the élite studied, arriving in a cloud of Chanel No. 5, 'wearing a new outfit every day'.

Stalin retained his control of these privileges, continuing to choose the cars for every leader so that Zhdanov received an armoured Packard, a normal Packard and a ZiS 110, Beria got an armoured Packard, a ZiS and a Mercedes, while Poskrebyshev got a Cadillac and a Buick. He consoled the family of Shcherbakov, the Moscow boss who died of alcoholism, with a shower of cash.† Stalin specified: 'Give them an apartment with a dacha, rights to the Kremlin Hospital, limousine ... NKVD special staff ... teacher for children ...' He awarded Shcherbakov's widow 2,000 roubles a

---

* Nina Adzhubei joined the élite herself when her son married Khrushchev's daughter, Rada. When Khrushchev became Soviet leader, Alexei Adzhubei became powerful as the leader's adviser and *Izvestiya* editor.
† Although Stalin was cynical about the renaming of places after his late magnates, he decided to build a statue and rename a region, street and factory after Shcherbakov. The original draft suggested naming a town after him, too, but Stalin crossed that out, scribbling: 'Give his name to a cloth factory.' On 9 December 1947, the Politburo set annual salaries of the Premier and President at 10,000 roubles; Deputy Premiers and CC Secretaries 8,000 roubles. Stalin's salary packets just piled up, unspent, in his desk at Kuntsevo.

month, his sons 1,000 a month until graduation, his mother 700 a month, his sister 300. His wife also received a lump sump of 200,000 roubles and his mother 50,000 roubles – sums of unthinkable munificence for the average worker. Here was Stalin's new imperial order.

* * *

'Crown Prince' Vasily set a new standard for corruption, debauchery and caprice. Even when officers complained about him to Stalin, they used a special formula to define Vasily's sacred place: 'He is close to the Soviet people because he is your son.' Yet beneath the arrogance, Vasily was the most terrified of all the courtiers: Stalin scoffed that he would 'walk through fire' if he ordered it. Vasily especially feared the future:

'I've only got two ways out,' he told Artyom. 'The pistol or drink! If I use the pistol, I'll cause Father a lot of trouble. But when he dies, Khrushchev, Beria and Bulganin'll tear me apart. Do you realize what it's like living under the axe?'

He callously abandoned his wife, Galina, taking their son Sasha to live with him at the House on the Embankment. She so longed to see Sasha that the nanny secretly met her so she could play with him. But Galina was too frightened to demand a flat or housekeeping from him. Vasily then married Marshal Timoshenko's daughter Ekaterina, 'a pretty Ukrainian'. His apartment was not grand enough for the scions of the Generalissimo and the Marshal so he demanded General Vlasik's elegant villa on Gogolevsky. He flew back from Germany with a plane filled with 'loot': 'golden ornaments, diamonds, emeralds, dozens of carpets, lots of lady's lingerie, a huge number of men's suits, overcoats, fur coats, fur wraps, astrakhan' until Vasily's house was 'bursting with gold, German carpets and cut glass'. There was so much that his wife Timoshenka gradually sold it and pocketed the money. When his marriage to Timoshenka collapsed, he married a swimming star, the statuesque Kapitolina Vasileva, with whom he was happiest. Svetlana thought he was looking for his mother in his wives because he called her 'mama' and she even wore her hair in a bun like Nadya.

Vasily commanded the Air Force in the Moscow Military District, a job beyond his capabilities. He demanded that his strutting entourage call him *Khozyain* like his father. 'Vasily drank heavily almost every day,' testified his adjutant later, 'didn't turn up for work for weeks on end and couldn't leave the women alone.'

Once Crown Princes proudly drilled their own regiments. Now, like a Western millionaire's son, Vasily was determined to make his own VVS (Air Force) football team top of the league. He immediately sacked the football manager, having decided to rescue Starostin, Russia's pre-eminent soccer manager exiled by Beria, for plotting to assassinate Stalin, from the Gulag. Starostin was called into his camp commandant's office and handed the *vertushka*: 'Hello, Nikolai, this is Vasily Stalin.' General Stalin's plane arrived and flew Starostin back to Moscow where Vasily hid him while he tried to get his sentence reversed.

Abakumov, now boss of the Dynamo team, was furious. The MGB kidnapped Starostin. Vasily, using Air Force intelligence officers, grabbed him back. Abakumov kidnapped him again. When Vasily phoned the Minister, he denied any knowledge of the footballer but Starostin managed to get a message to Vasily who despatched the head of Air Force security to bring him back yet again. That day, Vasily attended the Dynamo game in the government box, with Starostin beside him. The MGB brass were foiled. Vasily called Abakumov's deputy and shouted: 'Two hours ago you told me you didn't know where Starostin was ... He's sitting here right beside me. Your boys abducted him. Remember, in our family, we never forgive an insult. That's told to you by General Stalin!'*

When he visited Tiflis, he got drunk, took a fighterplane up over the city and caused havoc by swooping over the streets. If he did not get his way, he denounced officers to Abakumov or Bulganin. The only escape was to denounce him to Stalin himself:

'Dear Joseph Vissarionovich, I ask you to tell Vasily Josephovich not to touch me,' wrote the air-force officer N. Sbytov, who had spotted the first German tanks approaching Moscow. 'I could help him.' Sbytov revealed that Vasily was constantly name-dropping: 'When my father approved this job, he wanted me to have an independent command,' he whined.

---

* When Starostin was finally returned to his camp (where he ran the soccer team), Vasily hired the famous coach of Dynamo Tiflis and managed to make it to fourth place in 1950 and the semi-finals of the USSR Cup. He favoured Stalinist punishments and plutocratic incentives: when his team lost 0–2, he ordered their plane to dump them in the middle of nowhere, far from Moscow, as a punishment; when the team won, a helicopter landed on the field filled with gifts. When he bothered to turn up to his Air Force command, he ruled there too with wild generosity and grim terror. Thanks to Zurab Karumidze for these anecdotes of his father-in-law, Vasily's football manager.

Vasily certainly behaved like a boy brought up by Chekists: when some 'Enemies' were found in his command, he set up an impromptu torture-chamber in his own apartment and started 'beating the soles of the man's feet with a thin rod' until this *ersatz*-Lubianka broke up into a party.

* * *

Days after Zhukov's exile, President Kalinin, who was ill with stomach cancer, started to deteriorate. Stalin was fond of Papa Kalinin, personally arranging to send him down to recuperate in Abkhazia, calling the local boss to demand 'maximum care', and later ordering his bodyguards to look after him tenderly. Yet he also tormented the half-blind Kalinin, remembering 'Papa's' dissent in the twenties for which he had excluded him from active government for two decades. When Tito offered Kalinin some cigarettes at a banquet, Stalin quipped:

'Don't take any of those Western cigarettes!' Kalinin 'confusedly dropped them from his trembling fingers'.

The 71-year-old Kalinin lived with his housekeeper and two adopted children while his adored wife festered in the camps. Emboldened by his imminent death, Kalinin appealed to Stalin:

'I look calmly on the future of our country … and I wish only one thing – to preserve your power and strength, the best guarantee of the success of the Soviet State,' he started his letter. 'Personally I turn to you with two requests – pardon Ekaterina Ivanovna Kalinina and appoint my sister to bring up the two orphans living with me. With all my soul, a last goodbye. M. Kalinin.' Stalin, Malenkov and Zhdanov voted to pardon Kalinin's wife after she had admitted her guilt, the usual condition for forgiveness:

'I did bad things and was severely punished … but I was never an enemy to the Communist Party – pardon me!'

'It's necessary to pardon and free at once, and bring the pardoned to Moscow. J Stalin.'

Before he died, on 24 June, Kalinin wrote an extraordinary but pathetic letter to Stalin, inspired by his bitter need of Bolshevik redemption:

'Waiting for death … I must say that during all the time of the oppositions, no one from the opposition ever proposed hostility to the Party line. This might surprise you because I was friendly with some of them … Yet I was criticized and discredited … because Yagoda worked hard to imply my closeness to the oppositions.' Now he revealed a secret he had kept for twenty-two years: 'In the year after Lenin's death, after the row with Trotsky, Bukharin invited me to his flat to admire his hunting trophies and asked – would I consider "ruling without Stalin?"; I replied I couldn't contemplate such a thing. Any combination without Stalin was incomprehensible ... After the death of Lenin, I believed in Stalin's policy ... I thought Zinoviev most dangerous.' Then he again requested that Stalin care for his sister and the orphans, and 'commit this letter to the archive'.

At the funeral, when photographers hassled Stalin, he pointed at the coffin, growling: 'Photograph Kalinin!'

* * *

On 8 September, Stalin headed off on his holiday while Molotov shuttled around the world to attend meetings with the Allies to negotiate the new Europe. In Paris, he defended Soviet interests in Germany while still trying to win a protectorate over Libya, against the ever-hardening opposition of the Western allies. It seems that Stalin still hoped to consolidate his position by negotiations with his former allies.

Stalin, writing in code as 'Druzhkov' or *Instantsiya*, praised Molotov's indomitable defiance. Molotov was very pleased with himself too. When he found himself relegated to the second row at a French parade, he stormed off the podium but then wrote to Stalin for approval: 'I'm not sure I did the right thing.'

'You behaved absolutely correctly,' replied Stalin. 'The dignity of the Soviet Union must be defended not only in great matters but in minutiae.'

'Dear Polinka honey,' the vain Molotov wrote exultantly. 'I send greetings and newspaper pictures as I left the parade on Sunday! I enclose *Paris-Midi* which shows the three pictures of 1. me on the tribune. 2. I start to leave; and 3. I leave the tribune and enter my car. I kiss and hug you warmly! Kiss Svetusya for me!' Molotov flew on to another session in New York, which Stalin again supervised from Coldstream in Gagra: Stalin cared less about the details of Italian reparations than about Soviet status as a great power. Molotov was in favour again: on 28 November, Stalin wrote tenderly: 'I realize you are nervous and getting upset over the fate of the Soviet proposal ... Behave more calmly!' But faced with Ukrainian famine and American rivalry, the cantankerous *Vozhd* sensed dangerous weakness, corruption and disloyalty around him.

* * *

While Molotov was triumphant at having signed the peace treaties with the defeated nations, Stalin contrived another humiliation. Stalin was already a member of the Academy of Sciences and now Molotov was offered the same honour, with the *Vozhd*'s blessing. Molotov dutifully sent the Academy a grateful cable, upon which Stalin swooped with aquiline spite: 'I was struck by your cable ... Are you really so ecstatic about your election as an honorary Academician? What does this signature "truly yours, Molotov" mean? I never thought you could become so emotional about such a second-rate matter ... It seems to me that you, a statesman of the highest type, must care more about your dignity.'

Stalin continued to seethe about the inconvenience of his people starving, Hungry Thirty Three all over again.* First he tried to joke about it, calling one official 'Brother Dystrophy'. Then, when even Zhdanov reported the famine, Stalin blamed Khrushchev, his Ukrainian viceroy as he had done in 1932: 'They're deceiving you ...' Yet 282,000 people died in 1946, 520,000 in 1947. Finally he turned on the Supply maestro, Mikoyan. He ordered Mekhlis, resurgent as Minister of State Control, to investigate:

'Don't trust Mikoyan in any business because his lack of honest character has made Supply a den of thieves!'

Mikoyan was clever enough to apologize:

'I saw so many mistakes in my work and surely you see it all clearly,' he wrote to Stalin with submissive irony. 'Of course neither I nor the rest of us can put the issue as squarely as you can. I will do my best to study from you how to work as necessary. I'll do everything to learn lessons ... so it will serve me well in my subsequent work under your fatherly leadership.' Like Molotov, Mikoyan's old intimacy with Stalin was over. Khrushchev too fell into disfavour about his attitude to the famine: 'Spinelessness!' Stalin upbraided him and, in February 1947, sacked him as Ukrainian First Secretary (he remained Premier). Kaganovich, who now resembled 'a fat landowner', replaced him and arrived in Kiev to batter him into shape. Stalin's disfavour always brought debilitating stress to his grandees: Khrushchev collapsed with

---

* Not only could Stalin not feed his civilians but his correspondence with Beria and Serov (in Germany) shows that the Soviets were anxious that they could not feed their army in Germany, let alone the East Germans.

pneumonia. His name vanished from Ukrainian newspapers, his cult withered. But Kaganovich ordered doctors to treat Khrushchev with penicillin, one of the western medicines of which Stalin so disapproved. Even if he recovered, was Stalin's 'pet' doomed?

50

'The Zionists Have Pulled One Over You!'

In 1947, the American Secretary of State, George Marshall, unveiled a massive programme of economic aid to Europe that initially sounded attractive to the shattered Imperium. Molotov was immediately despatched to Paris to find out more. At first the leaders thought of the Plan like Lend-Lease with no strings attached, but Stalin soon grasped that it would resuscitate Germany and undermine his East European hegemony. Molotov initially favoured the Plan and still leaned towards a negotiated settlement but Stalin rejected Marshall.

Stalin and Zhdanov resolved to tighten their control over Eastern Europe. Simultaneously, Stalin supported the foundation of the Jewish state, which he hoped would become a Middle Eastern satellite. On 29 November, he voted for it at the UN and was the first to recognize Israel. He gave Mikhoels the Stalin Prize. But it soon became clear Israel was going to be an American ally, not a Russian one.

In the cauldron of Stalin's irrational prejudices, razor-sharp political instincts and aggressively Russian sensibilities, Mikhoels's dream of a Jewish Crimea became a sinister Zionist/American Trojan horse,* a Hebraic Marshall Plan. Zionism, Judaism and America became interchangeable in Stalin's mind. He was obviously supported by his magnates: even after Stalin's death, Khrushchev sympathetically explained to some Polish Communists, 'We all know Jews; they all have some connection with the capitalistic world because they have relatives living abroad. This one has a granny ... The Cold War began; the imperialists were

---

* Like so many of Stalin's febrile fears, there was substance here: the Ottoman Sultans had controlled the Black Sea through their control of Crimea. Catherine the Great and Prince Potemkin annexed the Crimea in 1783 for the same reason, just as the Anglo-French armies landed there in 1853 to undermine Russia. Khrushchev controversially donated Crimea to Ukraine in 1954, a decision that almost caused a civil war in the 1990s between Ukrainians and those who wished to be ruled by Russia.

plotting how to attack USSR; then the Jews want to settle in the Crimea ... here's the Crimea and Baku ... Through their connections, the Jews had created a network to carry out American plans. So he squashed it all.' This view was not only held in Stalin's councils: his nephew, Vladimir Redens, agreed with complaints that 'the Committee was giving off terrible Zionist propaganda ... as if the Jews were the only people who suffered.' Stalin's anti-Semitism dovetailed with his campaign of traditional nationalism. Even his prejudices were subordinate and complementary to *realpolitik*.

Stalin ordered Abakumov to gather evidence that Mikhoels and the Jewish Committee were 'active nationalists orientated by the Americans to do anti-Soviet work', especially through Mikhoels's American trip when 'they made contact with famous Jewish persons connected with the US secret service'. Mikhoels played into Stalin's hands.

Mikhoels, the Yiddish actor out of his depth in this duel with the Stalinist *Golem,* wanted to appeal to Stalin. He called the second most influential Jew after Kaganovich, Polina Molotova, to ask whether to appeal to Zhdanov or Malenkov.

'Zhdanov and Malenkov won't help you,' replied Polina. 'All power in the country's in Stalin's hands alone and nobody can influence him. I don't advise you write to Stalin. He has a negative attitude to Jews and won't support us.' It would have been unthinkable for her to speak in such a way before the war.

Mikhoels made the tempting but spectacularly ill-timed decision to reach Stalin through Svetlana. Stalin was already brooding about Svetlana's taste for Jewish men. After Kapler, there was Morozov whom she had married on the rebound from Sergo Beria. Stalin had nothing against Morozov personally, 'a good fellow', he said, but he had not fought in the war, and he was Jewish. 'The Zionists have pulled one over you,' Stalin told her. Malenkov's daughter Volya had just married the Jewish grandson of Lozovsky, who ran Mikhoels' Jewish Committee. Molotov proposed Mikhoels' Jewish Crimea letter and his wife Polina's brother was a Jewish American businessman. These American agents were everywhere. Now it got worse.

Mikhoels, frantic to protect the Jewish community, asked Zhenya Alliluyeva who mixed with the Jewish intelligentsia, if he could meet Svetlana. The élite children were wary of suitors using them for their connections: 'One of the unpleasant things of being daughter of a *chinovnik* was that I couldn't trust young people around me,' says Volya Malenkova. 'Many wanted to marry me. I didn't know if they wanted me or my father's influence.'

The Alliluyevs warned Zhenya against meddling in dangerous Jewish matters: 'All stirred together in this pot,' says Vladimir Redens. 'We knew it wasn't going to end well.' But it seems that Zhenya did introduce Mikhoels to Svetlana and Morozov. Stalin heard about this immediately* and erupted in a rage: the Jews were 'worming their way into the family'. Furthermore, Anna Redens was once again irritating Stalin, publishing a tactless memoir of his early days and nagging Vasily who complained to Stalin. Thus Mikhoels innocently stumbled into a hornets' nest.

Stalin ordered Abakumov to investigate the Alliluyev connection to American-Zionist espionage, muttering to Svetlana that Zhenya had poisoned her husband Pavel in 1938. Shrewd people began to divorce their Jewish spouses. Svetlana Stalin divorced Morozov: every history book repeats that Stalin ordered this and Svetlana's cousin Leonid Redens also claims that he did. But she herself explained, 'My father never asked me to divorce him', adding in more recent interviews that she had not been in love with Morozov: 'We divorced because I wasn't in love with him.' This rings true as far it goes: Leonid Redens adds that 'there were many men in Svetlana's life; she'd had enough of Morozov.' But Stalin himself told Mikoyan that 'if she doesn't divorce Morozov, they'll arrest him'. She left Morozov: 'No one would have left me,' said this Tsarevna. It seems that Stalin got his son to fix the matter. 'Vasily took Morozov's passport,'† says Redens, 'and brought him a new one without the wedding stamp.'

Abakumov started to arrest the Alliluyevs' Jewish circle. On 10 December, he arrested Zhenya Alliluyeva, once so intimate with Stalin, accusing her of 'disseminating foul slander about the Head of the Soviet Government'. Zhenya's husband, her vivacious actress daughter Kira, and Anna Redens joined her. Prominent Jews were pulled in.

The *Instantsiya*, that dread euphemism for the sacred eminence

---

* It was not long before Zhenya learned that her own husband was an MGB agent who had informed on her ever since their marriage, but every élite family had its informer. She divorced him.

† Grigory Morozov, who became a respected Soviet lawyer and always behaved with great discretion and dignity, refused to be interviewed for this book, saying, 'I never want to relive 1947 again.' He died in 2002.

in the Kremlin, believed the Jewish/Alliluyev set had 'expressed interest in the personal life of the Head of the Soviet Government, backed by foreign intelligence'. Stalin permitted 'methods of persuasion' to implicate Mikhoels. The 'French wrestling', as the torturers called it, was led by Komarov, a vicious anti-Semitic psychopath, who announced to his victims: 'Your fate's in my hands and I'm not a man, I'm a beast,' adding, 'All Jews are lousy bastards!' Abakumov supervised this diabolical sadist, ordering the prisoners 'a deadly beating!'

Goldshtein, who had introduced Mikhoels to the Alliluyevs, testified later how 'they started to beat me with a rubber baton on the soft parts of my body and my bare heels ... until I couldn't sit or stand.' They beat his head so hard 'my face was swollen terribly and my hearing affected. Exhausted by day and night-time interrogations, terrorized by beatings, curses and threats, I fell into a deep depression, a total moral confusion and began to give evidence against myself and others.'

'So you say Mikhoels's a swine?' Abakumov shouted.

'Yes he is,' replied the broken Goldshtein who admitted that Mikhoels had asked him to 'notice all the small details of the relationship between Svetlana and Grigory ... [to] inform our American friends.' When Stalin read this, it confirmed his worst fears about Mikhoels.

Vladimir Redens, at twelve, had now lost both mother and father. His young cousins, Zhenya's boys, had lost their parents and sister. Vladimir rushed to tell Olga, his grandmother, who had continued to live in the Kremlin after the death of her husband Sergei in 1946. To his amazement, she had never forgiven Zhenya for marrying so fast:

'Thank God!' she said on hearing about Zhenya's arrest, and crossed herself. But she called Stalin about Anna's arrest:

'They were used by the Enemy,' replied Stalin. When the family wished 'someone would tell Stalin', the old lady replied, 'nothing happened without him knowing.' They naïvely blamed Beria, not realizing that Abakumov reported only to Stalin.

Svetlana tried to intercede for the 'Aunties' but Stalin warned her 'they talked too much. You make anti-Soviet comments too.' Kira Alliluyeva, Svetlana's first cousin also arrested, claims that Stalin warned his daughter: 'If you act as their defender we'll also put you in jail.' Both she and Vasily cut dead the Alliluyev children.

* * *

Now that Svetlana was single again, Stalin started to talk about whom she should next marry, telling his magnates, 'She said she'd marry either Stepan Mikoyan or Sergo Beria.' The Politburo fathers were alarmed. The Tsarevna did not seem to mind that both boys were not only already married but in love with their wives. Stalin told the anxious Mikoyan and Beria:

'I told her neither one nor the other. She should marry Yury Zhdanov.' Simultaneously, this clumsy, tyrannical matchmaker told Yury to marry Svetlana.

On 16 July, Stalin embarked on a road trip to meet the people and see the country, something he had not done since 1933. It was to be a reflective and nostalgic three-month holiday, a mark of his exhaustion and his new style as a distant but paramount leader. He left the indecisive Bulganin in charge.

While Abakumov tortured Jews to create a new 'American' conspiracy and destroy Mikhoels, Stalin and his convoy of armoured ZiS110s headed south, accompanied by Valechka, towards Kharkov.

51

A Lonely Old Man on Holiday

The Generalissimo ordered that there was to be no tedious ceremony and all passed off 'without any sensationalism – which greatly pleased Stalin', wrote Vlasik, who found the expedition exhausting. Stalin himself had only slept for about two hours but he was 'in a good mood which made us all happy'. He inspected everything, muttering that he would not have seen anything 'from my desk'.

He even experienced some aspects of ordinary life: his car broke down near Orel. Stalin got out for a stroll, surrounded by his 'attachments', and came upon some parked trucks whose drivers were struck dumb when he introduced himself. At Kursk, Stalin stayed the night in the flat of a local Chekist. In the morning, he thought they should leave the couple a present so he left a bottle of scent on the lady's dressing table. At Kharkov, Stalin noticed people were still living in dugouts. He told Valechka that this upset him. When out-of-favour Khrushchev arrived, reassuring Stalin that the famine was much exaggerated and presented him with some juicy melons, Valechka was naïvely appalled, grumbling to Svetlana that they deceived 'your father – of all people!'

Finally, the relieved Vlasik loaded Stalin on to the special train that took them down to Yalta where he probably stayed at the Livadia before the cruiser *Molotov* conveyed him to Sochi. The weather was gorgeous, the crew thrilled by their passenger. Vlasik, court photographer, took so many photographs that Stalin, 'always sensitive', noticed:

'Vlasik's doing well but no one photographs him. Someone must photograph him with us.'

In Sochi, Stalin strolled around the town, followed by Vlasik, Poskrebyshev and the frantic bodyguards who struggled to control the campers holidaying on the coast. When some schoolchildren gathered round his car, he offered them a ride to the local café, the Riviera, where a little girl cried because she had not got any sweets. Stalin put her on his knee and told her to choose anything she liked. Porcine Vlasik paid the bill, then turned to the children and cried:

'Now children! A Pioneer Hurrah for Comrade Stalin' – the Soviet version of 'Hip hip hurrah!' One can imagine him punching the air as 'the children shouted a harmonious hurrah!'

* * *

They then drove down to Stalin's spiritual home in these twilight years, Abkhazia, where he believed the air and the food ensured longevity:

'Do you remember how amazed that English writer J. B. Priestley was when he met an Abkhazian peasant aged 150?' he reflected. 'If I lived here, I might live to 150!'* Stalin often told Molotov how he missed his homeland. Stalin had championed the Russian people as the ties that bound his empire; it was they who provided the dynamic power to promote Bolshevism and guaranteed his glory. His destiny was Russian. Hence Vasily said, 'Papa was once a Georgian.' But his personal Russianness has been exaggerated. His lifestyle and mentality remained Georgian. He talked Georgian, ate Georgian, sang Georgian, personally ruled Georgia through the local bosses, becoming involved in parochial politics, missed his childhood friends, and spent almost half of his last eight years in his own isolated, fantasy Georgia.

Stalin based himself at Coldstream but constantly moved to new houses. It is claimed that they were gloomy. Certainly the wood-panelling was sombre but when one visits them in the summer, they are delightful. Stalin usually ate and worked outside on the verandas and all had lush gardens full of flowers where he loved to walk. Above all, the houses were chosen for their vistas: the views from these grave houses are all breathtakingly beautiful.

He now started staying at the white mock-Baroque mansion in the lush gardens of Dedra Park at Sukhumi where Mandelstam had watched Yezhov dance the *gopak*. During the thirties, he had holidayed at a small dacha built by Lakoba, at New Athos; now he had another Cuban-style villa built next to it, all on one floor and

---

* Stalin had always taken a great interest in longevity. In 1937, he had sponsored Professor Alexander Bogomolov's work into the phenomenon of the extraordinary life-spans of the people of Georgia and Abkhazia. Stalin is said to have believed this was due to water from glaciers and their diet – he therefore drank special glacial water.

with a splendid sea view. There was already a CC sanatorium by the lake at the remote Lake Ritsa which could only be reached by a long drive through a scenic gorge beside a bubbling torrent. In 1948, he ordered a new house to be joined to the old.*

Stalin had access to any of the innumerable state dachas, but there seem to have been about five around Moscow, several in the Crimea, including two imperial palaces, three in Georgia proper, and about five in Abkhazia that he used regularly. At least fifteen were kept staffed. Yet in many ways, he remained the itinerant, restless Georgian revolutionary of his youth. Accompanied by Poskrebyshev, constantly supplied by air with the latest CC papers, summoning his potentates at will, despatching telegrams round the world, he was always the fulcrum of power.

* * *

When he arrived, there was one ritual that was an echo of older times: Stalin had hung Lenin's death-mask on the wall at Kuntsevo where it was illuminated like an icon with a burning lamp. Whenever he went on holiday, the icon would travel with him. He ordered his commandant Orlov 'to hang the face in the most visible place'.

As he moved in, the magnates and the entire Georgian leadership arrived simultaneously at their local houses, waiting to be summoned. Abakumov was ready to fly down at a moment's notice with news of the latest interrogations. If there were Politburo rows, he summoned the magnates for Solomonic judgement. They dreaded having to spend any time with Stalin on holiday, which 'was worse than the dinners', according to Khrushchev who once endured a whole month. Fighting the

---

* Most of Stalin's houses were reached through an archway of the security building (though not Lake Ritsa and New Athos) before emerging in a lush garden with privet hedges and a path that led up to a Mediterranean-style villa surrounded by a veranda. Their biggest room was always the high-ceilinged wood-panelled dining-room that boasted a long table that could be made smaller. All were painted a sort of military green, perhaps to camouflage them from the sky. All were virtually invisible, hidden up narrow lanes, and so concealed within palm and fir trees that it was hard to see them even from their own garden. Virtually all of them had their own jetties and all had summerhouses where Stalin worked and held dinners. All contained the tell-tale billiard room which was usually combined with a cinema, the film being projected out of little wooden windows across the billiard table on to the far wall. All had many bedrooms with divans and vast bathrooms with tiny baths made to fit Stalin's height. All had been built or refashioned for Stalin by his court architect Miron Merzhanov who lived with Martha Beria's mother, Timosha, Gorky's daughter-in-law and Yagoda's love. Merzhanov was arrested in the late forties like all of Timosha's previous lovers.

Ukrainian famine and separatism, Khrushchev remained under a temporary cloud as he recuperated. Stalin ordered Kaganovich to supervise Khrushchev and beat any nationalism out of the Ukrainians, a feat he had formerly achieved in the late twenties. Khrushchev and Kaganovich, long-time allies, lived cheek by jowl, their families going on walks every weekend. Inevitably, they soon became mortal enemies. Both appealed to Stalin who summoned them to Coldstream. Over dinner and a movie, he stoked their hatred, enforced peace and ultimately recalled Kaganovich to Moscow.

His East European vassals, especially Gottwald, Bierut and Hoxha, did not dare resist a summons. But the two favourites were the local chiefs with whom Stalin could relax, partly because both were in their mid-thirties, partly because they were Georgians. Confiding in them more than in his own children, he appeared divine to them but also paternal.

Candide Charkviani, the cultured Georgian First Secretary, visited him 'every second day'. It helped that Stalin had been taught the alphabet by a priest named Charkviani, even though he was no relation to Candide. He trusted Charkviani so much that he not only revealed his sleeping arrangements but when Candide told him about a Georgian prince who changed his underwear daily, Stalin showed him a chest of drawers full of 'white cotton underclothes': 'It's not hard for a prince,' Stalin quipped. 'But I'm a peasant and I do the same.'

The other confidant was Akaki Mgeladze, the ruthless and sleekly handsome boss of Abkhazia, whom Stalin nicknamed 'Comrade Wolf'. Stalin liked Charkviani for his knowledge of literature and Mgeladze for his political intriguing. He sometimes challenged Mgeladze to drive from his Sukhumi office to the dacha in seventeen minutes. Charkviani and Mgeladze hated each other, like their predecessors Beria and Lakoba.*

Valechka, Vlasik and Poskrebyshev, who stayed in nearby dachas, plus a stenographer and cipher officer, were his other regular companions. With his 'sad face, swivelling eyes and cunning', Poskrebyshev sorted out the papers that arrived each

---

* This is based on Charkviani's memoirs. Mgeladze's memoirs, that almost rank alongside Mikoyan's for their intimacy, have only just been published in Georgia. The Georgian and Abkhazian bosses were naturally rivals: in the case of Beria versus Lakoba, the Tbilisi boss destroyed the Sukhumi boss but it worked the other way round with Charkviani and Mgeladze.

day by plane from Moscow and then brought them up to the villa. Poskrebyshev, whom Stalin had lately nicknamed 'the Commander-in-Chief', defended the Generalissimo from unwanted callers. When Mikoyan phoned in October 1947, Poskrebyshev chided him:

'You've already been told you shouldn't bother Comrade Stalin on this question and you do it again.' To outsiders, for whom the Politburo was the holy of holies, this was a shocking display.

Stalin ate his meals outside, on the verandas, in the summer-house or by Lake Ritsa, reading the papers. There were open magazines and books on virtually every surface and piles of papers. Before he set off for the south, he scrawled to Poskrebyshev:

'Order all these books. Stalin. *Goethe's Letters*, *Poetry of the French Revolution*, Pushkin, Konstantin Simonov, Shakespeare, Herzen, *History of the Seven Years War* – and *Battle at Sea 1939–1945* by Peter Scott.' He still worked late into the evenings, starting his dinners late. Vlasik and Poskrebyshev did not always dine with the Boss but the *chef de cabinet* invited guests with the drear words:

'Stalin awaits you.' When Poskrebyshev shepherded the guests to the door, Stalin joked:

'So how's our Commander-in-Chief?' Sunburnt, grey-haired, with a bald patch, thin-faced with a pot belly and sloping shoulders, Stalin met them on the veranda like an affable Georgian countryman, wearing a civilian suit like a safari costume. When it was very hot, there was a sprinkler on the Coldstream terrace that cooled the air, spraying an arch of water over the roof.

Sometimes, the housekeeper pointed the guests down the garden where they found Stalin wielding a spade, weeding his lemon trees assisted by General Vlasik:

'I'm showing you how to work!' He showed off his lemons and roses: 'he was a romantic about nature,' wrote Mgeladze. But his favourite flower, the mimosa, was an organic metaphor for his own secretive sensitivity for when touched, it closed like a mouth. 'The mimosa's the earliest flower that anticipates the coming of spring,' Stalin told Mgeladze. 'How Muscovites love mimosas, they stand in queues for them. Think how to grow more to make the Muscovites happy!' They often went for walks and sometimes even strolled through Sukhumi where Stalin asked schoolchildren questions like: 'What do you want to do when you're grown up?'

* * *

At the Georgian feast often laid up outside, Stalin genially opened the bottles. The 'endless meals' were agonizing for the magnates but fascinating for the younger Georgians. Maps were brought in, empires admired, characters from the past discussed, jokes told, toasts raised. Poskrebyshev toasted Stalin for destroying Bukharin and Rykov:

'You were right, Comrade Stalin – if they'd won ...' Poskrebyshev could afford a certain levity with Stalin who often appointed him *'tamada'*. 'Now you'll drink to my health!' Poskrebyshev ordered. Stalin obeyed. Molotov hailed Stalin elaborately:

'If you weren't Stalin,' Iron Arse toasted, 'the USSR would not have beaten Trotsky, won the war, gained the Bomb or conquered such an Empire for Socialism.' This pleased the host. The drinking often turned nasty when the Politburo or foreign vassals were guests but with the Georgians, it was much more cheerful and nostalgic.

When Stalin sang, Poskrebyshev and Vlasik provided the harmonies like a pair of grotesque choirboys. After dinner the guests usually stayed the night. Stalin could be unsettlingly kind: when Mikoyan's brother Artyom, designer of MiG (Mikoyan-Gurev) aircraft, suffered angina and was put to bed, he was aware of someone coming into his room and tenderly laying a blanket over him. He was amazed to see it was Stalin.

One thing united virtually all his guests: the desire to escape this strange nervy old man with his alternation of vicious, dangerous explosions, self-pitying regrets and excruciatingly boring reminiscences. Their frantic and creative efforts to find excuses to leave their all-powerful but supersensitive host, without causing offence, provide a comical theme to these long nights.

That year, Svetlana was one of the first guests, staying for three weeks in her own smaller house. She found the awkward dinners with Beria and Malenkov tedious. Escape was easier for her but none the less a struggle: once at dinner with Molotov, Mikoyan and Charkviani, she suddenly asked:

'Let me go back to Moscow!'

'Why're you in such a hurry?' replied her hurt father. 'Stay ten days. Is it boring here?'

'Father, it's urgent! Please let me go!' Stalin became angry:

'Stop going on about it! You'll stay!' Then later, Svetlana started again.

'Go if you want!' barked Stalin. 'I can't make you stay!' He could not grasp the extent to which his political murders had sterilized and poisoned his world but perhaps he sensed it when he pathetically told Svetlana: 'You aren't in a stranger's house.' Svetlana was still there when Zhdanov arrived. She managed to depart on good terms, sending 'Father' a warm letter to which he replied:

'Hello Svetka ... It's good you haven't forgotten your father. I'm well ... I'm not lonely. I'm sending you some little presents – tangerines. A kiss.'

Zhdanov came to help work out Stalin's policy for securing his hold over Eastern Europe. Molotov's tendency to negotiate with the West had ended with the rejection of the Marshall Plan. Now Zhdanov seemed to gain ascendancy in foreign as well as domestic policy, or rather he was naturally closer to his master's voice. Their relationship remained almost paternal. Stalin marked Zhdanov's speeches with schoolmasterly notes: 'Must put in Lenin quotations!' he scrawled in brown crayon on one.

Together they created Zhdanov's speech that divided Europe into 'two camps', the ideological basis for the Iron Curtain over the next forty years. To counteract the Marshall Plan and the discomfiting independence of Tito's Yugoslavia, Stalin ordered Zhdanov to create a new Communist International, the Cominform, to enforce Soviet hegemony over Eastern Europe.

Zhdanov, accompanied by his hated rival Malenkov, recently recalled to a lower post, then flew up to the Polish town of Szklarska Poreba where the ruling Communist Parties from Poland to Yugoslavia awaited Moscow's instructions. The conference took place in a secret police convalescent home, with Zhdanov and the rest of the delegates staying upstairs. Apart from giving his 'two camps' speech on 25 September, Zhdanov behaved with all the blustering arrogance of an imperial viceroy. When Berman, one of the Polish leaders (the one who had waltzed with Molotov), expressed doubts about his Cominform, Zhdanov arrogantly replied,

'Don't start throwing your weight around. In Moscow we know better how to apply Marxism-Leninism.' At every stage, 'Comrade Filipov', or Stalin on holiday, instructed 'Sergeev and Borisov' (Zhdanov and Malenkov) on how to proceed. This was the high point of Zhdanov's career and his greatest lasting achievement, if it can be called that. It was appropriate that the meeting was held in a sanatorium because, by the end of it, 'the Pianist' was collapsing from alcoholism and heart failure. He may have triumphed over Molotov, Malenkov and Beria but he could not control his own strength. Zhdanov, only fifty-one but exhausted, knew 'he wasn't strong enough to bear the responsibility of succeeding Stalin. He never wanted power,' asserts his son. He flew back to the seaside to recover near Stalin, where the two called on each other, but then he suffered a heart attack.*

Zhdanov's illness created a vacuum that was keenly filled by Malenkov and Beria who became so close, they even sent their greetings to Stalin jointly that November, writing 'we derive great happiness from working under your rule ... Devoted to you, L. Beria and G. Malenkov.' Yet their friendship was always political: Beria really thought Malenkov 'spineless ... nothing but a billygoat!' None the less, Zhdanov noticed their resurgence, telling his son: 'A faction has been formed.' Resting until December, he was too weak to fight this vicious battle.

* * *

Once Molotov and Mikoyan, fresh from their recent humiliations, had also been to stay, Stalin found himself alone. He longed for the company of young people. Beria, according to his son, thought that Stalin's loneliness was an act. He wanted his associates around him 'to keep an eye on them, not from fear of solitude', but this does not explain his yearning for the companionship of unimportant youngsters. 'While everyone talks about the great man, genius in everything,' Stalin muttered to Golovanov, 'I have no one to drink a glass of tea with.' Zhdanov, on one of his visits, was accompanied by his son Yury, Stalin's ideal son-in-law. Stalin often telephoned him to give career advice:

'People say you spend lots of time on political activities,' he had once told Yury, 'but I want to tell you politics is a dirty business – we need chemists!' Yury qualified as a chemist then took a master's degree in philosophy.

Now twenty-eight, Yury and one of his aunts were driving along by the Black Sea and as they passed the road to the Gagra dacha,

---

* Zhdanov was not the only one: Andreyev, just fifty-two, fell ill in 1947 though he remained an active Politburo member until 1950; he lost his position in 1952.

they were surprised to see a number of guards running towards them:

'Comrade Stalin summons you, Comrade Zhdanov!' they said. Yury sent a message that he was with his aunt and the guard ran back: 'Both invited.' On the enclosed veranda, a suntanned, relaxed Stalin awaited them. After asking about his father's health, Stalin, pouring the wine, came to the point:

'Maybe you should work for the Party.'

'Comrade Stalin,' replied Yury, 'You once told me politics was a dirty business.'

'This is a different era. Times change. You'll do Party work, you'll travel and see the regions. You'll see how we make decisions and how they disagree with them immediately.'

'I'd better consult my mother and father,' said Yury Zhdanov who knew that no magnate wanted their children in the snakepit of Stalin's court. But Zhdanov agreed: Stalin appointed Yury to the important job – for such a young man – of Head of the CC Science Department. Unwittingly, Yury was placing his head inside the jaws of the crocodile at the very moment that the battle for succession was about to burst into blood-letting. 'I didn't fear him,' says Yury now, 'I knew him since childhood. Only later I realized that I *should* have been afraid.'

Yury did not have to stay, but another young man was less fortunate and endured nine days before he managed to escape. That October, Oleg Troyanovsky, a Foreign Ministry interpreter of twenty-six, was sent down to Gagra to interpret for Stalin at a meeting with some British Labour MPs.*

Handsome, brown-haired and erudite, Troyanovsky was another child of the élite. When Stalin first met young Troyanovsky, he liked him so much that he put on the Red Indian accent from *Last of the Mohicans*: 'Send my regards to pale-faced brother from leader of redskins!' When Stalin had seen off the British MPs, he said to Troyanovsky: 'Why don't you stay on and

* Stalin had stayed with Troyanovsky's father Alexander in Vienna in 1913, appointed him first Soviet Ambassador to Washington and protected him during the Terror. Stalin liked but never quite trusted Troyanovsky who was an ex-Menshevik. Once he crept up on him, put his hands over his eyes and whispered, 'Friend or foe?' In 1948, Troyanovsky's career as Stalin's interpreter came to an abrupt end when Molotov suddenly moved him in order to protect him. His father, the old diplomat, had been playing bridge and criticizing the leadership, with the indomitable Litvinov. It was a dangerous time. Later Troyanovsky interpreted for Khrushchev. This account is based on an interview with him.

live with us for a while. We'll get you drunk and then we'll see what sort of person you are.'

This was so unexpected and alarming that Troyanovsky stammered that surely it would be 'a burden to Comrade Stalin', but he insisted. Troyanovsky was understandably uneasy but Stalin summoned him to play billiards a few times, a game he played extremely well without even seeming to aim at the ball. They mainly met at dinner where they were sometimes joined by Poskrebyshev or Politburo members. The host personally served Troyanovsky. The conversation was 'never awkward, no silences', even though Troyanovsky was shrewd enough to ask no questions and proffer few opinions. Stalin did the talking, reminiscing about his stay with Oleg's father in Vienna in 1913, his 'first time with a Western-style family'. Otherwise Stalin just told him to rest but 'it was hardly possible to describe anything to do with Stalin as restful'.

Troyanovsky, like every other guest, fretted about how to escape without offending Stalin. After nine nights, he plucked up the courage to ask Stalin if he could leave. Stalin seemed surprised until Troyanovsky explained that he was returning to Moscow to become a Party member.

'An important event,' said Stalin. 'Good luck.' Presenting Troyanovsky with a basket of fruit, there was an awkward but telling moment as he saw him off: 'It's probably boring for you here. I've got used to loneliness. I got accustomed to it in prison.'

On his return to Moscow on 21 November, this genial old host ordered Abakumov to murder the Yiddish actor, Mikhoels. Nine days later, he supported the UN vote for the creation of Israel.

52

Two Strange Deaths: the Yiddish
Actor and the Heir Apparent

The Stalin Prize Committee sent Mikhoels to Minsk to judge plays at Belorussian theatres. When this was reported to Stalin, he verbally ordered Abakumov to murder Mikhoels on the spot, specifying some of the details with Malenkov present. Abakumov gave the task to his deputy, and the Minsk MGB boss, invoking the *Instantsiya*. Abakumov's plan was to 'invite Mikhoels to visit some acquaintances in the evening, provide him with a car ... bring him to the vicinity of [Belorussian MGB boss] Tsanava's dacha and kill him there; then take the corpse to a deserted street, place it across the road leading to the hotel and have a truck run over it ...' The plan has all the hallmarks of the clumsy, gangsterish games that Stalin used to devise with Beria to liquidate those too celebrated to be arrested. Tsanava passed the orders down the line, always dropping the magic word – *Instantsiya*.

On 12 January, Mikhoels and his friend Vladimir Golubov-Potapov, a theatre critic and MGB agent, spent the day meeting actors, then dined at their hotel. At 8 p.m. they left the hotel to meet Golubov's 'friend'. Presumably the MGB car took them to Tsanava's dacha where Mikhoels was probably injected with poison to stun him, another job for the MGB's doctors. Perhaps he fought back. This exuberant artist, the last connection with the intellectual brilliance of Mandelstam and Babel, loved life and must have struggled. He was smashed on the temple with a blunt object, and shot too. Golubov, the duplicitous bystander, was killed as well. The bodies were then driven into town, run over with a truck and left in the snow.*

* The man in charge of the operation was Lavrenti Tsanava, black-haired with a dapper moustache, one of the Georgians Beria had brought to Moscow. Like so many in the Cheka, he was a criminal. Those who knew him well could only say that 'he was a beast'. His real name was Djandjugava and he had been convicted of murder until Beria rescued him and he became boss of the Belorussian MGB. He did not prove a particularly loyal protégé since he was now close to Abakumov. After Stalin's death he was arrested and executed.

Stalin was informed of the killings probably before the bodies had been dumped in the street, and just as Svetlana was arriving to visit him at Kuntsevo. Stalin was on the phone, most likely to Tsanava: 'Someone was reporting to him and he listened. Then to sum up, he said, "Well, a car accident." I remember his intonation very well – it was not a question, it was a confirmation ... He was not asking, he was proposing it, the car accident.' When he had put down the phone, he kissed Svetlana and said, 'Mikhoels was killed in a car accident.'

At seven the next morning, two bodies were found sticking out of the snow. Mikhoels's body was returned to Moscow and delivered to the laboratory of Professor Boris Zbarsky, the (Jewish) biochemist in charge of Lenin's mummy: noticing the damaged head and the bullethole, he was ordered to prepare the victim of the 'road accident' for the lying-in-state in the Jewish Theatre, where no one was fooled by his 'broken face' and 'mutilated features made up with greasepaint'.

Mikhoels was an artistic hero to some of Stalin's courtiers as well as to the public: on the 15th, the night before the funeral, Polina Molotova, who had rediscovered her Jewish roots during the war, quietly attended the lying-in-state and muttered, 'It was murder.' After the funeral, Yulia Kaganovich, the niece of Lazar and daughter of Mikhail who had committed suicide in 1941, arrived at the Mikhoels' and led his daughter into the bathroom. Here, with taps running, she whispered: 'Uncle sends his regards,' adding an order from the anxious Kaganovich: 'He told me to tell you – never ask anyone about anything.' The Jewish Theatre was renamed for Mikhoels; a murder investigation was opened. The Jewish Committee continued, and Stalin would be the first to recognize Israel.

However, out of the public eye, Mikhoels's murderer, Tsanava, received the Order of Lenin 'for exemplary execution of a special assignment from the Government'. Zhenya Alliluyeva was sentenced to ten years, her daughter Kira to five years, 'for supplying information about the personal life of [Stalin's] family to the American Embassy'. Anna Redens also got five years. They were placed in solitary confinement.*

The MGB now started to build a case against Deputy Foreign

---

* The 'Aunties' were in Vladimir prison. Zhenya Alliluyeva wanted to commit suicide and swallowed stones but survived. Like so many others, she was kept alive by the kindness of strangers. A Polish prisoner in the neighbouring cell knocked in prison code 'Live for your children.'

Minister Solomon Lozovsky and other prominent Jews: Polina Molotova was quietly sacked from her job. Stalin openly joked about his own anti-Semitism, teasing Djilas about Jews in the Yugoslav leadership:

'You too are an anti-Semite, you too ...'

* * *

Zhdanov, despite his 'red puffy face and lively movements', recovered his heartiness and power: 'I might die at any moment and I might live a very long time,' he told Djilas. At dinners, he tried to resist alcohol and ate nothing but a plate of clear soup.

For a sick man, the next few months could hardly have been less restful: Stalin now encountered his first real opposition for almost twenty years. Marshal Tito was no vassal. His Partisans had fought valiantly against the Germans and not depended on the Red Army to liberate them. Now, the Yugoslavs bitterly denounced Zhdanov's 'dictatorial behaviour' at the Cominform conference. When Stalin read this, he could not believe the impertinence of it, scrawling in brown crayon: 'Very queer information!'

Stalin had agreed to leave Greece to the West, reserving the right to choose when and where to confront America. Tito disregarded his orders and started to supply the Greek Communists. Stalin was determined to test American resolve in Berlin, not in some obscure Balkan village. The final straw was the planned Balkan federation agreed between the Bulgarian leader, Dmitrov, and Tito, without Stalin's permission. As the row heated up, Tito sent his comrades, Milovan Djilas and Edvard Kardelj, to negotiate with Stalin. At grisly Kuntsevo dinners, Stalin, Zhdanov and Beria tried to overawe Yugoslavia with Soviet supremacy. Djilas was fascinated but defiant. So, on 28 January, *Pravda* denounced Dmitrov's plan.

On 10 February, Stalin summoned the Yugoslavs and Bulgarians to the Little Corner to humiliate them, as if they were impudent Politburo members. Instead of opposing the Bulgarian–Yugoslav plan, he proposed a collage of little federations, linking countries that already hated each other. Stalin was 'glowering and doodling ceaselessly'.

'When I say no it means no!' said Stalin who instead proposed that Yugoslavia swallow Albania, making gobbling gestures with his fingers and gulping sounds with his lips. The scowling threesome – Stalin, Zhdanov and Molotov – only hardened Tito's resistance.

Stalin and Molotov despatched an eight-page letter implying that Tito was guilty of that heinous sin – Trotskyism. 'We think

Trotsky's political career is sufficiently instructive,' they wrote ominously but the Yugoslavs did not care. On 12 April, they rejected the letter. Stalin decided to crush Tito.

'I'll shake my little finger,' he ranted at Khrushchev, 'and there'll be no more Tito!' But Tito proved a tougher nut than Trotsky or Bukharin.

* * *

At Kuntsevo dinners, Zhdanov, the heir apparent but increasingly a frail alcoholic with a sick heart, 'sometimes lost the willpower to control himself' and reached for the drink. Then Stalin 'shouted at him to stop drinking', one of the rare moments he tried to restrain the boozing, a sign of Zhdanov's special place. But at other times, the pasty-faced, sanctimonious Zhdanov, sitting prissily and soberly while Stalin swore at Tito and smirked at scatological jokes, outraged him:

'Look at him sitting there like Christ as if nothing was any concern to him! There – looking at me now as if he were Christ!' Zhdanov blanched, his face covered with beads of perspiration. Svetlana, who was present, gave him a glass of water but this was only a routine eruption of Stalin's blazing temper that usually passed as suddenly as it struck. None the less, Stalin was increasingly irritated by Zhdanov's over-familiar smugness and independence of mind. Beria and Malenkov were aided in their vengefulness from a surprising quarter.

Chosen by Stalin, growing closer to Svetlana and, at twenty-eight, Head of the CC Science Department, Yury Zhdanov was cock of the walk. He took his science as seriously as his father took culture. Yury resented the absurd dominance of Trofim Lysenko in the field of genetics: the scientific charlatan had used Stalin's backing during the Terror to purge the genetics establishment of genuine scientists.

'Yury, don't tangle with Lysenko,' Zhdanov jokingly warned his son. 'He'll cross you with a cucumber.' But Zhdanov may have been too ill to stop him.

On 10 April, 1948, young Zhdanov attacked both Lysenko's so-called creative Darwinism, and his suppression of scientists and their ideas, in a speech at the Moscow Polytechnic. Lysenko listened to the lecture through a microphone in a nearby office. This experienced courtier appealed to Stalin, attacking Yury's impudence in speaking for the Party 'in his own name'. Lysenko copied the letter to Malenkov who supported him. Wheels were turning. Malenkov sent the lecture to Stalin who now believed himself the 'Coryphaeus' – the 'choirmaster' – of science. He read Yury's lecture with mounting disdain:

'Ha-ha-ha!' he scribbled angrily. 'Nonsense!' and 'Get out!' The impertinent puppy had contradicted Stalin's views on heredity and evolution, and usurped his personal authority. When Yury claimed that these were his own personal views, Stalin exclaimed: 'Aha!' and forwarded his comments to a delighted Malenkov.

Frustrated by Yugoslav resistance, tension in Berlin, and Zionist intrigues, Stalin had decided this was the moment to challenge America in Europe. He demanded Party discipline; Yury had flouted it. In an Olympian flash that changed Soviet science and politics, Coryphaeus intervened. On 10 June, Stalin held one of his set-piece humiliation sessions in the Little Corner. Andrei Zhdanov humbly took notes at the front, his son lurked at the back while Stalin, pacing 'pipe in hand and puffing frequently', muttered:

'How did anyone dare insult Comrade Lysenko?' Zhdanov miserably noted Stalin's words in his exercise book: 'Report is wrong. ZHDANOV HAS BEEN MISTAKEN.' Then Stalin stopped and asked: 'Who authorized it?'

His gaze chilled the room. 'There was the silence of the grave,' wrote Shepilov, a Zhdanov protégé. Everyone looked down. Shepilov stood up to admit:

'The decision was mine, Comrade Stalin.'

Stalin walked up to him and stared into his eyes. 'I can honestly say,' recalled Shepilov, ' I never saw such a look ... His eyes seemed to possess some incredible force. Their yellow pupils transfixed me like ... a cobra coiled to strike.' Stalin 'did not blink for what seemed eternity'. Then he demanded:

'Why did you do it?' Shepilov tried to explain but Stalin interrupted: 'We'll set up a committee to clarify all the facts. The guilty must be punished. Not Yury Zhdanov, he's still young,' but he pointed his pipe at 'the Pianist': 'It's necessary to punish the fathers.' Then, in a terrible silence, slowly pacing, he listed the members of the committee – Malenkov ... but no Zhdanovs! Stalin deliberatedly waited until the end. Did this mean the *Zhdanovshchina* was over? 'After long thought, Stalin uttered, "And Zhdanov," leaving a long silence before adding, "Senior." '

Yury wrote an apology to Stalin, citing his own 'inexperience':

'I unquestionably committed a whole series of grave mistakes.' Malenkov masterfully manipulated the unintentional impudence of Zhdanov junior to pull himself back into the centre: the apology was published in *Pravda*. But Stalin himself had engineered Zhdanov's eclipse. The humiliation worsened Zhdanov's health: he must have wished he had emulated the Berias and Malenkovs who kept their children far from politics.

On 19 June, an exhausted Zhdanov, accompanied by his rival Malenkov, arrived at the second Cominform meeting in Bucharest to preside over the expulsion of Yugoslavia from the fold. 'We possess information,' Zhdanov declared absurdly, 'that Tito is an Imperialist spy.' The Yugoslavs were excommunicated.

On 24 June, Stalin imposed the Berlin Blockade, challenging the Western Allies and hoping to force them out by closing land supplies to their zone deep in Soviet East Germany. Both these challenges could only accelerate the vicious campaign against Jews in Moscow and the venomous fight for Stalin's succession. It is usually claimed that Zhdanov had supported the Yugoslavs and therefore was blamed for the rift. Zhdanov and Voznesensky had indeed known the Yugoslavs well since 1945 but they not only supported Stalin's stance but accelerated it by bringing Tito's antics to his notice.

The Yugoslav schism was the unnecessary result of Stalin's own obstinacy. While the country worshipped Stalin the God, familiarity bred contempt. By 1948, Djilas believed he was 'showing conspicuous signs of senility', comparing everything to distant memories of his childhood or Siberian exiles: 'Yes I remember the same things ...' then 'laughing at inanities and shallow jokes'. His own men observed his intellectual decline and dangerous unpredictability: 'old and addled, we started to lose respect for him,' said Khrushchev. Beria too had gone through the same 'evolution' – starting with zealous worship and ending with disillusion. But most of the magnates, particularly Molotov, Mikoyan, Kaganovich and Khrushchev, remained fanatical believers in Marxism-Leninism, while virtually all of them, including Malenkov who saw himself as a civil servant *chinovnik*, believed Stalin was still on the side of history, for all his faults.

In June, Zhdanov, back from Bucharest, suffered another cardiac crisis and a minor stroke, resulting in breathing difficulties and paralysis of the right side. 'I've been told to have medical care and rest,' he told a protégé. 'I don't think I'll be away for long.'

On 1 July, Stalin replaced Zhdanov with his nemesis, Malenkov, as Second Secretary. He was a useful scapegoat but, in Stalin's orbit, there was no need to destroy Zhdanov to promote Malenkov: it suited Stalin to run them in parallel. Zhdanov fainted on his way back from Kuntsevo: now, desperately ill, he could no longer perform his duties. Yury explains that his father 'wasn't dismissed – he simply fell ill and couldn't defend his interests', which is confirmed by the doctors: 'Comrade Zhdanov needs two months' rest, one in bed,' Professor Yegorov told Stalin in a Top Secret report on which Stalin wrote: 'Where vacation? Where treatment?'

Stalin, recalls Yury, 'became worried. Father's illness caused a change in the balance of power.' Mikoyan confirmed this. Indeed Zhdanov's allies, Voznesensky and Kuznetsov, remained ascendant. Yury kept his job.

Stalin sent his own doctors to supervise Zhdanov who was moved to a sanatorium at Valdai, near Novgorod. None the less, Zhdanov felt power slipping through his sclerotic fingers: when, on 23 July, Shepilov called to update him on Malenkov's return, Zhdanov shouted into the phone. That night, he had a heart attack. Stalin sent his deputy Voznesensky and his own physician Vinogradov to visit the patient.

Zhdanov's obvious symptoms of arteriosclerosis and heart failure were misdiagnosed. Instead of daily cardiograms and total rest, he was prescribed exercise and harmful massages. On 29 August, he had another severe attack. Once again Stalin sent Vinogradov and ordered Voznesensky and Kuznetsov to check the treatment. Before the politicians arrived, a row broke out over the patient. Dr Lydia Timashuk, the cardiographer, diagnosed a 'myocardial infarction' (a heart attack), and she was almost certainly right, but the distinguished professors made her rewrite her report to specify a much vaguer 'dysfunction due to arteriosclerosis and hypertension' in a typical piece of bureaucratic infighting. The doctors pooh-poohed her grave diagnosis and prescribed walking in the park. Hence, Zhdanov suffered another heart attack.

Timashuk denounced her superiors and had Zhdanov's chief bodyguard deliver the letter to General Vlasik to give personally to Stalin. When nothing happened, Timashuk, an MGB agent, wrote to the secret police. Abakumov forwarded the letter to Stalin that same day. Stalin signed it, wrote 'Into the archive', but did nothing. But he was 'very anxious and sent back Voznesensky to check on Father', says Yury who was already there.

On the 31st, Stalin's fallen favourite got out of bed to visit the lavatory and died of a massive coronary. On Poskrebyshev's orders, the post-mortem was carried out in an ill-lit, shoddy bathroom in Kuznetsov's presence. The professors were terrified that their misdiagnosis and cover-up would be exposed so they sacked and denounced Timashuk who then wrote more damning letters to Stalin and Kuznetsov, MGB *curator*. But this time, Vlasik did not deliver the letter and Kuznetsov ignored his.

Timashuk became the villainess of the Doctors' Plot because her letters were later used by Stalin but this was ironic since she was medically correct. Zhdanov may have been mistreated but the rumours of murder seem unlikely. The Kremlevka was meant to be the finest Soviet hospital but was so ruled by fear of mistakes, scientific backwardness and political competition that incompetent decisions were made by committees of frightened doctors. Famous patients, from Mekhlis to Koniev, were routinely mistreated. Even in democracies, doctors try to cover up silly mistakes. If Stalin had really wanted to murder Zhdanov, it would have not have taken five heart attacks over years but a quick injection. Zhdanov's widow and son were convinced he was not killed: 'Everything was simpler,' Yury recalls. 'We knew his doctors well. Father was very ill. His heart was worn out.'

Yet why did the manically paranoid Stalin ignore the denunciation? Zhdanov's illness was obviously serious and Stalin may well have been content to leave treatment to the top Kremlin doctors: besides he was irritated with Zhdanov. But at a deeper level, these medical squabbles were an opportunity for Stalin. He had used medical murder himself and forced doctors in the thirties to confess to killing Kuibyshev and Gorky. This meticulous opportunist and patient conspirator, older but still a genius for creating complex machinations, would exploit Zhdanov's death when he was ready to create the Terror he was convinced was necessary. A year later, his old comrade Dmitrov, the Bulgarian leader, died while being treated by the same doctor. Walking in the Sochi garden with his Health Minister, Stalin stopped admiring his roses and mused, 'Isn't it strange? One doctor treated them and they both died.' He was already considering the Doctor's Plot but it would take him three years to return to Timashuk's letters.

Stalin helped bear Zhdanov's open coffin at the funeral,

showing kindness to the family. At dinner afterwards, Stalin became drunk.*

It was said that the Aragvi restaurant was full of Beria's Georgians that night, toasting Zhdanov's death.

* * *

On 8 September, Stalin, delayed in Moscow by the Berlin crisis and Zhdanov's funeral, started a three-month holiday, moving restlessly from Sukhumi to the Livadia, where he entertained the Czech President Gottwald. At Museri, the old dacha built by Lakoba, he was visited by Molotov and Mikoyan. At dinner, Poskrebyshev rose and denounced Mikoyan:

'Comrade Stalin, while you're here resting in the south, Molotov and Mikoyan have prepared a plot against you in Moscow.'

Mikoyan leapt up, black eyes flashing: 'You bastard!' he yelled, raising his fist to punch Poskrebyshev.

Stalin caught his hand: 'Why do you shout like that?' he soothed Mikoyan. 'You're my guest!' Molotov sat 'pale as paper like a statue'. Mikoyan protested his innocence. 'If so, don't pay any attention to him,' Stalin added, having inspired Poskrebyshev in the first place.

Stalin declared that these veterans were too old to succeed him. Mikoyan, just fifty-two, much younger than Stalin, thought this silly but said nothing. The successor, said Stalin, had to be a Russian, not a Caucasian. Molotov remained 'the obvious person' but Stalin was disenchanted with him. Then, in a lethal blessing, Stalin pointed at the benign, long face of Zhdanov's protégé, Kuznetsov: 'here's the man' he wanted to succeed him as General Secretary. Voznesensky would succeed as Premier. Mikoyan sensed 'this was a very bad service to Kuznetsov, considering those who secretly dreamed of such a role'.

Stalin himself was bound to become suspicious of any anointed successor, especially given the failure of his Berlin Blockade, which had to be called off when the West energetically supplied their zones with a remarkable airlift. This only fuelled Stalin's seething paranoia, already stimulated by his own illness, Tito's defiance and Zionist stirrings among Russian Jews. Beria and Malenkov sharpened their knives.

---

* Perhaps Stalin was affected by Zhdanov's death. He named the dead man's birthplace, Mariopol on the Black Sea, Zhdanov. According to the bodyguards, after Zhdanov's funeral, Molotov was worried about Stalin's health and asked them not to let him garden. When Stalin discovered this interference in his private life, he mistrusted Molotov all the more.

Part Ten

The Lame Tiger, 1949–1953

53

Mrs Molotov's Arrest

While Stalin anointed successors in the south, the indomitable Envoy Extraordinary of the new State of Israel, Golda Myerson (known to history as Meir) arrived in Moscow on 3 September to tumultuous excitement among Soviet Jews. The Holocaust and the foundation of Israel had touched even the toughest Old Bolshevik internationalists like Polina Molotova. Voroshilov's wife (née Golda Gorbman) amazed her family by saying, 'Now we have our Motherland too.'

On Jewish New Year, Meir attended the Moscow Great Synagogue: jubilant Jews waited outside because the synagogue was full yet it was hardly a riot. Even Polina Molotova, now fifty-three, made an appearance. At Molotov's 7 November diplomatic reception, Polina met Golda Meir, two formidable, intelligent women from almost identical backgrounds.

Polina spoke Yiddish, the language of her childhood, which she always used when she met Mitteleuropeans, though she tactfully called it 'the Austrian language'. Meir asked how she knew Yiddish. '*Ikh bin a yidishe tokhhter*,' replied Polina. 'I'm a daughter of the Jewish people.' As they parted, Polina said, 'If things go well for you, then things will be good for Jews all over the world.' Perhaps she did not know how Stalin resented her pushy intelligence, snobbish elegance, Jewish background, American businessman brother and, as he told Svetlana, 'bad influence on Nadya'. Her sacking in May was a warning but she did not know that Stalin had considered murdering her in 1939.*

---

* Some Jews were sacked. Kaganovich continued as Deputy Premier and Politburo member but his elder brother Yuli lost his job. Like Polina, Kaganovich's grandson recalls that Lazar too remembered the Yiddish of his childhood: when he met the German Communist Ernest Thalman he tried to use it. The 'second lady of the state', Andreyev's wife Dora Khazan, was sacked as Deputy Minister of Textiles and General Khrulev's Jewish wife was arrested. Mekhlis, like Kaganovich, continued as Minister of State Control and only retired in 1950 after a stroke. The Jewish Boris Vannikov continued to run the First Directorate of Sovmin in charge of the nuclear project.

The synagogue 'demonstration' and Polina's Yiddish *schtick* outraged the old man on holiday, confirming that Soviet Jews were becoming an American Fifth Column. No wonder Molotov had supported a Jewish Crimea. On 20 November, the Politburo dismantled the Jewish Committee and unleashed an anti-Semitic terror, managed by Malenkov and Abakumov. Mikhoels's colleagues were now arrested, together with some brilliant Jewish writers and scientists, from the Yiddish poet Perets Markish to the biochemist Lina Shtern. They also arrested the father of Svetlana's newly-divorced husband: 'The entire older generation's contaminated with Zionism,' Stalin lectured her, 'and now they're teaching the young people too.'

Stalin ordered the prisoners to be tortured to implicate Polina Molotova while spending the steamy evenings over dinner at Coldstream, telling Charkviani folksy tales of his childhood. He suddenly missed his old friends, particularly a priest named Peter Kapanadze with whom he had studied at the seminary. After the Revolution, the priest had become a teacher but Stalin sometimes sent him money. Now he invited Kapanadze and MGB Lieut.-Gen. Sasha Egnatashvili, the Gori family friend whom Stalin called 'the innkeeper's son', to a dinner party. Charkviani hurried back to Tiflis to gather the guests. The seven old friends were soon singing Georgian songs led by the 'host with the sweet voice'. Stalin insisted that some of them stay for a week by which time, like all his guests, they were desperate to escape. Finally one of them displayed considerable ingenuity by singing a folk song at dinner with the refrain: 'Better go than stay!'

'Oh I see,' said Stalin, 'you're bored. You must be missing your grandchildren.'

'No, Soso,' replied the guest. 'It's impossible to be bored here but we've been here almost a week, wasting your time ...' Stalin let them go, returning on 2 December to Moscow, brooding about the dangerous duplicity of Molotov. He had discovered (probably from Vyshinsky) that Molotov had travelled alone in a special railway carriage from New York to Washington when he had perhaps received instructions to undermine the USSR with a Jewish homeland. It was Poskrebyshev, Stalin's alter ego, who 'started to hint' to Molotov:

'Why did they assign you a special car?' Molotov put 'two and two together' but there was nothing he could do.

Amazingly, it was an opera that finally convinced Stalin to

move against the Molotovs. Soon after his return, Stalin saw an Armenian opera, *Almast*, that told the story of a prince whose wife betrays him. 'He saw treason could be anywhere with anyone' but especially among the wives of the great. Stalin, fortified operatically and armed with Abakumov's testimonies, confronted Molotov with Polina's guilt. 'He and I quarrelled about it,' said Molotov.

'It's time for you to divorce your wife,' said Stalin. Molotov agreed, partly because he was a Bolshevik but partly because obedience might save the woman he loved. When he told her the charges against her, she shrieked:

'And you believe them! If this is what the Party needs, we'll divorce,' she agreed. In its queer way, it was a most romantic divorce, with both sacrificing themselves to save the other. 'They discussed how to save the family,' says their grandson. Polina moved in with her sister. They waited nervously but, said Molotov, 'a black cat had crossed our path.'

* * *

Stalin ordered Malenkov and Abakumov to put together the Jewish Case. Malenkov insisted to Beria that he was not anti-Semitic: 'Lavrenti, you know I'm Macedonian. How can you suspect me of Russian chauvinism?'

Since its centrepiece was the plan for the Jewish Crimea, on 13 January 1949 Malenkov summoned Lozovsky, ex-overlord of the Jewish Committee, to Old Square for an interrogation. This was already a matter of life and death for Lozovsky – but it also had its dangers for that punctilious but murderous 'clerk' Malenkov, because his eldest daughter Volya was married to the son of a Jewish official named Shamberg whose sister was married to Lozovsky.

'You sympathized ...' with the Jewish Crimea, said Malenkov, 'and the idea was vicious!' Stalin ordered Lozovsky's arrest.

Malenkov extricated his family from its Jewish connections. Volya Malenkova divorced Shamberg. Every history repeats that Stalin ordered this divorce and that Malenkov enforced it. Volya Malenkova vigorously denies this, claiming that the marriage had not worked because Shamberg had married her for the wrong reasons – and had 'bad artistic taste'. 'My father even discouraged me saying, "Think carefully and seriously. You rushed into the marriage. Careful before rushing out of it."' But this was not how it appeared to Shamberg, who was summoned to Malenkov's office. Just as Vasily Stalin accelerated Svetlana's divorce, so Malenkov's bodyguard fixed Volya's.*

As many as 110 prisoners, most of them Jews, were suffering 'French wrestling' at the hands of the vicious Komarov in the Lubianka. 'I was merciless with them,' boasted Komarov later, 'I tore their souls apart ... The Minister himself didn't scare them as much as me ... I was especially pitiless with (and I hated the most) the Jewish nationalists.' When Abakumov questioned the distinguished scientist Lina Shtern, he shouted at her: 'You old whore ... Come clean! You're a Zionist agent!' Komarov asked Lozovsky which leaders 'had Jewish wives', adding, 'no one is untouchable'. The prisoners were also encouraged to implicate the Jewish magnates, Kaganovich and Mekhlis, but Polina Molotova was the true target. Abakumov told Stalin that she had 'contacts with persons who turned out to be Enemies of the People'; she attended synagogue once, gave advice to Mikhoels, 'attended his funeral and showed concern for this family'.

Five days later, Stalin gathered the Politburo to read out the bizarre sexual-Semitic accusations against Polina. A young man testified about having had an affair and 'group sex' with this Bolshevik matron. Molotov could hardly believe this 'terrible filth' but, as Stalin read on, he realized that 'Security had done a thorough job on her!' Even the iron-bottomed Molotov was scared: 'My knees trembled.' Kaganovich, who disliked Molotov, and as a Jew had to prove his loyalty, viciously attacked Iron-Arse, recalling how 'Molotov couldn't say anything!'

Polina was expelled from the Party for 'close relations with Jewish nationalists' despite being warned in 1939, when Molotov had abstained on a similar vote. Now, remarkably, he abstained again but sensing the gravity of the case, he buckled. 'When the Central Committee voted on the proposal to expel PS Zhemchuzhina ... I abstained which I acknowledge to be politically incorrect,' he wrote to Stalin on 20 January 1949. 'I hereby declare that after thinking the matter over, I now vote in favour ... I

---

* Shamberg 'was heartbroken', according to his friend Julia Khrushcheva. Both Svetlana Stalin and Volya Malenkova are adamant that they ended unhappy marriages but there can have been no greater incentive to end an unhappy Jewish marriage than the seething anti-Semitic paranoia of Stalin. Stalin did not need to say a word. The young people knew what to do. To Malenkov's meagre credit, he managed to protect the Shambergs themselves, hiding the boy's father Mikhail in the provinces. 'Volya' was a name invented by Malenkov, meaning 'Will' as in the People's Will.

acknowledge I was gravely at fault in not restraining in time a person close to me from taking false steps and from dealings with such anti-Soviet nationalists as Mikhoels ...'

On 21 January, Polina was arrested in her squirrel-fur coat. Her sisters, doctor and secretaries were arrested. One of her sisters and a brother would die in prison. Her arrest was ominous for the other leaders who secretly sympathized with her.

Polina, who was not tortured, denied everything: 'I was not at the synagogue ... It was my sister.' But she also faced more accusations of sexual debauchery: the confrontation with Ivan X reads like a bad farce:

'Polina, you called me into your office [and] proposed intimacy!'

'Ivan Alexeevich!' exclaimed Polina.

'Don't deny it!'

'I had no relationship with X,' she asserted. 'I always regarded Ivan Alexeevich X as unreliable but I never thought he was a scoundrel.' But X appealed to her mercy:

'I remind you of my children and my broken family to make you admit your guilt towards me ... You forced me into an intimate relationship.' Meanwhile Polina continued to play the *grande dame* in the netherworld. Another prisoner heard her shouting,

'Phone my husband! Tell him to send my diabetes pills! I'm an invalid! You've no right to feed me this rubbish!'

No one heard anything more of Polina, who became Object No. 12. Many believed she was dead but Beria, who played little part in the Jewish Case, knew better from his contacts. 'Polina's ALIVE!' he whispered to Molotov at Politburo meetings.

Stalin and Abakumov discussed whether to make her the leading defendant in their Jewish trial but then decided Lozovsky would be the star. Polina was sentenced to five years in exile, a mild sentence considering the fates of her co-prisoners, in Kustanai, Central Asia. She turned to drink but overcame it. 'You need three things' in prison, she told her daughters later, 'soap to keep you clean, bread to keep you fed, onions to keep you well.' Ironically, she was befriended by some deported kulaks so that the innocent peasants, whom she and her husband had been so keen to liquidate, were the kind strangers who saved her life. She never stopped loving Molotov, for during her imprisonment, she wrote:

'With these four years of separation, four eternities have flowed over my strange and terrible life. Only the thought of you forces me to live and the knowledge that you may still need the remnants of my tormented heart and the whole of my huge love for you.' Molotov never stopped loving her: touchingly, he ordered his maids to lay a place for her at table every evening as he ate alone, aware that 'she suffered because of me ...'

Stalin now excluded Molotov from the highest echelons, scrawling that documents should be signed by Voznesensky, Beria and Malenkov 'but not Comrade Molotov who doesn't participate in the work of the Buro of the Council of Ministers'. However he still trusted Mikoyan just enough to send that worldly Armenian on a secret mission to size up Mao Tse-tung who was about to complete his conquest of China.

The Chinese Civil War was in its last throes. Stalin had miscalculated how quickly Chiang Kai-shek's regime would collapse. Until 1948, Mao Tse-tung's success was an inconvenience to Stalin's policy of a *realpolitik* partnership with the West but the Cold War changed his mind. He began to think of Mao as a potential ally even though he told Beria that the Chairman was a 'margarine Marxist'.

On 31 January 1949, in great secrecy, Mikoyan reached Mao's headquarters in Xibaipo in Hopei province where he met Mao and Chou En-lai and presented Stalin's gifts. One present was typically venomous: Mikoyan had to tell Mao that an American at his court was a spy and should be arrested. Stalin (Comrade Filipov) kept in contact with Mikoyan (Comrade Andreev) through Mao's Russian doctor, Terebin, who doubled as decoder. The visit was a success even though Mikoyan admitted that he had hoped for a rest from Stalin's nocturnal habits, only to find that Mao kept the same hours.

On his return, Mikoyan found a shock awaiting him. Stalin sacked Molotov and Mikoyan as Foreign and Foreign Trade Ministers, though both remained Deputy Premiers. Then he accused Mikoyan of breaking official secrecy about his Chinese trip. Mikoyan had only told his son Stepan: 'Did you tell anyone about my Chinese trip?' he asked him.

'Svetlana,' replied Stepan.

'Don't blab.' An innocent comment by Svetlana to her father had endangered the Mikoyans. Stalin had not forgotten the arrest of Mikoyan's children in 1943. They were still under surveillance.

'What happened to your children who were arrested?' Stalin

suddenly asked Mikoyan ominously. 'Do you think they deserve the right to study at Soviet institutions?' Mikoyan carefully did not reply – but he understood the threat, particularly after Polina's arrest. He expected the boys to be arrested, yet nothing happened. Stalin started to mutter that Voroshilov was 'an English spy' and hardly saw him* while the diminished Molotov and Mikoyan just hung on. But now Stalin's chosen successors succumbed to the brutal vendetta of Beria and Malenkov in a sudden blood bath.

---

* On 22 August 1946, Stalin listened to the weather forecast and was infuriated to hear that it was completely wrong. He therefore ordered Voroshilov to investigate the weather forecasters to discover if there was 'sabotage' among the weathermen. It was an absurd job that reflected Stalin's disdain for the First Marshal who reported the next day that it was unjust to blame the weather forecasters for the mistakes.

54

Murder and Marriage:
the Leningrad Case

The 'two scoundrels' played for only the highest stakes: death. But Stalin himself was always ready to scythe down the tallest poppies – those gifted Leningraders – to maintain his own paramountcy.

Stalin's heir apparent as Premier, Nikolai Voznesensky, 'thought himself the cleverest person after Stalin', recalled the Sovmin manager, Chadaev. At forty-four, the youngest Politburo member distinguished himself as a brilliant planner who enjoyed an unusually honest relationship with Stalin. However, this made him so brash that 'that he didn't bother to hide his moods' or his strident Russian nationalism. Rude to his colleagues, no one made so many enemies as Voznesensky. Now his patron Zhdanov was dead, his enemy Malenkov resurgent. Beria 'feared him' and coveted his economic powers. Voznesensky's arrogance and Stalin's touchiness made him vulnerable.

During 1948, Stalin noticed that production rose in the last quarter of the year but dipped in the first quarter. This was a normal seasonal variation but Stalin asked Voznesensky to level it out. Voznesensky, who ran Gosplan, promised he would. However, he failed to do so and, afraid of Stalin, he concealed the statistics. Somehow this *legerdemain* was leaked to Beria who discovered that hundreds of secret Gosplan documents had gone missing. One night at Kuntsevo, Beria sprung it on Stalin, who, observed Mikoyan, 'was astonished,' then 'furious'.

'Does it mean Voznesensky deceives the Politburo and tricks us like fools?' Beria then revealed the damning secret about Voznesensky that he had treasured ever since 1941: during Stalin's breakdown, Voznesensky had told Molotov,

'Vyacheslav, go forward, we'll follow you!' That betrayal clinched it. Andreyev, that relentless bureaucratic killer, was brought in to investigate. Frantic, Voznesensky called Stalin but no one would receive him. Sacked from the Politburo on 7 March 1949, he spent his days at his Granovsky flat writing an economics treatise. Once again, that dread duo, Malenkov and Abakumov, took over the Gosplan Case.

The other anointed heir was 'young handsome' Kuznetsov, who had helped Zhdanov remove Malenkov in 1946 and replaced Beria as *curator* of the MGB, thus earning their hatred. Sincere and affable, Kuznetsov was the opposite of Voznesensky: virtually everyone liked him. But decency was relative at Stalin's court: Kuznetsov had aided Zhdanov in anti-Semitic matters and forwarded Stalin a report on the sexual peccadilloes of Party officials. He worshipped Stalin, treasuring the note he had received from him during the war – yet he did not understand him. He made the mistake of examining old MGB files on Kirov's murder and the show trials. Kuznetsov's blundering into such sensitive matters aroused Stalin's suspicions.

Simultaneously, Malenkov alerted Stalin that the Leningrad Party had covered up a voting scandal and held a trade fair without Government permission. He managed to connect these sins with a vague plan mooted by Zhdanov to create a *Russian* (as opposed to a Soviet) Party alongside the Soviet one and make Leningrad the Russian capital. These trivialities may hardly sound like crimes punishable by death but they masked the fault lines in the Soviet Imperium and Stalin's dictatorship.* Besides, a Russian Party could not be led by a Georgian. Stalin championed the Russian people as the binding force of the USSR but he remained an internationalist. Voznesensky's nationalism worried the Caucasians: 'For him not only Georgians and Armenians but even Ukrainians aren't people,' Stalin told Mikoyan. Beria must have worried about his future under the Leningraders.

Malenkov had shrewdly amassed a collage of mistakes that touched all Stalin's sensitive places. 'Go there and take a look at what's going on,' Stalin ordered Malenkov and Abakumov who arrived in Leningrad with two trains carrying five hundred MGB officers and twenty investigators from the *Sled-Chast*, the department 'to Investigate Especially Important Cases'. When

---

* These dangers were perfectly demonstrated in 1991 when Boris Yeltsin used his Russian Presidency to demolish Gorbachev's USSR. The moving of the capital back to Leningrad, city of Zinoviev and Kirov, had been a deadly issue in Russian politics ever since Peter the Great. Men died for it in the eighteenth century and they would die for it in 1949. Stalin was also suspicious of the popular heroism of Kuznetsov and the city of Leningrad itself during WW2. It represented an alternative totem of military patriotism to himself and Moscow.

'Stalin orders him to kill one', Beria said, 'Malenkov kills 1,000!' Malenkov attacked the local bosses, stringing together disparate strands into one lethal conspiracy. The arrests began, but Voznesensky and Kuznetsov lingered at their flats in the pink Granovsky block, convinced that Stalin would forgive them: 1937 seemed a long time ago. Even Mikoyan thought blood-letting was a thing of the past.

* * *

He had reason to hope so because his youngest son Sergo, now eighteen, was engaged to Kuznetsov's 'charming, beautiful' daughter Alla. When her father fell, Alla gave Sergo the chance to avoid marrying an outcast:

'Does it change your intentions?' But Sergo loved Alla and his parents had come to adore her 'like our own daughter'. Mikoyan supported the marriage.

'And you allow this marriage? Have you gone crazy?' the pusillanimous Kaganovich whispered to Mikoyan. 'Don't you understand that Kuznetsov's doomed? Stop the marriage.' Mikoyan was adamant. On 15 February, 1949, Kuznetsov was sacked as Party Secretary and accused of 'non-Bolshevik deviation' and 'anti-State' separatism. Three days later, the couple got married. Kuznetsov was cheerfully oblivious, 'a courageous man,' thought Mikoyan, 'with no idea of Stalin's customs.' Mikoyan gave the couple a party at Zubalovo but Kuznetsov, finally realizing his plight, telephoned Mikoyan to say he could not come because he had an 'upset stomach'. Mikoyan would not hear of it:

'We've enough lavatories in the house! Come!'

'I've no car,' answered Kuznetsov. 'You do better without me.'

'It's indecent for a father to miss his daughter's wedding,' retorted Mikoyan who sent his limousine.* At the party, Kuznetsov could not relax. He felt he was endangering his daughter.

'I feel unwell,' he said, 'so let's drink to our children!' Then he left.

* * *

* Meanwhile just across the landing, in another apartment at Granovsky, a similar discussion in this tiny world was going on: Rada Khrushcheva, whose father was still in Kiev, was staying with her father's friends the Malenkovs. She wanted to go to the wedding, but Malenkov, who knew how doomed Kuznetsov was, refused to give her the limousine to take her there. 'I won't give you the car – you're not studying well.' But Rada went under her own steam.

That dangerous spring, poor Kuznetsov attended another Politburo marriage that involved the beleagured Zhdanov faction. 'Stalin had always wanted me to marry Svetlana,' recalls Yury Zhdanov, still at the Central Committee. 'We were childhood friends so it wasn't daunting.' But marrying a dictator's daughter was not so straight-forward: Yury was not sure to whom he should propose, the dictator or the daughter. He went to Stalin, who tried to dissuade him:

'You don't know her character. She'll show you the door in no time.' But Yury persisted. 'Stalin didn't give any lectures but told me that he trusted me to look after Svetlana,' says Yury.

Stalin now played matchmaker, according to Sergo Beria: 'I like that man,' Stalin told Svetlana. 'He has a future and he loves you. Marry him.'

'He made his declaration of love to you?' she retorted. 'He's never looked at me.'

'Talk to him and you'll see,' said Stalin.

Svetlana still loved Sergo Beria and told him: 'You didn't want me? Right, I'll marry Yury Zhdanov.'

However, she became fond of 'my pious Yurochka' and they agreed to marry. But 'my second marriage was the choice of my father', explained Svetlana, 'and I was tired of struggling so went through with it.'

The Generalissimo did not attend the wedding party at the Zhdanovs' dacha seven miles beyond Zubalovo along the Uspenskoye Road. The guests included another Politburo couple: Natasha, the daughter of Andreyev and Dora Khazan, was there with her husband, Vladimir Kuibyshev, the son of the late magnate. 'There were also schoolmates … from comparatively ordinary families too,' remembers Stepan Mikoyan who was also a guest. Then there was dancing and a feast: Yury, like his father, played the piano. It was natural that Kuznetsov was there because he had been Zhdanov's closest ally but everyone knew he was under a cloud.

Yury and Svetlana, along with her son Joseph Morozov, now aged four, lived with Zhdanov's widow in the Kremlin. 'I never saw my own father,' Joseph recalled. 'I called Yury "daddy". Yury loved me!'

A few days later, they were visiting Zubalovo when Vlasik called: Stalin was on his way. 'What do you want to move to the Zhdanovs' for?' he asked her. 'You'll be eaten alive by the women there. There are too many women in that house.' He wanted the young couple to move into Kuntsevo, adding a second floor but in his maladroit way he could not ask directly and probably did not want to be bothered.

Svetlana remained with the prissy widows of Zhdanov and Shcherbakov: soon she loathed her mother-in-law Zinaida who combined 'Party bigotry' with 'bourgeois complacency'. Her marriage was not loving: 'the lesson I learned was never to go into marriage as a deal.' Sexually it was, in her words, 'not a great success'. She never forgave Zinaida Zhdanova for telling her that her mother had been 'mad'. However they had a daughter, Katya, though Svetlana was so ill during the birth that she wrote to her father saying she felt abandoned and was delighted to receive his brusque reply.*

Besides, the wedding was not well timed for the Zhdanovs. Kuznetsov and Voznesensky were on the edge of the precipice. Yury sensed the Leningrad Affair 'was undoubtedly aimed at my father' but 'I wasn't afraid then. I discovered later I should have been destroyed ...' He was right: the prisoners were later tortured to implicate Zhdanov.

* * *

Stalin mulled over Kuznetsov's fate. Poskrebyshev invited the Leningrader to dinner at Kuntsevo but Stalin refused to shake his hand: 'I didn't summon you.' Kuznetsov 'seemed to shrink'. Stalin expected a letter of self-criticism from Kuznetsov but the naïve Leningrader did not send one. 'It means he's guilty,' Stalin muttered to Mikoyan.

Yet Stalin had doubts. 'Isn't it a waste not letting Vosnesensky work while we're deciding what to do with him?' he asked Malenkov and Beria who said nothing. Then Stalin remembered that Air Marshal Novikov and Shakhurin were still in jail.

'Don't you think it's time to release them?' But again the duo said nothing, whispering in the bathroom that if they released

---

*'Dear Svetochka,' Stalin wrote to Svetlana in hospital on May 1950. 'I got your letter. I'm glad you got off so lightly. Kidney trouble is a serious business. To say nothing of having a child. Where did you ever get the idea I'd abandoned you? It's the sort of thing people dream up. I advise you not to believe your dreams. Take care of yourself. Take care of your daughter too. The State needs people even those born prematurely. Be patient a little longer – we'll see each other soon. I kiss you my Svetochka. Your "little papa".' He did not devote all his time to the Leningrad Case. During these days, he also supervised the creation of the new Soviet Encyclopaedia, deciding every detail from its quality of paper to its contents. When the editor asked if he should include 'negative persons' such as Trotsky, he joked, 'We'll include Napoleon, but he was a big scoundrel!'

Shakhurin and Novikov, 'it might spread to the others' – the Leningraders. While he considered these matters of life and death, Stalin drove off to his dacha at Semyonovskoe, passing on the way a queue of bedraggled citizens waiting in the rain at a bus stop. Stalin stopped the car and ordered his bodyguards to offer the people a lift but they were afraid.

'You don't know how to talk to people,' growled Stalin, climbing out and ushering them into the limousine. He told them about the death of his son Yakov and a little girl told him of the death of her father. Afterwards Stalin sent her a school uniform and a satchel. Three weeks later, he ordered Abakumov to arrest, torture and destroy the Leningraders who had only recently been his anointed successors.

On 13 August, Kuznetsov was summoned to Malenkov's office. 'I'll be back,' he told his wife and son Valery. 'Don't start supper without me.' The boy watched him head down Granovsky towards the Kremlin: 'He turned and waved at me. It was the last time I ever saw him,' says Valery. He was arrested by Malenkov's bodyguard.

Yet Stalin hesitated about Voznesensky, whose arrest would leave him in the hands of Malenkov and Beria. Stalin still invited him to Kuntsevo for the usual dinners and talked of appointing him to the State Bank. On 17 August, Voznesensky wrote pathetically to Stalin, begging for work: 'It's hard to be apart from one's comrades … I understand the lesson of Partymindedness … I ask you to show me trust,' signing it, 'Devoted to you.' Stalin sent the letter to Malenkov. The duo kept up the pressure. The ailing but drear Andreyev exposed all manner of 'disorders in this organization': 526 documents had gone missing from Gosplan. This invented case was one of Andreyev's last achievements. Voznesensky admitted he had not prosecuted the culprits because there were 'no facts … Now I understand … I was guilty.' Khrushchev later accused Malenkov of 'whispering to Stalin' to make sure Voznesensky was exterminated. 'What!' Malenkov replied. 'That I was managing Stalin? You must be joking!' Stalin was unmanageable but highly suggestible: he remained in absolute command.

Four months later, Voznesensky was arrested in this sweep of Zhdanovites, joining Kuznetsov and 214 other prisoners who were tortured in a frenzy of 'French wrestling'. Brothers, wives and children followed them into the maw of Abakumov's MGB.

Kuznetsov was thrashed so badly his eardrums were perforated. 'I was beaten until the blood came out of my ears,' one prisoner, Turko, testified after Stalin's death. 'Komarov smashed my head against the wall.' Turko implicated Kuznetsov. The torturers asked Abakumov if they should beat prisoner Zakrizhevskaya who was pregnant:

'You're defending her?' bellowed Abakumov. 'The law doesn't ban it. Get on with your business!' She was tortured and miscarried:

'Tell us everything,' the torturers told her. 'We're the vanguard of the Party!'

The fallen vanguard, Kuznetsov and Voznesensky, were held in a Special Prison on Matrosskaya Tishina Street set up by Malenkov who arrived incognito with Beria and the Politburo to interrogate the prisoners.

The sinisterly genial Bulganin, who was also under threat, was given the duty of interrogating his old friend, Voznesensky's brother, Alexander, who had been Rector of Leningrad University. When the prisoner saw him, he thought he was saved: 'He rushed to me,' Bulganin admitted later, 'and cried, "Comrade Bulganin, my dear, at last! I'm not guilty. It's great you've come! Now Comrade Stalin will learn the truth!"' Bulganin snarled back at his erstwhile friend:

'The Tambov wolf's your friend', a Russian saying that meant 'no friend of yours'. Bulganin felt he had no choice: 'What could I do?' he whined. 'I knew Beria and Malenkov sat in the corner and watched me.' Like all of Stalin's cases, the guilt was elastic and could be extended on his whim: Molotov, who was close to Voznesensky, was vaguely implicated too.

* * *

By the time Kuznetsov's daughter Alla and her new husband Sergo Mikoyan rushed back from their honeymoon, just days later, her father had already been beaten into a signed confession. Anastas Mikoyan received his daughter-in-law in his Kremlin study. 'It was very hard for me to speak to Alla,' wrote Mikoyan. 'Of course I had to tell her the official version.' Alla ran out sobbing.

'I ran to follow,' Sergo recalls, 'afraid she'd kill herself.'* Mikoyan

---

* Sergo and Alla were convinced this was 'an intrigue by Malenkov and Beria who tricked Stalin. It's amazing we believed this,' recalls Sergo. 'But we NEVER ONCE spoke about the case until after Stalin's death.' His father allowed Sergo to see Kuznetsov's son but not his wife because he knew he too would be arrested. As for the Kremlin children who lived in Granovsky Street, they noticed that suddenly their neighbours, the Voznesenskys and Kuznetsovs, had gone. 'But no one mentioned it,' said Igor Malenkov, whose father was responsible. 'I just concentrated on reading about sport.'

called back Sergo and showed him Kuznetsov's confession, which Stalin had distributed. Sergo did not believe the charges.

'Every page is signed,' said Mikoyan.

'I'm sure the case will clear up and he'll return,' replied Sergo.

'I couldn't tell him,' wrote Mikoyan, 'that Kuznetsov's fate was already predetermined by Stalin. He would never return.'

* * *

The Leningrad Case was not Beria's only success: just after Kuznetsov's arrest in late August 1949, Beria set out in a special armoured train for a secret nuclear settlement amidst the Kazakh steppes. Beria was frantic with worry because if things went wrong, 'we would', as one of his managers put it, 'all have to give an answer before the people'. Beria's family would be destroyed. Malenkov comforted him.

Beria arrived in Semipalatinsk-21 for the test of the 'article'. He moved into a tiny cabin beside Professor Kurchatov's command post. On the morning of 29 August, Beria watched as a crane lowered the uranium tamper into position on its carriage; the plutonium hemisphere was placed within it. The explosives and the initiator were in place. The 'article' was then wheeled out into the night on to a platform where it would be raised to the top of the tower. Beria and the scientists left.

At 6 p.m., they assembled in the command post ten kilometres away with its control panel and telephones to Moscow, all behind an earthen wall to deflect the shock wave. Kurchatov ordered detonation. There was a bright flash. After the shock wave had passed, they hurried outside to admire the mushroom cloud rising majestically before them.

Beria was wildly excited and kissed Kurchatov on the forehead but he kept asking,

'Did it look like the American one? We didn't screw up? Kurchatov isn't pulling our leg, is he?' He was very relieved to hear that the destruction at the site was apocalyptic. 'It would have been a great misfortune if this hadn't worked out,' he said. He hurried to the telephone to ring Stalin, to be the first to tell

Julia Khrushcheva 'used to play with Natasha, Voznesensky's daughter. Soon after her father's arrest, I brought her home to our flat. But my mother said nothing.' The etiquette of unpersonage differed from family to family: while Natasha Poskrebysheva went on playing with Natasha Voznesenskaya, Nadya Vlasik 'crossed the road whenever she saw her'. I am especially grateful to Sergo Mikoyan for sharing his account of this story.

him. But when he rang, Stalin replied crushingly that he already knew and hung up. Stalin had his own sources. Beria punched the General who had dared tell Stalin first, shouting, 'You've put a spoke in my wheel, traitor, I'll grind you to pulp.' But he was hugely proud of his 'colossal achievement'. Four years after Hiroshima, Stalin had the Bomb.

Beria had another reason to be happy: he had met a good-looking woman named Drozhdova whose husband worked in the Kremlin. He may have had an affair with her before she introduced him to her daughter, Lilya, only fourteen but already a 'blue-eyed, long-legged paragon of Russian beauty with long blonde plaits', recalls Martha Peshkova. Beria was entranced: 'his last great love.' The mother wanted all the benefits:

'Don't let him do it until you've got a flat, car, dacha,' she said to Lilya, according to Peshkova. Beria set her up in style. Nina Beria tolerated this affair but in the summer when she and Martha were in Gagra, her husband entertained Lilya at the dacha. 'The whole of Moscow knew,' says Martha. Beria and Malenkov were riding high but it turned out that someone else would benefit most from the power vacuum left by the Leningraders.

* * *

Stalin summoned Khrushchev from Kiev. 'I couldn't help but feel anxious,' he admitted, when Kuznetsov and Voznesensky were being tortured. He called Malenkov who comforted him:

'Don't worry. I can't tell you now why you've been called but I promise you've got nothing to fear.' Khrushchev had governed the Ukraine since 1938, ruthlessly purging the kulaks before the war, crushing the Ukrainian nationalists, ordering the assassinations of Uniate bishops afterwards and, in February 1948, organizing the expulsion of 'harmful elements' from villages: almost a million were arrested on Khrushchev's initiative, a colossal crime which approached the deportation of the kulaks in brutality and scale. Small wonder that in retirement, he reflected, 'I'm up to my elbows in blood.' Apart from the short period in 1947 when Stalin sent Kaganovich to replace him in Kiev, Khrushchev, 'vital, pig-headed, jolly' but now bald and almost spherical in shape, was an enduring favourite. His plain speaking made his sycophancy sound genuine. Stalin regarded this dynamic cannonball of a man as a semi-literate peasant – 'Khrushchev's as ignorant as the Negus of Ethiopia,' he told Malenkov. Yet he did not completely underestimate his 'deep naturalness, pure masculinity, tenacious cunning, common sense and strength of character'.

'With him,' Stalin reflected, 'you need a short leash.' When Khrushchev arrived in Moscow, he hurried to Beria's house for further reassurance. There was a growing solidarity among Stalin's courtiers. Beria comforted him too.

Stalin appointed Khrushchev CC Secretary and Moscow boss but confided, 'things aren't going very well ... We've exposed a conspiracy in Leningrad. And Moscow's teeming with anti-Party elements.' He wanted Khrushchev to 'check it out'. As the Leningrad Case showed, the system encouraged Terror entrepreneurialism. The magnates could either douse a case or inflame it into a massacre: it was then up to Stalin to decide whether to protect the victims, save the evidence for later or slaughter them immediately.

'It's the work of a provocateur,' Khrushchev replied. Stalin accepted his judgement. He soon placed him in charge of Agriculture. 'Stalin treated me well.' Having destroyed the Leningrad connection, and undermined Molotov and Mikoyan, the 'two scoundrels' were perfectly placed for the succession. Khrushchev was recalled to balance their power. However, this plan did not quite work because Khrushchev became 'inseparable' from Beria and Malenkov. The Khrushchevs and the Malenkovs* lived close to one another at Granovsky while Beria's limousine seemed to be constantly parked on the street waiting for them. Sometimes he hailed the young Khrushchevs as they went to school:

'Look at you! The very image of Nikita!'

The threesome joked about Stalin's plan while betraying one another to him. After Malenkov had failed to master the impossible job of Agriculture, Andreyev took it over but was then discredited and forced to recant, marking the end of his career. Now Khrushchev was in charge but his plan for gigantic agricultural centres, 'agrotowns', rebounded on him. Stalin, Beria and Malenkov forced him to recant publicly. Molotov and Malenkov wanted him sacked but Beria, who underestimated the 'round-headed fool,' intervened to save him. Stalin protected Khrushchev, tapping his pipe on his head – 'it's hollow!' he joked.

---

* They were now the heart of Stalin's new inner 'quintet' along, with Beria and Bulganin. Kaganovich enjoyed a partial return to favour. On Sundays, those two fat bureaucrat friends, Khrushchev and Malenkov, took bracing walks up Gorky Street, surrounded by phalanxes of secret policemen.

* * *

On 5 September, Stalin began his holiday in Sochi where Beria joined him for a barbecue of *shashlyks* to celebrate the Bomb which, along with the destruction of the Leningraders, had temporarily returned him to favour. But it would not last. Stalin's distrust of the men around him was now overwhelming. He moved south to New Athos, the smallest and cosiest of his houses, where he spent most of his last holidays.

When the Supreme Soviet announced the Soviet Bomb, Stalin mused to his young confidant Mgeladze about the new world order:

'If war broke out, the use of A-bombs would depend on Trumans and Hitlers being in power. The people won't allow such people to be in power. Atomic weapons can hardly be used without spelling the end of the world.' He was so happy that he burst into song, singing 'Suliko' accompanied by Vlasik and Poskrebyshev, in a rendition that hit the notes perfectly, just like Beria's Bomb.

'Chaliapin sang it a little better,' beamed Stalin.

'Only a little bit better,' chorused his companions.

Old Stalin was thinking more and more about Nadya. Walking in the gardens with Mgeladze, Stalin lamented his disasters as a parent. First there was Yasha:

'Fate treated Yakov badly ... but he died a hero,' he said. Vasily was an alcoholic: 'He does nothing, but drinks a lot.' Then Svetlana, his feminine alter ego, 'does whatever she wants'. This most destructive of husbands was sensitive enough about Svetlana's marriages: 'Morozov was a good fellow but for Svetlana, it wasn't love ... It's just fun for her. She walked all over him ... Naturally this made the marriage unsuccessful. Then she got married again. Who knows what next? ... Svetlana can't even sew on a button, the nannies didn't teach her. If her mother had raised her, she'd be more disciplined. You understand, there was always too much pressure on me ... No time for the children, sometimes I didn't see them for months ... The kids didn't get lucky. Ekaterina!' He fondly mentioned his first wife Kato, then 'Oh Nadya, Nadya!' Mgeladze had never seen Stalin so sad. 'Comrade Wolf, I ask you not to say a word about what you've heard.'

55

Mao, Stalin's Birthday
and the Korean War

On 7 December 1949, Stalin arrived back in Moscow in time for two momentous events: the arrival of the new Chinese leader, Chairman Mao Tse-tung, and the celebration of his seventieth birthday. At noon on 16 December, Mao, who had taken Peking in January, arrived at Yaroslavsky Station where he was met by Molotov and Bulganin in his Marshal's uniform.* The visit started as awkwardly as it ended. Mao invited the Russians to a Chinese meal on the train but Molotov refused. Mao sulked, the beginning of a sulk as monumental in its way as the Great Wall itself. Over-awed by Stalin's greatness but also contemptuous of his consistent lack of support and misreading of China, the tall, gangling Mao was taken directly to one of Stalin's dachas, Lipki.

At 6 p.m., Mao and Stalin met for the first time at the Little Corner. The two Communist titans of the century, both fanatics, poets, paranoics, peasants risen to rule empires whose history obsessed them, careless killers of millions, and amateur military commanders, aimed to seal America's worst nightmare: a Sino-Soviet treaty that would be Stalin's last significant achievement. Yet they observed each other coolly from the Olympian heights of their own self-regard. Mao complained of being 'pushed aside for a long time'.

'The victors are never blamed,' answered Stalin. 'Any ideas or wishes?'

'We've come to complete a certain task,' said Mao. 'It must be both beautiful and tasty.'

A cantankerous silence followed. Stalin appeared baffled by this enigmatic allusion which meant a treaty that was both symbolic and practical, standing for both world revolution and Chinese

---

* Mao had brought a treasure trove of Chinese gifts and several carriages of rice. The lacquer ornaments still hang on the walls of Molotov's retirement flat on Granovsky and Stalin divided the rice amongst his courtiers. In return, Stalin presented him with the names of his Soviet agents in the Chinese Politburo. Back in Peking, Mao swiftly liquidated them.

national interests. Stalin's first priority was protecting his Far Eastern gains, agreed at Yalta and confirmed in the old Sino-Soviet Treaty. He would sign a new treaty if it did not alter the old one. Mao wished to save face, before signing away Chinese lands. This was stalemate. Mao suggested summoning Chou En-lai, his Premier, to complete the negotiations.

'If we cannot establish what we must complete, why call for Chou?' asked Stalin.

They parted: Mao claimed Stalin refused to see him but he had his own reasons to wait. He remained miserably in Moscow for several weeks before the two sides came together, grumbling bitterly that there was 'nothing to do there but eat, sleep and shit'. The prim Russians were shocked at Mao's scatological jokes both in person and on their bugs.

'Comrades,' said Stalin, 'the battle of China isn't over yet. It's only just beginning.' Beria joked to the others that Stalin was jealous of Mao for ruling a bigger nation.

Mao was not completely ignored: Molotov, Bulganin and Mikoyan visited him at the dacha. Stalin wondered if the Chinese enigma was a 'real Marxist'. Like an abbot testing a novice, Molotov patronizingly tested Mao's Marxist knowledge, deciding the Chairman was a 'clever man, a peasant leader, something like a Chinese Pugachev'* but not a real Marxist. After all, Molotov repeated prissily to Stalin, Mao 'confessed he had never read *Das Kapital*'.

* * *

On 21 December, Mao and the entire Communist world gathered at the Bolshoi to celebrate the birthday of their supreme pontiff. Something between a religious pilgrimage and an imperial triumph, a royal wedding and a corporate junket, the festivities cost 5.6 million roubles and attracted thousands of pilgrims. Stalin, torn between contempt for their worship and craving for it, played the modest curmudgeon as Malenkov, always at the forefront of the basest acts of idolatry, tried to persuade him that 'the people' expected a celebration – and a second Hero of the Soviet Union star.

'Don't even think of presenting me with another star,' he growled.

*Emelian Pugachev was the Cossack pretender claiming to be the dead Emperor Peter 111 who led a massive peasant rebellion against Catherine the Great in 1773–4.

'But Comrade Stalin, the people ...'

'Leave the people out of it.' But he finally accepted the second star and happily reviewed the arrangements. The archives contain the extraordinary preparations: President Shvernik headed the 'Committee for Preparations of Comrade Stalin's Birthday' which self-consciously contained 'ordinary workers', magnates, marshals and artists such as Shostakovich, who gravely debated the creation of an Order of Stalin, the guest-list, *placement* – and a Stalin gift-pack. At a total cost of 487,000 roubles, every delegate was to receive a dressing-gown, slippers, razor and a set of Moskva soap, talc and scent (the proudest creation of Polina Molotova, now in jail).

In *Pravda*, Khrushchev hailed Stalin's 'sharp intransigence to rootless cosmopolitans', the Jews. Poskrebyshev praised Stalin's brilliance at growing lemons. The wives of the magnates brought their own presents – Nina Beria made walnut jam 'as a little souvenir ... of your mother', to which Stalin wrote a thank-you letter:

'As I eat your jam, I remember my youth.'

Beria rolled his eyes: 'Now you'll be lined up for this chore every year.'

Famous artistes and élite children rehearsed their tributes. Parents had never been pushier: Poskrebyshev managed to land his daughter Natasha the plum role of reciting an idolatrous ditty, then presenting Stalin (who had ordered the death of her mother) a bouquet. At the Bolshoi, ballerinas practised 'curtsies to the God'.

At the Little Corner, the night before, Stalin changed the *placement* so that he was no longer in the centre but Malenkov insisted he had to be in the front row. He pointedly placed himself between Mao and Khrushchev, the new favourite. Later he felt pressure on his neck, then staggered from a dizzy spell, but Poskrebyshev steadied him. He would not call the doctors. Poskrebyshev prescribed one of his remedies.

The next night, the packed Bolshoi awaited the magnates. Stalin's exotic entourage, including Mao, Ulbricht of Germany, Rakosi of Hungary and Bierut of Poland, mingled in the *avant-loge* until everything was ready. When they trooped out, the audience applauded madly. Stalin sat to the left of centre under a jungle of scarlet banners and a giant portrait of himself. Then the endless speeches started, hailing the birthday boy as a genius. Stalin gestured to General Vlasik and whispered that guests were to speak in their own languages, an internationalist gesture by 'the father of peoples'. Togliatti spoke in Italian which he translated into Russian himself. Mao's address, in his surprisingly high-pitched voice, won a standing ovation. Stalin was exhausted from standing up so often. Then the schoolgirls, in their Pioneer dresses, emerged led by Natasha Poskrebysheva to recite their poem. Poskrebyshev winked at his daughter who scampered up and presented the bouquet of red roses: 'Papa and Stalin both loved red roses,' she says.

'Thanks *ryzhik*, redhead, for the roses!' Stalin said and pointed at his devoted Poskrebyshev who beamed with pride.

The party reassembled for a huge banquet at the Kremlin's Georgievsky Hall and for a concert starring the tenor Kozlovsky, the ballerina Maya Plisetskaya and the soprano Vera Davydova. Vlasik personally checked their dressing rooms for assassins or bombs. When she danced, Maya noticed 'the Emperor's bewhiskered face in the first row at the long festive table facing away from the stage and half turned to me [with] Mao next to him'.

Mao's superlative sulk was wearing thin. Face had been saved. When he tried to call Stalin, he was told he 'was not at home and it would be better to talk to Mikoyan'. Finally, on 2 January, Stalin sent Molotov and Mikoyan to begin negotiations. Chou En-lai* arrived on the 20th and started to negotiate with the new Foreign Minister, Vyshinsky, and Mikoyan. Mao and Chou were invited to the Kremlin only to be reprimanded by Stalin for not signing a critique of US Secretary of State Dean Acheson's recent speech. When Mao grumbled about Stalin's resistance to the treaty, Stalin retorted:

'To hell with that! We must go all the way.' Mao sulked even more. In the limousine out to Kuntsevo, the Chinese interpreter invited Stalin to visit Mao.

'Swallow your words!' Mao hissed in Chinese to the interpreter. 'Don't invite him!' Neither of the titans spoke for the entire thirty-minute drive. When Stalin invited Mao to dance to his gramophone, a singular honour for a visiting leader, he refused. It

---

* Stalin admired Chou and President Liu Shao-chi as the most 'distinguished' of Mao's men but he thought that Marshal Chu-Teh was a Chinese version of 'our Voroshilov and Budyonny'.

did not matter: the game of poker was over. While reserving for himself the supreme priesthood of international Communism, Stalin allowed Mao a leading role in Asia.

At the banquet at the Metropol Hotel on 14 February, after the treaty was signed, Stalin pointedly denounced Titoism – and Mao continued his heroic sulk. The two giants barely spoke: 'sporadic' exchanges subsided into 'endless pauses'. Gromyko struggled to keep the conversation going. Stalin may not have liked Mao but he was impressed: 'Of the Marxist world, the most outstanding is Mao ... Everything in his Marxist-Leninist life shows principles and drive, a coherent fighter.' The alliance was immediately tested on the battlefields of Korea.

* * *

Kim Il Sung, the young leader of Communist North Korea, now arrived in Moscow to ask Stalin's permission to invade South Korea. Stalin encouraged Kim but shrewdly passed the buck to Mao, telling the Korean he could 'only get down to action' after consulting with 'Comrade Mao Tse-tung personally'. In Peking, the nervous Mao referred back to Stalin. On 14 May, Stalin cunningly replied, 'The question should ultimately be decided by the Chinese and Korean comrades together.' He thus protected his dominant role but passed the responsibility. None the less, his magnates were worried by his reckless challenge to America and failing powers of judgement. At 4 a.m., on Sunday, 25 June 1950, North Korea attacked the south. Driving all before them, the Communists were soon poised to conquer.

On 5 August, a weary, ageing Stalin departed by special train for his longest holiday so far. It was to be four and a half months, brooding on his anti-Jewish case, on his anger towards Molotov and Mikoyan, distrust of Beria, and dissatisfaction with the ruthlessness of Abakumov's MGB – while the world teetered on the brink thousands of miles away in Korea.

No sooner had he arrived to rest than disaster struck in the faraway peninsula. Stalin had withdrawn from the UN to protest against its refusal to recognize Mao's China instead of Taiwan as the legitimate government but President Truman called Stalin's bluff by convening the Security Council to approve UN intervention against North Korea. The Soviet Union could have avoided this but Stalin wrongly insisted on boycotting the session, against Gromyko's advice. 'Stalin for once was guided by emotion,' remembered Gromyko. In September, the powerful US counter-attack at Inchon, under the UN flag, trapped Kim's North Koreans in the south and then shattered their army. Once again, Stalin's testing of American resolve had backfired badly – but the old man simply sighed to Khrushchev that if Kim was defeated, 'So what. Let it be. Let the Americans be our neighbours.' If he did not get what he wanted, Russia would still not intervene.

As the Americans advanced into North Korea towards the Chinese border, Mao desperately looked towards Stalin, fearing that if they intervened and fought the Americans, their Sino-Soviet Treaty would embroil Russia too. Stalin replied, with Nero-like nonchalance, that he was 'far from Moscow and some-what cut off from events in Korea'. But on 5 October, Stalin fired off a telegram of blunt *realpolitik* and shameless bluff: America was 'not prepared ... for a big war' but if it came to it, 'let it happen now and not in a few years when Japanese militarism will be restored'. Thus Stalin pulled the sting out of Mao's reservations and pushed his ally one step closer to war.

Mao deployed nine divisions but despatched Chou to Stalin's holiday house, probably New Athos, to discuss the promised Soviet air cover for the Chinese troops. On 9 October, a tense Chou, accompanied by Mao's trusted protégé, the fragile but talented Lin Piao, later his doomed heir apparent, faced Stalin, Malenkov, Beria, Kaganovich, Bulganin, Mikoyan and Molotov.

'Today we want to listen to the opinions and thinking of our Chinese comrades,' Stalin opened the meeting. When Chou stated the situation, Stalin replied that Russia could not enter the war – but China should. None the less, if Kim lost, he offered the North Koreans sanctuary. He could only help with military equipment. Chou, who had been counting on Soviet air cover, gasped. Afterwards, Stalin invited the Chinese to a Bacchanal from which only Lin Piao emerged sober. This was one of the occasions when Beria disagreed with Stalin and, as ever, he was the most daring in expressing himself. When he came out of the meeting on sending Chinese forces into Korea, he found the Georgian boss, Charkviani, waiting outside:

'What's he doing?' Beria, who understood the nuclear threat, exclaimed nervously. 'The Americans will be furious. He'll make them our enemy.' Charkviani was amazed to hear such heresy.

'It's hard for me to trust a man 100% but I think I can rely on him,' Stalin reflected to Mgeladze over dinner, having manoeuvred Mao into fighting the Americans without Soviet air cover.

On 19 October, Mao deployed his waves of Chinese cannon fodder to throw back the surprised Americans. Henceforth, even when the front finally stabilized along the 38th Parallel and the North Koreans begged for peace, Stalin refused to agree: attrition suited him. As he told Chou at a later meeting, in a phrase that illustrates Stalin's entire monstrous career, the North Koreans could keep on fighting indefinitely because they 'lose nothing, *except for their men*'.

* * *

While the old Generalissmo basked in the sun pulling the strings in Korea, he was also killing his own men. On 29 September, Kuznetsov and Voznesensky were tried at the Officers' Club in Leningrad before an MGB audience. Before the trial finally started, the accused were ordered to leave Zhdanov out of their testimony. The main accused were sentenced to death by shooting next day and the Politburo endorsed the sentences. 'He'd sign first,' admitted Khrushchev, 'and then pass it around for the rest of us to sign. We'd sign without even looking ...' Did they sign the death-list over dinner on the veranda?

Kuznetsov defiantly refused to confess, which outraged Stalin and embarrassed Abakumov:

'I'm a Bolshevik and remain one in spite of the sentence I have received. History will justify us.' The accused were said to have been bundled into white sacks by the Chekists and dragged out to be shot. They were killed fifty-nine minutes after midnight on 1 October, their families exiled to the camps. There is some evidence that Stalin marked the lists with symbols specifying how they were to die. Voznesensky may have been kept alive for a while because Stalin later asked Malenkov:

'Is he in the Urals? Give him some work to do!' Malenkov informed Stalin that Voznesensky had frozen to death in the back of a prison truck in sub-zero temperatures. After Stalin's death, Rada Khrushcheva asked what had happened to Kuznetsov:

'He died terribly,' replied her father, 'with a hook through his neck.'

This little massacre consolidated the power of Malenkov, Beria, Khrushchev and Bulganin – the last men standing as Stalin entered his final years – but it was the swansong of Abakumov. That sensuous, flashy sadist would soon roll up his bloody carpet for good. Perhaps it was over-confidence that led him to close the Jewish Case in March 1950: no one was released. The tortures were so grievous that one victim counted two thousand separate blows on his buttocks and heels.

Yet as that main case temporarily subsided, Stalin was orchestrating another anti-Semitic spasm from his holiday. Anti-Semitism now 'grew like a tumour in Stalin's mind', said Khrushchev, yet he himself praised it in *Pravda*. Stalin called in the Ukrainian bosses for a dinner at which he briefed them on orchestrating a similar anti-Semitic campaign in Kiev. The hunt for 'Zionist danger' was pursued through the Government with thousands of Jews being sacked.*

Stalin was particularly fascinated by a case against Jewish managers in the prestigious Stalin Automobile Plant that made his limousines: they had sent Mikhoels a telegram celebrating the foundation of Israel.

'The good workers at the factory should be given clubs so they can beat the hell out of those Jews at the end of the working day,' Stalin told Khrushchev in February.

'Well, have you received your orders?' Beria asked sardonically. Khrushchev, Malenkov and Beria, that inseparable threesome, summoned the Jewish ZiS managers to the Kremlin and accused them of 'loss of vigilance' and complicity in an 'anti-Soviet Jewish nationalistic sabotage group'. The terrified manager fainted. The three magnates had to resuscitate him with cold water. Stalin released the manager but two Jewish journalists, one a woman, who had written about the factory, were executed. His personal intervention made the difference between life and death. Another Jewish manager, Zaltsman, was saved because, during the war, he had sent Stalin a desk-set shaped like a tank with the pens forming the guns.

The Jews were not Stalin's only target: his suspicions of Beria were constantly fanned by the ambitious Mgeladze, his boss in Abkhazia, who shrewdly revealed Beria's crimes and vendettas of the late thirties. Stalin encouraged him and denounced Beria during their chats over dinner. Mgeladze's was only one voice that informed Stalin of how corruptly the Mingrelians ran Georgia. Beria was a Mingrelian, so was Charkviani who had run it since

---

* Even Svetlana's husband was now involved. In the Central Committee machine, Yury Zhdanov, Stalin's son-in-law, that highly qualified paragon of Soviet education, reported to the orchestrator of the anti-Semitic hunt, Malenkov, that some scientists 'had flooded theoretical departments of ... Institutes with its supporters, Jews by origin.'

1938. Stalin ordered Abakumov to check the notoriously venal Georgia, and build a case against the Mingrelians, not forgetting Beria himself: 'Go after the Big Mingrelian.'

On 18 November, towards the end of his holiday, Stalin agreed to arrest the first Jewish doctor. Professor Yakov Etinger, who had treated the leaders, was bugged talking too frankly about Stalin. Etinger was tortured about his 'nationalistic' tendencies by one of Abakumov's officers, Lieut.-Col. Mikhail Riumin, who forced him to implicate all the most distinguished Jewish doctors in Moscow but he somehow failed to please his boss. Abakumov ordered Riumin to desist but the officer tortured Etinger so enthusiastically that he died of 'heart paralysis' – a euphemism for dying under torture. Riumin was in trouble – unless he could destroy Abakumov first.

Abakumov was not guilty of idleness: Stalin was now redoubling the repression. Arrests intensified. In 1950 there were more slaves in the Gulags – 2.6 million – than ever before. But Abakumov knew too much about the Leningrad and Jewish cases. Worse, Stalin sensed the foot-dragging of the MGB – and Abakumov himself. It was Yagoda all over again – and he needed a Yezhov.

The brakes on the Jewish Case, the rumours of corruption, the whispers of Beria and Malenkov, possibly the strutting bumptiousness of the man himself, turned Stalin against Abakumov. There was no sudden break but when Stalin returned from holiday,* just after his seventy-first birthday, on 22 December, he did not summon Abakumov. The weekly meetings ceased, as they had for Yagoda and Yezhov. Within the MGB snakepit, the ebbing of Stalin's favour and the death of Etinger presented Riumin with an opportunity. 'Little Mishka' or, as Stalin nicknamed him, 'the Midget' or 'Pygmy' – the '*Shibsdik*', was the *Vozhd*'s second murderous dwarf.

---

* 'I want to delay my return because of bad weather in Moscow and the danger of flu. I'll be in Moscow after coming of frost,' Stalin wrote to Malenkov in December 1950.

56

The Midget and the Killer Doctors:
Beat, Beat and Beat Again!

Riumin, thirty-eight, plump and balding, stupid and vicious, was the latest in the succession of ambitious torturers who were only too willing to please and encourage Stalin by finding new Enemies and killing them for him. Unlike Yezhov, who had been so popular until he became an inquisitor, Riumin was already an enthusiastic killer even though he had passed eight school grades, qualifying as an accountant. As Malenkov showed, education was no bar to mass murder. He had his own problems. Dismissed for misappropriating money in 1937 – and now in danger for killing the elderly Jewish doctor, the Midget decided to act. Perhaps to his own surprise, he lit the fuse of the Doctors' Plot.

On 2 July 1951, Riumin wrote to Stalin and accused Abakumov of deliberately killing Etinger to conceal a Jewish medical conspiracy to murder leaders such as the late Shcherbakov. This brought together Stalin's fears of ageing, doctors and Jews. It was not Beria but Malenkov who sent Riumin's letter to Stalin. This is confirmed by Malenkov's assistant though he claimed that Riumin wrote the letter 'for his own reasons'. The Doctors' Plot worked against Beria and the old guard like Molotov but this swelling case could threaten Malenkov and Khrushchev too. So often at Stalin's court, a case would start coincidentally, be encouraged by some magnate and then be spun back at them by Stalin like a bloody boomerang. Malenkov sometimes allied himself with Khrushchev, sometimes with Beria, but it was always Stalin making the big decisions. Riumin's allegation of medical murder may have been prompted by Stalin himself – or it may have been the spark that inspired him to reach back to Zhdanov's death and create a maze of conspiracies to provoke a Terror that would unite the country against America outside and its Jewish allies within.

He now ordered Beria and Malenkov to examine the 'Bad Situation at the MGB', accusing Abakumov of corruption, ineptitude and debauchery. Around midnight on 5 July in the

Little Corner, Stalin agreed to Malenkov's suggestion to appoint Semyon Ignatiev, forty-seven, as the new boss. At 1 a.m., Abakumov was called in to hear of his downfall. At 1.40 a.m., Riumin arrived to receive his prizes: promotion to General and, later, Deputy Minister. Serving a short spell as a Chekist in 1920, Ignatiev was an eager, bespectacled CC bureaucrat who was a friend of Khrushchev and Malenkov. Indeed Khrushchev described Ignatiev as 'mild and considerate' though the Jewish doctors would hardly have agreed with him. Beria again failed to regain control over the secret police. Henceforth Stalin himself ran the Doctors' Plot through Ignatiev. Stalin sent Malenkov to tell the MGB that he wanted to find a 'grand intelligence network of the USA' linked to 'Zionists'.

The next day, 12 July, Abakumov was arrested. In the tradition of fallen secret policeman, his corruption was lovingly recorded: 3,000 metres of expensive cloth, clothes, sets of china, crystal vases – 'enough for a shop' – were found in his homes. In order to build his flats Abakumov removed sixteen families and spent a million roubles to make a 'palace' using two hundred workers, six engineers and the entire MGB Construction Department. Yet the downfall of monsters also destroyed the innocent: Abakumov's young wife, Antonina Smirnova, with whom he had a two-month-old son, had received 70,000 roubles-worth of presents, including an antique Viennese pram. So she was arrested: the destiny of the girl and the baby are unknown.*

Abakumov, no longer a Minister but just a number, Object 15, spent three months shackled in the refrigerator cell, being viciously interrogated by his nemesis, the Midget:

'Dear LP,' he wrote pitifully to Beria, 'I feel so terrible ... You're the closest man to me, and I wait for you to ask me back ... You will need me in the future.' Abakumov had been destroyed for failing to push the Jewish Case. Ignatiev and the egregious

---

* As in 1937, the Terror first destroyed the leadership of the MGB itself which was now arrested. Colonel Naum Shvartsman, one of the cruellest torturers since the late thirties and a journalist expert at editing confessions, testified that he had had sex not only with his own son and daughter, but also with Abakumov himself, and, at night when he broke into the British Embassy, with Sir Archibald Clark Kerr, a momentous diplomatic development in Anglo-Soviet relations that had mysteriously passed unnoticed at the Court of St James. Shvartsman claimed to have been poisoned with 'Zionist soup' – an idea that harks back to the infamous plot by Enemies in the Jewish Autonomous Oblast during the thirties to poison Kaganovich's gefilte. But he also delivered what Stalin wanted, implicating Abakumov, that unlikely Zionist sympathizer.

'Midget' Riumin set about torturing the Jewish officials of the JAFC and the doctors to 'substantiate the evidence of espionage and nationalistic activity'.

* * *

The impresario of this theatre of plots and pain was now ageing fast. He sometimes became so giddy that he fell over in his Kremlin apartment. The bodyguards had to keep a close eye on him because 'he didn't look after himself'. He hardly bothered to read all his papers. Kuntsevo was strewn with unopened boxes. He still corrected Bulganin's speeches like a schoolmaster but then forgot Bulganin's name in front of the rest of the Politburo:

'Look, what's your name?'

'Bulganin.'

'Right yes … that's what I meant to say.'

Riven by arthritis, diminished by raging arteriosclerosis, dazed by fainting spells, embarrassed by failing memory, tormented by sore gums and false teeth, unpredictable, paranoid and angry, Stalin left on 10 August for his last and longest holiday. 'Cursed old age has caught up with me,' he muttered. He was even more restless than usual, travelling from Gagra to New Athos, Tsaltubo to Borzhomi and back. At Lake Ritsa, the woods, lakeside and paths were peppered with strange green metal boxes, containing special telephones so Stalin could call for help if taken ill on a stroll.

But dizzy spells were not going to stop him cleansing his entourage:

'I, Molotov, Kaganovich, Voroshilov – we're all old … we must fill … the Politburo with younger … cadres,' he ominously told Mgeladze. Yet his paranoia gave him no rest: 'I'm finished,' he told Mikoyan and Khrushchev who, like all the magnates, were on holiday near by so they could visit Stalin twice a week. 'I don't even trust myself.'

At dinner, he surveyed his courtiers and 'puffing out his chest like a turkey', he embarked on that favourite but lethal subject – his successor. It could not be Beria because he 'wasn't Russian', nor Kaganovich, a Jew. Voroshilov was too old. He did not even mention Mikoyan (an Armenian) or Molotov. It could not be Khrushchev because he was a 'country boy' and Russia needed a leader from the intelligentsia. Then he named Bulganin, the very man whose name he tended to forget, as his successor as Premier. None was ideologically qualified to lead the Party but he had not mentioned Malenkov who perhaps took this as an encouraging sign. He ordered books and started frantically studying.

'Well, Comrade Stalin requires me to study political science.' Malanya, caught reading Adam Smith, asked a colleague, 'How long will it take to master?'

The magnates were convinced that Stalin was becoming senile but actually he was never more dangerous, determined and in control. He lashed out in every direction, at his comrades, Jews, Mingrelians, even banana importers. The story of the bananas sums up the governing style of the ageing Stalin.

Vlasik learned a shipment of bananas had just arrived and eager to soothe the bad teeth of the Master, he bought some for Stalin. At dinner at Coldstream with all the magnates, Vlasik proudly presented the bananas. Stalin peeled one and found it was not ripe. He tried two more. They too were not ripe. 'Have you tried the bananas?' he asked his guests. Stalin summoned Vlasik:

'Where did you get these bananas?' Vlasik tried to explain but Stalin shouted: 'These crooks take bribes and rob the country. What was the name of the banana ship?'

'I don't know,' said Vlasik, 'I didn't take an interest ...'

'Take an interest! I'll put you on trial with the rest of them!' bellowed Stalin. Poskrebyshev rushed off to find out the name of the ship and order arrests. Malenkov pulled out his notebook and took notes. Stalin ordered Mikoyan to sack the new Trade Minister. But Beria was eager to beat Mikoyan to the banana, as it were.

The dinner ended at 5 a.m. At 6 a.m., Stalin called Beria to tell him to sack the Minister. When Mikoyan called Moscow just after 6 a.m., he found that Beria had already reprimanded the unfortunate. A few days later, Mikoyan arrived to say goodbye and Stalin was still talking about those bananas. The Minister was sacked. Charkviani wrote that this was typical of Stalin's 'eruptions leading to irrelevant decisions'. Stalin, concluded Mikoyan drily, 'was simply very fond of bananas.'

Stalin's limbs ached but when he took the waters at Tsaltubo, the weather was too hot. He decided to take the waters at Borzhomi and visit a house with special memories. He had stayed at the Likani Palace, a neo-Gothic mansion owned by Grand Duke Michael, Nicholas II's brother, overlooking the Kura River, with Nadya in happier times. It had become a museum and was barely habitable, without bedrooms, which suited Stalin. It suited his magnates less: he ordered Khrushchev and Mikoyan to stay too. They rushed over from Sochi and Sukhumi but, without beds, they had to camp together, sharing a room like boy scouts.

Stalin ate every day at a table laid under a tree by the Kura in idyllic lush countryside. When he went for walks, he cursed at the bodyguards, bumping into them by suddenly changing direction. He decided to visit Bakuriani but the locals mobbed his car, placing carpets and banqueting tables across the road. The supreme curmudgeon had to dismount and join his overexcited fans for a Georgian feast. 'They open their mouths and yell like dunderheads!' he muttered, face twitching. He never made it to Bakuriani and returned to Abkhazia.

At the Palace, where Nadya had rested after Vasily's birth, Stalin brooded on his family. Vasily, now pitifully ill with alcoholism, visited. 'His health's so poor, his stomach's sick, he can't even eat,' Stalin confided in Charkviani. Like a Western millionaire booking his playboy son into the Betty Ford Clinic, Stalin intervened to enrol Vasily in a drying-out programme but here too he searched for a culprit and found one in the banana procurer:

'Vlasik and his friends did it, they turned his drinking into an addiction!' Stalin had been cursing Vlasik's corruption for years. A denunciation letter and Malenkov's investigation into MGB venality revealed Vlasik's orgies and shenanigans. Stalin was upset but felt mired in corruption. He finally sacked his most devoted retainer.*

Svetlana's marriage to Yury was over after just two years. In a letter to her father, she called Yury a 'heartless bookworm' and an 'iceberg'. Stalin told Mgeladze that Svetlana wore the trousers:

'Yury Zhdanov's not the head of that family – he can't insist on anything. He doesn't listen to her nor she to him. The husband should run a family ... that's the main thing.' But Yury himself would never dare ask Stalin for a divorce so Svetlana came to see him instead.

'I know what you want to say,' he said. 'You've decided to divorce him.'

'Father,' Svetlana answered in a begging tone. Charkviani, who was present, was embarrassed and excused himself but Stalin insisted he stay.

---

* Vlasik was despatched to be Deputy Commandant of a labour camp in the Urals whence he rashly bombarded Stalin with protestations of his innocence. But this did not place Beria in charge of his bodyguards who remained under Ignatiev's MGB.

'So why're you divorcing him?' Stalin asked.

'I can't live with my mother-in-law. She's impossible!'

'What does your husband say?'

'He supports his mother!'

Stalin sighed: 'If you've decided to divorce him, I can't change your mind, but your behaviour isn't acceptable.' She blushed and left, walking out of the Zhdanov family and moving into a flat in the House on the Embankment with her two children.

'Who knows what next?' muttered Stalin.

'Stalin wasn't too happy when it ended,' admits Yury, but he was not too surprised either. He did not hold it against Yury but invited him to stay at Lake Ritsa where they chatted half the night about Stalin's visit to London in 1907. When they naturally talked about the campaign against cosmopolitanism, Zhdanov, who had played his own role in hunting out Jewish scientists, asked Stalin if he thought it was 'assuming a lopsided national character', meaning it was aimed too much against the Jews.

'Cosmopolitanism's a widespread phenomenon,' replied Stalin. When he finally got up to go to bed in the early hours, he cited a Jewess he admired: 'Maria Kaganovich – there's a real Bolshevik! One should pay attention to social position, not national condition!' and he staggered off to sleep. In the morning the table was laid on the bank of Lake Ritsa and Yury watched Stalin peruse *Pravda*. 'What are they writing about?' he snarled, reading out, 'Long live Comrade Stalin, leader of all nations!' – and he tossed it away in disgust.

After entertaining other old friends, who complained that the Mingrelians were notoriously corrupt, Stalin headed back to New Athos and then dared Mgeladze to be there within seventeen minutes. The ambitious Abkhazian boss, who sensed his hours of chatting with the old man were about to bear fruit, made it in fifteen and finally convinced Stalin that Charkviani was running 'a bordello!'

He furiously summoned the Georgian MGB boss, the crude, barrel-chested Rukhadze. 'The Mingrelians are totally unreliable,' said Stalin, who in old age embraced the parochial hatreds of different regions of Georgia. Thousands of Mingrelians were arrested but Stalin wanted to destroy Beria. Perhaps he suspected that Lavrenti was no Marxist: 'He's become very pretentious ... he's not how he used to be ... Comrades who dine with him say he's utterly bourgeois.'

Stalin was 'afraid of Beria', thought Khrushchev, 'and would
have been glad to get rid of him but didn't know how to do it.'
Stalin himself confirmed this, sensing that Beria was winning
support: 'Beria's so wily and tricksy. He's become so trusted by the
Politburo that they defend him. They don't realize he's pulled the
wool over their eyes. For example – Vyacheslav [Molotov] and
Lazar [Kaganovich]. I think Beria has his eye on a future goal. But
he's limited. In his time, he did great work but as for now ... I'm
not sure he wouldn't misuse his power.' Then Stalin remembered
his closest allies: 'Zhdanov and Kirov thought poorly of him but
... we liked Beria for his modesty and efficiency. Later he lost these
qualities. He's just a policeman.'

Ignatiev sent sixty MGB interrogators and a torture specialist
carrying a special medical case filled with his instruments, down
to Tiflis. Stalin phoned Charkviani, with whom he had spent
hours discussing literature and family, and without saying hello,
threatened:

'You've closed your eyes to corruption in Georgia ... Things'll go
badly for you, Comrade Charkviani.' He hung up. Charkviani was
terrified.

The Beria family, Nina and Sergo, sensed this tightening
garrotte. Stalin appointed Beria to give the prestigious 6
November address but three days afterwards, he dictated an order
about a Mingrelian conspiracy that directly threatened Beria,
using his wife Nina's links to the Menshevik émigrés in Paris.

Vasily Stalin naïvely confided to Sergo Beria that relations
between their fathers were 'tense', which he blamed on
anti-Georgian Russians in the Politburo. Svetlana, who was so
close to Nina, warned her that something was afoot. Beria's
marriage to Nina was under strain because Lilya Drozhdova had
given birth to a daughter by Beria whom they named Martha after
his mother. Lilya was now about seventeen and she had lasted as
Beria's mistress for a couple of years. The bodyguards told Martha
Peshkova that when Lilya was at the dacha, the baby was placed
in the same cradles as Sergo's children. Not surprisingly, the
arrival of the baby upset Nina. She unhappily decided she needed
a separate life and built herself a cottage in Sukhumi.

* * *

On 22 December 1951, Stalin, like a lame, restless and hungry
tiger, returned to Moscow, clearly intent on enforcing a new
Terror, with specific anti-Semitic features. The torture chambers of

Ignatiev and Riumin groaned with new Jewish and Mingrelian victims to destroy Molotov and Beria. Stalin did know how to 'get rid' of Beria, but the 'master of dosage' had always worked with agonizing patience. But now he was old. Stalin loathed Beria yet Sergo recalls that 'when in a morose mood, he came to see us seeking human warmth'. Stalin admitted to Nina he could barely sleep any more:

'You can't know how tired I am. I have to sleep like a gundog.'

Beria played Stalin well: he shrewdly offered to purge Georgia himself. In March 1952, Beria sacked Charkviani,* replaced him with Mgeladze and publically admitted:

'I too am guilty.'

Stalin and Beria despised each other but were linked by invisible threads of past crimes, mutual envy and complementary cunning. Stalin still discussed foreign policy with Beria, even letting him write a paper proposing a neutral, reunified Germany. Beria could still manipulate the Generalissimo with what Khrushchev called 'Jesuitical shrewdness' but he was too clever by half, riling Stalin. 'You're playing with a tiger,' Nina warned him.

'I couldn't resist it,' replied Beria.

The gap between Beria's dreams and his reality had made him 'a deeply unhappy man', wrote his son. Without the ideological fanaticism that bound the others to Stalin, Beria now questioned the entire Soviet system: 'The USSR can never succeed until we have private property,' he told Charkviani. He despised Stalin, whom he considered 'no longer human. I think there is only one word that describes what my father felt in those days,' wrote Sergo Beria. 'Hatred.' Beria became ever more daring in his denunciations of Stalin: 'For a long time,' he sneered sarcastically, 'the Soviet State had been too small for Joseph Vissarionovich!' Always the most craven and most irreverent, he denounced Stalin but the other leaders were afraid to join in: 'I considered it an attempt to provoke us,' said Mikoyan.

Yet, gradually, their shared fears and Stalin's unpredictability

---

* Stalin protected Charkviani because the leader had been taught the alphabet as a boy by a Father Charkviani. Stalin moved him to work as a CC Inspector in Moscow. But Beria was powerless to defend himself or his protégés. When the Mingrelian secret policeman Rapava, who was a family friend of the Berias, was arrested, his wife bravely set off secretly to Moscow to ask Nina Beria's help. But when the desperate woman called Beria's house, Nina was too scared to come to the phone. The German housekeeper Ella said, 'Nina cannot come to the phone.' This was how the Mingrelians realized that Beria himself was in trouble.

created a 'sense of solidarity', a support system among ambitious killers who wanted to survive and protect their families. Even Beria became the unlikely avuncular comforter for bruisers like Khrushchev and Mikoyan in these uneasy times. The others revelled in Beria's eclipse – and shared his fears. Malenkov warned him, Khrushchev teased him. Molotov and Kaganovich were so impressed with Beria that even when Stalin criticized him, they defended him. Yet any and all were ready to destroy the others. It was not long before Ignatiev and his MGB torturers were even trying to link Stalin's two obsessions: Beria, they whispered, was secretly Jewish.

That spring, Stalin was examined by his veteran doctor, Vinogradov, who was shocked by his deterioration. He suffered from hypertension and arteriosclerosis with occasional disturbances in cerebral circulation, which caused minor strokes and little cysts in the brain tissue of the frontal lobe. This exacerbated Stalin's anger, amnesia and paranoia. 'Complete rest, freedom from all work,' wrote Vinogradov on the file but the mention of retirement infuriated Stalin who ordered his medical records destroyed and resolved to see no more doctors. Vinogradov was an Enemy.

On 15 February, Stalin ordered the arrests of more doctors who admitted helping to kill Shcherbakov, which in turn led to Dr Lydia Timashuk, the cardiologist who had written to Stalin about the mistreatment of Zhdanov. Stalin called in Ignatiev and told him that, if he did not accelerate the interrogations of the Jewish doctors already under arrest, he would join Abakumov in prison. The MGB were 'nincompoops!'

'I'm not a supplicant of the MGB!' barked Stalin at Ignatiev. 'I can knock you out if you don't follow my orders ... We'll scatter your group!' He now talked more to his bodyguards and Valechka than to his comrades. The death of the Mongolian dictator, Marshal Choibalsang, in Moscow that spring worried him enough to confide in his chauffeur: 'They die one after another. Shcherbakov, Zhdanov, Dmitrov, Choibalsang ... die so quickly!* We must change the old doctors for new ones.' The bodyguards could talk quite intimately to Stalin and Colonel Tukov replied that those doctors were very experienced. 'No, we must change them for new ones ... The MVD insists on arresting them as saboteurs.' Valechka heard

*Georgi Dmitrov, the Bulgarian leader, died in 1949.

him say he was not sure about the case. But Stalin was not for turning: he wanted the Jewish Crimea case to be tried imminently. Lozovsky and a distinguished cast of Jewish intellectuals again became the playthings of Riumin and Komarov.

Meanwhile, Vasily Stalin's treatment for alcoholism had failed completely. At the May Day parade, the weather was bad and the planes should not have been allowed to fly but a drunken Vasily ordered the flypast to proceed. Two Tupolev-4 bombers crashed. Stalin watched darkly from the Mausoleum and afterwards sacked Vasily as Moscow Air Force commander, sending him back to the Air Force Academy.

Eight days later, at midday on 8 May, the 'trial of the Jewish poets' starring Solomon Lozovsky, former Deputy Foreign Minister, and the Yiddish poet Perets Markish opened in the Dzerzhinsky Officers' Club at the Lubianka. Stalin had already specified that virtually all the defendants were to be shot.

Lozovsky had been tortured but his pride in his Bolshevik and, more surprisingly, Jewish pedigrees was unbroken. His speech shines out of this primordial darkness as the most remarkable and moving oration of dignity and courage in all of Stalin's trials. He also shredded Riumin's imbecilic Jewish-Crimean conspiracy.

'Even if I had wanted to engage in such activity ... would I have gotten in touch with a poet and an actor? ... After all, there is an American Embassy ... swarming with intelligence officers. The doorman at the Commissariat of Finance would not do such a thing, let alone the Deputy Foreign Minister!'

Lozovsky was so convincing that the judge, Lieut.-Gen. Alexander Cheptsov, stopped the trial, a unique happening which suggests that Stalin was forcing a new Terror onto an unwilling and no longer blindly obedient bureaucracy. Cheptsov complained of its flimsiness to Malenkov in the presence of a rattled Ignatiev – and humiliated Riumin. Malenkov ordered the trial to proceed. On 18 July, Cheptsov sentenced thirteen defendants to death (including two women), sparing only the scientist Lina Shtern, perhaps because of her research into longevity. But Cheptsov did not carry out the executions, ignoring Riumin's shrill orders to do so, and appealed to Malenkov.

'Do you want to bring us to kneel before these criminals?' Malenkov retorted. 'The Politburo has investigated this case three times. Carry out the Politburo's resolution.' Malenkov admitted later that he had not told Stalin everything: 'I did not dare!'

Stalin rejected official appeals. Lozovsky* and the Jewish poets were shot on 12 August 1952.

* * *

Stalin refused to take a holiday that August: instead, unhappy at the dominance of Malenkov and Khrushchev, he decided to call a Congress in October, the first one since 1939, to anoint new, younger leaders and destroy his old comrades.

By September, Ignatiev, assisted by 'Midget' Riumin, had tortured the evidence out of his prisoners to 'prove' that the Kremlin doctors, led by Stalin's own physician, had indeed murdered Zhdanov, Shcherbakov, Dmitrov and Choibalsang. A new crop were arrested but not yet Vinogradov. On the 18th, Stalin told Riumin to torture the doctors. Riumin, who possessed a macabre gift for primitive theatre, designed a special torture chamber at Lefortovo, furnished like a dissection room and operating theatre, to intimidate the doctors. Long before Laurence Olivier played the Nazi dentist in *Marathon Man*, Stalin was torturing his own doctors in a ghastly surgical parody.

'You're acting like a whore! You're an ignoble spy, a terrorist!' Riumin shouted at one of the doctors. 'We'll torture you with a red-hot iron. We have all the necessary equipment for that ...' Stalin's family was included in a bizarre medical melodrama, spawned by Stalin's furious imagination and Riumin's diabolical obedience: the doctors had deliberately subverted Vasily Stalin's treatment for 'nervous disorders' and had failed to prevent toxicosis in Svetlana Stalin after the birth of her child Katya Zhdanov in the spring of 1950. A surreal touch, if any was needed, was added by the case of Andreyev who had been ill since 1947: the doctors prescribed cocaine for his insomnia so it was hardly surprising he was unable to sleep. Andreyev† had become

---

* One of the survivors of Stalin's time, Maxim Litvinov, the Jewish ex-Foreign Commissar, managed to die in his bed on 31 December 1951. He was a perennial target of the MGB's anti-Semitic cases. Molotov admitted that Litvinov should have been shot for his rambunctious indiscretions in the late war years: 'It was only by chance that he remained among the living,' said Molotov chillingly. There was a plan to arrange a road accident à la Mikhoels but finally Litvinov died with his errant English wife by his bedside: 'Englishwoman go home!' were his last words. 'They did not get him,' said Ivy Litvinov who returned to London. Their daughter now lives in Brighton.
† Andreyev had appealed to Malenkov in January 1949 to 'check the treatment ... I don't feel good despite following doctors' orders. My head's dizzy ... I almost fall over. I'm disastrous. I feel the treatment and diagnosis is wrong ...' He was probably right since the cocaine was clearly the wrong medicine. He signed off: 'I'm devilishly unhappy to be out of work.'

dependent on the drug, one of history's more unlikely coke addicts.

Absurd as the details may sound, the Doctors' Plot had the beautiful enveloping symmetry of a panacea, one of Stalin's fantastical masterpieces: working alone, only informing his grandees when he had results, and keeping complete control over all the parallel threads through the 'Midget', he wove a tapestry that sewed together every intrigue and leading victim since the war, in order to mobilize the Soviet people against the external enemy, America, and its internal agents, the Jews, and therefore justify a new Terror. New research shows Stalin would toss into this cauldron various 'murderous' Jews and doctors, Abakumov and his 'unvigilant' Chekist 'nincompoops', and the executed Leningrader, Kuznetsov, who would be the link between the Jews, Zhdanov's death, and the magnates – especially Mikoyan, via their children's marriage. Just as in 1937 a man did not have to be a Trotskyite to be shot as one, so now the victims did not have to be Jewish to be accused of 'Zionism': Abakumov, no philo-Semite, was now smeared with Zionism. As for the sturdily Russian Molotov, Stalin had not nicknamed him 'Molotstein', in the twenties, for nothing.

Did Stalin really believe it all? Yes, passionately, because it was politically necessary, which was better than mere truth. 'We ourselves will be able to determine,' Stalin told Ignatiev, 'what is true and what is not.'

Stimulated by his labyrinth of secret investigations, Stalin did not give up his literary and scientific interests. As his brain atrophied, Stalin still 'swotted like a good pupil', as Beria put it, studying to dominate new fields and solve ideological problems. 'I am seventy yet I go on learning just the same,' Stalin boasted to Svetlana. He read all the entries for the Stalin Prize and chaired the Committee to choose the winners in his office. That year, pacing as usual, he decreed that a novelist named Stepan Zlobin should win. Malenkov however pulled out a file and said,

'Comrade Stalin, Zlobin conducted himself very badly when he was in a German concentration camp ...' Stalin walked round the table three times in dead silence then asked:

'To forgive?' He continued pacing the table in silence. 'Or not to forgive? To forgive or not to forgive?' Finally, he answered: 'Forgive!' Zlobin won the prize. Stalin then attacked anti-Semitism: he had lately insisted that Jewish writers must have their Semitic names published in brackets after their Russian pseudonyms. Now he asked the surprised Committee: 'What's this for? Does it give pleasure to someone to underline that this man is Jewish? Why? To promote anti-Semitism?' As usual the old fox was playing several games in parallel.

He had always been interested in the theory of linguistics: the field had been dominated by Professor Marr who had established Stalinist orthodoxy by arguing that language, like class, would ultimately disappear and merge into one language as Communism approached. A Georgian linguistics scholar, Arnold Chikobava, wrote to Stalin to attack the theory. Stalin, keen to buttress his national Bolshevism by overturning Marrism, summoned Chikobava to a dinner that lasted from 9 p.m. to 7 a.m. taking notes diligently like a student. He then held an open debate in *Pravda*, finally intervening with his own article, 'Marxism and the Problems of Linguistics' which immediately altered the entire field of Soviet science and ideology.*

Just before the Congress opened, Stalin proudly distributed the other fruit of his studies, his turgid masterpiece *Economic Problems of Socialism in the USSR*, which declared the 'objectivity' of economic laws and reasserted the orthodoxy that the imperialist states would go to war, but it also leapt some of the stages of Marxism, to claim that Communism was achievable in his lifetime. Faith in ideology was always vital to Stalin but those old believers Molotov and Mikoyan did not agree with this 'Leftist derivation'. When they came to dinner at Kuntsevo, Stalin asked:

'Any questions? Any comments!' Beria and Malenkov, never ideologists, praised it. But even now, in danger of his life, Molotov would not agree with an ideological deviation. He just mumbled and Mikoyan said nothing. Stalin noticed their silence and, later, smiled maliciously at Mikoyan:

'Ah, you've lagged behind! Right now, the time has come!' When they met to discuss the Presidium of the Congress, Stalin said,

---

* Chikobava told Stalin that some of his Armenian colleagues had been sacked for sharing his views so Stalin immediately got the Armenian boss, Arutinov, on the telephone and asked about the professors. 'They were removed from their posts,' replied Arutinov. 'You were in too much of a hurry,' replied Stalin and hung up. The professors were woken up immediately and restored to their positions. His meeting with Chikobava probably took place on 12 April 1950 just as he was discussing the timing of the Korean War; Stalin's article was published on 20 June that year. Chikobava's original letter was sent to Stalin by Candide Charkviani, then Georgian First Secretary, which shows the power of those with direct access to the *Vozhd*.

'No need to enter Mikoyan and Andreyev – they're inactive Politburo members!' Since Mikoyan was immensely busy, the Politburo chuckled.

'I'm not joking,' snapped Stalin. 'I suggest it seriously.' The laughter stopped instantly, but Mikoyan was included. Even at the height of his tyranny, Stalin had to feel his way in this close-knit oligarchy: Mikoyan and Molotov were prestigious Poltiburo titans, respected not only by their colleagues but by the public. Stalin proposed they expand the Politburo into a Presidium of twenty-five members. Mikoyan realized this would make it easier to remove the old Politburo members. 'I thought – "something's happening."' Mikoyan was suddenly afraid: 'I was just knocked off my feet.' They realized Stalin had meant it when he shouted:

'You've grown old! I'll replace you all!'

At 7 p.m. (to suit Stalin's own timetable) on 5 October 1952, the Nineteenth Congress opened. The leaders sat bunched together on the left with the ageing Stalin alone on the right. Stalin himself only attended the beginning and the end of the Congress but giving the major reports to Malenkov and Khrushchev placed them in pole position for the succession.* He only spoke at the end of the Congress for a few rambling minutes but a punch-drunk Stalin boasted to Khrushchev:

'There, look at that! I can still do it!' Khrushchev was ill during the Congress: when an old doctor visited him on Granovsky and treated him kindly, 'I was tormented because I already had the testimony against the doctor. I knew no matter what I said, Stalin would not spare him.' But the real action was on 16 October at the Plenum to elect the Presidium and Secretariat. No one was ready for Stalin's ambush.

---

* Molotov opened the Congress, Kaganovich spoke on the Party rules, and Voroshilov closed it, representing the status quo, which few guessed that Stalin was planning to radically overturn. But there were clues. Significantly Stalin changed the Party's name from Bolshevik to Communist Party. In the new Presidium, Beria slipped from his usual third place after Molotov, and Malenkov to fifth after Voroshilov. Beria's acolytes Merkulov and Dekanozov were dropped from the new CC.

57

Blind Kittens and Hippopotamuses:
the Destruction of the Old Guard

Stalin loped down to the rostrum two metres in front of the pew-like seats where the magnates sat. The Plenum watched in frozen fascination as the old man began to speak 'fiercely', peering into the eyes of the small audience 'attentively and tenaciously as if trying to guess their thoughts'.

'So we held the Party Congress,' he said. 'It was fine and it would seem to most people that we enjoy unity. However, we don't have unity. Some people express disagreement with our decisions. Why did we exclude ministers from important posts ... Molotov, Kaganovich, Voroshilov? ... Ministers' work ... demands great strength, knowledge and health.' So he was bringing forward 'young men, full of strength and energy'. But then he unleashed his thunderbolt: 'If we're talking unity, I cannot but touch on the incorrect behaviour of some honoured politicians. I mean Comrades Molotov and Mikoyan.'

Sitting just behind Stalin, their faces turned 'pale and dead' in the 'terrible silence'. The magnates, 'stony, strained and grave', wondered 'where and when would Stalin stop, would he touch the others after Molotov and Mikoyan?'

First he dealt with Molotov:

'Molotov's loyal to our cause. Ask him and I don't doubt he'd give his life for our Party without hesitation. But we cannot overlook unworthy acts.' Stalin dredged up Molotov's mistake with censorship: 'Comrade Molotov, our Foreign Minister, drunk on *chartreuse* at a diplomatic reception, let the British Ambassador publish bourgeois newspapers in our country ... This is the first political mistake. And what's the value of Comrade Molotov's proposal to give the Crimea to the Jews? That's a huge mistake ... the second political mistake of Comrade Molotov.' The third was Polina: 'Comrade Molotov respects his wife so much that as soon as we adopt a Politburo decision ... it instantly becomes known to Comrade Zhemchuzhina ... A hidden thread connects the

Politburo with Molotov's wife – and her friends ... who are untrustworthy. Such behaviour isn't acceptable in a Politburo member.' Then he attacked Mikoyan for opposing higher taxes on the peasantry: 'Who does he think he is, our Anastas Mikoyan? What's unclear to him?'

Then he pulled a piece of paper out of his tunic, and read out the thirty-six members of the new Presidium, including many new names. Khrushchev and Malenkov glanced at each other: where had Stalin found these people? When he proposed the inner Bureau, everyone was astonished that Molotov and Mikoyan were excluded.* Then, returning to his seat on the tribune, he explained their downfall: 'They're scared by the over-whelming power they saw in America.' He ominously linked Molotov and Mikoyan to the Rightists, Rykov and Frumkin, shot long before, and Lozovsky, just shot in August.

Molotov stood and confessed:

'I am and remain a loyal disciple of Stalin,' but the Generalissimo cupped his ear and barked:

'Nonsense! I've no disciples! We're all disciples of Lenin. Of Lenin!'

Mikoyan fought back defiantly: 'You must remember well, Comrade Stalin ... I proved I wasn't guilty of anything.' Malenkov and Beria heckled him, hissing 'liar' but he persisted. 'And as for the bread prices, I completely deny the accusation' – but Stalin interrupted him:

'See, there goes Mikoyan! He's our new Frumkin!'

Then a voice called out:

'We must elect Comrade Stalin General Secretary!'

'No,' replied Stalin. 'Excuse me from the posts of General Secretary and Chairman of the Council of Ministers [Premier].' Malenkov stood up and ran forward, chins aquiver, with the desperate grace of a whippet sealed inside a blancmange. His 'terrible expression' was not fear, observed Simonov, but an 'understanding much better than anyone else of the mortal danger that hung over all: it was impos-sible to comply with Stalin's request.' Malenkov, tottering on the edge of the stage, raised his hands as if he was praying and piped up:

'Comrades! We must all unanimously demand that Comrade

---

* Yet Stalin still remembered his loyalest retainer Mekhlis, who had suffered a stroke in 1949. Now dying at his dacha, all he longed for was to attend the Congress. Stalin refused, muttering that it was not a hospital but when the new CC was announced, he remembered him. Mekhlis was thrilled – he died happy and Stalin authorized a magnificent funeral.

Stalin, our leader and teacher, remain as General Secretary!' He shook his finger, signalling. The whole hall understood and began to cry out that Stalin had to remain at his post. Malenkov's jowls relaxed as if he had 'escaped direct, real mortal danger'. But he was not safe yet.

'One doesn't need the applause of the Plenum,' replied Stalin. 'I ask you to release me ... I'm already old. I don't read the documents. Elect yourselves another Secretary.' Marshal Timoshenko replied:

'Comrade Stalin, the people won't understand it. We all as one elect you our leader – General Secretary!' The cheering went on for a long time. Stalin waited, then, waving modestly, he sat down.

Stalin's decision to destroy his oldest comrades was not an act of madness but the rational destruction of his most likely successors. As Stalin remembered well, the ailing Lenin had attacked his likely successor (Stalin himself) and proposed an expanded Central Committee with none of the leaders as members. It was now that the magnates realized 'they were all in the same boat' because, Beria told his son, 'none of them would be Stalin's successor: he intended to choose an heir from the younger generation.' There was probably no secret heir: only a 'collective' could succeed Stalin.*

Stalin was satisfied by Molotov's ritual submission but asked him to return the secret protocols of the Ribbentrop Pact, clearly to form part of the case against him. As for Mikoyan, Stalin was shocked at his defiance. At Kuntsevo, in the absence of his two bugbears, Stalin grumbled to Malenkov and Beria:

'Look, Mikoyan even argued back!' In the days after the

---

* One of these heirs would probably have been Mikhail Suslov, fifty-one, Party Secretary, who combined the necessary ideological kudos (Zhdanov's successor as CC Ideology and International Relations chief) with the brutal commitment: he had purged Rostov in 1938, supervised the deportation of the Karachai during the war, suppressed the Baltics afterwards and presided over the anti-Semitic campaign. In 1948, he frequently met Stalin. Furthermore, he was personally ascetic. Beria loathed this 'Party rat', bespectacled, tall and thin as a 'tapeworm' with the voice of a 'grating castrate'. Roy Medvedev makes the educated guess that Suslov was 'Stalin's secret heir' in his new *Neizvestnyi Stalin* but there is no evidence of this. Suslov helped overthrow the de-Stalinizing Khrushchev in 1964 and became the éminence grise of the re-Stalinizing Brezhnev regime right up until his death in 1982. At the Plenum, Brezhnev himself was one of the young names elected to the Presidium. On his title, Stalin got his way: afterwards he appeared as the first 'Secretary' but no longer as 'General Secretary', a change that persuaded some historians that he lost power at the Plenum. Until recently, the only account of this extraordinary meeting was Simonov's but now we also have the memoirs of Mikoyan, Shepilov and Efremov.

Plenum, Molotov and Mikoyan continued to play their usual roles in the Government but Stalin was now supervising the climax of his Doctors' Plot, burning with fury against Professor Vinogradov for recommending his retirement. Yet it was typical of this stealthy old conspirator that he had suppressed his anger and waited eleven months to gather the evidence to destroy his own physician. Now it all came bursting out. Ordering Ignatiev to arrest Vinogradov, he shouted:

'Leg irons! Put him in irons!'

On 4 November, Vinogradov was arrested, touching every Politburo family because, as Sergo Beria wrote, he was 'our family doctor'.

* * *

Three days later, Svetlana, now entangled in another dangerous relationship, this time with Johnreed Svanidze, the son of those executed 'spies' Alyosha and Maria, brought over her two children to play with their grandfather. It was the Revolution holiday, the twentieth anniversary of Nadya's suicide. At the height of the Jewish Terror, Stalin really 'hit it off' with his half-Jewish grandson, Joseph Morozov, now seven, with his 'huge shiny Jewish eyes and long lashes'.

'What thoughtful eyes,' said Stalin, pouring the children thimbles of wine 'in the fashion of the Caucasus'. 'He's a smart boy.' Svetlana was touched. He had recently met Yakov's fifteen-year-old daughter, Gulia Djugashvili, whom he delighted by letting her serve the tea.

'Let the *khozyaika* do it!' he said, tousling her hair, kissing her. Gulia, better than anyone, catches his febrile excitement at the great enterprise of a new struggle: 'His face was very tired but he could hardly stay still.'

Stalin was infuriated by Riumin's slowness in beating the evidence out of the doctors, calling the MGB a herd of 'hippopotamuses'. He shouted at Ignatiev: 'Beat them! What are you? Do you want to be more humanitarian than Lenin who ordered Dzerzhinsky [founder of the Cheka] to throw Savinkov out of the window? ... Dzerzhinsky was no match for you but he didn't shirk the dirty work. You work like waiters in white gloves. If you want to be Chekists, take off your gloves.' Malenkov repeated Stalin's orders to use 'death blows'.

On 13 November, a few days after little Joseph's visit, he ordered the petrified Ignatiev to sack Riumin: 'Remove the Midget!' As for the doctors, 'Beat them until they confess! Beat, beat and beat again. Put them in chains, grind them into powder!' Stalin offered Vinogradov his life if he admitted 'the origins of your crimes ... You may address your testimony to the Leader who promises to save your life ... The whole world knows our Leader has always kept his promises.' Vinogradov knew no such thing.

'My situation is tragic,' the doctor replied. 'I have nothing to say.' He tried to name dead people whom his testimony could no longer harm. Stalin then lashed out at Ignatiev himself for his backsliding. Ignatiev suffered a heart attack and took to his bed.*

Now Stalin turned on his dogged retainer, Vlasik, destroying his debauched bodyguard just as he had the colourful Pauker in 1937. Vlasik had been on drinking terms with the homicidal doctors but he also knew too much, particularly that Stalin had been informed of Zhdanov's mistreatment and done nothing about it. Vlasik himself had probably only ignored Timashuk's letters on Stalin's lead. But now he was arrested, brought to Moscow and accused of concealing the evidence with Abakumov. He never betrayed the Boss. But his arrest was a cunning move because Vlasik's 'treason' helped cover Stalin's own role. All his mistresses and drinking cronies were arrested and questioned by Malenkov. Vlasik was tortured: 'My nerves were broken and I suffered a heart attack. I had months without sleep.' Stalin knew that Poskrebyshev, his other devoted old retainer, was best friends with Vlasik: had he played some role in suppressing the evidence against the killer doctors? He had distrusted Poskrebyshev ever since his article on Stalin's lemon-growing skills in 1949: was someone encouraging his grim amanuensis to step out of the shadows? But Stalin also learned that Poskrebyshev had shared Vlasik's orgies. He was mired in 'filthy affairs', said Molotov. 'Women can serve as agents!' Poskrebyshev arrived at Beria's house in a panic: everyone ran to Beria for reassurance but he himself was in equal danger.

Stalin sacked Poskrebyshev (his deputy, Chernukha, replaced him), moved him to be secretary of the Presidium and received

---

* The 'Midget' plunged with the same speed that he had risen to an obscure desk in the Ministry of State Control and was replaced by S. A. Goglidze. Earlier, Stalin turned against his instrument in the Mingrelian Case, Georgian MGB boss Rukhadze, who had boasted of his intimacy with the *Vozhd*. 'The question of Rukhadze's arrest is timely,' Stalin wrote to Mgeladze and Goglidze on 25 June 1952. 'Send him to Moscow where we'll decide his fate!' Riumin, Goglidze and Rukhadze were all shot after Stalin's death.

him for the last time on 1 December. He had removed his two most loyal servants. Stalin now had enough evidence to escalate the hysteria.

After seeing the heart-broken Poskrebyshev, Stalin unveiled the horror of what he called 'the killers in white coats' to the Presidium: 'You're like blind kittens,' he warned them at Kuntsevo. 'What will happen without me is that the country will die because you can't recognize your enemies.' Stalin explained to the 'blind kittens' that 'every Jew's a nationalist and an agent of American intelligence' who believes 'the USA saved their people'. He linked these killer doctors to the medical murderers of Gorky and Kuibyshev and repeated his mantra-like justification for 1937. A Great Terror was again imminent. He turned to the secret police: 'We must "treat" the GPU,' he said. 'They know they're sitting in shit!'

The magnates understood this ominous reference because an anti-Semitic trial was already underway in Prague where the Czech General Secretary, Rudolf Slansky, a Jew, was accused of 'anti-State conspiracy'. Three days later, he and ten other mainly Jewish Communists were hanged. Stalin planned something similar in Warsaw for he asked Bierut about his Jewish lieutenants:

'Who's dearer to you – Berman or Minc?'

Bierut to his credit replied:

'Both equally.'

Stalin ordered more schemes to assassinate Tito.

* * *

The Czech executions brought the noose closer to Molotov and Mikoyan who debated the court etiquette of condemned men. Stalin called them 'American or British spies'. 'To this day,' Molotov reminisced, 'I don't know precisely why. I sensed he held me in great distrust.'

They kept turning up for dinner as if nothing had happened. 'Stalin wasn't glad to see them', noticed Khrushchev. Finally Stalin banned Molotov and Mikoyan: 'I don't want those two coming around any more.' But the staff secretly told them when the dinners were taking place. So Stalin banned the staff from talking to them. Still, they kept turning up because Khrushchev, Beria, Malenkov and Bulganin, the Four, alerted them – a sign of growing sympathy, because they appreciated that 'they were trying to stay close to save themselves ... to stay alive.' Mikoyan asked Beria's advice:

'It would be better if you lay low,' he suggested.

'I'd like to see your face when ... you're sacked,' replied Mikoyan.

'That happened to me years ago,' said Beria.

Molotov and Mikoyan, realizing their lives were in danger, met in the Kremlin to decide what to do. Mikoyan had always trusted Molotov not to repeat his comments – and 'he never let me down or used my trust against me'. Both were hurt, and angry.

'It's practically impossible to rule a country in your seventies and decide all issues at the dinner-table,' Molotov said aloud at a meeting, a risky act of *lèse-majesté* that would have been unthinkable before the Plenum.*

The magnates would all have assisted in the liquidation of Molotov and Mikoyan. Stalin was old, raging, vindictive, paranoid and in a hurry. Yet his sense of the possible, the patience and charm that balanced his cruelty, and his roughness still worked, as he methodically, logically micromanaged the case. The unpredictable fury, frantic hastiness and implacable paranoia ironically drove the magnates closer together. Beria and Khrushchev were against Stalin's changes. Malenkov comforted Beria who comforted Mikoyan; Khrushchev and Beria comforted Molotov. During whispered consultations in the Kuntsevo lavatories, the Four laughed off Stalin's suspicions and mocked the Doctors' Plot.

'We should protect Molotov,' Beria told the other three, 'he's still needed by the Party.'

December 21 was officially Stalin's seventy-third birthday. Molotov and Mikoyan had not missed his birthday for thirty years. He rarely invited anyone – one just arrived for supper. The outcasts discussed what to do. Mikoyan thought that if they did not go, it would 'mean that we had changed our attitude to Stalin'. They phoned the Four, who told them they had to come.

So at 10 p.m. on the 21st, they arrived at Kuntsevo, where Stalin had hung plangent magazine photographs on the walls of children feeding lambs and famous historical scenes like Repin's *Reply of the Zaporozhian Cossacks*, his favourite picture. Svetlana was there too. Stalin was quiet but friendly, proud that he had given up smoking after fifty years. But he was already suffering from breathing difficulties. His face was livid and he had put on

* Voroshilov, sacked and humiliated, seems to have respectfully resented Stalin too. His wife used to whisper that Stalin was jealous of Klim's popularity – another unthinkable heresy.

weight, suggesting high blood pressure. He sipped light Georgian wine. As Svetlana was leaving, Stalin asked her:

'Do you need any money?'

'No,' she answered.

'You're only pretending. How much do you need?' He gave her 3,000 roubles for herself and for Yakov's daughter, Gulia, useful housekeeping money but Stalin thought it was millions. 'Buy yourself a car but show me your driving licence!' Underneath, Stalin was 'angry and indignant' that the Four had invited Molotov and Mikoyan.

'You think I don't realize you let Molotov and Mikoyan know? Stop this! I won't tolerate it,' he warned Khrushchev and Beria. He ordered them to give this message to the outcasts: 'It won't work: he's not your comrade any more and doesn't want you to visit him.' This really alarmed Mikoyan:

'It was becoming clear ... Stalin wanted to finish with us and that meant not only political, but physical destruction.'

The four last men standing decided, according to Beria's son, 'not to let Stalin set them against each other'. Stalin sometimes asked the Four: 'Are you forming a bloc against me?' In a sense they were, but none of them, not even Beria, had the will. Mikoyan discussed, probably with Molotov, the murder of Stalin but, as he later told Enver Hoxha, 'We gave up the idea because we were afraid the people and the Party would not understand.'

* * *

On 13 January 1953, after two, maybe even five, years' patient plotting, Stalin unleashed a wave of hysterical anti-Semitism by announcing the arrest of the doctors in *Pravda*: 'Ignoble Spies and Killers under the Mask of Professor-Doctors', a phrase that he had personally coined and scrawled on to the draft article which he annotated carefully.* On 20 January, Doctor Timashuk, Zhdanov's cardiologist, was called to the Kremlin where Malenkov gave her Stalin's personal thanks for her 'great courage' and the next day, she received the Order of Lenin. But Stalin was still using Ehrenburg as his decoy when a week later, on 27 January, he awarded him

---

* Stalin diligently added the following phrases in his handwriting: 'For a long time, Comrade Stalin warned us our success had shadows ... Thoughtlessness is good for our enemies who sabotage us ...' They were the 'slavemasters and cannibals of USA and England ... What about the people who inspired the killers? They can be sure we'll repay them ... As long as there is wrecking, we must kill thoughtlessness in our people.'

the Stalin Prize. Meanwhile throughout January and February, the arrests intensified.

The article revealed the lack of vigilance in the security services, a signal that Beria himself was a target. Not only were Beria's allies arrested in Georgia; his protégés in Moscow, such as the Chief of Staff, Shtemenko, were sacked. His ex-mistress V. Mataradze was also arrested. He 'expected the death-blow ... at any minute,' wrote his son. Beria 'expressed his disrespect for Stalin more and more boldly', noted Khrushchev, 'insultingly'. He even boasted to Kaganovich that 'Stalin doesn't realize if he tried to arrest me the Chekists would organize an insurrection.'

Apart from their fears for their own lives, the magnates were worried about nuclear war with America: Stalin, who was still stoking the Korean War, inconsistently swung between fear of war and the ideological conviction that it was inevitable. Beria, Khrushchev and Mikoyan feared the effect on America of Stalin's alarming unpredictability.* Stalin ringed Moscow with anti-aircraft missiles. As his own campaign inspired fear of American attack, he even discussed it with his bodyguards:

'What do you think – will America attack us or not?' he asked Kuntsevo's Deputy Commandant, Peter Lozgachev.

'I think they'd be afraid to,' replied the officer, at which Stalin suddenly flared up:

'Clear out – what are you doing here anyway? I didn't call you.' But he was sensitive to the guards in a way that was unthinkable with the politicians. He called in Lozgachev:

'Forget that I shouted at you but just remember: they will attack us. They're Imperialists, and they certainly will attack us. If we let them. That's the answer you should give.'

* * *

Stealing sleep on his sofas like 'a gundog', Stalin calmed himself by repeatedly playing Mozart's Piano Concerto No. 23. Visitors found him 'greatly changed' – a 'tired old man' who 'talked with difficulty' between 'long pauses' – but he managed his Terror tenaciously. Stalin orchestrated the drafting of a letter, to be signed by prominent Soviet Jews, begging for Jews to be deported

---

* After Stalin's death, Mikoyan told his sons that 'if we didn't have war when he was alive, we won't have war now.' This was ironic since for all Stalin's paranoia, inconsistencies and risk-taking in foreign policy, it was the clumsy and impulsive Khrushchev who brought the world closest to nuclear war during the Cuba Missile Crisis.

from the cities to protect them from the coming pogrom. The letter itself has never been found but Mikoyan confirmed that 'the voluntary-compulsory eviction of Jews' was being prepared. Kaganovich was hurt when he was asked to sign it but found a loyal way of refusing.

'Why won't you sign?' asked Stalin.

'I'm a member of the Politburo, not a Jewish public figure, and I'll only sign as a Politburo member.'

Stalin shrugged: 'All right.'

'If it's necessary, I'll write an article.'

'We might need an article,' said Stalin.

Even Kaganovich complained about Stalin, confiding in Mikoyan: 'It's so painful for me that I've always been consciously struggling against Zionism – and now I have to "sign off on it".' Khrushchev claimed that Kaganovich 'squirmed' but signed the letter. (Neither Kaganovich nor Khrushchev is a truthful witness when it comes to their own roles.) However Ehrenburg, who saw it and managed to avoid signing by appealing to Stalin, said it was addressed *to* the Politburo and signed by 'scholars and composers' which suggests that Kaganovich had managed to 'squirm' successfully. The latest evidence shows that two new camps were being built, perhaps for the Jews.

Stalin closely read the testimonies of the tortured doctors, sent daily by Ignatiev. He ordered the likely star in his Jewish Case, Object 12 (otherwise known as Polina Molotova), brought back to Moscow and interrogated. But the Jewish Case was not Stalin's only business during these weeks.

He rarely saw diplomats, but on 7 February, he received the young Argentine Ambassador, Leopoldo Bravo, who thought Stalin 'healthy, well-rested and agile in conversation'. Stalin admired Peron, offering generous loans because, despite his Fascist past, he appreciated Peron's anti-Americanism. But he was most interested in Eva Peron.*

'Tell me,' he asked Bravo, 'did she owe her rise to her character or her marriage to Colonel Peron?' Bravo was the second-last outsider to see Stalin alive.

Seven days later, at 8 p.m. on 17 February, Stalin visited the Little Corner for the last time to receive the Indian diplomat K. P. S. Menon. His mind was on his plots for he spent the

---

* Evita had died of ovarian cancer on 26 July 1952.

half-hour sketching wolves' heads on his pad, reflecting, 'The peasants are right to kill mad wolves.' At 10.30 p.m. Stalin left with Beria, Malenkov and Bulganin, probably for dinner at Kuntsevo.

He was still working up a case against Beria and his other Enemies: he ordered his new Georgian boss Mgeladze to get Beria to sign an order to attack the MGB, effectively against himself. Beria was not happy but had to agree. One of the Premier's last meetings was to order another assassination attempt on Tito.

At 8 p.m. on 27 February, Stalin arrived alone at the Bolshoi to watch *Swan Lake*. As he left, he asked his 'attachment', Colonel Kirillin, to thank the cast for him, speeding to Kuntsevo where he worked until about 3 a.m. He rose late, read the latest interrogations of the Jewish doctors and the reports from Korea, walked around the snowy garden and ordered Commandant Orlov:

'Brush the snow off the steps.' That afternoon, Stalin may have taken a steam bath. As he got older the heat eased the arthritis in his stiff arm, but Professor Vinogradov had banned *banyas* as bad for high blood pressure. Beria had told him he did not have to believe doctors. Now he threw caution to the winds. In the evening, he was driven into the Kremlin where he met his perennial companions, Beria, Khrushchev, Malenkov and Bulganin, in the cinema. Voroshilov joined them for the movie, noting Stalin was 'sprightly and cheerful'. Before he left, he arranged the menu with Deputy Commandant Lozgachev and ordered some bottles of weak Georgian wine.

At 11 p.m., Stalin and the Four drove out to the dacha for dinner. The Georgian buffet was served by Lozgachev and Matrena Butuzova (Valechka being off duty that night). Bulganin reported on the stalemate in Korea and Stalin decided to advise the Chinese and North Koreans to negotiate. Stalin called for more 'juice'. They talked about the doctors' interrogations. Beria is supposed to have said that Vinogradov had a 'long tongue', gossiping about Stalin's fainting spells.

'Right, what do you propose to do now?' said Stalin. 'Have the doctors confessed? Tell Ignatiev if he doesn't get full confessions out of them, we'll shorten him by a head.'

'They'll confess,' replied Beria. 'With the help of other patriots like Timashuk, we'll complete the investigation and come to you for permission to arrange a public trial.'

'Arrange it,' said Stalin. This is Khrushchev's account: he and Malenkov later blamed Beria for all Stalin's crimes but their own parts in the Doctors' Plot remain murky. It is unlikely that Beria was the only one encouraging Stalin.

The guests were longing to go home. Stalin was pleased with the suave Bulganin but growled that there were those in the leadership who thought they could get by on past merits.

'They are mistaken,' he said. In one account, he then stalked out of the room, leaving his guests alone. Perhaps he returned. The accounts seem contradictory – but then, so was his behaviour. At about 4 a.m., on the morning of Sunday, 1 March, Stalin finally saw them out. He was 'pretty drunk ... in very high spirits', boisterously jabbing Khrushchev in the stomach, crooning 'Nichik' in a Ukrainian accent.

The relieved Four asked the 'attachment', Colonel Khrustalev, for their limousines: Beria as usual shared his ZiS with Malenkov, Khrushchev with Bulganin. Stalin and the guard escorted them to their cars. Indoors, Stalin lay down on a pink-lined divan in the little dining room, with its pale wooden panelling, which was where this old itinerant conspirator had chosen to sleep that night – not helpless, not mad, but a brutal organizer of Terror at the awesome peak of his power.

'I'm going to sleep,' he cheerfully told Khrustalev. 'You can take a nap too. I won't be calling you.' The 'attachments' were pleased: Stalin had never given them a night off before. They closed the doors.

* * *

At midday that Sunday morning, the guards waited for the Boss to get up, sitting in their guardhouse that was linked to his rooms by a covered passageway twenty-five yards long. But there was 'no movement' all afternoon. The guards became anxious. Finally, at 6 p.m. Stalin switched on the light in the small dining room. He was obviously up at last. 'Thank God, we thought,' said Lozgachev, 'everything's all right.' He would call for them soon. But he did not.

One, three, four hours passed but Stalin did not appear. Something was wrong. Colonel Starostin, the senior 'attachment', tried to persuade Lozgachev to go in to check on the old man. 'I replied, "you're senior, you go in!"' recalled Lozgachev.

'I'm afraid,' said Starostin.

'What do you think I am? A hero?' retorted Lozgachev. They were not the only ones waiting: Khrushchev and the others expected the call to dinner. But the call did not come.

58

'I Did Him In!': the Patient and
his Trembling Doctors

At around 10 p.m., the CC mail arrived. The short, burly Lozgachev, gripping the papers, stepped nervously into the house, going from room to room. He was especially noisy because 'we were careful not to creep up on him … so he'd hear you coming.' He 'saw a terrible picture' in the small dining room. Stalin lay on the carpet in pyjama-bottoms and undershirt, leaning on one hand 'in a very awkward way'. He was conscious but helpless. When he heard Lozgachev's steps, he called him by 'weakly lifting his hand'. The guard ran to his side:

'What's wrong, Comrade Stalin?'

Stalin muttered something, 'Dzhh' but he could not speak. He was cold. There was a watch and a copy of *Pravda* on the floor beside him, a bottle of Narzan mineral water on the table. He had wet himself.

'Shall I call the doctor maybe?' asked Lozgachev.

'Dzhhh,' buzzed Stalin. 'Dzhhh.' Lozgachev picked up the watch: it had stopped at 6.30 when the stroke had hit him. Stalin gave a snore and seemed to fall asleep. Lozgachev dashed to the phone and called Starostin and Butuzova.

'Let's put him on the sofa, it's uncomfortable … on the floor,' he told them and the three lifted him on to the sofa. Lozgachev kept vigil – 'I didn't leave the Boss's side' – while Starostin telephoned MGB boss Ignatiev, in charge of Stalin's personal security since Vlasik's dismissal in May 1952. He was too frightened to decide anything. He had the power to call doctors himself but he had to act carefully. He ordered Starostin to call Beria and Malenkov. He probably also warned his friend Khrushchev because he needed protection against Beria who blamed him for the Doctors' Plot and the Mingrelian Case, and wanted his head. Beria was probably the last to find out.

Meanwhile the 'attachments' moved Stalin on to the sofa in the main dining room where the famous dinners took place, because it was airier there. He was very cold. They covered him with a blanket and Butuzova rolled his sleeves down. Starostin could not find Beria, probably entangled with his mistress somewhere, but contacted Malenkov who said he would search for him. Half an hour later, he called back:

'I haven't found Beria yet,' he admitted. After another half-hour, Beria called:

'Don't tell anybody about Comrade Stalin's illness,' he ordered, 'and don't call.' Lozgachev sat anxiously beside Stalin. He said his hair went grey that night. Malenkov had also called Khrushchev and Bulganin:

'The Chekists have rung from Stalin's place. They're very worried, they say something's happened to Stalin. We'd better get out there ...' Yet Khrushchev claimed that when they arrived at the guardhouse, they 'agreed' not to enter but to leave this sensitive matter to the guards. Stalin was now sleeping and would not want to be seen 'in such an unseemly state. So we went home.' The guards do not remember this visit. It seems more likely that Khrushchev, Bulganin, and probably Ignatiev, after frantic consultations, sent in Beria and Malenkov to find out if anything was really wrong. Somehow, during the night, the anti-Semitic campaign in *Pravda* was halted by someone – or was it Stalin's deliberate pause?*

At 3 a.m. on the morning of Monday 2 March, this little delegation arrived at Kuntsevo, over four hours after Starostin's first call to Malenkov. Both men acted in character: Beria was the dynamic, keyed-up (possibly drunk) adventurer, Malenkov, Stalin's punctilious, nervous clerk. While Beria marched into the hall, Malenkov noticed to his horror that his shoes were creaking and slipped them off. 'Malanya' tucked his shoes under his arm and tiptoed forward in his socks with the grace of a flabby dancer.

'What's wrong with the Boss?' They looked at the sleeping Generalissimo, snoring under his blanket, and then Beria turned on the 'attachments'.

'What do you mean ... starting a panic?' he swore at Lozgachev. 'The Boss is obviously sleeping peacefully. Let's go, Malenkov.'

'Malanya' tiptoed out in his socks while Lozgachev tried to

---

* Perhaps the other two waited outside in their ZiS. Ignatiev must also have been present. But already, it seems, Beria had taken control. No one knows who stopped the anti-Semitic media campaign that night. Suslov was the CC Secretary in charge of Ideology but who ordered him to put it on hold? It remains a mystery.

explain that 'Comrade Stalin was sick and needed medical attention'.

'Don't bother us, don't cause a panic and don't disturb Comrade Stalin!' The worried guards persisted but Beria swore:

'Who attached you fools to Comrade Stalin?'

The limousine drove away to meet the waiting Khrushchev and Bulganin. The bargaining for power surely started that night. Lozgachev returned to his vigil while Starostin and Butuzova went to sleep in the guardhouse.

Dawn broke over the firs and birches of Kuntsevo. It was now twelve hours since Stalin's stroke and he was still snoring on the sofa, wet from his own urine. The magnates surely discussed whether to call doctors. It was extraordinary that they had not called a doctor for twelve hours but it was an extraordinary situation. This is usually used as evidence that the magnates deliberately left Stalin without medical help in order to kill him. But in their fragile situation, at a court already bristling with spy-mania against the killer doctors, it was not just hyperbole to fear causing panic. Stalin's own doctor was being tortured merely for saying he should rest. If Stalin awoke feeling groggy, he would have regarded the very act of calling doctors as an attempt to seize power. Furthermore, they were so accustomed to his minute control that they could barely function on their own.

But the Four had those hours to divide power. The decision to do nothing suited everyone. Beria and Malenkov, Stalin's first deputies, in the Government and Party respectively, were legally in charge until a full meeting of the Politburo and then of the Central Committee. If Stalin was dying, they needed time to tie up power. Possibly for the same reasons, it was in the interests of Khrushchev and Bulganin to delay medical help until they had protected their position. They seem to have promised to protect Ignatiev and promote him to the CC Secretariat.

Beria, the only one of the Four fearing for his life at that time, had every reason to hope the hated Stalin would die. (Molotov and Mikoyan did not yet know Stalin was ill.) Yet Beria was never alone with Stalin – he took care that Malenkov was with him. He was not in control of the MGB, nor the Doctors' Plot, nor the bodyguards, hence his comment, 'Who attached you fools to Comrade Stalin?' Even though Beria has always been blamed for the delay, Khrushchev and Ignatiev may actually have been the cause of it.

Whatever their motives, the Four delayed calling a doctor until morning. We will never know if this was medically decisive or not. There was the possibility of an operation to clear the blood clot but doctors agree that it had to take place within hours of the stroke and who would have dared to authorize it? In the fifties, there was a remote chance of such an operation being successful: it was more likely to kill the patient. Melodramatic accounts of Stalin's death, of which there are no shortage, claim that Stalin was murdered. It is most likely that the denial of medical care made not the slightest difference. But Beria clearly thought it had:

'I did him in!' he later boasted to Molotov and Kaganovich. 'I saved you all!'

Recent research has suggested that he perhaps spiked Stalin's wine with a blood-thinning drug such as warfarin, which, over several days, might cause a stroke. Perhaps Khrushchev and the others were accomplices, hence the cover-up suited them all.

The Four now returned home to sleep, saying nothing to their families. At the imperial bedside, Lozgachev was desperate. He awoke Starostin and told him to call the Politburo – 'otherwise he'll die and it'll be curtains for you and me'. The terror that prevented the leaders calling the doctors now made the guards demand them. They phoned Malenkov who told them to send in Butuzova to take another look. She announced it was 'no ordinary sleep'. Malenkov called Beria.

'The boys have rung again from Stalin's place,' Malenkov told Khrushchev. 'They say there really is something wrong with Comrade Stalin. We'll have to go back again. We agreed the doctors would have to be called.' Beria and Malenkov were making all the decisions but which doctors to call? So they asked Tretyakov, Minister of Health, to select some *Russian* (not Jewish) doctors. Khrushchev arrived at Kuntsevo to tell the relieved 'attachments' the doctors were on their way. Colonel Tukov called Molotov, Mikoyan and Voroshilov, another sign that the Four had never approved of their exclusion.

'Call the Politburo. I'm on my way,' Molotov replied. When the phone rang in Voroshilov's home, the old Marshal was transformed: 'He became strong and organized,' wrote his wife in her unpublished diary, 'as I saw him in dangerous situations in the Civil and Great Patriotic Wars ... I understood unhappiness was coming. In great fear through running tears, I asked him, "What happened?" He embraced me. "Don't be afraid!"'

Voroshilov joined Kaganovich, Molotov and Mikoyan at the bedside. Molotov noticed 'Beria was in charge.' Stalin opened his eyes when Kaganovich arrived and looked at his lieutenants one by one – and then closed his eyes again. Unlike the overbearing Beria, Molotov and Kaganovich were deeply moved. Tears ran down their cheeks. Voroshilov reverently addressed the patient:

'Comrade Stalin, we're here, your loyal friends and comrades. How do you feel dear friend?'

Stalin's face was 'contorted'. He stirred but never fully regained consciousness. Khrushchev was 'very upset, I was very sorry we were losing Stalin'. He rushed home to wash and hurried back to Kuntsevo with no one in his family asking any questions. According to his son, Beria called home and told his wife about Stalin's illness: Nina burst into tears. Like most of the Politburo wives, even those about to be killed, she was inconsolable.

At 7 a.m., the doctors, led by Professor Lukomsky, finally arrived but they were a new team who had never worked with Stalin before. They were brought to the patient in the big dining room which must have reeked of stale urine. With their colleagues under torture, they were awestruck by the sanctity of Stalin and petrified by Beria's Mephistophelian presence lurking behind them. Their examination of the powerless, once omnipotent patient was a comedy of errors. 'They were all trembling like us,' observed Lozgachev. First, a dentist arrived to take out Stalin's false teeth but 'he was so frightened, they slipped out of his hands' and fell on to the floor. Then Lukomsky tried to take Stalin's shirt off in order to take his blood pressure. 'Their hands were trembling so much,' noticed Lozgachev, 'that they could not even get his shirt off.' Lukomsky was 'terrified to touch Stalin' and could not even get a grip on his pulse.

'Hold his hand properly!' Beria snapped at Lukomsky.

The clothes had to be cut away with scissors. 'I ripped open the shirt,' recalled Lozgachev. They began to examine the patient 'lying on a divan on his back, his head turned to the left, eyes closed, with moderate hyperaemia of the face ... There had been involuntary urination, [his clothes were soaked in urine.]' His pulse was 78; heartbeat 'faint'; blood pressure 190 over 110. His right side was paralysed while his left limbs quivered sometimes. His forehead was cooled. He was given a glass of 10 per cent magnesium sulphate. A neuropathologist, therapist and nurse stood vigil. The doctors asked the guards who had seen what. The guards now feared for their lives too: 'We thought, this is it then, they'll put us in a car and it's goodbye, we're done for!'

Stalin had suffered a cerebral catastrophe or, in their words, 'middle-left cerebral arterial haemorrhaging ... The patient's condition is extremely serious.' It was official at last. Stalin would not be able to work again.

The bodyguards stepped back and faded into the furniture. There was little the doctors could actually do. They recommended: 'Absolute quiet, leave the patient on the divan; leeches behind the ears (eight now in place); cold compress on the head ... No food today.' When he was fed, it was to be with a teaspoon 'to give liquid when there is no choking'. Oxygen cylinders were wheeled in. The doctors injected Stalin with camphor. They took a urine sample. The patient stirred. 'Stalin tried to cover himself.'

Svetlana, who had celebrated her birthday the night before, was called out of a French class and told, 'Malenkov wants you to come' to Kuntsevo. Khrushchev and Bulganin, both in tears, waved her car to a stop and hugged her.

'Beria and Malenkov will tell you everything.' It was again clear who was in charge. The bustle and noise astonished her: Kuntsevo had always been so quiet. She noticed that the doctors were strangers. When she came to the bedside, she kissed Stalin, realizing 'I loved my father more tenderly than I ever had before'.

When he was summoned, Vasily was so scared of his father that he thought he would have to present his work and pitifully arrived with his air-force maps. He was soon drunk. Throughout the next two days, he lurched in and out of the quiet sickroom, shouting:

'You swine haven't saved my father!' Svetlana was embarrassed to hear him. The leaders wondered whether to remove this loose cannon but Voroshilov took Vasily aside, soothing him:

'We're doing all we can to save your father's life.'

Once it was proved that he was incapacitated, Beria 'spewed forth his hatred of Stalin' but whenever his eyelids flickered or his eyes opened, Beria, terrified that he would recover, 'knelt and kissed his hand' like an Oriental vizier at a Sultan's bedside. When Stalin sank again into sleep, Beria virtually spat at him, revealing his reckless ambition, and lack of tact and prudence. The other magnates observed him silently but they were weeping for Stalin, their old but flawed friend, longtime leader, historical titan, and the supreme pontiff of their international creed, even as they sighed with relief that he was dying. Perhaps 20 million had been killed; 28 million deported, of whom 18 million had slaved in the Gulags. Yet, after so much slaughter, they were still believers.

At about ten, the entire old Politburo, from Beria and Khrushchev, to Molotov, Voroshilov and Mikoyan, headed to the Kremlin where they met at 10.40 a.m. in the Little Corner to agree a plan. Stalin's seat stood empty. They had restored themselves to power. For ten minutes, Dr Kuperin, the new Kremlevka chief, and Professor Tkachev nervously presented the report quoted above to the confused, upset and pent-up magnates. Afterwards, no one spoke, which made Kuperin even more nervous. It was perhaps too early to discuss what would happen next. Finally, Beria, who had already emerged as the most active leader, dismissed the doctors with this ominous order:

'You're responsible for Comrade Stalin's life. Do you under-stand? You must do everything possible and impossible to save Comrade Stalin!' Kuperin flinched, then withdrew. Malenkov, with whom Beria seemed to be co-ordinating everything, read out a decree for twenty-four hour vigils by the leaders in pairs. Then Beria and Malenkov sped back to Kuntsevo to watch over the patient. Molotov and Mikoyan were not asked to keep vigil: Beria ordered Mikoyan to stay in the Kremlin and run the country.

Back at Kuntsevo, when Malenkov was on vigil with Beria, they requested the doctor's prognosis. Kuperin displayed a chart of the blood circulation:

'You see the clotted blood vessel,' he lectured the Politburo as if to medical students. 'It's the size of a five-kopeck piece. Comrade Stalin would remain alive if the vessel had been cleared in time.'

'Who guarantees the life of Comrade Stalin?' Beria challenged the doctors to operate if they dared.

'No one dared,' said Lozgachev. Malenkov asked for the prognosis:

'Death is inevitable,' replied the doctors. But Malenkov did not want Stalin to die yet: there could be no interregnum.

At 8.30 p.m., the leaders, chaired now by Beria, met again for an hour at the Little Corner. Kuperin's official report did not present Stalin's condition as hopeless but the patient had deteriorated. His blood pressure was now 210 over 120, breathing and heartbeat irregular. Six to eight leeches were applied around his ears. Stalin received enemas of magnesium sulphate, and spoonfuls of sweet tea.

That evening, Lukomsky was joined by four more doctors including the eminent Professor Myasnikov: the Politburo knew the top doctors were all in prison.

At Kuntsevo, Dr Myasnikov found 'a short and fat' Stalin lying there 'in a heap ... His face was contorted ... The diagnosis seemed clear – a haemorrhage in the left cerebral hemisphere resulting from hypertension and sclerosis.' The doctors kept their detailed log, taking notes every twenty minutes. The magnates sat blearily in armchairs, stretching their legs, standing by the bedside, watching the doctors. These endless nights gave them the chance to plan the transfer of power.

'Malenkov gave us to understand,' wrote Myasnikov, 'he hoped that medical measures would succeed in prolonging the patient's life "for a sufficient period". We all realized he had in mind the time necessary for the organization of the new Government.'

There were no more official meetings in the Kremlin until 5 March. While Beria and Malenkov whispered about the distribution of offices, Khrushchev and Bulganin wondered how to prevent Beria grabbing control of the secret police. Beria's plans had been laid long before, probably with Malenkov: since no Georgian could rule Russia again, Malenkov planned to head the Government while remaining Secretary. Beria would seize his old fiefdom, the MGB/MVD.

Late at night, Mikoyan looked in on the dying man. Molotov was ill but he appeared from time to time, thinking of his Polina whom he hoped was alive in exile. He did not know she was being interrogated in the Lubianka. But that evening, on Beria's orders, her interrogations abruptly stopped. The interrogations of the doctors continued, however. The factotum of the Doctors' Plot, Ignatiev, was noticed nervously peering at the prone Stalin from the doorway. He was still terrified of him.

'Come in – don't be shy!' said Lozgachev. The next morning Khrushchev popped home to sleep and told his family that Stalin was ill.

There were moments when Stalin seemed to regain consciousness: they were feeding him with soup from a teaspoon, when he pointed up at one of the mawkish photographs on the wall of a girl feeding a lamb and then 'pointed at himself'. 'He sort of smiled,' thought Khrushchev. The magnates smiled back. Molotov thought it was an example of Stalin's self-deprecating wit. Beria fell to his knees and kissed Stalin's hand fervently. Stalin closed his eyes, 'never to open them again'. At 10.15 a.m. that morning the doctors reported that Stalin had worsened.

'The bastards have killed Father,' Vasily lurched in again. Khrushchev put his arm round this tiny terrified man, guiding him into the next room.

Beria, who went home for some lunch, was open about his relief. 'It will better for him to die,' he told his family. 'If he survives it will be as a vegetable.' Nina was still weeping about Stalin's death: 'You're a funny one, Nina. His death has saved your life.' Nina visited Svetlana daily to comfort her.

Late on the 4th, Stalin started to deteriorate, his breathing becoming shorter and shallower, the Cheyne-Stokes breathing pattern of a patient losing strength. Beria and Malenkov checked up on their Second Eleven of doctors. That night, three surprised prisoners, tortured daily in the Doctors' Plot, were led off for another session. But this time, their torturers was not interested in the Zionist conspiracy but politely asked their medical advice.

'My uncle is very sick,' said the interrogator, and is experiencing 'this Cheyne-Stokes breathing. What do you think this means?'

'If you're expecting to inherit from your uncle,' replied the professor, who had not lost his Jewish wit, 'consider it's in your pocket.' Another distinguished professor, Yakov Rapoport, was asked to name the specialists who should treat this 'sick uncle'. Rapoport named Vinogradov and the other doctors under arrest. But the interrogator asked if Doctors Kuperin and Lukomsky were good too. He was shocked when Rapoport replied, 'Only one of the four's a competent physician but on a much lower level than the men in prison.' The interrogations continued but the investigators had lost interest. Sometimes they fell asleep during the sessions. The prisoners knew nothing.

At 11.30 p.m. Stalin retched. There were long pauses between ragged breaths. Kuperin told the assembled grandees, who watched in awed silence, that the situation was critical.

'Take all measures to save Comrade Stalin!' ordered the excited Beria. So the doctors continued to struggle to keep the dying Generalissimo alive. An artificial respirator was wheeled in and never used but it was accompanied by young technicians who stared 'goggle-eyed' at the surreal things happening all around them.

On the 5th, Stalin suddenly paled and his breathing became shallower with longer intervals. The pulse was fast and faint. He started to wiggle his head. There were spasms in his left arm and leg. At midday, Stalin vomited blood. The latest research has uncovered a first draft of the doctors' medical notes, which reveal that his stomach was haemorrhaging, a detail deleted from the final report. Perhaps it was cut because it might suggest poisoning. Warfarin might well have caused such bleeding, which does indeed look suspicious, but it may just have marked the collapse of a sick old body.

'Come quickly, Stalin's had a setback!' Malenkov told Khrushchev. The magnates rushed back. Stalin's pulse slowed. At 3.35 p.m., his breathing stopped for five seconds every two or three minutes. He was sinking fast. Beria, Khrushchev and Malenkov had received the Politburo's permission to ensure that Stalin's 'documents and papers, both current and archival, are put in proper order'. Now, leaving the other two at the bedside, Beria sped into the Kremlin to begin the process of searching Stalin's safe and files for incriminating documents. First there may have been a will: Lenin had left a testament and Stalin had talked of recording his thoughts. If so, Beria now destroyed it. The files were filled with denunciations and evidence against all the leaders. There would have been evidence of Beria's dubious role in Baku during the Civil War and there would also have been the missing documents that revealed the bloody role of Malenkov and Khrushchev in the Great Terror, the Leningrad Case and the Doctors' Plot. That afternoon, these three began the destruction of documents. This successfully protected the historical reputation of Khrushchev and Malenkov, even if Beria's was already beyond repair.*

Beria returned. The doctors reported on the latest decline. An official meeting of the whole regime, three-hundred senior officials, was set for that evening. Now the magnates gathered informally in one of the other rooms to form the new Government. Beria and his 'billygoat' Malenkov had prearranged the 'collective leadership', taking turns proposing the appointments. Molotov and Mikoyan returned to the Presidium, shrunk

---

* Five telling letters were supposedly found under a sheet of newspaper in Stalin's desk, Khrushchev told A. V. Snegov, who could only remember three of them to the historian Roy Medvedev. The first was Lenin's letter of 1923 demanding that Stalin apologize for his rudeness to his wife, Krupskaya. The second was Bukharin's last plea: 'Koba, why do you need me to die?' The third was from Tito in 1950. It was said to read: 'Stop sending assassins to murder me ... If this doesn't stop, I will send a man to Moscow and there'll be no need to send any more.'

to its previous size. Molotov returned as Foreign Minister, Mikoyan as Minister of Internal and External Trade. Khrushchev remained one of the senior Secretaries but he was excluded from the Government. Beria was dominant, reuniting the MVD and MGB while remaining First Deputy Premier. Malenkov succeeded to both Stalin's posts of Premier and Secretary. Yet the military were also strengthened: Defence Minister Bulganin's new deputies were the old paladins, Zhukov and Vasilevsky. Voroshilov became President. No wonder Beria was exultant.

The illegitimate Mingrelian, trained as an architect but seasoned in the police, was already dreaming of ruling the Imperium, one of the nuclear superpowers, and becoming an international statesman, not just a secret policeman any more. He had survived against all the odds; he was free of fear. He could unleash his loathing of Stalin: 'That scoundrel! That filth! Thank God we're free of him!' He could expose that phoney Generalissimo: 'He didn't win the war!' he was soon telling his confidants. 'We won the war!' Furthermore, 'We would have avoided the war!' He harnessed the phrase 'the cult of personality' to denounce Stalin. He would free the nationalities, open the economy, liberate East Germany, empty the labour camps with a beneficent amnesty and expose the Doctors' Plot. He did not doubt for a moment that his superior intelligence and fresh anti-Bolshevik ideas would triumph. Even Molotov realized 'he was a man of the future'.

If his policies seemed to prefigure Gorbachev's reforms, Beria always remained 'just a policeman', in Stalin's words, for he was itching to avenge himself on those, such as Vlasik, who had betrayed him. He was not the successor, merely the strongman in a 'collective leadership'. But many of the new potentates feared him, his brutality and his bid for popularity by de-Bolshevizing the regime. Beria underestimated Khrushchev and the marshals. None the less, it was a remarkable achievement.

Afterwards, the magnates gathered beside the wheezing patient. Beria approached the bedside and announced melodramatically like a Crown Prince in a movie:

'Comrade Stalin, all the members of the Politburo are here. Speak to us!' There was no reaction. Voroshilov pulled Beria back:

'Let the bodyguards and staff come to the bedside – he knows them intimately.' Colonel Khrustalev stood by the bed and spoke to him. Stalin did not open his eyes. The leaders queued to bid goodbye, forming up in pairs like a crocodile of schoolchildren in order of importance, with Beria and Malenkov first, then Voroshilov, Molotov, Kaganovich and Mikoyan, followed by the younger leaders. They shook his hand ritually. Malenkov claimed that Stalin squeezed his fingers, passing him the succession.

Leaving just Bulganin at the bedside, the potentates then rushed to the Kremlin where the Presidium, Council of Ministers and Supreme Soviet Presidium gathered to rubber-stamp the new Government: they removed Stalin as Premier but strangely left him as a Presidium member. The three hundred or so officials confirmed the prearranged deal. There was a sense of 'relief' among the magnates.*

They expected a call from Bulganin to announce Stalin's death but none came. Stalin was still holding out and they headed back to Kuntsevo. After 9 p.m., he started to sweat. His pulse was weak, his lips turned blue. The Politburo, Svetlana Stalin, Valechka, the guards gathered round the sofa. The junior leaders crowded outside, watching from the doorway.

At 9.30 p.m., Stalin's breaths were forty-eight a minute. His heartbeat grew fainter. At 9.40 p.m. with everyone watching, the doctors gave Stalin oxygen. His pulse virtually disappeared. The doctors proposed an injection of camphor and adrenalin to stimulate his heart. It should have been Vasily and Svetlana's decision but they just watched. Beria gave the order. Stalin gave a shiver after the injection and became increasingly breathless. He slowly began to drown in his own fluids.

'Take Svetlana away,' commanded Beria to prevent her seeing this dread vision – but no one moved.

'His face was discoloured,' wrote Svetlana, 'his features becoming unrecognizable ... He literally choked to death as we watched. The death agony was terrible ... At the last minute, he opened his eyes. It was a terrible look, either mad or angry and full of the fear

* Khrushchev and Bulganin did protect Ignatiev who became a CC Secretary but Beria later managed to get him sacked for his part in the Doctors' Plot. Yet he was merely reprimanded and sent to Bashkiria as First Secretary before moving on to run Tataria. Khrushchev presented him as a victim not a monster in his Secret Speech. Most of the top Chekists of the Doctors' Plot, including Ogoltsov, who had commanded Mikhoels's murder, and Ryasnoi, were protected under Khrushchev, and later under Brezhnev. Khrushchev's punishment of Stalin's crimes was highly selective. Ignatiev received medals on his seventieth birthday in 1974. The luckiest of Stalin's MGB bosses, he was the only one to die, respected, in his bed aged seventy-nine in 1983.

of death.' Suddenly the rhythm of his breathing changed. His left hand rose. A nurse thought it was 'like a greeting'. He 'seemed either to be pointing upwards somewhere or threatening us all ...' observed Svetlana. It was more likely that he was simply clawing the air for oxygen. 'Then the next moment, his spirit after one last effort tore itself from his body.' A woman doctor burst into tears and threw her arms around the devastated Svetlana.

The struggle was not over yet. A Brobdingnagian doctor fell on the corpse and started artificial respiration, athletically massaging the chest. It was so painful to watch that Khrushchev felt sorry for Stalin:

'Stop it please! Can't you see the man's dead? What do you want? You won't bring him back to life. He's already dead,' Khrushchev called out, showing his impulsive authority in the first order not given by Beria or Malenkov. Stalin's features became 'pale ... serene, beautiful, imperturbable,' wrote Svetlana. 'We all stood frozen and silent.'

Once again they formed up in that uneasy crocodile: Beria darted forward and ritually kissed the warm body first, the equivalent of wrenching a dead king's ring off his finger. The others queued up to kiss him. Voroshilov, Kaganovich, Bulganin, Khrushchev and Malenkov were sobbing with Svetlana. Molotov cried, mourning Stalin despite his own imminent liquidation and that of his wife. Mikoyan hid his feelings but 'it may be said I was lucky'. Beria was not crying: indeed he was 'radiant' and 'regenerated' – a bulging but effervescent grey toad, glistening with ill-concealed relish. He strode through the weeping potentates into the hall. The sepulchral silence around the deathbed was suddenly 'shattered by the sound of his loud voice, the ring of triumph unconcealed', in Svetlana's words:

'Khrustalev, the car!' he bellowed, heading for the Kremlin.

'He's off to take power,' Mikoyan said to Khrushchev. Svetlana noticed 'they were all terrified of him.' They looked after him – and then with frenzied haste, 'the members of the government rushed for the door ...' Mikoyan and Bulganin remained a little longer but then they too called for their limousines. The *Instantsiya* had left the building. The colossus had vanished, leaving only the husk of an old man on a sofa in an ugly suburban house.

Just the servants and family remained: 'cooks, chauffeurs and watchmen, gardeners and women who waited at table' now emerged out of the background 'to say goodbye'. Many were sobbing, with rough bodyguards wiping their eyes with their sleeves 'like children'. A weeping old nurse gave them valerian drops. Svetlana watched numbly. Some servants started to turn off the lights and tidy up.

Then Stalin's closest companion, the comfort of the cruel loneliness of this unparalleled monster, Valechka, who was now aged thirty-eight and had worked with Stalin since she was twenty, pushed through the crying maids, 'dropped heavily to her knees' and threw herself on to the corpse with all the uninhibited grief of the ordinary people. This cheerful but utterly discreet woman, who had seen so much, was convinced to her dying day that 'no better man ever walked the earth'. Laying her head squarely on his chest, Valechka, with tears pouring down the cheeks of 'her round face', 'wailed at the top of her voice as the women in the villages do. She went on for a long time and nobody tried to stop her.'

Postscript

Stalin was embalmed. On 9 March 1953, Molotov, Beria and Khrushchev spoke at his funeral, after which he was laid in the Mausoleum beside Lenin. Polina Molotova was still in the Lubianka. The next day, Beria invited Molotov to his office there. When Molotov arrived, Beria rushed ahead to greet Polina: 'A heroine!' he declared. Her first question was 'How's Stalin?' She fainted when she learned he was dead. Molotov took her home.

Beria moved to liberalize the regime and arrested those responsible for the Doctors' Plot but his proposal to free East Germany provoked an uprising that alarmed the other magnates. Khrushchev began to plan Beria's destruction. He won over Premier Malenkov and Defence Minister Bulganin. Molotov still admired Beria but agreed to support Khrushchev because of the German crisis. Surprisingly, President Voroshilov supported Beria. When he was consulted, Mikoyan said he distrusted Khrushchev because he was so close to Beria and Malenkov. Khrushchev did not tell Mikoyan the whole story, but he agreed that Beria should be demoted to Petroleum Minister. Kaganovich typically sat on the fence. But Marshal Zhukov and his generals provided the muscle.

On 25 June, Beria was swinging gaily on his hammock at his dacha, singing Georgian songs. He had been called to a special meeting of the Presidium. Nina warned him to be careful but he was not worried because he explained that Molotov supported him. At about 1 p.m. next day, Khrushchev stood up at the meeting and attacked Beria. Bulganin joined in but Mikoyan was surprised to hear that Beria was to be arrested.

'What's going on, Nikita?' Beria asked. 'Why are you searching for fleas in my trousers?' When it was Malenkov's turn to support the coup, he lost his nerve and gave a secret signal to the generals waiting outside. Marshal Zhukov burst in and seized Beria.

Nina Beria, her son Sergo and daughter-in-law Martha Peshkova were also arrested and imprisoned. From his cell, Beria bombarded Malenkov with letters begging for his help and mercy for his family. On 22 December, he, along with Merkulov, Dekanozov and Kobulov, was sentenced to death by a secret political court for treason and terrorism, charges of which these killers were obviously innocent.

Beria was stripped to his underwear; hands manacled and attached to a hook on the wall. He frantically begged to be allowed to live, making such a noise that a towel was stuffed in his mouth. His eyes bulged over the bandage wrapped round his face. His executioner – General Batitsky (later promoted to Marshal for his role) – fired directly into Beria's forehead. He was cremated. His protégé and then rival, Abakumov, was tried for the Leningrad Case and shot in December 1954. Many of Stalin's crimes were blamed on them.

When the new leaders began to release prisoners, their reactions were often similar. Kira Alliluyeva, herself newly released, picked up her mother Zhenya from the Lubianka.

'So finally, Stalin saved us after all!' declared Zhenya.

'You fool!' exclaimed Kira. 'Stalin's dead!' Zhenya admired Stalin up to her death in 1974. Her sister-in-law Anna Redens, like Budyonny's second wife, Olga, had lost her mind in confinement and never recovered. Vlasik returned broken from prison but he and Poskrebyshev remained friends, both dying in the mid-sixties.

Khrushchev emerged as the dominant leader. Malenkov was removed as Premier and replaced by Bulganin. In 1956, Khrushchev, backed by Mikoyan, famously denounced Stalin's crimes in his 'Secret Speech'. Five years later, Stalin's body was removed from the Mausoleum and buried in the Kremlin wall.

In 1957, Molotov, Kaganovich and Malenkov, backed by Voroshilov and Bulganin, managed to overthrow Khrushchev in the Presidium. However Khrushchev mobilized the Central Committee, flying in his supporters in planes organized by Marshal Zhukov.

At a Plenum, Stalin's murderous magnates scrambled to blame one another for their crimes: 'Sleeves rolled up, axe in hand, they lopped off heads,' Zhukov accused them – and Khrushchev himself. Khrushchev attacked Malenkov who replied: 'Only you are completely pure, Comrade Khrushchev!' Kaganovich insisted 'the whole Politburo signed' the death lists. Khrushchev accused him back but Kaganovich roared: 'Didn't you sign death warrants in Ukraine?' Finally Khrushchev shouted: 'All of us taken together aren't worth Stalin's shit!' As a recent historian has written, 'this was certainly no Nuremberg' but it was the 'closest Stalin's henchmen came to a day of reckoning'. Molotov, Kaganovich and Malenkov were sacked. Kaganovich and Malenkov were despatched to run a potash factory and powerstation respectively in distant regions. Malenkov's daughter says her father found this minor job a calming relief; Kaganovich's grandson reports that 'Iron Lazar' immediately discarded his notorious temper and never shouted again, becoming a cosy grandfather.

Molotov became Soviet Ambassador to Mongolia and then, in 1960, Soviet Representative at the UN Atomic Agency in Vienna so that he was present, ignored in the background, when President Kennedy and Khrushchev met there with their delegations in June 1961.

Khrushchev, like Stalin before him, became Premier as well as First Secretary. Marshal Zhukov became Defence Minister as a reward for his help but his pugnacity and fame threatened the increasingly vainglorious Khrushchev who sacked him for 'Bonapartism'. By 1960, when the senile Voroshilov retired as President, Khrushchev and Mikoyan were the last of Stalin's magnates in power. During the Cuba Missile Crisis, it was Mikoyan who flew to Havana, accompanied by his son Sergo, to persuade Castro to agree to Khrushchev's compromise, and then on to Washington to talk to Kennedy. Mikoyan, who had helped carry Lenin's coffin, also attended JFK's funeral.

After the scare of the Missile Crisis and the autocratic folly of his agricultural panaceas, Khrushchev was overthrown in 1964 by a cabal of Stalin's young stars, Brezhnev, Kosygin and their *éminence grise*, Suslov, who ruled until their deaths in the eighties. Mikoyan survived even this upheaval and became President, retiring in 1965.

The old magnates found it hard to cope with their fall. They had expected to be arrested so were all relieved to be alive. When they left their apartments in the Kremlin in 1957, Kaganovich and Andreyev found they did not even own their own towels or sheets. Many of them were granted apartments in the palatial Granovsky buildings where the shrewd Molotov managed to secure two apartments as well as a dacha. Kaganovich and Malenkov retired to spartan but large apartments in another building on the

Frunze Embankment but avoided each other. These famous and blood-spattered old pensioners spent their retirements writing their memoirs, receiving Stalinist admirers, avoiding the hostile stares of former victims they encountered in the street, applying for readmission to the Party, and shuffling through papers in the Lenin Library: they were non-people but spotting them became a thrilling form of living archaeology.

Happily and lovingly reunited, Molotov and Polina remained unapologetic Stalinists: Svetlana wrote that visiting them was like entering a 'palaeontological museum'. The prickly disdain between Molotov and Kaganovich lasted until their deaths but was as nothing compared to their loathing for Khrushchev. He admitted being 'up to his elbows' in the blood of his victims and 'that burdens my soul'. He defied his successors by dictating his selectively honest memoirs, dying in 1971. Despite his illnesses, Andreyev died the same year: the commemorative plaque on the wall outside Granovsky makes him the last of Stalin's butchers to be celebrated. Mikoyan wrote frank but equally selective memoirs until his death in 1978.

Three others survived into another era: while Polina died in 1970, Molotov left his remorseless reminiscences, to posterity, in conversations with a sympathetic journalist. He survived to see the accession of Gorbachev, passing away in 1986. Malenkov remained a Stalinist but enjoyed the poetry of Mandelstam and rediscovered the Christian faith of his childhood that may have been a sort of repentance. In 1988, he was buried beneath a cross and the (utterly inappropriate) statue of the 'lion of justice', sculpted by his grandson. Kaganovich, ever the most cautious and pusillanimous, outlived everyone to witness the beginning of the end of the Soviet Union that he had helped build, dying in 1991.

Their families have enjoyed mixed fortunes and take very different views of Stalin and their parents' roles: most became editors, architects or scientists. Vasily Stalin was sent to prison, released, remarried and finally died tragically of alcoholism in 1962. His son Alexander, who uses his mother's name, is a respected theatrical designer in Moscow, but his two children by Marshal Timoshenko's daughter both died young – of alcoholism. Svetlana Alliluyeva defected and returned to Russia and then left again, married an American by whom she had a daughter, lived in Harvard and Cambridge, made and lost a fortune with her beautifully written memoirs, finally found herself without means in sheltered housing in Bristol and is now living alone in obscurity in the American Midwest. Having embraced liberalism and rejected Stalinism, she has displayed both her father's intelligence and his paranoia. Her Russian children, Joseph Morozov and Katya Zhdanova, are both doctors in Russia.

Yury Zhdanov remarried and returned to academia, becoming Rector of Rostov-on-Don University where he still lives as an honoured professor emeritus, admirer of Stalin and defender of his father. Artyom Sergeev remained in the military, rose to Lieutenant-General and lives outside Moscow. The rest of the Alliluyev family remains close: Kira Alliluyeva worked as an actress and is as as irrepressible today as she was when she refused to climb under Stalin's billiard table in 1937.

Stepan Mikoyan flourished as a test pilot and also rose to Lieutenant-General. His younger brother Sergo edited a magazine on Latin America. Both live in Moscow. Kaganovich's daughter Maya married and had children and cared for her father in old age, only outliving him for a few years.

Sergo Beria and Martha Peshkova were released and moved to Kiev with Beria's widow Nina, who never stopped loving her husband. In 1965, Martha divorced Sergo who continued to work as a missile scientist under his mother's name, Gegechkori. Shortly before his death in 2000, he published his memoirs and appealed to the Russian Supreme Court to rehabilitate his father. The Court upheld the trumped-up charges against Beria. Martha, who has kept her looks, still lives in her large dacha on the old estate of her grandfather, Gorky. Beria's charming grandchildren, who use the Peshkov name, are an interior decorator, an art academic and an electronics expert.

Lilya Drozhdova, Beria's 'last love', never betrayed him. She lives in Moscow and, in her early sixties, remains beautiful.

Budyonny's third wife still lives in his apartment on Granovsky filled with life-sized paintings of the Marshal on horseback. The apartments there are now worth over a million dollars so that the Molotovs rent out theirs to American investment bankers, perhaps proving right Stalin's suspicions of Vyacheslav's 'Rightist' tendencies. Molotov's grandson Vyacheslav Nikonov was one of the leading liberals of 1991, who helped open up the KGB archives and became one of President Yeltsin's top advisers, serving on his re-election team in 1996. He now runs one of Moscow's most respected political think-tanks and is writing his grandfather's biography.

Perhaps Stalin was right about the Mikoyans too: Anastas's grandson Stas became a Soviet rock star, set up his own record label during the nineties and is now the leading Russian rock impresario, their Richard Branson. Beria's hope that his grandchildren would study at Oxford was not realized but his great-grandson has just left the English public school, Rugby. Malenkov's daughter Volya, an architect, followed her father's later religious journey to become a builder of churches in her old age: her business cards feature pictures of the churches she has built. She and her brothers, both professors of science, remained convinced of their father's innocence.

Stalin's confidant Candide Charkviani survived to see an independent Georgia in 1991 and wrote his unpublished memoirs. His son Gela served as the chief political adviser to former President Shevardnadze since 1993.

To this day, the friendships and feuds of Stalin's reign survive among the children of the magnates. The families of the grandees who remained in power, Mikoyans, Khrushchevs and Budyonnys, are regarded as a Soviet aristocracy even now. Nina Budyonny, still a Stalinist, is best friends with Julia Khrushcheva, who is not. The friendship of Marshals Budyonny and Zhukov is not only enjoyed by their daughters but by their grandchildren too. Stepan Mikoyan remains friends with Natasha Andreyeva even though the former is a liberal, the latter a diehard Stalinist. Artyom Sergeev remains in contact with those close pals, Nadya Vlasik and Natasha Poskrebysheva. But the Malenkovs and Andreyevs still despise Khrushchev.

It is only natural that all defend their fathers' parts in the Terror. The Khrushchevs and Mikoyans have the courage and decency to admit the truth, reflecting their fathers' attempts to correct the worst of Stalin's (and their own) atrocities. None the less, many of the magnates' children still enthusiastically defend the Terror and many prefer to blame Beria for Stalin's own crimes.

Martha Peshkova, who was brought up with Gorky in Sorrento, who still believes her grandfather and father were murdered, who as a child played with Stalin, reflects that 'Stalin was as clever as he was cruel. Politics in Stalin's time was like a closed jar with intriguers fighting one another to the death. What a frightening time! But if Beria had had his way after Stalin, he'd have improved the lifestyle of the country and we'd probably have avoided the destruction and poverty of today!'

Vladimir Alliluyev (Redens), whose father was shot on Stalin's orders and whose mother lost her mind in his prisons, insists he was a 'great man with good and bad sides'. Natasha Poskrebysheva, whose mother was shot by Stalin, admires him enormously and claims to be his daughter. Natasha Andreyeva, who lives in straitened circumstances in an apartment filled with her father's art deco Kremlin furniture, remains the most aggressively Stalinist. 'I have inherited my mother's intuition,' she warned this author during his interview for this book. 'I can see an Enemy by their eyes. Are you an Enemy? Are you afraid of the Red Flag?' She still supports the Terror: 'We had to destroy spies before the war.' Despite the bulging file chronicling her father's murderous spree in 1937, she asserts his innocence and claims, 'Khrushchev's dirty hands killed far more in Ukraine!' The 'system', not Stalin, were to blame for any 'mistakes', Andreyeva concludes. 'But you Western capitalists have killed many more in Russia with your AIDS than Stalin ever did!'

Those who lived the extraordinary, terrible and privileged life as a child of Stalin's grandees remain linked together and it is no surprise that their attitudes defy time – and the fate of their own families. The passionately optimistic ideals of Marxism-Leninism-Stalinism and the imperial triumphs of the Generalissimo's armies remain as potent and persuasive as the presence of Stalin himself, of whom they are never free. Old Molotov was asked if he dreamed about Stalin: 'Not often but sometimes. The circumstances are very unusual. I'm in some sort of destroyed city and I can't find a way out. Afterwards, I meet HIM …'

Source Notes

The full and extremely extensive references for this book are available in the hardback edition and also on the author's website at:

http://www.simonsebagmontefiore.com

Many of the sources for this work are totally new. However, to make the paperback a manageable and readable size, the author and publisher have decided not to include them in the paperback. We hope the readers will agree that, for most, the balance of convenience is best served by this policy.

Select Bibliography

Primary

Antipenko, N. A. 'Tyl Fronta', *Novy Mir*, no. 8, 1965
Alanbrooke, Viscount, *War Diaries 1939–45*, London 2001
Alexandrov, G. V. *Epokha I kino*, Moscow 1983
Alliluyeva, Svetlana, *Twenty Letters to a Friend*, London 1967
Alliluyeva, Svetlana, *Only One Year*, London 1971
Alliluyev, Sergei, *Proidennyi put*, Moscow 1946
Alliluyeva, Anna S., *Vospominaniya*, Moscow 1946
Alliluyev, Sergei, and Anna Alliluyeva, (ed. David Tutaev), *The Alliluyev Memoirs*, London 1968
Babel, Isaac, *1920 Diary*, New Haven, CT 1990
Babel, Isaac, *Collected Stories*, London 1994
Baibakov, N. K., *Delo zhizni: zapiski neftyanika*, Moscow 1984
Bazhanov, Boris, *Bazhanov and the Damnation of Stalin*, Athens, OH 1990
Berezhkov, Valentin, *Kak ia stal perevodchikom Stalina*, Moscow 1963
Berezhkov, Valentin, *History in the Making, Memoirs of WW2 Diplomacy*, Moscow 1983

L. P. BERIA:

Beria, L. P., 'Lavrenty Beria: Pizma iz tyuemnogo bunkera', *Istochnik*, no. 4, 1994
Beria, L. P., *On the History of Bolshevik Organizations in Transcaucasia*, Moscow 1949
Beria, Nina, 'Letters to LP Beria', *Istochnik*, no. 2, 1994
Beria, Nina, 'Letter to Members of Presidium 7 January 1954', *Vlast*, no. 34, 2001
Beria, Sergo, *Beria My Father: Inside Stalin's Kremlin*, London 2001
The Beria Affair, The Meetings Signalling the End of Stalinism, (ed. D. M. Sickle), New York 1992.
Beria Affair, CC Plenum 12–7 July 1953, *Izvestiya TsK KPSS*, nos. 1 and 2, 1991
Bessedovsky, G., *Revelations of a Soviet Diplomat*, London 1931
Birse, A. H., *Memoirs of an Interpreter*, London 1967
Bohlen, Charles E., *Witness to History*, London 1973

Bolshakov, I. G., 'Letter to AN Poskrebyshev on film Tarzan', *Istochnik*, no. 4, 1999

Bukharin, Nikolai, *How It All Began*, New York 1998

Budyonny, S. M., *Proidennyi put*, Moscow 1968

Budyonny, S. M., (ed. Nina Budyonny), *Notes*, unpublished

Cadogan, Alexander, *The Diaries of Sir Alexander Cadogan*, London 1971

Charkviani, Candide, *Memoirs on Stalin*, unpublished

Chikobava, Arnold, 'Kogda ix kak eto bylo', *Ezhegodnik iberiysko-kavkazskogo yazykoznaniya*, vol. 12, 1985

W. S. CHURCHILL:

Churchill, Winston S., *Second World War*, London 1951

Churchill and Stalin, documents from British Archives, FCO Historians

Dan, Lydia, 'Bukharin o Staline', *Noviy Zhurnal*, 75 (Mar. 1964).

Davies, Joseph E., *Mission to Moscow*, London 1942

Dedijer, V., *Tito Speaks*, London 1953

Dekanozov, Reginald, *Some Episodes of the History of Soviet–German Relations Before the War*, unpublished

Deriabin, Peter, *Inside Stalin's Kremlin*, Dulles, VA 1998

Dmitrov, Georgi (ed. Ivo Banac), *The Diary of Georgi Dmitrov 1933–49*, New Haven, CT 2003

Dobrynin, Anatoly, *In Confidence: Moscow's Ambassador to Six Cold War Presidents*, Washington DC 2001

Djilas, Milovan, *Conversations with Stalin*, NY 1962

Djilas, Milovan, *Wartime*, London 1980

Djugashvili, Gulia, *Ded, Otets, Mat i Drugie*, Moscow 1993

Eden, A., *Memoirs, Facing the Dictators*, London 1962

Efimov, Boris, *Mikhail Koltsov, Kakim On Byl*, Moscow 1965

Efremov, L. N., Memoir of Plenum, *Dosye Glastnosty, Spetsvypusk* 2001

Ehrenburg, Ilya, *Men, Years, Life,* London 1966

Eisenhower, D. D., *Crusade in Europe*, London 1948

Fedorenko, N. T., 'Zapiski diplomata. Rabota s Molotovym', *Novaya i Noveishaya Istoriya*, no. 4, 1991

Gaulle, Charles de, *Memoires de Guerre*, Paris 1959

Gaulle, Charles de, *Complete War Memoirs of Charles de Gaulle 1940–46*, NY 1964

Ginsburg, Eugenia S., *Journey into the Whirlwind*, NY 1967

Gnedin, E. A., *Katastrofa I vtoroe rozhdenie*, Amsterdam 1997

Gromyko, Andrei, *Memoirs*, London 1989

Gromyko, Andrei, *Pamyatnoye*, Moscow 1990

Grossman, Vasily, *Life and Fate*, London 1985

Grossman, Vasily, 'Mama', *Znamya*, vol. 5, 1989

Guinzburg, S. Z., *O proshlom, dlya budushchego*, Moscow 1984

Gunther, John, *Inside Russia Today*, NY 1962

Harriman, Averell W., and Elie Abel, *Special Envoy to Churchill and Stalin, 1941–6*, NY 1975

Hilger, Gustav and Alfred Mayer, *Incompatible Allies: A Memoir History of German–Soviet Relations 1918–41*, NY 1953

Hoxha, Enver (ed. Jon Halliday), *Artful Albanian: the Memoirs of Enver Hoxha*, London 1986

Iskander, Fasil, *Sandro of Chegem*, London 1979

L. M. KAGANOVICH:

Kaganovich, L. M. (ed. Felix Chuev), *Tak Govoril Kaganovich*, Moscow 1992

Kaganovich, L. M., *Pamiatniye Zapiski*, Moscow 1997

Kennan, George, *Memoirs*, Boston 1967

Kamov, B., 'Smert Nikolaia Yezhova', *Iunost*, no. 8, 1993

Kavtaradze, Sergo, *Memoirs*, unpublished

Kavtaradze, Sergo, Interview, *Literaturnaya Rossiya*, no. 12, 1989

N. S. KHRUSHCHEV:

Khrushchev, N. S. (Jerrold Schecter and Vyacheslav Luchkov, eds), *Khrushchev Remembers: the Glasnost Tapes*, NY 1990

Khrushchev, N. S., *Khrushchev Remembers*, London 1971/London 1974

Khrushchev, N, S. 'Memuary Nikity Sergeevicha Khrushcheva', *Voprosy Istorii* 1990–95

Khrushchev, Sergei, *Nikita Khrushchev and the Creation of a Superpower*, Pennsylvania 2001

Koniev, I. S., *Sorok pyatyi*, Moscow 1966

Koniev, I. S., *Zapiski kommanduushchego frontom*, Moscow 1991

Kopelev, Lev, *No Jail for Thought*, London 1977

Krivitsky, Walter, *I Was Stalin's Agent*, London 1940

Kravchenko, Victor, *I Chose Freedom*, NY 1946

Krementsov, Nikolai, *Stalinist Science*, Princeton, NJ 1997

Kuznetsov, N. G., Memoirs, *Voprosy Istorii*, no. 4–5, 1965

Larina, Anna, *This I Cannot Forget, The Memoirs of Nikolai Bukharin's Widow*, London 1993

Lunghi, Hugh, *Minutes of Meeting between Generalissimo JV Stalin and Admiral Mountbatten at Babelsberg, Germany, 25 July 1945 at 12.45 hours*, unpublished

Lunghi, Hugh, *Tribute to Sir Winston Churchill at Churchill Memorial Concert*, Blenheim Palace 1 March 1997

Lunghi, Hugh, *Meeting Stalin*, European Service, General News Talk, BBC, 1 March 1963

Maisky, Ivan, *Memoirs of a Soviet Ambassador*, London 1967

Malenkov, Andrei, *O moem otse Georgie Malenkove*, Moscow 1992

Malyshev, V. A., Notes, *Istochnik*, no. 5, 1997

Mandelstam, Nadezhda, *Hope Against Hope*, London 1999

Meretskov, K. A., *Na sluzhbe narodu*, Moscow 1970

Mgeladze, Akaki, *Stalin, kakim ya ego znal*, Tbilisi 2001

A. I. MIKOYAN:

Mikoyan, Anastas, *Tak bylo*, Moscow 2000

Mikoyan, N., 'A Month at Beria's Dacha', *Forum*, no. 3, 1995

Mikoyan, Stepan, *Memoirs of Military Test-flying and Life with the Kremlin's Elite*, London 1999

V. M. MOLOTOV:

Molotov, V. M. (ed. Felix Chuev), *Molotov Remembers*, Chicago 1993

Molotov, V. M. (ed. Felix Chuev), *Sto Sorok Besed s Molotovym*, Moscow 1991

Muratov, E., '6 Chasov s I V Stalinym na Prieme v Kremle', *Neva*, no. 7, 1993

Myasnikov, A. I., Medical notes on JV Stalin's Illness, *Literaturnaya Gazeta*, 1 March 1989

Nutsibidze, Ketevan and Shalva, *Nakaduli*, Tbilisi 1993

Okunevskaya, Tatiana, *Tatianin den*, Moscow, 1998

Orlov, Alexander, *Secret History of Stalin's Crimes*, London 1954

Ortenberg, David, 'U Zhukova v Perkbushkogo', *Krasnaya Zvezda*, 30 Nov. 1991

Ortenberg David, *Stalin Shcherbakov Mekhlis i Drugie,* Moscow 1995

Pahlavi, HIM Mohammed Reza, *Mission for My Country*, London 1961

Parrott, Cecil, *The Serpent and the Nightingale*, London 1977

Patolichev, N. S., *Ispytanie na zrelost*, Moscow 1977

Pavlov, V. N., Avtobiographicheskie Zametki', *Novaya i Noveishaya Istoriya*, 2000, no. 4

Plisetskaya, Maya, and Tim Scholl, *I, Maya*, New Haven, CT 2001

Platonov, Andrei, *The Foundation Pit*, London 1996

Pronin, Vasily P., 'Gorod u linii fronta', in *Moskovskie Novosti*, no. 21, 26 Mar./2 Apr. 1995, p. 14

Pronin, Vasily P, *Gorod-voin, Bitva za Moskvu*, Moscow 1966

Pirozhkova, A. N., *At His Side, The Last Ten Years of Isaac Babel*, VT 1996

Putin, Vladimir, *First Person*, NY 2000

Rapoport, Yakov, *The Doctors' Plot, Stalin's Last Crime*, London 1991

Razgon, Lev, *Plen v svoem otechestve*, Moscow 1994

Roberts, Frank, *Dealing with Dictators*, London 1991

Rokossovsky, K., *Soldatskiy dolg*, Moscow 1968

Romanov, A. I., *The Nights are Longest There*, Boston 1972

Rosliakov, K., *Ubiistvo Kirova. Polititcheskie i ugolovnye prestupleniya v 1930 godakh*, Leningrad 1991

Rybin, A. G., *Stalin v Oktyabre 1941*, Moscow undated

Rybin, A. T., 'Ryadom s IV Stalinym', *Soziologicheskie Issledovaniya*, no. 3, 1988

Rybin, A. T., *Stalin i Zhukov*, Moscow 1994

Rybin, A. T., *Ryadom Stalinym v Bolshom Teatre*, Moscow undated

Rybin A. T., *Kto Otravil Stalina?*, Moscow undated

Rybin, A. T., *Next to Stalin: Notes of a Bodyguard*, Toronto, 1996

Rzhevskaya E., 'B tot den pozdhnei oseniu' in SS Smirnov, *Marshal Zhukov: kakim my ego pomnim*, Moscow 1988

Sakharov, Andrei, *Memoirs*, NY 1992

Sbornik zakonodatelnykh i normativnykh actov o repressiyakh i reabilitatsii, Moscow 1993

Serge, Victor, *From Lenin to Stalin*, London 1937

Shakhurin, A., 'Memoirs' *Voprosy Istorii*, no. 3, 1975

Shepilov, D., *Neprimknuvshii*, Moscow 2001

Shepilov, D., Vospominaniya, *Voprosy Istoriii*, 1998, vols 3, 4, 5, 6

Shreider, M., *NKVD iznutri. Zapiski chekisti*, Moscow 1995

Sholokhov, Mikhail, *Virgin Soil Upturned*, London 1988

Shostakovich, Dmitri, *Testimony The Memoirs of Dmitri Shostakovich As related to and edited by Solomon Volkov*, London 1981

Shtemenko, S. M., *Generalnyi shtab v gody voiny*, Moscow 1981

Simonov, K., 'Glazami cheloveka moego pokoleniya', *Znamya*, no. 3, 1988

Simonov, K., 'Conversations with Admiral IS Isakov,' *Znamya*, no. 5, 1988

Simonov K., 'Zametki k biografii GK Zhukova', *Voprosy Istorii*, nos. 6, 7, 8, 9, 10, 12, 1987

Simonov, K., *Diaries*, RGALI, Moscow

Smith, Walter Bedell, *My Three Years in Moscow*, NY 1948

Smirnoff, S. S., *G. K. Zhukov: Kakim My Ego Pomnium*, Moscow 1988

J. V. STALIN:

Lih, Lars T., Oleg V. Naumov, and Oleg V. Khlevniuk (eds), *Stalin's Letters to Molotov*, New Haven, CT 1995

O. V. Khlevniuk, R. W. Davies, L. P. Kosheleva, E. A. Rees, and L. A. Rogovaya, *Stalin i Kaganovich Perepiska 1931–36*, Moscow 2001

Stalin, J. V., *Sochineniya*, Moscow 1946–1952

Stalin, J. V., *Ekonomicheskiye problemy socializma v SSSR*, Moscow 1953

Stalin, *Vystuplenie na prieme v Kremle v chest kommanduyushchikh voiskami Krasnoi Armii* in *Works* (ed. Robert McNeal), vol. II 1941–5, Stanford, CA 1967

'Stalin, Molotov Zhdanov o vtoroy serii filma Ivan Grozny', *Moskovskie Novosti*, no. 37, 7 Aug. 1988

'Josif Stalin v obiatiiakh semyii: iz lichnogo arkiva', *Istochnik*, Moscow 1993

Starostin, Nikolai, *Futbol skvoz gody*, Moscow 1992

Sudoplatov, Pavel, and Anatoli Sudoplatov, with Jerrold I. and Leona Schecter, *Special Tasks, the Memoirs of an Unwanted Witness, a Soviet Spymaster*, London 1994

Sukhanov, N. N., *The Russian Revolution 1917. A personal record*, London 1955

Sukhanov, D. M., *Memoirs*, Library of Congress

Timashuk, Lydia, 'Tsel byla spasti zhizn bolnogo. Pisma Lidii Timashuk',
    Istochnik, no. 1, 1997
Trotsky, Leon, *My Life*, NY 1930
Trotsky, Leon, *Stalin*, London 1968
Trail, Vera, *Memoirs of Yezhov*, unpublished
Trifinov, Yury, *House on the Embankment*, Evansto, IL 1999
Troyanovsky, Oleg, *Cherez godiy rasstoyaniya*, Moscow 1997
Valedinsky, I., 'Vospominaniya o vstrechah s tov. Stalinym IV, *Muzei
    Revolutsii*, vol. 23, bk. 2, Moscow 1992
Vaschchenko, N., *Za Grani Istorii*, Moscow 1998
Vasilevsky, A. M., *Delo Vsey Moey Zhizni*, Moscow 1978
Vishnevskaya, Galina, *Galina, Russian Story*, London 1984

N. S. VLASIK:
Vlasik, N. S., 'Moya Biografiya', *Shpion*, vols 8, 9
'Vlasik Case: Interrogations', *VIZh*, no. 12, 1989
Voronov, N.V., *Memoir of NV Voronov*, Volkogonov Collection, Reel 8,
    6 June 1994

K. E. VOROSHILOV:
Voroshilov, K. E., *Stalin and the Armed Foces of the USSR*, Moscow 1951
Voroshilov, K. E., *Razzkaz o zhizni. Vospominaniya*, Moscow 1968
Werth, Alexander, *Year of Stalingrad*, London 1946
Werth, Alexander, *Russia at War*, London 1964

G. YAGODA:
Litvin, A. L., (ed.), *Genrikh Yagoda Narkom vnutrennikh del SSSR, Generalnyi
    kommissar gosudarstvennoy besopastnosti*, Kazan 1997
Yakovlev, A. S., *Tsel zhizni*, Moscow 1970
Yerofeev, Vladimir, 'Ten Years of Secretaryship', *International Affairs*,
    vol. 9, 1991
Zakharov, M. V., *Generalnyi shtab v predvoennye gody*, Moscow 1989
Zbarsky, Ilya, and Samuel Hutchinson, *Lenin's Embalmers*, London 1998

A. A. ZHDANOV:
A. A. Zhdanov, 'Doklad Zhdanova o zhurnalakh Zvezda i Leningrad',
    Bolshevik, nos. 17–18, September 1946
Zhdanov, Yury, 'O kritie i samokritike v nauchnoy rabote', *Bolshevik*,
    1951, no. 21. pp. 28–43
Zhdanov, Yury, 'Vo mgle protivorechii,' *Voprosy Filosofii*, 1993, no. 7,
    p. 74

G.K. ZHUKOV:
Zhukov, G. K., *Vospominaniya i razmyshleniya*, 10th edn, Moscow
    1990
Zhukov, G. K., 'Korotko o Staline', *Pravda*, 20 January 1989
Zhukov, G. K., 'Na Kurskoy Duge', *VIZh*, Aug. 1967

Secondary

Antonov-Ovseenko, Anton, *The Time of Stalin: Portrait of a Tyranny*, NY 1980

Antonov-Ovseenko, Anton, *Beria*, Moscow 1999

Applebaum, Anne, *GULAG: A History of the Soviet Concentration Camps*, London 2003

Aptekov, Pavel, and Olga Dudorova, 'Peace and statistics of losses: Unheeded Warning and the Winter War', *Slavic Military Studies*, vol. 10, no. 1, March 1997

Avtorkhanov, Abdurakhman, *Stalin and the Soviet Communist Party*, London 1959

Axell, Albert, *Stalin's War Through the Eyes of his Commanders*, London 1997

Babichenko, D., and M. Sidorov, 'Nevelika pobeda', *Itogi*, no. 31 (269), 2001

Barsukov, N., 'Mart 1953. Stranitsy Istorii KPSS', *Pravda*, 27 Oct. 1989

Barbosa, Adalberto Zelmar, *El Federalismo Bloquista: Bravo o el pragmatismo politico*, Buenos Aires 1988

Beevor, Antony, *Stalingrad*, London 1998

Beevor, Antony, *Berlin The Downfall 1945*, London 2002

Biagi, Enzo, *Svetlana: The Inside Story*, London, 1967

Bialer, Seweryn (ed.), *Stalin and his Generals*, NY 1969

Bloch, Michael, *Ribbentrop*, London 1994

Blotsky, Oleg, *Vladimir Putin The Story of My Life*, Moscow 2002

Bobrenov, V., and V. Wiazantsev, 'Marshal protiv Marshala', *Armia*, 1993 nos 8, 9, 10

Bortoli, Georges, *Death of Stalin*, London 1975

Bos, W. H., and E. M. Farber, 'Joseph Stalin's Psoriasis: Its Treatment and the Consequences', *Cutis*, vol. 59, Apr. 1997

Brackman, Roman, *The Secret File of Joseph Stalin*, London 2001

Brent, Jonathan, and Vladimir P. Naumov, *Stalin's Last Crime: The Doctors' Plot*, London 2003

Briukhanov, B. B., and E. N. Shoshkov, *Opravdaniyu ne podlezhit: Ezhov I ezhovshchina*, St Petersburg 1998

Bromage, Bernard, *Molotov*, London 1956

Brooks, Jeffrey, *Thank You Comrade Stalin*, Princeton 2000

Burleigh, Michael, *The Third Reich, A New History*, London 2000

Carlton, David, *Churchill and the Soviet Union*, London 2000

Carr, E. H., *What is History?* London 1964

Carswell, John, *The Exile, the Life of Ivy Litvinov*, London 1980

Chase, William J., *Enemies Within the Gates? The Comintern and the Stalinist Repression 1934–39*, New Haven, CT 2001

Chinsky, Pavel, *Staline archives inedites*, Paris 2001

Chisholm, Anne, and Michael Davie, *Beaverbrook: A Life*, London 1992

Chubariyan, Alexander O., and Vladimir O. Pechatnov, '"Molotov the Liberal": Stalin's 1945 Criticism of his Deputy', *Cold War History*, vol. 1, no. 1, Aug. 2000

Clark, Alan, *Barbarossa*, London 1996

Cohen, Stephen, *Bukharin and the Bolshevik Revolution, A Political Biography 1888–1938*, London 1973

Cohen, Y., 'Des lettres comme action: Stalin au début des années 1930 vu depuis les fonds Kaganovich', *Cahiers du Monde russe*, no. 3, vol. 38, July–September 1997

Conquest, Robert, *The Great Terror, Stalin's Purge of the Thirties*, London 1968

Conquest, Robert, *The Nation Killers*, London 1972

Conquest, Robert, *Inside Stalin's Secret Police: NKVD Politics 1936–1939*, Stanford, CA 1985

Conquest, Robert, *Harvest of Sorrow: Soviet Collectivization and the Terror/Famine*, London 1986

Conquest, Robert, *Stalin and the Kirov Murder*, Oxford 1989

Conquest, Robert, *Stalin: Breaker of Nations*, London 1991

Coox, Alvin D, 'L'affaire Liushkov: Anatomy of a Defector', *Soviet Studies*, 1967, vol. 8, no. 3

Coox, Alvin D., 'The Lesser of Two Hells: NKVD General GS Lyushkov's Defection to Japan 1938–45', *Slavic Military Studies*, vol. 11, no. 3, Sept. 1998

Curtis, J. A. E. , *Manuscripts Don't Burn: Mikhail Bulgakov A Life in Letters and Diaries*, London 1991

Dallin, Alexander, and F. I. Firsov (ed.), *Dmitrov and Stalin 1934–1943*, New Haven CT 2000

Davies, R. W. 'The Sypsov/Lominadze Affair', *Soviet Studies*, 33, no. 1, Jan. 1981

Easter, Gerald, *Reconstructing the State: Personal Networks and Elite Identity in Soviet Russia*, Cambridge 2000

Ebon, M., *Malenkov*, London 1953

Erickson, John, *Soviet High Command A Military/Political History 1918–41*, London 1962

Erickson, John, *The Road to Stalingrad*, London 1983

Erickson,John, *The Road to Berlin*, London 1996

Fairbanks, C. H., 'Clientilism and higher politics in Georgia 1949–1953', *Transcaucasia*, Ann Arbor, MI 1983

Fay, Laurel, *Shostakovich, A Life*, Oxford 2001

Figes, Orlando, *A People's Tragedy: The Russian Revolution 1891–1924*, London 1996

Figes, Orlando, *Natasha's Dance, A Cultural History of Russia*, London 2002

Fitzpatrick, Sheila, *The Cultural Front, Power and Culture in Revolutionary Russia*, Ithaca, NY 1992

Fitzpatrick, Sheila, *Everyday Stalinism, Ordinary Life in Extraordinary Times: Soviet Russia in the 1930s*, Oxford 1999

Fitzpatrick, Sheila, *Stalinism: New Directions*, London 2000

Garros, V., N. Korenevskaya, and T. Lahusen, *Intimacy and Terror: Soviet Diaries of the 1930s*, New Press 1995

Gazur, Edward P., *Secret Assignment: The FBI's KGB General*, NY 2001

Gendlin, L., *Confession of Stalin's Lover*, Moscow 1991

Getty, J. A., and R. T. Manning (eds), *Stalinist Terror. New Perspectives*, Cambridge 1993

Getty, J. Arch, *Origins of the Great Purges: the Soviet CP Reconsidered 1933–1938*, Cambridge 1985

Getty, J. Arch, and Oleg V. Naumov, *The Road to Terror: Stalin and the Self-Destruction of the Bolsheviks 1932–9*, New Haven, CT 1999

Gilbert, Martin, *Churchill: A Life*, London 1991

Glantz, David, 'The Kharkov Operation May 1942', *Slavic Military Studies*, vol. 5, Sept 1992, Dec 1992

Glantz, David, *Zhukov's Greatest Defeat: the Red Army's Epic Disaster in Operation Mars 1942*, Manchester 2000

Glantz, David, *Barbarossa: Hitler's Invasion of Russia 1941*, London 2001

Glantz, David, 'Forgotten Battles of German Soviet War – the Winter Campaign: the Crimean Counter-Offensive', *Slavic Military Studies*, vol. 14, March 2001

Gleason, Abbott, *Totalitarianism: The Inner History of the Cold War*, Oxford 2001

Gobarev, Victor, 'Soviet Military Plans and Actions During the First Berlin Crisis', *Slavic Military Studies*, vol. 10, Sept. 1997

Gobarev, Victor, 'Khrushchev and the Military: Historical and Psychological Analysis', *Slavic Military Studies*, vol. 11, 1998

Goncharov, Sergei N., John W. Lewis, and Xue Litai, *Uncertain Partners: Stalin, Mao and the Korean War*, Stanford, CA 1993

Gorlizki, Yoram, *Stalin's Cabinet: the Politburo and Decision-Making in the Post-War Years*, in Christopher Read, *The Stalin Years: A Reader*, London 2003

Gorlov, S. A., 'Peregovory VM Molotova v Berline v Noiabre 1940 goda', *VIZh*, vols. 6, 7, 1992

Gorodetsky, Gabriel, *Stafford Cripps' Mission to Moscow 1940–2*, London 1984

Gorodetsky, Gabriel, *Grand Delusion; Stalin and the German Invasion of Russia*, New Haven, CT 1999

Gromov, E., *Stalin: Vlast I Iskusstro*, Moscow 1998

Hahn, Werner, *Postwar Soviet Politics: the Fall of Zhdanov and the Defeat of Moderation 1946–53*, Ithaca, NY 1982

Harris, Jonathan, 'The Origins of the Conflict between Malenkov and Zhdanov 1939–1941', *Slavic Review*, vol. 35, no. 2, 1976

Holloway, David, *Stalin and the Bomb: the Soviet Union and Atomic Energy 1939–1956*, New Haven, CT 1994

Hosking, Geoffrey, *A History of the Soviet Union 1917–1991*, London 1992

Ivanov, S. P., *Shtab armeiskii, Shtab frontovoi*, Moscow 1990

Y. Izumov, 'Why Khrushchev took revenge on Stalin', *Dosye Glasnost*, no. 12, 2001

Jansen, Marc, and Nikita Petrov, *Stalin's Loyal Executioner: People's Commissar Nikolai Ezhov 1895–1940*, Stanford, CA 2002

Jeffery, Inez Cope, *Inside Russia: Life and Times of Zoya Zarubina*, Austin TX 1999

Jenkins, Roy, *Truman*, London 1986

Karpov, Vladimir, 'Tainaya rasprava nad marshalom Zhukovym', *Vestnik Protivovozdushnoy Oborony*, no. 7, 8, 17 and 19 August 1991

Karpov, Vladimir, 'Rasprava Stalina nad Marshalom Zhukovym', *Vestnik Protivovozdushnoy Oborony*, 7–8, 1992

Karpov, Vladimir, *Marshal Zhukov: Opala*, Moscow 1994

Karpov, Vladimir, *Rastrelyanniye Marshaly*, Moscow 2000

'Career of Communications Worker Vladimir Kazakov', *Nezavisimoe Voennoe Obrozenie*, vol. 19, 2002, p. 5

Kahan, Stuart, *Wolf of the Kremlin*, NY 1987

Kemp-Welch, A., *Stalin and the Literary Intelligentsia*, London 1991

Kenez, Peter, *Cinema and Soviet Society from the Revolution to the Death of Stalin*, London 2001

Khlevniuk, Oleg, *Stalin NKVD i sovetskoe obshchestvo*, Moscow 1993

Khlevniuk, Oleg, *In Stalin's Shadow, the Career of Sergo Ordzhonikidze*, NY 1993

Khlevniuk, Oleg, *Stalinskoe Politburo v 1930 gody. Sbornik dokumentov*, Moscow 1995

Khlevniuk, Oleg, *Le Circle du Kremlin, Staline et le bureau politique dans les années 30: les jeux du pouvoir*, Paris 1996

Khlevniuk, Oleg, Y. Gorlizki, A. I. Miniuk, M. Y. Prozymenshikov, L. A. Rogovaya, and S. V. Somonova (eds), *Politburo TsK BKP i Sovet Ministrov SSSR 1945–53*, Moscow 2002

Kirilina, A. A. *L'Assassinat de Kirov*, Paris 1995

Amy Knight, *Beria: Stalin's First Lieutenant*, Princeton, NJ 1993

Amy Knight, *Who Killed Kirov? The Kremlin's Greatest Mystery*, NY 1999

Kojevnikov, Alexei, *Games of Stalinist Democracy, Ideological discussions in Soviet sciences 1947–1952* in Sheila Fitzpatrick, *Stalinism: New Directions*, London 2000

Kotkin, Stephen, *Magnetic Mountain: Stalinism as a Civilization*, University of California, 1995

Korol, V. E., A. I. Sliusarenko, and I. U., Nikolaenko, 'Tragic 1941 and Ukraine: New Aspect of Problems', *Slavic Military Studies*, vol. 11, no. 1, March 1998

Kostyrchenko, Gennadi, *Out of the Red Shadows, Anti-Semitism in Stalin's Russia*, NY 1995

Kulikov, E., M. Miakgov, and O. Rzheshevsky, *Voina 1941–1945*, Moscow 2001

Kun, Miklos, *Stalin: An Unknown Portrait*, NY 2003

Kuznetsov, I. I., 'Stalin's Minister VI Abakumov', *Slavic Military Studies*, vol. 12, no. 1, March 1999

Kuznetsov, I. I., 'KGB General Naum Isakovich Eitingon 1899–1991',
    Slavic Military Studies, vol. 14, no. 1, Mar. 2001
Lakoba, S., Ocherki po politicheskoy istorii Abkhazii, Sukhumi 1990
Lastours, S. de, Toukhatchevski, Paris 1996
Lebedeva, N. S., Katyn, Moscow 1994
Levashov, Viktor, Mikhoels: Ubiystvo Mikhoelsa, Moscow 1998
Lewis, Jonathan, and Phillip Whitehead, Stalin: Time for Judgement,
    London 1990
Leyda, Jay, Kino: History of Russian and Soviet Film, London 1973
Likhanov, D., and V. Nikonov, 'La pochistil OGPU', in Sovershenno
    sekretno 1992, 4
Loguinov, V., Taini Stalina, General Vlasik i yego soratniki, Moscow 2000
Malia, Martin, The Soviet Tragedy: A History of Socialism 1917–2000,
    NY 1994
Marcucci, L., Il Commissario di Ferro di Stalin, Turin 1997
Mariamov, Grigory, Kremlevskiy tsenzor: Stalin smotrit kino, Moscow
    1986
McLoughlin, Barry, and Kevin McDermott, Stalin's Terror: High Politics
    and Mass Repression in the Soviet Union, London 2002
Medvedev, Roy, Let History Judge, London 1976
Medvedev, Roy, On Stalin and Stalinism, Oxford 1979
Medvedev, Roy, Khrushchev, NY 1983
Medvedev, Roy, All Stalin's Men: Six Who Carried the Bloody Purges,
    NY 1985
Medvedev, Roy, Neizvestnyi Stalin, Moscow 2001
Medvedev, Roy and Zhores, Politicheskiy dnevnik, Amsterdam 1975
Medvedev, Zhores, The Rise and Fall of T. D. Lysenko, NY 1969
Mee, Charles L. Jr, Meeting at Potsdam, London 1975
Merridale, Catherine, Night of Stone, Death and Memory in Russia, London
    2000
Merridale, C., Moscow Politics and the Rise of Stalin: the Communist Party in
    the Capital 1925–32, Basingstoke/London 1990
Morgan, Ted, FDR, London 1985
Munn, Michael, John Wayne: the Man Behind the Myth, London 2003
Naumov, V., 1941 god, Dokumenty, Moscow 2000
Nekrasov, V. F., Beria: Konets kariery, Moscow 1991
Nekrasov, V. F., Zhelezni Narkomy, Moscow 1995
Nenarakov, A, 'Shatbs/Kapitan, Marshall, Vrag Naroda, Yegorov', Rodina,
    no. 10, 1989
Nevakivi, Jukka (ed.), Finnish-Soviet Relations 1944–1948, Helsinki 1994
Nevezhin, V. A., 'Stalin's 5th May Address: the experience of
    Interpretation', Slavic Military Studies, vol. 11, no. 1, March 1998
Nove, Alex (ed.), The Stalin Phenomenon, New York 1993
Overy, Richard, Russia's War, London 1997
Papkov, S. A., Stalinsky Terror v Sibiri 1928–1941, Novosibirsk 1997

Parrish, Michael, *The Lesser Terror: Soviet State Securiy 1939–1953*, London 1996

Parrish, Michael, 'The Last Relic: Serov', no. 3, *Slavic Military Studies*, vol. 10, Sept. 1997

Parrish, Michael, 'Downfall of the Iron Commissar NI Yezhov 1938–1940', *Slavic Military Studies*, vol. 14, no. 2, June 2001

Pavlenko, N. G., 'GK Zhukov: Iz neopublikovanykh vospominaniy', *Kommunist*, vol. 14, Sept. 1988

Pavlenko, N. G., 'Razmyshleniya o sudbe polkovodtsa', *VIZh*, nos 10, 11, 12, 1988

Pechatov, Vladimir O., 'The Allies are pressing on you to break your will ...' *Foreign Policy Correspondence between Stalin and Molotov and other Politburo members, September 1945/December 1946*, Working Paper 26, Cold War International History Project, Woodrow Wilson International Centre for Scholars, Washington DC

Perrie, Maureen, *The Cult of Ivan the Terrible in Stalin's Russia*, London 2001

Perlmutter, Amos, *A Not So Grand Alliance 1943–45*, Columbia, MO 1994

Petrov, N. V., and K. V. Scorkin, *Kto Rukovodil NKVD 1934–41: Spravochnik*, Moscow 1999

Pipes, Richard, *The Formation of the Soviet Union: Communism and Nationalism 1917–1923*, Harvard 1954

Pipes, Richard, *Russia Under the Bolshevik Regime*, London 1994

Polianski, A., *Yezhov: Istoriya zheleznogo stalinskogo narkoma*, Moscow 2001

Pope, Arthur Upham, *Maxim Litvinov*, London 1943

Popov, B. S., and V. G. Oppokov, 'Berievshchina', *VIZh*, 1990, no. 3

Porter, Cathy, *Alexandra Kollantai*, London 1980

Povartsov, S. *Prichina smerti-rastrel*, Moscow 1996

Raanan, Gavriel D., *International Policy Formation in the USSR Factional 'Debates' during the Zhdanovshchina*, Hamden, CT 1983

Radosh, R., M. R. Habeck and G. Sevostianov (eds), *Spain Betrayed the Soviet Union in the Spanish Civil War*, New Haven, CT 2001

Radzinsky, Edvard, *Stalin*, London 1996

Read, Christopher, *The Stalin Years: A Reader*, London 2003

Read Anthony, and David Fisher, *The Deady Embrace: Hitler, Stalin and the Nazi-Soviet Pact 1939–1941*, London 1988

Rees, E. A., *Stalinism and Soviet Rail Transport 1928–1941*, London 1995

Reese, R. R., *Stalin's Reluctant Soldiers: A Social History of the Red Army*, Kansas 1996

Richardson, Rosamond, *The Long Shadow: Inside Stalin's Family*, London 1993

Rieber, Alfred J., 'Stalin Man of the Borderlands', *American History Review*, vol. 106, no. 5, December 2001

Riehl, Nikolaus, and Frederick Seitz, *Stalin's Captive Nikolaus Riehl and the Soviet Race for the Bomb*, London 1996

Rigby, T. H., 'Was Stalin a Disloyal Patron?', *Soviet Studies*, vol. 38, no. 3, July 1986

Rigby, T. H., *Political Elites in the USSR*, Aldershot 1990

Ritterspoon, G. T., *Stalinist Simplifications and Soviet Complications. Social Tensions and Political Conflicts in the USSR 1933–53*, Philadelphia 1991

Roberts, Andrew, *The Holy Fox: A Biography of Lord Halifax*, London 1991

Roberts, Geoffrey, 'Beware Greek Gifts: the Churchill/Stalin Percentages Agreement of October 1944', *Churchill and Stalin, FCO Historians' Conference 2002*

Rogovin, Vadim Z., *1937: Stalin's Year of Terror*, Oak Park, MI 1988

Rosenfeldt, N. E., *Knowledge and Power: the Role of Stalin's Secret Chancellery in the Soviet System of Government,* Copenhagen 1978

Rubenstein, Joshua, *Tangled Loyalties: the Life and Times of Ilya Ehrenburg*, London 1996

Rubenstein, Joshua, and Vladimir P. Naumov, *Stalin's Secret Pogrom, The Postwar Inquisition of the Jewish Anti-Fascist Committee*, New Haven, CT 2001

Rubtsov, Y., *Alter Ego Stalina: Stranitsy politicheskoi biografi LZ Mekhlisa*, Moscow 1999

Rubtsov, Y, *Marshay Stalina*, Rostov 2000

Rybakov, Anatoli, *Children of the Arbat*, Boston 1988

Rzheshevsky, O. A., *Vtoraya Mirovaya Voina*, Moscow 1995

Rzheshevsky, O. A. (ed.), *War and Diplomacy: the Making of the Grand Alliance*, NY 1996

Rzheshevsky, O. A., 'Winston Churchill in Moscow 1942', *Churchill and Stalin, FCO Historians' Conference 2002*

Sainsbury K., *The Turning Point*, London 1986

Salisbury, Harrison, *900 Days, The Siege of Leningrad*, London 1969 (r/p: 2000)

Seaton Albert, *Stalin as Military Commander*, Conshohocken, PA 1998

Service, Robert, *The Bolshevik Party in Revolution: A Study in Organizational Change 1917–23*, London 1979

Service, Robert, *A History of 20th Century Russia*, London 1997

Service, Robert, *Joseph Stalin, the Making of a Stalinist*, John Channon (ed.), *Politics, Sociey and Stalinism in the USSR*, London 1998

Service, Robert, *Lenin*, London 2000

Service, Robert, 'Architectural Problems of Reform: from Design to Collapse', *Totalitarian Movements and Political Religions*, vol. 2, no. 2, autumn 2001

Shapiro, Leonard, *The Communist Pary of the Soviet Union*, London 1970

Sheinis, Z, *Maxim Maksimorich Litvinov*, Moscow 1989

Shentalinsky, Vitaly, *The KGB's Literary Archive*, London 1995

Shentalinsky, Vitaly, 'Okhota v revzapovednike', *Novy Mir*, 1998, no. 12

Shukman, Harold (ed.), *Stalin's Generals*, London 1993

Shukman, Harold (ed.), *Stalin and the Soviet–Finnish War 1939–1940*, London 2002

Siegelbaum, Lewis, and Andrei Sokolov (eds), *Stalinism as a Way of Life, A Narrative in Documents*, New Haven, CT 2001

Smith, Edward Ellis, *Young Stalin*, New York 1967

Soyfer, Valery, *Lysenko and the Tragedy of Soviet Science*, NJ 1994

Spahr, William J, *Zhukov, The Rise and Fall of a Great Captain*, Novato, CA 1995

Spahr, William J., *Stalin's Lieutenants, A Study of Command under Duress*, Novato, CA 1997

Starr, S. Frederick, *Red and Hot, The Fate of Jazz in the Soviet Union 1917–80*, Oxford 1983

Stoliarov, K. A., *Golgofa*, Moscow 1991

Sukhomlinov, A., *Vasily: Syn Vozhdya*, Moscow 2001

Sulianov, Anatoli, *Arrestovat v Kremle. O zhizni i smerti marshala Beria: Povest*, Minsk 1991

Suny, Ronald Grigor, *The Making of the Georgian Nation*, Stanford, CA 1988

Suvenirov, O. F., *Tragediya RKKA 1937–8*, Moscow 1998

Taubman, William, *Khrushchev, The Man and His Era*, London 2003

Taubman, William, Sergei Khrushchev, and Abbott Gleason, *Nikita Khrushchev*, New Haven, CT 2000

Taylor, A. J. P., *Beaverbrook*, London 1972

Thomas, Hugh, *Armed Truce, The Beginnings of the Cold War 1945–6*, London 1986

Thurston, Robert W., *Life and Terror in Stalin's Russia 1934–41*, New Haven, CT 1996

Trepper, L., *Bolshaya igra*, Moscow 1990

Tolstoy, Nikolai, *Stalin's Secret War*, London 1981

Tolstoy, Nikolai, *The Tolstoys*, London 1983

Torchinov, B. A., and A. M. Lentiuk, *Vokrug Stalina*, St Petersburg 2000

Toranska, Teresa, *Oni, Stalin's Polish Puppets*, London 1987

Tucker, Robert, *Stalin as Revolutionary*, NY 1974

Tucker, Robert, *Stalin in Power: the Revolution from Above*, New York 1990

Tucker, Robert, *Stalinism: Essays in Historical Interpretation*, New Brunswick, NJ 2000

Ushakov, S., and A. A. Stukakov, *Front Voennykh Prokurorov*, Moscow 2000

Uspenski, V. D., *Taynyi Sovetnik Vozhdya*, Moscow 1992

Vaksberg, Arkady, *Stalin's Prosecutor, The Life of Andrei Vyshinsky*, NY 1991

Vaksberg, Arkady, 'Delo marshala Zhukova: nerazorvavshayasya bomba', *Literaturnaya Gazeta*, no. 32, 5, Aug. 1992

Vaksberg, Arkady, *Stalin Against the Jews*, NY 1995

Vasilieva, Larissa, *Kremlin Wives*, London 1994

Vasilieva, Larissa, *Kremlevskie Zheny*, Moscow 2001

Vasilieva, Larissa, *Deti Kremya*, Moscow 2001

Veiskopf, Mikhail, *Pisatel Stalin*, Moscow 2001

Volkogonov, Dmitri, *Stalin: Triumph and Tragedy*, London 1991

Volkogonov, Dmitri, *The Rise and Fall of the Soviet Empire*, London 1998

Watson, Derek, 'The Early Career of VM Molotov', *CREES Discussion Papers, Soviet Industrialisation Project Series*, Univ. of Birmingham, vol. 26, 1986

Watson, Derek, *Molotov and Soviet Government: Sovnarkom 1930–41*, Basingstoke 1996

Wheatley, Dennis, *Red Eagle. The story of the Russian Revolution and of Klimenty Efremovitch Voroshilov, Marshal and Commissar for Defence of the USSR*, London 1938

Yakovlev, Alexander, *A Century of Violence in Soviet Russia*, New Haven, CT 2002

Yakovlev, A. N., R. Pikhoya, and A. Geishtor, *Katyn*, Moscow 1997

Yakovlev, N. N., *Zhukov*, Moscow 1992

Young, Gordon, *Stalin's Heirs, Who's Who in Soviet Russia*, London 1953

Zenkovich, N. A., *Marshaly I genseki*, Smolensk 1997

Zhavoronkov, G., 'I snitsya nochyu den', *Sintaksis*, no. 32, 1992

Zhirnov, E., 'Gornichnyh Predstavit k Nagradam', *Vlast*, vol. 16, 2000

Zhirnov, E, 'Conversation with Office Manager of USSR Council of Ministers Mikhail Smirtukov', *Vlast*, vol. 11 (Molotov), vol. 7 (Bulganin), vol. 5 (Malenkov), vol. 25 (Stalin), 2000

Zhukov, Y. N., 'Borba za vlast v rukovodstve SSSR v 1945–1952', *Voprosy Istorii*, no. 1, 1995

Zhukov, N. Y., 'Tainy Kremlevskogo dela 1935 goda I sudba Avelia Yenukidze', *Voprosy Istorii*, no. 9, 2000

Zubkova, Elena, 'Obshchestvennaya atmosphera posle voiny (1945–1946)', *Svobodnaya Mysl*, no. 6, 1992

Zubok, Vladislav, and Constantine Pleshakov, *Inside the Kremlin's Cold War, From Stalin to Khrushchev*, Harvard 1996

Index